America's Heroes

AMERICA'S HEROES

*Medal of Honor Recipients from
the Civil War to Afghanistan*

James H. Willbanks, Editor

ABC-CLIO

Santa Barbara, California • Denver, Colorado • Oxford, England

Copyright 2011 by ABC-CLIO, LLC

All rights reserved. No part of this publication may be reproduced, stored in a retrieval system, or transmitted, in any form or by any means, electronic, mechanical, photocopying, recording, or otherwise, except for the inclusion of brief quotations in a review, without prior permission in writing from the publisher.

Library of Congress Cataloging-in-Publication Data

America's heroes : Medal of Honor recipients from the Civil War to Afghanistan / James H. Willbanks, editor.
      p. cm.
  Includes bibliographical references and index.
  ISBN 978-1-59884-393-4 (hard copy : acid-free paper) — ISBN 978-1-59884-394-1 (ebook) 1. Medal of Honor—Biography.   2. United States—Armed Forces—Biography.   3. Heroes—United States—Biography.   4. Courage—History—Anecdotes.   5. United States—History, Military—Anecdotes.   6. United States—History, Naval—Anecdotes.   I. Willbanks, James H., 1947–

  UB433.A57   2011
  355.0092'273—dc22   2010047130

ISBN: 978-1-59884-393-4
EISBN: 978-1-59884-394-1

15 14 13 12 11   1 2 3 4 5

This book is also available on the World Wide Web as an eBook.
Visit www.abc-clio.com for details.

ABC-CLIO, LLC
130 Cremona Drive, P.O. Box 1911
Santa Barbara, California 93116-1911

This book is printed on acid-free paper ∞

Manufactured in the United States of America

This book is dedicated to all those American men and women
who have taken up arms in defense of their nation.

This book is also dedicated to our daughter Jennifer,
who will live in our hearts forever.

CONTENTS

LIST OF ENTRIES

ACKNOWLEDGMENTS

I would like to thank several organizations and groups for the invaluable assistance they provided in the compilation of this encyclopedia. First I would like to thank the Congressional Medal of Honor Society, Mt. Pleasant, South Carolina, which was founded in 1958, according to its charter, to maintain "memory and respect" for those have received the nation's highest award for heroism. The society and its Web site have been critical sources of information about the medal and its recipients. Likewise, the Home of Heroes, Pueblo, Colorado, has a superb Web site that includes a treasure trove of information on the history of the medal and the heroes who received it. I would also like to recognize the US Army Center of Military History at Fort Lesley J. McNair in Washington, D.C., which maintains a comprehensive database that includes all the Medal of Honor citations.

Lastly, I would like to express my appreciation to the scholars who contributed to the biographical section of this encyclopedia; it has been a pleasure to work with them all.

PREFACE

The Medal of Honor is the ultimate symbol of courage and valor under fire and is awarded to only the bravest of the brave; it is an object of awe and veneration. More than 40 million men and women have served in the armed forces of the United States since the Continental Army was formed in 1775, but fewer than 3,500 men and one woman have been awarded the Medal of Honor. This rare honor is bestowed only upon those who have shown conspicuous bravery "above and beyond the call of duty." It is such an extraordinary honor that President Harry S. Truman, himself a soldier in World War I, reportedly said on several occasions, "I'd rather wear that medal than be President of the United States."

The Medal of Honor is the epitome of valor and selfless service, and many who received the medal made the supreme sacrifice—giving their lives—in that service. The recipients of the Medal of Honor are officers and enlisted men from all branches of the service. They come from all walks of life and from many different ethnic backgrounds and cultures; they come from all over the country, and even some foreign lands. They come from every armed service and have seen action in America's wars from the Civil War to Afghanistan. Despite all these differences, the recipients of the Medal of Honor all share one thing in common. At some point in their lives, they selflessly performed extraordinarily courageous acts in the face of almost insurmountable odds—deeds that were clearly "above and beyond the call of duty."

The recipients of the Medal of Honor are admired and looked upon as the best America has to offer, but none of them sought recognition. Those who survived to accept the medal, more often than not, accepted it in honor of their comrades who fought and sometimes died in the defense of their nation. Perhaps Canadian-born Peter Lemon, who received the medal for valor in Vietnam, summed up this idea best when he told a group of young students, "Whenever you see the Medal, you see millions of people out there who have given their service and sacrificed for your freedom."

This encyclopedia is meant to be a tribute to those Americans who have demonstrated uncommon valor in the face of great danger and have been recognized for their actions by being awarded the Medal of Honor. It is also a tribute to all those other Americans who Peter Lemon mentioned—those who have performed acts of valor and courage that have gone unrecognized. To them all, the nation owes a great debt of gratitude.

INTRODUCTION

The Medal of Honor is the nation's highest award for military valor, and it can be awarded to soldiers, sailors, airmen, marines, and coast guardsmen. It is presented by the president of the United States in the name of Congress and thus is often mistakenly referred to as the Congressional Medal of Honor. It is awarded for "conspicuous gallantry and intrepidity at the risk of life above and beyond the call of duty." Due to the nature of its criteria, it is often awarded posthumously.

The Medal of Honor did not exist until the Civil War. However, the idea of recognizing individual acts of bravery dates back to the Revolutionary War. The Badge of Military Merit was established by Gen. George Washington, commander in chief of the Continental Army, on August 7, 1782. The award, which consisted of a purple cloth heart, was designed to recognize "any singularly meritorious action," and records indicate that only three persons received the award.

The Badge of Military Merit fell into disuse after the Revolutionary War, although it would be revived in 1932 as the Purple Heart, which was awarded to those who had been wounded in World War I. In the interim, there were several efforts to devise a way to recognize individual valor on the battlefield. In 1847, after the outbreak of the Mexican-American War, a "certificate of merit" was established for those who distinguished themselves during battle; however, it was discontinued after the war.

Early in the Civil War, the idea of a medal for bravery on the battlefield was proposed to Gen. Winfield Scott, then Union general-in-chief, but he rejected the idea because he thought medals smacked of European affectation. However, a similar proposal was presented to Secretary of the Navy Gideon Welles, who endorsed the idea of creating a medal for valorous service for enlisted men in the Navy and Marine Corps. Senator James W. Grimes of Iowa introduced a bill in Congress that was signed by President Abraham Lincoln in December 1861. The next year, a "medal of honor" was created for the Army, largely due to the efforts of Edward D. Townsend, assistant adjutant general, and Massachusetts senator Henry Wilson. The bill creating the Army medal was signed into law in July 1862. It was to be awarded "to such noncommissioned officers and privates as shall most distinguish themselves by their gallantry in action, and other soldier like qualities."

Although proposed only for the Civil War, Congress made the medal permanent in 1863, extending provisions to include officers as well as enlisted men, and making the provisions retroactive to the beginning of the Civil War. The Medal of Honor has remained the highest and most prestigious award that can be earned by the US Armed Forces.

The first act of valor that would be recognized with the Medal of Honor occurred on February 13, 1861, a year before the Medal of Honor was proposed. Bernard J. D. Irwin, an Army assistant surgeon, led a group of 14 men into Apache Pass, Arizona, to rescue 60 soldiers surrounded by a band of Indians. However, he would not actually receive the medal until 1894, over 30 years later.

Army private Francis Edwin Brownell was the first to receive the Medal of Honor during the Civil War. On May 24, 1861, he found and killed the murderer of Union Colonel Elmer E. Ellsworth in Alexandria, Virginia.

John Williams, captain of the USS *Pawnee*, was the first to earn the Navy Medal of Honor for his bravery in leaving no man behind in a desperate battle in June of 1861. However, he would not receive the medal until April 1863.

On March 25, 1863, Secretary of War Edwin Stanton made the first presentation of the Medal of Honor to six of the surviving members of the famous Andrews Raiders. James J. Andrews, a civilian, led a force of 23 military and civilian volunteers deep into Confederate territory to Marietta, Georgia, where they captured an entire train pulled by the locomotive *General* in an effort to disrupt the lines of transportation between Atlanta, Georgia, and Chattanooga, Tennessee. They were pursued by locomotive and eventually captured, after which seven of the raiders, including Andrews, were hung as spies. Four of those hanged also received Medals of Honor, the first to receive the medal posthumously. In all, 19 of the 24 Andrews Raiders won the Medal of Honor, but not Andrews, the civilian leader of the raid.

2nd Lt. Thomas Custer, brother of the infamous Gen. George Armstrong, became the first to receive two Medals of Honor for two separate actions during the Civil War. Only 13 other people have received two distinct Medals of Honor for two separate actions (five others received both the Army and Navy medals for the same action).

During the Civil War, a total of 1,522 Medals of Honor were issued to Army and Navy personnel. However, there were no detailed criteria or time limits for presenting the award, so many went to individuals who had done nothing particularly heroic. For example, President Lincoln authorized the award of the medal to 864 members of the 27th Maine Volunteer Infantry Regiment for reenlisting.

As time went on, requirements for the Medal of Honor became more strict, and fewer people began to receive the award. In 1897, Congress passed legislation to ensure that the Medal of Honor could be awarded only for "gallantry and intrepidity." Furthermore, nomination for the award had to be made by someone other than the one who was being nominated for a valorous deed. Additionally, one or more eyewitnesses must testify under oath about the deed, and the recommendation had to be submitted with one year of the act for which the medal would be awarded.

In 1905, President Theodore Roosevelt issued an executive order outlining the basic policy for the actual presentation of the Medal of Honor. When possible, the recipient would be ordered to Washington, D.C., where the president as the commander in chief or his designated representative would present the medal in an appropriate ceremony. If it proved impractical for the recipient to come to Washington, as it would during World Wars I and II, the service chief of staff would designate the time and place for the award ceremony. President Roosevelt presented the first Medal of Honor at the White House to one of his old Rough Rider comrades, assistant surgeon James Robb Church, on January 10, 1906.

In April 1916, Congress approved legislation that provided for the creation of a "Medal of Honor Roll," which was to include all honorably discharged Medal of Honor recipients who earned the medal in combat and reached the age of 65. The primary purpose of this legislation was to give the recipients the same level of recognition afforded holders of similar British and French awards for valor.

Later that same year, the War Department established a Medal of Honor review board consisting of five retired general officers to consider all 2,625 medals presented by the Army up to that time with the intent of undoing what were seen as earlier abuses in the awarding of the medal. The board released its findings in 1917, striking the names of 911 Medal of Honor recipients, most from the Civil War, who the board felt did not deserve the Medal of Honor. The names of those struck included all the medals awarded to the 27th Maine for reenlisting, 29 members of President Lincoln's funeral guard, and 6 civilians whose courage was not questioned but who were deemed ineligible for the medal due to their civilian status. Among these were five scouts, including Buffalo Bill Cody, who had served in the Indian Campaigns, and Civil War assistant surgeon Mary Edwards Walker, the only woman ever to receive the Medal of Honor. The medals of Dr. Walker, Cody, and the other scouts would later be restored.

In 1918, several other medals were established by Congress, including the Distinguished Service Cross, the Distinguished Service Medal, and the Silver Star, constituting what became known as the "pyramid of honor" with the Medal of Honor at the apex. The lower-precedence awards were to recognize heroism or distinguished service of a "lesser degree" than that recognized by the Medal of Honor.

In the period from 1921 to 1923, by congressional legislation signed by the president, the Medal of Honor was awarded to the Unknown Soldiers of the United States, Britain, France, Italy, Belgium, and Rumania. Later, the Medal of Honor would be awarded to the American Unknown Soldier of World War II in 1948, the Korean War in 1957, and the Vietnam War in 1984.

During the period from 1918 to 1963, the award of the Medal of Honor continued to be a rare event, but regulations still permitted the medal to be awarded for peacetime bravery and distinguished acts not involving combat. During this period, Cdr. Richard E. Byrd, who flew over the North Pole in 1926, and Charles Lindbergh, who made his famous trans-Atlantic solo flight in May 1927, both received the Medal of Honor. In another case, four sailors were awarded the Medal of Honor for risking their lives to save the crew of the sunken American submarine USS *Squalus* in May 1939 (the Navy had long had a practice of awarding the Medal of Honor for noncombat actions, presenting, for example, 48 Medals of Honor during the period from 1901 to 1911 for actions involving boiler explosions onboard ships, shipboard fires, and saving lives).

With the outbreak of World War II, the award of the Medal of Honor once again focused on recognizing valor above and beyond the call of duty in combat against an armed enemy. The award of the Medal of Honor remained rare. Even though 13 million men served in World War II, less than 500 medals were awarded, more than half of them posthumously.

In 1947, President Harry S. Truman created the United States Air Force as a separate branch of the Armed Forces, doing away with the Army Air Corps. However, during the Korean War, members of the Air Force who received the Medal of Honor received the Army Medal. A total of 133 Medals of Honor were awarded for heroism in the Korean War, 95 of them posthumously.

In 1956, three years after the end of the Korean conflict, Congress passed legislation authorizing the Air Force Medal of Honor, distinct from the Army and Navy Medals of Honor. Marines continued to receive the Navy Medal of Honor.

In 1963, Congress again tightened the regulations governing the award of the Medal of Honor. The act for which the medal would be received had to be done while engaged in action against an enemy of the United States, while engaged in military operations involving conflict with an opposing force, or while serving with friendly foreign forces engaged in an armed conflict against an opposing armed force in which the United States is not a belligerent party.

During the Vietnam War, fewer than 250 Medals of Honor were awarded, almost half of them posthumously. During this period, there was one exception to the enemy-action rule. Captain William McGonagle received the Medal of Honor for his actions while in command of the USS *Liberty* when it was mistakenly attacked by the Israel Defense Forces in the eastern Mediterranean on June 8, 1967, during the Six-Day War.

Since the 1980s, a number of Medals of Honor have been belatedly awarded to correct past administrative errors and oversights or to consider previous recommendations as a result of new evidence. On July 19, 1980, President Jimmy Carter presented the Medal of Honor to Matt Urban some 36 years after he had performed numerous acts of valor during the fighting in France and Belgium during World War II. On February 24, 1981, President Ronald Reagan presented the Medal of Honor to Roy Benavidez for his valor during the Vietnam War.

On April 24, 1991, President George H. W. Bush presented the Medal of Honor to the family of World War I hero Cpl. Freddie Stowers for his extraordinary and inspirational valor during the Meuse-Argonne campaign of 1918; Stowers, an African American, was mortally wounded while attempting to destroy a machine gun that had pinned down his unit. The paperwork recommending Stowers for the award had been lost for over 70 years.

In 1993, a special study was commissioned to investigate racial discrimination in the awarding of medals in World War II; no African Americans had received the Medal of Honor for action during the war. The study concluded with a recommendation that several African American Distinguished Service Cross recipients be upgraded to the Medal of Honor. On January 13, 1997, President Bill Clinton presented the Medal of Honor to seven African Americans, all of which except the one to Vernon Baker were presented posthumously.

A similar study was conducted in 1998 to examine the records of Asian Americans who had served in World War II. On June 21, 2000, President Clinton presented the Medal of Honor to 22 Asian Americans for their acts of courage during World War II, including Senator Daniel Inouye and 19 Japanese Americans who had served in the famous 442nd Regimental Combat Team.

Periodically, there have been other additions to the Medal of Honor Roll of Heroes to correct past oversights. On January 21, 2001, President Clinton presented the Medal of Honor posthumously to Theodore Roosevelt for his bravery in the Spanish-American War. President Clinton also presented Medals of Honor to James Day for action in World War II, Robert Ingram and Alfred Rascon for action in Vietnam, and Andrew Smith posthumously for action in the Civil War. President George W. Bush presented Medals of Honor to Ed Freeman, Bruce Crandall, Jon Swanson, and Humbert Versace (the last two posthumously) for action in Vietnam; to Ed Salomon for action in World War II; and to Tibor Rubin and Woodrow Keeble, the first full-blooded Sioux to receive the Medal of Honor, for action in Korea. Rubin was a Jewish veteran and Holocaust survivor who some believed to have been overlooked for the medal originally because of anti-Semitism.

The award of the Medal of Honor has been exceedingly rare for conflicts since the end of the Vietnam War. There were no awards of the Medal of Honor during Grenada, Panama, Lebanon, or Desert Storm. Two Medals of Honor were awarded for action in Mogadishu, Somalia, in 1993. As of this writing, only four Medals of Honor were awarded for valor in the Iraq War and four for Afghanistan, all but one of them posthumously.

Having provided a brief history of the establishment and evolution of the Medal of Honor, this encyclopedia seeks to provide selected profiles of those who have earned this rare and prestigious honor with their bravery and selflessness. Each of them has a unique story that deserves to be heard. Unfortunately, however, space does not permit a full discussion of all those who have received the medal; therefore, a sampling of Medal of Honor recipients will have to suffice. What follows are selected biographical sketches of 200 recipients of the Medal of Honor, arranged alphabetically. The individuals selected for this biographical section were chosen to reflect the wide diversity of ethnic and cultural backgrounds, branches of service, and conflicts that mark the 3,454 individuals who have been awarded the Medal of Honor. Each biographical profile begins with a box that includes name (as shown on the Medal of Honor citation), birth date, date of death (where applicable), home state (at time of entry into the service), branch of service, conflict fought in, and age (at the time of the action for which the medal was awarded). The biographical narratives address each recipient's early years, military background, the act for which the Medal of Honor was awarded, and the recipient's later years. References are provided for each entry.

The biographical section also includes a number of sidebars distributed throughout the section meant to amplify the biographical profiles and provide interesting sidelights on the Medal of Honor and its recipients.

The biographical section is followed by tabular data that includes a listing of Medals of Honor awarded by service and conflict and a complete alphabetical listing of all individuals, indicating their service and conflict, who have received the Medal of Honor. The encyclopedia concludes with an extensive bibliography on the Medal of Honor and its recipients followed by a detailed index.

Adams, Lucian

Born: October 26, 1922
Died: March 31, 2003
Home State: Texas
Service: Army
Conflict: World War II
Age at Time of Award: 22

Lucian Adams was born on October 26, 1922, in Port Arthur, Texas. He was one of 12 children from a large, Mexican American family. Adams worked for two years in a wartime plant after his graduation from high school before joining the US Army in 1943. By the summer of 1944, Adams was serving as a staff sergeant with the 30th Infantry Regiment, 3rd Infantry Division. It was during that time that the 3rd Infantry Division invaded southern France, landing near Saint-Tropez and proceeding to move inland toward central France.

In late October of 1944, on a country road near the town of Saint-Dié, France, while attempting to make contact with two companies in his battalion that were cut off by the enemy, Adams found himself under heavy enemy fire. He quickly moved forward to scout for nearby German positions and discovered three machine gun nests in the area. Adams quickly notified his company commander and was subsequently ordered to break through enemy lines to retrieve the separated GIs.

Sergeant Adams, with a borrowed Browning Automatic Rifle (BAR) in hand, led his men down the country road and soon after was fired upon by the enemy machine gun positions. The opening enemy machine gun bursts instantly killed three of his soldiers and left six of his men wounded. Adams quickly moved forward from tree to tree, firing his BAR from the hip, while the remainder of his men took cover. Upon reaching the first German machine gun nest, with rounds passing just above his head, Adams used a grenade to kill the gunner. Soon after, another German appeared from his nearby foxhole only to be killed by a burst of fire from Sergeant Adams's weapon. Adams charged the second machine gun nest and destroyed it in similar fashion as the first, while also forcing two German infantrymen supporting the weapon to surrender. Adams continued into the woods, where he killed five more enemy soldiers and destroyed the third enemy machine gun, thus clearing the wooded area of the entire enemy opposition. Right after the action, Adams was told that he had been recommended for the Medal of Honor, but he did not think much about it, because he had heard the same thing after he had single-handedly destroyed a German machine gun position during the battle at Anzio.

Sergeant Adams remained in the war and fought his way through Germany until the spring of 1945, when he received official word that he was to receive the Medal of Honor from President Franklin D. Roosevelt. However, President Roosevelt died before Adams left Europe, so Lt. Gen. Alexander Patch presented Adams the medal in Nuremberg's Zeppelin Stadium. After the war, Adams returned to the United States and worked for the next 40 years with the Veterans Administration in San Antonio, Texas. On March 31, 2003, Lucian Adams died a humble hero after suffering from diabetes and heart problems. He is buried in the Fort Sam Houston National Cemetery in San Antonio.

Thomas D. Lofton Jr.

Further Reading

Collier, Peter, and Nick Del Calzo. *Medal of Honor: Portraits of Honor beyond the Call of Duty.* New York: Artisan, 2006.

Yeide, Harry, and Mark Stout. *First to the Rhine: The 6th Army Group in World War II.* St. Paul, MN: Zenith Press, 2007.

Baca, John P.

Born: January 10, 1949
Died:
Home State: California
Service: Army
Conflict: Vietnam War
Age at Time of Award: 21

Born in Providence, Rhode Island, on January 10, 1949, John P. Baca describes himself as a "problem kid," frequently appearing before juvenile authorities in the San Diego area where he grew up. Wanting to join the military at the age of 17, he was declared ineligible because he was on parole from the California Youth Authority. His wish came true, however, in 1969, when he was drafted into the US Army.

Baca's first unit assignment in Vietnam, just a few months after his induction into the Army, was to a heavy-weapons platoon with Company D, 1st Battalion, 12th Cavalry of the 1st Cavalry Division (Airmobile) operating along the Cambodian border in Phuoc Long Province. As a recoilless rifleman, his job was to use the weapon against enemy troops in bunkers or fortified positions. His job was to support rifle platoons in firefights by providing firepower not normally available to the platoon.

On February 10, 1970, Baca's unit returned to base after having been in the field for approximately one month. The normal rotation for such a unit would have required a few days to repair equipment, alter and repair uniforms, and spend time preparing for the next operation. However, that same afternoon his platoon was ordered back into the field to set up a night ambush near a trail where there was suspected enemy activity. They were helicoptered into position at dusk.

The standard operating procedure for such a mission was to set up warning devices such as claymore mines (M18A1) connected to trip wires that would explode when activated by an enemy soldier, thus providing an early warning that the enemy was in the area. One such mine was detonated, and an accompanying patrol went to the site of the explosion to investigate. They came under heavy fire from an enemy patrol that had set up an ambush along the trail, and Baca ran to the aid of his fellow soldiers. He fired one round from his weapon as a grenade landed near his firing position. With several friendly troops in the area, Baca had to make an immediate decision, and his instincts motivated him to remove his helmet, cover the grenade, and then cover the helmet with his body. The grenade exploded, ripping Baca's stomach and internal organs. He recalls seeing his intestines outside his fatigue shirt as his buddies removed him from the battlefield and placed him against a tree. Nearly two hours elapsed before he was medevaced to a hospital in Long Binh. His wounds were extensive, and he spent one year in rehabilitation in Vietnam, Japan, and the United States. His mother came to Japan because he was not expected to recover from the extensive surgery associated with his wounds.

Baca, however, recovered and left the Army after his wounds healed. He had entered college when he was notified that he had been awarded the Medal of Honor. President Richard Nixon presented him the medal at the White House on June 15, 1971.

In 2002, a park in Huntington Beach, California, was named in his honor, and at the dedication ceremony he minimized his actions by saying, "I am an ordinary citizen who answered my country's call to duty and performed to the very best of my ability."

John Baca has returned to Vietnam to help build medical clinics for the Vietnamese as part of the Veteran's Vietnam Restoration Project. One of the Vietnamese who worked with him on the project was a soldier Baca had captured, rather than killed, on Christmas Day, 1969. That is the story he wants to tell more than the story of his being awarded the Medal of Honor. As of 2010 he works for the cause of homeless veterans and participates in the annual motorcycle Run for the Wall in support of the Rolling Thunder parade in Washington, D.C.

Ron Milam

Further Reading

Collier, Peter, and Nick Del Calzo. *Medal of Honor: Portraits of Valor beyond the Call of Duty.* New York: Artisan, 2006.

Murphy, Edward F. *Vietnam Medal of Honor Heroes.* New York: Ballantine Books, 2005.

Smith, Larry. *Beyond Glory: Medal of Honor Heroes in Their Own Words—Extraordinary Stories of Courage from WWII to Vietnam.* New York: W. W. Norton, 2003.

Bacon, Nicky Daniel

Born: November 25, 1945
Died: July 17, 2010
Home State: Arizona
Service: Army
Conflict: Vietnam War
Age at Time of Award: 22

Born November 25, 1945, in Caraway, Arkansas, Nicky Daniel Bacon was the son of a poor cotton sharecropper. Bacon was raised in relative poverty, which caused his family to move to Arizona when he was six. He dropped out of high school after the ninth grade. Bacon, although underage at 17, joined the Arizona National Guard in 1963 after signing his mother's name to his enlistment papers. He attended basic training at Fort Ord, California. After Bacon volunteered for active duty in 1964, he was assigned to the 8th Infantry Division in Germany. He received orders for Vietnam at Christmastime of 1965.

While in Vietnam on his very first mission, the helicopter he was on was involved in a midair collision with another helicopter. Bacon was one of only two survivors. His first tour of duty ended in 1967, and Bacon was assigned to Hawaii, where he trained troops for Vietnam. He volunteered to join those men for his second tour in 1968.

In Vietnam in the fall of 1968, Staff Sergeant Bacon was serving as a squad leader with 1st Platoon, Company B, 4th Battalion, 21st Infantry, 11th Infantry Brigade, Americal Division, which was engaged in the interdiction of supplies funneling into South Vietnam via the Ho Chi Minh Trail. On August 26, 1968, Bacon's unit returned to base camp after a month of fighting in the field. Instead of the expected rest and rehabilitation time, his company was quickly ordered to board helicopters en route to Tam Ky, where a 1st Cavalry Division unit under enemy attack needed relief.

Bacon's platoon was ordered to attack a hillside where North Vietnamese Army regulars, estimated to be at regimental strength, had opened up on the US troops. Bacon assaulted an enemy bunker, which he knocked out of action with hand grenades. When his platoon leader was wounded, Bacon moved his wounded officer to safety and took over command of the platoon. He returned to action to destroy a machine gun. When another platoon joined the hillside attack, its platoon leader was also wounded, and Bacon took command of that unit as well.

Heavy rocket fire slowed friendly tanks from reaching the action to evacuate American wounded. Bacon attacked again and killed at least four enemy soldiers and knocked an antitank weapon out of action. This allowed the friendly tanks to move forward. Staff Sergeant Bacon climbed on board a tank and directed fire against enemy positions, while the American wounded were evacuated. Finally, air strikes were called in, which permitted Bacon's unit to move up the hill.

Bacon originally received the Distinguished Service Cross for his actions at Tam Ky, but his medal came under review for upgrade thanks to reports from pilots who had observed his actions from the air. While stationed at Fort Hood, Texas, he received word that he was to be awarded the Medal of Honor. President Richard M. Nixon presented the medal to Bacon at the White House on November 24, 1969. Bacon had hopes of returning to Vietnam for a third tour of duty, but his request was eventually denied. In addition to his post-Vietnam service at Fort Hood, Bacon also served in Germany and at Fort McClellan, Alabama.

First Sergeant Bacon retired after 21 years of service in June 1984. In addition to his Medal of Honor and Distinguished Service Cross, Bacon also earned the Legion of Merit, two Bronze Stars, the Purple Heart (which he only received in 2008), and the Combat Infantryman's Badge. In retirement, Bacon served as the 16th president of the Congressional Medal of Honor Society. He also served as the director of Veterans Affairs for his home state of Arkansas from 1993 to 2005, and he was also a civilian aide to the secretary of the Army. Bacon was in high demand as a speaker and remains an advocate for his fellow veterans. He credited his faith in God, his hardship as a youngster in Arkansas, and his friends for enabling him to survive the difficulties of two tours in the jungles of Vietnam.

Nick Bacon died on July 17, 2010, following a struggle with throat cancer. He was buried July 24 at the Arkansas State Veterans Cemetery in North Little Rock.

Thomas Dwight Veve

Further Reading

Collier, Peter, and Nick Del Calzo. *Medal of Honor: Portraits of Valor beyond the Call of Duty.* New York: Artisan, 2006.

Coy, Jimmie Dean. *Valor: A Gathering of Eagles.* Mobile, AL: Evergreen Press, 2003.

Smith, Larry. *Beyond Glory: Medal of Honor Heroes in Their Own Words—Extraordinary Stories of Courage from WWII to Vietnam.* New York: W. W. Norton, 2003.

Baker, Vernon

Born: December 17, 1919
Died: July 13, 2010
Home State: Wyoming

Service: Army
Conflict: World War II
Age at Time of Award: 26

Vernon Joseph Baker was born on December 17, 1919, in Cheyenne, Wyoming. Orphaned at a young age, he and his two older sisters were raised by their maternal grandparents in Cheyenne. Despite being a high school graduate—no small accomplishment for an African American during the Great Depression—he could not find any good jobs. After working as a shoeshine boy, menial laborer, and porter for the Union Pacific Railroad, he enlisted in the US Army in June 1941. Baker had hoped to serve in the Quartermaster Corps because he had heard that they had the easiest job, but the recruiter signed him up for the infantry.

After his initial training at Camp Wolters, Texas, Baker was transferred to the 25th Infantry Regiment at Fort Huachuca, Arizona. Since he could read, write, and type, Baker became a company clerk and corporal and soon thereafter a supply sergeant. After the attack on Pearl Harbor, Hawaii, on December 7, 1941, he was promoted again to staff sergeant. Baker's rapid rise caused anger among long-serving troops, white and black, who might have been privates or privates first class for almost 20 years in the Army. Not long after being physically assaulted by three white corporals who resented his status (the corporals were never apprehended or court-martialed for their crime), Baker's regimental commander recommended him for Officer Candidate School (OCS). After graduating from the infantry OCS at Fort Benning, Georgia, Baker was commissioned a second lieutenant on January 11, 1943.

After serving as an airbase security officer at Camp Rucker, Alabama, he was transferred to Company C, 370th Infantry Regiment, 92nd Infantry Division. The 92nd Infantry Division was made up of African American enlisted men and noncommissioned officers (NCOs) with some African American junior officers. The majority of officers, however, were white, mostly of Southern extraction, because the Army believed that Southerners knew how to "handle" African Americans. Unfortunately, African American units not only received predominantly white Southern officers but also generally

Vernon Baker, US Army (US Army).

received the worst of these officers (based on standardized Army training and testing), as the better officers were sent to white units.

The 370th Infantry Regiment arrived in Italy on July 24, 1944, a full three months before the rest of the division, and was temporarily attached to the 1st Armored Division. When the remainder of the division arrived, the division took its place in the Allied lines.

On April 5 and 6, 1945, near Viareggio, Italy, Baker's company was part of a divisional assault on the German strongpoint of Castle Aghinolfi in the mountainous and heavily defended hills of Italy. In the predawn hours of April 5, Baker and his weapons platoon led the company advance, despite losing his mortars to American artillery fire. During this advance, Baker personally destroyed three machine gun nests and an artillery observation position, as well as cutting German communication wire in more than a dozen places. Once the seriously depleted company established a position within 100 yards of the castle, they were hit by a heavy German mortar barrage. During the barrage, Baker's white company commander led the company's wounded executive officer to safely, leaving the company leaderless. Despite desperate calls for artillery support and reinforcements to the regimental headquarters, no help arrived. His original 26-man platoon reduced to fewer than 10, Baker had no choice but to retreat. During the retreat, Baker destroyed three machine gun positions that had been missed during the initial advance. When he finally reached the American lines, only 6 men from the original 26 remained alive. The next day, Baker was ordered to guide the lead company of the 473rd Infantry Regiment back to the forward-most position his platoon had occupied the day before. Recommended for the Medal of Honor by his battalion commander for his actions, Baker's award was downgraded to the Distinguished Service Cross (DSC), the Army's second highest award for valor.

Remaining in the Army after the war, Baker lost his commission in 1947 because he did not have a college education. As a master sergeant, he worked as a Signal Corps photographer for several years. During the Korean War, Baker became a first lieutenant again and volunteered for combat. As one of the few African Americans with the DSC, he was not allowed to return to combat. Instead, Baker was given command of a company in the 11th Airborne Division at Fort Campbell, Kentucky. After the Korean War, he again reverted to NCO status and served until his retirement in 1968 with 28 years of active service. After retiring from the Army, Baker worked for the American Red Cross for 19 years, serving a tour in Vietnam, before retiring to northern Idaho.

In 1993, the US Army commissioned a study to determine why no African Americans had been awarded the Medal of Honor during World War II. The study found widespread racism, and Army records revealed a number of Medal of Honor recommendations that had been downgraded to the DSC. On the basis of this evidence, seven African Americans awarded the Silver Star or DSC during

World War II had their awards upgraded to the Medal of Honor. Only one of them, Baker, was still alive on January 13, 1997, when the medals were presented by President Bill Clinton in a White House ceremony.

In April 1997, Baker was invited by the Italian government to return to Italy on the 52nd anniversary of the battle for Castle Aghinolfi. There, people turned out to honor Baker and celebrate the African American soldiers who freed them from the Nazi occupation.

After a long battle with brain cancer, Vernon Baker died at the age of 90 at his home south of St. Maries, Idaho, on July 13, 2010; he was buried at Arlington National Cemetery.

Alexander M. Bielakowski

Further Reading

Baker, Vernon J., and Ken Olsen. *Lasting Valor*. Columbus, MS: Genesis Press, 1997.

Collier, Peter, and Nick Del Calzo. *Medal of Honor: Portraits of Valor beyond the Call of Duty*. New York: Artisan, 2006.

Kingseed, Cole C. *Old Glory Stories: American Combat Leadership in World War II*. Annapolis, MD: Naval Institute Press, 2006.

Mikaelian, Allen, and Mike Wallace. *Medal of Honor: Profiles of America's Military Heroes from the Civil War to the Present*. New York: Hyperion, 2002.

Smith, Larry. *Beyond Glory: Medal of Honor Heroes in Their Own Words—Extraordinary Stories of Courage from WWII to Vietnam*. New York: W. W. Norton, 2003.

Baldwin, Frank D.

Born: June 26, 1842
Died: April 22, 1923
Home State: Michigan
Service: Army
Conflict: Civil War, Indian Campaigns
Age at Time of Award: 22, 32

Frank Dwight Baldwin, one of the most decorated US Army officers of the 19th century and the first American soldier to earn the Medal of Honor in two different wars, was born near Manchester, Michigan, on June 26, 1842. He started his military career in 1861, serving briefly as a second lieutenant in the Michigan Horse Guards. In September 1862, he was commissioned a first lieutenant in the 19th Michigan Infantry and served with that unit throughout the Civil War. In March 1863, Baldwin was captured during the battle of Thompson's Station in Tennessee. For a brief period before he was exchanged, he was confined at Libby Prison near Richmond.

THE MEDAL OF HONOR AND THE BATTLE OF
THE LITTLE BIGHORN, JUNE 25–26, 1876

The US Army's disastrous defeat at the Little Bighorn in June 1876 played a pivotal role in establishing the rational for awarding the Medal of Honor, an important step in maintaining the prestige of the medal. While the men under Brevet Maj. Gen. George A. Custer fought and ultimately died on what has become known as Last Stand Hill, the remaining elements of the 7th Cavalry—three companies under Maj. Marcus Reno—moved to a ridge four miles to the southeast. The battalion under Capt. Frederick Benteen and the pack train soon joined them. For the remaining daylight hours on June 25, the surviving 400 men of the 7th Cavalry held off repeated Sioux and Cheyenne attacks. The Indian attacks tapered off after dark, and the cavalrymen dug hasty positions with cups, bayonets, and the few shovels in the pack train, preparing for the inevitable attacks the next day. Throughout June 26, repeated Indian attacks pinned the men in their positions. The surgeon established a hasty collection point for the wounded in a small depression in the center of the position. Without a water source, canteens were soon empty in the June heat, and the wounded men suffered immensely. Four men volunteered to occupy an exposed position, and for 20 minutes, their firing drew Indian attention away from other men who rushed down to the river to fill canteens for the wounded men's relief. After 36 hours in contact, the Sioux and Cheyenne packed up their villages and departed to the west. Shortly after, the relief column arrived at the battlefield.

After the battle, with no other award for valor, company commanders of the Reno-Benteen force nominated large numbers of their men, sometimes entire companies, for the Medal of Honor. Brig. Gen. Alfred Terry, commanding the expedition, rejected the mass nominations, noting, "Medals of Honor are not intended for ordinary good conduct, but for conspicuous acts of gallantry." Col. S. F. Curtis convened a board of officers to review the recommendations, with one criteria being "the conduct which deserves such recognition should not be the simple discharge of duty, but such acts beyond this that if omitted or refused to be done, should not justly subject the person to censure as a shortcoming or failure." While this system was not formally adopted in the future, the board established the precedent that the medal was to be awarded only for extraordinary deeds.

The board recommended the approval of 24 medals for the actions of June 25–26. The four men who drew the Indian attention to the ridge, Sgt. George Geiger, blacksmith Henry Mechlin, saddler Otto Voit, and Pvt. Charles Windolph, were awarded the medal. Congress also recognized the 14 men who went for the water— privates Neil Bancroft, Abram Brant, Thomas Callen, Frederick Deetline, Theodore Goldin, David Harris, William Harris, James Pym, Roy Stanislaus, George Scott, Thomas Stivers, Peter Thompson, Frank Tolan, and Sgt. Charles Welch. Three men, Sgt. Benjamin Criswell, Pvt. Henry Holden, and Sgt. Thomas Murray, brought up ammunition from the pack trains under heavy fire. Sgt. Richard Hanley single-handedly recaptured an ammunition-laden pack mule that had panicked and ran into the Indian lines. Cpl. Charles Cunningham declined to leave the line after bring wounded and continued to direct his men while Sgt. Rufus Hutchinson was recognized for leading his men throughout the action as well as being part of the group that went for the wounded soldiers' water.

Mark T. Gerges

During the battle at Peachtree Creek, Georgia, on July 12, 1864, Baldwin was in command of the 19th Michigan's Company D. He was nominated for his first Medal of Honor for leading his company in a counterattack against heavy fire, during which he single-handedly penetrated the Southern positions and captured and returned with two Confederate officers, plus the colors of a Georgia regiment. He did not, however, receive that Medal of Honor until December 3, 1891.

Mustered out of Federal service as a captain in June 1865, Baldwin received a Regular Army commission as a second lieutenant in the 19th Infantry in February 1866. Seven months later, he transferred to the 37th Infantry and spent the next three years serving with that unit on the Kansas frontier. In 1869, Baldwin was assigned to the 5th Infantry, then under the command of Col. Nelson A. Miles.

Baldwin served as Miles's chief of scouts during the Red River War in the Texas Panhandle. He was nominated for a brevet promotion to captain for his actions during a battle on the Salt Fork of the Red River on August 30, 1874. Two months later at McClellan's Creek, Texas, he led two companies of the 5th Infantry in a surprise attack against a vastly larger Cheyenne force to rescue two settler girls who had been captured several months earlier when the rest of their family had been killed by the Cheyenne. Baldwin was again nominated for a brevet promotion, and on November 27, 1894, he received his second Medal of Honor for that action.

Following the Little Bighorn massacre in 1876, the 5th Infantry was transferred to Montana. On December 18, 1876, Baldwin commanded a force that dispersed Sitting Bull's camp on the Red Water River. Less than a month later, on January 8, 1877, Baldwin led 5th Infantry troops in an attack against forces under Crazy Horse at Wolf Mountain. Baldwin received brevet promotion nominations for each of those actions. Later that year, Baldwin participated in the Lame Deer expedition and the campaign against Chief Joseph's Nez Percés.

For more than 20 years following the Civil War, all action on brevet promotions was stalled by restrictive statutes enacted by Congress in 1869 in reaction to the wholesale distribution of such promotions during the Civil War. On February 27, 1890, Congress finally passed a new law specifically authorizing the president to confer brevet promotions for gallant service during the Indian Campaigns. Even then, it was more than four years before President Grover Cleveland sent to Congress the consolidated list of the brevet nominations since 1869. The list of 158 officers was submitted on April 20, 1894, but the brevets were confirmed and entered in the officers' records with an effective date of February 27, 1890. Baldwin's four nominations were consolidated into two brevet promotions, one to captain and one to major. Baldwin had already held the substantive rank of captain since 1879, and he would be promoted to the substantive rank of major in 1898.

Baldwin continued serving on the western frontier in various capacities throughout the remainder of the 19th century. Between October 1894 and May 1898, he was the resident agent at the Anadarko Agency in Indian Territory, today's state of Oklahoma. Upon his promotion to lieutenant colonel in December 1899, Baldwin was assigned to the 4th Infantry, stationed at Cavite on the Philippine Island of Luzon. In July 1901, he was promoted to colonel and assumed command of the 27th Infantry. On Mindanao on May 2, 1902, Baldwin's troops defeated a large Moro force at Bayan.

Frank Baldwin was promoted to brigadier general on June 9, 1902. The following February, he was appointed commander of the US Army's Department of the Colorado. He retired from the Army in 1906 shortly after being promoted to major general. During World War I, Baldwin also served as the adjutant general of the state of Colorado. Baldwin died in Denver on April 22, 1923. He is buried at Arlington National Cemetery.

David T. Zabecki

Further Reading

Baldwin, Alice Blackwood, ed. *Memoirs of the Late Frank D. Baldwin, Major General, U.S.A.* Los Angeles: Wetzel, 1929.

Neal, Charles M., Jr. *Valor across the Lone Star: The Congressional Medal of Honor in Frontier Texas.* Austin: Texas State Historical Association, 2002.

Ballard, Donald E.

Born: December 5, 1945
Died:
Home State: Missouri
Service: Navy
Conflict: Vietnam War
Age at Time of Award: 23

Donald E. Ballard was born on December 5, 1945, in Kansas City, Missouri. At the age of 20, already married and working in a dental lab, Ballard joined the US Navy in 1965. He went to basic training and then, because dental assistants were plentiful, he was offered the opportunity to attend surgical assistant school. After serving as an assistant in the operating room, he was "volunteered" to serve as a medic with the Marine Corps. He sailed with his unit for amphibious training in the Mediterranean ocean, where they conducted a mock landing on the island of Corsica.

In 1967, Hospital Corpsman Second Class Ballard was sent to Vietnam. There he joined Company M, 3rd Battalion, 4th Marines in the 3rd Marine Division. In Quang Tri Province during his unit's first combat action, Ballard was wounded, receiving the first of his three Purple Hearts (he would be wounded five other times during his tour of duty but treated these wounds himself).

On May 16, 1968, Ballard had just treated two marines for heat exhaustion and was returning from assisting in their evacuation by helicopter when he and his company were attacked by a North Vietnamese Army unit. In the ensuing battle, Ballard repeatedly exposed himself to enemy fire to provide aid to wounded marines. As he went about his work, an enemy grenade landed among the casualties. Ballard unhesitatingly threw himself on the grenade and cradled it to his body to protect his comrades from the deadly blast. The grenade failed to explode, so he rolled over and hurled the grenade away, returning to his treatment of the wounded. The grenade, which apparently had a defective fuse, exploded in midair where it could not do any damage.

Ballard was wounded again in the fall of 1968 and was evacuated to Okinawa. After two months, he returned to the United States, where he was assigned to work in a surgical clinic in the naval hospital in Memphis.

In 1970, Ballard left the Navy and enlisted in the Army to attend officer candidate school. In May of that year, Ballard was summoned to the White House, where he was presented the Medal of Honor by President Richard Nixon and Gen. William Westmoreland. General Westmoreland offered Ballard a direct commission in the Army, but he turned it down for family reasons and later joined the Kansas National Guard. During the course of his career in the Kansas Guard, he served as an ambulance platoon leader, medical company commander, and a number of other key positions. On April 5, 1998, Ballard was promoted to colonel in the Guard. He served as special assistant to the Kansas adjutant general until he retired in 2000 after 35 years of active and reserve component service. He and his wife now live in his hometown of Kansas City, Missouri. Ballard was inducted into the National Guard Hall of Fame in November 2001.

James H. Willbanks

Further Reading

Collier, Peter, and Nick Del Calzo. *Medal of Honor: Portraits of Valor beyond the Call of Duty.* New York: Artisan, 2006.

Jordan, Kenneth N., Jr. *Heroes of Our Time: 239 Men of the Vietnam War Awarded the Medal of Honor 1964–1972.* Atglen, PA: Schiffer Publishing, 2004.

Murphy, Edward F. *Vietnam Medal of Honor Heroes.* New York: Ballantine Books, 2005.

Barfoot, Van T.

Born: June 15, 1919
Died:
Home State: Mississippi

Service: Army
Conflict: World War II
Age at Time of Award: 25

Van T. Barfoot was born in Edinburg, Mississippi, on June 15, 1919. Barfoot was unaware of his Native American heritage and grew up not knowing he was an official member of the Choctaw tribe. He enlisted in the Army in 1941 and was initially assigned to the 1st Infantry Division, serving with the division in Louisiana and Puerto Rico. He earned a promotion to sergeant in December 1941 and served with the Amphibious Force Atlantic Fleet at Quantico, Virginia. After the Army inactivated this unit, Barfoot transferred to the 157th Infantry, 45th Infantry Division and was shipped to Europe.

Barfoot participated in a series of amphibious landings, beginning with the Allied invasion of Sicily in July 1943, the invasion of Italy at Salerno in September, and the landings at Anzio in late January 1944. His unit pushed in from the Anzio beachhead and, by May 1944, has taken up defensive positions around the town of Carano. During this time, Barfoot led numerous day and night patrols, during which he created a mental map of the German minefields and defenses. On the morning of May 23, his unit received orders to attack the German positions. Barfoot volunteered to lead a squad attack through the German minefields. Using his knowledge of the German positions and terrain, he maneuvered himself within range to destroy a German machine gun with a grenade attack. Barfoot continued the attack, advancing along the German line and eliminating two other machine gun positions. During this attack, he killed 7 German soldiers and captured an additional 17 enemy troops.

After the morning assault, Barfoot's unit consolidated its position. Seeing three German tanks maneuvering to counterattack his unit, Barfoot used a bazooka to destroy the lead tank, forcing the two trail tanks to reverse direction. He killed the crew of the destroyed tank as they dismounted; then, he advanced into enemy territory and destroyed a field piece using a demolition charge. Finally, Barfoot evacuated two seriously injured members of his squad to safety, which required him to move the soldiers nearly a mile.

Following his heroic actions, Barfoot received a battlefield commission. Four months later, he learned that he would receive the Medal of Honor for his actions at Carano in May. Although he had the option of receiving the award in the United States, Barfoot chose to receive the medal on the battlefield so his men could see the ceremony. On September 28, 1944, Lt. Gen. Alexander Patch, commanding general of VII Corps, awarded Barfoot the Medal of Honor at a ceremony in Epinal, France.

After World War II, Barfoot remained in the Army. He trained as a helicopter pilot and in the Vietnam War flew over 30 combat missions. Barfoot retired as a colonel in 1974. Barfoot served as the military advisor to the Virginia National Guard. On September 27, 2007, he attended the dedication of a Veterans Administration (VA) Alzheimer's unit at the VA center that bears his name. The Sitter and Barfoot Veterans Care Center in Richamond houses 160 patients. At the dedication, Barfoot gave a speech where he emphasized his determination to spend his remaining years supporting soldiers and veterans.

In October 2009, Mississippi named a section of State Highway 16 "Van T. Barfoot Medal of Honor Highway." Van Barfoot is one of five Native Americans to receive the Medal of Honor after World War I. Of the five Native Americans awarded the Medal of Honor, Barfoot is one of two still alive. As of 2010 he lives in Ford, Virginia.

Gates M. Brown

Further Reading

Atkinson, Rick. *The Day of Battle: The War in Sicily and Italy, 1943–1944*. New York: Henry Holt, 2007.

Collier, Peter, and Nick Del Calzo. *Medal of Honor: Portraits of Valor beyond the Call of Duty*. New York: Artisan, 2006.

Barnum, Harvey C., Jr.

Born: July 21, 1940
Died:
Home State: Connecticut
Service: Marine Corps
Conflict: Vietnam War
Age at Time of Award: 25

Harvey C. Barnum Jr. was born on July 21, 1940, in Cheshire, Connecticut. In school, he excelled in sports. He also participated in the Boy Scouts and was elected president of his senior class in high school. Upon graduation from high school, Barnum attended St. Anselm's College in Manchester, New Hampshire, where he graduated with a bachelor of arts degree in economics in June 1962. While still in college, Barnum had joined the Marine Corps Platoon Leaders Class (PLC) program and, upon graduation, was offered a commission as a second lieutenant in the Marine Corps Reserve.

Barnum graduated from the Marine Corps' basic school in December 1962 and received the military occupational specialty of artillery officer. Ordered to Okinawa, Japan, Barnum served as a forward observer for Battery A, 1st Battalion, 12th Marines. He later completed an assignment as a liaison officer for the battalion as well. Promoted to first lieutenant in December 1964, Barnum served a career-broadening tour with the 2nd Marine Air Wing and participated in Operation Steel Pike, a division-sized amphibious operation in Spain. In March 1965, Barnum transferred to Hawaii and was assigned as guard officer, Marine Barracks, US Naval Base, Pearl Harbor, Hawaii.

In December 1965, Barnum was assigned to temporary duty in Vietnam and acted as an artillery forward observer with Company H, 2nd Battalion, 9th Marines. On December 18, 1965, Barnum and the marines of Company H were engaged in combat against Viet Cong forces near the village of Ky Phu in Quang Tri Province. At the time, Barnum's company was attached to the 2nd Battalion, 7th Marines then conducting Operation Harvest Moon. Barnum's company was assigned to act as the rear guard for the battalion when his unit was suddenly pinned down by a barrage of extremely accurate enemy mortar, machine gun, and small arms fire. Disregarding his own safety, Barnum reported to his rifle company commander at the very moment an enemy shell happened to strike. The explosion mortally wounded the commander and killed the radio operator. Giving aid to his dying commander, Barnum removed the radio from the deceased radio operator and strapped it to his own back. He later used this radio to call in supporting artillery and air strikes. As the senior surviving officer, Barnum immediately assumed command of the rifle company and quickly set about giving encouragement to and directing the fire of the surviving marines of the company. Pointing out targets, Barnum coolly directed the fire of him men, quickly gaining fire superiority over the enemy. When two armed helicopters were sent to assist him, Barnum personally directed their fire at the entrenched enemy and organized a platoon-sized counterattack against their positions while simultaneously arranging for the transportation and evacuation of his wounded marines. Leading by personal example, Barnum led the assault against the remaining enemy positions and routed the Viet Cong. For his actions at Ky Phu, Barnum was recommended for the Medal of Honor. The medal was presented to him by Secretary of the Navy Paul H. Nitze on February 27, 1967.

Following the expiration of his temporary duty assignment in Vietnam, Barnum returned to Marine Barracks at Pearl Harbor. He was eventually transferred to Headquarters Marine Corps in Washington, D.C. as aide de camp to Lt. Gen. Lewis Walt, then the assistant chief of staff for manpower and later assistant commandant of the Marine Corps. Returning to Vietnam in October 1968, Barnum served as the commanding officer of Battery E, 2nd Battalion, 12th Marines. For his service in this capacity, he was awarded the Bronze Star with Combat "V," the Navy Achievement Medal with Combat "V," and the Purple Heart for wounds received in action.

Following his second tour in Vietnam, Barnum served in a number of successive assignments in the Marine Corps in the United States and Okinawa. Promoted to the rank of lieutenant colonel in December in 1978, he attended the Naval War

College in Newport, Rhode Island. Barnum later served at the US Central Command, where he helped plan and execute the first US/Jordanian joint exercise and twice planned and executed Operation Bright Star. One of his final assignments was as the military secretary to the commandant of the Marine Corps. Barnum retired from the Marine Corps as a colonel in 1989. Following retirement, Barnum served as the principal director, Drug Enforcement Policy, Office of the Secretary of Defense. He was also a past president of the Congressional Medal of Honor Society and as of 2010 serves as the deputy assistant secretary of the Navy for reserve affairs and resides in Reston, Virginia.

Charles P. Neimeyer

Further Reading

Collier, Peter, and Nick Del Calzo. *Medal of Honor: Portraits of Valor beyond the Call of Duty*. New York: Artisan, 2006.

Smith, Larry. *Beyond Glory: Medal of Honor Heroes in Their Own Words—Extraordinary Stories of Courage from World War II to Vietnam*. New York: W. W. Norton, 2003.

Barrett, Carlton W.

Born: November 24, 1919
Died: May 3, 1986
Home State: New York
Service: Army
Conflict: World War II
Age at Time of Award: 24

Born in Fulton, New York, on November 24, 1919, Carlton W. Barrett entered active duty service in Albany, New York, on October 29, 1940. Upon completion of initial entry training, Private Barrett was assigned as a rifleman in the 18th Infantry Regiment of the 1st Infantry Division—the "Big Red One."

Barrett was perhaps the smallest man in his regiment, standing only five feet, four inches tall and weighing 125 pounds. On the morning of June 6, 1944, D-Day, he found himself part of a three-man reconnaissance team assigned the task of establishing a rally point on Omaha Beach for their regiment's forces upon making their landing. His team was supposed to arrive on the beach, radio the location of the rally point to the ship transporting their regiment, and then wait for their unit to arrive.

Events conspired to change the nature of Private Barrett's mission that day. Arriving around midday as a reserve regiment, the 18th expected to find the beach secure and the assault moving inland. Instead, reinforced German positions had survived the American preparatory bombardment relatively unscathed, leaving them in place to pour a devastating volume of fire upon the soldiers attempting to wade ashore and causing many American landing craft to unload their passengers in the wrong sector or in deep water far from the beach.

Barrett, deposited in neck-deep water, made his way onto a beach near Saint-Laurent-sur-Mer that was immersed in chaos. Instead of the relatively simple reconnaissance mission he had expected to perform, the young private found himself in a fight for his life. Reacting quickly to these desperate circumstances, Barrett, repeatedly exposing himself to intense small arms and mortar fire, returned to the surf, where he carried several wounded comrades to evacuation craft waiting offshore, saving the lives of many men who would almost surely have died if left on the beach to await medical care.

Barrett next returned to the beach, where he continued to expose himself to the sustained German fire that inflicted 2,500 American casualties that day. Demonstrating leadership far beyond that expected of a young private, Barrett performed duties as a guide, assisted shocked and wounded soldiers, and repeatedly carried messages the length of the beach between officers attempting to regain control of the situation.

Private Barrett earned his Medal of Honor that day not for killing enemy soldiers, but for saving American lives and continuously risking his own life to help restore a situation that for at least part of the "longest day" seemed beyond hope. Although one of only four men awarded the Medal of Honor for their heroism on D-Day, Barrett never achieved fame, and his fellow soldiers said life darkened for him after the war. Private Barrett remained in the Army, serving as a cook and a supply specialist and eventually rising to the rank of staff sergeant before his retirement on June 30, 1963.

Sergeant Barrett's memory inspires Americans to this day, including the young boy who chose Barrett as the subject of an essay on human courage and sacrifice; the boy's essay won the middle school prize in a 2008 contest sponsored by the Congressional Medal of Honor Society.

Sergeant Barrett died on March 3, 1986, and his Medal of Honor joined the other artifacts preserved at the 1st Division Museum at Cantigny in Wheaton, Illinois.

Mark T. Calhoun

Further Reading

Allen, Thomas B. "Savior at Omaha Beach." *Military History* 26, no. 2 (June/July 2009): 19.

Balkoski, Joseph. *Omaha Beach: D-Day, June 6, 1944.* Mechanicsburg, PA: Stackpole Books, 2004.

Harrison, Gordon A. *Cross-Channel Attack: US Army in World War II: European Theater of Operations.* Reprint, Washington, D.C.: Department of the Army Historical Division, 2007.

Lang, George, Raymond L. Collins, and Gerard F. White. *Medal of Honor Recipients, 1863–1994*. New York: Facts on File, 1995.

Lewis, Adrian R. *Omaha Beach: A Flawed Victory*. Chapel Hill: University of North Carolina Press, 2001.

Tillman, Barrett. *Heroes: U.S. Army Medal of Honor Recipients*. New York: The Berkley Group, 2006.

Basilone, John

Born: November 4, 1916
Died: February 19, 1945
Home State: New Jersey
Service: Marine Corps
Conflict: World War II
Age at Time of Award: 26

Born in Buffalo, New York, on November 4, 1916, and raised in Raritan, New Jersey, John Basilone was 1 of 10 children born to an Italian American tailor. Not an especially gifted student, John decided to forgo high school after finishing eighth grade and worked as a caddie at the Raritan Valley Country Club until he turned 18. He enlisted in the Army and found an aptitude for machine guns; he could assemble and disassemble the weapon quickly, even while blindfolded. During his Army enlistment he served overseas in the Philippine Islands, which earned him the nickname Manila John. While enjoying his tour in the Far East, Basilone longed for his family and friends and returned home to Raritan after a three-year enlistment. He went back to caddying and also worked as a driver until he became bored with civilian life, and in 1940 he decided to join the Marines.

Starting his Marine Corps career at Quantico, Virginia, he saw service at Cuba; Parris Island, South Carolina; and Camp Lejeune, North Carolina. After the attack on Pearl Harbor, Basilone volunteered for duty in the Pacific and, in April 1942, deployed to Western Samoa. On September 18, Basilone landed on the island of Guadalcanal as part of Operation Hightower with the 1st Marine Division. Serving in legendary Marine "Chesty" Puller's battalion, Basilone was the noncommissioned officer in charge of two machine gun sections and was set in place to defend Henderson Airfield. During the night of October 24–25, Basilone and his marines laid their guns in defensive positions in preparation for an expected a Japanese assault. By 2200 hours, a forward listening post reported a large enemy movement. As the Japanese approached the marine positions, Basilone ordered his men to hold their fire until the enemy was about 30 yards away. Once the marines opened up, they inflicted serious damage to multiple waves of attacking Japanese forces. Still, a few

Japanese attackers managed to make it to the defensive positions, where Basilone dispatched them with his pistol.

Upon hearing that both machine guns to his right were out of action and fearing an enemy flanking maneuver, Basilone took one of the guns from his position and began carrying it to the exposed flank. While moving to the new position, he ran into a Japanese patrol and sprayed the enemy with the searing-hot machine gun in his hands. When he arrived at the defensive position, he found only two marines alive and the guns out of action. Almost immediately, the Japanese initiated another attack. With no time to set up the machine gun's tripod, Basilone initiated a grazing fire that cut down the advancing enemy. Before the next assault wave, he moved to one of the guns that was out of action and repaired it just in time to repel another assault. For hours, the Japanese continued to attack in groups of 15 to 20, and Basilone and his marines continued to mow them down.

With ammunition and water running short, Basilone made two trips to obtain the much-needed resupply. During these trips, while draped in ammunition belts, he was under constant enemy sniper fire and at one time was knocked down by a Japanese grenade. Between ammunition runs, Basilone repaired another machine gun and quickly had it employed. As a result of their withering fire, it was estimated that Basilone and his marines alone killed 2,900 Japanese soldiers. For his actions that night, he was awarded the Medal of Honor and was ordered home to participate in the war bond effort.

After months of public appearances back in the United States, Basilone was assigned barracks duty at the Washington Naval Yard. Uncomfortable with his celebrity, Basilone requested a return to the war in the Pacific. Shortly afterward, Basilone got his wish and was part of the assault force landing on the island of Iwo Jima on February 19, 1945. During the landings, Basilone single-handedly put a Japanese pillbox out of action and exposed himself to enemy fire while killing a Japanese sniper targeting marines escaping from a disabled tank. While conjecture surrounds the actual cause of his death, the most accepted version is that he was killed by enemy artillery fire, dying in the black ash of Iwo Jima with his marines surrounding him. As a result of his actions on Iwo Jima, Basilone was posthumously awarded the Navy Cross. He remains the only enlisted marine in World War II to hold the Medal of Honor, the Navy Cross, and the Purple Heart. John Basilone's story is portrayed prominently in the HBO series *The Pacific*, which began airing on the network in 2010.

John M. Curatola

Further Reading

Ambrose, Hugh. *The Pacific*. New York: NAL Caliber, 2010.

Brady, James. *Hero of the Pacific: The Life of Marine Legend John Basilone*. Hoboken, NJ: John Wiley and Sons, 2010.

Cerasini, Marc. *Heroes: U.S. Marine Corps Medal of Honor Winners*. New York: Berkley Books, 2002.

Hargis, Robert, and Ramiro Bujeiro. *World War II Medal of Honor Recipients: Navy & USMC*. Oxford, UK: Osprey, 2003.

Jordan, Kenneth. *Men of Honor: Thirty-Eight Highly Decorated Marines of World War II, Korea, and Vietnam*. Atglen, PA: Schiffer Publishing, 1997.

Benavidez, Roy P.

Born: August 5, 1935
Died: November 29, 1998
Home State: Texas
Service: Army
Conflict: Vietnam War
Age at Time of Award: 23

Roy P. Benavidez was born on August 5, 1935, in Lindenau, near Cuero, Texas. His parents were of Mexican and Yaqui Indian ancestry. When he was two years old, his father died of tuberculosis and his mother remarried. However, she died five years later, also from tuberculosis. He and his younger brother and half-sister moved to El Campo to live with an uncle. He dropped out of middle school in order to help support the family by working in the fields, picking beets and cotton.

Benavidez enlisted in the Texas Army National Guard in 1952 and enlisted in the Regular Army in June 1955. After completion of airborne school, he was assigned to the 82nd Airborne Division at Fort Bragg, North Carolina. In 1964, he was sent to Vietnam, where he was assigned as an advisor to a South Vietnamese infantry regiment. During a patrol, he was severely injured by a land mine and was evacuated to Brooke Army Medical Center in San Antonio, Texas. Doctors there feared he would never walk again, but he proved them wrong and walked out of the hospital under his own power in July 1966. He returned to Fort Bragg, where he underwent training to become a Green Beret.

On his second tour in Vietnam in 1968, Benavidez, now a staff sergeant, was assigned to the super-secret MACV Studies and Observations Group (MACV-SOG) based at Loc Ninh, near the Cambodian border. On May 2, 1968, a 12-man Special Forces reconnaissance patrol was surrounded by a North Vietnamese Army battalion. Benavidez heard the radio call for help and boarded a helicopter to go to the aid of the beleaguered patrol. Once in the area, he directed the helicopter to a nearby clearing and leaped from the hovering aircraft. Carrying several medical bags, he made his way under heavy enemy fire to the US patrol. By this time, the team members were already dead or too injured to make it to an extraction zone. During the six-hour battle that ensued, Benavidez continually exposed himself to withering fire to come to the aid of his comrades, suffering a total of 37 separate bayonet, bullet, and shrapnel wounds while simultaneously directing the defense of the unit and trying to organize an emergency extraction. The first extraction ended in tragedy when the helicopter was shot down just after Benavidez and the survivors of the patrol got on board. Despite his wounds, Benavidez established a hasty defense around the downed aircraft and called in tactical air support and attack helicopters to help hold back the enemy forces. Finally, he was able to get his surviving comrades on a second extraction helicopter. He was the last man on the aircraft. When they arrived back at the base, his comrades thought Benavidez was dead. He was being placed into a body bag when he came to and was evacuated to Saigon, where he underwent surgery. Somehow, he survived his multiple wounds.

Benavidez was awarded the Distinguished Service Cross for his heroic actions; he was credited with saving eight American lives. In 1973, the full extent of Benavidez's actions would become known, and he was nominated for the Medal of Honor. However, the time limit on the medal had expired. An appeal to Congress resulted in an exemption for Benavidez, but he was still denied the medal because the board required an eyewitness account. In 1980, however, a witness was located—an old friend who Benavidez thought had been killed in the battle. The man, radioman Brian O'Connor, who learned by chance about the effort to have his friend awarded the Medal of Honor, submitted a 10-page sworn statement on the battle and Benavidez's actions to save his companions. Finally, on February 24, 1981, President Ronald Reagan presented the Medal of Honor to Benavidez in a White House ceremony.

Shortly after the ceremony, the Social Security Administration, as part of cost-cutting moves, terminated Benavidez's disability benefits, along with those of thousands of other veterans. Retired from the Army in 1976, he still suffered from shrapnel in his heart and a punctured lung, but he was deemed "able to work." Benavidez subsequently testified before the House Select Committee on Aging about how veterans needed their benefits to get by. Shortly thereafter, his Social Security benefits were reinstated when the Social Security Administration abandoned the effort to terminate veterans' disability benefits.

In retirement, Benavidez was very active as an inspirational speaker at schools and civic events. He also frequently spoke to troops at US installations in the United States and around the world.

Roy Benavidez died from complications from diabetes on November 29, 1998, in San Antonio, and he was buried with full military honors at the Fort Sam Houston National Cemetery. A number of installations and buildings have been named in Benavidez's honor in Texas, Oklahoma, and Colorado. Additionally, the US Navy named one of its Bob Hope–class roll-on roll-off vehicle cargo ships the USNS *Benavidez*.

James H. Willbanks

Further Reading

Benavidez, Roy P., and John R. Craig. *Medal of Honor: A Vietnam Warrior's Story*. Washington, D.C.: Brassey's, 1995.

Benavidez, Roy P., John R. Craig, and Oscar Griffin. *The Three Wars of Roy Benavidez*. San Antonio, TX: Corona Publishing, 1986.

Jordan, Kenneth N., Jr. *Heroes of Our Time: 239 Men of the Vietnam War Awarded the Medal of Honor 1964–1972*. Atglen, PA: Schiffer Publishing, 2004.

Murphy, Edward F. *Vietnam Medal of Honor Heroes*. New York: Ballantine Books, 2005.

Plaster, John. *SOG: The Secret Wars of America's Commandos in Vietnam*. Boulder, CO: Paladin, 2008.

Birkhimer, William E.

Born: March 1, 1848
Died: June 10, 1914
Home State: Iowa
Service: Army
Conflict: Philippine Insurrection
Age at Time of Award: 51

William E. Birkhimer was born on March 1, 1848, in Somerset, Ohio, but was raised in Iowa. In March 1864, he joined the 4th Iowa Volunteer Cavalry at the age of 16 and saw extensive service with that regiment through the last year of the Civil War. He was mustered out in August 1865, having received nine commendations for bravery. In the summer of 1866, he was appointed from the state of Iowa to the US Military Academy.

Birkhimer excelled at West Point and graduated 19th in a class of 58. He chose field artillery as his branch and was commissioned a second lieutenant in the 3rd Artillery Regiment. He attended the artillery school at Fort Monroe and graduated first in his class. In 1884, he published an important work on artillery titled *Historical Sketch of the Organization, Administration, Material, and Tactics of the Artillery, United States Army*.

Birkhimer later transferred to the judge advocate branch. He served as the judge advocate of the Department of Columbia from 1886 to 1890. In 1889, Birkhimer earned a law degree from the Law School of the University of Oregon. He later was admitted to practice law before the Supreme Court of the United States. With his legal knowledge, Birkhimer became one of the army's foremost experts on military law, the law of war, and the issue of military government. In 1892, he first published his book *Military Government and Martial Law*. The book subsequently went through three editions (1892, 1904, and 1915). It was considered the most important work on the subject and was a standard text at both West Point and the Army Staff College at Fort Leavenworth for more than 20 years. It was a key doctrinal reference guiding US military government operations in Cuba, Puerto Rico, and the Philippines after the Spanish-American War.

In the summer of 1898, Captain Birkhimer deployed to the Philippines with the 3rd Artillery Regiment. He subsequently served as aide to Gen. Henry Lawton. In that capacity, in May 1899, Captain Birkhimer accompanied Lawton's elite scout force to reconnoiter and sketch enemy positions. On May 16, Birkhimer and 18 scouts were investigating the defenses of San Miguel de Mayumo. They discovered 300 Filipino troops in the defensive position. A dozen scouts, including Birkhimer, charged across 150 yards of open ground and flanked the enemy position. The enemy then retreated across a bridge into the town, closely followed by Birkhimer and the scouts. With the scouts in hot pursuit, the enemy quit the town. Birkhimer and the small force of scouts then held the bridge and town for several hours until following infantry companies came up to support them. Birkhimer and 11 soldiers received the Medal of Honor for the action at San Miguel. Birkhimer's actions also led to his appointment as the colonel of the 28th Volunteer Infantry Regiment. He led that regiment in combat in the Philippines for 18 months and was cited numerous times for bravery.

The 28th Volunteer Infantry mustered out of service in May 1901. After that date, Birkhimer returned to his duties as a captain in the 3rd Artillery. He was promoted to major in August 1901 and lieutenant colonel in 1905. William Birkhimer was appointed brigadier general and retired from active service after 35 years because of ill health in 1906. Birkhimer died on June 10, 1914, and is buried in Arlington National Cemetery.

Louis A. DiMarco

Further Reading

Linn, Brian McAllister. *The Philippine War, 1899–1902.* Lawrence: University Press of Kansas, 1902.

McClernand, E. J. "William E. Birkhimer." *Forty-Sixth Annual Reunion of the Association of Graduates of the United Sates Military Academy.* New York: Association of Graduates, 1915.

Blake, Robert

Born: Born into slavery; date uncertain
Died: Unknown
Home State: Attributed to Virginia; emancipated in South Carolina
Service: Navy

Conflict: Civil War
Age at Time of Award: Unknown

Robert Blake was born into slavery, so his actual date and place of birth are unknown. He was among 400 slaves captured during a Civil War raid by the US Navy on South Carolina's Santee River in 1862. The Navy relocated Blake and the other so-called contrabands to North Island in Winyah Bay. While there, he answered a call for "20 single men" to serve on USS *Vermont*, a 2,633-ton storeship. Blake later transferred to USS *Marblehead*, a 691-ton Unadilla-class screw steam gunboat, where he served as a steward with the rank of contraband. Blake's service on *Vermont* and *Marblehead* was not unique; the US Navy was the most integrated service at the time.

At around 5:00 a.m. on Christmas Day, 1863, USS *Marblehead*, short 30 of her normal complement of 100 crewmen, was anchored in the Stono River off Legareville near Charleston, South Carolina. Suddenly, the ship shuddered from the impact of a Confederate howitzer shell fired from a hidden battery. As the crew of *Marblehead* rushed to their battle stations and the ship prepared to get under way, the vessel's captain, Lt. Cdr. Richard W. Mead Jr., appeared on deck dressed in his nightclothes. Robert Blake followed, bearing the captain's uniform. In quick succession, more rounds hit the ship, killing at least three sailors and wounding six more, including a powder boy. With no official battle station, Blake could have sought shelter below deck. Instead, on his own initiative, he pitched into the fight by supplying the ship's Dahlgren and Parrott guns with powder. By all accounts, Blake's fearless, calm, and good-natured execution of this duty inspired the sweating gun crews. Although initially surprised, *Marblehead* eventually suppressed the Confederate battery and caused its abandonment. Blake and two other crew members of USS *Marblehead*—Boatswain's Mate William Farley and Quartermaster James Miller—received the Medal of Honor for this action. Blake received a promotion to seaman and, after reenlisting, served again on USS *Vermont*.

Blake was the first African American recipient of the Navy's Medal of Honor and the first African American serviceman actually awarded the medal; however, Sgt. William Harvey Carney of the 54th Massachusetts Infantry Regiment was awarded the Medal of Honor in 1900 for an action that occurred on July 18, 1863, four months before the action that led to Blake's award. In all, 25 African Americans—18 soldiers and 7 sailors—received the Medal of Honor during the Civil War.

We know nothing of Robert Blake's post–Civil War life or his burial place, but his service represents the important contribution that African Americans made to the Union war effort.

Gregory S. Hospodor

Further Reading

Beyer, W. F., and O. F. Keydel, eds. *Deeds of Valor: How America's Heroes Won the Medal of Honor.* Vol. 2. Detroit, MI: The Perrien-Keydel Company, 1906.

Hanna, Charles W. *African American Recipients of the Medal of Honor: A Biographical Dictionary.* Jefferson, NC: McFarland, 2002.

Bleak, David B.

Born: February 27, 1932
Died: March 23, 2006
Home State: Idaho
Service: Army
Conflict: Korean War
Age at Time of Award: 20

David B. Bleak was born on February 27, 1932, in the high farm country of eastern Idaho. He grew up to be a mountain of a man—six foot, five inches tall and 250 pounds. Bleak dropped out of high school and worked for a time in ranching and farming but enlisted in the US Army on November 1, 1950, wanting to see the world. Bleak trained at Fort Riley, Kansas, and was assigned to a medical company attached to the 223rd Infantry Regiment, 40th Infantry Division. The division was a California National Guard unit called to active service for the Korean War. At Camp Cook in California, Bleak received more intensive medical training before he and his division were shipped out to Korea in January 1952. Soon afterward, he was promoted to sergeant.

Arriving in Korea, the 40th Division was ordered to defend a mountainous area around Minari-gol, near the 38th parallel. The result was trench warfare not unlike that of World War I,

David B. Bleak, US Army (US Army Medical Department Regiment).

with constant low-level combat. To determine whether the opposing Chinese communists were planning an offensive, the 2nd Battalion of the 223rd Infantry was ordered to scout enemy positions and obtain one or more prisoners for questioning. Bleak volunteered to accompany the Intelligence and Reconnaissance (I&R) platoon on this dangerous mission up Hill 499.

The patrol, consisting of 20 enlisted men under a technical sergeant, set out from UN lines at 0430 hours on June 14, 1952. Cover consisted of only low bushes and the broken nature of the land. An attack by Company F to their left had jumped off at 0245 hours, intended to distract the enemy from Bleak's patrol. As the I&R platoon climbed the hill, they were hit by heavy automatic weapons fire. From his position at the end of the line, Bleak quickly made his way forward to the wounded soldiers. After applying field dressings and stabilizing the men, he followed the remainder of the patrol toward the crest of the hill.

Bleak saw an American soldier go down, hit by fire from an unspotted Chinese position. The medic rushed the trench and flung himself into it. Bleak tackled one Chinese soldier and broke his neck with his bare hands. When Bleak jumped up, he was confronted by another soldier. Grabbing the man by the neck with both hands, Bleak used his massive strength to crush his windpipe. A third Chinese soldier ran up, and Bleak stabbed him through the chest with his combat knife.

Bleak then returned to his mission of mercy, running to treat the wounded American soldiers. While Bleak was standing next to one soldier, a Chinese hand grenade bounced off the soldier's helmet and landed nearby. Bleak knocked his comrade down and threw himself over him. The grenade's explosion did not harm the other soldier, but it shook Bleak up. Even so, he continued to treat the wounded.

When a hidden machine gun opened up on the platoon as it made its way down Hill 499, three American soldiers were wounded. Ignoring the enemy fire, Bleak ran to treat the men. A bullet hit him in the leg, but he continued onward after applying a field dressing to his own wound. Two of the men were able to walk toward American lines after being treated, but the third could not move. Despite the enemy fire, Bleak hoisted the man on his shoulders and began carrying him to safety. Two Chinese soldiers armed with rifles and bayonets suddenly confronted the pair. Bleak gently laid his comrade down and charged the enemy. Despite his wound, he avoided their thrusts and grabbed both their heads in his massive hands. In a move rarely seen in real life, Bleak smashed the soldiers' heads together, cracking their skulls. After tossing their limp bodies off the path, the medic once again picked up the wounded American and resumed his journey.

All 20 men from the I&R patrol returned to American lines, bringing with them several prisoners. A third were wounded, but recovered, thanks to Bleak's administrations. Bleak himself soon returned to duty even though he suffered nerve damage in his leg. Although his tour in Korea soon ended, Bleak volunteered to remain in Asia. While posted to Japan, he learned that he had been awarded the Medal of Honor for his courage under fire in ministering to the wounded and disabling or killing five enemy soldiers. Bleak received his Medal of Honor at the White House on October 27, 1953, from President Dwight D. Eisenhower.

After the war, Bleak left the Army and returned to Idaho. He and his wife, Lois, had four children. Bleak refused to use his status as a war hero to get jobs. Instead, he worked at a number of professions, eventually becoming a janitor at the Idaho National Engineering Laboratory. Bleak worked his way up to chief hot cell technician, disposing of radioactive fuel rods. He retired in the mid-1990s. He died on March 23, 2006, in Arco, Idaho, of emphysema, Parkinson's disease, and complications from a broken hip.

Although David Bleak remained humble about his achievements, others remembered what he had done. On April 20, 1995, the Sergeant David B. Bleak Troop Medical Clinic was dedicated at Fort Sill, Oklahoma. After Bleak's death, the governor of Idaho declared June 14, 2007, as "Sergeant David Bruce Bleak Day," marking the 55th anniversary of his accomplishments.

Tim J. Watts

Further Reading

Jacobs, Bruce. *Korea's Heroes: The Medal of Honor Story.* New York: Berkley Publishing, 1961.
Murphy, Edward F. *Korean War Heroes.* Novato, CA: Presidio Press, 1992.

Boyington, Gregory

Born: December 4, 1912
Died: January 11, 1988
Home State: Washington
Service: Marine Corps
Conflict: World War II
Age at Time of Award: 31

Born on December 4, 1912, in Coeur d'Alene, Idaho, Gregory "Pappy" Boyington graduated from the University of Washington in 1934 with a degree in aeronautical engineering. Joining the Marine Corps in 1935, he became a naval aviator two years later. Excessive drinking, marital estrangement, financial difficulties, and disrespect for superior officers characterized his next four years of service; nevertheless, he was recognized as an excellent pilot. In late 1941, Boyington volunteered for service with Col. Claire Chennault's American Volunteer Group (the Flying Tigers) in China.

Flying in defense of Burma and later in China during the spring of 1942, Boyington was credited with two aerial victories, although he maintained he had downed six Japanese aircraft. Transferred to the South Pacific in early 1943, he was promoted to major and ordered to form a new squadron to take the place of the refitting VMF-214 unit. This new unit, also designated VMF-214 and operating in the Solomon Islands, became legendary as the Black Sheep Squadron.

Between September 1943 and January 1944, the Black Sheep Squadron claimed it destroyed or damaged 197 Japanese aircraft. Boyington, nicknamed "Gramps" by his men and "Pappy" by the press because he was 30 years old, became something of a folk hero in the United States, immortalized in lavish news coverage. He himself downed 22 Japanese aircraft during this period. Combined with his earlier 6 in China and Burma, his 28 aerial victories made him the leading Marine Corps ace of all time.

Boyington was shot down on January 3, 1944, on a fighter sweep over Rabaul after being jumped by more than 20 Japanese aircraft. Picked up by a Japanese submarine, he spent the remainder of the war in prisoner-of-war camps. On his return to the United States in 1945, he was promoted to colonel and awarded the Medal of Honor for extraordinary heroism while serving as squadron commander of the Black Sheep; he also received the Navy Cross.

Boyington left the service in 1947. He then held a succession of jobs, constantly struggling with alcoholism and marital problems. In 1958, he wrote *Baa Baa, Black Sheep*, detailing his war experiences. In the 1970s, he produced the short-lived television series *Baa Baa Black Sheep*, based loosely on his book. Boyington died in Fresno, California, on January 11, 1988.

Luke B. Kingree

Further Reading

Boyington, Gregory. *Baa Baa, Black Sheep*. New York: G. P. Putnam, 1958.

Gamble, Bruce. *Black Sheep One: The Life of Gregory "Pappy" Boyington*. Novato, CA: Presidio Press, 2000.

Walton, Frank E. *Once They Were Eagles*. Lexington: University Press of Kentucky, 1986.

Brady, Patrick Henry

Born: October 1, 1936
Died:
Home State: Washington
Service: Army
Conflict: Vietnam War
Age at Time of Award: 31

Born in Philip, South Dakota, on October 1, 1936, Patrick H. Brady attended O'Dea High School in Seattle, Washington, where he was active in sports. While at Seattle University, he hated the compulsory ROTC course and was eventually booted out. However, reasoning that he would probably have to serve in the Army and that it would be better to be an officer than an enlisted man, he reentered the program and, upon graduation in 1959, was commissioned a second lieutenant in the Army Medical Service Corps. His first assignment was as a medical platoon leader in Berlin, but he applied for flight school and was accepted. He graduated from the US Army Aviation School at Fort Rucker, Alabama, as a helicopter pilot in 1963.

Patrick Henry Brady, US Army (US Army Medical Department Regiment).

He first reported to Vietnam in January 1964. He was assigned as a medical evacuation pilot with the 57th Medical Detachment (Helicopter Ambulance), then under the command of Maj. Charles L. Kelly. After Kelly was killed in action on July 1, Brady assumed command of the 57th's Detachment A, operating out of the Mekong Delta.

In August 1967, Brady returned to Vietnam for a second tour of duty, this time as a major serving as the operations officer and later commander of the 54th Medical Detachment. Brady instilled in his new unit the ethos of his old mentor Kelly: "No compromise. No rationalization. No hesitation. Fly the mission. Now!" Patients came above all else.

On January 5, 1968, piloting "Dust Off 55," Brady flew an incredible series of medevac missions in the fog-wrapped mountains near Chu Lai, south of Da Nang. Under intense enemy fire, Brady flew nine different missions and evacuated 51 wounded soldiers. He went through three different helicopters, which together contained over 400 bullet holes. For his actions that day, Brady initially received the Distinguished Service Cross (DSC). However, once back in the United States, he received a call from Gen. William Westmoreland, who informed him that his DSC had been upgraded to the Medal of Honor. He was presented the medal by President Richard Nixon on October 9, 1969. During his two tours in Vietnam, Brady flew over 2,000 combat missions and evacuated more than 5,000 wounded; Brady also received the Distinguished Service Cross and the Distinguished Flying Cross with five Oak Leaf Clusters.

Patrick Brady retired from the US Army as a major general in September 1993 after 34 years of service. One of his last assignments was as the US Army's chief of public affairs.

David T. Zabecki

Further Reading

Brady, Patrick H. "When I Have Your Wounded." *ARMY* (June 1989): 64–72.

Collier, Peter, and Nick Del Calzo. *Medal of Honor: Portraits of Valor beyond the Call of Duty.* New York: Artisan, 2006.

Dorland, Peter, and James Nanney. *Dust Off: Army Aeromedical Evacuation in Vietnam.* Washington, D.C.: U.S. Army Center of Military History, 1982.

Britt, Maurice L.

Born: June 29, 1919
Died: November 26, 1995
Home State: Arkansas
Service: Army
Conflict: World War II
Age at Time of Award: 24

Maurice L. Britt was born in Carlisle, Arkansas, on June 29, 1919. As a child, he acquired the unlikely nickname of Footsie, which stuck with him his entire life. A talented athlete, he attended the University of Arkansas with athletic scholarships in both football and basketball, becoming an All-American in football. He graduated in 1941 with a degree in journalism and a reserve commission as a second lieutenant through the ROTC program. That same year, he played as a rookie end for the Detroit Lions. His teammate and the Lions' star running back was Byron White, the future US Supreme Court justice.

Although he had received a partial deferment so he could play during the 1941 football season, Britt was called to active duty in early 1942. Reporting to Camp Robinson, Arkansas, he was assigned as a platoon leader in the 3rd Infantry Division's Company L, 3rd Battalion, 30th Infantry. He continued to serve with Company L until his medical evacuation from Italy two years later.

The 3rd Infantry Division landed at North Africa near Fedala on November 8, 1942. Britt's company helped silence the 128-mm coastal defense guns at Fort Blondin. Britt then led his platoon as the 30th Infantry moved across the top of the North African coast from Casablanca to Oran to Algiers to Tunis. Britt and his platoon landed at Sicily on July 10, 1943. They took part in the capture of Palermo and marched overland to Messina. On September 19, Britt's unit made its third combat amphibious landing in less than a year, reaching the Italian mainland at Salerno as part of a follow-on assault wave.

Shortly after the Salerno landing, L Company's commander was wounded and evacuated. Britt assumed command of the company as the 3rd Infantry Division advanced to the Volturno River. During the attack to secure the town of Acerno, Britt earned a Silver Star and his first Purple Heart for crawling to within 50 yards of a German machine gun position and eliminating it with rifle grenade fire. Several weeks later, he earned the Bronze Star Medal with "V" Device for rescuing one of his wounded men under enemy fire during the attack against the German positions on Monte San Nicola.

Following two days of bitter fighting, the 30th Infantry on November 8 secured Monte Rotundo, which controlled one of the key mountain approaches to Cassino. True to their tactical doctrine, the Germans immediately launched fierce counterattacks to retake the decisive position. After two more days of intense combat, Britt's Company L was down to only 55 effectives when more than 100 Germans attacked his 600-yard-wide sector. During the fierce fighting, Britt was hit in the side by a rifle bullet and suffered multiple grenade fragmentation wounds to his face, chest, and hands. His canteen was shot full of holes, and his field glasses were shattered. After expending all his carbine ammunition, he threw 32 hand grenades, killing five Germans, wounding many more, and capturing four. Once the German attack had been stopped, Britt refused to go back to the aid station for treatment until his battalion commander gave him a direct order to do so. Even then, he refused the battalion surgeon's evacuation order. Britt was nominated for the Medal of Honor for his heroic actions. He also later received the British Military Cross.

A little more than two months later, Britt, still in command of Company L, landed at Anzio on January 22, 1944. The following day, Britt's company attacked across the Mussolini Canal to secure a key road junction. The battle for the position raged all day. At one point in the fighting, Britt purposely exposed himself to draw fire from a concealed German machine gun. Once he had a fix on the position, he called in artillery and mortar fire to knock it out. As the grim, close-quarters fighting dragged on, Britt directed more artillery fire to eliminate three more enemy machine guns and two personnel carriers. Even while his Medal of Honor nomination for his actions on November 10, 1943, was working through the system, he was nominated for a Distinguished Service Cross for the battle of January 23, 1944.

Britt's war came to an end the following day while he was calling in artillery fire on advancing German tanks. One of the Panzers sent a round crashing into the stone farmhouse he was using as an observation post. The resulting blast tore off his right arm at the elbow and broke one of his legs. He also sustained chest injuries that eventually cost him his right lung. This time Britt finally was medically evacuated, with his third Purple Heart of the war.

On June 5, 1944, Captain Britt received the Medal of Honor at the University of Arkansas Commencement Ceremony; he accepted the medal on behalf of his men who served alongside him. While recovering from his wounds, he toured the United States to sell war bonds. Medically discharged in late December 1944, he returned to Arkansas and went on to study law at his alma mater. He subsequently spent 20 years working in business and industry. In the late 1960s, he served two terms as Arkansas lieutenant governor, and then he served as Arkansas district director for the Small Business Administration from 1971 to 1985. Maurice Britt's World War II wounds afflicted him for the rest of his life. On November 26, 1995, one of America's most gallant soldiers died of heart failure at the age of 76. He is buried in Little Rock National Cemetery.

David T. Zabecki

Further Reading

Feng, Patrick. "Maurice 'Footsie' Britt." *On Point: The Journal of Army History* 15, no. 4 (Spring 2010): 18–20.

Murphy, Edward F. *Heroes of World War II*. Novato, CA: Presidio Press, 1990.

Taggart, Donald G., ed. *History of the Third Infantry Division in World War II*. Washington, D.C.: Infantry Journal Press, 1947. Reprint, Nashville, TN: Battery Press, 1987.

Brown, Bobbie E.

Born: September 2, 1907
Died: November 8, 1971
Home State: Georgia
Service: Army
Conflict: World War II
Age at Time of Award: 37

Robert Evan Brown Jr. was born in Dublin, Georgia, on September 2, 1907. Enlisting at Columbus, Georgia, in 1922, he signed the enlistment papers as "Bobbie E. Brown"— the name he would be known by for the rest of his life. Standing at over six feet at age 15, the recruiting sergeant didn't question Brown's age. Brown, a talented athlete at 175 pounds, became an excellent soldier. He qualified expert on all the infantry small arms, earning the extra stipend in his monthly pay for superior marksmanship.

Brown played a number of sports, earning a berth on the All-Army football squad and boxing. His reputation as a competent soldier and outstanding athlete earned him the position of headquarters company first sergeant of Maj. Gen. George S. Patton's 2nd Armored Division at Fort Benning, Georgia.

When the war began, Brown was transferred to the 18th Infantry Regiment, 1st Infantry Division. Fighting through North Africa with the 18th Infantry, he earned a "mustang" battlefield commission to lieutenant. As a platoon leader, he led his unit in combat in Sicily and then on to England to prepare for the D-Day invasion.

After landing on Omaha Beach in June 1944, the 1st Infantry Division pushed inland. Crossing France later that summer, Brown assumed command of Company C when the company commander was killed. He was promoted to captain just as his unit reached the German border. Figuratively and literally he was now the "Old Man" of the company. On October 8, Brown's unit was poised to attack Aachen, the first major city in Germany to be reached by the Allies. C Company was assigned to attack a series of seven bunkers guarding the entry into the city, all part of the Siegfried Line.

The German bunker system was an extensive fortification line built from 1938 to 1942 to protect Germany's western frontier. The bunkers were designed to hold up to platoon-sized units and had multiple gun ports, some with rotating armored cupolas. One of the seven bunkers assigned to Company C had an 88-mm gun in an armored turret.

At midday, October 8, C Company was poised to assault the bunkers in its assigned zone of action. The majority of the bunkers were on a hill marked by a large Christian cross monument; the hill became known as Crucifix Hill. Shortly after taking their positions at the base of the hill, C Company was pinned down by heavy fire even though fighter-bombers made several bombing runs against the bunker system. Brown sensed that the German resistance was not affected by the bombing and determined that only direct ground attack would suffice to eliminate the resistance. Ordering flamethrowers forward and personally grabbing explosive demolitions, Brown leaped forward and took the lead.

Moving to the closest of the bunkers, Brown threw satchel charges through the rear door to destroy the bunker. A pole charge jammed into the firing port of the second bunker destroyed it. Moving to the third bunker, Brown threw another set of charges through a door a German soldier had opened to go to the adjoining ammunition bunker. The destruction of the third bunker ended German resistance in the bunker complex, clearing the way into Aachen. Although wounded by a mortar shell, Brown refused treatment in order to stay and lead his troops in turning back two German counterattacks, inflicting heavy losses on the enemy. For this action, Brown was recommended for the Medal of Honor.

Brown continued to lead his unit until the end of the war. President Harry Truman presented the Medal of Honor to Brown in a White House ceremony on August 23, 1945. In addition to the Medal of Honor, he also received two Silver Stars, a Bronze Star, and eight Purple Hearts.

After the war, Robert Brown was selected among 100 captains to attend the first Infantry Officer Advanced Course at Fort Benning, Georgia. His lack of formal education past the grade-school level hindered Brown's advancement, but he was able to retire from the Army in 1952 after 30 years' service. Brown accepted an entry-level position at West Point in the cadet mess hall and soon earned the supervisor's position. He died at his home in Flushings, New York, on November 8, 1971, and is buried in Arlington National Cemetery.

Edwin L. Kennedy Jr.

Further Reading

Lang, George, Raymond L. Collins, and Gerard F. White. *Medal of Honor Recipients 1863–1994.* Vol. 2, *WWII to Somalia.* New York: Facts on File, 1995.

Schott, Joseph L. *Above and Beyond: The Story of the Congressional Medal of Honor.* New York: G. P. Putnam's Sons, 1963.

Bucha, Paul William

Born: August 1, 1943
Died:
Home State: Missouri
Service: Army
Conflict: Vietnam War
Age at Time of Award: 24

Born on August 1, 1943, at the height of World War II, Paul William Bucha's parents were first-generation Americans of Croatian heritage. His parents instilled in him an expectation for excellence and the need to be self-sufficient. Bucha's childhood and youth reflected the life of a military family. His father was an army colonel, and Bucha's family moved frequently, including spending three years each in Germany and Japan. He graduated from Horton Watkins High School in St. Louis, Missouri, in 1961.

Bucha was an outstanding swimmer, and Yale University offered him a scholarship to compete on its swim team. But a chance detour to West Point after visiting Yale changed Bucha's educational path and life. Neither of his parents encouraged him to attend the US Military Academy, but Bucha was determined to do so following his brief visit. He obtained a presidential appointment and entered with the class of 1965.

Bucha excelled at West Point. Twice named an All-American, Bucha captained the swim team and was regimental commander of the Corps of Cadets his senior year, graduating in the top 3 percent of his class. West Point taught him the principles of leadership he would use throughout his life: integrity, confidence, competence, compassion, and humility. After graduation, the army sent Bucha to Stanford University, where he earned his MBA in 1967.

Promoted to captain, Bucha became commander of Delta Company, 3rd Battalion, 187th Infantry Regiment, 3rd Brigade, 101st Airborne Division at Fort Campbell, Kentucky, as the division prepared to deploy to Vietnam. Delta Company, however, had no men. For the first six weeks after his assignment, Bucha literally was a company of one. Although Bucha recruited his first sergeant, unneeded clerks, administrative personnel, and soldiers released from the stockade otherwise formed Delta Company. Bucha's company became known as the "clerks and jerks." He trained them hard to impart the skills they would need in combat, to instill trust in his leadership, and to build esprit de corps.

Delta Company arrived in South Vietnam in late November 1967. For the first few months, the company led a charmed existence. Despite being sent into some of the most dangerous areas, the unit returned from missions virtually unscathed. Then, on March 16, 1968, Delta Company was inserted into dense jungle near Phuoc Vinh in Binh Duong Province, tasked with seeking out and engaging enemy forces. For the first two days, the unit met only light resistance. But late on March 18, the lead reconnaissance platoon ran into a North Vietnamese battalion many times the size of the 89-man company.

The lead element became pinned down by heavy enemy fire. Bucha crawled through intense fire and single-handedly destroyed an enemy machine gun position firing from the fork of a tree. Bucha returned to the company perimeter and directed the defense. He encouraged his men throughout the night, directing artillery and airborne gunship fire onto enemy positions. He did everything he could to convince the enemy his force was larger than it was—throwing grenades from different positions at set times and changing the firing patterns along the edges of the perimeter. When part of his company was cut off, he ordered them to turn off their radios and feign death. He declined reinforcements from another company, believing it too dangerous for them to move to Delta Company's position. Using flashlights and in complete view of enemy snipers, Bucha ensured the evacuation of three helicopter loads of seriously wounded soldiers. At daybreak, he led a rescue party to the men who had been cut off. By then, the North Vietnamese had withdrawn, leaving behind over 150 dead.

Bucha commanded Delta Company for several more months before being reassigned to the brigade staff. After rotating home in late 1968, he spent the next year at the advanced armor officer's school at Fort Knox. Bucha then returned to West Point as an instructor, where he taught accounting from 1969 to 1972. While at West Point, he learned he would receive the Medal of Honor. Bucha considered declining the medal, believing he had not done anything special or particularly courageous. However, a conversation with a sergeant coordinating the award ceremony convinced Bucha that he should accept the decoration in recognition of his men. On May 14, 1970, Bucha received the Medal of Honor from President Richard M. Nixon.

Paul Bucha left the Army in 1972 and embarked on a successful career in business. He spent six years working around the world for Electronic Data Systems, managing various international business operations. In 1979, he entered the real estate business. Bucha formed his own company and continues as a real estate developer and consultant, devoting his work to environmentally or historically sensitive projects. Bucha has served as president of the Congressional Medal of Honor Society and as a director of various corporations and foundations. He still swims every day, is an advocate for veterans' rights, and lectures on ethics in business and government. In his public appearances, Bucha makes it clear that he wears the Medal of Honor for his men and all those who have served, especially those who died without recognition. In 2008, Bucha advised then presidential candidate Barack Obama on foreign policy issues. Bucha is the father of four children and resides with his wife in Ridgefield, Connecticut.

Alan M. Anderson

Further Reading

Collier, Peter, and Nick Del Calzo. *Medal of Honor: Portraits of Valor beyond the Call of Duty.* New York: Artisan, 2006.

Flanagan, E. M. *Rakkasans: The Combat History of the 187th Airborne Infantry.* New York: Presidio Press, 1997.

Jones, Robert. *101st Airborne Division.* 2nd ed. Paducah, KY: Turner Publishing, 2001.

Burke, Lloyd L.

Born: September 29, 1924
Died: June 1, 1999
Home State: Arkansas
Service: Army
Conflict: Korean War
Age at Time of Award: 27

Lloyd Leslie "Scooter" Burke was born on September 29, 1924, in the small town of Tichnor, Arkansas. Seen as too small for sports, Burke joined his high school band as a drummer. A talented and dedicated musician, Burke won a state drum solo championship while in school. Burke also served as the president of his high school's honor society and was named president of his senior class. Burke attended Henderson State College after graduating high school, but in 1943 he left college to enlist in the Army.

During World War II, Burke served in an engineering battalion in Italy. Upon his discharge in 1946, Burke returned to Henderson State to complete his degree.

While in college, Burke joined the ROTC, and after his graduation in 1950 he received a commission in the US Army as a second lieutenant. It was during this time that Burke also earned his nickname, Scooter. Burke reported for duty in Korea as an infantry officer on October 28, 1950. He joined a platoon in G Company, 2nd Battalion, 5th Cavalry Regiment of the 1st Cavalry Division. When the Chinese launched a counterattack across the Yalu River, Burke led his platoon to safety, an action for which he was awarded the Silver Star, the Distinguished Service Cross, and a Purple Heart.

In October 1951, the UN Command launched Operation Commando, the last major UN offensive of the Korean War. On October 28, 1951, Burke, now commanding Company G, and his men were attempting to cross the Yokkok-chon River but were pinned down by a well-entrenched Chinese force on Hill 200. G Company had been tasked with getting supplies to the front as other units of the 2nd Battalion attempted to take the hill. When the attack to take the hill stalled, G Company was called in to assist in the attack. Burke led his men toward the front and began an assault against enemy positions on the hill.

During the fight, Lieutenant Burke found himself on the hill positioned directly under a group of entrenched Chinese soldiers. The enemy began to drop grenades straight down on Burke, who managed to catch several grenades and throw them back at the Chinese before they could detonate. Burke's men quickly came up to support him, and they quickly took the enemy position. Burke's company soon came under fire from yet another enemy bunker. Burke personally scouted the enemy position and returned to his unit. Taking a machine gun and several drums of ammunition, Burke moved to a vantage point from which he could engage the enemy.

Once in position, Burke opened fire, killing the majority of the enemy soldiers in the bunker. The rest of G Company moved up to support Burke. The Chinese troops, caught in Burke's fire, soon attempted to abandon their bunker and retreat. Although wounded from shrapnel, Burke led his men forward, firing as he moved. Under his leadership, G Company succeeded in taking Hill 200 and routing the Chinese forces entrenched there. At the end of the battle, over 200 Chinese lay dead. Burke was credited with killing at least 100 of the enemy through his actions alone. For his leadership and personally bravery, Lieutenant Burke was awarded the Medal of Honor by President Harry S. Truman on April 11, 1952.

Following his service in Korea, Burke remained in the US Army. Assigned to the 1st Infantry Division, Burke reported to Vietnam in July 1965. Ten days after his arrival, a helicopter in which he was riding crash-landed, and Burke was injured by a Viet Cong grenade. He was evacuated to the United States and underwent a long period of hospitalization. After recovering from his wounds, Burke became the Army liaison to the House of Representatives, a post he held from 1967 to 1978. Burke retired from the Army as a colonel in 1978 with 35 years of service. After his retirement, Burke served as a president of the Congressional Medal of Honor Society. He also helped raise funds for the Korean War Memorial in Washington, D.C.

Lloyd Burke died on June 1, 1999, at his home in Hot Springs, Arkansas, at the age of 74. Burke passed away shortly after attending a Memorial Day ceremony honoring Medal of Honor winners in Indianapolis, Indiana. Burke, a veteran of three wars, was buried in Arlington National Cemetery.

John Sager

Further Reading

Jacobs, Bruce. *Korea's Heroes: The Medal of Honor Story*. New York: Berkeley Publishing, 1961.

Tillman, Barrett. *Heroes: U.S. Army Medal of Honor Recipients*. New York: The Berkley Group, 2006.

Bush, Robert Eugene

Born: October 4, 1926
Died: November 8, 2005
Home State: Washington
Service: Navy
Conflict: World War II
Age at Time of Award: 18

Robert Eugene Bush, a logger's son, was born on October 4, 1926, in Tacoma, Washington. His parents divorced when he was four, and he was raised by his mother, a nurse, in Raymond, Washington. Upon starting his junior year in high school, Bush gained his mother's permission to join the US Navy at the age of 17. After entering the Navy, he was assigned to the duty of a medical corpsman. To Bush, his placement was fate considering his mother ran the local hospital back in Raymond, where he had assisted with the disposal of limbs from amputee patients.

In 1944, after turning 18, Bush received orders to ship out to the Russell Islands in the Pacific as a corpsman with a rifle company in the US Marine Corps. He joined the 2nd Battalion, 5th Marines, 1st Marine Division two days before Christmas for training on Pavuvu Island. Then, in early 1945, Bush and his outfit participated in the invasion of Okinawa in the Ryukyu Islands.

On May 2, 1945, Bush's company was assaulting an enemy hill in an attempt to advance on Japanese forces well fortified on the island. Soon after the marines started the attack, the enemy opened fire on them. Nearly a dozen marines were killed or wounded, among them a lieutenant. With heavy machine gun fire and mortar rounds landing all around him, Bush ran from one marine to another in order to render aid. Eventually working his way to the lieutenant, Bush began to administer plasma in an attempt to revive him.

As Bush worked on the wounded lieutenant, the Japanese rushed toward them. Taking hold of the plasma bottle with one hand, Bush used his other hand to fire his .45 caliber automatic pistol at the charging Japanese. When his pistol ran out of ammunition, Bush grabbed the lieutenant's carbine and continued to fire at the enemy. Several Japanese grenades landed near the two men, piercing Bush's body with shrapnel and blinding him in one eye as he shielded the lieutenant. Despite his wounds, Bush continued firing at the Japanese force until he killed them all. After the area was secured from the enemy, Bush returned to caring for the wounded marines, refusing medical attention until finally collapsing on the way to the nearest aid station.

After several months in the hospital, Bush returned home to finish high school and marry his childhood sweetheart. Soon after their engagement, he received a call that he was to report to Washington, D.C. in order to receive the Medal of Honor for his courageous actions on Okinawa. Bush and his wife-to-be moved up the wedding date in order to make the trip their honeymoon. On October 5, 1945, President Harry Truman presented Robert E. Bush with the Medal of Honor only one day after Bush's 19th birthday.

Bush continued his education, enrolling at the University of Washington in order to study business. In 1951, he started his own lumber company, which eventually became a multimillion-dollar business. He also became very active in supporting veterans' causes and served as the president of the Congressional Medal of Honor Society. In 1998, Bush was honored with a monument in South Bend, Washington, depicting his heroic actions on Okinawa. The Navy Hospital in Twentynine Palms, California, and the clinic at Camp Courtney in Okinawa were also named in his honor. On November 8, 2005, Robert Bush died after a tough battle with cancer. Although he has passed, his actions of courage and bravery during the fighting on Okinawa will never be forgotten.

Thomas D. Lofton Jr.

Further Reading

Alexander, Joseph H. *The Final Campaign: Marines in the Victory on Okinawa.* Marines in World War II Commemorative Series. Washington, D.C.: Marine Historical Center, 1995.

Brokaw, Tom. *The Greatest Generation.* New York: Random House, 1998.

Collier, Peter, and Nick Del Calzo. *Medal of Honor: Portraits of Valor beyond the Call of Duty.* New York: Artisan, 2006.

Murphy, Edward F. *Heroes of WWII.* New York: Ballantine Books, 1990.

Butler, Smedley Darlington

Born: July 30, 1881
Died: June 21, 1940
Home State: Pennsylvania
Service: Marine Corps
Conflict: Mexican Campaign (Veracruz); Haiti Campaign, 1915
Age at Time of Award: 33, 36

Smedley Darlington Butler was born into a prominent Quaker family in West Chester, Pennsylvania, on July 30, 1881. His father, Thomas Stalker Butler, was a lawyer and, for 31 years, a US congressman. Butler attended the Haverford School but dropped out when the war with Spain began, joining the Marine Corps on April 8, 1898, while still 16. His first assignment was to the Philippines, and, in 1900, he participated in the expedition to Peking (Beijing) to crush the Boxer Rebellion, during which he was wounded twice. For a singular act of heroism helping wounded comrades during the campaign, Butler received the Marine Corps Brevet Medal, at the time the highest Marine Corps medal for officers, as well as a brevet promotion to captain. In 1908, he was diagnosed with a nervous condition and went on leave for nine months before returning to the Marine Corps.

Butler won two Medals of Honor as a major. The first was for his activities during the US occupation of Veracruz, Mexico, in 1914. Major Butler returned his medal to the Navy Department, explaining that he had done nothing to deserve the nation's highest decoration for valor. The Navy Department responded that he was not only to retain the medal, but also to wear it.

In 1915, the United States intervened in Haiti. On November 17, Major Butler led an attack that resulted in the capture of Fort Riviere from the Caco bandits. For that action, he received his second Medal of Honor. He was the only Marine Corps officer ever to win the Marine Corps Brevet Medal and two Medals of Honor for two different actions.

Much to his disappointment, Butler did not see combat during World War I. Advanced to temporary brigadier general in 1918, he commanded the debarkation depot of Camp Pontanezen, Brest, France, from October 1918 to July 1919. He was appointed permanent brigadier general on March 5, 1921. As commandant of the Marine Corps Barracks, Quantico, Virginia, from 1919 to 1924, Butler was an enthusiastic advocate of enlisted education.

During January 1924–December 1925, Butler was on temporary leave of absence from the Marine Corps to serve as director of the Department of Safety in Philadelphia, Pennsylvania, where he achieved considerable success in a full-scale assault on crime in the city. From 1927 to 1929, Butler commanded the Marine Expeditionary Force in China. He returned from China to be promoted to major general on July 5, 1929, and resumed the direction of Quantico, which he made the show-place of the Marine Corps.

Many expected Smedley Butler, as the senior Marine general, to be named commandant in 1930, but he failed to receive the appointment and retired from the Marine Corps at his own request on October 1, 1931. An outspoken opponent of US interventions abroad, Butler was one of the first to write about the military-industrial complex (*War Is a Racket*, 1935). A frequent speaker at meetings organized by pacifists and church groups, Butler spoke out against war profiteering and what he regarded as the growth of fascism in the United States. For a time in the mid-1930s, he acted as a spokesman of the American League against War and Fascism. Butler ran unsuccessfully as a candidate for the Republican nomination for the US Senate from Pennsylvania in 1932. In 1934, he claimed that a group of wealthy industrialists planned to overthrow the US government. Butler died in the Philadelphia Naval Hospital on June 21, 1940.

Spencer C. Tucker

Further Reading

Heinl, Robert Debs, Jr. *Soldiers of the Sea: The United States Marine Corps, 1775–1962.* Baltimore, MD: The Nautical & Aviation Publishing Company of America, 1991.

Millett, Allan R. *Semper Fidelis: The History of the United States Marine Corps.* New York: The Free Press, 1982.

Schmidt, Hans. *Maverick Marine: General Smedley D. Butler and the Contradictions of American Military History.* Lexington: University Press of Kentucky, 1987.

Venzon, Anne Ciprion. *General Smedley Darling Butler: The Letters of a Leatherneck, 1898–1931.* New York: Praeger, 1992.

Butterfield, Daniel

Born: October 31, 1831
Died: July 17, 1901
Home State: New York
Service: Army
Conflict: Civil War
Age at Time of Award: 31

Born on October 31, 1831, in Utica, New York, Daniel Butterfield attended school in New York City and then embarked on a business career. Shortly after the Civil War began in April 1861, he enlisted in the Union Army as a first sergeant and experienced a meteoric rise through the ranks. Two weeks after his induction, he was promoted to colonel of the 12th New York Infantry Regiment. He ably commanded his troops at the July 21, 1861, First Battle of Bull Run/Manassas. In July 1861, he received command of a brigade, and that September he was promoted to brigadier general of volunteers.

Butterfield then joined Maj. Gen. George B. McClellan and his Army of the Potomac for the Peninsula Campaign (March–August 1862). Butterfield was severely wounded on June 17, 1862, in the Battle of Gaines' Mill but had distinguished himself so greatly that he was later awarded the Medal of Honor for this action.

Butterfield became a division commander after the Second Battle of Bull Run/Manassas (August 29–30, 1862) and the Battle of Antietam (September 17, 1862). During the Battle of Fredericksburg (December 13, 1982), he was again advanced, this time to V Corps commander as a major general. His corps took part in the bloody assault on Marye's Heights. When Maj. Gen. Joseph Hooker took command of the Army of the Potomac in January 1863, he made Butterfield his chief of staff. In this position, which Butterfield continued to hold under Hooker's successor, Maj. Gen. George Gordon Meade, Butterfield made a number of enemies due to his officiousness and hot temper.

On July 3, 1863, Butterfield was struck by a shell fragment during the third day of the Battle of Gettysburg, forcing him to leave the Army to recover. In the fall of that same year, he returned to duty as chief of staff for Hooker, now commanding the Army of the Cumberland at Chattanooga, Tennessee. Butterfield then took command of the 3rd Division in XX Corps, which he led during the first half of the Atlanta Campaign (May 1–September 2, 1864), receiving brevet Regular Army appointments to brigadier and major general. Sickness then forced him to leave the Army to recuperate. He ended the war on special service at Vicksburg, Mississippi.

Daniel Butterfield remained in the Army after the war, and until 1870 he headed its recruiting service and was colonel of the 5th Infantry Regiment. He is known for having developed the haunting bugle call known as "Taps." He also developed the designs for the system of corps insignia for the Union Army. Butterfield died at his home in Cold Spring, New York, on July 17, 1901.

Jeannine M. Loftus

Further Reading

McPherson, James M. *The American Heritage New History of the Civil War.* New York: Metro Books, 2001.

Williams, David. *A People's History of the Civil War: Struggles for the Meaning of Freedom.* New York: New Press, 2005.

Cafferata, Hector A., Jr.

Born: November 2, 1929
Died:
Home State: New Jersey

Service: Marine Corps
Conflict: Korean War
Age at Time of Award: 21

Hector A. Cafferata Jr. was born on November 2, 1929, in New York City. He grew up and attended school in New Jersey and enlisted in the Marine Corps Reserve on February 15, 1948. Initially, Cafferata was assigned to the 21st Reserve Infantry Battalion located at Dover, New Jersey. However, following the outbreak of hostilities in Korea, he was called to active duty on September 6, 1950.

Given just two weeks precombat training at Camp Pendleton, California, Cafferata was assigned as a Marine rifleman with Company F, 2nd Battalion, 7th Marines, 1st Marine Division. During the early winter months of 1950, Cafferata and his company were part of the historic retreat of the 1st Marine Division at Chosin Reservoir. During an especially intense period of combat in and around Toktong Pass, Cafferata's company was attacked by communist Chinese forces intent on cutting off the line of retreat of the 1st Marine Division. Company F's mission was to deny the strategic Toktong Pass to the Chinese, which was critical to the successful withdrawal of the 1st Marine Division with all its men and equipment as they made their way toward the sea.

During the early morning hours of November 28, 1950, Cafferata's company position was suddenly and violently attacked by a large group of communist Chinese soldiers. Cafferata noted that the Chinese attack was so unexpected that he literally leaped out of his sleeping bag firing his weapon at his attackers at point-blank range. It was not until much later that Cafferata realized that he had been fighting for a significant period of time in freezing weather in just his socks and wearing only a light jacket. All other members of Cafferata's fire team had become casualties in this initial assault. This situation had created a temporary gap in Company F's interconnected defensive line. As a result, Cafferata was forced temporarily to fight alone with grenades and his own service weapon against charging communist Chinese soldiers intent on overrunning his position. Disregarding his own personal safety, Cafferata moved up and down the line, frequently exposing himself to direct enemy fire while he killed at least 15 of the enemy and wounded many others, forcing the Chinese to briefly withdraw their attacking force. His actions enabled other Company F reinforcements to reach his location just in time to blunt yet another assault by the enemy. The following morning, Cafferata continued the fight to keep the Chinese from breaking through his position when a hostile grenade was thrown into a shallow gully filled with his wounded comrades.

Unhesitatingly, Cafferata jumped into the gully, again under heavy enemy fire, and tossed out the grenade. However, the weapon blew up as he hurled it forward out of the gully. The resultant explosion severed part of one of his fingers, and he was grievously wounded in the left hand and arm. Nonetheless, his fellow wounded marines in the gully were not injured by the blast. Ignoring the pain of his wounds, Cafferata continued to fight on until wounded again by a sniper's bullet and forced to evacuate for further medical treatment.

Cafferata's "stouthearted and indomitable" conduct during the fighting at Toktong Pass and his "dauntless perseverance in the face of almost certain death" in "saving the lives of several of his fellow Marines" merited him a recommendation for the Medal of Honor. However, due to the nature of his wounds, Cafferata had to be medically evacuated to Japan in December 1950, and he returned to the United States in early 1951 for further treatment. He was retired from the Marine Corps on September 1, 1951. On November 24, 1952, Cafferata received the Medal of Honor from President Harry S. Truman during ceremonies at the White House.

Following the Korean War, Hector Cafferata worked in sales in Port Murray, New Jersey. He also once owned a bar called the Cliffside and later worked for the New Jersey State Fish and Game Department. In October 1988, Cafferata was selected to represent disabled veterans at the eighth Paralympics held in Seoul, Korea. As of 2010 he spends his time between family and home in New Jersey and Florida. An elementary school in Cape Coral, Florida, was named in his honor.

Charles P. Neimeyer

Further Reading

Collier, Peter, and Nick Del Calzo. *Medal of Honor: Portraits of Valor beyond the Call of Duty*. New York: Artisan, 2006.

Montross, Lynn. *The Chosin Reservoir Campaign: U.S. Marine Corps Operations in Korea, 1950–1953*. Nashville, TN: Battery Press, 1987.

Russ, Martin. *Breakout: The Chosin Reservoir Campaign, Korea 1950*. New York: Penguin Books, 2000.

Simmons, Edwin H. *Frozen Chosin: U.S. Marines at the Changjin Reservoir*. Washington, D.C.: Headquarters Marine Corps, History and Museums Division, 2002.

Smith, Larry. *Beyond Glory: Medal of Honor Heroes in Their Own Words—Extraordinary Stories of Courage from WWII to Vietnam*. New York: W. W. Norton, 2003.

Carney, William H.

Born: February 29, 1840
Died: December 8, 1908
Home State: Massachusetts
Service: Army
Conflict: Civil War
Age at Time of Award: 23

Born a slave in Virginia on February 29, 1840, William H. Carney attended a secret school conducted by a local minister and learned to read and write. Later, he was emancipated when his master died. He moved to New Bedford, Massachusetts, and was studying for the ministry when he learned that the first regiment of African American soldiers was being formed to fight for the Union. President Abraham Lincoln had issued the Emancipation Proclamation on January 1, 1863, and, for the first time, African Americans were being encouraged to enlist in the Union Army. Carney joined the 54th Massachusetts Colored Infantry's C Company, saying he "could best serve my God by serving my Country and my oppressed brothers."

In July of that same year, the 54th Massachusetts spearheaded the assault on Fort Wagner in South Carolina, the first real test of the young African Americans who had volunteered for service in the Union Army. When the company's flag bearer was fatally shot, 23-year-old Carney threw down his rifle and grabbed the flag before it fell and then carried it throughout the remainder of the battle.

Although he suffered multiple gunshot wounds in the head, chest, legs, and one arm, Carney carried the flag to safety when the 54th was driven back by a Confederate counterattack. Seeing his predicament, a soldier from another regiment offered to take the flag so Carney could seek medical aid. Carney replied, "No one but a member of the 54th should carry the colors!"

Later, Carney miraculously carried the regiment's flag into camp after the battle to the rousing cheers of his battered comrades. He responded, "Boys, I only did my duty. The flag never touched the ground." He then fell to the ground in a dead faint, weak from the wounds he had received. For these feats, he became the first African American to perform action in combat that resulted in the awarding of the Medal of Honor, but he would not receive the medal until long after the action at Fort Wagner.

The following year, Carney was discharged due to the disabilities of his wounds. He returned to New Bedford and worked as a mail carrier and later as a messenger in the Massachusetts legislature in Boston. On May 23, 1900, nearly 40 years after his valor during the Civil War, Carney was awarded the nation's highest honor for heroism, the Medal of Honor. Though by this time several other African Americans had already received the award for heroism during the Civil War and the Indian Campaigns, Sergeant Carney's action at Fort Wagner was the first to merit the award.

William Carney died at his home in New Bedford on December 8, 1908, and is buried in Oak Grove Cemetery there. His final resting place bears a distinctive stone—an engraved white marble stone with the gold image of the Medal of Honor, a tribute to a courageous soldier and the flag he loved so dearly.

James H. Willbanks

AFRICAN AMERICANS AND THE MEDAL OF HONOR

Since the founding of the Medal of Honor, 87 African Americans have earned this decoration. In the first conflict during which it was available, the Civil War, 25 African Americans earned the Medal of Honor—18 of whom were soldiers and the remaining 7 sailors. Oddly enough, there seems to have been little racial prejudice in the awarding of the Medal of Honor during that conflict.

Interestingly, although the first African American whose actions resulted in the Medal of Honor, William H. Carney, performed his actions in 1863, he did not receive his decoration until 1900. On the other hand, Robert Blake became the first African American to actually be awarded the Medal of Honor in 1864. During this earlier period of the Medal of Honor, it was not uncommon for individuals to recommend themselves for the medal even years after their actions. Soldiers and sailors could use official reports or solicit written testimony from living witnesses to their actions. The most extreme example of awarding the medal years after the action was Andrew Jackson Smith, an African American soldier who was not awarded his Medal of Honor for actions in 1864 until 2001.

The post–Civil War period from 1866 to the outbreak of the Spanish-American War in 1898 found the US Army heavily engaged in combat with Native Americans on the frontier. During this time, African Americans made up the enlisted and noncommissioned officers of four regiments in the regular US Army—the 9th and 10th Cavalry regiments and the 24th and 25th Infantry regiments. As a group, these African American soldiers were nicknamed "Buffalo Soldiers" by the Native Americans they fought.

During this post–Civil War period, 18 Medals of Honor were awarded to African Americans—14 to "Buffalo Soldiers" and the remaining 4 to Seminole Indians of African descent who served as US Army Indian scouts. In addition, at least 4 white officers were awarded the medal while serving alongside African American soldiers. Also during this era, 8 African American sailors earned the medal for saving the lives of drowning shipmates. One sailor, Robert A. Sweeney, was the only African American to earn the Medal of Honor twice—both times for rescuing a shipmate in danger of drowning.

Despite lasting less than four months, the Spanish-American War was long enough for six African Americans—five soldiers from the 10th Cavalry Regiment and one sailor from the US Navy—to earn the Medal of Honor. Attitudes toward both African Americans and the Medal of Honor began to change in the early 20th century. Fewer medals were awarded to African Americans, and their roles in the military also started to change. For instance, from the Civil War through the Spanish-American War, African Americans were able to serve as regular sailors aboard US Navy vessels. However, as the 20th century progressed, the Navy increasingly "encouraged" African Americans to serve as stewards and cooks in ship kitchens. This unofficial policy culminated when African Americans were completely barred from enlisting in the Navy between 1919 and 1932, and, when enlistments resumed, African Americans were specifically prohibited from any jobs other than cooks and stewards. Attitudes toward the Medal of Honor also changed with the creation of other decorations for valor. As a result, the medal was only earned for the most extreme acts of heroism.

Despite the great accomplishments and fame of the "Harlem Hellfighters" and other African American units in World War I, the Army's attitude toward African

American soldiers had definitely changed. The African American 93rd Infantry Division was loaned out to the French Army for the duration of the war, and, although the French were generous in decorating these soldiers, their own nation was not. Only one African American soldier, Freddie Stowers, earned the Medal of Honor during World War I, and, though recommended for the medal at the time, his decoration was not approved until 1990.

Unfortunately, World War II followed the same pattern as World War I; due to widespread racism and discrimination, the nation failed to recognize African American valor, and no Medals of Honor were earned by African Americans during the war. Finally, in 1993, a special study was commissioned to investigate racial discrimination in the awarding of medals in World War II; the study recommended that several African American Distinguished Service Cross recipients be upgraded to the Medal of Honor. On January 13, 1997, seven Medals of Honor were awarded to World War II African American soldiers for their heroic actions. Unfortunately, only one of the seven men, Vernon J. Baker, was still alive by the time of the award, as the other six men had died in the intervening years or had been killed in action during the war.

By the outbreak of the Korean War in 1950, the Armed Forces had finally begun to desegregate. However, even though President Truman signed Executive Order 9981 in 1948, the last US Army units were not integrated until 1954. Two African Americans, both of whom served with the still-segregated 24th Infantry Regiment, earned the Medal of Honor during the Korean War. When the United States entered the Vietnam War, African Americans served on a fairly even footing with other Americans. This is confirmed by the fact that 20 African Americans were awarded the Medal of Honor for actions in the Vietnam War.

No African Americans have been awarded the Medal of Honor since the Vietnam War, but this is not surprising since only 10 Medals of Honor have been awarded for actions during this period.

Alexander M. Bielakowski

Further Reading

Hanna, Charles W. *African American Recipients of the Medal of Honor: A Biographical Dictionary, Civil War through Vietnam War*. Jefferson, NC: McFarland, 2002.

Owens, Ron. *Medal of Honor: Historical Facts and Figures*. Paducah, KY: Turner Publishing, 2004.

Cavaiani, Jon R.

Born: August 2, 1943
Died:
Home State: California
Service: Army
Conflict: Vietnam War
Age at Time of Award: 27

Born in Royston, England, on August 2, 1943, Jon R. Cavaiani came to the United States with his parents in 1947 at the age of four. Though he was originally classified 4-F for medical reasons, Cavaiani managed to enlist in the US Army at Fresno, California, in 1968. He became a naturalized citizen shortly after enlisting. Cavaiani volunteered for the Special Forces and, after completion of his training, was sent to Vietnam in June 1970.

Staff Sergeant Cavaiani was assigned to Military Assistance Command, Vietnam's Studies and Observation Group (SOG) Command and Control North (CCN) and served as advisor to Montagnards in extreme northwestern South Vietnam as part of the Vietnam Training Advisory Group. In June of 1971, Cavaiani commanded a small garrison at a radio relay station known as Outpost Hickory. The base, actually an important radio monitoring post, was deep inside enemy-dominated territory, at least 20 miles from friendly firebases Fuller and Carroll. Cavaiani commanded the base—held by 27 Americans, including a squad of American Rangers and 67 indigenous troops—though Cavaiani was outranked by several others. An enemy attack by North Vietnamese Army (NVA) regulars was believed imminent.

On the morning of June 4, a surprise attack was prevented when Cavaiani spotted enemy movement and opened fire first with an M-60 machine gun. He then led the fight to hold the camp against a superior force throughout the day. Air strikes were called in, but when the fight appeared lost, Cavaiani requested evacuation helicopters. He carried a wounded American captain to the helipad and even took the time to write a medal commendation for an American soldier. Though the attack appeared to be faltering in later afternoon, the enemy threat caused the evacuation to be called off at around 4:30 p.m., before all the remaining men were removed.

During the evening, Cavaiani organized a defense around the helipad with the remaining 25 men. The group held off at least eight separate attacks until the helipad was finally overrun after midnight. A circling AC-119 gunship refused Cavaiani's final request to fire into friendly positions. Cavaiani, now wounded, ordered his remaining men to try to escape and evade, but he and another remaining American sergeant, James Jones, fought on from a bunker. When the badly wounded Jones left the bunker and attempted to surrender, he was killed by the NVA. Cavaiani chose to try and fake his death in the bunker, which was later burned by the enemy. Early the next morning, June 5, Cavaiani managed to escape into the jungle, though he had suffered severe burns and numerous wounds. After eluding the enemy for 11 days, Cavaiani had nearly reached the safety of Camp Fuller when he was captured. He later said it was an old man with a bolt-action rifle that stopped him from reaching friendly lines.

Several of those who had been last rescued from Hickory had reported his death, and Cavaiani was reported as missing in action. A year later, his name was released over the Viet Cong "Liberation Radio" net as a prisoner. He was moved northward to the prisoner-of-war camp known as Plantation Gardens for interrogation, then on to the Zoo, and was finally transferred to the infamous Hanoi Hilton in December of 1972. Cavaiani remained a prisoner until he was released in accordance with the Paris Peace Accords on March 27, 1973. Shortly thereafter, Cavaiani learned that he had been recommended for the Medal of Honor, which was presented to him on December 12, 1974, by President Gerald R. Ford.

Jon Cavaiani remained in active military service. Among his variety of postings, Cavaiani was an instructor at Fort Bragg, served with both the 10th and 11th Special Forces groups, and was assigned to the Allied Staff in West Berlin. His final posting was as a ROTC instructor at University of California-Davis. He retired from active service on May 31, 1990, at the rank of sergeant major. Cavaiani's other decorations include the Legion of Merit, the Bronze Star, and the Purple Heart. As of 2010 he resides in California.

Thomas Dwight Veve

Further Reading

Collier, Peter, and Nick Del Calzo. *Medal of Honor: Portraits of Valor beyond the Call of Duty*. New York: Artisan, 2006.

Coy, Jimmie Dean. *Valor: A Gathering of Eagles*. Mobile, AL: Evergreen Press, 2003.

Plaster, John L. *SOG*. New York: Simon & Schuster, 1997.

Steinman, Ron. *The Soldiers' Story: Vietnam in Their Own Words*. New York: Barnes & Noble, 2002.

Chamberlain, Joshua L.

Born: September 8, 1828
Died: February 24, 1914
Home State: Maine
Service: Army
Conflict: Civil War
Age at Time of Award: 35

Joshua Lawrence Chamberlain was born on September 8, 1828, in Brewer, Maine. He attended Bowdoin College in Brunswick, Maine, and graduated in 1852. An aspiring minister, he later earned a master's degree from Bangor Theological Seminary. He then returned to Bowdoin as a professor of rhetoric and modern languages. When the Civil War began, Chamberlain accepted a commission as a lieutenant colonel of the 20th Maine Volunteers Infantry Regiment, which became part of the Army of the Potomac.

Chamberlain and the 20th Maine were present at, but did not participate in, the September 17, 1862, Battle of Antietam, having formed part of the reserve held back by Maj. Gen. George McClellan. The unit engaged Confederate forces three days later at Shepherdstown (in western Virginia), where Chamberlain had the first of six horses shot out from under him during the war. Chamberlain then fought in the Battle of Fredericksburg (December 11–15, 1862) and the Battle of Chancellorsville (May 1–4, 1863). He was promoted to colonel that same month. He then took part in the Battle of Gettysburg, beginning on July 1, 1863.

At Gettysburg on July 2, Chamberlain was assigned to Little Round Top, one of two small, critical hills on the Union's left flank. If the Confederates could control these, they could enfilade the Union line. Immediately realizing its critical importance, Chamberlain was determined to hold Little Round Top. After turning back several Confederate charges that day and extending his line, and with ammunition running low, Chamberlain ordered a downhill bayonet charge. This action shocked the Confederates and forced their retreat. Chamberlain was wounded in the action. For his heroism and tenacity, he would be awarded the Medal of Honor 30 years later, on August 11, 1893.

Chamberlain was promoted to brigadier general in June 1864 and brevetted to major general in March 1865. He participated in the Spotsylvania Court House Campaign (May 7–18, 1864), the Second Battle of Cold Harbor (June 1–3, 1864), and the Petersburg Campaign (June 15, 1864–April 3, 1865). During another intrepid assault at Petersburg in June 1864, he was wounded for a fourth time, this time nearly fatally. Defying all odds, he recovered sufficiently to return to duty. For his actions, he secured a brevet promotion to brigadier general in June 1864.

Upon the surrender of Gen. Robert E. Lee's Army of Northern Virginia at Appomattox, Virginia, Gen. Ulysses S. Grant selected Chamberlain to preside over the ceremony and receive the Confederate surrender on April 12, 1865. As the Confederate troops passed by and laid down their arms, Chamberlain saluted them. Although criticized by some in the Union for this, he was remembered in the South as one of the most gallant soldiers of the Union Army.

After the war, Joshua Chamberlain served as a Republican governor of Maine (1866–1870) and as president of Bowdoin College (1871–1883). He died in Portland, Maine, on February 24, 1914. Chamberlain was a central figure in Michael Shaara's 1975 Pulitzer Prize–winning historical novel *The Killer Angels*, which treats the Battle of Gettysburg.

Claude G. Berube

Further Reading

Desjardin, Thomas A. *Stand Firm Ye Boys from Maine: The 20th Maine and the Gettysburg Campaign.* New York: Oxford University Press, 1995.

Perry, Mark. *Conceived in Liberty: Joshua Chamberlain, William Oates, and the American Civil War.* New York: Viking, 1997.

Wallace, Willard R. *Soul of the Lion: A Biography of General Joshua L. Chamberlain.* New York: Thomas Nelson and Sons, 1960.

Childers, Ernest

Born: February 1, 1918
Died: March 17, 2005
Home State: Oklahoma
Service: Army
Conflict: World War II
Age at Time of Award: 25

A Creek Indian, Ernest L. Childers was born in Broken Arrow, Oklahoma, on February 1, 1918. Raised on the family farm, he learned to shoot after his father, a lawyer, died and Childers became responsible for providing food—in the form of rabbits and other wild game—for his mother and four brothers. After graduating from the Chilocco Indian Agricultural School in north-central Oklahoma, Childers joined the Oklahoma National Guard in 1937 to earn extra money for his family. Mobilized with the rest of the National Guard in 1940, his unit, the 180th Infantry Regiment, 90th Infantry Brigade, became part of the 45th Infantry Division.

In early September 1943, Childers, by then a second lieutenant who had already seen combat in Sicily, arrived on the beaches of Salerno on the mainland of Italy. On September 22, while leading a patrol of eight men near Oliveto, he broke his ankle when he jumped into a shell crater while under mortar fire. Attempting to crawl to a nearby aid station, Childers saw the station destroyed by the same mortars that had indirectly caused his injury. He then returned to his men and ordered them to cover him as he crawled toward those German positions most likely responsible for the mortar fire.

Despite the covering fire provided his men, Childers was fired upon by two German snipers located in a farmhouse. He dispatched each of them in turn and continued to crawl toward the German positions. Since he could not stand and ascertain his exact position, Childers did not realize that he had luckily crawled around to the side of two German machine gun nests. When the first German position noticed him, they attempted to swing their gun around to engage him, but Childers shot first, killing the gunner and assistant gunner. The second German position was better protected, so he threw a large rock into it to flush out the gunners. Again, his luck held out, as the Germans mistook the rock for a hand grenade. As the Germans jumped out of their position, Childers killed one while a member of his patrol shot the second. Childers continued to advance up the hill toward a German observation post located in another farmhouse. At the top of the hill, Childers single-handedly captured a German artillery observer even though he was out of ammunition at the time.

After recovering from his wounds in North Africa, Childers returned to his unit and fought in the Battle of Anzio, where he was again wounded. While recovering from this second wound at a hospital in Allied-occupied Naples, he was ordered to report to Lt. Gen. Jacob Devers, commander of the 6th Army Group. Childers assumed he was in trouble but could not understand why. Instead, he discovered that he had been awarded the Medal of Honor. On July 13, 1944, Childers was officially presented the medal by Devers in Naples; he was the first Native American to earn the medal since the Indian Wars of the 1800s. Childers was later sent to Washington, D.C., where he met with President Franklin D. Roosevelt.

Childers decided to remain in the US Army after World War II. Later postings included the Jungle Operations Training Center in Panama and US Army Cold Weather and Mountain School in Alaska before his retirement in 1965 as a lieutenant colonel with 28 years of total service.

After the terrorist attacks of September 11, 2001, Childers wrote a widely circulated statement urging Americans not to take their outrage out on Arab Americans.

"Even though I have darker skin than some Americans, that doesn't mean I'm any less patriotic than any other American," he wrote. "I am appalled that people who call themselves 'Americans' are attacking and killing other Americans simply because of their hair and skin color."

Ernest Childers died at age 87 on March 17, 2005, and was buried in the same town where he had been born—Broken Arrow, Oklahoma.

Alexander M. Bielakowski

Further Reading

Collier, Peter, and Nick Del Calzo. *Medal of Honor: Portraits of Valor beyond the Call of Duty.* New York: Artisan, 2006.

Owens, Ron. *Medal of Honor: Historical Facts and Figures.* Paducah, KY: Turner Publishing, 2004.

Tillman, Barrett. *Heroes: U.S. Army Medal of Honor Recipients.* New York: The Berkley Group, 2006.

Cody, William F.

Born: February 26, 1846
Died: January 10, 1917
Home State: Kansas
Service: Scout

Conflict: Indian Campaigns
Age at Time of Award: 26

William F. Cody was born in Iowa Territory on February 26, 1846. About 1853, Cody's family moved near Leavenworth, Kansas. His father's outspoken abolitionist views brought him into violent conflict with pro-slavery radicals, and he was assaulted and stabbed by an angry mob while giving a speech. Young William, age 9, helped rescue his father, who never fully recovered, and from the age of 11 Bill became the principal breadwinner for the family. He was employed as a "boy extra" on the overland freight lines of Russell, Waddell, and Majors, where he demonstrated early the acumen, grit, and marksmanship that ultimately made him famous.

At age 12, on a freight run to Utah, Cody single-handedly killed an Indian warrior attempting to ambush another teamster. At 14, he joined the Pony Express and immediately became one of its boldest and most celebrated riders. In 1861, he attempted to join the Union Army but was refused because he was too young. Instead, he worked as a teamster, supplying distant Fort Laramie until finally enlisting as a private in the 7th Kansas Volunteer Cavalry in 1863. He became a scout operating in western Missouri and Arkansas but saw little combat. After 1865, he undertook a variety of odd jobs and entrepreneurial schemes without much success until, in 1868, he was hired as scout/hunter for the Kansas Pacific Railroad then under construction. In the space of four months, in addition to other duties, he killed almost 4,700 bison, earning his sobriquet, Buffalo Bill. His skills brought him to the attention of the Army, and he was hired as a civilian scout.

From 1868 to 1872, Cody was continually engaged scouting for the Army, much longer than most white scouts and remarkable given the poor pay, arduous conditions, and hazards of the work. He soon came to the attention of the department commander, Gen. Philip Sheridan, when, after several other experienced scouts had refused, he volunteered to carry dispatches from Fort Leavenworth to Fort Laramie, a distance of 700 miles, over a route where several riders had disappeared and were presumed dead. He quickly became relied upon for the most dangerous

William F. Cody, US Army Scout (New York Historical Society).

missions and on numerous occasions saved other detachments and dispatch riders from ambush. As a reward, he was appointed chief of scouts for the 5th and later 3rd Cavalry, where he demonstrated a singular and invaluable understanding of the Plains Indians and earned a reputation for reckless courage in several engagements.

Although Cody's Medal of Honor is often mistakenly attributed to the battle of Summit Springs in 1869 or to his famous duel with "Yellow Hand" in 1876, the date of the award citation, April 26, 1872, indicates that it was based on a poorly documented engagement on the North Platte River. Three other soldiers, all of Company B, 3rd Cavalry, also received the medal, and all were cited for "Gallantry in Action."

The only known descriptions of the event are from Cody himself, whose versions vary. Cody appears to have been leading an advanced detachment of about 40 troopers when they encountered and were attacked by a much larger force of Sioux. Company B conducted an aggressive defense under Cody's direction for several hours until the Sioux withdrew at the advance of the main body. Casualties for either side are unknown.

By the turn of the century, Buffalo Bill Cody was perhaps the most famous man in the world due to his genius for showmanship and self-promotion. So exaggerated were his exploits by publicist Ned "Buntline" Judson and other pulp writers and stage producers that it was inevitable more sober-minded observers would question the validity of Cody's Medal of Honor.

The ambiguity of both the citation and Cody's status as civilian contractor contributed to the award being revoked by the Miles Commission in 1916, which significantly raised the standards for award of the medal. Cody, in declining health and diminished circumstances, made no public objection. He died less than a year later, on January 10, 1917.

The Medal of Honor was restored to William Cody and five other civilian scouts by a special act of Congress in 1989. Although Buffalo Bill's fame and place in American legend probably made the return of his award inevitable, it can be confidently stated that, by the standards then prevailing, he earned his medal as much as any soldier in the West. What is clear, despite the hoopla and controversy surrounding Cody's life, is that Cody was a frontiersman of extraordinary ability and courage who commanded the genuine respect of his peers in the hard world of the 19th-century American West.

Edward L. Bowie

Further Reading

Cody, William F. *The Life of Hon. William F. Cody Known as Buffalo Bill the Famous Hunter, Scout, and Guide. An Autobiography.* Lincoln: University of Nebraska Press, 1978.

Wetmore, Helen Cody. *The Last of the Great Scouts: The Life Story of Col. William Cody "Buffalo Bill."* Lincoln: University of Nebraska Press, 1899.

Cohn, Abraham

Born: June 17, 1832
Died: June 2, 1897
Home State: New Hampshire
Service: Army
Conflict: Civil War
Age at Time of Award: 33

Abraham Cohn was born June 17, 1832, in the East Prussian town of Guttentag. The former University of Berlin medical student and self-described teacher immigrated to New York at the age of 28 at a time when many Jews fled Germany during the mid-19th century. Living in New York at the outbreak of war between the North and the South, Cohn enlisted with the 68th New York Regiment as a private until poor health conditions forced him out of the Army. In January 1864, he reenlisted as a private in the 6th New Hampshire and served with that regiment for the remainder of the war.

Cohn rose through the ranks quickly after joining the 6th New Hampshire volunteer regiment. By March 1864, less than three months after his reenlistment, he was promoted to sergeant major. The following May, as part of Gen. Ulysses S. Grant's campaign in Virginia, Cohn's regiment guarded the rebuilt railroad running from Manassas Junction to Rappahannock Station. Not long afterward, fighting between Union and Confederate troops ensued in that region in what became known as the Battle of the Wilderness, the first of several battles in General Grant's Overland Campaign that eventually led to Gen. Robert E. Lee's surrender the following spring.

On May 6, Confederate forces under Gen. James Longstreet arrived near Plank Road just in time to repulse a Union attack that had pushed Confederate forces back more than a mile earlier that morning. Longstreet's successful counterattack allowed the Confederates to regain some of the ground they lost and created confusion among Federal soldiers from Maj. Gen. James Wadsworth's V Corps, which included Cohn's 6th New Hampshire.

The situation worsened after Wadsworth fell with a fatal head wound while rallying his soldiers to counter the Confederate attack. Because of Wadsworth's death and the Confederate advance, most V Corps soldiers immediately retreated from the battle. At that moment, Sergeant Major Cohn rallied soldiers from various units to stand and resist the Southern offensive, coaxing and coercing many of them from leaving the battlefield altogether. Cohn's motley group of "disorganized and fleeing troops of different regiments" eventually formed a defensive line that stopped the Confederate assault and created a standstill between the two armies.

Cohn's actions almost three months later along the Petersburg lines also factored into his receiving the Medal of Honor. Following the Union's failed attempt to explode Confederate fortifications on the Petersburg lines on July 30, 1864, otherwise known as the Battle of the Crater, Confederate forces regrouped and began firing on the helpless Union soldiers, who fell and wound up trapped in the crater. Despite suffering a severe shoulder injury, Cohn still managed to deliver orders to the advanced IX Corps generals under exposure to the heavy Confederate fire. According to the citation for his award, Cohn responded "bravely and coolly" despite the Union's vulnerable position.

Cohn's regiment mustered out July 17, 1865, almost three months after Gen. Robert E. Lee's surrender at Appomattox Courthouse. Cohn left the Army as a first lieutenant before disbanding; he had been one of an estimated 9,000 Jewish soldiers who fought for the Union Army and was one of only six to earn the Medal of Honor for his actions during the Civil War.

Following the war, Abraham Cohn moved to New York City, where he was active in business affairs. He died June 2, 1897, at the age of 65, leaving behind his wife and eight children. He was buried in New York's Cypress Hills Cemetery.

Jeremy Prichard

Further Reading

Shaffer, Duane E. *Men of Granite: New Hampshire's Soldiers in the Civil War.* Columbia: University of South Carolina Press, 2008.

Slotkin, Richard. *No Quarter: The Battle of the Crater, 1864.* New York: Random House, 2009.

Cole, Robert G.

Born: March 19, 1915
Died: September 18, 1944
Home State: Texas
Service: Army
Conflict: World War II
Age at Time of Award: 29

Robert George Cole was born at Fort Sam Houston in San Antonio, Texas, on March 19, 1915, the son of an Army doctor. He graduated from Thomas Jefferson High School in San Antonio in 1933 and joined the US Army on July 1, 1934. On June 26, 1935, he was honorably discharged to accept an appointment to the US Military Academy at West Point.

Cole graduated with the class of 1939 and returned home to marry Allie Mae Wilson. He was appointed a second lieutenant to the 15th Infantry at Fort Lewis, Washington, in 1939 and remained there until his transfer to the 501st Parachute Infantry Regiment at Fort Benning, Georgia. In March 1941, he received his jump wings and rapidly advanced through the ranks at Fort Benning. On D-Day, June 6, 1944, the date of his unit's first combat jump, Cole was a lieutenant colonel commanding the 3rd Battalion of the 502nd Parachute Infantry Regiment.

After being in division reserve, Cole's battalion guarded the right flank of the 101st Airborne during the attempt to take the approaches to Carentan, France. On the afternoon of June 10, Cole led 400 men of his battalion single file down a long causeway, with marshes at either side, later to be known as Purple Heart Lane. A hedgerow behind a large farmhouse on the right was occupied by well dug-in German troops. At the far end of the causeway was the last of four bridges over the Douve River flood plain. Beyond the last bridge was Carentan, which the 101st had been ordered to seize to affect a linkup with the 29th Infantry Division coming off Omaha Beach.

Cole's entire unit was suddenly pinned down by intense and withering enemy rifle, machine gun, mortar, and artillery fire placed upon them from well-prepared and heavily fortified positions within 150 yards of the foremost elements. The devastating and unceasing enemy fire prevented any move and inflicted numerous casualties. Several attempts to force the position proved fruitless, and the battalion took up defensive positions for the night.

At dawn the next morning, after having taken more casualties from German mortars and a strafing attack by two German aircraft, Lieutenant Colonel Cole called for artillery support, which failed to dislodge the German defenders. Cole then called for smoke on the dug-in Germans and issued orders to fix bayonets. With utter disregard for his own safety and completely ignoring the enemy fire, he rose to his feet in front of his battalion and, with drawn pistol, shouted to his men to follow him in the assault. Catching up a fallen man's rifle and bayonet, he charged on and led the remnants of his battalion across the bullet-swept open ground and into the enemy position, engaging at close range and in some cases fighting hand-to-hand. The German survivors retreated, taking more casualties as they withdrew.

The assault, which came to be known as Cole's Charge, proved costly, as 130 of Cole's 265 men became casualties. With his battalion exhausted, Cole called for the 1st Battalion to pass through his lines and continue the attack.

However, they were also severely depleted by mortar fire crossing bridge #4 such that they took up positions with 3rd Battalion rather than proceeding. On the edge of Carentan, they were subjected to strong counterattacks by the German 6th Parachute Regiment during the morning and afternoon. At the height of the attack, at approximately 1900 hours, Cole's artillery observer managed to break through radio jamming and called down a concentration by the entire Corps artillery that broke up the attacks for good. Lieutenant Colonel Cole was recommended for a Medal of Honor for his actions that day but did not live to receive it.

On September 18, 1944, during Operation Market Garden, Cole called for air support and was in the process of laying out identification panels when his life was ended by a German sniper. Cole's widow accepted his Medal of Honor at a presentation ceremony at Fort Sam Houston on October 30, 1944. Along with Cole's wife was his two-year-old son, a son Cole had never seen in person. Lieutenant Colonel Cole is buried at Netherlands American Cemetery and Memorial in Margraten, the Netherlands.

Robert G. Cole High School at Fort Sam Houston is named after Robert Cole, as is a housing area, Cole Park, in Fort Campbell, Kentucky. On September 18, 2009, a monument was unveiled in Best in the Netherlands near the place of his death. Cole's son was present at the ceremony along with members and veterans of the 101st Airborne Division.

Jason M. Sokiera

Further Reading

Ambrose, Stephen E. *Citizen Soldiers.* New York: Simon & Schuster, 1997.

Murphy, Edward F. *Heroes of World War II.* Novato, CA: Presidio Press, 1990.

Ryan, Cornelius. *A Bridge Too Far.* New York: Simon & Schuster, 1974.

Ryan, Cornelius. *The Longest Day.* New York: Simon & Schuster, 1959.

US Senate. Committee on Veterans Affairs. *Medal of Honor Recipients, 1863–1973.* Washington, D.C.: Government Printing Office, 1973.

Craft, Clarence B.

Born: September 23, 1921
Died: March 28, 2002
Home State: California
Service: Army
Conflict: World War II
Age at Time of Award: 23

Clarence B. Craft was born on September 23, 1921, in San Bernardino, California. He joined the Army in Santa Ana, California. After completing basic training in the United States, he became an army truck driver. By May 31, 1945, Craft was serving as a private first class with G Company in the 382nd Infantry Regiment of the US 96th Infantry Division.

The 96th Infantry Division, known as the Deadeyes, was part of the US Army's XXIV Corps. It took part in two major campaigns in the Pacific War—first with Gen. Douglas A. MacArthur's leapfrogging campaign in the Southwest Pacific Theater. In October of 1944, the 96th Infantry Division fought through fierce Japanese resistance in the jungles and mountains of Leyte Island in the Philippines. In 1945, the XXIV Infantry Corps was transferred to the Central Pacific Theater as part of the newly formed US 10th Army.

In April of 1945, the US 10th Army, commanded by Gen. Simon B. Buckner Jr., invaded Okinawa. The 10th Army consisted of the US Army's XXIV Corps (96th Infantry Division, 7th Infantry Division, and 77th Infantry Division) and the US Marine III Amphibious Corps (1st Marine Division, 6th Marine Division, and 2nd Marine Division).

After meeting slight resistance on April 1, 1945 (L-Day), the US Marines turned north, while the US Army wheeled south. The Japanese Army decided to defend the southern portion of the island. Japanese soldiers spent months building several lines of defense in depth. These positions, built upon a series of hills and larger hill masses, would cost American soldiers and eventually marines thousands of lives over a three-month period. One of those death traps was the Shuri Line.

In late May 1945, after 12 days of fierce fighting, the 96th Infantry Division was stalled on the Shuri Line. Fanatical Japanese resistance, defensive topography, foul weather, and large numbers of causalities were the enemies of the Deadeyes.

The 96th Division needed replacement troops for the front line. Pfc. Clarence Craft was transferred from the motor pool to Company G. The mild-mannered Californian, however, took to combat with great ease.

On May 31, 1945, G Company commander tapped Craft and five other US soldiers to probe the area near Hen Hill. The Japanese had dug into the reverse slope of Hen Hill and waited for the Americans in a six-foot-deep trench. As Craft's patrol ascended Hen Hill, the soldiers were hit with a volley of rifle fire, machine gun bursts, and hand grenades. Several soldiers were wounded in the attack. Immediately, Craft initiated a one-man assault on Japanese positions, killing the enemy with rifle fire as he climbed the hill mass. Craft fired his rifle and threw hand grenades into the trench on the reverse slope, killing dozens of stunned Japanese soldiers. Craft motioned to his fellow soldiers to join him and continued his attack on the disorganized enemy. Pfc. Walter Hilik and Pvt. Joseph W. Kronbau assisted Craft by forming a chain to pass several cases of hand grenades and ammunition to the top of Hen Hill during his one-man battle with the Japanese Army.

Soon, Craft and his comrades were joined by the rest of G Company. He then moved forward and knocked out a machine gun position and sealed many Japanese soldiers inside a cave with a satchel charge. Craft was credited with killing at least 25 Japanese soldiers during his fearless assault on Hen Hill. Within hours, the 96th Infantry Division had advanced 1,200 yards. By nightfall, Hen, Hector, and Bard Hills fell to the Deadeyes, assuring the collapse of the eastern sector of Shuri Line.

Private First Class Craft's exploits that day on Hen Hill were among the most unique and extraordinary of a battle considered by many military historians the most brutal battle of the Pacific War. After the war, Craft was invited to the White House, where he was presented the Medal of Honor by President Harry S. Truman on November 1, 1945.

Craft's gallantry was forever etched into Deadeye and US Army lore by combat artist Technical Sergeant Arthur Foremen. Foreman's vivid watercolor painting *The Hero of Hen Hill* was published, among a dozen others, in the division's postwar history: *The Deadeyes: The Story of the 96th Infantry Division.*

Clarence Craft stayed in the Army and reached the rank of sergeant first class, serving in the Korean War before leaving the service. He died in 2002 at age 80 and was buried at Fayetteville National Cemetery in Fayetteville, Arkansas.

Erik D. Carlson

Further Reading

Belote, James H., and William M. Belote. *Typhoon of Steel.* New York: Bantam Books, 1984.

The Deadeyes: The 96th Infantry Division. 2nd rev. ed. Nashville, TN: Turner Publishing, 1999.

James, Clayton D., and Anne Sharp Wells. *From Pearl Harbor to V-J Day: The American Armed Forces in WWII.* Chicago: Ivan R. Dee, 1995.

Crandall, Bruce P.

Born: February 17, 1933
Died:
Home State: Washington
Service: Army

Conflict: Vietnam War
Age at Time of Award: 32

Bruce P. Crandall was born on February 17, 1933, and raised in Olympia, Washington. At Olympia High School, he became All-State and All-American in baseball. He was drafted into the Army in 1953. Crandall was commissioned in 1954 from engineer officer candidate school and went directly to fixed-wing flight school followed by helicopter flight school. His early assignments included eight years flying mapping missions in the Arctic, North Africa, and the jungles of Central and South America. He also commanded two separate combat engineer companies.

In 1963, he was reassigned to the 11th Air Assault Division at Fort Benning, Georgia, helping develop helicopter air-assault techniques and doctrine. In early 1965, he deployed to the Dominican Republic with the XVIII Airborne Corps as the aviation liaison officer for the division's helicopters that were attached to the corps.

The 11th Air Assault was redesignated the 1st Cavalry Division (Airmobile) in July 1965 and began to deploy to Camp Radcliffe, near An Khe in the Republic of Vietnam. Upon his return from the Dominican Republic, Major Crandall assumed command of A Company, 229th Assault Helicopter Battalion and deployed to Vietnam to join the rest of the division. In this position, he commanded a company of 20 lift helicopters supporting combat assaults for 13 months in the Central Highlands. During the year, he flew the lead helicopter on over 750 missions. He also volunteered and flew a number of medical evacuation missions when medevac pilots refused to fly because of intense enemy fire.

On November 14, 1965, Crandall, call sign "Ancient Serpent 6," led his flight of helicopters in lifting troops for a search-and-destroy mission from Plei Me to Landing Zone (LZ) X-Ray in the Ia Drang Valley. On the fourth troop lift, the airlift began to take heavy enemy fire, and by the time Crandall and his flight had refueled and returned for the next troop lift, the enemy had LZ X-Ray targeted. As Major Crandall and the first eight helicopters landed to discharge troops on his fifth troop lift, his helicopter came under such intense enemy fire that the ground commander, Lt. Col. Hal Moore, ordered the second flight of helicopters to abort their mission.

When Major Crandall returned to his base, he was told that Lieutenant Colonel Moore and his troops were in heavy contact and desperately needed ammunition. Knowing that the unit on the ground had suffered serious casualties, Crandall asked for volunteers and led two aircraft back to LZ X-Ray. Despite the fact that the LZ was still under relentless enemy fire, Crandall landed, delivered the much-needed ammunition, and supervised the loading of seriously wounded soldiers onto his aircraft. Crandall's decision to land on the hot LZ inspired the other pilots, who then landed and picked up more wounded. Crandall and his wingman, then Capt. Ed W. Freeman, continued to fly in and out of the LZ throughout the day and into the evening, completing 22 flights, most under intense enemy fire. For this action, Crandall received the Distinguished Service Cross.

Crandall continued to fly for the rest of his tour. In January 1966, he rescued 12 wounded soldiers during Operation Masher, twice dropping his helicopter through dense jungle canopy while under heavy enemy ground fire to affect the rescue. For his courage in that incident, Crandall received the Aviation and Space Writers Helicopter Heroism Award for 1966.

After his first tour was complete, Crandall returned to the United States, served an assignment in Colorado, and then attended the Armed Forces Staff College. He then went back to Vietnam for his second tour, this time flying Huey gunships in the 1st Cavalry Division. In January 1968, four months into his tour, Crandall's helicopter was downed during another rescue attempt due to Air Force bombs going off too close to where he was flying. He sustained a broken back and several other injuries. After five months in the hospital, he went to the University of Nebraska to complete his bachelor's degree. He went on to serve in successive assignments in Thailand, Missouri, and California. He was scheduled for reassignment to Argentina as an aviation adviser when he suffered a stroke, which ended his flying career. He recovered and was reassigned to Caracas, Venezuela, working on the Inter-American Geodetic Survey. His final assignment was as senior engineer adviser to the California Army National Guard. He retired from the service in 1977 as a lieutenant colonel. In retirement, Crandall worked as a city manager in California and a public works manager in Arizona before settling down in Washington State.

Ultimately, the battle of the Ia Drang would be immortalized first in the book *We Were Soldiers Once . . . and Young*, written by Hal Moore and Joe Galloway, who was also on the ground at LZ X-Ray. Later, the story was retold in the Mel Gibson movie *We Were Soldiers*. Crandall was portrayed by actor Greg Kinnear.

In July 2001, Ed Freeman received the Medal of Honor for his valor in the Battle of the Ia Drang. At the time, Freeman said that Crandall's lack of a medal for the same action made his award ceremony bittersweet.

That situation was rectified several years later when Bruce Crandall's Distinguished Service Cross was upgraded to the Medal of Honor. President George W. Bush presented Bruce Crandall the medal in a White House ceremony on February 26, 2007, 41 years after his heroic actions in the Ia Drang Valley.

James H. Willbanks

Further Reading

Moore, Harold G., and Galloway, Joseph L. *We Were Soldiers Once . . . and Young: Ia Drang—the Battle That Changed the War in Vietnam.* New York: Random House, 1992.

Moore, Harold G., and Galloway, Joseph L. *We Were Soldiers Still: A Journey Back to the Battlefields of Vietnam.* New York: Harper, 2008.

Custer, Thomas W.

Born: March 15, 1845
Died: June 25, 1876
Home State: Ohio
Service: Army
Conflict: Civil War
Age at Time of Award: 20

Born in New Rumley, Ohio, on March 15, 1845, Thomas Ward Custer was the first service member awarded the Medal of Honor twice. Both awards came within a week of each other during the Civil War.

Shortly after the Civil War started, 16-year-old Tom Custer attempted to enlist. Unbeknownst to Custer, his father had already notified the recruiting officer that Tom was underage. Undeterred by the setback, Custer, characteristically, refused to give up on his pursuit to join the Army. Returning home, he continuously harangued and pestered his parents about enlisting until they finally relented. On September 2, 1861, Tom Custer reported to the recruiting officer in Gilead, Ohio. Once again, Custer listed his age as 18, and he enlisted as a private in Company H, 21st Ohio Volunteer Infantry.

Custer saw his first action at Stones River on December 31, 1862. He did nothing to distinguish himself during the battle but did demonstrate an aptitude for soldiering. Throughout his first enlistment, Tom Custer proved himself a very capable soldier and rose to the position of runner for the brigade commander. This assignment required him to demonstrate initiative and courage as he performed his duties under enemy fire. Custer reenlisted on January 1, 1864, and continued to serve as a runner in the brigade staff through the capture of Atlanta in 1864.

In the meantime, his brother George had risen to the rank of brigadier general of volunteers and, in the fall of 1864, assumed command of the 3rd Cavalry Division. One of George's first actions was to secure a commission for Tom along with a transfer to his command. In November 1864, 2nd Lt. Tom Custer reported for duty with the 6th Michigan Cavalry with special duty on the division staff.

Custer was awarded his first Medal of Honor for his actions at the Battle of Namozine Church in Virginia. On the morning of April 3, 1865, the lead elements of the 3rd Cavalry Division ran into three Confederate cavalry regiments forming a rearguard in the woods at a road intersection near Namozine Presbyterian Church.

As part of the division staff, Custer rode with the lead brigade and joined in their charge on the Confederate position. Riding at a full gallop, Custer leaped over the Confederate barricades. As the confused Confederates fell back, Custer noticed a color bearer directly in front of them. Urging his horse forward, he seized the colors of the 2nd North Carolina cavalry and took 3 officers and 11 enlisted men prisoner. Having seized one set of regimental colors, Custer was anxious to repeat his feat, and, one week later, he would get the opportunity at Sayler's Creek.

Once again, Custer rode with a lead brigade, and at the command "Charge!" Custer spurred his horse and galloped toward the rebel line. As in the earlier action at Namozine Church, Custer leaped over the barricades but found himself surrounded by Confederate soldiers. Firing in all directions, Custer's one-man assault forced the confused Confederates to fall back. A Confederate battle flag caught Custer's eye, and he quickly bore down on the color bearer. The color bearer stood his ground and shot Custer in the face with his pistol. The bullet entered Custer's right cheek and exited under his right ear. Reeling from the wound, Custer shot the color bearer with his pistol. As the color bearer collapsed, Custer snatched the colors from his hands and rode back toward the Union lines. The bloodied Custer sought out his brother to present his trophy. As he approached George Armstrong Custer, Tom Custer shouted, "Armstrong, the damned rebels have shot me, but I've got my flag." An aide quickly grabbed the flag, and George ordered his brother to the hospital. The Battle of Sayler's Creek was Tom Custer's last action of the Civil War. On April 24, 1865, he received his first Medal of Honor from Secretary of War Edwin M. Stanton, and he received his second Medal of Honor on May 22, 1865, making him the first American service member to be awarded two Medals of Honor.

Custer continued to serve in the Army at the conclusion of the war on occupation duty in Louisiana and Texas before securing an appointment in the 1st US Infantry. However, his service in the 1st Infantry would be brief. His brother George secured a commission as a lieutenant colonel in the new 7th Cavalry and once again managed to have Tom transferred to his command. From 1866 to 1876, Tom Custer would serve with the 7th Cavalry patrolling the western plains. On June 25, 1876, Custer, along with his brothers George and Boston and 220 other troopers of the 7th Cavalry, died at the Battle of the Little Bighorn. Tom Custer's remains were recovered from the battlefield and are interred at the National Cemetery at Fort Leavenworth, Kansas.

Marlyn R. Pierce

Further Reading

Day, Carl F. *Tom Custer: Ride to Glory.* Spokane, WA: The Arthur Clarke Company, 2003.

Urwin, Gregory J. W. *Custer Victorious.* Rutherford, NJ: Associated University Press, 1993.

Utley, Robert. *Cavalier in Buckskins.* Norman: University of Oklahoma Press, 1988.

Dahlgren, John Olof

Born: September 14, 1872
Died: February 11, 1963
Home State: California
Service: Marine Corps
Conflict: China Relief Expedition
Age at Time of Award: 28

John Olof Dahlgren was born on September 14, 1872, in Kahliwar, Sweden. After joining the US Marine Corps, Dahlgren was sent to China, where the situation was becoming contentious. Badly strained relations between various foreign governments and the Manchu Dynasty had grown steadily worse in the 1890s.

In 1898, US Naval forces had been ordered into several areas of China to protect life and property of various groups composed of governmental, commercial, and religious entities. The Manchu Dynasty, while not officially sanctioning the behavior of those who eventually become known as the "Society of Righteous and Harmonious Fists" and who became popularly known as the "Boxers," turned a blind eye to their violent behavior toward foreigners.

By late May 1900, events in China had become so volatile that additional military forces were needed to protect not only American interests, but also those of the Japanese, British, Russian, French, Italian, German, and Austrian governments. US Naval forces of the US Asiatic Fleet responded to this call for assistance with the dispatching of the USS *Oregon*, the USS *Newark*, and the USS *Raleigh*.

Cpl. John Dahlgren served as a member of the marine detachment, USS *Oregon*, a US marine detachment of one officer, Capt. John T. Meyers; one sergeant, Edward A. Walker; two corporals, Dahlgren and Martin Hunt; and 22 privates and five "Blue Jackets" (US Navy).

Disembarking at Taku (now called Dagu), China, on May 29, 1900, after being in receipt of orders/mission for only one hour, this force, along with armed forces of other nationalities with besieged legations in contested areas, made its 90-mile trip to Peking (Beijing) by foot and rail in two days. They arrived on May 31, 1900, just before the city was encircled by the Boxers.

Each member of that detachment took with them only their weapons, the appropriate cleaning kit, and the few personal items they could carry in their packs. The remainder of their baggage train was to be brought up by rail at a subsequent date. This never transpired, as the Boxers tore up the tracks, an event leading to much depravation of the marines and sailors, who were in need of footwear and clothing by the time the siege was lifted several months later. Upon arrival in Peking, however, each element of the multinational force marched directly to their legations and set up defenses as best as could be established with materials that could be found in the immediate area.

With each passing day the intensity of Boxer actions, including direct attacks on the various national forces, increased in magnitude and sophistication. By way of illustration, at one point the Boxers built a tower that provided positions for delivering plunging fire into the multinational force positions. Something had to be done about the tower, so a marine night attack was launched that successfully dislodged the Boxers from that position, at which point it ceased to be a threat to legation forces.

US marines and sailors, while hard pressed, held their positions, literally standing back-to-back with allied German soldiers. The battle was often characterized as hand-to-hand combat with the Boxers, a fight in which success was a foregone conclusion.

It was not uncommon for multinational forces to transport the wounded of other nationalities to their parent units when recovered from combat actions. With Boxer forces numbering around 50,000, the allied forces, never exceeding 16,000 at their high point, had to rely on teamwork, professionalism, soldierly bearing, and personal bravery every bit as much then as now.

It was in this setting that John Dahlgren was recognized by General Order of the Navy Department Number 55 on July 19, 1901, awarding him the Medal of Honor for distinguished "meritorious conduct" during the battle of Peking, June 20 to July 16, 1900.

Upon being honorably discharged from the US Marine Corps in 1901, John Dahlgren made his home in Vallejo, California. He died on February 11, 1963, and is buried in Golden Gate National Cemetery, San Bruno, California.

Wilburn E. Meador Jr.

Further Reading

The Congressional Medal of Honor: The Names, the Deeds. Forest Ranch, CA: Sharp & Dunnigan, 1984.

Metcalf, Lt. Col. C. H. "The Marines in China." *Marine Corps Gazette* 22, no. 3 (September 1938): 35–37, 53–58.

Skelly, Anne. "Marines in the Boxer Rebellion." *Leatherneck* 20, no. 9 (September 1987): 20–25.

Daly, Daniel Joseph

Born: November 11, 1873
Died: April 27, 1937
Home State: New York

Service: Marine Corps
Conflict: China Relief Expedition, Haiti Campaign, 1915
Age at Time of Award: 26, 31

Daniel Joseph Daly was born in Glen Cove, Long Island, New York, on November 11, 1873, and he joined the US Marine Corps in January 1899 at the age of 25. The following May he sailed for Asia and was posted in Beijing as part of the American legation guard. China was then in the throes of the bloody Boxer Rebellion, a violent reaction against foreigners, and the rebels closely besieged the European quarter of the city. On the night of August 14, 1900, Daly was the sole sentry guarding the Tartar Wall when several dozen Chinese suddenly attacked. Defending himself with rifle fire, bayonet, and rifle butt, he single-handedly held his ground for several hours while the Chinese kept shouting "Quon fay! Quon fay!" This, Daly was amused to learn, meant "very bad devil." Reinforcements forced the rebels to withdraw, and for this conspicuous display of bravery, he received his first Medal of Honor.

Daly spent the next 15 years abroad, seeing service in the Philippines and Veracruz, Mexico. In 1911, he distinguished himself by putting out a fire on board the USS *Springfield* that threatened the ship's magazine. This act won him commendations from the secretary of the navy and the major general commandant. In 1915, marines landed on the island of Haiti to wrest control from a group of marauding bandits known as the Cacos. On October 24, Daly was part of a 35-man patrol under Maj. Smedley D. Butler that was ambushed by 400 rebels while crossing a river. Numerous pack animals carrying valuable equipment were lost in midstream, but Daly dove in and retrieved a machine gun and ammunition under fire. At daybreak, he then led one of three squads that attacked the Cacos from different directions, routed them, and captured their stronghold. This affair earned Daly his second Medal of Honor.

The advent of World War I found Daly as first sergeant of the 73rd Company, 6th US Marines. He was actively engaged in combat in the Toulon sector (March–May 1918), the Aisne Operation (June 1918), and the Chateau-Thierry sector (June 1918). He further embellished his already legendary standing in Marine Corps history during intense fighting at Belleau Woods. When his company became pinned down under heavy machine gun fire, they refused to advance. Daly suddenly jumped up and exclaimed, "Come on, you sons of bitches! Do you want to live forever?" and carried the German emplacements. The quiet and soft-spoken sergeant later denied ever using such language but continued to distinguish himself in further action.

On June 5, 1918, Daly single-handedly extinguished a dangerous fire threatening the ammunition dump at Lucy de Bocage. Two days later, he ignored a tremendous German artillery bombardment and visited his company's machine gun crews to keep up their spirits. Finally, on June 10, Daly attacked an enemy machine gun nest with a pistol and hand grenades, capturing it single-handedly. This seemingly invincible sergeant was seriously wounded on June 21 and evacuated under protest. Three months later, he rejoined the 4th Marine Brigade, fought in the capture of Mont Blanc ridge, and received two more wounds. Daly's heroism culminated in more decorations, including a Distinguished Service Medal, the Navy Cross, the French Medaille Militaire, and the Croix de Guerre with palm. He was one of the most heavily decorated solders of World War I.

Daniel Daly completed a brief tour of occupation duty in Germany after the war and returned home a hero. Celebrity, however, never appealed to him, and he publicly denied any glory seeking on his part. "I was only doing my job," Daly insisted to the press, "I wanted to be a good sergeant of marines." He requested to be placed on the Fleet Marine Reserve soon after, and, in 1919, Daly retired and went to work as a bank guard on Wall Street. He held the position without fanfare for 17 years and died of a heart attack on April 27, 1937, at the age of 64. This legendary marine was commemorated in 1942 by having the destroyer *Daly* named in his honor. His superior, the equally valorous Gen. Smedley D. Butler, also a Medal of Honor double award recipient, considered Daly "the fightin'est Marine I ever knew" and said, "It was an object lesson to have served with him."

John C. Fredriksen

Further Reading

Millett, Allan R. *Semper Fidelis: The History of the United States Marine Corps.* New York: The Free Press, 1982.

Tassin, Ray. *Double Winners of the Medal of Honor.* Canton, OH: Daring Books, 1986.

Davila, Rudolph B.

Born: April 27, 1916
Died: January 26, 2002
Home State: California
Service: Army
Conflict: World War II
Age at Time of Award: 28

Born to a Spanish father and a Filipino mother in El Paso, Texas, on April 27, 1916, Rudolph Blanco Davila was raised and educated in Watts, California. He enlisted in the Army in Los Angeles. During World War II, he served as an infantryman assigned to Company H, 7th Infantry Regiment, 3rd Infantry Division. In 1944, Staff Sergeant Davila and his company were part of the Allied force trapped in the Anzio pocket. The invasion of Anzio (Operation Shingle) had been an effort by the Allies to flank the German positions in Italy by landing a force between the main enemy lines and the city of Rome. In theory, the Germans would be forced to abandon their defensive positions in order to defend Rome and protect their rear area. In reality, the slow, methodical pace of the Allied forces after the landing allowed the Germans time to regroup and counterattack. As a result, what should have been a rapid flanking movement by the Allies resulted in continued stalemate both along the main front line and in the defensive pocket created around the city of Anzio.

The final, successful breakout from the Anzio pocket started on May 23, 1944. On May 28, 1944, Davila and his company were near Artena, Italy, when they were caught in an exposed position on a hillside by German machine guns. Rather than engage the German positions, the American machine gunners (Company H was the heavy-weapons company of the 2nd Battalion, 7th Infantry Regiment) were reluctant to move for fear of drawing fire on themselves. The result was that the Americans were trapped—unable to move forward or backward. Realizing the seriousness of the situation, Davila crawled 50 yards under fire to the nearest American machine gun and put it into action. In order to observe the effect of his shots, he fired from the kneeling position despite the fact that enemy rounds struck the machine gun's tripod and passed between his legs. His efforts inspired the other machine gunners of the company, who also opened fire on the German positions. Davila then ordered his weapon's original gunner to take over so that he could crawl forward, still under enemy fire, and direct all of the American guns until both of the German positions had been destroyed.

With these enemy strong points eliminated, Company H continued advancing until they were again engaged by German troops. Despite being wounded in the leg, Davila mounted a burning American tank and, though drawing a considerable amount of German fire in this exposed position, eliminated this second group of enemy soldiers with the tank's .50 caliber machine gun. Dismounting the tank, Davila advanced 150 yards toward a German-held farmhouse where two more enemy machine guns were firing on American troops. Using two hand grenades and his rifle, he killed the five Germans who occupied the main floor of the house. Davila then climbed up to the attic, where he destroyed two more enemy machine gun teams with rifle fire.

For his actions, Davila was given a battlefield commission to second lieutenant and recommended for the Medal of Honor by his company commander. The award was downgraded to the Distinguished Service Cross (DSC), the Army's second highest award for valor. After recovering from his leg wound, Davila returned to combat. A few months later, when the 3rd Infantry Division found itself fighting in the Vosges Mountains of France, he and his men were taken under fire by a German tank. The shell struck a nearby tree, and Davila was hit by shrapnel, which pierced his lung and severed nerves on his left side. This wound caused permanent damage to his arm, which would remain partially paralyzed and withered despite 13 operations. While he was being treated for his wounds at a hospital in Modesto, California, he met a nurse named Harriet, and three months later they were married.

After being medically discharged from the US Army, Davila used the GI Bill to attend the University of Southern California, receiving bachelor's and master's degrees in sociology, and subsequently taught high school in Los Angeles.

In 1996, in the wake of an independent report that found significant racism in decisions not to award the Medal of Honor to African Americans in World War II, Hawaii senator Daniel Akaka requested that a similar study be performed regarding Asian Americans. This report returned similar conclusions, leading the US Army to upgrade 22 of the 104 DSCs awarded to Asian Americans in World War II to Medals of Honor. On June 21, 2000, President Bill Clinton presented the medals to Rudolph Davila and 21 other recipients, only 7 of whom were still alive. Davila died of cancer on January 26, 2002, and was buried with full military honors at Arlington National Cemetery.

Alexander M. Bielakowski

Further Reading

Collier, Peter, and Nick Del Calzo. *Medal of Honor: Portraits of Valor beyond the Call of Duty.* New York: Artisan, 2006.

Tillman, Barrett. *Heroes: U.S. Army Medal of Honor Recipients.* New York: The Berkley Group, 2006.

Davis, Charles W.

Born: February 21, 1917
Died: January 18, 1991
Home State: Alabama
Service: Army
Conflict: World War II
Age at Time of Award: 25

Charles W. Davis was born February 21, 1917, in Gordo, Alabama, where he spent most of his younger years. However, he graduated from high school in Montgomery, Alabama. He attended the University of Alabama on a baseball scholarship. He had completed three years of a prelaw course and one year of law school when he entered the Army as a second lieutenant of infantry in July 1940. He was transferred to Fort Sam Houston, Texas, in November 1940, where he met, courted, and married his wife, Joan. They were reassigned to Hawaii in July 1941.

Davis was on duty with the 25th Infantry Division at Schofield Barracks on Oahu when the Japanese attacked Pearl Harbor on December 7, 1941. After the attack, troops of the division moved to the beaches for the defense of Honolulu and Ewa Point. Following an intensive period of training, the 25th Division shipped out for Guadalcanal in November 1942 to relieve the marines near Henderson Field. The 25th Division, commanded by Maj. Gen. J. Lawton Collins, arrived in December and joined the Army's Americal Division and the 2nd Marine Division as part of the newly formed XXIV Corps, commanded by Maj. Gen. Alexander M. Patch. The division entered combat on January 10, 1943.

In preparation for a planned general offensive to destroy all the Japanese forces remaining on Guadalcanal, General Patch ordered the Americal Division to clear the Japanese troops from the Mount Austin complex, high ground overlooking Henderson Field. The American soldiers, most in their first combat experience of the war, initially had a difficult time with the Japanese. Patch ordered the 25th Division into the fight to finish clearing Mount Austin and nearby hills and ridgelines.

The 27th Infantry Regiment "Wolfhounds" were given the mission of clearing a ridgeline the Americans called Galloping Horse Ridge. On January 12, 1943, the 2nd Battalion was advancing on its assigned objective. The two leading companies quickly became intermingled and were pinned down by enemy machine guns. With the attack faltering, Captain Davis, executive officer of 2nd Battalion, volunteered to go forward to straighten out the intermingled companies and locate the strongpoint that was holding up their advance. Accompanied by two other men, Davis crawled along the east side of the ridge until he was able to spot the location of the enemy strongpoint. He took measures to untangle the two companies and scouted out the Japanese strongpoint. He then radioed for mortar fire, but the shells failed to destroy the strongpoint; it was still in action, keeping the American infantry in place. Joined by his battalion commander, Lt. Col. Herbert V. Mitchell, they remained in the forward, exposed position during the night, devising a plan to break the stalemate the next morning.

When the attack was launched the next morning, it was stymied almost immediately by enemy machine gun fire coming from a knoll on the southern edge of the ridge. Captain Davis and four other men volunteered to try to take out the Japanese strongpoint. Crawling on their bellies and covered by friendly mortar fire, Davis and his party crept to within 10 yards of the enemy position. The Japanese defenders threw two grenades at them, but the grenades failed to explode. Davis and his men threw eight grenades into the Japanese position. As soon as the grenades exploded, Davis jumped to his feet and fired one burst from his rifle, which promptly jammed; he switched his rifle to his left hand, pulled out his pistol, and began shooting at the startled Japanese in the strongpoint.

While still firing his pistol, Davis led the assault up the hill, "running like a halfback," dodging back and forth to avoid the fire directed against him as he advanced over open ground. As Davis led the charge, he was in full view of most of the 2nd Battalion and the Japanese defenders, and his actions had "an electrifying effect on the battalion." Inspired by Davis's actions, the American troops "came to life" and stormed over the ridge, routing the defenders and killing or chasing away the rest of the Japanese on the knoll. By noon, the last Japanese stronghold on the Galloping Horse had fallen. The capture of this position broke Japanese resistance, and the battalion was then able to proceed and secure the corps' objective. The Americans counted the bodies of 170 Japanese soldiers on and around the Galloping Horse. The Americans suffered less than 100 killed.

Davis was subsequently promoted to major, and, on July 17, 1943, in a ceremony on Guadalcanal, he received the Medal of Honor for this action on Galloping Horse Ridge. Lt. Col. Mitchell and the other volunteers who accompanied Davis received the Distinguished Service Cross.

Charles Davis reached the rank of colonel and served in the Korean and Vietnam wars before retiring. In retirement, he remained active in community and military affairs, serving on the Board of Directors of the National Football Foundation and Hall of Fame and as president of the Congressional Medal of Honor Society. He died at the age of 73 on January 18, 1991, and is buried in Arlington National Cemetery.

James H. Willbanks

Further Reading

Collins, Gen. J. Lawton. *Lightning Joe: An Autobiography*. Baton Rouge: Louisiana State University Press, 1980.

Frank, Richard B. *Guadalcanal*. New York: Random House, 1990.

Miller, John Jr. *Guadalcanal: The First Offensive*. Washington, D.C.: Historical Division, Department of the Army, 1949.

Murphy, Edward F. *Heroes of World War II*. Novato, CA: Presidio Press, 1990.

Davis, Raymond G.

Born: January 13, 1915
Died: September 3, 2003
Home State: Georgia
Service: Marine Corps
Conflict: Korean War
Age at Time of Award: 35

Born in Fitzgerald, Georgia, on January 13, 1915, Raymond G. Davis graduated in 1933 from Atlanta Technical High School. He then entered Georgia School of Technology, graduating in 1938 with a bachelor's degree in chemical engineering. While in college, Davis participated in ROTC, but after graduation he resigned his commission in the Army Reserve to accept an appointment as a Marine second lieutenant on June 27, 1938.

In the prewar years, Davis served in a number of successive assignments, including service aboard the USS *Portland*; shore duty at Quantico, Virginia, and Aberdeen, Maryland; and with the 1st Marine Division at Guantánamo Bay, Cuba.

During World War II, he participated in the Battle for Guadalcanal, the Eastern New Guinea and Cape Gloucester campaigns, and the Pelilu operation. In April 1944, while commanding a battalion of the 1st Marine Division as a major on Pelilu, he was awarded the Navy Cross and Purple Heart.

During the Korean War, Davis, then a lieutenant colonel, commanded 1st Battalion, 7th Marines from August to December 1950. During the period from December 1 to 4, he led his battalion through heavy snow and subzero temperatures against heavy enemy resistance in the relief of a beleaguered rifle company and then seized and held a vital mountain pass controlling the only route available for two Marine regiments in danger of being cut off by the enemy against repeated enemy attacks. For this action, he was nominated for the Medal of Honor. He continued to command his battalion, receiving two Silver Stars and the Legion of Merit with Combat "V" for subsequent action. Davis served as executive officer of the 7th Marines from December 1950 to June 1951, when he returned to the United States. The recommendation for the Medal of Honor had been lost in a fire, and it took two years for it to be resubmitted, but on November 24, 1952, President Harry S. Truman presented Davis the Medal of Honor in a White House ceremony.

Following his service in the Korean War, Davis served in a number of key Marine billets at Marine Corps Headquarters and attended several Marine schools and the National War College.

In July 1963, Davis was promoted to brigadier general and assigned as assistant division commander, 3rd Marine Division on Okinawa. In December 1964, he was reassigned to Headquarters Marine Corps. He was promoted to major general in November 1966. Ordered to Vietnam, Davis served briefly as deputy commanding general, Provisional Corps, before assuming command of the 3rd Marine Division in May 1968. Under Davis, Marine tactics changed from staffing fixed defensive positions to conducting highly mobile operations throughout western Quang Tri Province. For his Vietnam service, he received the Distinguished Service Medal.

In March 1971, Raymond Davis received his fourth star and appointment as assistant commandant of the Marine Corps. Davis retired from active duty on March 31, 1972, after more than 33 years in the Corps. In 1975, he became president of RGMV, Inc., a land development company in Stockbridge, Georgia. In 1987, President Ronald Reagan asked Davis to serve on the Korean War Veterans Memorial Board, and, in 1995, he assisted in the dedication of the completed memorial. General Davis died of a heart attack at the age of 88 on September 3, 2003. He was buried at Forest Lawn Memorial Gardens in College Park, Georgia. In a fitting tribute, the funeral detail and honor guard was commanded by the then commandant of the Marine Corps, Gen. Michael W. Hagee.

James H. Willbanks

Further Reading

Collier, Peter, and Nick Del Calzo. *Medal of Honor: Portraits of Valor beyond the Call of Duty.* New York: Artisan, 2006.

Fehrenbach, T. R. *This Kind of War.* Dulles, VA: Brassey's, 1963.

Russ, Martin *Breakout: The Chosin Reservoir Campaign, Korea 1950.* New York: Penguin Books, 1999.

Davis, Sammy L.

Born: November 1, 1946
Died:
Home State: Indiana
Service: Army
Conflict: Vietnam War
Age at Time of Award: 21

Sammy L. Davis was born November 1, 1946, in Dayton, Ohio. In 1965, Davis enlisted in the US Army immediately after high school and entered the service in Indianapolis, Indiana. He volunteered for the artillery because his father had been an artilleryman in World War II. Soon after completing basic training, he requested to be sent to Vietnam. On November 18, 1967, Davis's unit, Battery C, 2nd Battalion, 4th Artillery of the 9th Infantry Division, consisting of 42 men and 11 guns, was deployed by helicopter into an area west of Cai Lay. Their objective was to create a forward fire–support base called Firebase Cudgel. In this position, only a canal separated the Viet Cong (VC) from the Americans. After midnight, Viet Cong in the area attacked Battery C with heavy mortar attack while approximately 1,500 VC launched a ground assault.

Private First Class Davis and the rest of his unit responded to this advance with beehive rounds, each containing 18,000 metal darts per shell, from their 105-mm howitzers. In an attempt to protect the gun crew, Davis took over a machine gun to provide covering fire. As Davis was firing, a VC recoilless rifle round struck the howitzer, knocking the crew from the firing position and blowing Davis into a foxhole. Davis realized that they were about to be overrun, so he struggled to his feet and made his way to the now-damaged howitzer. He rammed a shell into the gun and fired point-blank into the VC who were advancing five deep directly into his position. The beehive round devastated the attackers, stopping them in their tracks, but an enemy mortar round exploded nearby, knocking Davis to the ground.

He got up and kept firing the howitzer until he had expended all the traditional rounds. Then he fired a white phosphorous shell, and then the last shell he had, a "propaganda shell" that was filled with pamphlets.

Davis heard his fellow soldiers across the canal and realized that somehow they had been separated from the rest of the unit. Even though he did not know how to swim, Davis took an air mattress and paddled across the canal; several other soldiers followed him. On the other side of the canal, Davis found three wounded soldiers and gave them morphine. Davis provided covering fire as another soldier took the most severely wounded of the three across the water. Davis then placed the other two wounded soldiers on the air mattress and transferred them across the canal to an American fire base for treatment. Davis made his way back to his original position with the howitzer crew and continued to fight against the VC, but in the early morning hours, he sustained serious injuries in his back and buttocks.

Due to the severity of his wounds, Davis received notice while in the hospital that he was going to return to the United States. He petitioned Gen. William Westmoreland, commander of US forces in Vietnam, asking to stay with his unit. Westmoreland granted him permission, but Davis, still hobbled by his wounds, was not able to return to the line and returned as a cook.

Almost exactly one year later, on November 19, 1968, President Lyndon B. Johnson presented Davis with the Medal of Honor. Angelo Liteky, James Allen Taylor, Dwight H. Johnson, and Gary Wetzel also received the award that day. In addition to his Medal of Honor, Davis also received a Silver Star and two Purple Hearts. He retired from the military in 1984.

The 1994 film *Forrest Gump* is loosely based on Sammy Davis's Medal of Honor citation. In the film, Gump's face is imposed over the actual footage from Davis's medal ceremony. On October 2, 1996, President Bill Clinton signed Congressional Law H.R. 3186, which renamed the United States Army Publications Center in St. Louis, Missouri, to the Sammy L. Davis Federal Building. Davis continues actively to support the troops of the United States. During December of 2000, Davis toured US troop bases in Europe and the Balkans. He played the harmonica for the troops in memory of his sergeant during the Vietnam War, Johnston Dunlop. In 2001, Davis gave an address titled "Promise" to his daughter and her graduating class at Sheppard Air Force Base in Wichita Falls, Texas. In July 2005, Davis's Medal of Honor was stolen out of his locked car in Indianapolis, Indiana. It was recovered at the bottom of the White River and returned to Davis within days.

Denise M. Carlin

Further Reading

Collier, Peter, and Nick Del Calzo. *Medal of Honor: Portraits of Valor beyond the Call of Duty*. New York: Artisan, 2006.

Lowry, Timothy. *And Brave Men, Too*. New York: Crown Publishers, 1985.

Day, George E.

Born: February 24, 1925
Died:
Home State: Iowa
Service: Air Force
Conflict: Vietnam War
Age at Time of Award: 42

Born in Sioux City, Iowa, on February 24, 1925, George Everett "Bud" Day left high school prior to graduation in order to join the Marine Corps during World War II. He served on active duty for two-and-a-half years, posted to an artillery battalion on Johnson Island in the South Pacific. Upon returning from the war, he attended Morningside College and then the University of South Dakota School of Law.

Day was admitted to the South Dakota bar in 1949. The next year, Day received a direct commission as a second lieutenant in the Iowa Air National Guard. Called to active duty in 1951 during the Korean War, he underwent flight training. He then saw combat in two tours as a pilot flying the Republic F-84 Thunderchief fighter-bomber in Korea.

Promoted to captain, Day remained in the Air Force. In 1967, with the anticipation of retiring the next year, Major Day requested assignment to Vietnam. In April 1967, he was assigned to the 31st Tactical Fighter Wing at Tuy Hoa Air Base in the Republic of Vietnam (South Vietnam). Shortly after his arrival, Day took command of Detachment 1, 416th Tactical Fighter Wing. His men flew North American F-100 Super Sabres out of Phu Cat Air Base. His aircraft served as "Fast FACs" (forward air controllers) in missions over Laos and the Democratic Republic of Vietnam (North Vietnam).

On August 26, 1967, in the course of his 65th mission—directing an air strike against a North Vietnamese surface-to-air missile (SAM) site west of Dong Hoi, 20 miles north of the demilitarized zone (DMZ)—Day's aircraft was shot down. During his ejection, Day's right arm was broken in three different places, and he sustained eye and back injuries. The other member of his crew ejected safely and was subsequently picked up by a rescue helicopter. Day, however, was taken prisoner by local militia forces shortly after he landed.

On the fifth night of his captivity, Day escaped, and, despite his injuries and the fact that the North Vietnamese had taken his boots, he was able to cross the DMZ back into South Vietnam. Unfortunately for Day, after 12 days of successful evasion and just two miles from the US Marine firebase at Con Thien, he was again captured, this time by a Viet Cong patrol that wounded him in the leg and hand. Returned to his original prison camp, Day was tortured for having escaped, and his right arm was again broken. He was then moved to a succession of prison camps near Hanoi, where he was starved, beaten, and tortured. In December 1967, Day shared a cell with Navy Lt. Cdr. John S. McCain III.

Following the Paris Peace Accords and after five years and seven months as a North Vietnamese prisoner, Day was released on March 14, 1973. He had been promoted to colonel while a prisoner, and he decided to remain in the Air Force in hopes of earning a promotion to general. After a year in physical rehabilitation and with 13 medical waivers, he was finally returned to flying status. He subsequently served as vice commander of the 33rd Tactical Fighter Wing at Eglin Air Force Base, Florida.

On March 4, 1976, President Gerald R. Ford awarded George Day the Medal of Honor for his personal bravery while a captive in North Vietnam. Day retired from active duty in 1977. He then took up the practice of law in Florida. In 1996, Day took the lead in filing a class-action lawsuit against the US government on behalf of military retirees who had been stripped of their medical benefits. He won the case in district court in 2001, but the decision was overturned by the US Court of Appeals in 2002. During the 2004 US presidential election, Day appeared in a Swift Boat Veterans for Truth advertisement, speaking against Democratic presidential candidate John F. Kerry.

James H. Willbanks

Further Reading

Collier, Peter, and Nick Del Calzo. *Medal of Honor: Portraits of Valor beyond the Call of Duty.* New York: Artisan, 2006.

Coram, Robert. *American Patriot: The Life and Wars of Colonel Bud Day.* New York: Little, Brown. 2007.

Day, George E. *Return with Honor.* Mesa, AZ: Champlin Museum Press, 1991

Newman, Rick, and Don Shepperd. *Bury Us Upside Down: The Misty Pilots and the Secret Battle for the Ho Chi Minh Trail.* Novato, CA: Presidio Press, 2007.

Dean, William F.

Born: August 1, 1899
Died: August 26, 1981
Home State: Illinois
Service: Army
Conflict: Korean War
Age at Time of Award: 51

Born in Carlyle, Illinois, on August 1, 1899, William F. Dean failed to gain admission to West Point and enrolled at the University of California at Berkeley, graduating in 1922. Dean had secured a Reserve commission in May 1921, but in

October 1923 he was granted a Regular Army commission as a second lieutenant of infantry.

Dean served with the 38th Infantry Regiment at Fort Douglas, Utah, during 1923–1926. He then saw service in Panama with the 42nd and 33rd Infantry regiments. In 1929 he rejoined the 38th Infantry, and in 1934 he was assigned to the 30th Infantry Regiment at the Presidio of San Francisco, California. During 1935–1936, Dean attended the Army Command and General Staff School at Fort Leavenworth, Kansas. Following a tour with the 19th Infantry Regiment at Schofield Barracks, Hawaii, he returned to the United States and attended the Army Industrial College in Washington, D.C., graduating in June 1939. He served briefly at the Chemical Warfare School at Edgewood Arsenal, Maryland, before returning to Washington, D.C. that September to attend the Army War College, from which he graduated in June 1940. He then served in the Operations and Training Division of the War Department General Staff and was appointed assistant to the secretary of the general staff in January 1941.

In March 1942, Dean was reassigned to Headquarters, Army Ground Forces, where he served as assistant chief, then chief, of the Requirements Section. He was promoted to brigadier general in December 1942, and in February 1944 he became assistant commander of the 44th Infantry Division in Louisiana. He moved with the division to Camp Phillips, Kansas, and from there to southern France in August 1944. He remained with the 44th Infantry Division throughout its campaigns in southern France and Germany. Named to command the division in December 1944, he was promoted to major general in March 1945, and in July 1945 he redeployed the division to the United States in preparation for its reassignment to the Pacific Theater.

In September 1945, General Dean joined the faculty of the Army Command and General Staff School at Fort Leavenworth; he became assistant commandant of the school in June 1946. In October 1947, he was reassigned as military governor of South Korea. He supervised the first free elections there and the inauguration of the Republic of Korea in August 1948. Dean then assumed command of the 7th Infantry Division in Korea and took it to Japan in January 1949. The following June, he became chief of staff of the 8th US Army in Japan. In October 1949, he was reassigned to command the 24th Infantry Division, which subsequently became the first US ground combat unit to respond to the North Korean invasion of South Korea on June 25, 1950. General Dean arrived at Taejon airfield on July 3, 1950, and immediately assumed command of all US forces in Korea.

Striving to stem the North Korean advance, Dean personally led his division in the bitter defense of Taejon on July 19–20, on one occasion attacking a Korean People's Army (KPA, North Korean) tank with only a hand grenade and his .45 caliber pistol. Given the near total disintegration of his division under heavy KPA attack and the lack of communications, Dean's actions can only be characterized as "leading by example" in desperate circumstances.

Separated from the rest of his command in the confused withdrawal from Taejon, Dean wandered alone and injured in the hills until he was betrayed by two South Koreans on August 25, 1950. He thus became the highest-ranking United Nations Command (UNC) officer taken prisoner by the communists. Dean's courageous conduct in captivity was equal to his bravery at Taejon, for which he was awarded the Medal of Honor in February 1951. He was released from captivity on September 3, 1953, and returned a hero, although he was criticized later for his defense of those US prisoners of war (POWs) who had cooperated with the communists.

In December 1953, William Dean became deputy commander of the 6th US Army at the Presidio. When he retired from active duty in October 1955, he was awarded the coveted Combat Infantryman's Badge by Army chief of staff Gen. Maxwell D. Taylor, thus becoming only the second general officer, after Gen. Joseph W. Stilwell, to be so honored. Dean died at Berkeley, California, on August 26, 1981.

Charles R. Shrader

Further Reading

Ancell, R. Manning, and Christine M. Miller. *The Biographical Dictionary of World War II Generals and Flag Officers: The U.S. Armed Forces.* Westport, CT: Greenwood, 1996.

Appleman, Roy E. *South to the Naktong, North to the Yalu.* Washington, D.C.: Office of the Chief of Military History, Department of the Army, 1961.

Dean, William F., with William L. Worden. *General Dean's Story.* New York: Viking, 1954.

DeBlanc, Jefferson Joseph

Born: February 15, 1921
Died: November 22, 2007
Home State: Louisiana
Service: Marine Corps
Conflict: World War II
Age at Time of Award: 22

Born in Lockport, Louisiana, on February 15, 1921, Jefferson J. DeBlanc attended Southwestern Louisiana Institute and studied mathematics and physics. At the end of his junior year, he left school and enlisted in the US Navy and eventually entered the aviation cadet program in October 1941. Earning his wings at Corpus Christi, Texas, in May 1942, DeBlanc opted for the Marines and was commissioned a second lieutenant. Undergoing carrier training in the Grumman F4F Wildcat fighter, he was eventually assigned to Marine Fighting Squadron (VMF) 112 and sent overseas.

Arriving at Guadalcanal on November 1, he wasted no time in downing Japanese aircraft. On November 12, he claimed two Japanese GM4 "Betty" bombers, and, on December 18, DeBlanc added a third victory by destroying an F1M "Pete" floatplane. On January 31, 1943, he was the section leader of eight F4Fs escorting a strike force of SBD "Dauntless" dive-bombers raiding the Japanese fleet near the island of Kolombangara. Two F4F pilots claimed engine problems and left the formation, leaving a force of only six fighters. Despite problems with his own aircraft's fuel system, DeBlanc continued on, thinking that he might have enough fuel to make it back to base after the raid.

Over the target, the SBDs dove at the enemy ships while DeBlanc remained at 14,000 feet to protect the bombers from pursuing Japanese. Coming under attack at lower altitude, the SBDs called for assistance. Diving down to 1,000 feet, DeBlanc rolled in on two Petes attacking an SBD. He opened fire on the trailing fighter and sent it spiraling down. Next he set his sights on the lead Japanese fighter. Flying slightly below the Pete's flight path so the rear gunner could not see him, DeBlanc again closed on the fighter and fired. The Japanese plane exploded. These two kills, combined with his previous three, officially made DeBlanc an ace.

Climbing to his right and clearing his tail of any enemy fighters, DeBlanc heard someone yell "Zeros!" over the radio. DeBlanc saw that he was 500 feet below 10 Japanese A6M fighters and climbed straight toward them. Due to his lower altitude, the Zeros had no idea DeBlanc was closing on them. He aimed at the lead Zero and fired on the unsuspecting fighter. However, the Zero rolled out of DeBlanc's sights during the pursuit, and the kill could not be confirmed. Following this attack, DeBlanc locked onto another Zero. As the enemy climbed, the marine matched the Zero's movements. When the enemy rolled level, DeBlanc fired, causing the Zero to explode. Following the victory, DeBlanc was engaged by several Zeros and maneuvered defensively.

Eventually clearing himself of enemy fighters, he assessed his plane's own damage and started his return to base. He took stock of his fuel status and then saw two more Zeros approaching. At this point, DeBlanc could have joined with the returning SBDs, preserved his fuel supply, and hoped the bomber's gunners could fend off the attackers, or he could have engaged the enemy himself and forgone any chance of returning to base. He chose the latter and turned into the attackers. While closing head-on into one Zero, DeBlanc waited until he was in optimal range and then fired. DeBlanc hit the enemy aircraft; the Japanese pilot attempted to ram the marine fighter, but DeBlanc kept firing until the Zero exploded. With debris all around, DeBlanc banked his fighter to engage the other Zero, but the enemy already began maneuvering into a firing position. Fortunately for DeBlanc, the enemy pilot misjudged the Wildcat's airspeed, overshot his prey, and inadvertently flew in front of the marine's aircraft. DeBlanc fired a short burst, scored direct hits, and downed the Zero.

After these two kills, DeBlanc found himself under attack from other Zeros and sustained substantial damage. His F4F caught fire and began disintegrating, and he bailed out, landing in Vella Gulf. Swimming ashore at Kolombangara, DeBlanc was given refuge by friendly natives and treated for his injuries. He was picked up by a Navy PBY Catalina on February 12 and returned to his squadron.

Later in the war, Jefferson DeBlanc flew in the Marshall Island and Okinawa campaigns, finishing the war with nine victories. He was presented the Medal of Honor by President Harry S. Truman in a White House ceremony on December 6, 1946. Following the war, he continued his studies and remained in the Marine Corps Reserve and retired as a colonel in 1972. DeBlanc died on November 22, 2007, from pneumonia complications. He is buried in Saint Michael's Cemetery in Saint Martinville, Louisiana.

John M. Curatola

Further Reading

Collier, Peter, and Nick Del Calzo. *Medal of Honor: Portraits of Valor beyond the Call of Duty*. New York: Artisan, 2006.

DeBlanc, Jefferson. *The Guadalcanal Air War*. Grenta, LA: Pelican Publishing, 2008.

Hammel, Eric. *Marines at War: 20 True Heroic Tales of U.S. Marines in Combat, 1942–1983*. Pacifica, CA: Pacifica Press, 1999.

Mersky, Peter. *Time of Aces: Marine Pilots in the Solomons, 1942–1944*. Washington, D.C.: Marine Corps Historical Center, 1993.

Dix, Drew Dennis

Born: December 14, 1944
Died:
Home State: Colorado
Service: Army
Conflict: Vietnam War
Age at Time of Award: 24

Born at West Point, New York, on December 14, 1944, and raised in Pueblo, Colorado, Drew D. Dix enlisted in the US Army at the age of 17 in 1962 after a very positive experience in his high school Junior ROTC program. He joined the US Army, hoping to become a member of the Special Forces thanks in some measure to the fame given the relatively young organization by President John F. Kennedy. However, at that time, Special Forces required that a volunteer be at least 21 years of age, which Dix was not. Dix found his way to the other side of Fort Bragg, North Carolina, joining the 82nd Airborne Division and serving as a military policeman before transferring to a similar assignment in Fort Carson, Colorado. Dix returned to Fort Bragg with a 122-day temporary duty assignment in support of US operations in the Dominican Republic. Once back at Fort Bragg, now 21-year-old Sergeant Dix tried again to gain entry into Special Forces and this time around was accepted for the qualification course. He graduated in June of 1967 and received assignment to 6th Special Forces Group (SFG), but his time in the 6th Group proved short. By September 1967, Dix had orders to 5th SFG South Vietnam. Initially assigned as an individual replacement for a Special Forces A-team then in the Republic of Vietnam, Dix soon found himself reassigned as an American advisor to what was to be a 136-man Vietnamese Reconnaissance Unit operating in Chau Doc Province along the Cambodian border in the Mekong Delta. Dix's reconnaissance team was itself under the control of the Central Intelligence Agency (CIA) with its primary mission being that of capturing key Viet Cong (VC) leaders.

Two VC battalions had successfully infiltrated Chau Phu City prior to the start of the Tet Offensive. On January 31, 1968, the two battalions were in position to seize control of the city, threatening various US and South Vietnamese installations with capture or destruction. Dix, along with a small team of US Navy SEALs, undertook the task of getting threatened US and Allied personnel to safety. At the Provincial Tactical Operations Center (TOC), he learned that eight American and two Philippine workers with the US Agency for International Development (USAID) were trapped. Dix understood that to reach them would require additional firepower beyond what he had. Finding out that a machine gun–mounted jeep was available a kilometer away at the US Embassy house (the real center of US operations and the area logistics base), Dix made his way alone and on foot to the vehicle. Returning to the TOC, Dix took six of his team in several jeeps to the American nurses' quarters. The effort resulted in the rescue of one nurse. While the rescue was going on, Dix and the others held off two VC companies.

Moving to the USAID compound, Dix's men next rescued the eight Americans. Successful in this, Dix became aware that the Vietnamese Military Security Service building in the center of the city was in enemy hands. Although one of the Navy SEALs died heroically in the effort, Dix and his men cleared the building and then returned to the TOC. At the TOC, Dix lost use of the SEAL team to higher command. Not to be deterred, Dix ordered 10 of his Vietnamese security team to accompany him on foot back into center city, where they thought the remaining two Philippine USAID workers were being held. Assaulting the building, Dix and his recon team killed six more VC while also finding and securing the missing USAID workers.

The following day, Dix and 20 Vietnamese soldiers cleared other buildings in the downtown area under VC control. During the afternoon hours of the fight, Dix and his men captured 20 prisoners, including a VC general officer who was supposed to take over and administer Chau Phu. By the end of the second day, significant sections of the city were once again in Allied hands due in large part to the actions of Dix and his men. Dix alone received credit for killing 14 enemy soldiers. For these actions, Dix was recommended for the Medal of Honor.

President Lyndon B. Johnson presented the medal to Staff Sergeant Dix on January 16, 1969, as one of the last official acts of his presidency. Drew Dix returned to Special Forces, eventually accepting a direct commission as a captain in the infantry. Dix returned one last time to Vietnam as an infantry officer in the 101st Airborne Division in 1971. Returning to the United States and Fort Bragg, he attended Methodist College in Fayetteville, North Carolina, earning a bachelor's degree. Assigned again to Special Forces, he became involved in the initial organizational efforts to create a viable counterterrorism capability inside of the US military. Toward the end of his active duty career, he was among those pushing for and laying the groundwork for a joint special operations headquarters. Having achieved the rank of major and completing 20 years of service, Dix retired to civilian life. He did not end his interest in the defense of his nation, however. As a civilian, he would go on to be director of homeland security in Alaska before returning to retirement in the mountains of New Mexico.

Joseph R. Fischer

Further Reading

Collier, Peter, and Nick Del Calzo. *Medal of Honor: Portraits of Valor beyond the Call of Duty.* New York: Artisan, 2006.

Dix, Drew. *The Rescue of River City.* Mimbres, NM: Drew Dix Publishing, 2000.

Faranacci, Donald. *Last Full Measure of Devotion: A Tribute to America's Heroes of the Vietnam War.* Bloomington, IN: AuthorHouse, 2007.

Sutherland, Lt. Col. Ian D. W. *Special Forces of the United States Army.* San Jose, CA: R. James Bender Publishing, 1990.

Donlon, Roger Hugh C.

Born: January 30, 1934
Died:
Home State: New York
Service: Army
Conflict: Vietnam War
Age at Time of Award: 30

Roger Hugh C. Donlon was born in Saugerties, New York, on January 30, 1934. In 1953, he enlisted in the US Air Force with the intention of flying, but he failed his second physical examination because of cataracts. Discharged from the Air Force in 1955, he was admitted to the US Military Academy, West Point that same year. He resigned from West Point in April 1957 and returned to military service in February 1958, when he joined the US Army.

Donlon secured a commission through officer candidate school (OCS). He spent the first few years of his army career at Fort Jackson, South Carolina, progressing in responsibility from company officer to instructor, company commander, and finally staff officer. In September 1961, he served as platoon leader in the 9th Infantry Division at Fort Jonathan Wainwright, Alaska, until he became aide-de-camp to Brig. Gen. Lester L. Wheeler.

In August 1963, Donlon joined the 5th Special Forces Group (Airborne) at Fort Bragg, North Carolina, but later transferred to the 7th Special Forces Group (Airborne) because of his training in Alaska. He assumed command of Detachment A-726, C Company of the 7th Special Forces Group (Airborne) in January 1964 and began preparations for deployment to the Republic of Vietnam (South Vietnam).

Captain Donlon arrived in South Vietnam with his 12-man detachment on May 27, 1964, and took over the camp at Nam Dong, 35 miles west of Danang. In the early morning of July 6, 1964, a reinforced Viet Cong (VC) battalion attacked the camp with mortar and small arms fire, threatening to overrun the defending American, one Australian, South Vietnamese, and Nung forces guarding Nam Dong. During the nearly five-hour battle for Nam Dong, Donlon received wounds in the stomach, left shoulder, leg, and face, as well as other minor wounds over his body as a result of shrapnel. Throughout the fight, and despite his wounds, Donlon regrouped his troops, administered first aid, directed counterfire with the camp's mortars, and rallied his men against the VC assault. Two members of Detachment A-726, Gabriel R. Alamo and John L. Houston, died in the battle, along with the Australian adviser, Kevin Conway, the first Australian to be killed in action in the Vietnam War. Donlon returned to the United States shortly thereafter to recuperate. On December 17, 1964, President Lyndon B. Johnson presented him with the Medal of Honor for his actions during the Battle of Nam Dong, making him the first recipient of the nation's highest decoration for valor during the Vietnam War.

After the war, Roger Donlon held a variety of assignments before retiring to Kansas from the army as a colonel on December 14, 1988. He has written two books about his Vietnam experiences: *Outpost of Freedom* (1965) and *Beyond Nam Dong* (1998). Donlon is also the executive director of the Westmoreland Scholarship Foundation and is active in numerous veterans' activities and programs.

Ronald B. Frankum Jr.

Further Reading

Collier, Peter, and Nick Del Calzo. *Medal of Honor: Portraits of Valor beyond the Call of Duty*. New York: Artisan, 2006.

Donlon, Roger. *Beyond Nam Dong*. Leavenworth, KS: R and N Publishers, 1998.

Donlon, Roger, with Warren Rogers. *Outpost of Freedom*. New York: Avon Books, 1966.

Proft, Robert J. *United States of America's Congressional Medal of Honor Recipients: Their Official Citations*. Columbia Heights, MN: Highland House II, 2007.

Donovan, William Joseph

Born: January 1, 1883
Died: February 8, 1959
Home State: New York
Service: Army
Conflict: World War I
Age at Time of Award: 35

William Joseph "Wild Bill" Donovan was a second-generation Irish Catholic born on January 1, 1883, in Buffalo, New York. A star quarterback at Columbia, Donovan received his undergraduate and then law degrees from there in 1908. He practiced law in Buffalo, where he met and married socialite Ruth Rumsey in 1914. In 1916, as commander of I troop, 1st Cavalry Regiment of the New York National Guard, Captain Donovan led his cavalry troop along the Mexican border as part of Brig. Gen. John J. Pershing's Punitive Expedition chasing the Mexican revolutionary Pancho Villa.

Within days of redeploying from the border, Donovan was mobilized once again, this time to command 1st Battalion of the 69th "Fighting Irish" Infantry Regiment of the New York National Guard. As part of the National Guard's 42nd "Rainbow" Division, the 69th was redesignated the 165th Infantry, but the men of Donovan's command still referred to their unit as the "Old 69th." By February 28, 1918, Donovan's men entered the firing line in a sector close to Lunéville, France. Their first significant battle occurred July 27–28, 1918, on the river Ourcq, and it was to be a fierce small-unit action that would fully test Donovan's combat leadership. Although wounded, he performed superbly under fire. For his heroism and leadership, Donovan received the Distinguished Service Cross from General Pershing and earned the nickname Wild Bill from his men.

By October, Donovan was a lieutenant colonel and in command of the regiment. He prepared his regiment for a major attack on the Kriemhilde Fortress, a German stronghold in the Argonne Forest, as part of General Pershing's 1,250,000-strong Meuse-Argonne Offensive to break the entire Kriemhilde Line and get to Sedan and into Germany. On October 14, Donovan's regiment attacked the experienced German 41st Infantry Division near Landres-et-St. Georges. Against dug-in machine guns, gas, and enemy aircraft, the regiment lost 400 men on the first day. Cut off from all communications, Lieutenant Colonel Donovan personally continued to lead his men against the Kriemhilde Fortress, moving from position to position, reorganizing decimated units and leading them forward. Wounded just below the right knee by a machine gun, Donovan refused to be evacuated for over five hours, instead consolidating his gains and preparing his unit for an enemy counterattack. When the German counterattack came, it was violent and sudden. Donovan, although severely wounded, personally positioned his mortars and forces and then encouraged them to rout the enemy. Rout they did, forcing the remaining Germans back into the fortress in total disarray. Only then would Donovan allow his own evacuation, knowing his men would hold their gains. After his recovery, he would lead his regiment, now known as the "Fighting 69th," back to New York in April 1919. In 1922, Lieutenant Colonel Donovan was awarded the Medal of Honor for his dauntless courage and battle command under fire against the Kriemhilde Fortress, becoming one of the most decorated officers in the war.

Wild Bill Donovan continued to excel in life after the war. He was an accomplished federal attorney and even ran for the governorship of New York. In 1942, he became the founder and commander of the direct antecedent of the Central Intelligence Agency, the Office of Strategic Services (OSS). The OSS was technically a military organization, and Donovan would rise to the rank of major general. After the war and the liquidation of the OSS by President Truman, Donovan became ambassador to Thailand in 1953 and 1954. In the end, he went back to his first occupation, that of lawyer. He attracted some of the finest legal talent in the country and founded the acclaimed Donovan Leisure Newton & Irvine, the great Rockefeller Plaza law firm. In 1957, President Eisenhower awarded Donovan the highest honor a civilian can earn, the National Security Medal. Donovan became the first American to earn the nation's four top decorations: the Medal of Honor, the Distinguished Service Cross, the Distinguished Service Medal, and finally the National Security Medal. Wild Bill Donovan died at Walter Reed General Hospital in Washington, D.C., on February 8, 1959, at the age of 76, and is buried in Arlington National Cemetery.

Scott A. Porter

Further Reading

Brown, Anthony Cave. *Wild Bill Donovan: The Last Hero*. New York: The New York Times Book Company, 1982.

Dunlop, Richard. *Donovan: America's Master Spy*. Chicago: Rand McNally, 1982.

Harris, Stephen L. *Duffy's War: Fr. Francis Duffy, Wild Bill Donovan, and the Irish Fighting 69th in World War I*. Dulles, VA: Potomac Books, 2006.

Doolittle, James H.

Born: December 14, 1896
Died: September 27, 1993
Home State: Alaska
Service: Army

Conflict: World War II
Age at Time of Award: 46

Born on December 14, 1896, in Alameda, California, James Harold "Jimmy" Doolittle grew up in Nome, Alaska. He attended Los Angeles Community College and the University of California, but he left school following the entry of the United States into World War I and enlisted as a flying cadet in the Signal Corps Reserve. He attended flight school, became a pilot, and was commissioned a second lieutenant. He then served as a flight-gunner instructor at Rockwell Field in San Diego, California. His request for assignment to France was denied because of the armistice of November 1918.

In 1920, Doolittle secured a Regular Army commission, and, on September 4, 1922, he made the first transcontinental flight in less than 24 hours. He then studied at the Massachusetts Institute of Technology, where he received master's and PhD degrees in aeronautical engineering. A leader in advances in both military and civilian aviation, Doolittle helped develop horizontal and directional gyroscopes and pioneered instrument flying.

Doolittle gained prominence through stunt flying, racing, and demonstrating aircraft. In 1930, he left the army to become aviation manager for Shell Oil, where he helped develop new high-octane aviation fuels that greatly benefited the United States in World War II. He won the Harmon (1930) and Bendix (1931) trophies, and in 1932 he broke the world airspeed record.

In July 1940, Doolittle returned to the army as a major. Following US entry into World War II, he was promoted to lieutenant colonel in January 1942. On April 18, 1942, Doolittle commanded the first American air strike on the Japanese mainland. The raid was a great fillip for US morale, and for it he was awarded the Medal of Honor and promoted to brigadier general.

In July 1942, Doolittle took command of the 12th Air Force in England, which he led in Operation Torch in North Africa. In November 1943, he was given command of the 15th Air Force in the Mediterranean Theater, directing it in raids against German-held Europe. In January 1944, he assumed command of the 8th Air Force in the European Theater, and that March he was promoted to temporary lieutenant general. On Germany's surrender in May 1945, Doolittle moved with the 8th Air Force to Okinawa, although the 8th arrived in the Pacific Theater too late to see much action.

In May 1946, James Doolittle returned to the civilian sector as a vice president for Shell Oil, and later he became its director. He also served on the National Advisory Committee for Aeronautics, the Air Force Science Advisory Board, and the President's Science Advisory Committee. In June 1985, Doolittle was promoted to general on the retired list by act of Congress. He died on September 27, 1993, in Pebble Beach, California.

Sean K. Duggan

Further Reading

Doolittle, James H., with Carroll V. Glines. *I Could Never Be So Lucky Again: An Autobiography by General James H. "Jimmy" Doolittle.* Atglen, PA: Schiffer, 1991.

Glines, Carroll V. *Doolittle's Tokyo Raiders.* Salem, NH: Ayer, 1964.

Merrill, James M. *Target Tokyo: The Halsey-Doolittle Raid.* New York: Rand McNally, 1964.

Thomas, Lowell, and Edward Jablonski. *Doolittle: A Biography.* Garden City, NY: Doubleday, 1976.

Doss, Desmond T.

Born: February 7, 1919
Died: March 23, 2006
Home State: Virginia
Service: Army
Conflict: World War II
Age at Time of Award: 26

Born in Lynchburg, Virginia, on February 7, 1919, Desmond T. Doss was raised a Seventh-Day Adventist. His devout religious beliefs were an essential part of his character, with the sixth commandment, "Thou shalt not kill," becoming one of the central themes of his life. Believing in serving both God and his country, Doss registered for the draft at the age of 18.

War found Doss working in a shipyard; he had the opportunity for a deferment, which he refused. Despite his registration as a conscientious objector (a term Doss did not like, preferring conscientious co-operator), the army assigned Doss as a medical aid man to a rifle company in the 77th

Desmond T. Doss, US Army (US Army Medical Department Regiment).

Infantry Division. Doss had to get the help of the chaplain to have his status as a conscientious objector officially accepted, and his fellow soldiers regularly derided him for this, as well as for his habit of praying at his bunk and his refusal to carry a weapon. One officer threatened him with a court-martial and a medical discharge as a mental case, and Doss had to endure almost constant derision from his officers and fellow soldiers. Despite these incidents, he insisted on continuing to do his duty.

Doss first saw action during the invasion of Guam, July 21–August 8, 1944, regularly accompanying the men on patrols even when he was not required to do so. After a short rest, the 77th Infantry Division went back into action in the Philippines on December 7, 1944, on the island of Leyte. There, Doss received a Bronze Star for his repeated bravery in treating the wounded while under fire.

Doss's division was in action in the Philippines until the beginning of February 1945. They were then sent to Okinawa in late March. There, they took part in some of the fiercest fighting of the Pacific War. Troops from 77th Division's 1st Battalion, 307th Regiment were tasked with clearing the Maeda Escarpment, a strategic ridge dominating access to the southern portion of Okinawa. During the night of April 30–May 1, the battalion fought its way up a 40-foot cliff and onto the edge of the escarpment itself. It was here, within a few days, that Doss earned his Medal of Honor.

On May 5, after pushing further onto the ridge, the men of the 307th Regiment were counterattacked by the Japanese and driven back. Doss stayed on the ridge to treat and evacuate the wounded. Under almost constant fire over the next several hours, Doss worked his way among the wounded, carrying them back to the edge of the cliff and lowering them to safety below. The litter that he used initially was not up to the task, so he instead tied a double bowline in the rope, a knot he had learned as a boy at summer camp. Under rifle and grenade attack, and crawling to within feet of the Japanese positions, Doss rescued the wounded one by one. He claimed that he did not know how many wounded he rescued that day, though the Army settled on the number of 75. Doss's battalion—1st Battalion, 307th Regiment—suffered nearly 500 casualties from the 800 men who had gone into action a week previously.

After securing the escarpment, the unit captured another rise called Chocolate Drop. In the night attack on this position, a grenade badly wounded Doss, but he still found the strength to aid other wounded soldiers. While carried back to the aid station, he gave up his place on a stretcher so that another man might be taken instead. Making his way back with the help of another soldier, Doss was again wounded. His arm was badly broken, which took him out of the war.

President Truman awarded Desmond Doss the Medal of Honor on October 12, 1945. He spent most of the next six years in and out of the hospital, being treated for complications resulting from his wounds. Eventually, he had a lung and several ribs removed. Unable to work regularly, Doss suffered from financial hardship. This was somewhat alleviated after appearing as a guest on the television program *This Is Your Life* in February 1959. He spent most of his remaining years helping others through his local church. Doss died on March 23, 2006, and was buried at Chattanooga National Cemetery in Tennessee.

Nicholas A. Murray

Further Reading

Appleman, Roy E., et al. *Okinawa: The Last Battle.* Washington, D.C.: Historical Division, Department of the Army, 1948.

Collier, Peter, and Nick Del Calzo. *Medal of Honor: Portraits of Valor beyond the Call of Duty.* New York: Artisan, 2006.

Smith, Larry. *Beyond the Glory: Medal of Honor Heroes in Their Own Words—Extraordinary Stories of Courage from World War II to Vietnam.* New York: W. W. Norton, 2003.

US Congress. Senate. Committee on Veterans Affairs. *Medal of Honor Recipients, 1863–1978: "In the Name of the Congress of the United States."* Washington, D.C.: Government Printing Office, 1979.

Dunham, Jason L.

Born: November 10, 1981
Died: April 22, 2004
Home State: New York
Service: Marine Corps
Conflict: Iraq
Age at Time of Award: 23

Born in Scio, New York, on November 10, 1981, Jason L. Dunham joined the Marine Corps in 2000. In early 2004, he deployed to Iraq, where he served with the 3rd Battalion, 7th Marine Regiment. On April 14, Corporal Dunham was leading a patrol in the town of Karabila when they heard a firefight erupt approximately two kilometers to the west. Corporal Dunham led his team toward the engagement to provide fire support to his battalion commander's convoy, which had been ambushed by insurgents as it was traveling to Camp Husaybah. Dunham and his marines dismounted and stopped a group of seven Iraqi vehicles trying to depart the area. One insurgent left his vehicle and engaged Dunham in hand-to-hand combat, during which the insurgent dropped a hand grenade. In an attempt to save his fellow marines from injury, Dunham threw himself on the grenade, using his helmet to try to shield himself and his comrades. Severely wounded in the ensuing explosion, Dunham was evacuated from Iraq. He died at the Naval Medical Center, Bethesda, Maryland, on April 22, 2004.

On November 10, 2006, President George W. Bush announced on the occasion of the dedication of the National Museum of the Marine Corps at Quantico, Virginia, that Jason Dunham had been awarded the Medal of Honor. Bush formally presented the medal to Dunham's family in a ceremony at the White House on January 22, 2007. Dunham was the first marine to receive the medal in the Iraq War and the first marine to be so honored since the Vietnam War. The navy's newest Arleigh Burke–class destroyer (DDG-109), which was commissioned in November 2010, was named in his honor.

Spencer C. Tucker

Further Reading

Fuentes, Gidget. "Medal of Honor Is First for a Marine since Vietnam." *Marine Corps Times,* November 20, 2006.

North, Ollie, and Chuck Holton. *American Heroes: In the Fight against Radical Islam.* Nashville, TN: B&H Books, 2009.

Phillips, Michael M. *The Gift of Valor: A War Story.* New York: Broadway Books, 2005.

Dunham, Russell E.

Born: February 23, 1920
Died: April 6, 2009
Home State: Illinois
Service: Army
Conflict: World War II
Age at Time of Award: 25

Russell E. Dunham was born in East Carondelet, Illinois, on February 23, 1920, but grew up around Fosterburg, Illinois. As a teenager, he moved to St. Louis to live with his brother Ralph, where the two sold soup and tamales to survive in an area still affected by the Depression. Dunham enlisted in the US Army in 1941 and was assigned to I Company, 30th Infantry, 3rd Infantry Division. He participated in campaigns in North Africa (1942), Sicily (1943), Italy (1943), and France (1944–1945) during which time he earned the Medal of Honor in addition to the Silver Star, the Bronze Star, the Croix de Guerre, the Purple Heart, and the Combat Infantryman's Badge.

T/Sgt. Dunham's finest hour occurred on January 8, 1945, when his unit was fighting on the outskirts of Kaysersberg, France, during Army operations to clear the Colmar Pocket in the Alsace. The Americans were opposed by the 708th Volksgrenadier and 189th Infantry divisions of the German Army.

While leading a platoon of Company I as part of a local breakthrough, Dunham's unit came under withering machine gun fire from entrenched German positions firing down a slope into the American unit. Enemy artillery rounds landed immediately behind the Americans; retreat wasn't an option. Taking the initiative in an effort to save his men, T/Sgt. Dunham single-handedly rushed the German gun nearest him. He was wearing a white camouflage vest made from a discarded mattress cover, which provided minimal concealment as he crept closer to the gun. As he approached, a German bullet tore into his back, spinning him around, and he fell back down the hill. Dunham recovered and again moved forward when a German grenade landed at his feet. He instinctively kicked it away and continued toward the enemy position. Firing at point-blank range, he killed the gunner and assistant gunner before finding himself out of rifle ammunition. He jumped into the emplacement and hauled out a third German by the collar and sent him flying down the hill. "The captain said we needed prisoners," he later remarked.

Now taking fire from a second machine gun nest, Dunham picked up a rifle and carefully moved close enough to throw two grenades, destroying both the German gun and its crew. When this second position also came under enemy fire, Dunham repeated his now-successful formula and low crawled 50 yards until he was within range of the third machine gun. Waiting until the Germans were forced to stop firing to change barrels, Dunham threw more grenades and killed the members of this crew, as well. In all, during an episode lasting perhaps 10 minutes, he had killed nine Germans, wounded seven, and captured two. Despite a serious wound to his back, which had now bled until it showed through his makeshift snow-camouflage smock, Dunham resisted going for medical attention. He later said, "I was exhausted, but didn't want to go back. We still had more to do."

Amazingly, T/Sgt. Dunham's trials were not yet over. Returning to his unit before his wounds had fully healed, Dunham was captured along with most of his battalion on January 22 during a brief German armored counteroffensive near Holtzwihr, France. He was discovered hiding in a sauerkraut barrel, but when his captors found a pack of cigarettes, they became distracted, stopped the search, and neglected to find Dunham's pistol. While in transport to a prisoner-of-war holding facility, the German driver stopped for a drink, and Dunham took advantage of the lapse. He shot his remaining guard and escaped on foot, suffering severe frostbite in his trek back to American lines.

Russell Dunham was awarded the Medal of Honor on May 11, 1945, for his actions at Kaysersberg. Gen. Alexander Patch noted that Dunham's actions saved the lives of 120 US soldiers.

Following the war, Dunham worked for 32 years as a benefits counselor with the St. Louis office of the Veterans Administration. He regularly gave talks to schoolchildren and veterans' groups about that day in January 1945 but was nevertheless conspicuously modest about his accomplishments. "You're never proud of killing anybody, and you don't win a medal. It's not a contest. You just receive it. And you don't receive it for how many you kill but for how many you save." Dunham died on April 6, 2009, at Godfrey, Illinois, and is buried in Godfrey's Valhalla Memorial Park.

Mark M. Hull

Further Reading

Collier, Peter, and Nick Del Calzo. *Medal of Honor: Portraits of Valor beyond the Call of Duty.* New York: Artisan, 2006.

Jordan, Kenneth N. *Yesterday's Heroes: 433 Men of World War II Awarded the Medal of Honor, 1941–1945.* Atglen, PA: Schiffer Military History, 1996.

Owens, Ron. *Medal of Honor: Historical Facts and Figures.* Paducah, KY: Turner Publishing, 2004.

Dyess, Aquilla James

Born: January 11, 1909
Died: February 2, 1944
Home State: Georgia
Service: Marine Corps
Conflict: World War II
Age at Time of Award: 35

Aquilla James Dyess was born on January 11, 1909, in Andersonville, Georgia. As a youth, he attained the rank of Eagle Scout in the Boy Scouts and also was awarded the Carnegie Medal for saving two swimmers off the coast of Charleston, South Carolina, in July 1928. He attended Clemson College in South Carolina, where he served as a cadet major in ROTC; in 1931, he was appointed an infantry second lieutenant in the US Army Reserve. After graduation from Clemson with a bachelor's of science in architecture, Dyess worked as a general contractor building houses in Georgia and as an assistant director for a boy's summer camp. In November 1936, Dyess learned that the Marine Corps was going to form a reserve unit in Augusta, Georgia; at this point, he decided to become a Marine. In December 1936, Dyess, having resigned his Army Reserve commission, accepted a commission as a first lieutenant in the US Marine Corps Reserve. Strongly interested in marksmanship, in 1937 Dyess was awarded the Bronze Medal as a member of the Marine Corps Rifle Team, which won the Hilton Trophy in the national matches that year, and he helped the team win the award again in 1938. While in the Marine Corps Reserves, Dyess worked hard to perfect his military skills and was promoted to the rank of captain shortly before being recalled to active duty in November 1940.

Despite Dyess's strong desire for duty with the infantry, he was instead assigned to the barrage balloon training school at Quantico, Virginia. This was a time of great frustration for Dyess as he was given a number of barrage balloon assignments at locations such as Lake Hurst, New Jersey; Parris Island, South Carolina; and New River, North Carolina. However, by March 1943, Dyess was finally able to get away from balloon units and was appointed executive officer for the 1st Battalion, 24th Marines. In October 1943, he assumed command of the battalion. At the time, Dyess was one of the few Marine Corps Reservists without any previous combat experience to be given command of an infantry battalion. Known to his officers and men as Big Red for his shock of red hair, Dyess walked with a pronounced limp due to a prewar football injury. He gained a reputation as a stern but fair taskmaster, working his men hard to get them ready for combat operations. By January 1944, Dyess and his yet-to-be-tested 1st Battalion, 24th Marines were in the South Pacific getting ready for an amphibious assault against Roi-Namur, a small island near Kwajalein in the Marshall Islands chain. On February 1, 1944, Dyess and his men had been assigned to seize Green Beach on the Namur side of the two-island chain. Dyess's performance on the first day of fighting was extraordinary, and he personally led repeated assaults against Japanese defensive positions. During the second day of fighting on Namur, Dyess continued his furious assault against the enemy. Moving against one of the last remaining Japanese positions, he positioned himself between the opposing lines to point out objectives and avenues of approach as he personally led the advancing marines against the enemy. While standing on the parapet of an antitank trench directing his men at an exposed point in the northern part of the island, he was mortally wounded by a burst of enemy machine gun fire.

For his "conspicuous gallantry and intrepidity," Lieutenant Colonel Dyess was posthumously awarded the Medal of Honor by President Franklin D. Roosevelt. The citation that accompanied the award stated that "his daring and forceful leadership and his valiant fighting spirit in the face of terrific opposition were in keeping with the highest traditions of the United States Naval Service." Dyess is the only American to have received both the Carnegie Medal for civilian heroism and the Medal of Honor. He is also one of only seven known Eagle Scouts who received the Medal of Honor.

Lieutenant Colonel Dyess was initially buried in the 4th Marine Division Cemetery on Roi-Namur Island, Kwajalein Atoll, Marshall Islands. In 1948, his remains were reinterred in Westover Memorial Park Cemetery, Augusta, Georgia. Aquilla Dyess and his heroism have been honored in a number of ways. In 1945, the destroyer USS *Dyess* (DD-880) was named in his honor. In October 1998, the Naval and Marine Corps Reserve Center in Augusta, Georgia, was dedicated to Lieutenant Colonel Dyess. The four-lane highway from Interstate 20 in Augusta, Georgia, to Fort Gordon is named the Jimmy Dyess Parkway in honor of Lieutenant Colonel Dyess.

Huong T. D. Nguyen

ANDREWS RAIDERS

The first recipients of the Medal of Honor were participants in one of the most colorful and dramatic operations of the Civil War—the "Andrews raid" of April 12, 1862. James J. Andrews, a civilian, planned and led the expedition; he hoped to seize a train near Atlanta, Georgia, and drive it north along the Western and Atlantic Railroad to Chattanooga, Tennessee, destroying track and bridges along the way. With its rail artery severed, Chattanooga would supposedly be vulnerable to capture by Federal forces in Tennessee.

Andrews and 23 volunteers (22 soldiers and 1 other civilian), all dressed in civilian clothes, infiltrated Confederate lines near Shelbyville, Tennessee, on April 7, 1862, and made their way to Chattanooga. Two of the would-be raiders, intercepted by suspicious Confederate soldiers, enlisted in the Confederate army so as to avert suspicion, but they subsequently deserted and returned to Federal lines. From Chattanooga, the remaining 22 men traveled by rail to Marietta, Georgia, where, early on the morning of April 12, 20 raiders boarded a northbound passenger train pulled by the locomotive *General*. (Two men overslept and missed the train.) Eight miles up the track from Marietta—at a place called Big Shanty, today known as Kennesaw—Andrews and his men commandeered the train and steamed north on their campaign of destruction. Closely pursued and lacking proper tools, the raiders inflicted only minor damage and never succeeded in setting fire to any bridges. The raid soon became a desperate race to escape from Confederate territory. Two miles north of Ringgold, Georgia, after a run of 89 miles, the *General* ran out of fuel. Andrews and his men scattered into the woods, but all were soon captured, including the two in Marietta who had missed the train.

Of the 22 raiders captured, 8, including Andrews and the other civilian, were hanged as spies. Eight other men escaped from prison and returned to Federal lines. The remaining six men were exchanged as prisoners of war. On March 25, 1863, Secretary of War Edwin M. Stanton presented to each of the six exchanged soldiers the newly authorized Army Medal of Honor. The first recipient was 19-year-old private Jacob Parrott from Fairfield County, Ohio. Eventually, the eight men who had escaped from captivity also received the medal, including the two who overslept at Marietta. One of the two men who had temporarily joined the Confederate army requested and obtained the medal. Four of the eight executed men received the award posthumously, though four did not. Andrews and the other civilian were not eligible, but no clear explanation exists for why two of the executed soldiers never got the medal. In sum, 19 of the 24 Andrews Raiders received the Medal of Honor.

Christopher R. Gabel

Further Reading

Simmons, Thomas E. *Forgotten Heroes of World War II: Personal Accounts of Ordinary Soldiers*. Nashville, TN: Cumberland House Publishing, 2002.

Smith, Perry M. *A Hero among Heroes: Jimmie Dyess and the 4th Marine Division*. Quantico, VA: Marine Corps Association, 1998.

Spector, Ronald. *Eagle against the Sun: The American War with Japan*. New York: Vintage Books, 1985.

Townley, Alvin. *Legacy of Honor: The Values and Influence of America's Eagle Scouts*. New York: Thomas Dunne Books, 2007.

Ehlers, Walter D.

Born: May 7, 1921
Died:
Home State: Kansas
Service: Army
Conflict: World War II
Age at Time of Award: 23

Walter D. Ehlers was born in Junction City, Kansas, on May 7, 1921. He and his brother Roland enlisted in the US Army at the outset of World War II in Europe. Walter admitted that his brother Roland was his hero and inspiration and that he might have quit if Roland had not encouraged him. They both grew up on a farm in Manhattan, Kansas, a short distance from Fort Riley. As young men during the Depression, they often hunted for game to eat. Hard outdoor living and shooting inured them both to tough conditions and honed skills they would practice in the coming war. Walter later attributed his ability to survive in the Army to his life on the farm.

Walter and Roland enlisted together and requested to be assigned to the same unit. Both men were originally sent to the 7th Infantry Division and then transferred to the 3rd Infantry Division. In North Africa, their company was transferred to the 18th Infantry Regiment, 1st Infantry Division. When Roland was wounded on Sicily and sent to a hospital in North Africa, Walter went on to England to prepare for the D-Day invasion. Roland rejoined his brother but was assigned to another company when the K Company commander determined there was too great a possibility of the men both becoming casualties during the beach assault on D-Day.

On June 6, both young men found themselves on the fire-swept shores of Omaha Beach as part of the 18th Infantry, 1st Infantry Division. Unbeknownst to Walter, Roland's landing craft suffered a direct hit from a German mortar round. In the meantime, Walter landed with his company and began the bitter fighting through the bocage of Normandy.

June 9 found Staff Sergeant Ehlers leading his squad after fighting inland from the beaches for about eight miles. Near Goville, he aggressively led his unit from the front through heavy German defenses. Ehlers unhesitatingly attacked multiple German machine guns and mortars in a fortified defensive position that was blocking his unit's advance. Despite heavy fire from interlocking German machine gun positions, Ehlers led his squad in eliminating the mortar crews and then turned his attention to the machine gun nests. Supported by fire from his unit, he single-handedly knocked out the machine guns.

The next day, Ehlers and his platoon found themselves far in advance of friendly units. Heavily engaged by withering fire from German positions to the front and flanks, his platoon was ordered to withdraw. Ehlers remained behind to cover the withdrawal of his men, standing conspicuously in order to draw fire away from his men. When his squad's automatic rifleman was hit and wounded, Ehlers went to his assistance and carried him to safety despite being shot in the torso himself. After evacuating his automatic rifleman, Ehlers returned under heavy German fire to recover the Browning Automatic Rifle.

Ehlers's actions allowed his unit to disengage successfully while saving the life of his automatic rifleman. After having his wound treated, Ehlers insisted on returning to lead his unit rather than be evacuated.

Shortly after the battles around Goville, Walter attempted to find his brother, whom he had not seen since landing in France. His brother had initially been listed as missing, but an officer came to notify Walter that Roland had unfortunately been killed in action when his craft received a direct hit from a mortar round. In the meantime, Ehlers's heroic actions were noticed by his chain of command, and he earned a battlefield commission as a lieutenant and was given a platoon to lead. Upon being recommended for promotion, Staff Sergeant Ehlers was transferred from Company K to Company C. His lieutenant bars were pinned on his uniform by Capt. Bobby Brown, the company commander who had already been recommended for, and would subsequently be awarded, the Medal of Honor.

Wounded again during subsequent fighting, Ehlers was evacuated but requested to return to his unit. A few days prior to the Battle of the Bulge, Ehlers was en route to rejoin his unit when he read in *Stars and Stripes* newspaper that he was to be awarded the Medal of Honor for his actions in Normandy. He received the medal on December 19, 1944.

Walter Ehlers survived the war to return home and work for the Veterans Administration and other veterans' organizations for over 37 years. An ardent patriot, he continues to actively support veterans and veterans' organizations.

Edwin L. Kennedy Jr.

Further Reading

Collier, Peter, and Nick Del Calzo. *Medal of Honor: Portraits of Valor beyond the Call of Duty*. New York: Artisan, 2006.

Lang, George, Raymond L. Collins, and Gerard F. White. *Medal of Honor Recipients 1863–1994*. Vol. 2, *WWII to Somalia*. New York: Facts on File, 1995.

Phillips, Col. James H., and Maj. John F. Kane, eds. *The Medal of Honor of the United States Army*. Washington, D.C.: Government Printing Office, 1948.

Evans, Ernest Edwin

Born: August 8, 1908
Died: October 25, 1944
Home State: Oklahoma

Service: Navy
Conflict: World War II
Age at Time of Award: 36

Ernest Edwin Evans, part Cherokee, was born on August 8, 1908, in Pawnee, Oklahoma. In 1931, Evans graduated from the US Naval Academy, where he was nicknamed Chief by his classmates, partially due to his heritage and partly due to his leadership abilities. As a naval officer, Evans excelled in the "Treaty Navy" of the 1930s and served on a wide variety of ships. Evans's 10-year experience in the interwar US military prepared him for success in the approaching conflict between the United States and Japan.

After America's entry into World War II in December 1941, Lieutenant Commander Evans served aboard the destroyer USS *Alden* (DD-211) in the Pacific Theater, participating in the Battle of the Java Sea in February 1942. Two weeks after the battle, he assumed command of the *Alden*.

On October 27, 1943, the Navy tapped Evans to become the skipper of the USS *Johnston* (DD-557). Evans helped to commission the ship in Seattle, Washington, and took the *Johnston* from the West Coast of the United States to the Western Pacific. The *Johnston* first saw combat during the campaign for the Marshall Islands when the ship took part in the bombardment of the beaches on Kwajalein on February 1, 1944. On May 15, while performing antisubmarine patrols off Bougainville, Commander Evans depth charged and sank the Japanese submarine I-16. Evans was awarded the Bronze Star for meritorious achievement for this action.

Meanwhile, the Joint Chiefs of Staff authorized Gen. Douglas A. MacArthur to launch his long-awaited return to the Philippines. MacArthur charged Gen. Walter Krueger's US 6th Army with the task of seizing Leyte Island in the middle of the enormous archipelago. On October 20, 1944, four US Army infantry divisions landed on the eastern coast of Leyte. MacArthur had fulfilled his pledge to return, but the battle for this large mountain- and jungle-laced island took months of bitter fighting and cost thousands of American lives.

While US soldiers fought to subdue the island, the US Navy waged a titanic battle with the Japanese Imperial Navy in the seas surrounding Leyte and Samar Island. An engagement on October 23–25, 1944, determined the fate of the American invasion of Leyte and resulted in the largest battle in naval history—the Battle of Leyte Gulf.

The Japanese plan was simple; the Combined Japanese Fleet was divided into several sections. The Northern Force, consisting of empty aircraft carriers, would lure Adm. William Halsey's Third Fleet north of the Leyte invasion beaches. Then the larger Central and Southern Forces would steam in and destroy the American invasion force.

Only Adm. Clifton A. F. Sprague's 7th Fleet, consisting of destroyers, submarines, battleships, and escort carriers, protected the vulnerable US landing forces. On October 25, 1944, Task Unit 77.4.3, also known as Taffy 3, which included Commander Ernie Evans and USS *Johnston*, took on the much-larger Japanese Central Forces off Samar Island steaming toward the American invasion fleet anchored off Leyte.

The *Johnston* was the first ship to lay a smoke screen in front of the approaching enemy fleet. The *Johnston*, severely outnumbered and outgunned, then engaged the Japanese fleet with her five-inch guns and torpedo tubes, damaging the heavy cruiser *Kumano*. With this action, Evans drew enemy fire away from the lightly armored escort carriers and transports, but the destroyer was severely damaged by three direct hits by Japanese 14-inch battleship shells, which destroyed the bridge and caused the *Johnston* to lose power and communications. Evans, who had been severely wounded during the exchange with the Japanese ships, shouted steering commands through an open hatch to the crew below deck and continued to fight the enemy ships as best he could.

During the next three hours of battle, the crippled *Johnston* continued to support the attacks by the other ships in Taffy 3 but drew so much fire from the Japanese fleet that it was finally completely put out of action.

Commander Evans ordered his crew to abandon the lifeless ship. Some of the *Johnston's* crew were able to climb into lifeboats; however, many officers and men had to jump into the water. Most sailors floating in the water died from their injuries or exposure to the unforgiving ocean. Soon the crippled ship rolled over and sank into the deep blue waters of the Leyte Gulf. Commander Evans was the last man off the ship. He and several dozen men were never found and died at sea.

Ultimately, the US Navy won the Battle of Leyte Gulf, and the Japanese Navy never recovered from the loss of ships and men. The US 6th and 8th armies conquered Leyte by early 1945 and prepared for the invasion of Luzon.

For his heroic leadership during the battle off Samar, Ernest Evans was posthumously awarded the Medal of Honor. The crew of the USS *Johnston* shared in the Presidential Unit Citation awarded Taffy 3. After World War II, the US Navy honored Commander Evans's memory and gallantry by naming the destroyer escort USS *Evans* (DE-1023) in his honor.

Erik D. Carlson

Further Reading

James, Clayton D., and Anne Sharp Wells. *From Pearl Harbor to V-J Day: The American Armed Forces in WWII*. Chicago: Ivan R. Dee, 1995.

Stewart, Adrian. *The Battle of Leyte Gulf*. New York: Scribner's, 1980.

Faith, Don C., Jr.

Born: August 26, 1918
Died: December 1, 1950
Home State: Indiana
Service: Army
Conflict: Korean War
Age at Time of Award: 32

Don C. Faith Jr. was born in Washington, Indiana, on August 26, 1918. He was the son of an Army general and, in his early years, traveled with his family to various postings in the United States and around the world. He graduated from high school in Kentucky. When he failed to win admission to West Point due to a dental disqualification, he enrolled in Georgetown University in Washington, D.C.

When the United States entered World War II, he immediately enlisted and was commissioned from officer candidate school (OCS) in February 1942. Faith was assigned to the 82nd Airborne Division and served in line and staff positions, as well as aide to Gen. Matthew Ridgeway. He participated in every combat jump made by the 82nd and received the Silver Star and Bronze Star with "V" device.

Faith was among a select group of OCS officers offered regular commissions after World War II. By the summer of 1950, with less than nine years in the Army, he was commanding the 1st Battalion, 32nd Infantry, 7th Infantry Division in Japan.

When North Korea invaded South Korea in June 1950, Faith's was among the battalions culled to round out Task Force Smith, which was rushed to Korea in July. The personnel from Faith's battalion were backfilled by inductees straight from basic training, and Faith began to prepare them for movement to Korea.

Faith and his battalion landed at Inchon in September 1950 and then moved up to take their place on the line. The battalion, largely due to Faith's leadership, performed reasonably well in the fighting around Seoul after Inchon.

Hastily thrown into the headlong pursuit to the Yalu without time to reconstitute and unequipped for winter operations, November 26 found the battalion in an isolated position beyond effective support range and in contact with Chinese forces. As late as November 28, Faith was being exhorted by Gen. Ned Almond, X Corps commander, to continue the attack, but for five terrible days, Faith and his battalion could do nothing but endure massive attacks by at least two Chinese divisions.

Throughout these desperate days and hours, Faith unhesitatingly exposed himself to intense enemy fire as he moved about directing the defense of his position, personally leading counterattacks when necessary to restore his lines.

During an attempt by his battalion to link up with another unit, Faith reconnoitered the route and personally directed the elements of his command across the ice-covered reservoir in breaking through to the friendly units. Then he assumed command of the force his unit had joined, and he was ordered to launch an attack to join more friendly elements to the south.

On December 1, 1950, Faith, although physically exhausted in the bitter cold, organized and launched the attack, but it was soon halted by enemy fire. He ran forward under enemy small arms and automatic weapons fire, got his men on their feet, and personally led them in blasting their way through the enemy ring.

As they came to a hairpin curve, enemy fire from a roadblock again pinned them down. Faith organized a group of men and directed their attack on the enemy positions on the right flank. He then placed himself at the head of another group of men and, in the face of direct enemy fire, led an attack on the enemy roadblock, firing his pistol and throwing grenades. When he had reached a position approximately 30 yards from the roadblock, he was mortally wounded, but he continued to direct the attack until the roadblock was overrun.

Shortly after forcing the roadblock, Faith quietly bled to death. From that point, the task force dissolved as fighting units. Several hundred soldiers, however, eventually made it back to friendly lines, every one of whom owed their lives in large measure to Faith.

Faith's remains were never recovered, but he is memorialized with a headstone at Arlington National Cemetery. On August 2, 1951, Lt. Col. Don Faith was posthumously awarded the Medal of Honor. In 1976, Faith was inducted into the OCS Hall of Fame at Fort Benning, Georgia.

Edward L. Bowie

Further Reading

Appleman, Roy E. *East of Chosin: Entrapment and Breakout in Korea, 1950.* College Station: Texas A&M University Press, 1987.

Hammel, Eric. *Chosin: Heroic Ordeal of the Korean War.* Novato, CA: Presidio Press, 1981.

Finn, John William

Born: July 24, 1909
Died: May 27, 2010
Home State: California
Service: Navy
Conflict: World War II
Age at Time of Award: 31

John W. Finn was born July 24, 1909, in Los Angeles County, California, the son of a plumber. He dropped out of school and joined the Navy just a few days before turning 17. He received recruit training in San Diego and spent a brief assignment

John William Finn, US Navy (Naval History and Heritage Command).

with a ceremonial guard company. He attended General Aviation Utilities training at Naval Station Great Lakes, graduating in December 1926. He was reassigned to Naval Air Station North Island in San Diego, where he initially worked in aircraft repair before becoming an aviation ordnance-man and working on antiaircraft guns. He then served on a succession of ships. He was promoted to chief petty officer in 1936 and served with patrol squadrons in San Diego, Washington State, and Panama.

By December 1941, Finn was stationed at Naval Air Station Kaneohe on the island of Oahu, Hawaii, 15 miles from Pearl Harbor and Battleship Row. At the time, he was responsible for a section of 20 men whose mission was to maintain the weapons of a PBY Catalina flying boat squadron.

When the Japanese attacked Hawaii on the morning of December 7, he was at home in bed with his wife when he heard the rumble of low-flying aircraft and a popping noise coming from the base about a mile away. At first, he thought someone had decided to conduct firing practice on a Sunday morning, but the wife of one his men pounded on his front door and told him they needed him at the base. Still not completely aware of what was happening, he threw on his dungarees and drove as calmly as he could toward the base and the hangars, at first observing the base speed limit of 20 miles per hour. However, when a fighter plane buzzed him, he looked up and saw the "red meatball" of the Japanese insignia and "threw it into second gear," racing as fast he could drive to the hangars. Arriving there, he commandeered a .50 caliber machine gun and set it up on a makeshift tripod of spare pipes out in the open, where he had a clear field of fire on the attacking aircraft. Firing at wave after wave of strafing Japanese Zeroes and dive bombers for more than two-and-a-half hours, he was credited with bringing down one plane on his own and probably hit several of the slower bombers, but that could not be confirmed in the confusion. While trying to fight off the Japanese attack, he sustained a number of injuries, including a bullet wound in his left arm; a broken left foot; shrapnel to his chest, stomach, right elbow, and thumb; and a laceration to his scalp. He refused to leave his post until he was ordered to seek medical attention for his wounds. After getting bandaged up, he returned to the hangar to help rearm returning planes. He later spent two weeks in the hospital recovering from his wounds.

On September 15, 1942, Finn received the Medal of Honor from Adm. Chester W. Nimitz, commander in chief of the Pacific Fleet, in a ceremony aboard the carrier USS *Enterprise* moored in Pearl Harbor. Nimitz cited Chief Finn for his "magnificent courage in the face of almost certain death."

Finn served stateside after recovering from his wounds. He was promoted to lieutenant in 1944 and later served on the carrier USS *Hancock*. After the war, he remained in the Navy until he retired in 1956. He and his wife, Alice, moved onto a 93-acre ranch in the desert outside San Diego. They became foster parents to five Native American children, causing the Finns to be embraced by the Campo Band of Diegueño Mission Indians, a tribe of Kumeyaay people in the San Diego area.

In 1999, Finn was among a number of Pearl Harbor veterans invited to Hawaii to attend the premiere of the Hollywood movie *Pearl Harbor*. In his later years, he was very active in participating in events celebrating veterans. On March 25, 2009, he attended National Medal of Honor Day ceremonies at Arlington National Cemetery. With the aid of canes, he stood beside President Barack Obama during a wreath-laying ceremony at the Tomb of the Unknown Soldier and later that day was a guest of the president and his family at the White House.

Finn died on May 27, 2010, at a nursing home in Chula Vista, California, the last survivor of the 15 Navy men who received the Medal of Honor for heroism during the Japanese attack on Pearl Harbor. He was 100 years old and was the oldest living recipient of the medal at the time of his death; he was preceded in death by his wife, who passed away in 1998. John W. Finn was buried at the Campo Indian Reservation cemetery.

James H. Willbanks

Further Reading

Collier, Peter, and Nick Del Calzo. *Medal of Honor: Portraits of Valor beyond the Call of Duty*. New York: Artisan, 2006.

Murphy, Edward F. *Heroes of World War II*. Novato, CA: Presidio Press, 1990.

Smith, Larry. *Beyond Glory: Medal of Honor Heroes in Their Own Words—Extraordinary Stories of Courage from WWII to Vietnam*. New York: W. W. Norton & Company, 2003.

US Senate. Committee on Veterans Affairs. *Medal of Honor Recipients, 1863–1973*. Washington, D.C.: Government Printing Office, 1973.

Fletcher, Frank Jack

Born: April 29, 1885
Died: April 25, 1973
Home State: Iowa

Service: Navy
Conflict: Mexican Campaign (Veracruz)
Age at Time of Award: 29

Born in Marshalltown, Iowa, on April 29, 1885, the son of Rear Admiral Thomas Jack Fletcher, Frank Jack Fletcher graduated from the US Naval Academy in 1906. Commissioned an ensign in 1908, Fletcher commanded the destroyer *Dale* in the Asiatic Torpedo Flotilla in 1910. Fletcher saw action in the 1914 US intervention at Veracruz, Mexico. For his bravery in moving more than 350 refugees to safety, he was awarded the Medal of Honor. Lieutenant Fletcher then served in the Atlantic Fleet.

Following US entry into World War I in 1917, he won promotion to lieutenant commander and commanded the destroyer *Benham* on convoy escort and patrol operations. Fletcher's postwar commands included submarine tenders, destroyers, and a submarine base in the Philippines, where he helped suppress an insurrection in 1924.

Fletcher attended both the US Naval War College (1929–1930) and US Army War College (1930–1931). From 1933 to 1936, he served as aide to the secretary of the Navy. From 1936 to 1938, Fletcher commanded the battleship *New Mexico* and then served in the Navy's Bureau of Personnel. Following his promotion to rear admiral, Fletcher commanded Cruiser Division 3 in the Atlantic Fleet.

On December 15, 1941, Fletcher took command of the Wake Island relief force centered on the carrier *Saratoga,* but he moved cautiously, and the island fell on December 23 before he could arrive. In January 1942, Fletcher received command of Task Force 17, which was centered on the carrier *Yorktown.* He participated in carrier raids on the Marshall and Gilbert islands and joined Task Force 11 in attacks on Japanese shipping in the Solomon Islands. Fletcher commanded US forces in the May 1942 Battle of the Coral Sea. Following his return to Pearl Harbor for hasty repairs to the *Yorktown,* Fletcher raced back with her to join the US force near Midway, where he helped orchestrate the dramatic US victory on June 3–6, 1942, in which four Japanese carriers were lost in exchange for the *Yorktown.*

Fletcher then commanded the three-carrier task force supporting 1st Marine Division assaults on Tulagi and Guadalcanal (Operation Watchtower). Unwilling to risk his carriers, Fletcher made the controversial decision to withdraw them before the transports had completed unloading supplies to the marines, forcing the transports to depart as well. He then committed his forces against the Japanese counterattack toward Guadalcanal, resulting in the Battle of the Eastern Solomons. Fletcher was wounded when his flagship, the carrier *Saratoga,* was torpedoed, and he returned to the United States.

After his recovery, Fletcher commanded the 13th Naval District and the Northwestern Sea Frontier. Fletcher's reputation for caution led chief of naval operations

Adm. Ernest J. King to assign him to command the North Pacific area in 1943. Following Japan's surrender in August 1945, Fletcher oversaw the occupation of northern Honshu and Hokkaido.

In 1945, Frank Fletcher joined the navy's General Board, which advised the secretary of the Navy; he served as its chairman from May 1946 until May 1947, when he was promoted to full admiral and retired. Fletcher died in Bethesda, Maryland, on April 25, 1973.

Stephen Patrick Ward

Further Reading

Hammel, Erich. *Carrier Clash: The Invasion of Guadalcanal and the Battle of the Eastern Solomons, August 1942*. Pacifica, CA: Pacifica Press, 1997.

Morison, Samuel E. *History of United States Naval Operations in World War II*. Vol. 3, *The Rising Sun in the Pacific, 1931–April 1942*; Vol. 4, *Coral Sea, Midway and Submarine Actions, May 1942–August 1942*. Boston: Little, Brown, 1948, 1949.

Regan, Stephen. *In Bitter Tempest: The Biography of Frank Jack Fletcher*. Ames: Iowa State Press, 1994.

Fluckey, Eugene Bennett

Born: October 5, 1913
Died: June 28, 2007
Home State: Washington, D.C.
Service: Navy
Conflict: World War II
Age at Time of Award: 31

Eugene Bennett Fluckey was born in Washington, D.C., on October 5, 1913. He was commissioned an ensign upon graduation from the US Naval Academy, Annapolis, in June 1935 and then served on the battleship *Nevada* and the destroyer *McCormick* before being assigned to the submarine school at New London, Connecticut. Upon completion of the course there, he was assigned first to S-42 and then to the submarine *Bonita* (SS-165), in which he completed five World War II patrols. In August 1942, he returned to Annapolis, where he completed graduate instruction in naval engineering.

In November 1943, Fluckey reported to Submarine Base New London, where he graduated from the prospective commanding officer school. Following one war patrol as the prospective commander of the submarine *Barb* (SS-220), Fluckey assumed command of that submarine on April 27, 1944, and soon established himself as one of the most effective submarine commanders of all time. Fluckey revolutionized submarine tactics, including carrying out the only US landing in the Japanese home

Eugene Bennett Fluckey, US Navy (Naval History and Heritage Command).

islands during the war. While cruising off Otasamu on the east coast of Karafuto, Fluckey noted a railroad on the coast and sent ashore a landing party with demolition charges; the team blew up a 16-car Japanese train. He also fired what he termed five-inch rockets into the towns of Shiritori and Kashiho and bombarded two other towns, destroying a lumberyard and sampans.

Fluckey was awarded four Navy Crosses for each of his 8th, 9th, 10th, and 12th war patrols. On his 11th war patrol of December 19, 1944, to February 15, 1945, he attacked two convoys, sinking a large ammunition ship in the first convoy. In the second engagement, on January 25, 1945, Fluckey attacked 30 Japanese ships anchored in Nankuan Chiang Harbor in only five fathoms of water. Despite knowing his escape would mean a high-speed run in shallow, mined waters from pursuing Japanese escort ships, he attacked and obtained eight direct hits on six of the merchant ships. Managing to clear the area in a high-speed run, he escaped two pursuing Japanese destroyers. Fluckey was subsequently awarded the Medal of Honor for this daring attack.

Known as the "Galloping Ghost of the China Coast," Fluckey was fourth on the list of Japanese ships sunk (16 and one-third) but first in shipping tonnage sunk, at 95,360 tons. This latter figure is more than any other US warship captain of the war—submarine, aircraft carrier, cruiser, or destroyer.

In August 1945, Fluckey returned to Groton, Connecticut, to oversee completion of the submarine *Dogfish* (SS-350) and to become its commanding officer, but on its commissioning he was ordered to the office of Secretary of the Navy James V. Forrestal. In December 1945, he became the personal aide to Fleet Admiral Chester W. Nimitz. In June 1947, Fluckey assumed command of the submarine *Halfbeak* (SS-352) before helping establish the Submarine Naval Reserve Force. During 1950–1953, he was US naval attaché in Portugal. In September 1953, he took command of the submarine tender *Sperry*. He commanded Submarine Flotilla 7 during 1955–1956 before becoming chairman of the Electrical Engineering Department at the Naval Academy. In July 1960, Fluckey was appointed rear admiral and then assumed command of Amphibious Group 4. During 1966–1968, he was director of Naval Intelligence before heading the Military Assistance Advisory Group in Portugal.

Eugene Fluckey retired from the Navy as a rear admiral in 1972. He later ran an orphanage in Portugal for a number of years. Fluckey died in Annapolis, Maryland, on June 28, 2007. On January 24, 2008, his remains were buried in the South China Sea from the US Navy nuclear attack submarine *Pasadena* near the site of his daring September 17, 1944, rescue of 14 Australian and British prisoners of war who were being transported to Japan when their ship sank. Some 450 miles distant at the time of the sinking, the *Barb* had managed to locate and rescue the survivors in spite of a typhoon.

Spencer C. Tucker

Further Reading

Blair, Clay, Jr. *Silent Victory: The U.S. Submarine War against Japan*. Philadelphia: J. B. Lippincott, 1975.

Collier, Peter, and Nick Del Calzo. *Medal of Honor: Portraits of Valor beyond the Call of Duty*. New York: Artisan, 2006.

Fluckey, Eugene B. *Thunder Below! The USS Barb Revolutionizes Submarine Warfare in World War II*. Urbana: University of Illinois Press, 1992.

Hargis, Robert, and Ramiro Bujeiro. *World War II Medal of Honor Recipients: Navy & USMC*. Oxford, UK: Osprey, 2003.

Lavo, Carl. "Fitting Ceremony for Navy Legend." *Naval History* 22, no. 3 (June 1008): 63.

Foley, Robert F.

Born: May 30, 1941
Died:
Home State: Massachusetts
Service: Army
Conflict: Vietnam War
Age at Time of Award: 25

Born May 30, 1941, in Newton, Massachusetts, Robert F. Foley grew to stand six feet, seven inches tall. A basketball star, Foley received 15 college scholarship offers by his senior year of high school. Passing through Massachusetts, the West Point hockey coach saw Foley score 44 points in a game and told the basketball coach about him. Impressed by the tradition and sense of purpose at the Academy when he visited at the invitation of the basketball coach, Foley decided to attend West Point even though it meant foregoing a potential professional basketball career.

Foley captained the West Point basketball team his senior year, graduated with the class of 1963, and was commissioned into the infantry. By 1966, he had completed Airborne and Ranger schools and was a 25-year-old captain commanding A Company, 2nd Battalion, 27th Infantry (the "Wolfhounds"), 25th Infantry Division in Vietnam.

In early November 1966, Foley and his company returned to base, tired after a 10-day search-and-destroy mission. But another company in his brigade had run into a North Vietnamese regiment, had been surrounded, and had suffered major casualties. So instead of receiving needed rest, A Company was ordered to go to the aid of the surrounded unit near Quan Dau Tieng, Republic of Vietnam.

Early on the morning of November 5, Foley and his company began their advance through dense, "triple canopy" jungle, which prevented the use of friendly artillery or air support. Foley led two platoons in a direct attack on strongly fortified enemy positions. When two radio operators were wounded, Foley ignored the heavy enemy fire and helped them to a position where they could receive medical aid. He then returned to the center of the action to encourage his men to maintain the momentum of the attack.

Foley was angry that his men were being hit. When one of his machine gunners went down, he picked up the machine gun, draped the ammunition belt over his shoulders, and charged the enemy positions. Firing the machine gun from the waist, Foley single-handedly destroyed three enemy machine gun emplacements. He found himself alone and nearly out of ammunition in the last bunker. But then his men caught up with him, and he continued to encourage and lead them forward. When the company encountered resistance on another flank, Foley moved to that area and, despite being wounded by an enemy grenade, refused medical treatment and again pushed his men forward for the next several hours. Foley's company accomplished its mission and relieved the encircled company.

Recommended by his men for the Medal of Honor, Foley received the decoration from President Lyndon B. Johnson on May 1, 1968. At the same time, Sgt. John F. Baker Jr., a former private in Foley's company, received the Medal of Honor for his distinguished valor during the same action.

Foley remained in the Army, serving 37 years until his retirement in 2000 and attaining the rank of lieutenant general. During his time in service, Foley commanded at the battalion and brigade levels with the 3rd Infantry Division in Germany and served as chief of staff for the 7th Infantry Division at Fort Ord, California, and as the assistant commander of the 2nd Infantry Division in Korea. In 1992, Foley returned to West Point as the 63rd commandant of cadets. While at West Point, he established a core-value program to inspire cadets to treat others with respect and dignity, initially called "Consideration for Others" and now called "Respect." It became an army-wide program and remains an integral part of leadership training at West Point.

After his tour as commandant of cadets, Foley was the assistant commander of the 2nd Army, commanding general of the US Military District of Washington, and finally, commanding general of the 5th Army at Fort Sam Houston, Texas.

Following retirement, Foley became president of the Marion Military Institute in Marion, Alabama, the nation's oldest military preparatory school and junior college. In 2005, Foley became the director of Army Emergency Relief, a private, nonprofit organization that provides emergency financial assistance to soldiers and their families. He continues to hold that position.

Robert Foley has an MBA from Fairleigh Dickenson University and also attended the Army Command and General Staff College and the Naval War College. In 2009, he received the Distinguished Graduate Award from the West Point Association of Graduates. He is a married father of two sons and one daughter. His two sons serve in the military, and his son in the Army recently commanded Foley's old unit—A Company, 2nd Battalion, 27th Infantry Regiment. Foley and his wife reside in Virginia.

Alan M. Anderson

Further Reading

Bergerud, Eric M. *Red Thunder, Tropic Lightning: The World of a Combat Division in Vietnam.* Boulder, CO: Westview Press, 1993.

Collier, Peter, and Nick Del Calzo. *Medal of Honor: Portraits of Valor beyond the Call of Duty.* New York: Artisan, 2006.

Foley, Robert F. *Consideration of Others.* Washington, D.C.: US Army Military District of Washington, 1997.

Stanton, Shelby L. *The Rise and Fall of an American Army: U.S. Ground Forces in Vietnam, 1965–1973.* New York: Presidio Press, 1985.

Foss, Joseph Jacob

Born: April 17, 1915
Died: January 1, 2003
Home State: South Dakota
Service: Marine Corps
Conflict: World War II
Age at Time of Award: 27

Joseph Jacob Foss was born April 17, 1915, on a farm near Sioux Falls, South Dakota. As a boy of 11, he fell in love with flying when his father took him to see Charles Lindbergh at an airport near his home. Several years later, he paid for his first airplane ride with a barnstormer. The pilot put his aircraft in a series of aerobatics to see if he could make the boy sick, but young Foss loved everything about the flight.

Foss's father died in 1933. Foss entered the University of South Dakota but had to drop out to help his mother run the family farm. Later, he entered the University of South Dakota, paying for tuition and books by working at a service station.

He also scraped together enough money to pay for a civilian pilot training program. In 1940, he graduated with a degree in business administration and a private pilot's license. Shortly thereafter, he enlisted in the Marine Corps to join the naval aviation cadet program in order to become a naval aviator.

Graduating from flight school at 26, Foss was considered too old for combat, so he was assigned as a flight instructor at the Navy's Pensacola Training Center in Florida. Later, he attended the Navy School of Photography before joining Maine Photographic Squadron 1, which was stationed at Naval Air Station North Island in San Diego, California. All the time, Foss was lobbying for a combat assignment. He qualified in Grumman F4F Wildcats and was eventually transferred to Marine Fighting Squadron 121 (VMF-121) as executive officer.

In October 1942, Foss and VMF-121 deployed to Noumea in the South Pacific, where he and his squadron were loaded aboard the escort carrier *Copahee*. On the morning of October 9, he and his squadron mates were catapulted off the deck in what was to be Foss's only carrier mission of the war. They landed at Henderson Field on Guadalcanal, becoming part of the Cactus Air Force in the continuing campaign to secure the island.

As exec of the squadron, Foss led a flight of eight Wildcats, which would become known as Foss's Flying Circus, in defending against the Japanese, who sent large numbers of aircraft in daily raids against Henderson Field and the marines fighting on the island. On October 13, Foss shot down a Japanese Zero on his first combat mission. During the next five weeks, he shot down a total of 23 Japanese planes and damaged a number of others. He was shot down himself four times during this period, once spending five hours in the water until rescued by Catholic missionaries in an outrigger canoe.

On January 23, 1943, as the battle of Guadalcanal wound down, Foss led a group of 12 American airplanes against a much larger Japanese formation of bombers and fighter escorts. His squadron downed four Zeros, with Foss accounting for three, forcing the bombers to turn back.

In the spring of 1943, Foss was ordered back to the United States; by this time, Foss had 26 confirmed kills, with 14 probables. He was in San Diego awaiting orders when he was notified that he would receive the Medal of Honor. On May 18, 1943, he was presented the medal by President Franklin D. Roosevelt in an Oval Office ceremony. As he left the office wearing the medal, a photographer from *Life* magazine snapped a photo that later appeared on the cover of the magazine.

After the ceremony, Foss served a short stint as a training advisor at the Santa Barbara Marine Corps Air Station in California. He returned to the Pacific in 1944 as commander of Marine Fighting Squadron 115.

After the war, Foss was commissioned in the South Dakota Air National Guard. Later, he turned to politics and was elected to the South Dakota House of Representatives. During the Korean War, Foss, then a colonel, was recalled to active duty and served as director of operations and training for the Central Air Defense Command. After the war, he reverted to the Air National Guard, eventually retiring with the rank of brigadier general.

In 1954, Foss was elected governor of South Dakota, serving two terms. In 1958, he made an unsuccessful bid for the US House of Representatives. After that, he served as the first commissioner of the American Football League from 1959 to 1966. During part of that time, he also hosted the ABC television show *The American Sportsman*. He was president of the National Rifle Association from 1988 to 1990. He and his wife were very active in the Easter Seals campaign and a number of other charities. In 2000, Foss was a consultant on the popular computer game *Combat Flight Simulator 2* by Microsoft.

In January 2002, at the age of 86, Foss again received national attention when he was stopped by security screeners at Phoenix Sky Harbor International Airport because he was carrying his Medal of Honor (which has pointed edges), a clearly marked dummy-bullet key chain, and a commemorative nail file with Medal of Honor insignia. He was on his way to attend a National Rifle Association meeting and to speak to cadets at the US Military Academy. After a 45-minute delay, he was allowed to board his plane with the Medal of Honor, but he had to mail home the key chain and nail file. This incident was used in a number of media articles about the issues involved in increased air travel security standards.

In late 2002, Joe Foss suffered a severe stroke. He died on New Year's Day 2003 and was buried at Arlington National Cemetery on January 21, 2003.

James H. Willbanks

Further Reading

Brokaw, Tom. *The Greatest Generation*. New York: Random House, 1998.

Collier, Peter, and Nick Del Calzo. *Medal of Honor: Portraits of Valor beyond the Call of Duty*. New York: Artisan, 2006.

Foss, Joe, and Donna Wild Foss. *A Proud American: The Autobiography of Joe Foss*. Novato, CA: Presidio Press, 2002.

Simmons, Walter. *Joe Foss, Flying Marine: The Story of His Flying Circus*. Whitefish, MT: Kessinger Publishing, 2008.

Tillman, Barrett. *Wildcat Aces of World War 2*. London: Osprey, 1995.

Fox, John Robert

Born: May 18, 1915
Died: December 26, 1944
Home State: Ohio
Service: Army

Conflict: World War II
Age at Time of Award: 29

Born in Cincinnati, Ohio, on May 18, 1915, John Robert Fox grew up in Ohio and graduated from Wyoming High School in 1934. Fox enlisted in Ohio's 372nd Infantry Regiment, where he served until graduating from Wilberforce University (located in Wilberforce, Ohio). Upon graduation, he received his Army ROTC commission in 1940.

Following his commissioning, Fox attended training at Fort Devens, Massachusetts, and later the Infantry School at Fort Benning, Georgia. Upon completion of his training, he was assigned to Cannon Company of the 366th Infantry Regiment. The 366th was deployed to North Africa and assigned to the 15th Air Force to secure airfields. In November of 1944, the 366th was attached to the 5th Army, 92nd Infantry Division (the historically all-black Buffalo Soldiers) and moved to Italy to participate in the liberation of Europe.

In November 1944, the 366th entered combat with the 92nd Infantry Division in the Serchio Valley. During the Battle of the Serchio Valley, in the vicinity of Sommocolonia, Italy, Lieutenant Fox was attached to the 598th Field Artillery Battalion to serve as a forward artillery observer. In this role, Lieutenant Fox was to call in adjustments to bring effective artillery fire on the enemy. On the evening of December 25, 1944, Lieutenant Fox set up his observation post on the second floor of a house in the village. The next morning, the village came under heavy fire from German and Italian forces that had infiltrated the area during the night. The Allied troops, who were greatly outnumbered, were forced to withdraw. Lieutenant Fox stayed in his position to adjust friendly artillery fire to cover the withdrawal of his comrades. As the Germans advanced to pursue the retreating Americans, Fox adjusted the artillery closer and closer to his position. Finally facing overwhelming odds, Fox called in an artillery barrage onto his own position. The fire direction center advised him that he would not survive the barrage; he insisted, saying, "Fire it!" During the ensuing barrage, Fox was killed, but his selfless act delayed the enemy advance. Later, when a counterattack retook the position, they found Lieutenant Fox's body along with the bodies of approximately 100 Axis soldiers.

Although Lieutenant Fox was recommended for the Distinguished Service Cross (DSC) at the time, the paperwork was lost. It was not until April 15, 1982, that Fox was awarded the DSC posthumously. His family had previously received the Bronze Star and Purple Heart he had earned.

Following an investigation commissioned by the Department of Defense in 1993, it was determined that a number of African Americans had not been awarded the Medal of Honor for actions during World War II due to their race. In 1996, Congress approved granting the Medal of Honor to seven African American soldiers from World War II. Lieutenant Fox was one of these men. On January 13, 1997, more than 50 years after Fox gave his life for his comrades, President Bill Clinton presented the Medal of Honor to Fox's widow, Arlene, in a White House ceremony honoring the seven African American World War II veterans whose earlier awards had been upgraded. The only one of the seven still living was Vernon Baker.

In 2005, the Hasbro Toy Company released an action figure commemorating Lt. John Fox in their GI Joe Medal of Honor series.

Christopher S. Trobridge

Further Reading

Astor, Gerald. *The Right to Fight: A History of African Americans in the Military.* Cambridge, MA: Da Capo Press, 1998.

Converse, Elliott V., III. *The Exclusion of Black Soldiers from the Medal of Honor in World War II.* Jefferson, NC: McFarland, 1997.

Hargrove, Hondon B. *Buffalo Soldiers in Italy: Black Americans in World War II.* Jefferson, NC: McFarland, 1985.

Freeman, Ed W.

Born: November 20, 1927
Died: August 20, 2008
Home State: Mississippi
Service: Army
Conflict: Vietnam War
Age at Time of Award: 38

Born in Neely, Mississippi, on November 20, 1927, Edward W. "Too Tall" Freeman was the sixth of nine children. He grew up in nearby McLain and graduated from Washington High School. He joined the Army and served in World War II, Korea, and Vietnam. He achieved the rank of master sergeant at the outbreak of the Korean War and was assigned to the Corps of Engineers.

However, combat requirements sometimes negate one's military occupational specialty (MOS), and Freeman was assigned to an infantry unit that was fighting at the Battle of Pork Chop Hill, where he earned a battlefield commission; his lieutenant's bar was pinned on by Gen. James Van Fleet personally.

Although he had served as an engineer and an infantry soldier, it was Freeman's desire to fly that would keep him in the service after Korea. Since he was an officer, he was eligible for flight school, and the emerging role of helicopters attracted him to apply. There was a problem, however, in that he was "too tall to fly" until the height limitation was raised in 1955. Trained first in fixed-wing aircraft, Freeman eventually switched to helicopters and was assigned to units that had army mapping responsibilities over some of the roughest terrain in the world; his flying responsibilities would take him to the Artic, the deserts of the Middle East and North Africa, and the jungles of Central and South America. This aerial observation job also brought him into contact with Bruce Crandall, with whom he would share incredible experiences as the war in Vietnam began to heat up.

On November 14, 1965, Captain Freeman and the pilots of the 229th Assault Helicopter Battalion of the 1st Cavalry Division (Airmobile) transported a battalion of troopers into the Ia Drang Valley of the Central Highlands, southwest of Pleiku in the Republic of Vietnam. This operation was designed to engage a North Vietnamese regiment of unknown size in what would become the first major battle between American and People's Army of Vietnam (PAVN) forces. The insertion of troops into Landing Zone (LZ) X-Ray was initially without incident, and Freeman and his fellow pilots returned to the base camp to pick up more soldiers. In the interim, a major battle had developed at X-Ray, and evacuation of wounded personnel suddenly became the most critical mission. However, the medical evacuation helicopters were not allowed, by standard operating procedures of the division, to fly into hot landing zones. Freeman and his commander, Maj. Bruce Crandall, volunteered to fly their lightly armed UH-1 Huey helicopters into X-Ray in support of the embattled American troops. Freeman made 14 trips into hot landing zones over the next three days, bringing ammo and water and evacuating many critically wounded soldiers. This battle would test the operational effectiveness of helicopters on the battlefield as both a troop transport system and a logistics support system. Freeman and his men passed the test, and the helicopter became the workhorse of the American military in Vietnam. The Americans prevailed at Ia Drang, although outnumbered 2,000 to 400, not in small part due to the heroism of men like Ed Freeman and Bruce Crandall.

Freeman returned to the United States in 1966 and retired from the military the next year. He settled in the Treasure Valley area of Idaho, his wife Barbara's home state. Freeman became a freelance pilot working for the state and federal government, fighting wildfires, performing animal censuses, and herding wild horses. He retired in 1991 having accumulated 17,000 hours flying in helicopters and 8,000 in fixed-wing aircraft.

Freeman was nominated for the Medal of Honor for his actions in the Ia Drang by his commander, Bruce Crandall, but the nomination was not submitted within the two-year time limit that was then in effect. Instead, Freeman received the Distinguished Flying Cross. In 1995, the two-year restriction was removed, at which time Freeman's nomination became eligible for reconsideration. On July 16, 2001, President George W. Bush presented Freeman with the Medal of Honor, nearly 36 years after the Battle of the Ia Drang Valley.

Ed Freeman's performance at Ia Drang was memorialized in the book *We Were Soldiers Once...and Young* by Lt. Col. Hal Moore and Joe Galloway, which then became the basis for the film *We Were Soldiers.* Freeman died of complications from Parkinson's disease on August 20, 2008. He is buried in the Idaho State Veterans Cemetery in Boise.

Ron Milam

Further Reading

Collier, Peter, and Nick Del Calzo. *Medal of Honor: Portraits of Valor beyond the Call of Duty.* New York: Artisan, 2006.

Faranacci, Donald. *Last Full Measure of Devotion: A Tribute to America's Heroes of the Vietnam War.* Bloomington, IN: AuthorHouse, 2007.

Moore, Harold G., and Galloway, Joseph L. *We Were Soldiers Once... and Young: Ia Drang—the Battle That Changed the War in Vietnam.* New York: Random House, 1992.

Moore, Harold G., and Galloway, Joseph L. *We Were Soldiers Still: A Journey Back to the Battlefields of Vietnam.* New York: Harper, 2008.

Funston, Frederick

Born: November 9, 1865
Died: February 19, 1917
Home State: Kansas
Service: Army
Conflict: Philippine Insurrection
Age at Time of Award: 33

Although Frederick Funston was born in New Carlisle, Ohio, on November 9, 1865, he hailed from Kansas. His father, a Civil War veteran named Edward Hogue Funston, moved the family to Iola, Kansas, in 1867, and Funston grew up there. His small stature and average grades kept him out of West Point, so instead he taught in a local schoolhouse and then enrolled at the University of Kansas. He left without taking a degree; became a reporter in Kansas City and Fort Smith, Arkansas; worked as a railroad collector on the Santa Fe Railroad; and then became an explorer on a botanical expedition to Death Valley. He moved on to a series of journeys to Alaska—the first to Yakutat Bay, and then the next year over the Chilkoot Pass to the Yukon River, a detour to above the Arctic Circle, and then down the Yukon to the sea.

In 1896, he joined the Cuban revolution against Spain as a filibustering volunteer. He became an artilleryman and fought in several of the small sieges of Spanish-held towns in the war. His participation gained him fame in Kansas, and he returned home and physically recovered from malaria he had contacted in Cuba just as the Spanish-American War began. The governor gave him command of the 20th Kansas Volunteer Regiment, and they headed to the Philippines in late 1898.

Upon arrival, the regiment took up position in the American lines on the northwest side of Manila, and the Philippine Insurrection broke out in February 1899.

The Kansans were among the vanguard in the conventional campaign that drove north from Manila. After falling back, the Filipino insurgents made a strong stand at Calumpit on the Rio Grande de Pampanga. There, on April 27, 1899, Funston and 45 of his men crossed the river on a raft and turned the enemy position. It was for this action that Funston earned the Medal of Honor.

He also gained a promotion to brigadier general in the Volunteers, and, as the insurgents, led loosely by Emilio Aguinaldo, switched to a guerilla war, Funston took command of a military district in central Luzon (4th District, Department of Northern Luzon). He developed an extensive intelligence network and focused on excursions into the countryside to strike quickly at guerrilla bands and supplies.

Along the way, his men captured intelligence giving the location of Aguinaldo's hideout at Palanan on the northeast coast of Luzon, and Funston came up with a plan to capture the insurrection's leader. Aguinaldo expected reinforcements, so Funston had a detachment of native Macabebe scouts pretend to be those troops while he and a handful of Americans posed as prisoners to get into the rebel camp. In March 1901, the detachment landed on the coast south of Palanan, marched north, took Aguinaldo prisoner, and escaped to the coast for transport back to Manila. Aguinaldo wrote a statement calling for an end to the insurrection, and other insurgent leaders began to follow suit. The insurrection petered out, and Funston became a national hero.

For his efforts, he became a brigadier general in the Regular Army. As it happened, Funston was in charge in San Francisco on April 18, 1906, when a terrible earthquake struck. He helped as much as he could to contain the damage by impeding the fire and stopping looting, and he also provided aid to the victims. Some criticized him for taking too heavy a hand, but mostly he earned plaudits for his efforts.

Thereafter, he cycled through a variety of commands throughout departments in the United States, in Cuba, at the Army service schools at Fort Leavenworth, and back to the Philippines, although it was not until 1914 that he finally received his promotion to major general. That spring, he took command of the American occupation of the Mexican city of Veracruz, performed well, and then moved on to the Southern Department, where he took responsibility for most of the border with Mexico. When the Mexican Revolution spilled over the border, most famously with Pancho Villa's raid of Columbus, New Mexico, in March 1916, Funston oversaw the American response, including Gen. John J. Pershing's expedition in pursuit of Villa.

Frederick Funston's successes in all these endeavors made him a strong candidate for command of the American forces in World War I. However, on February 19, 1917, the general died suddenly of a heart attack in San Antonio; he is buried in San Francisco.

Thomas Bruscino

Further Reading

Crouch, Thomas W. *A Leader of Volunteers: Frederick Funston and the 20th Kansas in the Philippines, 1898–1899.* Lawrence, KS: Coronado Press, 1984.

Crouch, Thomas W. *A Yankee Guerrillero: Frederick Funston and the Cuban Insurrection, 1896–1897.* Memphis, TN: Memphis State University Press, 1975.

Funston, Frederick. *Memories of Two Wars: Cuban and Philippine Experiences.* Introduction by Thomas Bruscino. Lincoln, NE: Bison Books, 2009.

Linn, Brian McAllister. *The U.S. Army and Counterinsurgency in the Philippine War, 1899–1902.* Chapel Hill: University of North Carolina Press, 1989.

Galer, Robert Edward

Born: October 24, 1913
Died: June 27, 2005
Home State: Washington
Service: Marine Corps
Conflict: World War II
Age at Time of Award: 29

Robert E. Galer was born on October 24, 1913, in Seattle, Washington, where he attended school, ultimately receiving a degree in engineering from the University of Washington in 1935. Galer was both an athlete and an academic. Galer held a job at the campus bookstore to help pay his way through university. He also played basketball for the university, leading his team to a division championship and earning All-America honors as a forward. He was later inducted into the Husky Hall of Fame.

While at the university, Galer served in the naval ROTC unit on campus and became interested in Marine Corps aviation. After graduation, he reported to the Naval Reserve Aviation Base at Seattle for flight training. Just over a year later, he was commissioned as a second lieutenant in the US Marine Corps. In April 1937, he was designated a naval aviator.

In the years between earning his wings and the attack on Pearl Harbor, Galer served with the 1st Marine Brigade in Quantico, Virginia; attended a course of instruction in Philadelphia; was attached to the New York Naval Yard; and finally served with Marine Scouting Squadron 3 based at Saint Thomas in the US Virgin Islands in 1939. It was here Galer earned his promotion to first lieutenant.

In 1940, he was transferred to San Diego, California, where he was assigned to the 2nd Marine Aircraft Wing, Marine Fighter Squadron 2 (VMF-2). On August 29, he and his squadron mates were trying to carrier qualify off San Diego. On the downwind leg of his approach, his engine failed and he had to ditch his Grumman F3F.

In January 1941, Galer's squadron moved to Marine Corps Air Station Ewa on the island of Oahu in Hawaii. There the squadron was redesignated Marine Fighter Squadron 224 (VMF-224). During this period, Galer served as the landing signal officer for his unit and played a key role in getting all the pilots in the squadron carrier qualified.

When the Japanese attacked Pearl Harbor on the morning of December 7, 1941, Galer rushed to his airfield only to find all the aircraft on fire. He and the other pilots took cover in a nearby swimming pool that was under construction and fired back at the attacking aircraft with their rifles.

When VMF-211 was sent to Wake Island, where all members were killed or captured, Galer was left behind because he was the only spare landing signal officer in the Pacific. Just before the Battle of Midway in June 1942, Galer, now a captain, was given command of VMF-224, a largely paper squadron that initially consisted on only one other pilot, a few enlisted men, and one plane. He scrounged up more men and equipment and began to train his unit.

In August 1942, Galer and VMF-224 were ordered to Guadalcanal, where American forces had established a beachhead. He and his unit landed at Henderson Field as the airstrip was still under construction by Naval Construction Battalions (Seabees) and in danger of being overrun by the Imperial Japanese Navy.

Galer's mission was to protect the American ground forces from Japanese aerial attack. His squadron and his old squadron, VMF-211, along with several carrier-based naval planes, formed what became known as the Cactus Air Force. Taking off daily from the dusty airstrip, they took their toll on the Japanese bombers, even though they were usually outnumbered. They were assisted in this effort by Australian coast watchers, who provided early warning that proved critical to the survival of the small number of American flyers.

During the month of September, Galer's squadron shot down 27 Japanese planes, with Galer accounting for 11 himself, earning him the designation as fighter ace, 1 of only 16 American aces to have served in the Pacific Theater (he would shoot down a total of 14 enemy aircraft before the war was over). During this period, Galer was shot down three times; each time, he went back into action immediately.

After Guadalcanal, Galer returned to the United States. In the spring of 1943, while attending the Army Command and General Staff College at Fort Leavenworth, Kansas, he received word that he would be awarded the Medal of Honor. On March 24, 1943, Galer received the medal from President Franklin D. Roosevelt in a White House ceremony.

Galer served as commandant of cadets at Naval Air Station Corpus Christi, Texas, before returning to the Pacific in 1944. During the Korean War, Galer, then a colonel, flew Corsairs as commander of Marine Air Group 12. He was shot down in June 1952 by enemy antiaircraft fire 100 miles behind communist lines but was saved by a daring helicopter rescue.

Galer was subsequently promoted to brigadier general and worked on guided missile development before his retirement in July 1957.

As one might imagine, Galer's impressive list of decorations was not limited only to the Medal of Honor. He was also the recipient of the Navy Cross, the Legion of Merit with a Flying "V," the Distinguished Flying Cross, and a Purple Heart, as well as the British Flying Medal. Despite these achievements, Galer remained a humble man throughout his long and distinguished career in the Marine Corps. This may be related to another unique distinction held by the major general. "Before WW II started, I lost an airplane while carrier qualifying off San Diego. At Guadalcanal, I got shot down three times. In Korea, I was a group leader and got shot down about 100 miles behind enemy lines, and the Navy came in and got me. My smart-aleck son, who is an Air Force pilot, says, 'That's five airplanes you lost. You're an enemy ace.' "

After his career as one of America's most decorated aviators, he worked in the missile industry and sold real estate in Dallas, Texas. On June 27, 2005, a stroke claimed the life of Robert Galer. He is buried near his home in Dallas.

Jason Everitt Foster

Further Reading

American Fighter Aces Album. Mesa, AZ: The American Fighter Aces Association, 1996.

Collier, Peter, and Nick Del Calzo. *Medal of Honor: Portraits of Valor beyond the Call of Duty.* New York: Artisan, 2006.

García, Macario

Born: January 20, 1920
Died: December 24, 1972
Home State: Texas
Service: Army
Conflict: World War II
Age at Time of Award: 24

Macario García was born in Villa del Castaño in the state of Coahuila, Mexico, on January 20, 1920. Like so many other poor Mexican sharecroppers, his family immigrated to the United States in search of a better life. After working at various jobs in south Texas towns, the Garcías established themselves as farm workers near the town of Sugar Land, Texas. The immigrant worker lifestyle was not conducive to a proper education, and young Macario's formal schooling ended at the third grade.

Although he was not an American citizen at the time, García enlisted in the US Army in 1942 because he felt he had to do his part to help his adopted country win the war against tyranny. Macario, or Mac as he was known to his buddies, was assigned as a rifleman with Company B, 22nd Infantry Regiment, 4th Infantry Division. He was wounded in action early in the Normandy campaign but soon rejoined his unit, which was fighting its way through France and into the enemy's homeland.

His date with destiny came on November 27, 1944, as his unit was advancing near the town of Grosshau, Germany. Suddenly, the advance was stalled by heavy machine gun, artillery, and mortar fire. Although painfully wounded by shrapnel, García, who was serving as acting squad leader, refused evacuation and crawled forward toward the enemy on his own initiative. When he felt he was within striking distance, García stood up and assaulted the enemy machine gun position, firing his rifle and hurling grenades as he advanced. He destroyed the weapon and killed three enemy soldiers, thus allowing his unit to continue the advance. Shortly thereafter, another machine gun blocked the American advance; again, Private García took the initiative and assaulted the enemy position. This time, he killed three more enemy soldiers and took four others prisoner. He continued fighting with his unit until they took their objective. Only then did he accept medical treatment and allow himself to be evacuated to the rear. For this action, he was recommended for the Medal of Honor.

On August 23, 1945, President Harry Truman presented then staff sergeant García the Medal of Honor in a ceremony at the White House. He also received the Purple Heart, the Bronze Star for valor, and the Combat Infantryman's Badge. After the war, the Mexican government too recognized García's wartime heroism by conferring on him the Medalla al Mérito Militar—Mexico's highest award for valor— and allowing him to wear the medals he earned in American service without loss of his Mexican citizenship. Despite his wartime heroism and love for his adopted country, García was not a stranger to ethnic prejudice. In September 1945, García was refused service at a restaurant in Richmond, Texas, because he was Hispanic. Furious at this blatant act of racism, García fought with the restaurant's owner. The ensuing publicity pointed at the contradictions in American society that still permitted discrimination based solely on a person's ethnicity. After a much-publicized trial, García was acquitted; he soon put the ugly incident behind him.

García accepted a job offer from President Truman and took a position as a counselor at the Veterans Administration, where he worked for 25 years. Despite his pride in his Mexican birth and ethnicity, and occasional instances of discrimination, García also loved his adopted country. He became an American citizen in 1947 and continued his education, earning a high school diploma in 1951. The following year, he married Alicia Reyes, and the couple had three children. In 1953, the Medal of Honor hero joined the US Army Reserve. His leadership abilities and work ethic commended him to his superiors, and he was promoted to the highest enlisted rank—sergeant major.

Ironically, despite having survived the horrors and dangers of ground combat, Macario García was killed in an automobile accident on December 24, 1972.

He is buried in the National Cemetery in Houston, Texas. An Army Reserve Center, a stretch of highway in Houston, and a middle school in Sugar Land, Texas, bear the hero's name. His portrait hangs in the rotunda of the Fort Bend County Courthouse in Richmond—the same town where he was denied service many years ago because of his ethnicity.

Prisco R. Hernández

Further Reading

Collier, Peter, and Nick Del Calzo. *Medal of Honor: Portraits of Valor beyond the Call of Duty.* New York: Artisan, 2006.

Smith, Larry. *Beyond Glory: Medal of Honor Heroes in Their Own Words.* New York: W. W. Norton, 2003.

US Congress. Senate. Committee on Veterans Affairs. *Medal of Honor Recipients, 1863–1978.* Washington, D.C.: Government Printing Office, 1973.

Gonsalves, Harold

Born: February 28, 1926
Died: April 15, 1945
Home State: California
Service: Marine Corps
Conflict: World War II
Age at Time of Award: 19

Harold Gonsalves was born on February 28, 1926, in Alameda, California. He attended school in Alameda but quit high school in his junior year to take a job as a stock clerk with Montgomery Ward in Oakland. He volunteered for the US Marine Corps in May 1943, and, after boot camp, he was assigned to the 2nd Pack Howitzer Battalion in Hawaii. In May 1944, his battalion was attached to the 22nd Marines, which then saw combat in the campaign for the Marshall Islands and participated in the recapture of Guam. After Guam, Gonsalves's unit was detached from the 22nd Marines and joined the 15th Marines of the US 6th Marine Division. With victory over Japan in August of 1945, Operation Iceberg—the invasion of the Ryukyu Islands—would be the 6th Marine Division's first and last combat action in World War II.

Operation Iceberg was the culmination of the US Navy's drive through the Central Pacific. By 1944, Adm. Chester W. Nimitz believed the invasion of Okinawa was the correct strategic decision. Once captured, Okinawa would become a vital emergency landing field for crippled US 20th Army Air Force B-29s returning from bombing missions. In addition, Okinawa provided a staging and supply area for the future invasion of Japan.

Admiral Nimitz assigned Gen. Simon B. Buckner Jr.'s US 10th Army with the task of breaching Japan's inner-defense ring. Buckner's forces consisted of the US Army's XXIV Infantry Corps (US 96th Infantry Division, US 7th Infantry Division, and US 77th Infantry Division) and the US Marine's III Amphibious Corps (US 1st Marine Division, US 6th Marine Division, and US 2nd Marine Division).

US soldiers and marines landed on Okinawa on April 1, 1945—both an Easter Sunday and an April Fool's Day. Four infantry divisions landed abreast near the lower third of the elongated island. The III Amphibious Corps under the command of Maj. Gen. Roy S. Geiger landed to the north of Gen. John R. Hodge's XXIV Corps. Much to the surprise of General Buckner and corps commanders, the invasion force encountered only token resistance. Because of this situation, Buckner altered his original plans for Operation Iceberg. For the US marines and Pfc. Harold Gonsalves, this meant a drive to the north.

While the US marines wheeled north, the US army drove south. Most of the Japanese Army was concentrated in the southern portion of the island. The Japanese defense consisted of concentric rings of heavily fortified lines—for example, the Shuri Line. Coupled with fanatical resistance, it ultimately took four US Army infantry and two US Marine divisions to capture the island.

As the US marines marched north, the terrain became more rugged, and Japanese resistance grew. However, there was no coordinated defense in depth. By the second week of April the Japanese decided to defend the Motubu Peninsula in northern Okinawa. The terrain was mountainous, and the Japanese resistance was growing fierce.

On April 15, 1945, Japanese artillery bombarded US 6th Marine Division positions on the Motubu Peninsula. Gonsalves was in a forward observation post helping direct artillery fire on Japanese positions. Gonsalves and his fellow marines advanced forward through withering fire. As Gonsalves and the marines approached the front line, a grenade landed near he and his comrades. In an instant, Gonsalves jumped on the grenade, covering the explosion with his body. Gonsalves saved his fellow marines but was killed by his selfless action.

Harold Gonsalves was buried in a temporary US 6th Marine Division cemetery on Okinawa. On June 19, 1946, Gonsalves was posthumously awarded the Medal of Honor for "conspicuous gallantry and intrepidity at the risk of his own life above and beyond the call of duty." President Harry S. Truman presented the award to Gonsalves's sister in the presence of his parents in a White House ceremony. After the war, the US military removed his body from the overseas cemetery. Gonsalves was reburied in the Golden Gate National Cemetery near San Francisco with full military honors on March 20, 1949.

Erik D. Carlson

Further Reading

Belote, James H., and William M. Belote. *Typhoon of Steel: The Battle for Okinawa.* New York: Bantam Books, 1984.

James, Clayton D., and Anne Sharp Wells. *From Pearl Harbor to V-J Day: The American Forces in WWII.* Chicago: Ivan R. Dee, 1995.

Moskin, Robert J. *The U.S. Marine Corps Story.* 3rd rev. ed. New York: Little, Brown, 1992.

Gonzalez, Alfredo

Born: May 23, 1946
Died: February 4, 1968
Home State: Texas
Service: Marine Corps
Conflict: Vietnam War
Age at Time of Award: 21

Born in Edinburgh, Texas, in 1946, the only son of Dolia Gonzalez, Alfredo Cantu "Freddy" Gonzalez made it clear to his mother and friends that he wanted to be a Marine. True to his word, Gonzalez enlisted in the Marines in May 1965, just after graduating from high school, where he had excelled as an All-District football player. After boot camp, he served a one-year tour in Vietnam during 1966–1967, where he finished with the rank of corporal. When he returned to the United States, Gonzalez learned of a particularly bad ambush that had claimed several of his former comrades' lives and believed that he would have saved them had he been there. Ignoring the pleas of friends who claimed he had done enough, Gonzalez signed on for another term.

Now a sergeant in Alpha Company in the First Battalion/First Marines (Alpha/1/1), Gonzalez earned the moniker of "old-timer" because he already had served one tour of duty. By the time the Tet Offensive erupted in 1968, Gonzalez had earned a reputation for heroism and an uncanny calm under fire. It was Lt. Col. Marcus "Mark" Gravel, commander of the First Battalion/First Marines, who first labeled Gonzalez the "perfect Marine" because of his devotion to duty and the loyalty he earned from his men. Reckless, perhaps, with his own life, the old-timer took great care to protect the lives of the marines under his command.

On the morning of February 3, 1968, five days after more than 10 battalions of Viet Cong (VC) and North Vietnamese Army troops had overrun Hue, the old imperial capital of Vietnam, Alpha/1/1 was ordered to move by truck convoy to Hue to help clear the city. The 21-year-old Gonzalez had taken command of the 3rd Platoon several days earlier because Alpha/1/1 suffered from a dearth of officers.

At the outset of the battle, Alpha/1/1's commander, Capt. Gordon Batcheller, suffered serious wounds outside of the city and turned command over to Lt. Ray Smith, who in turn was impressed with Gonzalez's leadership and fighting abilities; Smith later said of Gonzalez, "He was a real quiet person, but he always had a smile on his face. He was a little restrained in his emotions, but that was probably because he was truly one of the 'grown-ups' in our organization."

Gonzalez's calm under fire served his fellow marines well as the battle for Hue began in earnest. As his convoy neared the city, it came under heavy fire. He led his men in clearing the area. Exposing himself to enemy fire, he took out a Viet Cong machine gun bunker with two grenades. Gonzalez then retrieved a wounded marine from the ditch beside the road and hauled the larger man to safety, during which Gonzalez sustained shrapnel wounds. The old-timer refused a Navy corpsman's admonitions and an order from Lieutenant Smith to medevac in order to stay with his marines.

The next day, February 4, Alpha/1/1 encountered fire from rockets and machine guns near the St. Joan of Arc Church and School complex in the older part of the city. Smith's company attempted to secure the complex by blowing holes in the walls and then engaging in room-to-room combat.

During this fight, 3rd Platoon came under heavy enemy fire from rockets and automatic weapons. Gonzalez was hit again but, continuing to ignore his wounds, grabbed a handful of LAWs (M-72 light antitank weapons) and ran to the second floor of one of the nearby buildings. He fired on the enemy gunners from the second floor of the complex, knocking out one of the enemy rocket positions. Unfortunately, Gonzalez's luck ran out when the VC targeted his position and fired a rocket that caught the marine in the midsection, mortally wounding him.

Smith and Gravel both submitted Gonzalez's name for the Medal of Honor. In 1969, President Nixon signed the citation and Vice President Spiro Agnew awarded the posthumous medal to Gonzalez's mother, Dolia, in a White House ceremony on October 31 of that year.

Alfredo Gonzalez was laid to rest in his hometown of Edinburgh, Texas. An elementary school and a major road in Edinburgh now bear his name. In 1996, the US Navy commissioned the guided missile destroyer USS *Gonzalez* in honor of the fallen marine, and naval personnel have unofficially adopted Gonzalez's mother as "ship's mother."

John D. Fitzmorris III

Further Reading

Above and Beyond: A History of the Medal of Honor from the Civil War to Vietnam. Boston, MA: Boston Publishing Company, 1985.

Hammel, Eric. *Fire in the Streets: The Battle for Hue, Tet 1968*. Pacifica, CA: Pacifica Press, 1991.

Gordon, Gary I.

Born: August 30, 1960
Died: October 3, 1993
Home State: Maine
Service: Army
Conflict: Somalia
Age at Time of Award: 33

Gary I. Gordon was born in Lincoln, Maine, on August 30, 1960. Known as Bugsy to his friends while growing up, he demonstrated an early interest in the military. After graduating from high school, Gordon enlisted in the US Army in February 1978. After completing basic training, he was assigned to the combat engineers and selected for US Army Special Forces two years later. He was eventually assigned to the 2nd Battalion of the 10th Special Forces Group garrisoned at Fort Carson, Colorado. M.Sgt. Gordon's military career reached its zenith with his selection to the 1st Special Forces Group Detachment-Delta.

In December 1992, US forces deployed to Somalia to aid UN forces in Operation Restore Hope, tasked with restoring order in Somalia and feeding victims of a multiyear famine. The operation took a more violent turn on June 5, 1993, when rebel forces loyal to Mohammed Farrah Aideed killed 24 Pakistani troops in an ambush in Mogadishu. The next day, the United Nations Security Council issued Resolution 837, calling for the arrest of Aideed and anyone else responsible for the ambush. Toward that end, the United States deployed Task Force Ranger commanded by Maj. Gen. William F. Garrison in Operation Gothic Serpent. Task Force Ranger included Detachment Delta as well as other Army, Navy, and Air Force elements. The task force conducted several successful nighttime raids. The next raid, however, occurred during daylight hours, with disastrous results.

On October 3, 1993, Task Force Ranger received intelligence that several members of Aideed's clan were meeting at a location in Mogadishu. The task force immediately launched a daylight raid, against established practices. The initial capture was successful; however, during the extraction that followed, two Lockheed UH-60 Black Hawk helicopters were shot down. The first crash site was secured by Army Rangers. The second crash site was further away, and there were no available combat and rescue units to secure it. In an MH-6 Little Bird helicopter orbiting the area, Delta operators Sgt. Randy Shughart and Master Sergeant Gordon asked twice for permission to land and secure the crash site. The pair finally received permission after a third request. Shughart and Gordon removed the crew, including Chief Warrant Officer Mike Durant, to relative safety. The pair then set up a perimeter and engaged Somali clansmen. The firefight lasted until the Delta men ran out of ammunition and were killed. Their bodies and those of the dead from the downed

Black Hawk helicopter were later desecrated and dragged through the streets of Mogadishu. Durant was taken captive and later released.

For heroic action in the defense of a fellow serviceman, Gary Gordon and Shughart were both awarded the Medal of Honor. Gordon's family was presented the post-humous award by President Bill Clinton on May 23, 1994. The heroics of Gordon and Shughart were featured in the book and movie *Black Hawk Down*. Two further honors were bestowed upon Gordon: the naming of US Navy transport USNS *Gordon* (T-AKR 296) and the naming of the Shughart Gordon Military Operations Urbanized Terrain Complex [MOUT] training center at Fort Polk, Louisiana.

Shawn Livingston

Further Reading

Anderson, Cindy. "Leaving Lincoln." *Yankee* 59, no. 11 (1995): 56–68.

Bowden, Mark. *Black Hawk Down: A Story of Modern War*. New York: Atlantic Monthly Press, 1999.

Eversmann, Matt Schilling. *The Battle of Mogadishu: Firsthand Accounts from the Men of Task Force Ranger*. Novato, CA: Presidio Press, 2004.

Hagemeister, Charles Chris

Born: August 21, 1946
Died:
Home State: Nebraska
Service: Army
Conflict: Vietnam War
Age at Time of Award: 20

Charles C. Hagemeister was born August 21, 1946, in Lincoln, Nebraska. He grew up in Lincoln and attended college for a year and a half but became bored with academics. He worked for a while as a warehouseman before being drafted into the Army in March 1966. He entered the Army in May and went through basic training at Fort Polk, Louisiana. He then went to Fort Sam Houston, Texas, where he completed training as a combat medic in November of 1966.

Hagemeister was then reassigned to 1st Battalion, 5th Cavalry of the 1st Cavalry Division in the Republic of Vietnam. On March 20, 1967, Specialist 4th Class Hage-meister was supporting a platoon from A Company during combat operations in Binh Dinh Province when the unit came under heavy fire from three sides by an enemy force occupying well-concealed, fortified positions supported by machine guns and mortars.

Two of Hagemeister's comrades were seriously wounded in the initial contact; with total disregard for his own safety and well being, he raced through the deadly enemy fire to provide medical aid. His platoon leader and several other soldiers were wounded as the battle continued to rage; once again, Hagemeister continued to brave enemy fire to render lifesaving treatment to the wounded. He was taken under fire at close range from enemy soldiers; realizing that his unit's position was about to be overrun, he grabbed a rifle from a fallen comrade and killed four enemy soldiers who were attempting to encircle his position. He then silenced the enemy machine gun that was raking the perimeter.

Unable to move the wounded to a less exposed position, he ran through heavy fire to secure help from a nearby sister platoon. Returning with help, he placed the men in positions to cover the group and began to evacuate the wounded. He continued to move the wounded to safety until about midnight, when his unit was withdrawn to a new defensive position. Through his repeated and selfless actions, Hagemeister saved the lives of many of his comrades and inspired their actions in repelling the enemy assault.

After completing his tour in Vietnam, Hagemeister, promoted to specialist 5th class, was serving at McDonald Army Hospital in Fort Eustis, Virginia, when, only days from being discharged from the Army, he received word that he would be awarded the Medal of Honor. On May 14, 1968, he was presented the medal by President Lyndon B. Johnson in a White House ceremony. During the course of the conversation, Hagemeister told the president that he had just 72 hours left on his enlistment. Johnson turned to the senior Army officers present and told them that he wanted them to try to change the young man's mind. Apparently they did, because Hagemeister subsequently reenlisted.

Charles Hagemeister later received a direct commission in the US Army Reserve as an armor officer. After completing training at Fort Knox, Kentucky, he was assigned to Fort Hood, Texas, where he served as a platoon leader, a cavalry troop executive officer, and a squadron liaison officer. He served successive tours in Germany, Fort Hood, and Fort Knox, becoming a Regular Army officer along the way. Promoted to major, he attended the Army Command and General Staff College (CGSC) at Fort Leavenworth, Kansas. After graduation, he remained at Fort Leavenworth, serving on the CGSC faculty in the tactics department. Lieutenant Colonel Hagemeister retired from the Army in June 1990 but continues to serve as a contractor supporting computer battle simulations at Fort Leavenworth.

James H. Willbanks

Further Reading

Collier, Peter, and Nick Del Calzo. *Medal of Honor: Portraits of Valor beyond the Call of Duty.* New York: Artisan, 2006.

Murphy, Edward F. *Vietnam Medal of Honor Heroes.* New York: Ballantine Books, 2005.

Harmon, Roy W.

Born: May 3, 1916
Died: July 12, 1944
Home State: Oklahoma
Service: Army
Conflict: World War II
Age at Time of Award: 28

Roy William Woodrow Harmon was born in Talala, Oklahoma, on May 3, 1916. He was one of 14 siblings from a large loving family who knew him simply as Bill. Although not officially listed as Native American, Harmon's father claimed the family was part Cherokee. This lack of official documentation was quite normal because of the stigma then attached to being a Native American. During the 1930s, the family, like many during the Great Depression, struggled to make ends meet, and they moved to the fruit-farming valleys of California in order to find work. Ultimately it was from Pixley, California, that Roy entered the US Army during World War II.

By July 1944, Harmon was serving as a sergeant in Company C, 362nd Infantry Regiment, of the 91st Infantry Division. This division trained initially in Oregon, then in Washington State, before shipping to North Africa in April 1944. The men underwent further training there before they again sailed, this time for the fighting in Italy. The 91st Division, as a whole, went into action for the first time on July 12, 1944. The division's main objective was the high ground overlooking the Arno River. On the route of advance was the small town of Chianni, southeast of Livorno. In the approach to the town, elements of the division had a difficult time moving forward due to the Germans' extensive use of mines and their destruction of the local bridges.

Company C of the 362nd Regiment first made contact with the enemy at 4:15 a.m. on July 12, when heavy enemy machine gun fire met their advance about two miles southeast of Chianni. Three well-camouflaged German positions commanded the ground, and the lead platoon of Company C faced certain annihilation. Acting squad leader Harmon led his men forward, along a draw, in order to try to neutralize the German threat. Initially, his squad tried to set fire to the haystacks the Germans were using to conceal their positions. Despite the use of tracer rounds, the attempt did not succeed. At this point, Harmon decided to do something to rectify the situation. The ground was open and lacked good cover, but Harmon skillfully crawled forward until he was about 20 yards from the first German position. From there, and under intense fire, he was able to throw a grenade and set fire to the haystack, forcing the Germans into the open, where he killed them. He then set off for the second machine gun, about 100 yards farther away than the first. Here he was wounded for the first time but continued his attack until he was close enough to throw his grenades and destroy the enemy position. From there, he set off for the last machine gun nest. The approach to the final German position was devoid of all cover; he ran forward at first and then dropped to the ground and crawled straight into the teeth of the enemy fire. Again, the Germans shot him, and he hesitated briefly before continuing to push forward, trailing blood. When within range, he raised himself to throw a grenade, and German bullets hit him for the third time, knocking him down. However, with one final supreme effort, he got up and threw his last grenade at the enemy. Riddled by enemy fire, he fell to the ground, dead. His last grenade destroyed the German machine gun. His heroic actions opened the route of advance for his company and greatly assisted the whole attack.

President Truman posthumously awarded Roy Harmon the Medal of Honor on October 2, 1945. Later, the town of Pixley, California, named its airport Harmon Field in honor of his memory, and, at the Presidio Camp in California, a building was dedicated in his name. More recently, the students of Oologah-Talala High School in his hometown raised money to erect a monument to commemorate his bravery and service. Harmon is buried in the Florence American Cemetery in Italy.

Nicholas A. Murray

Further Reading

Brooks, Thomas. *The War North of Rome: June 1944–May 1945*. New York: Sarpedon, 1996.

Robbins, Major Robert. *The 91st Infantry Division in World War II*. Washington, D.C.: Infantry Journal Press, 1947.

US Congress. Senate. Committee on Veterans Affairs. *Medal of Honor Recipients, 1863–1978*. Washington, D.C.: Government Printing Office, 1979.

Harrell, William George

Born: June 26, 1922
Died: August 9, 1964
Home State: Texas
Service: Marine Corps
Conflict: World War II
Age at Time of Award: 21

William G. Harrell was born in Rio Grande, Texas, on June 26, 1922. After graduating from high school in 1939, he worked as a pipe fitter and attended the Agricultural and Mechanical College of Texas (later Texas A&M University) for two years, where he was in the Corps of Cadets. In July 1942, Harrell enlisted in the US Marines and completed basic training at the Marine Corps Recruit Depot, San

William George Harrell, US Marine Corps (Naval History and Heritage Command).

Diego, California. He then served in the depot's 1st Guard Company. He was promoted to corporal and transferred to Headquarters and Service, 2nd Battalion, at Camp Elliott in San Diego.

In February 1943, Corporal Harrell went overseas with Company A, 1st Battalion, 28th Marines, 5th Marine Division. After being promoted to sergeant, he participated in the assault on Saipan in June and July of 1944.

In February and March 1945, Sergeant Harrell took part in the Iwo Jima campaign as an assault group leader. On March 3, 1945, he and another marine were holding a position protecting the company command post. The surrounding area was studded with caves and ravines. During the early hours before dawn, Japanese troops infiltrated Marine lines and attacked. Awakened by the sudden attack, Harrell quickly opened fire with his carbine and killed two of the enemy as they emerged from a ravine. Disregarding the Japanese grenades that were landing near his position, he waged a fierce battle against the attackers until an exploding shell tore off his left hand and fractured his thigh. He was vainly attempting to load his weapon when his fellow marine returned from the command post with another weapon. Wounded again by a Japanese who rushed his foxhole wielding a sword, Sergeant Harrell managed to draw his pistol and kill his opponent. Exhausted and bleeding profusely, he was then locked in contact with two more Japanese soldiers, who charged his position and tossed a grenade in his hole. He killed one man with his pistol and grasped the sputtering grenade with his good right hand, pushing it toward the enemy soldier; the grenade exploded, killing the Japanese soldier, but in the process also severing Harrell's right hand.

At dawn, Sergeant Harrell was evacuated from his position, which was ringed by the bodies of 12 dead Japanese soldiers, at least 5 of whom he had personally dispatched in his self-sacrificing defense of the command post.

For his "conspicuous gallantry and intrepidity" and "indomitable fighting spirit against almost insurmountable odds," Harrell received the Medal of Honor from President Harry Truman at the White House on October 5, 1945.

After completing rehabilitation at Mare Island in California, he was discharged from the Marine Corps in February 1946. Equipped with hooks on both arms, he returned to Mercedes, Texas. In 1949, he moved to San Antonio, where he became the chief of the prosthetics division of the local Veterans Administration. During the night of August 9, 1964, Harrell shot and killed Mr. and Mrs. Ed Zumwalt with a rifle and then killed himself. The cause of the killings is still unknown. Harrell is buried at Fort Sam Houston National Cemetery in San Antonio.

In May 2010, the family of William Harrell donated his medal to the Sanders Corps of Cadets Center at Texas A&M University. A total of seven former students of Texas A&M have been awarded the Medal of Honor.

James H. Willbanks

Further Reading

Alexander, Joseph H. *Closing In: Marines in the Seizure of Iwo Jima*. Marines in World War II Commemorative Series. Washington, D.C.: Marine Historical Center, 1994.

Dethloff, Henry C. *Texas Aggies Go to War in Service of Their Country*. College Station: Texas A&M University Press, 2006.

Miller, Donald L. *D-Days in the Pacific*. New York: Simon & Schuster, 2005.

Neal, Charles M., Jr. *Valor across the Lone Star: The Congressional Medal of Honor in Frontier Texas*. Austin: Texas State Historical Association, 2002.

Woodall, James R. *Texas Aggie Medals of Honor: Seven Heroes of World War II*. College Station: Texas A&M University Press, 2010.

Hatch, John P.

Born: January 9, 1822
Died: April 12, 1901
Home State: New York
Service: Army
Conflict: Civil War
Age at Time of Award: 40

John Porter Hatch was born on January 9, 1822, in Oswego, New York. He graduated from the US Military Academy, West Point, in 1845 and was commissioned a second lieutenant in the Mounted Rifles, serving with distinction in the Mexican-American War (1846–1848). After that war, he held a variety of posts in the West and the Southwest.

Following the beginning of the Civil War in April 1861, Hatch was recalled to the East, where he subsequently commanded a cavalry brigade under Maj. Gen. George B. McClellan. In September, Hatch was promoted to the rank of brigadier general of volunteers and became chief artillerist, serving under Maj. Gen. Nathaniel P. Banks. Hatch saw action under Banks during Thomas J. "Stonewall" Jackson's 1862 Shenandoah Valley Campaign (May–June 1862).

In the run-up to Maj. Gen. John Pope's Second Bull Run Campaign, Hatch was given orders to disrupt and destroy a key section of railroad track between Gordonsville and Lynchburg, Virginia (part of the Virginia Central Railroad). Both of his attempts in this regard failed, the first because he had too many men and a supply train that slowed his progress and the second because, he claimed, the roads were muddy. Although he was an intrepid soldier, he seemed unable to execute a cavalry assault in which speed and surprise were paramount. Angered by Hatch's two failed attempts to disrupt the rail line, Pope gave him charge of an infantry brigade, which he commanded at the Second Battle of Bull Run (August 29–30, 1862).

Within days after Second Bull Run, Hatch was reassigned to Maj. Gen. Joseph Hooker's I Corps. Hatch took command of the 1st Division and was seriously wounded during the September 14, 1862, Battle of South Mountain. After he recovered, he took numerous administrative commands in the Southeast. These included the departments and districts of Florida, Hilton Head, and Morris Island (South Carolina). He also headed the Coast Division from November 1864 to March 1865. By war's end, he was in command of the District of Charleston.

With the end of the war, John Hatch continued in the Regular Army as a major in the 4th Cavalry, engaging in numerous skirmishes with Native Americans in the West. By 1881, he had attained the rank of colonel, which he would hold for the remainder of his career. That same year, he commanded the 2nd Cavalry. He retired in 1883 and moved to New York City. In 1893, Congress awarded him the Medal of Honor for bravery at the Battle of South Mountain. Hatch died in New York City on April 12, 1901.

Paul G. Pierpaoli Jr.

Further Reading

Cozzens, Peter, and Robert Girardi. *The Military Memoirs of General John Pope*. Chapel Hill: University of North Carolina Press, 1998.

Hennessey, John. *Return to Bull Run: The Second Campaign and Battle of Manassas*. New York: Simon & Schuster, 1992.

Hayashi, Shizuya

Born: November 28, 1917
Died: March 12, 2008
Home State: Hawaii
Service: Army

Conflict: World War II
Age at Time of Award: 26

Born in Waialua, Oahu, Hawaii, on November 28, 1917, Shizuya Hayashi was a soldier in the 65th Engineers on December 7, 1941, when the Japanese bombed US military bases on Pearl Harbor. A Nisei (second-generation Japanese American) soldier, he was removed from that unit because of his heritage. The US government became increasingly concerned about the security risks associated with Japanese American soldiers and placed them in roles where they could not affect the war effort negatively, such as picking up trash and working in the plantations of Hawaii. Their families were placed in 11 concentration camps around America and 1 in Hawaii.

In June 1942, the 100th Infantry Battalion, made up of 1,400 Nisei soldiers, was formed at Camp McCoy in Wisconsin. All the soldiers had been classified 4-C, enemy alien, by their respective selective service boards, and they were motivated to prove their allegiance to the nation. The formation of the battalion required an executive order by President Franklin D. Roosevelt due to the sensitive security issues, and soldiers like Hayashi felt relieved when they were finally offered an opportunity to serve their country.

The 100th became one of the four battalions of the 442nd Regimental Combat Team sent to Camp Shelby in Hattiesburg, Mississippi, to train for overseas deployment. They were ultimately sent to Italy and participated in the battles of Salerno, Anzio, Monte Cassino, Rome, and Arno. In the fall of 1943, the 100th landed at Salerno and immediately engaged German troops in some of the fiercest fighting of the war. Casualties were high due to the German 88-mm artillery known as "screaming mimis" because of the shrill sound made by the shells prior to impact.

On November 29, 1943, Private Hayashi and his platoon were attempting to find cover from an artillery bombardment when they stumbled into a German minefield that caused many casualties among the Nisei soldiers. Separated from his platoon as darkness fell, Hayashi wandered into a German emplacement, where a firefight ensued. Armed with a Browning Automatic Rifle (BAR), he was equipped with a weapon that could provide maximum firepower when engaging the enemy. Hayashi attacked the German machine gun position alone, killing the nine German soldiers who occupied the bunker. As German reinforcements came from another direction, he engaged them with the BAR, killing an additional nine enemy soldiers and taking four prisoners.

This action was recognized by his fellow squad members and eventually led to Hayashi being awarded the Distinguished Service Cross, the nation's second highest battlefield award. The presentation was made on the eve of the 100th's fiercest engagement of the war at Anzio.

Nearly 50 years after the Nisei soldiers' experiences in Italy, the Department of Defense began an exhaustive search of the battlefield performances of Japanese

American soldiers to determine if racial prejudice may have resulted in the downgrading of decorations. The result of this investigation was the upgrading of 21 Distinguished Service Crosses to Medals of Honor. Shizuya Hayashi's performance on the battlefield was one of those recognized by President Bill Clinton, who presented him the Medal of Honor at a White House ceremony on June 21, 2000.

In subsequent years, Hayashi's interviews with military historians and peers revealed a man who was proud not only of his service to his country but also of the humanity he had shown when confronted by the opportunity to kill a very young German soldier. Finding the young soldier on the battlefield curled up on the ground and crying, Hayashi had taken the boy prisoner because he did not believe he deserved to die. He told this story repeatedly when asked about his wartime service.

Hayashi's unit, the 442nd Regimental Combat Team, was known as the Purple Heart Regiment because of the awarding of 9,000 such awards. Their dedication, bravery, and persistence under fire have earned them the recognition as the most decorated unit of its size in American military history.

Shizuya Hayashi died of complications associated with a brain tumor on March 12, 2008.

Ron Milam

Further Reading

Collier, Peter, and Nick Del Calzo. *Medal of Honor: Portraits of Honor beyond the Call of Duty*. New York: Artisan, 2006.

Smith, Larry. *Beyond Glory: Medal of Honor Heroes in Their Own Words*. New York: W. W. Norton, 2003.

Hayes, Webb C.

Born: March 20, 1856
Died: July 26, 1934
Home State: Ohio
Service: Army
Conflict: Philippine Insurrection
Age at Time of Award: 43

James Webb C. Hayes was born in Cincinnati, Ohio, on March 20, 1856, the second son of Rutherford B. Hayes, who would become the 19th president of the United States. During the Civil War, Hayes's father commanded the 1st Brigade of the Kanawha Division in the Army of West Virginia, and the young man spent several winters in his father's military encampments, where he became a favorite of Gen. George Crook. After the Civil War, when Crook was establishing his reputation as the Army's premier Indian fighter, Hayes made a number of visits to the West, where the two took long hunting trips and Hayes sometimes accompanied patrols in pursuit of Apaches.

Hayes's formal military training began as a volunteer in the First (Cleveland) Troop of the Ohio cavalry. At the outbreak of the Spanish-American War in 1898, Hayes, at 41, was an established, highly successful businessman. His connections secured him an appointment as major in the 1st Ohio Volunteer Cavalry. He deployed to Cuba in time for the Santiago Campaign, in which he was wounded during the assault on San Juan Hill.

Always eager to be in on the action and with the connections to make it happen, he hastily arranged a transfer to Gen. Nelson Miles's command and was wounded again during the invasion of Puerto Rico. When the American annexation of the Philippines triggered a general insurrection, Hayes sought and received a commission as lieutenant colonel in the 31st Infantry US Volunteers, which shipped out from San Francisco bound for Manila in early November 1899.

In October, General Elwell Otis launched an attack intended destroy the Philippine "republican" army of Gen. Emilio Aguinaldo. The campaign was troubled from the start by command problems, bad weather, difficult terrain, and inadequate logistics. Despite these daunting challenges, the poorly trained and equipped Philippine forces were rapidly disintegrating under American pressure. Aguinaldo broke his remaining units into smaller regional groups to continue a guerilla war.

In order to shore up the faltering northern drive, the 31st Regiment, delayed by heavy weather, was redirected to the port of Vigan. The port had been occupied by the Navy and used to stage Army supplies. On December 3, 1899, Army lieutenant colonel James Parker, with a reduced company of the 33rd Infantry Regiment and along with the unit's sick and wounded, assumed security for the supply depot. Parker could muster perhaps 120 fighting men, including ambulatory patients.

The supplies at Vigan were a powerful draw to Philippine general Tinio, whose army, reduced to less than 500 ill-equipped and hungry men, was desperately trying to oppose the American advance. On the afternoon he assumed command, Parker unknowingly gave Tinio and several of his officers, disguised as local gentry, a tour of the depot in an effort to sway the local elite with a demonstration of American power. Tinio quickly planned a raid for that very night intended to overwhelm the Americans and seize the supplies. After dark, several hundred insurgents began infiltrating; shortly before midnight, a small group was challenged by an American patrol and their alarm roused the garrison, who stumbled blearily from their bunks into a confused firefight. Parker rapidly organized an ad hoc defense. Backed by over 50,000 rounds of rifle ammunition, fire discipline, at least, was not an issue.

The fighting could be heard at the docks where the 31st had been disembarking since early in the afternoon. A number of contradictory and wild reports reached the officers at the quayside, but no dispatch was received from Parker. Webb Hayes, having arrived only hours before, nevertheless elected to go forward alone to assess the situation and report back to his unit on the beach. He managed to penetrate the insurgent perimeter and, having determined that the garrison was holding its own, remained with them until morning, when Tinio hastily withdrew.

Hayes continued to serve in Luzon until June 1900, when, ever restless, he volunteered to command a detachment of the 31st dispatched to China as part of the international relief force assembling to deal with the Boxer Rebellion.

In 1902, Hayes, Parker, and two enlisted soldiers were awarded the Medal of Honor for their actions at Vigan. Hayes served as an official observer during the Russo-Japanese War and left the Army in 1905 but was reactivated and promoted to colonel in 1916. He finally retired as a brigadier general in 1919. Hayes went on to a very successful career in business, cofounding Union Carbide. He was also the driving force behind the founding of the Rutherford B. Hayes Presidential Center, the first presidential library. Hayes died on July 26, 1934, and was buried at the Rutherford B. Hayes home, Spiegel Grove, in Fremont, Ohio.

Given the lack of substantive evidence or detailed narrative supporting his Medal of Honor recommendation, it is arguable that Webb Hayes's award should have been revoked by the revised standards of the Miles MOH Review Commission convened in 1917. But his status at the time as a serving regular officer, his family connections, and his personal relationship with Gen. Miles made that outcome improbable.

Edward L. Bowie

Further Reading

Linn, Brian McAllister. *The Philippine War 1899–1902*. Lawrence: University Press of Kansas, 2000

"Webb C. Hayes: Biographical Sketch." Visitor Brochure, 2001, Rutherford B. Hayes Presidential Center, Spiegel Grove, Fremont, Ohio.

Heard, John W.

Born: March 27, 1860
Died: February 4, 1922
Home State: Mississippi
Service: Army
Conflict: Spanish-American War
Age at Time of Award: 38

John W. Heard was born on the eve of the Civil War on March 27, 1860, in Woodstock, Mississippi. His father rode with Nathan Bedford Forrest during the war.

Heard was appointed to West Point and graduated with the class of 1883. Assigned to the 3rd US Cavalry, the young officer spent years in Western frontier posts. Heard served on the Mexican border in 1892 and 1893, helping to suppress local disturbances. In 1894, he was sent to Chicago to help break the Pullman strike that threatened railroad traffic throughout the United States. Along with US Marshals, over 12,000 Regular Army troops were called in to force the railroad workers back to their jobs. By 1898, Heard was stationed at Fort Ethan Alan in Vermont.

In April 1898, Spain and the United States declared war on each other because of events in Cuba. Most of the US Regular Army, supplemented by state militia and regiments hurriedly raised for federal service, gathered in and around Florida for an invasion of Cuba. While most of the 3rd Cavalry shipped out to Cuba, First Lieutenant Heard was part of a small contingent of troops from the regiment who remained in Florida. Anxious to share in the opportunities offered by combat, he gladly volunteered to participate in a mission in July 1898 that brought him the Medal of Honor.

Heard and about a dozen soldiers from the 3rd Cavalry were assigned to guard a shipment of supplies for insurgents being shipped to northern Cuba. The supplies were carried on the *Wanderer*, a wooden fruit transport based out of New Orleans and hired by the Army Transport Service. On the morning of July 23, the ship and cargo arrived off the mouth of the Mani-Mani River. Bahia Honda, a major Spanish stronghold west of Havana, was only 10 miles east of the beach. The route to the beach was narrow and twisting, with reefs on either side. After the ship's captain anchored the vessel about 400 yards from shore, soldiers and crewmen began rowing the weapons, food, and clothing to the beach. A group of insurgents waited and began stacking the supplies.

Unknown to Heard or his colleagues, a large number of Spanish cavalrymen were hidden in the nearby forest. Either warned by informants or alerted by insurgent activity, the Spanish surprised the Americans. After most of the cargo had been unloaded, a force of around 1,000 Spanish cavalry charged the Americans and insurgents on the beach. Heard, on the *Wanderer*, ordered his men to lie down and open fire on the Spanish. This encouraged the insurgents, who also joined the fray, forcing the Spanish to retreat into the forest. From there, they poured heavy fire into the insurgent positions and the *Wanderer*. Heard later noted their aim was unusually good, and the upper works of the wooden ship were soon riddled with bullets. Despite the incoming fire, Heard stood and pointed out targets. Although a number of his men were seriously wounded, Heard did not receive a scratch.

The *Wanderer*'s position was untenable, and the captain ordered the anchor raised. Raising steam, the ship quickly turned and began working its way out to sea. The captain soon realized, however, that the electrical telegraph that carried directions to the engine room had been shot away by Spanish bullets. Without the telegraph, the *Wanderer* risked running aground and being captured by the Spanish.

Heard ordered two of his men to relay orders from the wheelhouse to the engine room, but they were both quickly wounded by Spanish bullets. Heard refused to order anyone else to risk their lives and decided to do the job himself. He stood outside the wheelhouse and took orders from the captain, and then ran back to the grating above the engine room and told the engineers what the captain wanted. Despite being targeted by the Spanish, Heard remained untouched, and the *Wanderer* was able to return to the open sea.

The Americans who had been ferrying supplies to the beach had rowed their boat out to sea in the meantime and were picked up by the *Wanderer*. The insurgents used the distraction of the ship's escape to haul off most of the supplies and escape into the forest. Although seven of Heard's detachment were seriously wounded, the mission was considered a success.

For his actions, John Heard received the Medal of Honor on June 21, 1899. He was promoted and sent to the Philippines to fight insurgents. He later returned to the United States as a recruiter before serving another tour of duty in the Philippines between 1905 and 1907. Heard served as commander of Army forces in Hawaii and received a brevet promotion to brigadier general on October 1, 1918. He reverted to his permanent rank of colonel at the end of his assignment in August 1919. The Hawaiian legislature extended its official thanks to Heard for increasing the efficiency of the Hawaiian National Guard. Heard died in New Orleans, Louisiana, on February 4, 1922.

Tim J. Watts

Further Reading

Above and Beyond: A History of the Medal of Honor from the Civil War to Vietnam. Boston, MA: Boston Publishing Company, 1985.

O'Brien, John, and Horace Herbert Smith. *A Captain Unafraid: The Strange Adventures of Dynamite Johnny O'Brien as Set Down by Horace Smith.* New York: Harper, 1912.

Hendrix, James R.

Born: August 20, 1925
Died: November 14, 2002
Home State: Arkansas
Service: Army
Conflict: World War II
Age at Time of Award: 19

Born on August 20, 1925, in Lepanto, Arkansas, to a sharecropper, James Richard Hendrix quit school after the third grade to work in the cotton fields to help support his family. In 1944, at age 18, he was drafted into the US Army. After basic training, he was sent to Europe as a private in the 53rd Armored Infantry Battalion of the 4th Armored Division. On December 26, 1944, with Patton's 3rd Army at the Battle of the Bulge near Assenois, Belgium, Hendrix, now aged 19, performed heroic deeds during the battle that earned him the Medal of Honor.

After Allied forces landed on the beaches of France on D-Day, June 6, 1944, and began to push the Germans back, there was hope that the war would soon be over. However, the Germans launched a surprise attack on American and British forces in the Ardennes region of Belgium and Luxembourg in December, and the Battle of the Bulge ensued, halting the Allied advance and inflicting severe casualties.

Three days before Christmas, the 101st Airborne Division was surrounded by German forces in Bastogne, Belgium. Patton's 4th Armored Division was ordered to break through to relieve the besieged paratroopers.

Hendrix's unit was in the forward element as the 4th Armored Division advanced toward Bastogne. As his unit approached Assenois, Belgium, a few miles south of Bastogne, they came under enemy combined small arms and artillery fire. The unit stalled when it was blocked by a German Tiger tank blocking the road. Hendrix dismounted from his M16 half-track and disabled the tank with a bazooka.

Hendrix remounted his half-track as the column began to move again. However, his vehicle was hit by artillery fire. He jumped out and took shelter in a shell crater. However, he saw two German 88-mm field gun positions. With artillery shells landing all around him, he charged forward with his rifle. He poured fire into the two-gun position until the crews surrendered; in all, he killed 1 German soldier and captured 13 others.

Later in the same engagement, he again left his half-track to silence two German machine guns and rescue two wounded American soldiers. Still later in the battle, Hendrix faced enemy fire to rescue a fellow soldier trapped in a burning half-track and move him to safety. For these actions, Private Hendrix was nominated for the Medal of Honor by General Patton.

On August 23, 1945, Hendrix received the Medal of Honor from President Harry S. Truman at the White House. However, the day before the ceremony, an incident received national attention in the media. The Willard Hotel in Washington, an official host for Medal of Honor recipients arriving in the city for a mass awards ceremony at the White House, had refused the Hendrix family entry to its Crystal Room for dinner because they said his father was not wearing the required coat and tie.

Hendrix, by then a sergeant, was quoted by United Press as saying his father had, in fact, worn a coat and tie, but the family settled for dinner at a nearby cafeteria. The story of this incident brought many letters of support to the Hendrix family.

After the war, Hendrix remained in the Army and joined the paratroopers. In September 1949, he survived another harrowing experience when his main and reserve parachutes failed to open during a training jump at Fort Benning, Georgia.

After falling more than 1,000 feet, he managed to land on his feet when he hit a newly plowed field and received only minor bruises. President Truman heard about the incident and contacted Hendrix, saying, "That was the second miracle of this world." When Hendrix asked what was the first, the president replied, "That I ever got elected president."

Hendrix volunteered for service again in the Korean War and in Vietnam. He retired from the US Army in 1965 as a master sergeant.

James Hendrix lived in Davenport, Florida, with his wife and four daughters. He died from throat cancer at the age of 77 on November 14, 2002, and is buried in Florida National Cemetery, Bushnell, Florida.

Debra J. Sheffer

Further Reading

Collier, Peter, and Nick Del Calzo. *Medal of Honor: Portraits of Valor beyond the Call of Duty.* New York: Artisan, 2006.

The Congressional Medal of Honor: The Names, the Deeds. Forest Ranch, CA: Sharp & Dunnigan, 1984.

Hernández, Rodolfo P.

Born: April 14, 1931
Died:
Home State: California
Service: Army
Conflict: Korean War
Age at Time of Award: 20

Rodolfo P. Hernández was born on April 14, 1931, in Colton, California, the son of migrant workers. His parents moved their five boys and three girls to Fowler, a small agricultural town in the middle of the state. Rodolfo was an active boy who showed little interest in school. He made it to eighth grade and then took on various odd jobs while looking for something better. At 17, he persuaded his mother to let him join the Army. Private Hernández completed basic training at Fort Ord, California, and volunteered for airborne training. When the Army reorganized for the Korean War, Hernández was assigned to the 187th Regimental Combat Team (RCT Airborne) and issued a Browning Automatic Rifle (BAR). Rodolfo, called Rudy by his fellow soldiers, took a liking to the weapon because you could "walk and fire it at the same time." He named his BAR "Baby Doll."

The 187th RCT (Airborne) was shipped to Korea and posted near Seoul. In October 1950, the unit made a combat jump near Sukchon, behind enemy lines, and was involved in hard fighting. The following February, Hernández's unit was once more committed to heavy combat. It was during this period that Hernández became aware of what he called his "inner man," a part of his self that took over during combat and allowed him to perform bravely and effectively under fire.

On Valentine's Day 1951, Rudy's platoon was pinned down by heavy enemy fire; suddenly, his inner man took over, and he led a charge uphill while firing his BAR. His example proved contagious, and the group of soldiers who followed him killed 50 of the enemy and captured three enemy positions. Soon thereafter, the bitter cold took its toll. Hernández was evacuated to Japan when he could not even walk because frostbite had damaged his feet. After convalescing in an Army hospital, Rudy asked to return to his unit in Korea.

Once reunited with his company, Rudy was promoted to corporal and squad leader and continued to participate in heavy combat. When his unit was assaulted by a strong North Korean force that pushed them off Hill 420 near Wontong-ni, the paratroopers counterattacked and retook their positions. They dug in for a miserable night of rain and cold. Two hours after midnight on May 31, 1951, the exhausted troops were startled by heavy artillery fire and the sound of bugles announcing an imminent assault by the North Koreans. Although most soldiers withdrew in the face of overwhelming odds, Rudy and his foxhole buddy fired round upon round at the advancing enemy; they were both wounded almost immediately. Bleeding and with a ruptured round choking his weapon, Rudy jumped out of his foxhole with fixed bayonet. Instantly, his inner man took over as he charged the enemy until falling to bullet, shrapnel, and bayonet wounds.

After US forces successfully counterattacked, Corporal Hernández's "body" was found by his comrades in front of his position, surrounded by the bodies of six enemy soldiers. He was evacuated in a body bag. Fortunately, a medic noticed that some of his fingers were moving and saved his life.

Hernández was presented the Medal of Honor by President Harry Truman in a ceremony in the White House Rose Garden. After the war, Rudy began a lifelong journey in rehabilitation. He had to relearn even the most basic of human functions. Even the simple act of swallowing was at first impossible. But he eventually managed to talk, walk, and use most of the left side of his body. His inner struggle was masked by the permanent smile he wore when surgeons sewed up his lips. Eventually, Rudy married and fathered three children. He worked for 17 years as counselor for the Veterans Administration, where he helped wounded veterans cope with the aftermath of the war.

After retiring from the Veterans Administration, he divorced and moved to Fayetteville, North Carolina, to be near his old unit's home station. He has continued to participate in many commemorative veterans' events. At the dedication of the North Carolina Korean War Memorial, he was spotted by the medic who had saved his life in that distant Korean battlefield. He has since remarried and continues to serve as an advocate for veterans and is active in his church community.

Although the lives of those who have earned the Medal of Honor are permanently shaped by the events that led to this distinction, the story of Rudy Hernández's life is one of continued courage, fortitude, and grace in the face of adversity. His lifelong struggle against disabilities and the courage of his example are at least as remarkable and commendable, if not more so, than his courageous actions when, on a barren godforsaken hill in Korea, he felt in the grip of his inner man.

Prisco Hernández

Further Reading

Collier, Peter, and Nick Del Calzo. *Medal of Honor: Portraits of Valor beyond the Call of Duty*. New York: Artisan, 2006.

Smith, Larry. *Beyond Glory: Medal of Honor Heroes in Their Own Words—Extraordinary Stories of Courage from WWII to Vietnam*. New York: W. W. Norton, 2003.

US Congress. Senate. Committee on Veterans Affairs. *Medal of Honor Recipients 1863–1978*. Washington, D.C.: Government Printing Office, 1979.

Herrera, Silvestre S.

Born: July 17, 1917
Died: November 26, 2007
Home State: Arizona
Service: Army
Conflict: World War II
Age at Time of Award: 27

Although his Medal of Honor citation lists El Paso, Texas, as his birthplace, Silvestre S. Herrera was born in Camargo, a rural village in the northern Mexican state of Chihuahua, on July 17, 1917. When he became an orphan in early infancy, an uncle took him under his care and crossed the border to El Paso, Texas, in search of a better life. There, Herrera struggled for survival as a farm laborer and worked at odd jobs. Herrera's uncle concealed the fact that he was not Herrera's real father and also kept his Mexican citizenship a secret. Later, Herrera moved to Phoenix, Arizona, where he married and found work as a mechanic at a dairy farm.

In 1944, Herrera received a draft notice. The news triggered a series of confessions. His uncle revealed to Herrera that he had been born in Mexico and, since he was not an American citizen, could not be drafted. He also informed Herrera that he was not his real father. Despite these shocking revelations and the fact that he was a married man with three children and one on the way, Herrera decided to answer the call to duty and joined the US Army. He felt that he could not ask another man to take the place fate had reserved for him. Private Herrera was assigned as an infantryman to Company E, 142nd Infantry Regiment, 36th Infantry Division. The 36th Division was a Texas National Guard unit that was slated for combat in the European Theater. Private Herrera spent some time in Italy and then participated in the invasion of Southern France. At first, resistance was light, but as the Germans retreated through mountainous terrain, their resistance stiffened.

On March 15, 1945, as his platoon was advancing along a forest trail near Mertz-willer, France, a German machine gun opened fire, pinning down the unit. On his own initiative, Private Herrera stood up and assaulted the enemy position, firing his M-1 rifle from the hip and throwing hand grenades. Eight stunned enemy soldiers surrendered, and the position was captured. When the platoon continued its advance, it was once more pinned down by heavy enemy machine gun fire. Again, Private Herrera advanced against the enemy position even though it was protected by a wide minefield. Unfortunately, he stepped first on one mine, then on another, and lost both feet. Despite the terrible pain and severe blood loss, Herrera continued to fire accurately at the enemy, forcing them to seek cover and allowing his squad to outflank and capture the enemy machine gun emplacement. After this action, he was evacuated to the United States.

On August 23, 1945, President Harry Truman presented the Medal of Honor to Herrera in a moving White House ceremony in which the wounded soldier wheeled his wheelchair forward to meet the president. He returned to Phoenix to a hero's welcome. As a sign of their pride and gratitude for the valor of the first Arizonan to be awarded the Medal of Honor, the citizens of the state raised $14,000 to provide for him and his family. He was honorably discharged from the Army as a sergeant in 1946. When the truth of his alien status became known, he was granted US citizenship.

After the war, Herrera lived in Phoenix, raising five children with his wife, Ramona, and earning his living as a skilled leather artisan. He was fitted with prosthetic legs, which allowed him some measure of mobility. When the Mexican government found out about his story, he was awarded the Order of Military Merit First Class, the highest military decoration for valor bestowed by Mexico. Though lacking formal education, Herrera was an advocate of education for his children and other disadvantaged youth. Appropriately, his story appears in the US Army's official *Soldier's Guide* as an example of honor and soldierly values.

In many ways, Silvestre Herrera's life story is the quintessential Mexican American immigrant story carried to heroic proportions. His illegal immigrant status, work ethic, love for both his Mexican heritage and his chosen country, and a life centered on traditional values such as family and faith are all central to the Mexican American defining narrative and its members' self-identity. Despite his natural modesty and quiet dignity, Herrera has been publicly honored by military and civic groups. An elementary school in Phoenix and the Army Reserve's 164th Corps Support Group Headquarters in Mesa, Arizona, bear his name. He died in Glendale,

Arizona, on November 26, 2007, at the age of 90 and is buried at the city's Resthaven Park Cemetery.

Prisco Hernández

Further Reading

Collier, Peter, and Nick Del Calzo. *Medal of Honor: Portraits of Valor beyond the Call of Duty.* New York: Artisan, 2006.

The Soldier's Guide FM 7–21.13. Washington, D.C.: Headquarters, Department of the Army, February 2004.

Tillman, Barrett. *Heroes: U.S. Army Medal of Honor Recipients.* New York: Berkeley, 2006.

US Congress. Senate. Committee on Veterans Affairs. *Medal of Honor Recipients 1863–1978.* Washington, D.C.: Government Printing Office, 1979.

Hooper, Joe R.

Born: August 8, 1938
Died: May 6, 1979
Home State: Washington
Service: Army
Conflict: Vietnam War
Age at Time of Award: 30

Born in Piedmont, South Carolina, on August 8, 1938, Joe Ronnie Hooper moved as a boy to Washington State with his family. There he attended—but did not complete—high school. In 1956, he enlisted in the US Navy, serving a three-year tour of duty. Serving on the aircraft carriers *Hancock* and *Wasp*, he left the Navy in 1959 with the rank of petty officer 3rd class.

Less than a year later, in May 1960, Hooper enlisted in the US Army and was trained as a paratrooper with the 82nd Airborne Division at Fort Bragg, North Carolina. After a tour of duty in South Korea, he was stationed at Fort Hood, Texas, and Fort Campbell, Kentucky. Promoted to platoon sergeant, Hooper also served with the 508th Infantry Regiment in the Panama Canal Zone. By the summer of 1967, however, Hooper had been demoted to corporal because of his penchant for getting into trouble. In October of that year, he was advanced to staff sergeant and was deployed to South Vietnam as a squad leader in the 501st Infantry Regiment, 101st Airborne Division.

During the Tet Offensive, on February 21, 1968, in the Battle of Hue, Hooper was credited with having killed 22 enemy combatants; in the process of the vicious firefight, he was wounded seven times. Despite his injuries, he left a field hospital to rejoin his outfit while still badly injured because he was concerned about the welfare of the young recruits under his charge. Returning stateside in June 1968, he was discharged from the service but promptly reenlisted in the Army in September 1968. On March 7, 1969, President Richard M. Nixon presented him with the Medal of Honor for his gallantry at Hue. Hooper subsequently served as a public relations specialist and served another tour of duty in Panama before returning to Vietnam for a second time, a posting he himself requested.

Hooper was commissioned a second lieutenant in December 1970 while in Vietnam, a highly unusual advancement for an enlisted man who had not yet attained a top noncommissioned officer's rank. He then served out the remainder of his tour as a platoon leader in the 101st Airborne Division. In April 1971, he returned to the United States. By this point, it is estimated that he had 115 enemy kills, including the 22 in the Battle of Hue. In addition to the Medal of Honor, he also received two Silver Stars, six Bronze Stars, and eight Purple Hearts. Back home, Hooper was restless and had grown disillusioned by the lack of discipline in the Army and American policy toward the Vietnam War. In 1972, he resigned his commission; two years later, he left the service.

Hooper stayed active by giving speeches and granting interviews about his combat experiences, and he joined a US Army Reserve outfit in Washington State. In March 1977, he attained the rank of captain, but his absences and infrequent presence at drills did not endear him to his superiors. In September 1978, he left the Reserves. This ended his military career, during which he had received 37 citations. Unable to adjust fully to civilian life—some say he suffered from posttraumatic stress disorder (PTSD)—Hooper became increasingly despondent. He was certainly disillusioned over the defeat of South Vietnam in 1975 and the vicious antiwar politics of the 1970s. He held a secession of civilian jobs and began to drink heavily. Hooper died of a stroke on May 6, 1979, at the age of 40, in Louisville, Kentucky. He is buried in Arlington National Cemetery.

Many have argued, with considerable justification, that Joe Hooper fell victim to the poisonous atmosphere that greeted returning Vietnam veterans; others have argued with similar justification that Hooper never gained the celebrity status enjoyed by someone like Audie Murphy, a highly decorated World War II veteran, because Vietnam was an unpopular war that most Americans wanted to forget.

Paul G. Pierpaoli Jr

Further Reading

Above and Beyond: A History of the Medal of Honor from the Civil War to Vietnam. Boston, MA: Boston Publishing Company, 1985.

Maslowski, Peter, and Don Winslow. *Looking for a Hero: Staff Sergeant Joe Ronnie Hooper and the Vietnam War.* Lincoln: University of Nebraska Press, 2005.

Howard, Oliver O.

Born: November 8, 1830
Died: October 26, 1909
Home State: Maine
Service: Army
Conflict: Civil War
Age at Time of Award: 32

Oliver O. Howard was born in Leeds, Maine, on November 8, 1830. Graduating from Bowdoin College in 1850 and the US Military Academy, West Point, in 1854, Howard was teaching mathematics at West Point when the Civil War began. Commanding the 3rd Maine Regiment, he led a brigade at the First Battle of Bull Run/Manassas on July 21, 1861, where he helped cover the Union retreat. His performance won him promotion to brigadier general. In the spring of 1862, Howard was conspicuous for his bravery at Seven Pines during the Peninsula Campaign on May 31, where he was wounded twice. His right arm was amputated close to the shoulder; for this action, Howard would receive the Medal of Honor in 1893.

During his convalescence, Howard became convinced that God had spared his life for the purpose of liberating slaves. Back in command, Howard fought with distinction at the battles of Second Bull Run/Manassas on August 28–30, 1862, and at Antietam/Sharpsburg. Promoted to major general of volunteers, Howard led his division in the desperate frontal assault at Marye's Heights, Fredericksburg, on December 13, 1862.

On April 2, 1863, Howard took command of the XI Corps, composed largely of German Americans. Hit on May 2 by Confederate lieutenant general Thomas J. "Stonewall" Jackson's flank attack in the Battle of Chancellorsville, Howard's corps virtually disintegrated. Notwithstanding this defeat and the considerable controversy about his role in it, Howard retained his command. During Confederate general Robert E. Lee's second invasion of the North, on the morning of July 1, 1863, Howard selected Cemetery Ridge as the key defensive position at Gettysburg. Although the performance of his "Dutchmen" over the next two days of battle could best be called mediocre, Howard enjoyed the ultimate satisfaction of receiving the thanks of Congress for his actions in the Battle of Gettysburg.

Howard then shifted to the Western Theater, commanding at Lookout Mountain, Missionary Ridge, and Knoxville. During the subsequent Atlanta Campaign, Maj. Gen. William T. Sherman chose him to command the Army of the Tennessee following the death of Maj. Gen. James McPherson. Having been at West Point with Confederate lieutenant general John Bell Hood, Howard became convinced that the Southern general would attack and ordered fortifications constructed. At both Ezra Church and Jonesboro, his army won easy defensive victories.

When Sherman marched from Atlanta for Savannah in November 1864, he assigned Howard the honor of commanding the right wing of the army. Howard's men carried out the assault that assured the capture of Savannah. Into the Carolinas, Howard's army impressed all with the rapidity of its movement over flooded swamp country. Although Howard publicly justified the harsh treatment meted out to Southerners during the march, he attempted to keep a check on gratuitous violence. At Columbia, for instance, when much of the city was in flames, he organized fire-fighting efforts, brought in regiments to control looters, and provided rations for the destitute citizens. Following the army's departure from Columbia, Howard became concerned over the misbehavior of Federal forces, in part for the detrimental effects that such depredations had on the discipline of his entire army. In North Carolina, Howard's army fought at Bentonville and Goldsboro. When Sherman negotiated surrender terms with Joseph E. Johnston on April 18, 1865, Howard was present. He was also a prominent figure in Sherman's Grand Review of the Army in Washington on May 24, 1865.

Throughout the war, Howard won the admiration of his men for his great personal bravery. He also attracted attention for his churchgoing and for his puritanical ways—he opposed profanity, drinking, and gambling. Some admirers characterized Howard as "the Christian general." Skeptics called him "Old Prayer Book." Certainly, Howard saw more than his share of battle, and he was, in Sherman's eyes, the consummate team player.

Oliver Howard's straight-laced demeanor led President Abraham Lincoln to appoint him in May 1865 the head of the Bureau of Refugees, Freedmen, and Abandoned Lands. While in this post, Howard championed African Americans in various ways. In 1867, he became the key figure in the establishment of one of the earliest black institutions of higher education, which was named in his honor (now Howard University); he served as its first president until 1874. Howard also played an active role in the settlement of the last remaining frontier, campaigning against Chief Cochise's Apaches in 1872, the Nez Percés in 1877, and the Bannocks and Paiutes in 1878. After various peacetime assignments, he retired from active duty in 1894. Howard died in Burlington, Vermont, on October 26, 1909.

Malcolm Muir Jr.

Further Reading

Castel, Albert. *Decision in the West: The Atlanta Campaign of 1864.* Lawrence: University Press of Kansas, 1992.

Howard, Oliver O. *Autobiography of Oliver Otis Howard.* New York: Baker & Taylor, 1908.

Howard, Robert L.

Born: July 11, 1939
Died: December 23, 2009
Home State: Alabama
Service: Army
Conflict: Vietnam War
Age at Time of Award: 31

Robert Lewis Howard was born on July 11, 1939, in Opelika, Alabama. He enlisted in the Army at Montgomery, Alabama, in 1956 and joined the 101st Airborne Division, following in the footsteps of his father and four uncles, who had been paratroopers in World War II. In 1965, he went to Vietnam for the first of his five tours in the war zone. He was subsequently wounded by a rifle bullet that ricocheted off a tree and hit him in the face. While recuperating in the hospital, he met a Special Forces officer who was visiting one of Howard's fellow patients. The officer convinced Howard to transfer to Special Forces. After completing training, he donned his Green Beret and returned to Vietnam in 1966 for an assignment with 5th Special Forces Group.

In December 1968, then sergeant first class Howard was serving in the highly classified Military Assistance Command, Vietnam—Studies and Observations Group (MACV-SOG). He had already been nominated for the Medal of Honor for two separate earlier actions. On December 28, Howard was second in command of a platoon of American and Vietnamese Special Forces that was tasked with rescuing a wounded Green Beret in Cambodia. The platoon was to be inserted by helicopter, but the landing zone was hot. It was several hours before they could clear the area and get the entire unit on the ground. By that time, it was dusk, so the platoon was moving to a nearby hilltop when a force of 250 North Vietnamese Army (NVA) soldiers opened fire on them. Howard and his lieutenant were at the head of the column when the NVA triggered a claymore mine against them. The blast knocked Howard unconscious, destroyed his rifle, and left him with shrapnel wounds in his hands.

When he came to, Sergeant Howard smelled the stench of burning flesh as an NVA soldier was using a flamethrower to torch the bodies of the American and South Vietnamese casualties. Howard lobbed a grenade at the NVA soldier and made his way toward his lieutenant, who had been badly wounded.

Howard administered first aid to his officer and began to drag him toward a ravine where several survivors of the ambush had taken refuge. There, he used a pistol from one of his comrades to kill three NVA soldiers who were advancing on the ravine. During this fight, a bullet struck Howard's ammunition pouch, detonating several magazines and knocking him down. Undaunted, he continued to aid his lieutenant, using the pistol to fend off the enemy soldiers.

With his officer down, Howard assumed command of the platoon and organized the outnumbered troops into a defensive perimeter. He crawled from position to position, distributing ammunition and directing fire against the surrounding enemy while calling in air support from airborne gunships. After two days of almost constant firefights, the stranded platoon was evacuated by US helicopters. Howard was the last man on the helicopters.

As a result of this action, Sergeant Howard received a direct promotion to first lieutenant. Two years later, in February 1971, while commanding a Special Forces company in Vietnam, his unit was in heavy contact with the enemy when he received a call on a field phone from Gen. William Westmoreland, senior US commander, who told him he had been awarded the Medal of Honor and would be pulled out to return to the United States to receive the medal. On March 2, 1971, President Richard Nixon draped the pale blue ribbon of the Medal of Honor around Howard's neck in a White House ceremony.

Howard remained in the Army after Vietnam. He served in a number of infantry, airborne, Ranger, and Special Forces assignments in the United States and overseas. Along the way, he attended the Army Command and General Staff College at Fort Leavenworth, Kansas, and the National War College at Fort McNair in Washington, D.C. While on active duty, he also received a bachelor's degree in police administration from Texas Christian University in 1973 and later two master's degrees. Howard retired at Fort Sam Houston in San Antonio, Texas, in 1992, after 36 years service; he was the last Vietnam Special Forces Medal of Honor recipient still on active duty when he retired.

During the course of his long Army career, he received, in addition to the Medal of Honor, two Distinguished Service Crosses, the Silver Star, four Bronze Stars, and eight Purple Hearts, making him one of the most highly decorated soldiers of the Vietnam War. After retiring from the Army, he made his home in Texas and worked at the Department of Veterans Affairs until January 2006, when he retired after 52 years of federal service. He frequently made trips around the country and also overseas to combat zones like Iraq and Afghanistan to visit with the troops. He served as president of the Congressional Medal of Honor Society from 2007 to 2009.

Robert Howard died on December 23, 2009, of pancreatic cancer at a hospice in Waco, Texas. He was buried in Arlington National Cemetery on February 22, 2010.

James H. Willbanks

Further Reading

Collier, Peter, and Nick Del Calzo. *Medal of Honor: Portraits of Valor beyond the Call of Duty.* New York: Artisan, 2006.

Murphy, Edward F. *Vietnam Medal of Honor Heroes.* New York: Ballantine Books, 2005.

Plaster, John. *Secret Commandos: Behind the Lines with the Elite Warriors of SOG.* New York: Simon & Schuster, 2004.

Plaster, John. *SOG: The Secret Wars of America's Commandos in Vietnam.* Boulder, CO: Paladin, 2008.

Inouye, Daniel K.

Born: September 7, 1924
Died:
Home State: Hawaii
Service: Army
Conflict: World War II
Age at Time of Award: 21

Daniel K. Inouye was born on September 7, 1924, in Honolulu, Hawaii, the child of Japanese immigrants. On December 7, 1941, the day the Japanese bombed Pearl Harbor, Inouye was a senior in high school. Having taught first aid at the local community center prior to the attack, Inouye spent the remainder of December 7 working at a Red Cross Station. He completed high school and tired to enlist in the Army; however, the War Department was not accepting Japanese Americans into service. In September 1942, he enrolled as a student in the University of Hawaii with aspirations to become a doctor. However, once the War Department lifted the restriction on Nisei (second-generation Japanese Americans) serving in the Armed Forces, Inouye dropped out of the university and enlisted in the US Army.

In March of 1943, Inouye was assigned to the 442nd Regimental Combat Team and took part in the Rome-Arno Campaign, where he established himself as an outstanding patrol leader. Inouye further distinguished himself in combat in October 1944 when elements of the 442nd were tasked by Gen. Alexander "Sandy" Patch to assist in aiding the 1st Battalion of the 141st Infantry regiment (the Lost Battalion), which had become surrounded by German units in the wooded area of Domaine de Champ. For approximately two days, Inouye and other members of 442nd fought savagely to break through to their comrades in the Lost Battalion. The 442nd succeeded in rescuing 211 of 275 members of the Lost Battalion, at a cost of 140 of their own. During the rescue of the Lost Battalion, Inouye distinguished himself as a skillful platoon leader, which the Army subsequently recognized with a battlefield commission to second lieutenant.

Back in Italy in 1945, Second Lieutenant Inouye would again prove himself a brave and courageous soldier. On April 21, 1945, while leading his platoon near San Terenzo, Inouye and his soldiers came under heavy German fire. Rallying his troops, Inouye and his men captured the German artillery and mortar positions

442ND REGIMENTAL COMBAT TEAM

Soon after the bombing of Pearl Harbor, Japanese Americans living on the West Coast were relocated and incarcerated in internment camps located in desolate, windswept desert areas in the western United States. Despite this treatment, Japanese Americans would eventually join up to fight for America and would establish an incredible record of bravery under fire and service to the nation under the banners of the 442nd Regimental Combat Team (RCT) and the 100th Infantry Battalion. These two units were formed independently at different times and did not share a common lineage, but the 100th Battalion would eventually become the first battalion of the 442nd RCT in June 1944.

The 100th Battalion (Separate) deployed first on August 11, 1943, bound for North Africa. On September 22, 1943, the battalion, assigned to the 34th Infantry Division, took part in the allied landing at Salerno. Seven days later, Sergeant Shigeo Takata from B Company became the first member of the unit to be killed in action. After obtaining its initial objective of Monte Milleto, the 100th continued to fight until it was relieved in early November. During that time, the men of the 100th earned 19 Silver Stars, but the casualties were high—3 officers and 75 enlisted men were killed during the unit's initial baptism by fire.

The 100th then joined the assault on Monte Cassino, suffering additional heavy casualties in the bitter fighting. By February 1944, the battalion was down to 521 men but had won the respect of fellow American soldiers for their bravery and refusal to leave a comrade behind. Correspondents called the Japanese American soldiers "little men of iron."

The depleted battalion received 200 Nisei replacements, joined the defense of the beachhead at Anzio until May 1944, and then participated in the push for Rome, halting only 10 miles from the city. Some believe that the 100th was halted deliberately to allow non-Nisei soldiers to liberate Rome.

Meanwhile, the 442nd Regimental Combat Team was activated on February 1, 1943, at Camp Shelby, Mississippi. It was comprised of the 442nd Infantry Regiment, the 522nd Field Artillery Battalion, the 232nd Combat Engineer Company, the 206th Army Ground Force Band, an antitank company, a cannon company, a service company, a medical detachment, and a headquarters company. The 442nd RCT chose "Go for Broke" as its motto, a Hawaiian slang term from the dice game craps meaning to risk everything, to give everything you have—all or nothing.

Upon completion of its training, the 442nd RCT set sail for Italy from Hampton Roads, Virginia, on May 1, 1944, arriving in Naples in June 1944, where it was attached to the 34th Division. The men of the 442nd were anxious to prove themselves in combat. On June 10, 1944, the 100th Battalion was attached to the 442nd to take the place of the regiment's missing 1st Battalion, which had remained in the United States to train replacements.

The 442nd RCT went right into the line and saw its first day of combat on June 26, 1944. After heavy fighting at Belvedere, Luciana, and Livorno, the unit was pulled back for a rest, having sustained 239 killed in action and 972 wounded. During those bloody battles, the men of the 442nd earned 11 Distinguished Service Crosses. In addition, the RCT was presented a Presidential Unit Citation (the nation's top award for combat units).

After fighting at the Arno River in August 1944, the 442nd moved to France for an attack in the Vosges Mountains, where they took the town of Bruyeres, capturing over 200 German soldiers. The unit was then attached to the 36th Infantry Division (formerly a Texas National Guard unit). Shortly thereafter, the 100th Battalion of the 442nd RCT broke through to rescue 211 members of a battalion from the 36th Division that had been cut off behind enemy lines. During the 34 days of almost continual fighting in the Vosges, the 442nd RCT suffered 216 killed in action and more than 856 wounded.

The 442nd RCT went back into combat in late March 1945. Attached to the 92nd Infantry Division, the RCT saw action against the Gothic Line in the Po Valley Campaign, seizing Monte Belvedere on April 7, Carrara on April 10, and Aulla on April 25, helping to break the back of the stiff German defense. Less than two weeks later, on May 7, 1945, Germany surrendered.

The troops of the 442nd Regimental Combat Team fought in eight major campaigns in Italy, France, and Germany. The total casualties in the 442nd RCT were 650 killed in action and 3,713 wounded.

In less than two years of combat, the 442nd Regimental Combat Team earned more than 18,000 individual decorations for valor, including 53 Distinguished Service Crosses, 588 Silver Stars, 5,200 Bronze Star Medals, 9,486 Purple Hearts, and an unprecedented 8 Presidential Unit Citations. Although the 442nd was one of the most decorated units of the war, only one Japanese American, Pfc. Sadao Munemori, Company A, 100th Battalion, was awarded the Medal of Honor, which he received posthumously for action near Seravezza, Italy, on April 5, 1945.

It took 50 years for the United States to recognize the other Nisei soldiers who were deserving of the country's highest award for valor. This was a result of a reexamination of the files of dozens of Japanese American soldiers to see if any might have been denied awards because of racial prejudice. In June 2000, President Bill Clinton awarded an additional 22 Medals of Honor to Asian Americans, 20 of which went to members of the 100th Battalion and 442nd RCT. One of these recipients was Hawaii's US senator Daniel Inouye, whose right arm was shattered by a grenade during his successful destruction of three German machine gun nests on a fortified ridge named Colle Musatello during the Po Valley Campaign. Although 13 of the 20 Japanese American Medals of Honor were given posthumously, the ceremony in the White House demonstrated that the United States fully acknowledged the important contribution made by the Japanese American soldiers to the defense of the nation.

James H. Willbanks

and reached the main German line of resistance. Facing heavy machine gun fire, Inouye charged the German bunker and took out one of the three machine gun emplacements with grenades and submachine gun fire. Hit by a German sniper, Inouye continued to lead and direct his men toward the other two German machine guns. Although wounded, Inouye inched forward and lobbed two grenades under sustained machine gun fire into the second gun emplacement. Although two of the three German gun emplacements had been silenced, the unit still faced heavy fire from the third position. Inouye found himself within range to throw his last grenade into the remaining gun emplacement. As he stood to throw his grenade, a German soldier launched a rifle-propelled grenade at Inouye. The rifle grenade hit Inouye's left arm as he was about to throw the grenade at the German position. Inouye quickly pulled the grenade from his mangled left hand and threw it at the Germans with his right hand. The grenade exploded and killed the German soldier, and Inouye charged the machine gun position with his submachine gun and was hit in his right leg by German fire. For his action on April 21 1945, Inouye became the only officer of the 442nd to earn the Distinguished Service Cross.

After numerous surgeries and approximately two years of recovery, the Army discharged Inouye as a captain. Inouye went back to college, graduating from the University of Hawaii in 1950. He then attended George Washington University Law School, graduating in 1952. He began a life in politics when he was elected in 1959 as the first congressman for Hawaii in the 86th Congress. Inouye continued to serve as a congressman until 1962, when the state elected him to the US Senate, a seat for which he was re-elected in 2010.

In 2000, President Bill Clinton directed the Department of Defense to review service records of Asian Americans and Pacific Islanders who had received the Distinguished Service Cross during World War II to ascertain if the records merited upgrades. Senator Inouye and 22 other Asian American veterans (15 posthumously) received the Medal of Honor after 50 years.

Sean N. Kalic

Further Reading

Collier, Peter, and Nick Del Calzo. *Medal of Honor: Portraits of Valor beyond the Call of Duty*. New York: Artisan, 2006.

Gomez-Granger, Julissa. *CRS Report for Congress: Medal of Honor Recipients: 1979–2008*. Washington, D.C.: Congressional Research Service, RL 30011, November 13, 2007.

Smith, Larry. *Beyond Glory: Medal of Honor Heroes in Their Own Words—Extraordinary Stories of Courage from WWII to Vietnam*. New York: W. W. Norton, 2003.

Yenne, Bill. *Rising Sons: The Japanese American GIs Who Fought for the United States in World War II*. New York: St. Martin's Press, 2007.

Irwin, Bernard J. D.

Born: June 24, 1830
Died: December 15, 1917
Home State: New York
Service: Army
Conflict: Indian Campaigns
Age at Time of Award: 30

Bernard J. D. Irwin, US Army (US Army Medical Department Regiment).

Bernard J. D. Irwin was born on June 24, 1830, in Ireland. In early 1861, Irwin was serving with the 7th Infantry at Fort Breckinridge in the Arizona Territory. What became known as the Bascom Affair began on January 27 when an Indian party raided a ranch at Sonoita Creek, stealing livestock and kidnapping a young boy from the ranch. The commander at nearby Fort Buchannan directed 2nd Lt. George N. Bascom and a mounted contingent of 60 men from the 7th Infantry to recover the boy. Bascom and his men were unable to find the raiders but determined, wrongfully as it turned out, that Apaches had conducted the raid and carried off the boy. They headed east and made contact with Cochise, the Chiricahua Apache chief, who agreed to meet with them. Cochise brought with him his brother, his two nephews, his wife, and his two children. At the meeting, Cochise claimed he had not conducted the raid, but Bascom, not believing him, tried to take Cochise and his family into custody to hold as hostages. Cochise escaped and captured four Americans, whom he offered to trade for his family. When the exchange was refused, Cochise killed the white men, and Bascom responded by hanging Cochise's brother and nephews before he and his troops began their journey home. Several days later, word was received at Fort Breckinridge that the greatly superior Apache force had surrounded Bascom and his men near Apache Pass, in southeastern Arizona.

Assistant Surgeon Irwin volunteered to lead a small force (only 14 men could be spared from the garrison) to ride to Bascom's rescue. On February 13, 1861, Irwin and his men, without horses, set out on mules to make the 100-mile march to relieve the Bascom party. After encountering a band of Indians, Irwin's group engaged and captured several of them, recovered stolen horses and cattle, and then continued the march. Eventually, Irwin and his men reached Bascom's column and helped break the siege. The Bascom Affair started a war with the Apaches that lasted until 1872.

Irwin eventually served as a surgeon in the Civil War. He was on the staff of Gen. William Nelson, commanding the 4th Division of the Army of Ohio. Irwin has been credited by some authorities with establishing the first tent field hospital during the Battle of Shiloh in 1862.

Irwin would eventually be awarded the Medal of Honor for his actions to rescue Bascom and his men in 1861. However, the Medal of Honor did not exist at the time of his action; it was not established until 1862, but Irwin's actions were not forgotten. Ultimately, he received the Medal of Honor on January 21, 1894. His action on February 13–14, 1861, was the first Medal of Honor action in history.

After the Civil War, Bernard Irwin went on to a long career in medicine. He died on December 15, 1917, and is buried at US Military Academy Post Cemetery, West Point, New York.

James H. Willbanks

Further Reading

Fahey, John H. "Bernard John Dowling Irwin and the Development of the Field Hospital at Shiloh." *Military Medicine* 171, no. 5 (May 1, 2006): 345–351.

Owens, Ron. *Medal of Honor: Historical Facts and Figures.* Paducah, KY: Turner Publishing, 2004.

Roberts, David. *Once They Moved Like the Wind: Cochise, Geronimo, and the Apache Wars.* New York: Simon & Schuster, 1993.

Sweeney, Edwin R. *Cochise: Chiricahua Apache Chief.* Norman: University of Oklahoma Press, 1995.

Wachtel, Roger. *The Medal of Honor: Cornerstones of Freedom.* New York: Scholastic, 2009.

Izac, Edouard Victor Michel

Born: December 18, 1891
Died: January 18, 1990
Home State: Iowa
Service: Navy
Conflict: World War I
Age at Time of Award: 26

Edouard Victor Michel Izac was born in Cresco, Iowa, on December 18, 1891. His last name at birth was Isaacs because a US immigration officer had changed the name arbitrarily from Izac in 1850 when his father, Balthazar, entered the United States from the German-speaking area of French Alsace. Although Izac's mother had been born in Philadelphia, her family came from the Baden-Württemberg area of Germany, where the particular dialect of German was similar to that spoken in Alsace. The young Izac grew up speaking Alsatian-Badisch German at home.

Izac graduated from the US Naval Academy at Annapolis in 1915. At 24, he was somewhat older than the rest of the graduates, and according to some reports he had shaved two years off his real age to get into the Academy. After an

Edouard Victor Michel Izac, US Navy (Naval History and Heritage Command).

initial assignment to the battleship USS *Florida* (BB-30), Izac transferred to the Naval Transport Service when America entered World War I. In July 1917, he was assigned to the troopship USS *President Lincoln*, originally a Hamburg-American Line German ship of the same name that the US government had seized in New York harbor when America declared war on Germany.

Starting in October 1917, Izac made five voyages from New York to France on the *President Lincoln*, which carried some 23,000 American troops in the process. By the fifth voyage, Lieutenant Izac was the ship's executive officer. The *President Lincoln* landed her fifth load of troops at Brest, France, on May 23, 1918, and six days later started the return trip to New York as part of a convoy escorted by destroyers. At sundown on May 30, the escorts left the convoy as it passed beyond what was supposed to be the limit of German U-boat operating range. However, at 9:00 the following morning, the *U-90* intercepted the convoy and fired three torpedoes into the *President Lincoln*.

Izac's ship sank within 20 minutes. Almost all of the 715 people on board managed to get off, while the *U-90* surfaced and approached the survivors in the lifeboats. The Germans demanded the surrender of the captain of the *President Lincoln* so they could take him back to Germany as proof of the sinking, but the crew feared the Germans would summarily execute him. As the crew hid their captain, Izac, speaking and gesturing in English, told them that the captain had been killed by one of the torpedo blasts. The ruse worked, but the *U-90* took Izac prisoner instead.

During the voyage back to Germany, Izac carefully concealed his knowledge of German while listening and noting everything that was taking place on the *U-90*. As an experienced naval officer, he acquired a detailed understanding of German submarine tactics and operations by the time the *U-90* got back to its base. Izac knew he had critical operational intelligence that could be used against the U-boats, but he could only get it back to Allied authorities by escaping captivity.

Izac made his first escape attempt even before he reached the prisoner-of-war (POW) camp, jumping from a rapidly moving train as his guards fired at him.

Quickly recaptured, one of the guards broke the stock of his rifle when he smashed it across Izac's head. Almost as soon as he was interred at the POW camp, Izac made another escape attempt. This time he slipped through gaps in the barbed wire, but once he was on the outside he purposely drew fire from the guards in an attempt to create a diversion so other POWs could escape. Izac then made his way through southwestern Germany, where his ancestors had come from, hiding in the woods by day and living on raw vegetables. Reaching the Rhine, he evaded the German sentries and swam the swift river toward Switzerland at night and then made his way to the American Embassy in Bern. Quickly returned to the United States, he reported to the US Navy Bureau of Navigation in Washington on November 11, 1918, the day the war ended.

Izac's intelligence was dated by the time he got it back, but that in no way detracted from his heroic actions during his more than five months as a POW. He received the Medal of Honor on November 11, 1920, from then assistant secretary of the navy Franklin D. Roosevelt. Several months later he was medically retired at the rank of lieutenant commander because of injuries he received while a POW. He also received the Croce di Guerra from Italy and the Cross of Montenegro.

During the 1920s, Izac moved to San Diego, California, and worked in journalism. From 1937 to 1947, Izac served in the US House of Representatives as a Democrat representing California's 20th congressional district. He was a prominent member of the House Naval Affairs Committee and served on a delegation of 12 representatives and senators that inspected the liberated Buchenwald, Dachau, and Dora concentration camps in the spring of 1945. He later coauthored the congressional report *Atrocities and Other Conditions in Concentration Camps in Germany.*

Throughout his later life, Izac continually downplayed his Medal of Honor, insisting that he had never done anything heroic. Nonetheless, the burden of the Medal of Honor was too much to bear for at least one member of his family. In 1953, his second-youngest child, Forrest, committed suicide at age 19, leaving behind a note saying he could never live to be the sort of hero his father was. Devastated by his son's death, Izac focused on gardening and writing. In 1965, he published a travel book about Israel, *The Holy Land, Then and Now.*

Edouard Izac died at the age of 98 on January 18, 1990, survived by 5 children, 19 grandchildren, and 25 great-grandchildren. He is buried at Arlington National Cemetery.

David T. Zabecki

Further Reading

Izac, Edouard. *Prisoner of the U-90*. Boston: Houghton Mifflin, 1919.

Mikaelian, Allen, and Mike Wallace. *Medal of Honor: Profiles of America's Military Heroes from the Civil War to the Present*. New York: Hyperion, 2003.

Jackson, Joe M.

Born: March 14, 1923
Died:
Home State: Georgia
Service: Air Force
Conflict: Vietnam War
Age at Time of Award: 45

Joe M. Jackson was born in Newman, Georgia, on March 14, 1923, and grew up during the Great Depression. After graduating from high school in 1940, Jackson attended a Christian trade school in Taquoa Falls, Georgia, where he trained to be an airplane mechanic. He completed the course in spring 1941. To gain experience, he enlisted in the Army Air Corps and was serving at Orlando Army Air Base in Florida when the Japanese attacked Pearl Harbor. By January 1942, his unit transferred to Westover Field, Massachusetts. Poaching a ride on a training flight as a "flight engineer" on a B-25, Jackson had to tell the pilot of the aircraft to feather the propeller when one of the engines caught fire during the flight. Jackson recounts that at that instant he figured, "I can fly an airplane." After being told by the Army Air Corps that he needed a college degree to fly, Jackson went back to work as an aviation mechanic. However, the Army Air Corps later instituted a program for enlisted men to test into the aviation cadet program. Jackson passed the examination, completed preflight training, and received his wings and commission as a second lieutenant in April 1943. He served the remainder of World War II as an instructor pilot and gunnery instructor in P-47, P-51, and P-63 fighter aircraft.

Although he did not fly any combat missions in World War II, Jackson stayed in the Army Air Corps, which became the US Air Force (USAF) in 1947, and finally got his chance to fly combat missions during the Korean War. He flew 105 missions in F-84s and earned a Distinguished Flying Cross. Between the end of the Korean War and the start of Vietnam, the Air Force promoted Jackson to captain, and later to major. Meanwhile, he graduated from the University of Omaha and the Air War College at Maxwell Air Force Base in Alabama. After these accomplishments, Jackson was assigned to Headquarters US Air Forces in Europe. It was during this assignment that Jackson received orders for South Vietnam.

Prior to leaving for Vietnam, Jackson trained to fly C-123 transport aircraft. Once in the country, Jackson flew with the 311th Air Commando Squadron, which resupplied Special Forces camps through South Vietnam. Later, he would command a detachment of aircraft flying from Da Nang airbase that flew supply missions in support of Allied troops in I Corps Tactical Zone.

On May 12, 1968, Jackson had a flight check scheduled for the day. During the course of this routine mission, Jackson and his aircraft were recalled to Da Nang and told that North Vietnamese Army (NVA) regular forces had overrun the Special Forces camp at Kham Duc, South Vietnam, and that the situation required his assistance. Three USAF combat controllers were trapped at the camp, where they had just finished overseeing the evacuation of South Vietnamese and soldiers from the base. Jackson and his crew flew to Kham Doc and reported in to the airborne command post. The airborne command post told Jackson to "orbit his aircraft at the southwest end of the base and await further instructions." Several aircraft (both rotary and fixed wing) had been shot down or destroyed on the ground as they tried to evacuate the personnel from the besieged base.

Jackson made one pass over the camp and then, under heavy enemy fire, landed his aircraft on the 2,200 feet of the runway that weren't already littered with burning and destroyed aircraft. Jackson brought his aircraft to a stop as the enemy continued to fire at it; the three combat controllers ran for the aircraft, and Jackson's crew assisted them aboard the C-123. Jackson promptly started his take-off roll as rockets and mortar fire continued to impact on the runway. Just before the aircraft lifted off, the NVA fired a 122-mm rocket at Jackson's aircraft, but luckily the rocket broke apart before it hit the aircraft and failed to explode. Jackson successfully got the C-123 airborne, passing through a withering enemy crossfire as the aircraft speeded down the runway.

For his brave and courageous action that day at Kham Duc, President Lyndon B. Johnson awarded Joe Jackson the Medal of Honor on January 16, 1969. Jackson continued to serve in the Air Force for several more years, including service in the Pentagon and on the faculty of the Air War College. He retired from the Air Force after 33 year of service in 1973 and worked as a consultant for Boeing until 1985. He and his wife reside in Kent, Washington.

Sean N. Kalic

Further Reading

Collier, Peter, and Nick Del Calzo. *Medal of Honor: Portraits of Valor beyond the Call of Duty*. New York: Artisan, 2006.

Smith, Larry. *Beyond Glory: Medal of Honor Heroes in Their Own Words—Extraordinary Stories of Courage from WWII to Vietnam*. New York: W. W. Norton, 2003.

US Congress. Senate. Committee on Veterans Affairs. *Medal of Honor Recipients, 1863–1979*. Washington, D.C.: Government Printing Office, 1979.

Jacobs, Jack H.

Born: August 2, 1945
Died:
Home State: New York

Service: Army
Conflict: Vietnam War
Age at Time of Award: 22

Jack Howard Jacobs was born on August 2, 1945, in Brooklyn, New York. A slight man of Jewish heritage, Jacobs grew up in Queens near LaGuardia Airport and then moved with his family to Woodbridge Township, New Jersey, in the mid-1950s. He was a 1962 graduate of Woodbridge High School and entered military service through Rutgers University's Army ROTC program, where he earned BA and MA degrees. With a wife and a daughter and no job, Jacobs joined the Army, planning to attend law school when his three-year commitment was completed. After completing officer and airborne training, he was assigned to Vietnam in 1967 as an assistant battalion advisor to the 2nd Battalion, 16th Infantry, 9th Infantry Division of the Army of the Republic of Vietnam (ARVN).

By the time the Tet Offensive began in 1968, First Lieutenant Jacobs and his two fellow American advisers had forged a close comradeship with the war-weary ARVN soldiers. On March 9, 1968, the South Vietnamese unit was advancing to contact along the Mekong River in Kien Phong Province when they made contact with a Viet Cong (VC) battalion situated in a series of well-disguised and fortified bunkers.

As Jacobs and his comrades advanced across rice paddies toward the enemy, deadly machine gun and mortar fire soon engulfed the battalion. A first attack against the bunkers failed in the face of greatly intensified fire, so Jacobs called in air support to facilitate a second attack. When the South Vietnamese company commander was critically wounded and the ARVN troops became disorganized, Jacobs, although wounded in the head by shrapnel from a mortar round that had landed nearby and had left most of the bones in his face broken, assumed command and ordered a retreat from the exposed position and organized a hasty defensive perimeter.

Then, in a scene Winston Groom might have used while writing *Forrest Gump*, Jacobs ignored the blood pouring into his eyes from his wounds and left the perimeter to retrieve a fellow wounded adviser, to whom he administered first aid. Then, he ran again into the face of heavy fire to rescue the wounded company commander. Time and again, the diminutive Jacobs braved enemy fire to retrieve the wounded and their weapons. In the process, he also single-handedly drove off three VC squads, killing three and wounding several others. In all, Jack Jacobs saved the lives of 1 US adviser and 13 ARVN soldiers. Gravely wounded during the fighting, Jacobs was evacuated by helicopter to a field hospital. He would undergo a dozen surgical operations to repair the damage to his face and skull.

After recovering from his wounds, Jacobs was assigned as commander of an officer candidate company at Fort Benning, Georgia. While in command, he received an order to report to Washington, D.C. On October 9, 1969, in a White House ceremony, Captain Jacobs received the Medal of Honor from President Richard Nixon for "conspicuous gallantry and intrepidity above and beyond the call of duty."

Remaining on active duty, Jacobs then attended graduate school at Rutgers University, where he earned a master's degree in international relations. He then returned for a second tour in Vietnam after promising he would avoid combat. He arrived in Vietnam in July 1972 and, despite his promise, got himself assigned as an advisor with the Vietnamese Airborne Division at Quang Tri in the thick of the fighting brought about by the 1972 North Vietnamese Eastertide Offensive. Jacobs was unhurt when the helicopter taking him to his unit was shot down, but he was later wounded again.

After the war, Jacobs became an instructor at the US Military Academy at West Point and the National War College in Washington, D.C. Despite his original plans to spend only 3 years in the service, Jacobs retired from the Army in 1987 with 20 years of active duty.

After retirement, Jack Jacobs pursued an active career in finance. In 2008, he penned his memoir, *If Not Now, When?: Duty and Sacrifice and America's Time of Need*, which won the 2010 Colby Award for outstanding military writing. He now serves as a member of the Council on Foreign Relations, as vice chairman of the Medal of Honor Foundation, and as a military analyst for MSNBC. Jacobs continues to participate in Memorial Day parades and graveside services, stating that such obligations "come with the medal."

John D. Fitzmorris III

Further Reading

Collier, Peter, and Nick Del Calzo. *Medal of Honor: Portraits of Valor beyond the Call of Duty.* New York: Artisan, 2006.

Jacobs, Jack H., and Douglas Century. *If Not Now, When?: Duty and Sacrifice and America's Time of Need.* New York: Penguin Books, 2008.

Smith, Larry. *Beyond Glory: Medal of Honor Heroes in Their Own Words—Extraordinary Stories of Courage from World War II to Vietnam.* New York: W. W. Norton, 2003.

Joel, Lawrence

Born: February 22, 1928
Died: February 4, 1984
Home State: North Carolina
Service: Army
Conflict: Vietnam War
Age at Time of Award: 37

Lawrence Joel, US Army (US Army Medical Department Regiment).

Born on February 22, 1928, Lawrence Joel spent his youth in Winston-Salem, North Carolina, growing up on the east side of the city, a predominantly African American section of the city at the time. Although only 17 years old when World War II ended, he nevertheless joined the Merchant Marines during the war and served for one year. In 1946, after completing his stint in the Merchant Marines, Joel joined the US Army. As a result of the Army's still-segregationist policies, he did not have many career opportunities during the early part of his service, though he did see combat during the Korean War.

In November 1965, Specialist Five Joel was a medic in the Headquarters and Headquarters Company (HHC), 1st Battalion, 503rd Infantry Regiment, 173rd Airborne Brigade in South Vietnam. On November 8, he took part in Operation Hump, a large search-and-destroy mission involving his battalion and the 1st Battalion, Royal Australian Regiment. After a 20-minute helicopter ride from Bien Hoa, Joel's unit was prepared for a full day of searching for the Viet Cong (VC) insurgents. Joel thought that the day began "fairly routine...just like back at Ft. Bragg—going to play war games." Unfortunately, the day would prove to be anything but routine.

Shortly before 8:00 a.m., Company C, 1st Battalion, 503rd Infantry Regiment encountered a dug-in VC regiment on Hill 65. Rather than easily overwhelming these enemy troops, the American forces quickly realized that they were facing a much larger and determined foe. The 1st Battalion's Company B was ordered to assist Company C and, without realizing it, managed to strike the VC regiment on their right flank. While many of the VC soldiers retreated in the face of this unexpected assault, the VC commander realized retreat would result in annihilation by superior American air and artillery fire. Instead, he ordered his men to close with the enemy in order to negate the American air and artillery advantage. If the VC moved in close enough, the Americans would be unable to use air and artillery fire without hitting their own troops. During the hand-to-hand fighting that followed, the VC used their superior numbers—they outnumbered the Americans by approximately six to one—to isolate and almost overrun the American units.

Throughout the battle, Joel repeatedly risked his life to provide medical aid to wounded American soldiers. When hit in the right calf by an enemy rifle round, he simply bandaged himself, administered a dose of morphine, and continued to help the casualties around him. After administering aid to all the nearby wounded, Joel fashioned a makeshift crutch and, under heavy fire, hobbled to a nearby unit to assist with more injured soldiers. Completely ignoring the warnings of other Americans, the bullets striking the ground around him, and his own pain, he knelt while holding up plasma bottles, completely engrossed in his mission. After receiving a second wound—this time in the right thigh—Joel continued to drag himself from casualty to casualty. Displaying resourcefulness when his medical supplies ran out, he saved the life of one soldier by placing a plastic bag over a severe chest wound to congeal the blood. When the 24-hour battle finally ended, more than 400 VC were dead, but at least 13 Americans had been saved by Joel's efforts.

Joel spent three months recuperating from his injuries in American hospitals in Saigon and Tokyo. Initially, he only received the Silver Star, the third highest US decoration for valor, for his actions. It took more than a year for the paperwork for his Medal of Honor to be processed and approved. On March 9, 1967, President Lyndon B. Johnson presented the medal to him in a White House ceremony. In his speech, President Johnson referred to Joel's bravery as a "very special kind of courage—the unarmed heroism of compassion and service to others." Joel was both the first medic to receive the Medal of Honor for service in Vietnam and the first living African American to receive the Medal of Honor since the Spanish-American War in 1898.

On April 8, 1967, his hometown of Winston-Salem held a parade in Lawrence Joel's honor that the *New York Times* called the biggest tribute the city had ever staged to honor an individual. Joel retired from the US Army in 1973 after 27 years of active service. He died of complications from diabetes on February 4, 1984, and is buried at Arlington National Cemetery.

Alexander M. Bielakowski

Further Reading

Murphy, Edward F. *Vietnam Medal of Honor Heroes.* New York: Ballantine Books, 1987.

Tillman, Barrett. *Heroes: U.S. Army Medal of Honor Recipients.* New York: Berkley, 2006.

Kaufman, Benjamin

Born: March 10, 1894
Died: February 5, 1981
Home State: New York
Service: Army
Conflict: World War I
Age at Time of Award: 25

Born on a small farm near Buffalo, New York, on March 10, 1894, Benjamin Kaufman spent his first eight years helping work the land. After his father became ill in 1902, the family moved into a small apartment in a rough Brooklyn neighborhood. He grew up tough and smart, and he was determined to make something of his life. He earned a scholarship to Syracuse University only to drop out to play professional baseball in a minor league. Kaufman's life would change forever when he was drafted into the Army in 1917. Once at Camp Upton near Yaphank Long Island, New York, Private Kaufman joined Company K, 308th Infantry, of the 77th "Statue of Liberty" Division. The division was a melting pot of ethnicities, mainly recent immigrants. Living and fighting alongside such a diverse mix of soldiers would profoundly affect Kaufman's views on equality.

Private Kaufman flourished in the Army. He became the regimental boxing champion and quickly rose in rank to become the first sergeant of his company. In April of 1918, his unit deployed to France, where the British Army trained the New Yorkers before sending them off to the Lorraine Sector just west of Verdun. This is where Kaufman experienced his first taste of combat, and he met the challenge by proving himself a capable leader. His superior officers recommended him for officer training, but he declined the opportunity.

During the next campaign in the Champagne sector, Kaufman impressed his superiors so much that he was once again recommended for officer training. However, an officer's commission meant a transfer to another unit, and Kaufman once again declined the opportunity so he could stay with Company K.

During the Aisne-Marne Offensive in August 1918, Kaufman was helping evacuate wounded soldiers during an artillery-delivered gas bombardment. He took off his gas mask to help dig out a soldier who had been buried by an explosion. As he was digging, a gas shell landed close by, gassing and partially blinding Kaufman. Although badly wounded, he continued to help evacuate other soldiers until ordered by his company commander to also be evacuated. His fierce loyalty to his men would not stop with his evacuation to a field hospital in the rear. By early October, Kaufman, still partially blind, went absent without leave from the hospital when he slipped away to rejoin Company K. This nearly earned him a court-martial, but the officers of his regiment were so glad to have him back they looked the other way, and for good reason—the division was preparing for the upcoming Meuse-Argonne Offensive.

During the Meuse-Argonne Offensive, the 77th Division attacked strong German defensive positions in the Argonne Forest. On October 2, 1918, Maj. Charles Whittlesey and his so-called Lost Battalion (who were not actually lost, nor a battalion) were cut off from the rest of the division and trapped in a deep ravine. Two days later, Kaufman and his company became part of the effort to reach Whittlesey and his command, along with some soldiers from the 308th Infantry. The Argonne was a hilly and dense forest full of German machine gun nests, and Kaufman's company was unable to continue their advance. Undeterred, Kaufman led a patrol of three soldiers to attack the machine gun emplacements. While advancing on the machine gun positions from the flank, Kaufman and two of his soldiers were wounded. From 25 yards away, a machine gun bullet had shattered Kaufman's right arm. He continued to advance on the machine gun alone, throwing grenades with his left arm while holding an unloaded pistol in his right hand. The machine gun crew withdrew except for one German, whom Kaufman took prisoner. Kaufman turned over his prisoner at the first aid station and then fainted from loss of blood. Kaufman had cleared the way for his company to continue their advance only to be evacuated once again to a field hospital, this time for the remainder of the war.

In 1919, Benjamin Kaufman received the Medal of Honor for his valorous actions in the Argonne Forest. Receiving the medal propelled him into the limelight. He became the national commander and later the director of the Jewish War Veterans. He also became a commander of the New Jersey Council of the Disabled American Veterans of the World War and a national vice commander of the National Legion of Valor. In World War II, he was a director of the War Manpower Commission in New Jersey. He was not only an advocate for Jewish soldiers, but also a staunch supporter for all veterans' rights. Above all, because of his experiences in the 77th Division, Kaufman was an activist for a multiracial American military and society. Benjamin Kaufman died on February 5, 1981, at the age of 86.

Scott A. Porter

Further Reading

Miles, L. Wardlaw. *History of the 308th Infantry: 1917–1919.* New York and London: The Knickerbocker Press, 1927.

Slotkin, Richard. *Lost Battalions: The Great War and the Crisis of American Nationality.* New York: Henry Holt, 2005.

Keeble, Woodrow W.

Born: May 16, 1917
Died: January 28, 1982
Home State: North Dakota
Service: Army
Conflict: Korean War
Age at Time of Award: 34

Woodrow W. Keeble was born on May 16, 1917, on the Sisseton-Wahpeton Sioux reservation in Waubay, South Dakota. While a young boy, his family moved to Wahpeton, North Dakota, where his mother worked at the Indian school. As a youth, Keeble excelled at sports, especially baseball. In 1942, he joined the North

Dakota National Guard. Keeble was being recruited by the Chicago White Sox when he was called to active duty in World War II.

Keeble was a member of North Dakota National Guard's 164th Infantry Regiment. After training in Louisiana, Keeble and his unit shipped out for the South Pacific. They saw action at Guadalcanal, Bougainville, Leyte, Cebu, and Mindanao. Ultimately, they landed in Japan and participated in the occupation of the Yokohama area. Keeble received two Purple Hearts for wounds received in the heavy Pacific fighting.

After the war, he returned to Wahpeton, married, and worked at the Indian school. When the Korean War broke out, the 164th was activated. The commander held a lottery to see who would be sent to the front lines and assigned training duties. Keeble, at 34, volunteered to go to the front lines.

As an individual augmentee from the National Guard, Keeble was assigned to George Company, 2nd Battalion, 19th Infantry Regiment, 24th Infantry Division. Given his leadership abilities and combat experience, he soon rose to the rank of master sergeant. In October 1951, his unit was ordered to take several mountains surrounding a Chinese base. During the subsequent fighting, Keeble was wounded on October 15 and then again on October 18, actions for which he would receive the Silver Star. With his body literally peppered with shrapnel, he was ordered to the rear for treatment. He refused and went forward to assume command of the company, as all the officers had been killed. On October 20, when his company assaulted the last mountain protecting the base, he was wounded yet again, and the company suffered heavy casualties from the devastating fire coming from the enemy in entrenched positions and three pillboxes. Keeble called in mortar and artillery support, decimating the enemy soldiers in the trenches, but the pillboxes continue to fire. Using his Browning Automatic Rifle and an arm-load of grenades, Keeble single-handedly engaged the pillboxes one at a time, ultimately taking out all three and dispatching 23 Chinese soldiers.

After the battle, Keeble's chain of command nominated him for the Medal of Honor. Every surviving member of Keeble's company signed letters of support. However, he received the Distinguished Service Cross instead.

After the war, Keeble returned home and took up his old teaching job. However, he contracted tuberculosis; doctors had to remove one lung, and, over the years, his health continued to deteriorate, and he suffered a series of strokes that left him partially paralyzed and unable to speak. Then his wife passed away, and he was left alone to care for his son, Earl. Unable to work and financially destitute, he was forced to pawn his medals.

He remarried in 1967 and gained a stepson, Russell. His wife, Blossom Iris Crawford-Harris, was the first Sioux woman to complete a doctorate in education at the University of South Dakota. Woodrow W. Keeble died January 28, 1982, and is buried in Sisseton, South Dakota.

Over the years, beginning in 1972, there was a steady effort to get the Medal of Honor for Keeble. Friends, fellow soldiers, family, and four US senators from North and South Dakota continued the fight even after Keeble's death. More recently, Senator John Thune (R-SD) was instrumental in getting the time restrictions on awarding the Medal of Honor waived so Keeble's Distinguished Service Cross could be upgraded. Despite failing health, Keeble's wife, Blossom, was determined to hang on to accept the long-awaited medal for her husband, but she died on June 3, 2007, before her dream could be realized.

Finally, on March 3, 2008, in a White House East Room ceremony, President George W. Bush presented the Medal of Honor to Woodrow E. Keeble posthumously for his valor in the Korean War. Keeble's stepson Russell Hawkins accepted the medal for his stepfather, 26 years after his death.

James H. Willbanks

Further Reading

Gomez-Granger, Julissa. *CRS Report for Congress: Medal of Honor Recipients: 1979–2008.* Washington, D.C.: Congressional Research Service, RL 30011, June 4, 2008.

Kelly, Charles E.

Born: September 23, 1920
Died: January 11, 1985
Home State: Pennsylvania
Service: Army
Conflict: World War II
Age at Time of Award: 22

Born on September 23, 1920, in Pittsburgh, Pennsylvania, Charles E. Kelly was one of nine brothers. His father was a blacksmith. He grew up in a tough neighborhood on the north side of Pittsburgh and had to leave school at age 14 to take a job as a house painter.

Kelly enlisted in the Army in May 1942, but before he saw action, he had already been in the stockade twice for going AWOL (absent without leave). Nevertheless, by the fall of 1943, he was serving in Company L, 143rd Infantry Regiment in the 36th Infantry Division. He saw his first combat during Operation Avalanche, the amphibious assault at Salerno on the Italian peninsula launched on September 9, 1943. Once ashore, the division moved inland.

Four days after the landing and a week before his 23rd birthday, Kelly volunteered to crawl two miles under German mortar, artillery, and sniper fire to reconnoiter an enemy-occupied hill that would be his battalion's next objective. During this mission, he silenced a German machine gun with his Browning Automatic Rifle (BAR).

After returning with his report, he led three men on a second mission near the town of Altavilla, 20 miles inland. Coming under fire from several machine gun nests and as many as 70 German soldiers, Kelly wiped out one nest and was credited by the other men with killing as many as 40 of the enemy.

Later that day, he was told to secure a three-story house at one end of the town square in Altavilla that had been serving as an ammunition storehouse. Kelly spent the night guarding the rear of the house. Early on the morning of September 14, the Germans launched an attack with infantry and armor on the town from three sides, effectively isolating Kelly and the other Americans there from the rest of their unit. Kelly spent the day fighting off the attackers with a variety of weapons, including his BAR, a Thompson submachine gun, a bazooka, and several rifles. At one point during the battle, he used a 37-mm antitank gun in the house's courtyard to take out a sniper in a nearby church steeple. Back inside the house, he lobbed a phosphorous grenade onto the roof of a nearby building that the Germans had infiltrated, setting it on fire.

Later, while rummaging through the building he was defending, he found several 60-mm mortar shells. He did not have a mortar, but he removed the two safety pins and began heaving the shells by hand at a group of Germans who were approaching his position through a ravine outside the rear of the house. Seven or eight of the shells exploded, killing five Germans and blunting the attack. That night, when the order was given for the Americans to pull back, he provided covering fire for his comrades until darkness fell, when he was able to make his way back to friendly lines.

Kelly was promoted to corporal after the fight in Altavilla. During the next several months, he was in the thick of other battles, including the assault on San Pietro and the bloody three-day crossing of the Rapido River, where he was promoted to sergeant in January 1944.

In the spring of 1944, a story about his combat exploits was published in the US military newspaper *Stars and Stripes*, referring to him as "Commando Kelly." By this time, he had been approved for the Medal of Honor. Gen. Mark W. Clark presented the medal to him on March 11, 1944. Soon after, Kelly returned home to the United States to a hero's welcome. He was given a parade in his hometown of Pittsburgh, and the mayor gave him a key to the city. The Army sent him on a goodwill tour pushing war bonds and demonstrating infantry battle techniques. After the tour, he was assigned to Fort Benning, Georgia.

After being honorably discharged in 1945, things started to go badly for Kelly. He failed in several business ventures, his young wife died of cancer, he lost his home in foreclosure, and his younger brother, who he had helped to enlist in the army at 17, went missing in action in Korea and was never seen again. Kelly worked at a number of jobs, but none for any length of time. He remarried and had several children with his new wife but continued to struggle with financial difficulties and holding a job. When people found out about his situation, donations and offers came rolling in due to fame as a war hero, but he could not or would not take advantage of the offers. He worked for the Kentucky Highway Department for three years, and then he abandoned his family in 1961. He was out of touch with them for almost 15 years while he drifted from one place to another, becoming a heavy drinker. Sadly, it is likely that Kelly suffered from what we now recognize as posttraumatic stress from his wartime experiences.

In late 1984, Charles Kelly was admitted to the Veterans Hospital in Pittsburgh suffering from kidney and liver failure. He died on January 11, 1985, and is buried in Highwood Cemetery in Pittsburgh.

In 1987, the Oakdale Army Support Element in Oakdale, Pennsylvania, was redesignated the Charles E. Kelly Support Facility.

James H. Willbanks

Further Reading

Kelly, Charles E. *One Man's War*. New York: Knopf, 1944.

Proft, Robert J. *United States of America's Congressional Medal of Honor Recipients: Their Official Citations*. Columbia Heights, MN: Highland House II, 2007.

Sinton, Starr, and Robert Hargis. *World War II Medal of Honor Recipients*. Vol. 2, *Army & Air Corps*. Oxford, UK: Osprey Publishing, 2003.

Tillman, Barrett. *Heroes: U.S. Army Medal of Honor Recipients*. New York: Berkley Caliber, 2006.

Kerrey, Joseph R.

Born: August 27, 1943
Died:
Home State: Nebraska
Service: Navy
Conflict: Vietnam War
Age at Time of Award: 25

Joseph Robert (Bob) Kerrey was born in Lincoln, Nebraska, on August 27, 1943. He attended Nebraska public schools and graduated from the University of Nebraska at Lincoln with a degree in pharmacology in 1966. Despite health problems, Kerrey was drawn to follow the family tradition of military service, and he volunteered for the US Navy's officer candidate school (OCS). His attendance at OCS was followed by additional training in the rigorous underwater demolition school at Coronado Island, California. After completing the challenging underwater program, Kerrey went on to more advanced training, ultimately becoming a member of the Navy's elite fighting force, the Navy Sea, Air, and Land Forces (SEALs).

In 1968, Lieutenant Kerrey was assigned to the Republic of Vietnam (South Vietnam) in SEAL Team One. He and his men patrolled the Mekong Delta, where he led his men on an attack of a suspected Viet Cong meeting at Thanh Phong on February 29, 1969. However, as was often the case, by the time Kerrey's unit arrived, the enemy was no longer present. Nonetheless, the SEAL attack at night on the village resulted in a number of civilian causalities. In recent years, Kerrey has been criticized for his role in what some have called the Thanh Phong Massacre. Awarded the Bronze Star for his actions, Kerrey has said that he deeply regrets what occurred at Thanh Phong and the loss of innocent lives. Some villagers later charged that civilians there had been rounded up after dark and summarily shot, something that Kerrey and his team adamantly deny.

Kerrey's unit carried out another attack, this time at Nha Thang, on March 14, 1969, capturing local political leaders there. Kerrey and his unit scaled a 350-foot cliff to drop unnoticed into the village, but during the descent, the team's cover was compromised and the unit came under fire. Kerrey sustained a serious leg wound when a grenade exploded at his feet. In spite of his grave injuries, Kerrey continued to direct his unit until he was transported from the field of battle. The raid was held a success, with several of the captured Viet Cong leaders providing vital intelligence. Kerrey, meanwhile, was treated for his wounds, resulting in the amputation of the lower part of one of his legs. Returned to the United States for recuperation, Kerrey was awarded the Medal of Honor by President Richard M. Nixon in May 1970.

After receiving a medical discharge from the Navy, Kerrey went into business, operating a chain of restaurants and fitness facilities. His success in business was soon matched by his achievements in politics. Kerrey, a political novice, came from nowhere to challenge incumbent Republican governor Charles Thone of Nebraska in the 1982 gubernatorial election. Kerrey waged an effective campaign and won the election. He took office in January 1983. After serving one four-year term as governor, Kerrey ran successfully for the US Senate in 1988, taking office in 1989.

Bob Kerrey distinguished himself in the Senate, and in 1992 he campaigned to secure the Democratic presidential nomination. He lost to Governor Bill Clinton from Arkansas, who went on to win the presidential election. Kerrey left the Senate in 2001. This did not mean an end to his public service, however. He subsequently served on the 9/11 Commission and, as a long-time advocate of higher education, accepted the presidency of the New School University in New York in 2001.

Jeffery B. Cook

Further Reading

Caldwell, Christopher. "Review of *When I Was a Young Man.*" *The Financial Times,* May 31, 2002, 19.

Collier, Peter, and Nick Del Calzo. *Medal of Honor: Portraits of Valor beyond the Call of Duty*. New York: Artisan, 2006.

Faranacci, Donald. *Last Full Measure of Devotion: A Tribute to America's Heroes of the Vietnam War*. Bloomington, IN: AuthorHouse, 2007.

Kerrey, Robert. *When I Was a Young Man: A Memoir*. New York: Harcourt, 2002.

Smith, Larry. *Beyond Glory: Medal of Honor Heroes in Their Own Words—Extraordinary Stories of Courage from WWII to Vietnam*. New York: W. W. Norton, 2003.

Kisters, Gerry H.

Born: March 2, 1919
Died: May 11, 1986
Home State: Indiana
Service: Army
Conflict: World War II
Age at Time of Award: 24

Gerry Herman Kisters was born in Salt Lake City, Utah, on March 2, 1919. His father had immigrated to the United States from Germany and was a furrier, a trade handed down from generation to generation in the Kisters family. Kisters's family moved to Bloomington, Indiana, in 1937, and he graduated from Bloomington High School the same year. After graduation, Kisters worked for his father for one year and then opened his own furrier shop in Vincennes, Indiana. Kisters closed the store two years later when he was drafted and inducted into the Army on January 17, 1941, at Fort Benjamin Harrison, Indiana. The Army sent Kisters to Fort Bliss, Texas, where he was assigned to the still-developing reconnaissance cavalry, which then was part of the 1st Cavalry Division. He was within weeks of completing his one year of required service and had just returned from church services when he learned of the Japanese attack on Pearl Harbor.

Kisters admittedly was not a good garrison soldier, and, as a consequence, he spent his first 18 months in the Army as a buck private, the lowest possible rank. Kisters's unit became an independent outfit in 1942 and was redesignated the 91st Cavalry Reconnaissance Squadron. The unit participated in the Louisiana Maneuvers in 1942, became mechanized, and trained to probe and search for the enemy on the battlefield, usually by drawing their fire.

When the 91st Cavalry arrived in Casablanca, North Africa, on December 24, 1942, Kisters was a corporal assigned to a demolitions squad. Attached to various divisions in April and May 1943, Kisters and the 91st Cavalry fought primarily as dismounted infantry, leading the final attack to drive the enemy from Tunisia. On May 7, 1943, Kisters was a staff sergeant scouting for an armored column with his unit. As the column advanced, it came under fire from German artillery. Looking over the crest of a hill, Kisters spotted a German 88-mm gun firing away. He crawled unnoticed to the rear of the emplacement and threw three grenades, wiping out the enemy crew. For his actions, Kisters received the Distinguished Service Cross.

Kisters next saw combat in Sicily. On July 31, 1943, Kisters and a new second lieutenant were leading nine other enlisted men near Gagliano, Sicily, in taking out a roadblock on a winding mountain road. Rounding a bend, the group discovered a culvert the Germans had destroyed, creating a crater in the road. Kisters and his lieutenant dismounted from their jeeps and cautiously advanced until they drew the Germans' fire. Somehow, they walked right up to a German machine gun nest. After Kisters lobbed several grenades, the four Germans in the emplacement surrendered, unable to turn their weapon toward the two soldiers quickly enough.

Another machine gun then started firing on Kisters and his lieutenant. Kisters left the lieutenant guarding the prisoners and advanced alone. Out of grenades and armed only with his carbine, Kisters moved toward the enemy position, but German snipers spotted Kisters and hit him three times in each leg. Despite his wounds, Kisters continued to crawl forward. When the gun crew started to remove sandbags to be able to lower their weapon on Kisters, he fired his carbine through the gap and killed three of the enemy. While the fourth German gunner ran away, a sniper's bullet hit Kisters in his right arm, causing nerve damage and knocking him unconscious. When he regained consciousness, the rest of his men had advanced, driving the snipers away. Kisters's wounds were so numerous that the first aid bandages carried by the German prisoners had to be used in addition to those carried by the Americans. The German prisoners helped carry Kisters to an aid station.

Shipped home, Kisters spent months recovering from his wounds. Still in the hospital in early February 1944, Kisters was promoted to second lieutenant and told that he would receive the Medal of Honor. On February 8, 1944, Gen. George C. Marshall pinned the Distinguished Service Cross on Kisters in Washington, D.C. Less than an hour later, President Franklin D. Roosevelt presented Kisters with the Medal of Honor. Kisters was the first American serviceman in World War II to receive both the Medal of Honor and the Distinguished Service Cross. (Kisters's decorations often are inaccurately credited to units other than the 91st Cavalry Reconnaissance Squadron.)

Feted by his hometown of Bloomington, Gerry Kisters was described as the "Sergeant York" of the war and America's "No. 1 Hero." He was featured in war bond drives and had the local county airfield named after him. Following additional medical treatment, Kisters taught reconnaissance at the cavalry school at Fort Riley, Kansas. Having married his high school sweetheart just before shipping out to North Africa, Kisters returned to his trade as a furrier after the war ended, had children, and lived in Bloomington for the rest of his life. He died at age 67 on May 11, 1986, and is buried in Rose Hill Cemetery in Bloomington.

Alan M. Anderson

Further Reading

Above and Beyond: A History of the Medal of Honor from the Civil War to Vietnam. Boston, MA: Boston Publishing Company, 1985.

Atkinson, Rick. *The Day of Battle: The War in Sicily and Italy, 1943–1944.* New York: Henry Holt, 2007.

D'Este, Carlo. *Bitter Victory: The Battle for Sicily, 1943.* New York: E. P. Dutton, 1988.

Salter, Fred H. *Recon Scout.* New York: Ballantine Publishing, 2001.

Kouma, Ernest R.

Born: November 23, 1919
Died: December 19, 1993
Home State: Nebraska
Service: Army
Conflict: Korean War
Age at Time of Award: 30

Born in Dwight, Nebraska, on November 23, 1919, Ernest R. Kouma grew up on the family farm until he enlisted in the Army in June 1940. After serving in the United States, Kouma saw combat in the European Theater as a tank commander in the 9th Armored Division, which found itself in the path of the German offensive through the Ardennes in December 1944. Despite their lack of combat experience, the division delayed the German advance toward Saint Vith and Bastogne. Following the fighting in the Ardennes, Kouma and the rest of the division conducted offensive operations into Germany, where they crossed the Roer River and attacked to the Rhine River. The division captured the Remagen bridge and then drove to Frankfurt, where they assisted in closing the Ruhr pocket. The division next participated in the encirclement of Leipzig. When the war ended, they found themselves in Czechoslovakia.

Following the war, Kouma decided to stay in the army. He served with the US forces in South Korea and the occupation forces in Japan before returning to the United States, where he was assigned as a tank commander in Company A, 72nd Tank Battalion assigned to the 2nd Infantry Division.

Following the invasion of South Korea by the North Korean People's Army, the United States decided to commit forces to the conflict. In addition to the occupation forces in Japan, the United States also began deploying stateside units. One of the units activated for combat in Korea was the 2nd Infantry Division along with the 72nd Tank Battalion. Kouma and the other members of the battalion embarked for Korea in August 1950. When the 2nd Infantry Division arrived, they were immediately thrown into the fighting to stabilize the Pusan Perimeter.

On the night of August 31, Kouma was occupying a defensive position with his tank, another M26 Pershing tank, and several antiaircraft vehicles near the hamlet of Agok in an area called the Naktong Bulge. They were on the left flank of the 9th Infantry Regiment, guarding the river crossing in the vicinity. The night began with fog covering the area and obscuring the river. About midnight, the fog lifted to reveal an enemy bridge already two-thirds of the way across the river. Kouma immediately opened fire and was soon joined by the second tank and the antiaircraft vehicles. Their combined fire destroyed the bridge, but the North Koreans had established a bridgehead in the 9th Infantry area.

Facing increasing pressure, the 9th Infantry began to fall back. When Kouma received word of the withdrawal, he immediately recognized that he needed to stay in position to cover the infantry. While reloading ammunition, Kouma's tank was taken under fire. Wounded in the foot, Kouma managed to return fire and engage an enemy machine gun position that began firing from the flank. The North Korean attack had destroyed one of the antiaircraft vehicles, and the other was damaged and forced to withdraw. Kouma and the other tank decided to move to open ground and engage the enemy. The two tanks fought for over an hour before the other tank, damaged from enemy fire, was forced to retreat. Kouma and his crew stayed behind to cover the tank's withdrawal.

Kouma and his crew held the flank against the North Koreans for another seven hours. Kouma repeatedly engaged the enemy with the tank's .50 caliber machine gun, exposing himself to enemy fire and receiving a second wound in the shoulder. After daybreak and with their ammunition supply dwindling, Kouma and his crew began their withdrawal through eight miles of enemy territory, engaging enemy positions along the way.

Upon reaching the company command post (CP), Kouma immediately began to replenish his ammunition and did not seek medical aid until ordered to do so. He again tried to rejoin the fight but was ordered to the evacuation station. On May 19, 1951, President Harry S. Truman presented the Medal of Honor to Master Sergeant Kouma in a White House ceremony.

After receiving the medal, Ernest Kouma continued a distinguished career in the Army. He served as a recruiter in Omaha, Nebraska, and finished the war as a tank gunnery instructor. After the war, he served another assignment as a recruiter and then served in tank battalions at Fort Carson, Colorado, and Germany. Kouma retired after 31 years and lived in McDaniel, Kentucky. He died on December 19, 1993, and is buried at the Post Cemetery on Fort Knox. The US Army's Tank Platoon Gunnery Excellence Competition at Fort Knox is named in Kouma's honor.

Robert J. Rielly

Further Reading

Fehrenbach, T. R. *This Kind of War*. Washington, London: Brassey's, 1963.

Murphy, Edward F. *Korean War Heroes*. Novato, CA: Presidio Press, 1992.

Lang, George C.

Born: April 20, 1947
Died: March 16, 2005
Home State: New York
Service: Army
Conflict: Vietnam War
Age at Time of Award: 19

Born in Flushing, New York, on April 20, 1947, George Charles Lang was raised in Hicksville, New York. He lost his father when he was seven and spent many years working at a luncheonette to help support his mother. After completing high school, he worked in a New York defense plant for a while before enlisting in the US Army after receiving his draft notice.

He arrived in Vietnam in the fall of 1968 as a specialist fourth class and was subsequently assigned to Company A, 4th Battalion, 47th Infantry, 9th Infantry Division in the Mekong Delta. By the following spring, Lang's unit was part of the Mobile Riverine Force, living in Navy transport ships and conducting search-and-destroy operations against the Viet Cong along the Mekong River network.

On February 22, 1969, there were reports that the enemy had concentrated in an area within Kien Hoa Province. Lang, who was scheduled for R&R that day but had not departed because of an admin error, joined his unit as they moved to the area in their boats. When Lang's platoon landed on shore, Lang, who had been promoted to squad leader due to his performance in earlier missions, took the point. Almost immediately, the unit came under intense enemy fire from a strongly fortified bunker complex. Lang immediately attacked and destroyed the first part of the fortification with rifle fire and grenades. As the Americans advanced, they came under fire from a second bunker. Lang sprinted forward and took out the enemy soldiers in the bunker with rifle fire and grenades.

His squad, in the process of securing a large enemy ammunition cache, again came under fire. Lang single-handedly took out the third bunker, only to have the squad receive heavy fire from a fourth bunker, this time including a crossfire using rockets and automatic weapons. During this fourth attack, Lang's squad suffered six casualties, and Lang himself was seriously wounded. He was hit in the back with a large piece of shrapnel, which paralyzed him. Still trying to direct his men, he was struck again by a bullet that hit his elbow and exited his shoulder. Despite his serious wounds, he refused to be evacuated until ordered to do so.

The next thing Lang remembered was waking up in the hospital with a priest about to give him last rites before he went in for a second surgery. He survived the surgery, but his spinal cord had been severed by the shrapnel. He spent several months in a hospital in Japan before returning to the United States, where he spent an additional 10 months in the hospital. He would remain in a wheelchair until his death.

After rehabilitating from his wounds, Lang received the Medal of Honor from President Richard M. Nixon on March 2, 1971. After the war, he lived in Seaford on Long Island, New York, where he worked as a bookkeeper and fished. Lang shunned the spotlight, but he worked behind the scenes to support his fellow veterans, visiting wounded soldiers at Walter Reed Army Medical Center. He also interviewed many other Medal of Honor recipients and contributed to a two-volume history entitled *Medal of Honor Recipients, 1863–1994*, published in 1995.

George Lang died from cancer at the age of 57 at his home in Seaford on March 16, 2005. He is buried in Cemetery of the Holy Rood in Westbury, New York. After Lang's death, the Wounded Warrior Project founded the George C. Lang Award for Courage in his memory to honor wounded veterans who best exemplify Lang's spirit and virtue.

Debra J. Sheffer

Further Reading

Collier, Peter, and Nick Del Calzo. *Medal of Honor: Portraits of Valor beyond the Call of Duty*. New York: Artisan, 2006.

Murphy, Edward F. *Vietnam Medal of Honor Heroes*. New York: Ballantine Books, 2005.

Lemon, Peter C.

Born: June 5, 1950
Died:
Home State: Michigan
Service: Army
Conflict: Vietnam War
Age at Time of Award: 19

Born in Toronto, Canada, on June 5, 1950, Peter C. Lemon became a US citizen at the age of 12. In February 1969, he enlisted in the US Army. Upon assignment to South Vietnam, Lemon volunteered to go through reconnaissance training, and, after completion of that training, he joined the 1st Infantry Division's Ranger company. Soon afterward, Lemon was transferred to Ranger Company E (RECON) in the 2nd Battalion, 8th Cavalry of the 1st Calvary Division. This unit conducted long-range reconnaissance and raids from their base in Tay Ninh Province into enemy-held territory.

On April 1, 1970, Lemon and his 18-man unit returned to Fire Support Base Illingworth, 50 miles northwest of Saigon. Approximately 300 to 400 members of the North Vietnamese Army attacked Killingworth that night. As the battle unfolded, Lemon moved along the perimeter and began shooting at the advancing enemy. The commanding officer, Lt. Greg Peters, ordered Lemon and a fellow soldier to take over an abandoned .50 caliber machine gun to better defend their position. However, the gun failed, and North Vietnamese mortar shells wounded Lemon and killed his fellow soldier. Lemon used his rifle to engage the enemy until the rifle too malfunctioned, and then he used hand grenades to fend off the enemy attackers. After eliminating all but one of the enemy soldiers in his assigned sector, he pursued and dispatched the remaining enemy in hand-to-hand combat. When a comrade was wounded, Lemon disregarded incoming fire to carry the fallen soldier to the aid station. He returned to his fighting position but was wounded a second time by enemy fire. Nevertheless, he continued to fight as the North Vietnamese Army troops were very near to overrunning the American position. Spotting a North Vietnamese rocket-propelled grenade (RPG) gunner, Lemon, although wounded a third time, climbed to the top of the defensive berm in an exposed position and successfully destroyed the gunner's position with an M-60 machine gun. Lemon, now wounded in his leg, neck, and head, continued to fight until he collapsed from his multiple wounds and exhaustion. After regaining consciousness at the aid station, he refused medical evacuation until his more seriously wounded comrades had been evacuated.

Lemon was finally evacuated that evening and spent a month in the hospital recovering. He was later reassigned to a support unit. Lemon received the Combat Infantryman Badge, two Bronze Stars, two Air Medals, the Army Commendation Medal, and a Purple Heart. On December 4, 1970, Sergeant Lemon was honorably discharged and returned to Michigan.

When word was received the following spring that Lemon was to receive the Medal of Honor, he seriously considered turning down the medal, maintaining that there had been 18 heroes that night at the fire base, 3 of whom had died. However, the Army convinced Lemon to accept the award. On June 15, 1971, 10 days after his 21st birthday, Lemon was presented the Medal of Honor by President Richard M. Nixon in a White House ceremony. Upon the presentation of the award, Lemon dedicated the honor to his unit and the three comrades he had lost in battle—Casey Waller, Nathan Mann, and Brent Street.

In 1976, Lemon entered Colorado State University, where he received a bachelor's degree in speech and a master's in business administration. He continues to be active in sharing his experiences as a motivational speaker, sculptor, and successful businessman. Lemon owned and operated the American Hospitality Association, an insurance organization, and Darnell-Lemon, Inc., a contracting firm. As of 2010 he is the president and owner of Lemco Enterprises, Inc., where he is a speaker, author, and executive film producer.

In March 1997, Lemon's book *Beyond the Medal: A Journey from Their Hearts to Yours* was published. It details the stories and accounts of other Medal of Honor recipients and their experiences in the service and life after. Over 32,000 copies of his book were donated to middle and high schools throughout the United States. He also was the executive producer of the PBS documentary *Beyond the Medal of Honor*.

On May 1, 2009, President Barack Obama presented Lemon, the only Canadian-born recipient of the Medal of Honor, with the Outstanding American by Choice award. This award is given by the US Citizenship and Immigration Services to honor a naturalized US citizen who has attained civic and professional achievements, as well as demonstrated exceptional commitment to the nation.

Peter Lemon continues to travel the country, inspiring enthusiasm and patriotism and sharing his humor and stories. As of 2010 he resides in Colorado and has three children.

Denise M. Carlin

Further Reading

Lemon, Peter C. *Beyond the Medal: A Journey from Their Hearts to Yours.* Golden, CO: Fulcrum Publishing, 1997.

Tillman, Barrett. *Heroes: U.S. Army Medal of Honor Recipients.* New York: Berkley Caliber, 2006.

Levitow, John L.

Born: November 1, 1945
Died: November 8, 2000
Home State: Connecticut
Service: Air Force
Conflict: Vietnam War
Age at Time of Award: 23

John L. Levitow was born November 1, 1945, in Hartford, Connecticut. He initially planned to join the Navy because the Army and Marines required too much walking. However, when he went to the recruiting station, the Navy recruiters were busy, so he went next door and joined the Air Force. Entering the Air Force in 1966, he first trained in the civil engineering field as a power line specialist. His first assignment was at McGuire Air Force Base in New Jersey. He later cross-trained as a loadmaster and served for a short period of time as a loadmaster on C-130s.

In July 1968, Levitow was sent to Vietnam, where he joined the 3rd Special Operations Squadron, which flew armed AC-47 gunships, based at Nha Trang. These gunships were modified C-47 cargo planes that had been fitted with 7.62-mm side-mounted Gatling "miniguns." Their mission was to provide fire support for American and South Vietnamese ground troops in contact with the enemy. After arriving in Nha Trang, Levitow was subsequently assigned to the squadron's forward operating base at Bien Hoa.

On February 24, 1969, Levitow was substituting for the regular loadmaster on "Spooky 71," who had become ill. Spooky 71, with a crew of eight, was scheduled to fly a night mission in the Tan Son Nhut Air Base area. However, during the course of the mission, as the gunship was conducting a patrol over the village of Lai Khe, the US Army base at Long Binh came under heavy attack, and Spooky 71 was dispatched to provide support. During the course of the mission, the aircraft fired thousands of rounds of ammunition at enemy forces and dropped M-24 magnesium flares to illuminate the battlefield.

Levitow, on his 180th combat mission, was responsible for removing the flares from a rack, setting their controls, and passing them to a gunner, who would pull the safety pins and then throw them out the cargo door. The flares, dangling from small parachutes, ignited in midair 20 seconds later.

In the fifth hour of the mission, the aircraft flew in the path of a Viet Cong 82-mm mortar shell, which hit the plane's right wing and exploded, opening a hole two feet in diameter and sending shrapnel through the aircraft's skin. Airman Levitow was hit by 40 pieces of shrapnel in his back and legs and was stunned by the concussion of the exploding shell. The other four crewmen in the cargo compartment were also wounded as the pilot, Maj. Kenneth Carpenter, tried to get the plane under control.

The gunner, Airman Ellis Owen, was about to throw out a flare when the mortar shell hit the aircraft; he was wounded by the blast, and the flare was torn from his grasp. The flare, now fully armed, was capable of burning through the plane's metal skin if it ignited. As Levitow was moving another wounded crewman away from the open cargo door, he noticed the smoking flare rolling around the inside of the aircraft among thousands of rounds of ammunition. If the flare ignited, it would fill the cargo bay with toxic smoke and, burning at 4,000°F, would no doubt cause the ammunition to explode. Additionally, the intense heat of the flare would eventually burn through the aluminum floor of the cargo bay and drop on the empennage control cables, causing the aircraft to go out of control.

With the plane in a 30-degree bank, Levitow tried vainly to pick up the flare as it skidded around the floor, but it kept rolling away from him. In desperation, Levitow threw himself on the flare, hugged it to his body, and, trailing blood and partially paralyzed from his wounds, dragged himself and the flare to the rear of the aircraft, where he hurled it out the open cargo door just as it ignited.

Despite his wounds, Levitow helped secure the cargo bay as the pilot struggled to get the crippled aircraft back to base. After landing at Bien Hoa, the extent of the damage became only too clear; the AC-47 had more than 3,500 holes in the wings and fuselage, one measuring more than three feet long.

Levitow was flown to the big Air Force hospital at Tachikawa, Japan. After spending two months in Japan recovering from his wounds, he returned to Vietnam and flew two more combat missions. However, upon showing up for his third mission, he was told by his squadron commander that he was grounded because he had been nominated for the Medal of Honor. After departing Vietnam, he was assigned as a C-141 loadmaster at Norton Air Force Base, California, where he completed his enlistment and separated from the Air Force. Back home in Connecticut, he was notified that his Medal of Honor had been approved.

On Armed Forces Day, May 14, 1970, President Richard Nixon presented the Medal of Honor to Sergeant Levitow at the White House. He was the first enlisted man in the Air Force to receive this honor.

After leaving the Air Force, John Levitow worked for federal and state veterans' agencies for more than two decades. He died from cancer at the age of 55 on November 8, 2000, at his home in Rocky Hill, Connecticut. He was buried at Arlington National Cemetery. As of 2010 the John Levitow Award is the highest honor presented to a graduate at the US Air Force Airman Leadership School. Levitow willed his Medal of Honor to the Enlisted Heritage Research Institute at the Senior Noncommissioned Officer Academy at Maxwell Air Force Base, Alabama, where it is now prominently displayed along with his uniform, ribbons, and other memorabilia.

James H. Willbanks

Further Reading

Collier, Peter, and Nick Del Calzo. *Medal of Honor: Portraits of Valor beyond the Call of Duty.* New York: Artisan, 2006.

Correll, John T. "20 Seconds Over Long Binh." *Air Force Magazine* 88, no. 4 (April 2005): 69–73.

Frisbee, John L. "The Saving of Spooky 71." *Air Force Magazine* 67, no. 10 (October 1984): 108.

Liteky, Angelo J.

Born: February 14, 1931
Died:
Home State: Florida
Service: Army

Conflict: Vietnam War
Age at Time of Award: 34

Angelo J. (Charles) Liteky was born on February 14, 1931, in Washington, D.C. The son of a career Navy petty officer, he grew up in Jacksonville, Florida. A gifted football and basketball player, Liteky received an athletic scholarship to the University of Florida. After two years of college, he entered seminary and was ordained a Catholic priest in the Missionary Servants of the Most Holy Trinity in 1960. Six years later, Liteky volunteered to become an Army chaplain.

On December 6, 1967, Liteky was on his first combat patrol, accompanying two platoons from the 4th Battalion, 12th Infantry of the 199th Infantry Brigade on a search-and-destroy mission near Phuoc Lac, in Bien Hoa province, Republic of Vietnam. While pursuing what they thought was a small band of guerillas through a rice paddy, the unit stumbled across the base camp of a Viet Cong battalion. An intense firefight broke out, killing one medic, wounding another, and forcing the Americans to take cover. In the ensuing chaos, Liteky—according to the official citation—crawled "to within 15 meters of an enemy machine gun position" to tend to two wounded soldiers, dragging them to safety. Liteky's actions inspired an American rally during which he continued to minister to the dead or dying, dragging other soldiers to safety, at times walking upright under enemy fire. Wounded in the neck and foot by shrapnel, Liteky continued to expose himself in order to aid his men and "personally directed the medivac helicopters in and out of the area." By the time the fighting ended, Liteky "had personally carried over 20 men to the landing zone for evacuation," all the while under heavy fire. For these actions, President Lyndon B. Johnson presented the Medal of Honor to Chaplain Liteky at a White House ceremony on November 19, 1968. He became only the fifth chaplain since the Civil War to receive the Medal of Honor and the only nonposthumous chaplain recipient during the Vietnam War.

Following receipt of the medal, Liteky volunteered for a second Vietnam tour. He served as chaplain to the 17th Field Hospital in An Khe in 1969 until his return to the United States in June 1970.

Troubled by the Catholic Church's requirement of priestly celibacy, Liteky took a leave of absence from the priesthood—thereby ending his duty as an Army chaplain—in 1971. Liteky eventually left the priesthood in 1975. His 1983 marriage to a former nun, Judy Blanch, precipitated a shift in Liteky's social consciousness.

On July 29, 1986, Liteky placed his medal in an envelope at the Vietnam Veteran's Memorial in Washington, D.C. Accompanying the Medal was a letter addressed to President Ronald Reagan renouncing the award in protest of US military involvement in Central America. In doing so, he became the only recipient to publicly renounce and return his medal.

Later in 1986, Liteky joined two other Vietnam veterans, and one from World War II, in a public fast on the US Capitol steps as part of a "Campaign of Conscience" against US foreign policy. Later, Liteky's 1990 fast outside, and subsequent acts of civil disobedience inside, Fort Benning, Georgia, aimed at the "School of the Americas" led to several arrests and periods of incarceration for trespassing and destruction of federal property. As a result of his civil disobedience, Liteky is also the only Medal of Honor recipient to be a named appellant in a US Supreme Court decision (*Liteky v. United States*). Liteky appealed his 1991 federal criminal conviction for destruction of government property during a protest at Fort Benning, Georgia, to the US Supreme Court, which upheld his conviction in 1994.

In 2002 and 2003, Angelo Liteky joined other peace activists in Baghdad to oppose the then-impending US invasion of Iraq. As of 2010 Liteky lives in San Francisco, California, with his wife, Judy, where he is writing his memoir and continuing to speak out against US military intervention abroad.

Bradley L. Carter

Further Reading

Ackermann, Henry F. *He Was Always There: The U.S. Army Chaplain Ministry in the Vietnam Conflict*. Washington, D.C.: Office of the Chief of Chaplains, Department of the Army, 1989.

Venzke, Rodger R. *Confidence in Battle, Inspiration in Peace: The United States Army Chaplaincy 1945–1975*. Washington, D.C.: Office of the Chief of Chaplains, Department of the Army, 1977.

Livingston, James E.

Born: January 12, 1940
Died:
Home State: Georgia
Service: Marine Corps
Conflict: Vietnam War
Age at Time of Award: 28

James E. Livingston was born January 12, 1940, in Towns, Georgia. He graduated from Lumber City High School in 1957. He entered North Georgia College and State University, where he was a member of the Corps of Cadets, but ultimately transferred to Auburn University to pursue a degree in civil engineering. Upon graduation and receiving his degree, Livingston was commissioned as a second lieutenant in the Marine Corps Reserve on June 6, 1962. Much of his early assignments included service as a platoon commander, an intelligence officer, and a Recruit Training Regiment series commander. In June 1966, Livingston served as commanding officer of the Marine detachment on the USS *Wasp*. In August 1967, he was assigned to the 3rd Marine Division in the Republic of Vietnam.

In March 1968, Livingston, having been promoted to captain, was awarded the Bronze Star Medal while serving as commanding officer, Company E, 2nd Battalion, 4th Marines, 9th Marine Amphibious Brigade in action against North Vietnamese troops in Quang Tri Province, Vietnam.

Less than two months later, on May 2, 1968, Captain Livingston once again distinguished himself in combat by demonstrating exceptional bravery and leadership on the battlefield as he led an attack on enemy forces at the heavily fortified village of Dai Do. A few days before, Livingston and his company had been ordered to defend a strategic bridge near Dong Ha, the headquarters of the 3rd Marine Division. At the time, elements of the North Vietnamese 320th Division had been threatening the undermanned Marine headquarters. During intense fighting in and around the village of Dai Do, Livingston moved his men over open rice paddies, all the while under enemy fire, to aid fellow marines of the 2nd Battalion, 4th Marine Regiment. As Livingston's company neared the village, they encountered fierce enemy resistance. After his first two platoons were unsuccessful in breaking through the enemy line, Captain Livingston—although wounded by grenade fragments—personally led the reserve platoon forward and eventually broke through the enemy defenses. He then led his men in destroying nearly 100 bunkers, driving the North Vietnamese from their positions.

Upon securing Dai Do, Livingston was left with only 35 out of the more than 100 who had been involved in the assault. As efforts were being made to care for the wounded, Livingston received word that Company H was pinned down near the small village of Dinh To. On his own volition, he immediately ordered his remaining men to follow him in reinforcing the embattled marines. Counterattacked by North Vietnamese forces, Livingston and his men remained engaged in intense close combat with the enemy. During this battle, Livingston was again wounded, this time in the thigh by an enemy machine gun bullet. Again refusing to be evacuated but unable to stand, Livingston continued to fire from a prone position, making sure all his troops got out before two of his own marines pulled him to safety.

Captain Livingston was awarded the Medal of Honor for his actions at Dai Do by President Richard Nixon on May 14, 1970. After serving as an instructor at the Army's Infantry School, director of division schools for the 1st Marine Division, and S-3 Operations Officer of the 3rd Battalion, 7th Marines, in 1975, Livingston returned to Vietnam as operations officer in charge of evacuation operations in and around Saigon.

After assignments in the United Kingdom as commanding officer of the Marine Barracks in London, service at the US Marine Corps recruit depot at Parris Island, and command of the 6th Marine Regiment, 2nd Marine Division, Livingston was promoted to brigadier general in 1988 and served as deputy for operations at the

National Military Command Center in Washington, D.C. He commanded the Marine Air Ground Combat Center in California during operations Desert Shield and Desert Storm, and he was instrumental in developing the Marine Corps Desert Warfare Training Program. In 1991, he was promoted to major general and took command of the Marine Reserve Force in New Orleans, Louisiana.

Having retired from active duty in 1995, Maj. Gen. James Livingston serves on the boards of numerous businesses and philanthropic organizations, including the Red Cross, the Boy Scouts of America, the National World War II Museum, and the Medal of Honor Foundation. He has also appeared before Congress as an advocate for early intervention for veterans with posttraumatic stress disorder.

Margaret L. Albert

Further Reading

Bartlett, Merrill L., and Jack Sweetman. *Leathernecks: An Illustrated History of the United States Marine Corps.* Annapolis, MD: Naval Institute Press, 2008.

Collier, Peter, and Nick Del Calzo. *Medal of Honor: Portraits of Valor beyond the Call of Duty.* New York: Artisan, 2006.

Livingston, James E., Colin D. Heaton, and Anne-Marie Lewis. *Noble Warrior: The Life and Times of Maj. Gen. James E. Livingston, USMC (Ret.), Medal of Honor.* New York: Zenith Press, 2010.

Nolan, Keith. *The Magnificent Bastards: The Joint Army-Marine Defense of Dong Ha, 1968.* Novato, CA: Presidio Press, 2007.

Shulimson, Jack, Leonard A. Blaisol, Charles R. Smith, and David A. Dawson. *U.S. Marines in Vietnam: The Defining Year, 1968.* Washington, D.C.: Headquarters Marine Corps, History and Museums Division, 1997.

Lopez, Jose M.

Born: June 1, 1912
Died: May 16, 2005
Home State: Texas
Service: Army
Conflict: World War II
Age at Time of Award: 32

Born on June 1, 1912, Jose M. Lopez was raised by his mother in Veracruz, Mexico. When he was eight years old, his mother died of tuberculosis, and he relocated to Brownsville, Texas, to live with his uncle's family. Growing up, Lopez worked at a number of jobs until he caught the attention of a boxing promoter; he then traveled the country, fighting 55 fights during his seven-year career as a boxer. He later joined the Merchant Marine.

Lopez first learned about the attack on Pearl Harbor by radio while he working as a deckhand on passenger liners en route from Hawaii to California. Upon docking in Los Angeles, his ethnically Hispanic features caused confusion, and he was arrested as a Japanese foreign agent. Thankfully, Lopez was able to convince federal officers that he was a Mexican American and not of Japanese descent.

In early 1942, Lopez received his draft card, enlisted in the army, and eventually became a sergeant in the 23rd Infantry Regiment, 2nd Infantry Division. He landed on Omaha Beach during the Normandy invasion and from there began a long journey of fierce fighting that ultimately led to an assault on Germany. But before entering the German homeland, Lopez found himself in the middle of the largest battle of US Army history, the Battle of the Bulge.

On December 17, 1944, the day after the start of the German offensive, Sergeant Lopez and his unit were in the forest area near Krinkelt, Belgium. The day was very cold, forcing GIs in some areas to struggle as they made their way through wet, icy, and snowy terrain. Suddenly, German tanks and infantry appeared in front of Lopez and his men, almost rolling right over their positions. With his company's left flank in danger of being overrun, he quickly sprang into action.

Lopez grabbed his heavy machine gun and ran to the exposed left flank while enemy bullets sliced the snow and dirt at his feet. From this position, he held his ground and constantly prayed. He was then forced to jump into a shallow hole offering little protection, and, as the enemy approached, he mowed down at least 10 of the German soldiers. Soon after, Lopez killed 25 more Germans who were attempting to push back his flank. With tank fire erupting all around him, a dazed Lopez moved his gun to the rear of his sector and opened fire on the enemy again. At one point, a shell landed nearby and rattled him, but he regained his senses, reset his gun, and commenced firing.

The enemy quickly maneuvered in such a way that they almost surrounded Lopez. He hurriedly packed up his heavy machine gun and ran to a group of nearby GIs who were setting up a defensive position. He fired from this position until all of his ammunition was exhausted. Then, Lopez retrieved his gun and made his way back toward the town.

Lopez single-handedly killed over 100 Germans while defending his company from being overrun by the enemy. His actions also allowed troops to build up a defensive line in order to repel the German attack. Lopez received a battlefield commission from his commanding officer but turned it down because he wanted to remain a sergeant. He continued to fight with the 2nd Infantry Division through Germany and into Czechoslovakia, where the war eventually ended for them. While in Czechoslovakia, Lopez received word that he was being sent to Nuremberg, Germany, to be awarded the Medal of Honor.

On June 18, 1945, Maj. Gen. James Van Fleet III presented Lopez the medal at a ceremony in Nuremberg. After returning to the United States, Lopez received a discharge from the Army after the war and took a job with the Veterans Administration in San Antonio, Texas. Jose Lopez lived in San Antonio until his death from cancer on May 16, 2005.

Thomas D. Lofton Jr.

Further Reading

Cavanagh, William C. C. *The Battle East of Elsenborn and the Twin Villages.* South Yorkshire, UK: Pen & Sword Books, 2004.

Collier, Peter, and Nick Del Calzo. *Medal of Honor: Portraits of Valor beyond the Call of Duty.* New York: Artisan, 2006.

Tillman, Barrett. *Heroes: U.S. Army Medal of Honor Recipients.* New York: The Berkley Group, 2006.

Lucas, Jacklyn Harold

Born: February 14, 1928
Died: June 5, 2008
Home State: North Carolina
Service: Marine Corps
Conflict: World War II
Age at Time of Award: 17

Jacklyn Harold Lucas was born on February 14, 1928, in Plymouth, North Carolina. He was cadet captain, the highest-ranking soldier in the junior barracks, at Edwards Military School in Salemburg, North Carolina, and excelled at numerous sports. Although only 14 years old, Lucas was big for his age and forged his mother's signature on an enlistment waiver to join the Marine Corps Reserve on August 6, 1942. He completed basic training at Marine Corps Recruit Depot, Parris Island, South Carolina, in early October 1942 and was then assigned to the Marine Barracks and Naval Air Station Jacksonville in Florida. He was subsequently transferred to the Replacement Battalion at New River, North Carolina, in June 1943, where he completed his military training and became a heavy machine gun crewman.

Sent to the 6th Base Depot of the Fifth Amphibious Corps toward the end of 1943, Lucas's true age was subsequently discovered by a military censor after he wrote a letter to his 15-year-old girlfriend. Threatened with discharge, Lucas was assigned administrative duties in and around a Hawaiian military supply depot until an ultimate determination could be made as to his future in the Marine Corps. During this time, he was often in trouble with military authorities and, due to his age, was told he would not be allowed to join a combat unit. Refusing to stay behind and anxious to get into combat, he stowed away on the USS *Deuel*, a transport ship then

UNCOMMON VALOR: MARINE MEDALS OF HONOR AT IWO JIMA

In the annals of Marine Corps history, Iwo Jima holds a place of almost mythical honor due to the fact that more Medals of Honor were awarded there than for any other comparable campaign that the Marines fought during the war. A total of 27 Medals of Honor were awarded, half of them posthumous. Of those, 22 were awarded to Marines, representing almost one-fourth of the total of Medals of Honor awarded to Marines for all of World War II.

The first of the medals awarded for Iwo Jima was presented for action that occurred two days prior to D-Day, February 17, 1945, to a landing craft commander, Lt. Rufus G. Herring, US Navy Reserve, captaining LCI (Landing Craft Infantry)-449. Herring's LCI, supporting underwater demolition team (UDT) swimmers, got into a hot engagement with the coastal guns on Mount Suribachi. Lieutenant Herring was wounded after a direct hit to the ship but was able to con the ship and crew to safety. For this action, he was later awarded the Medal of Honor.

Once the landings began in earnest on February 19, the intensity of the action can be traced by the numbers of Medals of Honor awarded. Including Lieutenant Herring's medal, one-third of the medals awarded for Iwo Jima were earned in the first five days of fighting.

Representative of the heavy fighting was the action that earned Pfc. Jacklyn Lucas his award on February 20. Lucas, of the 26th Marines, found himself and his buddies in support of a tank crew assaulting a pillbox. As Lucas's squad advanced, 11 enemy soldiers came up behind them from a tunnel. Lucas killed two before shielding his buddies from two grenades that had been thrown by the attackers. Miraculously, he survived due to the heroic efforts of on-scene Navy hospital corpsmen. One of them even shot an oncoming Japanese soldier while trying to patch Lucas up.

The remaining two-thirds of the Medals of Honor were awarded for the vicious fighting against the teeth of the Japanese defenses in the plateau north of the airfield. By March 14, the battle had been officially declared over, but the bitter fighting continued, and two Medals of Honor were awarded that day to two more marines. Pvt. Franklin Sigler earned his after his squad leader was wounded and he single-handedly annihilated the entire garrison of a Japanese strong point. Like most of the others awardees, he was wounded and refused evacuation while evacuating others until forcibly ordered to medically evacuate. The second Medal of Honor awarded that day would go posthumously to Pvt. George Phillips, who paid with his life for smothering a grenade with his body to save his buddies.

The fighting continued even after the Army's 147th Regiment arrived to take over from the Marines; however, all formal resistance was assumed at an end on March 25, when the last Japanese stronghold in "Death Valley" was taken. Nevertheless, the next day, a group 300 Japanese survivors launched an early morning Banzai attack on the airfield. Marine 1st Lt. Harry L. Martin of the 5th Pioneer Battalion organized a hasty defense and then led a key counterattack until he was mortally wounded by an enemy grenade. Martin's posthumous award would be the last Medal of Honor given for the battle on Iwo Jima, but, incredibly, it was not the last of the fighting. The Army fought on into the summer, killing another 1,600 Japanese hiding out in caves throughout the island.

John T. Kuehn

Jacklyn Harold Lucas, US Marine Corps (Naval History and Heritage Command).

carrying 5th Division marines to the western Pacific for the invasion of Iwo Jima. After a month of hiding on board the *Deuel,* he turned himself in to Capt. Richard H. Dunlap. Lucas's will to fight so impressed the Marine officer that Lucas was allowed to join the 1st Battalion, 26th Marine Regiment as a rifleman.

On February 19, 1945, Lucas and his fellow marines landed on Iwo Jima. The following day, while creeping through a twisting ravine near an uncertain front line, Lucas and three other marines were attacked by Japanese soldiers. Two hand grenades landed in Lucas's foxhole. He threw himself over one and then pulled the second beneath his body shortly before they exploded. While Lucas saved his comrades from certain death, he was severely wounded; his fellow marines believed he was dead and moved forward. However, he was later found to be alive and was evacuated for medical treatment.

Only six days after his 17th birthday, Lucas's valiant actions and spirit of self-sacrifice at Iwo Jima earned him the Medal of Honor. On October 5, 1945, Lucas was presented with the medal by President Harry S. Truman. He was the youngest Marine ever to receive this award.

With more than 250 pieces of shrapnel in his body and in every major organ, Lucas spent months in various field hospitals and endured dozens of surgeries while recovering from his wounds. He was medically discharged from the Marine Corps Reserve on September 18, 1945.

Following the end of the war, Lucas became a symbol of patriotism, meeting presidents and traveling the world to speak with frontline soldiers and fellow veterans. He left the military, completed high school, and earned his business degree from High Point University in North Carolina. He later became a successful businessman in the suburbs of Washington, D.C.

In 1961, Jack Lucas joined the Army and was commissioned as a second lieutenant and assigned to the 82nd Airborne Division. He was discharged at the rank of captain four years later. Speaking regularly to various groups all over the country, he made inspirational appearances before active duty service personnel and veterans. His book, *Indestructible*, was published in 2006. He died at the age of 80 at Hattiesburg, Mississippi, on June 5, 2008, after a battle with cancer.

Huong T. D. Nguyen

Further Reading

Bartley, Whitman S. *Iwo Jima: Amphibious Epic*. Washington, D.C.: US Marine Corps Historical Branch, Headquarters Marine Corps, 1954.

Collier, Peter, and Nick Del Calzo. *Medal of Honor: Portraits of Valor beyond the Call of Duty*. New York: Artisan, 2006.

Lucas, Jacklyn, with D. K. Drum. *Indestructible: The Unforgettable Story of a Marine Hero at Iwo Jima*. Cambridge, MA: Da Capo Press, 2006.

Ross, Bill D. *Iwo Jima: Legacy of Valor*. New York: Vintage Books, 1986.

Luke, Frank, Jr.

Born: May 19, 1897
Died: September 29, 1918
Home State: Arizona
Service: Army
Conflict: World War I
Age at Time of Award: 21

Frank Luke Jr. was born in Phoenix, Arizona, on May 19, 1897. After completing high school, he joined the US Army Signal Corps in September 1917 after US entry into World War I. He received flight training at Rockwell Field in San Diego, California, and took to flying readily; he was the first member of his class to fly solo without an instructor. In January 1918, Luke was commissioned a second lieutenant and pilot before being shipped to France. After several weeks of additional training at the aviator's school in Issoudun, he ferried aircraft for several months while continually seeking a combat assignment. Finally, in July 1918, the 22-year-old Luke was posted with the 27th Aero Squadron, 1st Pursuit Group, along the Aisne-Marne sector.

Luke quickly established a reputation for being a fine pilot who combined expert flying and superb marksmanship with reckless daring. Ever the loner, he made his first kill in August by leaving formation to fight alone. This resulted in the first of several official reprimands. Luke, however, continued racking up his score by adding three additional planes and 14 observation balloons in only six weeks.

The extremely dangerous practice of balloon busting became something of a career specialty for Luke. These lumbering craft were not only difficult to set afire, but they were also protected by antiaircraft batteries below and usually possessed a squadron of fighter planes circling above. Luke's practice was to stalk them near dusk when the balloons were being reeled in for the night, destroy them, and depart before German defenses could react. His tactic proved extremely effective, and, in a single week during September 1918, he downed 13 of these German craft. In mute testimony to the dangerous nature of this work, five of his SPAD XIII fighters returned so peppered by bullets that they were scrapped.

Luke, however, was a solitary individual who preferred to fly and fight alone. His maverick habits made him unpopular with other fliers and occasioned many official reprimands. At length, he was teamed up with Lt. Joseph Wehner, who, to the surprise of many, became a close friend. The two men made an efficient aerial team and together shot down several additional balloons and aircraft. On one occasion, Gen. Billy Mitchell observed the two in action from the ground and counted 50 bullet holes in their craft following their return.

Their lucky streak ended on September 19, 1918, when Luke and Wehner split up to engage some balloons and a flight of Fokkers. In a sizzling 10 minutes of combat, Luke flamed two balloons and three German craft. However, Wehner was killed, and thereafter Luke flew with a vengeance.

Luke's last flight occurred on September 29, 1918, when he took off alone and against orders for a sortie behind enemy lines. There, in a spectacular dogfight, he downed three additional balloons and two German Fokkers before his plane was damaged and he was forced to land. En route, Luke strafed an infantry column, killing several soldiers, and crashed near the village of Murvaux. Though called on to surrender, Luke fought back desperately with his pistol until he was killed. For this display of gallantry and self-sacrifice, he was posthumously awarded the Medal of Honor, the first given to an airman.

Frank Luke's score of 18 kills (4 airplanes and 14 balloons) is second only to Capt. Eddie Rickenbacker, and he is commemorated by Luke Air Force Base in Arizona. In 1975, he received the additional honor of being inducted into the National Aviation Hall of Fame in Dayton, Ohio.

John C. Fredriksen

Further Reading

Fredette, Raymond H. "Watch for Burning Balloons." *Air Force Magazine* 56 (1973): 78–82.

Haiber, William P., and Robert Haiber. *Frank Luke: The September Rampage.* La Grangeville, NY: Info Devels Press, 2003.

Hall, Norman S. *The Balloon Buster: Frank Luke of Arizona.* New York: Bantam, 1966.

Jordan, H. Glenn. "Frank Luke, Jr., Balloon Buster." *Military History of Texas and the Southwest* 13 (1976): 5–10.

Pardoe, Blaine. *Terror of the Autumn Skies: The True Story of Frank Luke, America's Rogue Ace of WWI.* New York: Skyhorse, 2008.

Whitehouse, Arthur G. *Hun Killer: Frank Luke, the Ace from Arizona.* New York: Award Books, 1966.

Mabry, George L., Jr.

Born: September 14, 1917
Died: July 13, 1990
Home State: South Carolina
Service: Army
Conflict: World War II
Age at Time of Award: 27

Born in Stateburg, South Carolina, on September 14, 1917, George L. Mabry Jr. graduated from Presbyterian College in Clinton, South Carolina, in 1940. He earned a reserve commission as a US Army second lieutenant and volunteered for active duty, serving initially with the 2nd Battalion, 8th Infantry Regiment, 4th Infantry Division.

On the morning of June 6, 1944, D-Day, Capt. George Mabry was among the first wave of 600 infantrymen scheduled to assault Utah Beach. Weather, smoke, and enemy mines conspired to throw the landing schedule into disarray, but the American soldiers managed to establish a foothold and began moving toward their assigned objectives. Crossing the dunes inland from the beach, Captain Mabry found himself and a group of soldiers in the middle of a minefield. Where some leaders might have withdrawn, Mabry chose to continue the attack. He led his men through the mines and then began clearing enemy foxholes and pillboxes. Due to the speed and determination of his attack, by mid-morning Mabry linked up with American paratroopers near Pouppeville, who took him to meet Maj. Gen. Maxwell Taylor, commanding general of the 101st Airborne Division. Captain Mabry earned the Distinguished Service Cross for his actions that day. He had served with distinction on his first day in combat and would continue to do so in the coming months.

By September 1944, American forces broke through the hedgerows of Normandy and were moving east toward Germany. Retreating German units reconstituted in defensive positions along the Siegfried Line, which ran roughly parallel to the German border. The Siegfried Line varied in strength from a thin belt of improved positions in some areas to parallel lines of antitank obstacles and powerful concrete pillboxes in others. One of the strongest points in the Siegfried Line lay in a densely forested area southeast of the city of Aachen called the Huertgen Forest. The forest became the focal point of a five-month-long campaign that was among the costliest of the war, devastating seven infantry divisions and one armored division before the Americans finally broke through the German lines. In this challenging terrain, Lieutenant Colonel Mabry, having earned two promotions since D-Day, would again distinguish himself as one of America's greatest combat heroes.

On November 16, 1944, the 2nd Battalion, 8th Infantry, with Mabry serving as its battalion executive officer, began an attack toward the Roer River crossing near Duren. The battalion commander, Lt. Col. Langdon A. Jackson Jr., requested infantry reconnaissance patrols and tactical air to support his battalion's attack, but no units were available to assist with reconnaissance, and bombing was ineffective in the dense woods. After a day of intense fighting and heavy American casualties, the battalion had gained almost no ground and regrouped to its original line of departure. The battalion received nearly identical attack orders for the second day and met with similar results. Upon receiving orders to continue the attack the next day, Jackson convinced his regimental commander, Col. Richard McKee, to replace his battalion with a fresh unit, but McKee simultaneously relieved Jackson of his command, replacing him with Lieutenant Colonel Mabry.

Mabry, hearing of his sudden promotion, refused to accept McKee writing off his battalion so abruptly. He requested a day to reconstitute, spending November 18 hastily assembling about 200 replacements in preparation for a renewed attack the next morning. Mabry adjusted the tactics that had failed his battalion in its previous attacks, seeking to surprise the German defenders rather than giving away his intentions with noisy armor support and preparatory artillery fires. More importantly, he realized he faced a significant leadership challenge in restoring his battalion's morale. As November 19 dawned, Mabry conducted a hasty reconnaissance to bypass an enemy machine gun position. After this initial success, Mabry found himself and his men once again in the midst of a minefield, but he kept up the momentum of the assault by clearing mines with his bayonet, opening a path for his battalion to continue its attack. Mabry then led his soldiers from one emplacement to the next, shooting or bayoneting German soldiers who resisted and sending the rest to the rear as prisoners. After clearing a third enemy bunker under heavy enemy fire, Mabry rallied the remnants of his battalion around him and halted the attack for the night. For his actions that day, Lieutenant Colonel Mabry was awarded the Medal of Honor.

George Mabry survived the war and continued to serve on active duty, with assignments including four years as commander of the Panama Canal Zone and a tour as an assistant division commander in Vietnam. His soldiers routinely commented on his exceptional qualities of leadership, his gift for storytelling, and his humble willingness to ask of his soldiers only what he was willing to accomplish himself. He retired in 1975 as a major general, ending a long and distinguished career that culminated in his distinction as the country's second most highly decorated soldier, after Audie Murphy. Major General Mabry died at the age of 72 on July 13, 1990, and was buried at Holy Cross Episcopal Church in Stateburg, South Carolina.

Mark T. Calhoun

Further Reading

Ambrose, Stephen E. *The Victors: Eisenhower and His Boys: The Men of World War II*. New York: Simon & Schuster, 1998.

Astor, Gerald. *The Bloody Forest: Battle for the Huertgen: September 1944–January 1945*. Novato, CA: Presidio Press, 2000.

Lang, George, Raymond L. Collins, and Gerard F. White. *Medal of Honor Recipients, 1863–1994*. New York: Facts on File, 1995.

MacDonald, Charles B. *The Siegfried Line Campaign. US Army in World War II: European Theater of Operations*. Reprint, Washington, D.C.: Historical Division, Department of the Army, 2001.

Tillman, Barrett. *Heroes: U.S. Army Medal of Honor Recipients*. New York: The Berkley Group, 2006.

MacArthur, Arthur, Jr.

Born: June 2, 1845
Died: September 5, 1912
Home State: Wisconsin
Service: Army
Conflict: American Civil War
Age at Time of Award: 18

Arthur MacArthur Jr. was born June 2, 1845, in Springfield, Massachusetts, the first son of Arthur MacArthur, a Scottish immigrant, and Aurelia Belcher MacArthur. By age 13, Arthur MacArthur Jr. had decided to become a soldier.

When the Civil War came, MacArthur pestered his father for permission to join the swelling ranks of the Union Army. Finally, after failing to secure his son a West Point appointment for 1862, Judge MacArthur relented and used his political influence to garner his now 17-year-old son an appointment as adjutant and first lieutenant in the 24th Wisconsin US Volunteer Infantry Regiment. Young Arthur stood roughly five feet tall and weighed about 90 pounds as he marched off to war.

MacArthur proved to have a knack for soldiering. At Perryville, Kentucky (October 8, 1862), he received a citation for bravery and a promotion to brevet captain. In the vicious fighting at Murfreesboro, Tennessee (December 30, 1862–January 3, 1863), MacArthur again distinguished himself. Later, as major and commander of the 24th, MacArthur cemented his reputation as one of the finest and youngest combat commanders in the West during the 1864 Atlanta Campaign and at Franklin (November 30, 1864), where his second wound sustained in combat ended his Civil War career. In March 1865, MacArthur received a promotion to brevet lieutenant colonel.

However brilliant MacArthur's battlefield performance had been at the afore-mentioned actions, he is best remembered for what he did at Missionary Ridge outside Chattanooga, Tennessee (November 25, 1863). The once-proud Army of the Cumberland had been humiliated at Chickamauga, Georgia (September 19–20, 1863), while MacArthur had been at home in Wisconsin on sick leave. Upon his re-turn, MacArthur found the regiment in bad shape—underfed, understrength (less than 150 men), and under siege. The Confederate Army of Tennessee held the high ground surrounding Chattanooga, including the imposing 500- to 800-foot-high Missionary Ridge. The situation looked and, indeed, was desperate. It fell to Maj. Gen. Ulysses S. Grant, fresh from his victory at Vicksburg, to break the siege. Grant sent reinforcements to Chattanooga and reestablished a supply route into the city. It remained only to break the Confederate lines.

Meanwhile, the Army of the Cumberland hungered to redeem its tarnished reputation in the fighting that lay ahead. On November 25, MacArthur's 24th Wis-consin got its chance.

Grant ordered units of the Army of the Cumberland, including the 24th Wis-consin, to take the Confederate entrenchments at the base of Missionary Ridge. Successful in accomplishing this mission, the 24th found itself subjected to a galling fire from above. Without orders and with its fighting blood up, the 24th advanced up the slope. When the regimental color sergeant went down halfway up the slope, the 18-year-old adjutant, MacArthur, picked up the flag. Shouting "On Wisconsin," he led the regiment to the crest, leaped over the Confederate breastworks with the flag in one hand and a pistol in the other, and planted the flag in front of Confeder-ate general Braxton Bragg's headquarters. Some claimed that the 24th's flag was the first upon the ridge. In any case, 27 years later, MacArthur, then 45, would receive the Medal of Honor for his intrepid act.

A question remains: Why was MacArthur awarded the Medal of Honor 27 years after his actions? Like all Civil War officers, MacArthur believed the medal was for noncommissioned officers and enlisted men only. This was certainly true of the ini-tial 1862 Act of Congress authorizing the creation of the medal. However, in 1863, Congress amended this legislation to include officers. The problem was that almost no one was aware of this fact. Their supposed ineligibility for the medal rankled MacArthur and a legion of other Civil War officers. In April 1890, MacArthur, at that time working in the Army's adjutant general's office, discovered the truth of the matter when the Medal of Honor recommendation paperwork for Matthias W. Day, an Indian War cavalry officer, crossed his desk. He acted promptly by doing some research and then submitted an application to the board meeting to consider Day's award. Approval followed. MacArthur had the list of Medal of Honor recipi-ents, which included six officers, published in the *Army Register*, which opened the door for others to apply. The result was that between 1891 and 1896, 67 officers received the Medal of Honor for actions during the Civil War.

Arthur MacArthur Jr. died on September 5, 1912, after a long and distinguished career in the Army. His son, Douglas MacArthur, would also become a soldier. Like his father, Douglas, too, would receive his nation's highest decoration for valor. The MacArthurs are one of only two father-son combinations to receive the Medal of Honor—the other was Theodore and Theodore Roosevelt Jr.

Gregory S. Hospodor

Further Reading

Cozzens, Peter. *The Shipwreck of Their Hopes: The Battles for Chattanooga.* Urbana: University of Illinois Press, 1994.

McDonough, James Lee. *Chattanooga—A Death Grip on the Confederacy.* Knoxville: University of Tennessee Press, 1984.

Spiller, Roger J., ed. *Dictionary of American Military Biography.* Vol. 2, *H–P.* Westport, CT: Greenwood, 1984.

Sword, Wiley. *Mountains Touched with Fire: Chattanooga Besieged, 1863.* New York: St. Martin's Press, 1995.

Young, Kenneth Ray. *The General's General: The Life and Times of Arthur MacArthur.* Boulder, CO: Westview Press, 1994.

MacArthur, Douglas

Born: January 26, 1880
Died: April 5, 1964
Home State: New York
Service: Army
Conflict: World War II
Age at Time of Award: 62

Douglas MacArthur was born at the Arsenal Barracks in Little Rock, Arkansas, on January 26, 1880, the third and last son of Arthur MacArthur Jr. and Mary Pinkney Hardy MacArthur. His father was a career military officer who rose to the rank of lieutenant general and received the Medal of Honor for his actions at Missionary Ridge in 1863.

Douglas MacArthur spent his early life moving from one military post to another. While his father was stationed in San Antonio, Douglas attended the West Texas Military Academy. In 1899, he entered West Point, a place that became his spiritual home. He graduated first in his class in 1903 and was commissioned a second lieutenant of engineers.

Douglas MacArthur, US Army (Library of Congress).

MacArthur's pre–World War II career included service in the Philippines, Panama, Mexico, Europe, and the United States. During World War I, he served primarily with the 42nd Division, eventually commanding the unit as a brigadier general. He was twice wounded in action and earned numerous decorations for heroism, including the Distinguished Service Cross and three Silver Stars.

After the war, MacArthur held positions of increasing responsibility. In 1930, he was promoted to general and appointed chief of staff of the Army, a post he held until 1935. In 1935, he went to the Philippines, first as military advisor and, later, as field marshal in the Philippine Army. When war came, MacArthur, who had retired from the US Army in 1937, returned to active duty and took command of the US forces in the Far East.

MacArthur received the Medal of Honor for his actions while commanding the valiant, if ill-fated, defense of the Philippines during 1941–1942. Pearl Harbor sealed the fate of the 140,000-man combined American and Philippine Army, although this was not clear to many at the time. After the Japanese attack at Pearl Harbor, the United States lacked the land, naval, and air power to effect a relief expedition to the Philippines, as called for in prewar plans. The tragic lot of the troops in the Philippines was to resist as long as possible. Douglas MacArthur led this effort.

As defeat in the Philippines approached, Gen. George C. Marshall, Army chief of staff, with the direct support of President Roosevelt, ordered MacArthur to leave the Philippines to set up a new Southwest Pacific command in Australia. MacArthur complied but made it clear that his preference was to share the fate of his beleaguered army.

The decision to order MacArthur to leave the Philippines as well as to award him the Medal of Honor for his service there was fundamentally political. The War Department feared the effect the capture of MacArthur, perhaps the most popular military figure in the United States and certainly the best known, would have upon the morale of the American people and the Army. An important, but secondary, consideration was the loss of MacArthur's services should he stay in the Philippines. However, Japanese propaganda made much of the "abandonment" of the forces in the Philippines by their commander (some American veterans of the campaign still harbor resentment over MacArthur's departure). George C. Marshall anticipated the Japanese propaganda. For Marshall, presenting MacArthur with the Medal of Honor was the obvious response; on January 31, 1942—MacArthur would not leave the Philippines until March 11—Marshall first brought up the subject in a cable to Maj. Gen. Richard K. Sutherland, MacArthur's chief of staff. MacArthur had been nominated twice previously for the medal and already held every other major American decoration. During the dark times of early 1942, the nation, in Marshall's opinion, badly needed a hero to rally behind; with the presentation of the Medal of Honor to MacArthur, it would have one.

Marshall wrote MacArthur's Medal of Honor citation with solicited input from Sutherland. The citation focused specifically upon the effect of MacArthur's leadership on the morale of the army and the people of the Philippines, paralleling the intended effect of the award's announcement upon the homefront in 1942. MacArthur went on to command Allied forces in the Southwest Pacific, to serve as military governor of occupied Japan, and to command UN forces in Korea. He died at Walter Reed Army Medical Center on April 5, 1964, at the age of 84. He was laid to rest in the rotunda of the MacArthur Memorial in Norfolk, Virginia.

Douglas MacArthur and his father, Arthur MacArthur Jr., are one of only two father-son combinations to receive the Medal of Honor—the other was Theodore Roosevelt and Theodore Roosevelt Jr.

Gregory S. Hospodor

Further Reading

James, D. Clayton. *The Years of MacArthur*. 3 vols. Boston: Houghton Mifflin, 1970–1985.

Morton, Louis. *The Fall of the Philippines. United States Army in World War II: The War in the Pacific*. Washington, D.C.: US Army Office of the Chief of Military History, 1952.

Perret, Geoffrey. *Old Soldiers Never Die: The Life of Douglas MacArthur*. New York: Random House, 1996.

Spiller, Roger J., ed. *Dictionary of American Military Biography*. Vol. 2, *H–P*. Westport, CT: Greenwood, 1984.

Mackie, John F.

Born: October 1, 1835
Died: June 18, 1910
Home State: New York
Service: Marine Corps
Conflict: Civil War
Age at Time of Award: 26

John Freeman Mackie was born on October 1, 1835, in New York City. Working there as a silversmith, he enlisted in the US Marine Corps at the Brooklyn Navy Yard on April 24, 1861. His first assignment was on the USS *Savannah* as part of the ship's Marine Detachment. The *Savannah* was mainly assigned to blockade duty off Cape Hatteras, North Carolina. During this time, the *Savannah* assisted in the capture of the Confederate forts Hatteras and Clark. The *Savannah* later participated in the capture of Port Royal, South Carolina, and other small islands and ports on the coast of Florida.

On March 1, 1862, Mackie was promoted to the rank of corporal and was assigned to the ironclad USS *Galena* under the command of Cdr. John Rodgers. The *Galena* was sent initially sent to Fort Monroe, Virginia, to possibly counter the dreaded Confederate ironclad CSS *Virginia* (Merrimac). During this time frame, Mackie saw a significant amount of action and participated in the Union naval assault and capture of Norfolk, Virginia, and witnessed the eventual destruction of the *Virginia* following the capture of Norfolk by Union naval forces.

On May 15, 1862, a small Union Navy flotilla that included the *Galena, Aroostook, Port Royal, Naugatuck,* and the famous USS *Monitor* attacked Confederate Fort Darling, located about four miles below Richmond, Virginia, near a bend in the James River called Drewry's Bluff. Fort Darling, sited on top of the bluff, guarded the river entrance to the Confederate capital and was of tremendous strategic importance to the rebel cause. During the fighting that followed, the *Galena*, mounting seven large-caliber naval guns, anchored about 400 yards from the fort while the other vessels anchored 800 yards further back. At 0600 hours, *Galena* opened fire on the well-defended fort, but the attack was strongly resisted by the Confederates. Almost immediately, Commander Rodgers was severely wounded by a Confederate shell. Early on in the fighting, it was obvious that the Union ships were at a clear disadvantage. The well-armored USS *Monitor* was unable to elevate its guns to properly target the fort, and a 100-pound gun on the *Naugatuck* exploded and forced that ship to also retire out of range. The *Port Royal* and *Aroostook* were both wooden hulls unable to withstand the plunging fire from the fort. Thus, the lone remaining ironclad, *Galena*, was forced to fight alone for over four hours.

While the *Galena* was indeed considered an ironclad ship, its armor was still fairly thin compared to that of the more powerful USS *Monitor*. Confederate rounds from the fort repeatedly penetrated *Galena's* armor plating and caused a significant number of casualties. To make matters worse, Confederate marines manning rifle pits on the nearby riverbank used sharpshooters to pick off any exposed personnel. While Corporal Mackie and other US marines of the *Galena* detachment returned fire, they had little effect on the amount of enemy fire coming from the riverbank. At the height of the fighting, a 10-inch round once again penetrated Galena's armor belt and smashed into one of its 100-pound Parrot guns, killing nearly its entire crew. Shouting "Come on boys, here's a chance for the Marines," Mackie and a number of nearby comrades quickly manned the Parrot rifle and kept the weapon in action.

By noon, *Galena's* gunner reported that the ship was entirely out of ammunition, and Commander Rodgers moved the vessel downriver and safely out of range. During the intense fighting in front of Fort Darling, the *Galena* had been hit an estimated 132 times by solid shot. Twelve sailors and one marine had been killed, and 11 more men were wounded.

For his conspicuous performance in combat at the battle of Drewry's Bluff, Mackie was promoted to sergeant and recommended for the Medal of Honor. Reassigned to the USS *Seminole*, Mackie received the medal on July 10,1863, while anchored off Sabine Pass in Texas.

From September 1, 1863, until February 1864, John Mackie and the *Seminole* remained at Sabine Pass on blockade duty. In August 1864, he and his *Seminole* shipmates took part in the Battle of Mobile Bay. Mackie was honorably discharged from the Marine Corps on August 23, 1865, in Boston, Massachusetts, after having served over four years of continuous service. He participated in 16 major battles and was in dozens with skirmishes in his role as a marine assigned to Union Navy ships. The only wartime injury he received occurred in January 1864 when he was struck in the head with a chain hook while trying to quell a group of drunken *Seminole* sailors. Mackie was the first US Marine to receive the Medal of Honor. He later married and settled outside of Philadelphia, Pennsylvania, where he lived the remainder of his life. He died on June 18, 1910, and was buried in Arlington Cemetery in Drexel Hill, Pennsylvania.

Charles P. Neimeyer

Further Reading

Field, Ron, and Richard Hook. *American Civil War Marines, 1861–1865*. New York: Osprey, 2004.

McPherson, James M. *Battle Cry of Freedom: The Civil War Era*. New York: Oxford University Press, 2003.

Sullivan, David M. *The United States Marine Corps in the Civil War*, Vol. 2, *The Second Year*. Shippensburg, PA: White Mane Publishing Company, 1997.

Mallon, George H.

Born: June 15, 1877
Died: Aug 2, 1934
Home State: Kansas
Service: Army

Conflict: World War I
Age at Time of Award: 41

Born on June 15, 1877, in Ogden, Kansas, just outside Fort Riley, George H. Mallon served with the 132nd Infantry, 33rd Division, an Illinois National Guard division activated in July 1917. He trained with the unit at Camp Logan, Texas, before being sent overseas in May 1918 as part of the American Expeditionary Force.

Mallon's company participated in the great Meuse-Argonne Offensive, which began on September 26, 1918. The 33rd Division was ordered to take heavily forti-fied positions at Montfaucon and Bois-de-Forges, which were considered impreg-nable by the Germans. On that day, and after becoming separated from the bulk of his company due to heavy fog, Captain Mallon led his nine remaining soldiers forward until he encountered a string of emplaced German machine guns. Lead-ing the attack, he captured all nine enemy guns without the loss of a single one of his soldiers. As his small party continued, they next came upon a German battery of 155-mm howitzers. Again taking the initiative, Mallon rushed the guns, captur-ing the battery and its crew. During this action, Mallon even disabled one German defender with his fists in hand-to-hand combat.

Despite two heroic acts already, Mallon was not through. His squad-sized party next ran into two additional German machine guns. He sent men on flank attacks while he pushed toward the center of enemy fire; he reached the gunners first and eliminated the threat. During the course of his advance, Mallon had captured 100 prisoners, 11 machine guns, four 155-mm howitzers, and one antiaircraft gun. In 1919, Captain Mallon received the Medal of Honor for this action.

George Mallon died on August 2, 1934, at St. Cloud, Minnesota, but was reinterred in 1939 as the first burial at the Fort Snelling National Cemetery in Minneapolis.

Mark M. Hull

Further Reading

Harris, Barnett W. *33rd Division: Across No-Man's Land.* Whitefish, MT: Kessinger Publishing, 2006.

Lang, George, Raymond Collins, and Gerald White. *Medal of Honor Recipients, 1863–1994.* New York: Facts on File, 1995.

Marm, Walter Joseph, Jr.

Born: November 20, 1941
Died:
Home State: Pennsylvania
Service: Army

Conflict: Vietnam War
Age at Time of Award: 23

Walter Joseph Marm Jr. was born November 20, 1941, in Washington, Pennsylvania, 30 miles southwest of Pittsburgh. He was the son of a state trooper. He was a Boy Scout who disliked hunting but enjoyed target practice with a rifle.

Marm graduated from Duquesne University in 1964 with a degree in finance. However, with the United States beginning to increase its commitment in Southeast Asia, he decided to enlist in the Army. He went to Fort Gordon, Georgia, for basic and advanced training before going on to officer candidate school and the Ranger course at Fort Benning, Georgia.

After being commissioned a second lieutenant in the infantry, Marm was assigned to Company A, 1st Battalion, 7th Cavalry, 1st Cavalry Division (Airmobile). The new division was to test the theory that helicopters could function as the modern equivalent of the horse, carrying men into battle. Marm deployed to Vietnam with the 7th Cavalry, George Armstrong Custer's old unit, and the rest of the division in September 1965.

During his first two months in Vietnam, he saw little combat. He participated in an ambush and helped secure a crash site where a US helicopter had gone down. On November 14, 1965, Second Lieutenant Marm was serving as a platoon leader during his battalion's sweep through the Ia Drang Valley in the Central Highlands in search of the North Vietnamese Army (NVA). The enemy was dug in around the Chu Pong Massif, a mountainous area adjacent to the Cambodian border.

The elements of 1st Battalion, 7th Cavalry, commanded by Lt. Col. Hal Moore, were inserted by helicopter into a landing zone on the valley floor designated "X-Ray." It did not take long for a pitched battle to develop. A platoon from B Company found itself isolated, surrounded by the NVA, and under heavy fire. Moore directed Company A to relieve the beleaguered platoon, which was in imminent danger of being overrun. Marm and his platoon took the lead, but the surrounding jungle was teeming with North Vietnamese soldiers. The Americans soon found themselves taking withering fire from every direction and were forced to take cover. Realizing that his platoon could not hold very long under these conditions and seeing four enemy soldiers moving toward his men, Marm got up and charged forward, firing at the attackers and killing all four. Then seeing that a concealed machine gun was placing devastating fire on his men, he deliberately exposed himself to draw its fire so he could determine the gun's position. Locating the gun behind a large termite hill, he attempted to destroy it with an antitank weapon but was unable to silence the enemy fire. Disregarding the intense fire, he charged 30 meters across open ground, hurled grenades into the enemy position, and took the survivors under fire with his rifle, killing eight enemy soldiers. When he turned to wave his platoon forward, he was shot in the left jaw by an NVA soldier, the bullet exiting out the right side of his neck. Two of his men rushed to his aid and got him to the battalion command post;

he was evacuated by helicopter later that night. Within days, he was recovering from his wounds in Valley Forge Hospital in Chester County, Pennsylvania. His jaw was wired shut, and he was on a diet of baby food until his wound healed.

The Medal of Honor was presented to Marm by Secretary of the Army Stanley Resor at the Pentagon on December 19, 1966. He was among 10 western Pennsylvanians who earned the Medal of Honor in Vietnam, all posthumously except for Marm and one other recipient.

In 1969, Marm asked to go back to Vietnam for a second tour. He was allowed to do so but only after he signed a waiver stipulating that going back to Vietnam was his own choice.

Walter Marm eventually retired from the Army in 1995 as a colonel with 30 years of service. He subsequently settled in North Carolina, where he became involved in the hog-farming business. Marm has been actively involved in the Congressional Medal of Honor Society and public speaking. A humble man, he always makes it clear that he wears the Medal of Honor for all those brave men in battle whose actions went unsung.

Ultimately, the battle of the Ia Drang was the first large-scale pitched battle between American and North Vietnamese troops. It would later be immortalized first in the book *We Were Soldiers Once... and Young*, written by Hal Moore, commander of the 1st Battalion, 7th Cavalry, and Joe Galloway, a reporter who was also on the ground at Landing Zone (LZ) X-Ray. Later the story was retold in the Mel Gibson movie *We Were Soldiers*.

James H. Willbanks

Further Reading

Collier, Peter, and Nick Del Calzo. *Medal of Honor: Portraits of Valor beyond the Call of Duty*. New York: Artisan, 2006.

Faranacci, Donald. *Last Full Measure of Devotion: A Tribute to America's Heroes of the Vietnam War*. Bloomington, IN: AuthorHouse, 2007.

Moore, Lt. Gen. (Ret) Harold G., and Joseph L. Galloway. *We Were Soldiers Once... and Young*. New York: Random House, 1992.

Moore, Lt. Gen. (Ret) Harold G., and Joseph L. Galloway. *We Are Soldiers Still: A Journey Back to the Battlefields of Vietnam*. New York: Harper, 2008.

Murphy, Edward F. *Vietnam Medal of Honor Heroes*. New York: Ballantine Books, 2005.

Martinez, Joe P.

Born: July 27, 1920
Died: May 26, 1943
Home State: Colorado

Service: Army
Conflict: World War II
Age at Time of Award: 22

Born in Taos, New Mexico, on July 27, 1920, to Mexican immigrants, Joseph Pantillion Martinez was one of nine children. In 1927, the Martinez family moved to Ault, Colorado. It was in Colorado that Martinez received his elementary and secondary education. Martinez was drafted by the US Army in August of 1942. Following his enlistment, Martinez was sent to Camp Roberts in California to complete his basic training.

Upon completion of his basic training, Martinez was assigned to Company K, 32nd Infantry Regiment, 7th Infantry Division. The division was training for the liberation of the Aleutian Islands at Fort Ord and San Luis Obispo.

In June of 1942, the Japanese had landed and occupied a number of islands in the Aleutian Islands. The US feared that the Japanese would use the islands as bases to launch air attacks against the West Coast. The campaign to liberate the Aleutian Islands began on May 11, 1943, when elements of the 7th Infantry Division landed at Holtz Bay and Massacre Bay, Attu. The initial landings faced determined defense by the Japanese Army.

One of the key locations on the island of Attu was Chichagof Harbor, where the Americans had to attack and overcome Japanese defenses in several mountain passes leading into the harbor. By May 26, the attack by the 32nd Infantry had stalled near Fish Hook Ridge in the face of intense enemy fire. Firing his Browning Automatic Rifle (BAR) and throwing hand grenades, Private Martinez assaulted the nearest enemy position. After taking the first Japanese position, Martinez gathered his comrades around him and proceeded to lead an attack on the main pass through heavy fire from both flanks. When Martinez reached the final trench, he was mortally wounded by Japanese fire, and he died the next day. Due to Martinez's actions, the Americans were able to take and hold the passes. With the successful attack on the passes, the path for American liberation of Chichagof Harbor, and later the entire island of Attu, was cleared, and the island was completely liberated by May 30.

For his actions in the battle for Attu, Private Martinez was posthumously awarded the Medal of Honor. He was the first of 13 Hispanics to receive the Medal of Honor during World War II. Joseph Martinez was also the first soldier from Colorado to receive the Medal of Honor during World War II. In recognition of his valor, the State of Colorado and the cities of Ault and Greeley, Colorado, have erected statues in his honor. The US Navy named a troop transport in Martinez's honor. The US Army also named an Army Reserve installation in Denver after him. Martinez is buried in Ault, Colorado.

Christopher S. Trobridge

Further Reading

Bartoletti, Lee F. "Battle of the Aleutian Islands: Recapturing Attu." *World War II*, November 2003.

Garfield, Brian. *The Thousand-Mile War: World War II in Alaska and the Aleutians.* New York and Toronto: Bantam Books, 1988.

US Congress. Senate. Committee on Veterans Affairs. *Medal of Honor Recipients, 1863–1973.* Washington, D.C.: Government Printing Office, 1973.

McCool, Richard Miles, Jr.

Born: January 4, 1922
Died: March 5, 2008
Home State: Oklahoma
Service: Navy
Conflict: World War II
Age at Time of Award: 23

Richard Miles McCool Jr. was born January 4, 1922, in Tishomingo, Oklahoma. He graduated from high school at the age of 15. At 19, he graduated from the University of Oklahoma with a degree in political science. After the bombing of Pearl Harbor in December 1941, he was accepted into the Navy ROTC program but then received an appointment to the US Naval Academy at Annapolis, Maryland, entering with the class of 1945. Because the war was on and there was a need for junior naval officers, his class was graduated a year early in 1944. Before graduating and receiving his commission, McCool signed up to serve in amphibious craft because he liked the idea of commanding his own vessel, rather than having to serve as a junior staff officer on a much larger ship. After graduation, McCool picked up his ship, a Landing Craft Support (LCS), in Boston, and then he and his crew of 70 men sailed for San Diego.

By June 1945, McCool and his ship were part of the fleet supporting operations on the island of Okinawa. His ship was part of a force of other LCS craft and destroyers manning a picket line to protect the rest of the fleet from Japanese kamikazes.

On June 10, McCool's ship, *LCS-122*, was closest to the USS *William D. Porter* (DD-579) when it was hit by a kamikaze and began to sink. McCool's crew helped rescue 99 surviving crew members from the *Porter* and carried them to another American ship.

The next day, McCool's vessel itself came under attack. The crew successfully fought off the first of two kamikazes, shooting it down. However, the second kamikaze, despite being hit by fire from *LCS-122*, struck the vessel's conning tower about eight feet below where McCool was standing. McCool, suffering chest wounds and burns, was knocked unconscious. When he came to, the vessel was on fire. Despite his wounds, he quickly rallied his crew and began to fight the fire. When he heard that two of his crew were trapped in the burning deckhouse, he rushed in to rescue them, carrying one of them to safety on his back despite the pain from his severe burns. He continued to command his ship until one of his lungs collapsed and he passed out again.

He spent two months recuperating from his wounds in the hospital on Guam. He was transferred to the Oak Knoll Naval Hospital in California and ultimately back to his home in Norman, Oklahoma. President Harry S. Truman presented McCool with the Medal of Honor on December 18, 1945, in a White House ceremony.

McCool recovered from his wounds and went back on active duty in mid-1946. He served in the Korean and Vietnam wars; additionally, he served on the staff of several fleets and shore stations and did tours of duty in Thailand and Japan. He retired in 1974 as a Navy captain after a 30-year career. After leaving the service, Captain McCool and his wife settled on Bainbridge Island, a 30-minute ferry ride across Puget Sound from Seattle in Washington State. There, he became active in local Democratic Party affairs, serving two terms as chair of the Kitsap County Democratic Party. He and his wife were active supporters of the arts on Bainbridge Island and in Seattle. McCool was inducted into the Oklahoma Military Hall of Fame in 2007.

McCool died of natural causes at the age of 86 on March 5, 2008, in a hospital in Bremerton, Washington.

James H. Willbanks

Further Reading

Collier, Peter, and Nick Del Calzo. *Medal of Honor: Portraits of Valor beyond the Call of Duty.* New York: Artisan, 2003.

Rielly, Robin L. *Kamikazes, Corsairs, and Picket Ships: Okinawa 1945.* Drexel Hill, PA: Casemate, 2008.

McGinnis, Ross A.

Born: June 14, 1987
Died: December 4, 2006
Home State: Pennsylvania
Service: Army
Conflict: Iraq
Age at Time of Award: 19

Ross Andrew McGinnis was born in Meadville, Pennsylvania, on June 14, 1987, the youngest of three siblings. When he was three, his family moved to Knox,

Pennsylvania, a tight-knit community 70 miles northeast of Pittsburgh. McGinnis was active in both the Cub Scouts and Boy Scouts and in his younger years enjoyed playing basketball and soccer through the YMCA. He also played Little League Baseball through the Knox Association. McGinnis was a 2005 graduate of Keystone Junior-Senior High, where his diversions included video games, mountain biking, and concert choir. More hands-on than academic, McGinnis in his spare time worked at a fast food restaurant and took classes in automotive technology at Clarion County Career Center, where he served as secretary and treasurer. When asked in kindergarten what he wanted to be when he grew up, McGinnis drew a picture of a soldier. Not surprisingly, McGinnis enlisted in the Army on his 17th birthday via the delayed entry program.

After basic and advanced infantry training at Fort Benning, Georgia, McGinnis was assigned to the 1st Battalion, 26th Infantry Regiment of the 1st Infantry Division in Schweinfurt, Germany. The youngest member of his unit, he excelled at soldiering. During training, the left-handed McGinnis qualified as expert with his rifle while shooting left-handed and as a sharpshooter while shooting right-handed. He had a reputation for making others laugh, and he generally wore a broad smile.

In mid-2006, the rangy youth would put his skills to work as a soldier with the 1st Platoon, C Company, 1st Battalion, 26th Infantry Regiment (attached to the 2nd Brigade Combat Team, 1st Infantry Division). The locale was eastern Baghdad, and the mission was to quell growing sectarian violence. During its time in Iraq, the 1st Battalion would suffer 31 KIAs (killed in action), nearly half of them belonging to C Company, McGinnis's unit.

He served as an M2 .50 caliber machine gunner in Charlie Company, then occupying Combat Outpost Apache in Adhamiya. Prior to the unit's arrival, the area had not witnessed any American combat presence for eight months. In November 2006, after Saddam Hussein was found guilty of crimes against humanity, Charlie Company fought five hours against insurgents attempting to overrun the outpost.

On the afternoon of December 4, McGinnis was riding in the last Humvee of a convoy, acting as rear guard security for an element patrolling to interdict insurgents and to deliver a generator. With two-story buildings on either side of the march route, the convoy motored past Abu Hanifa Mosque and took a turn to the southeast, at which juncture an unidentified insurgent threw a grenade into McGinnis's Humvee. He tried to deflect the grenade, but it nonetheless entered the vehicle through the gunner's hatch, coming to rest near the radio mount. The other four crewmen in the vehicle were unaware of the grenade's presence. McGinnis shouted "grenade" over the vehicle's intercom system to alert his fellow soldiers. Although McGinnis could have exited the vehicle at any time, he elected to throw himself on the grenade. His body absorbed nearly all of the grenade's fragments, which killed him instantly. McGinnis's warning allowed fellow crew members to assume protective positions. His gallantry and utter disregard for his own safety ensured the survival of his comrades.

In recognition of his bravery and wounds, McGinnis was posthumously awarded the Silver Star, the Bronze Star, and the Purple Heart. He was also promoted to specialist and nominated for the Medal of Honor, which was presented in a ceremony at the White House on June 2, 2008. The date was less than two weeks short of what would have been McGinnis's 21st birthday. Sfc. Cedric Thomas, S.Sgt. Ian Newland, Sgt. Lyle Buehler, and Spc. Sean Lawson—the four soldiers whose lives McGinnis saved—were in attendance.

Ross McGinnis is survived by his mother, Romayne, and his father, Thomas, as well as his sisters, Beck and Katie. After a memorial ceremony in Knox, McGinnis's remains were transferred to Arlington National Cemetery. The machine gun range at Fort Benning was named in his honor, as was the Clarion Veterans of Foreign Wars (VFW) Post. McGinnis was the second soldier to receive the Medal of Honor during the Iraq War.

Anton A. Menning

Further Reading

Ricks, Thomas E. *The Gamble.* New York: The Penguin Press, 2009.

Robinson, Linda. *Tell Me How This Ends.* New York: Public Affairs, 2008.

"Spc. Ross A. McGinnis." *Soldiers* 65, no. 3 (March 2010): 6–7.

West, Bing. *The Strongest Tribe.* New York: Random House, 2009.

McGinty, John J., III

Born: January 21, 1940
Died:
Home State: Kentucky
Service: Marine Corps
Conflict: Vietnam War
Age at Time of Award: 28

John J. McGinty III was born in Boston, Massachusetts, on January 21, 1940, but grew up in Louisville, Kentucky. McGinty enlisted in the Marine Corps Reserve in 1957, after he finished high school. He went on active duty in March 1958. Prior to his service in Vietnam, McGinty served as a drill instructor and a brig warden. He volunteered for Vietnam service in 1966 in an effort to give meaning to his time in uniform.

In Vietnam, McGinty served with the 3rd Battalion, 4th Marines. On July 15, 1966, as part of Operation Hastings, the battalion moved by helicopter to the demilitarized zone (DMZ) to interdict enemy action detected by aerial reconnaissance. Once on the ground, McGinty realized his unit faced North Vietnamese Army (NVA) regulars and not Viet Cong guerillas. US intelligence had underestimated the size of the enemy force in the area. McGinty's battalion faced a regimental-size element mounting an attack; his platoon, of approximately 30 marines, faced approximately 800 North Vietnamese soldiers.

During a lull in the fighting, the battalion received orders to withdraw. McGinty's company came under attack on July 18 while conducting rear guard activities to cover the battalion's withdrawal. At the beginning of the attack, enemy fire injured McGinty's radio operator and three other marines near his position. McGinty quickly took cover and began to organize his platoon's defense.

McGinty, then a staff sergeant and acting platoon leader, rallied his platoon to withstand wave after wave of North Vietnamese Army attacks. In the chaos of the battle, the platoon lost contact with two of its squads. McGinty, with no regard for his own safety, moved through heavy enemy fire to the separated squads. The two squads sustained 20 wounded men as well as the death of their corpsman. McGinty reloaded rifle magazines for the wounded and encouraged the men to continue to resist the attack. While encouraging these men, McGinty suffered shrapnel injuries in his leg, back, and left eye from a grenade. Through the pain, McGinty continued to conduct the defense of the platoon against further NVA attacks. The NVA forces retreated to reorganize for another assault. When the enemy approached from the rear, McGinty killed five enemy soldiers at very close range with his pistol.

McGinty continued to coordinate indirect fire and air support to maintain his defensive position. Only 9 of the 50 members of his platoon were combat ready when the unit's relief arrived. Because of McGinty's leadership, the NVA left over 500 dead soldiers on the battlefield.

McGinty continued to serve in the Marines. After his service in Vietnam, McGinty received a commission as a second lieutenant on August 8, 1967. After earning his commission, McGinty continued to serve at Parris Island as a series commander, supervising the training of recruits and the performance of their drill instructors.

While serving at Parris Island, McGinty learned that he had earned the Medal of Honor. President Lyndon B. Johnson presented the Medal of Honor to McGinty and his company commander, Capt. Robert Modrezejewski, in a joint ceremony at the White House on March 12, 1968.

John McGinty retired from the Marine Corps in 1976 after he lost his left eye due to the injuries sustained in 1966. He maintains his involvement with the Marine Corps. In 1999, McGinty served on a task force appointed by the governor of California to assess the quality of care in California veterans' homes. In 2005, he visited marines deployed to Afghanistan. In 2006, McGinty traveled to Iraq to speak to service members on Veterans Day. In 2008, he participated in an Armed Forces Entertainment tour that visited soldiers deployed throughout the Middle East. During this tour, McGinty, accompanied by other Medal of Honor recipients, spoke to soldiers about his service in the Marines. He currently resides in San Diego, California.

Gates M. Brown

Further Reading

Collier, Peter, and Nick Del Calzo. *Medal of Honor: Portraits of Valor beyond the Call of Duty.* New York: Artisan, 2006.

Murphy, Edward F. *Vietnam Medal of Honor Heroes.* New York: Ballantine Books, 2005.

McKinney, John R.

Born: February 26, 1921
Died: April 4, 1997
Home State: Georgia
Service: Army
Conflict: World War II
Age at Time of Award: 24

John R. "J. R." McKinney was born in Woodcliff, Georgia, on February 26, 1921, the son of a poor Georgia sharecropper. He quit school after third grade to use his hunting and fishing skills to provide food for his family during the difficult years of the Great Depression. He was drafted into the US Army and, upon completing training, joined Company A, 123rd Infantry, 33rd Infantry Division, known as the Golden Cross Division, headed to the Pacific Theater.

McKinney served with the Golden Cross Division during the hard-fought campaign for New Guinea. In February 1945, the division landed in the Philippines. Early on the morning of May 11, 1945, an elite strike force of approximately 100 Japanese Imperial soldiers attacked the unit's encampment near Dingalan Bay in Tayabas Province on the island of Luzon. The focus of the enemy attack was a machine gun position manned by three American soldiers. Private McKinney had just completed guard duty and was resting a short distance away when the attack began. In the course of the attack, McKinney suffered a glancing blow to the head with a saber, but he did not hesitate to join his comrades in the defense of his unit. When 10 Japanese soldiers overpowered the machine gun and were turning the gun around to use it against the American troops, McKinney charged headlong into the position, killing seven with rifle fire and three with the butt of his rifle. The machine gun was rendered inoperable, leaving him only with his rifle to defend the position against the advancing Japanese, who were hurling grenades and firing knee mortar shells into the American position. McKinney secured additional ammunition and continued to hold off the attacking Japanese troops using rifle fire, his rifle as a club, his knife, and his fists in hand-to-hand combat. When relief arrived, they discovered 40 dead Japanese soldiers in the immediate area of the machine gun. McKinney had single-handedly defended the unit's perimeter and saved the company from possible defeat. For this event, he was awarded the Medal of Honor on February 4, 1946, by President Harry S. Truman in a White House ceremony.

In addition to McKinney, two other men from the 33rd Division earned the Medal of Honor for bravery: Pfc. Dexter J. Kerstetter, who survived the war but died in an accident in 1972, and S.Sgt. Howard E. Woodward, who died in battle. In 1995, McKinney, the lone Medal of Honor survivor of the division, was the guest of honor at a 50-year reunion. He reluctantly attended and uncomfortably sat through dinner in a stiff new suit. When they introduced McKinney as the guest of honor, he was discovered absent from the banquet hall. His family found him outside in a nearby stand of trees. He told his family that he did not understand why he had survived when so many had not. He said he had probably survived because he used his wilderness skills and that he sometimes still heard the screams of the Japanese soldiers he had killed.

Fellow soldiers from McKinney's company and people from his hometown in Screven County, Georgia, remembered J. R. as a private, shy, uncomplaining, and uneducated man who did his duty and followed orders but kept to himself after the war. He returned home to Sylvania, Georgia, and his family after the war, but neighbors rarely saw him. He spent his time fishing, hunting, and farming. He never married. He left no personal papers and remained a private man until his death on April 4, 1997. The State of Georgia honored him in 1995 by renaming a highway the John R. McKinney Medal of Honor Highway. He was buried at Doubleheads Baptist Church in Sylvania, Screven County, Georgia.

Debra J. Sheffer

Further Reading

Johnson, Forrest Bryant. *Phantom Warrior: The Heroic True Story of Pvt. John McKinney's One-Man Stand against the Japanese in World War II.* New York: Berkley Publishing, 2007.

Tillman, Barrett. *Heroes: U.S. Army Medal of Honor Recipients.* New York: The Berkley Group, 2006.

Merli, Gino J.

Born: May 13, 1924
Died: June 11, 2002
Home State: Pennsylvania
Service: Army
Conflict: World War II
Age at Time of Award: 21

Gino J. Merli was born in Scranton, Pennsylvania, on May 13, 1924. The son of a coal miner, he entered the service of the US Army in his hometown of Peckville,

Pennsylvania. He served in Company H, 2nd Battalion, 18th Infantry Regiment, 1st Infantry Division during World War II as a private first class. Merli and the 1st Infantry Division, after training in the United States, traveled to England prior to the D-Day invasions in preparation for Operation Overlord. The division landed at Omaha Beach during D-Day on June 6, 1944. Merli fought with the 1st Infantry Division through the north of France.

On the night of September 4, 1944, Sars la Bruyere, Belgium, Merli was serving as a machine gunner when his company was attacked by a superior German force. The company was overrun, and he and several of his compatriots were surrounded when the other American troops were driven back by overwhelming numbers and firepower. They tried to cover the withdrawal of the other soldiers, but the assistant machine gunner was killed, and Merli's position was overwhelmed by the enemy; the other eight members of the section were forced to surrender. Merli slumped down beside the dead assistant gunner and feigned death. No sooner had the enemy group withdrawn than he was up and firing in all directions. Once more, his position was taken, and the captors found two apparently lifeless bodies. Merli again feigned death and then turned his weapon on the Germans when they left him for dead.

By daybreak, the enemy had suffered heavy losses, and as the American troops began a counterattack, the Germans asked for a truce. The Americans sent forward a negotiating party to accept the German surrender; they found Private First Class Merli still at his gun. On the battlefield lay 52 enemy dead, 19 of whom were directly in front of the gun. Merli had survived the night by outwitting the Germans until American forces could successfully retake his unit's position.

Merli was later wounded during the Battle of the Bulge; he was hospitalized in England for several weeks and then sent home on a troop ship. After surgery to remove shrapnel he had received at the Bulge, Merli learned that he was to receive the Medal of Honor. He was presented the medal by President Harry S. Truman on June 15, 1945, in a White House ceremony. Along with the Medal of Honor, Merli also received two Purple Hearts, the Bronze Star, the Battle of the Bulge Medal, and the Humanitarian Award of the Chapel of Four Chaplains for his actions during World War II.

Merli decided to assist fellow veterans after World War II by working as an adjudication officer at the Veterans Administration Center in Plains Township, Pennsylvania. Another one of Merli's contributions to his fellow veterans stems from his 1984 trip to Normandy alongside Tom Brokaw. Brokaw and NBC news were working on a 50th anniversary documentary about D-Day, and the network sent Brokaw along with these veterans to the beaches of Normandy. Merli, Brokaw, and other World War II veterans traveled to Normandy, France, to visit the site of their landings on D-Day. Merli and the other veterans walked and talked with Brokaw and each other about their experiences on that day, while Brokaw talked with the men about what it was like to not only live through such an event but their life experiences in general. Brokaw credited Merli as one of his many inspirations for his book *The Greatest Generation*. Brokaw wrote in his book: "In the spring of 1984, I went to the northwest of France, to Normandy, to prepare an NBC documentary on the fortieth anniversary of D-Day, the massive and daring Allied invasion of Europe that marked the beginning of the end of Adolf Hitler's Third Reich. There, I underwent a life-changing experience. As I walked the beaches with the American veterans who had returned for this anniversary, men in their sixties and seventies, and listened to their stories, I was deeply moved and profoundly grateful for all they had done. Ten years later, I returned to Normandy for the fiftieth anniversary of the invasion, and by then I had come to understand what this generation of Americans meant to history. It is, I believe, the greatest generation any society has ever produced."

Following Gino Merli's death on June 11, 2002, the Veterans Center in Scranton, Pennsylvania, was named after Merli and another Pennsylvania Medal of Honor recipient, Joseph Sarnoski. Another honor accorded the decorated World War II veteran is Gino Merli Drive, one of the main roads in his hometown of Peckville, Pennsylvania.

Jason M. Sokiera

Further Reading

Brokaw, Tom. *The Greatest Generation*. New York: Random House, 1999.

Collier, Peter, and Nick Del Calzo. *Medal of Honor: Portraits of Valor beyond the Call of Duty*. New York: Artisan, 2006.

Murphy, Edward F. *Heroes of World War II*. Novato, CA: Presidio Press, 1990.

US Congress. Senate. Committee on Veterans Affairs. *Medal of Honor Recipients, 1863–1973*. Washington, D.C.: Government Printing Office, 1973.

Miles, L. Wardlaw

Born: March 23, 1873
Died: June 26, 1944
Home State: New Jersey
Service: Army
Conflict: World War I
Age at Time of Award: 45

Louis Wardlaw Miles was born on March 23, 1873, in Baltimore, Maryland. His father was a Confederate Army doctor in the Civil War. After Miles graduated from Johns Hopkins University in 1894, his father urged him to become a doctor. Therefore, in 1897, he received an MD from the University of Maryland. However, Miles preferred English over medicine, so in 1902 he completed a PhD from Johns

Hopkins with a dissertation titled *King Alfred in Literature*. That same year, he obtained an appointment at Princeton. Woodrow Wilson, then president of the university, promoted Miles to preceptor in 1906, and in 1915 he received tenure.

Miles supported the Preparedness Movement and joined the Plattsburgh program in 1915 and 1916. In 1917, he resigned from Princeton and participated in the last Plattsburgh training session. When President Wilson declared war in April 1917, Miles enlisted as a lieutenant in the American Expeditionary Force. He joined the 77th Infantry Division, an Army division comprised of men mostly from New York City. His regiment was the ethnically diverse 308th.

From September 1917 to April 1918, the division trained at Camp Upton, Long Island, New York. On April 21, Miles arrived in France, where his regiment spent the next few weeks training under British tutelage around Flanders, then with the French in Lorraine. In June, Miles inspired the men of his platoon by keeping his wits and calm demeanor while enduring a heavy bombardment of gas and explosives in a German raid. He calmly walked along his line, directing his men's rifle fire to cover the flank of the neighboring unit, the target of the German raid, as well as his own exposed flank in anticipation of the same.

While in defensive positions on the Vesle River on August 17, Miles claimed to have captured the division's first German prisoner even though the official record accredited this distinction to the 307th Regiment the following day. For the remainder of August, the regiment endured constant artillery shelling and fierce hand-to-hand combat. Miles assumed command of Company B when his dear friend, Capt. Belvedere Brooks, was killed. Then, on September 4, the division finally stepped out of its stationary defensive positions and began to advance toward the Aisne River, some 9 to 10 kilometers away.

Two days earlier, the Germans began an orderly, planned withdrawal to fortified positions on the Aisne River. As ordered, the 77th Division harassed them the entire way. However, on September 7, the 308th Regiment ran into stiff resistance in front of the town of Revillon, approximately seven kilometers from where they had started a few days earlier. For the following week, the regiment struggled to fight its way up the slopes in front of the town, to no avail. There was a dearth of officers after numerous failed assaults; some companies were left with sergeants in command.

On September 13, Miles was promoted to captain; he volunteered to lead the next attack on the town, which was ordered for the following day. The assault had no artillery support, and Miles led the first wave of the attack himself. As he reached the German wire, he was hit by machine gun fire. However, he persisted, tackling the entanglement with wire cutters. In the process, he was shot again. In all, he was hit five times; both his arms and one of his legs were fractured. When the second wave arrived at his position, he ordered two men to carry him forward on a makeshift stretcher. His men drove the Germans out of their trench, only 18 inches deep, and prepared for the inevitable counterattack. They held on against continuous shelling from mortars, machine gun fire, and an assault. After a few hours, Miles was ordered, against his will, to be carried to the rear, where his leg was amputated. Unfortunately, the remaining soldiers withered under a daylong artillery barrage, were eventually driven from their hard-won position, and were forced to retake it again. On September 16, the division was relieved from the front, leaving it to another unit to drive the Germans from Revillon.

Miles was awarded the Medal of Honor for his deeds on September 14. Upon his return to the United States in 1919, Miles rejoined the staff at Princeton as an assistant professor. Later that year, he resigned and became the headmaster of the Gilman School in Baltimore, where he remained until 1926. The following year, he published the *History of the 308th Infantry, 1917–1919* and became a collegiate professor of English at Johns Hopkins. Louis Wardlaw Miles died on June 26, 1944, and was buried in Green Mount Cemetery, Baltimore.

Lon Strauss

Further Reading

Adler, J. O., M. Leonard G. McAneny, and Kaiser August. *History of the 77th Division: August 25, 1917 to November 11, 1918*. New York: 77th Division Association, 1919.

Miles, L. Wardlaw. *History of the 308th Infantry, 1917–1919*. New York: G. P. Putnam's & Sons, 1927.

Slotkin, Richard. *Lost Battalions: The Great War and the Crisis of American Nationality*. New York: Henry Holt, 2005.

Miles, Nelson A.

Born: August 8, 1839
Died: May 15, 1925
Home State: Massachusetts
Service: Army
Conflict: Civil War
Age at Time of Award: 23

Nelson A. Miles was born August 8, 1839, on his family's farm in Westminster, Massachusetts. He was working as a crockery store clerk in Boston when the Civil War broke out and joined the Union Army on September 9, 1861, and became a lieutenant in the 22nd Massachusetts Volunteer Infantry Regiment. On May 31, 1862, he was commissioned a lieutenant colonel in the 61st New York Infantry Regiment. After the Battle of Antietam, he was promoted to colonel. He participated in the Battle of Fredericksburg, and, during the Battle of Chancellorsville on May 3, 1863, he distinguished himself by commanding an advanced position against repeated Confederate assaults despite sustaining severe wounds to the neck and abdomen. For this action, Miles would receive the Medal of Honor on July 23, 1892.

MEDAL OF HONOR REVIEW BOARD

In 1916, the US Army convened a special board of five retired general officers to review each of the 2,625 Army Medals of Honor that had been awarded to that date. The board's specific mission was to identify those awards that did not meet the criteria for inclusion in the Roll of Honor, recently established by Section 122 of the National Defense Act, passed by Congress on June 3, 1916. The president of the board was Lt. Gen. Nelson A. Miles, himself a Medal of Honor recipient, and it included Lt. Gen. Samuel B. M. Young, a former chief of staff of the US Army. The board met from October 16, 1916, to January 17, 1917, and in its final report identified 911 Army Medals of Honor that did not fit the criteria of Section 122. As a result of those findings, the awards of 905 US Army soldiers and six civilians, including Dr. Mary E. Walker and William F. Cody (a.k.a. Buffalo Bill), were revoked, and their names were stricken from the Roll of Honor. All six of the civilian Medals of Honor were reinstated, but only many years later.

The earliest Medals of Honor awarded during the Civil War had been poorly documented, and the initial criteria were vaguely defined for what later evolved into America's premier recognition for combat heroism. In establishing the Roll of Honor, Section 122's language explicitly restricted membership to individuals "having in action involving actual conflict with an enemy, distinguished himself conspicuously by gallantry and intrepidity, at the risk of his life, above and beyond the call of duty." Section 122 also included "and who was honorably discharged from service." That last phrase was the foundation of the board's most controversial finding.

The 911 Medals of Honor identified by the Board fell into four broad categories. The least controversial group was the en-mass award to the entire 27th Maine Infantry Regiment. During the days leading up to the battle of Gettysburg in 1863, the 27th Maine was one of the few units left in Washington to defend the national capital. However, that unit's term of enlistment expired on June 30, and most of the troops intended to return home immediately. In an act of desperation, Secretary of War Edwin Stanton offered the Medal of Honor to any member of the regiment who volunteered to serve beyond the discharge date. Only 311 soldiers of the 27th Maine agreed, and even then they only served an additional four days until the fighting at Gettysburg was over. During the entire period of its Federal service, the 27th Maine never once served in combat. Nonetheless, when it came time to issue the promised Medals of Honor to the 311 volunteers, no accurate list could be produced. The War Department then compounded the error by issuing medals to all 864 of the individuals listed on the regiment's mustering-out roster. All of those awards clearly fell outside the criteria of Section 122.

Another noncontroversial group was the funeral detail of four officers and 25 senior noncommissioned officers who, in April 1865, escorted the body of President Abraham Lincoln from Washington, D.C. to Springfield, Illinois, for burial. Clearly, no combat action or contact with the enemy was involved.

The third group included 12 individuals who were determined to be unqualified for various reasons. Some awards, such as the one to Capt. Asa B. Gardner, undoubtedly had been frivolous. In 1872, Gardner had sent a letter to Secretary of War William Belknap requesting a medal "as a souvenir of memorable times past." Other cases were a little harder to judge. Pvt. Thomas Gilbert and Quartermaster Storekeeper

James M. Hawkins, for example, had both performed acts of heroism, but not in the presence of the enemy. Pvt. Robert Storr was an especially interesting case. Assigned to an engineer regiment that constructed a bridge over the James River, Storr died in 1862 after contracting a fever. He was awarded the Medal of Honor in 1871 at the request of his father in England. Storr's actions clearly did not qualify, but the board primarily disqualified him because he was a British citizen, thereby reinforcing the precedent that only US citizens were eligible for the Medal of Honor.

The most controversial of the disqualified groups included the six civilians: contract acting assistant surgeon Dr. Mary E. Walker and civilian scout William H. Woodall from the Civil War; and civilian scouts William F. Cody, Amos Chapman, William Dixon, and James B. Dozier from the Indian Wars. Section 122's "honorably discharged from service" clause was the basis for including the civilians on the disqualified list. Contrary to popular belief, there is no evidence to support the widely held conviction that Dr. Walker was targeted for disqualification specifically because of her gender.

Generals Miles and Young and their fellow board members agonized over the disqualification of the civilians. Even before the board officially convened, Miles wrote a letter to Secretary of War Newton D. Baker on July 19, 1916, pointing out, "If the provisions of Section 122 are strictly complied with, the Board is of the opinion that a grave injustice would be done to a class of public servants who have rendered most conspicuous acts of heroism that would be recognized by any army in the world." Miles asked Baker to approach Congress and request a modification of the language in Section 122. For whatever reason, Congress refused to reconsider, and the six Army civilians lost their Medals of Honor. Ironically, the same standards were never applied to three civilian boat pilots who received the Navy Medal of Honor during the Civil War: John H. Ferrell, Martin Freeman, and Perry Wilkes.

On May 4, 1977, the Army Board for Correction of Military Records submitted a recommendation to Secretary of the Army Clifford L. Alexander Jr. for the restoration of Dr. Walker's Medal of Honor. Alexander approved the recommendation on June 10, and her name was returned to the Roll of Honor. The precedent established in Dr. Walker's case also led to the restoration of the five civilian scouts, whose Medals of Honor were restored on June 12, 1989.

David T. Zabecki

After Chancellorsville, he was appointed brigadier general of volunteers and served in that capacity in the battles of the Wilderness and Spotsylvania Court House. By the end of the war, he had been wounded four times, had participated in every major battle of the Army of the Potomac except Gettysburg, and had commanded at every level, including regimental, brigade, division, and even briefly at corps.

Following the Civil War, Miles, as a colonel in the Regular Army, served as the commandant of Fort Monroe, Virginia, where he had custody, and was criticized for his treatment of former Confederate president Jefferson Davis.

In 1869, he became commander of the 5th US Infantry and played a major role in the Army's campaign against the American Indian tribes of the Great Plains. He led successful campaigns against the Kiowa, Comanche, and the Southern Cheyenne in the Red River War of 1874 to 1875. During 1876–1877, he led the campaign against the Lakota Sioux in the aftermath of the massacre of Lt. Col. George Armstrong Custer and his men at the Battle of the Little Bighorn, driving Sitting Bull into Canada. In the winter of 1877, he and his troops marched across Montana and defeated the Nez Percés, capturing Chief Joseph. Miles, vain and ambitious, would quarrel for the rest of his life with Gen. Oliver O. Howard over the credit for Joseph's capture. In 1886, he replaced Gen. George Crook as Army commander in Arizona and orchestrated the final surrender of Geronimo. Although not directly involved, Miles was criticized for his actions during the Wounded Knee massacre in 1890.

Miles was also criticized for his command of the troops mobilized to suppress the Pullman strike in Chicago in 1894. In 1895, upon the retirement of Lt. Gen. John M. Schofield, Miles became the general-in-chief of the Army, a post he held during the Spanish-American War. After the surrender of Santiago de Cuba, Miles personally led the invasion of Puerto Rico and served as the first head of the military government on the island, acting both as head of the army of occupation and administrator of civilian affairs. During this time, he had a very public quarrel with the secretary of war and attacked the commissary general of the Army, charging that he had provided rancid "embalmed beef" to Army troops in the field.

In 1900, Miles was promoted to lieutenant general based on his performance in the Spanish-American War, but, criticizing US policy in the Philippines, he ran afoul of President Theodore Roosevelt, who called Miles a "Brave Peacock." Miles also publicly opposed the long-overdue reform of the War Department, which called for converting the commanding general post to chief of staff. Reaching the mandatory retirement age of 64, he retired in August 1903, stepping down as the last commanding general of the Army. In 1904, he received a handful of votes at the Democratic National Convention from supporters who wanted him to become their party's nominee for president. In his late 70s, he volunteered for service during World War I but was turned down by President Woodrow Wilson due to his advanced age.

Nelson Miles lived out his remaining years quietly in Washington, D.C. He died on May 15, 1925, at age 85 from a heart attack. He was one of the last surviving Civil War soldiers on either side to serve as a general officer during that conflict. Miles is buried in Arlington National Cemetery in one of only two mausoleums in the cemetery (the other belongs to Gen. Thomas Crook Sullivan). Miles City, Montana, was named in Miles's honor.

James H. Willbanks

Further Reading

Amchan, Arthur J. *The Most Famous Soldier in America: A Biography of Lt. Gen. Nelson A. Miles, 1839–1925*. McLean, VA: Amchan Publications, 1989.

DeMontravel, Peter R. *A Hero to His Fighting Men: Nelson A. Miles, 1839–1925*. Kent, OH: Kent State University Press, 1998.

Johnson, Virginia Weisel. *The Unregimented General: A Biography of Nelson A. Miles*. New York: Houghton Mifflin, 1962.

Miles, Nelson Appleton. *Personal Recollections and Observations of General Nelson A. Miles, Embracing a Brief View of the Civil War, or, From New England to the Golden Gate: And the Story of his Indian Campaigns, with Comments on the Exploration, Development, and Progress of Our Great Western Empire*. Ann Arbor: University of Michigan Library, 2009. First published in 1897 by The Werner Company, Chicago.

Warner, Ezra J. *Generals in Blue: Lives of the Union Commanders*. Baton Rouge: Louisiana State University Press, 1964.

Wooster, Robert. *Nelson Miles and the Twilight of the Frontier Army*. Lincoln: University of Nebraska Press, 1996.

Millett, Lewis L.

Born: December 15, 1920
Died: November 14, 2009
Home State: Maine
Service: Army
Conflict: Korea
Age at Time of Award: 31

Lewis L. Millett was born in Mechanic Falls, Maine, on December 15, 1920; he grew up in rural Maine and was athletically inclined. His background made him well suited to become a soldier. In 1940, he left high school after joining the US Army National Guard. Believing that the United States would not enter the war against the Axis powers, Millett deserted after having been trained as an Air Corps gunner. He went to Canada. Unlike a later generation, it was not to avoid service but rather to join the Canadian Army, which was already fighting with the British. He was assigned to an antiaircraft unit in London but requested transfer to the US Army after the Japanese attack on Pearl Harbor.

In 1942, Millett joined an artillery battalion and landed in North Africa. He earned a Silver Star in Tunisia for driving a burning ammunition-filled half-track away from Allied soldiers, jumping to safety just as it exploded. He later shot down a German fighter using a half-track mounted machine gun. He fought with his unit during the Italian campaign in battles for Salerno and Anzio. However, it was after Anzio that the Army discovered Millett's 1941 desertion to Canada; he was subsequently court-martialed and convicted. He was fined $52 and forfeited his leave privileges. Only weeks later, he received a "Mustang" battlefield promotion to second lieutenant for his valor in combat. He eventually ended the war as a first lieutenant artillery forward observer and returned to Maine, where he joined the Army National Guard.

Voluntarily returning to active duty in 1949, he was assigned to the 25th Infantry Division on occupation duty in Japan. When the war broke out in Korea, Millett served both as an aerial artillery observer and liaison officer. Wanting to get into action, Millett volunteered to lead an infantry company that had recently lost its commander. He replaced another outstanding officer, Capt. Reginald B. Desiderio, who had been killed the previous November in hand-to-hand combat. Desiderio was subsequently awarded the Medal of Honor. This was a unique and completely coincidental event for both commanders of Company E, 27th Infantry Regiment.

As the new company commander for Company E, Millett was intent on training his soldiers to use their bayonets. This was not a personal quirk but related to a captured Chinese communist report that asserted that Americans did not like to fight in close combat. Millett took exception to the Chinese document and was eager to prove it wrong.

Captain Millett was enthusiastic about his new command. Physically fit and aggressive, he was able to lead from the front and did so. His unit went on the offensive as part of UN Operation Thunderbolt in January–February 1951, a counteroffensive operation to drive the Chinese north of the Han River. On February 7, 1951, Millett's company was advancing along a road at the base of a line of hills. Rice paddies bordered the road to the west and southwest. Steep hills to the east and north watched over the winding road. E Company had two tanks attached from the regimental tank company. As the first infantry platoon reached the bottom of a steep hill near Soam-Ni (now Osan Air Base), it came under intense small arms and antitank fire.

Captain Millett ordered both tanks to use their turret-mounted machine guns to lay a base of fire and suppress Chinese infantry firing down on the road from the crest of the hill. With the first platoon pinned down, Captain Millett ordered the third platoon to move forward to join the first platoon. With both platoons on line, Millett moved to the head of his troops and, shouting and yelling encouragement, led his understrength company uphill with fixed bayonets.

As Millett bounded up the hill, he threw grenades, clubbed, and then bayoneted any unfortunate Chinese soldiers who did not run away. Confronting two Chinese soldiers in a trench who refused to surrender, he bayoneted both before moving on. The ferocity of attack broke the Chinese defense, and those who had not been wounded or killed ran off the back side of the hill to escape. Over 47 dead Chinese littered the hill. At least 18 had been killed with bayonets.

Despite shrapnel wounds from Chinese grenades, Millett reorganized his company to continue the attack. He subsequently led his company to the Han River line and, after a couple of weeks, was replaced with another commander. He had been recommended for a valor award, and his superiors did not want him to be killed before it was presented. On July 5, 1951, Captain Millett was awarded the Medal of Honor by President Harry S. Truman.

Lewis Millett continued to serve in a variety of command and staff positions, eventually serving in yet another war, this time in Vietnam. He retired from the Army in 1973 but stayed extremely active in Army affairs, visiting training installations to lecture on bayonet fighting. He was honored with the position of "Honorary Colonel of the Regiment" of the 27th Infantry—the "Wolfhounds," his old unit. He was admitted to the Jerry L. Pettis Memorial Veterans Affairs Medical Center in Loma Linda, California, with congestive heart failure on Veterans Day in 2009, where he died a few days later. He was buried at Riverside National Cemetery in Riverside, California.

Edwin L. Kennedy Jr.

Further Reading

Collier, Peter, and Nick Del Calzo. *Medal of Honor: Portraits of Valor beyond the Call of Duty*. New York, Artisan, 2006.

Lang, George, Raymond L. Collins, and Gerard F. White. *Medal of Honor Recipients, 1863–1994*. Vol. 2, *WWII to Somalia*. New York: Facts on File, 1995.

Smith, Larry. *Beyond Glory: Medal of Honor Heroes in Their Own Words—Extraordinary Stories of Courage from WWII to Vietnam*. New York: W. W. Norton, 2003.

Miyamura, Hiroshi H.

Born: October 6, 1925
Died:
Home State: New Mexico
Service: Army
Conflict: Korean War
Age at Time of Award: 25

Hiroshi Miyamura's parents emigrated from Japan and settled in Gallup, New Mexico, in 1906. Miyamura was born on October 6, 1925, in Gallup. He graduated from high school in June 1943 and was drafted into the Army in 1944 and sent to Camp Blanding, Florida. Assigned to the 442nd Infantry Regiment, the famous Japanese American unit, Miyamura initially could not be sent overseas to join his unit because he had not reached the minimum age for overseas duty. He then was diagnosed with a hernia and required surgery. He finally embarked on a ship overseas, but five days out of Naples the war ended, and he never saw combat.

Miyamura stayed with the 442nd Regiment as part of the occupation forces, and, in July 1946, he returned with the members of the unit and participated in a parade for President Truman, where the regiment received its seventh Presidential Unit Citation. Miyamura was discharged shortly after and enlisted in the Army Reserve. He went home to Gallup and started a career as an auto mechanic.

When the Korean War erupted, Miyamura was recalled to active duty in September 1950. After refresher training, he flew to Japan and joined his unit. He was assigned to Company H, 7th Infantry Regiment of the 3rd Infantry Division as a machine gun squad leader. In November 1950, the 7th Regiment landed on the northeastern coast of North Korea. They initially protected the port facilities, airfields, and supply lines in the Wonsan and Hungnam areas for X Corps, which at the time was driving for the Yalu River. After the Chinese entered the war and X Corps began its withdrawal to the coast, the 3rd Infantry Division assisted the corps and covered the evacuation by defending a shrinking perimeter. Miyamura and his unit were among some of the last troops to leave the port of Hungnam before its destruction.

After evacuation from Hungnam, the 3rd Infantry Division was immediately placed into the line, and, by April 1951, the United States and its allies were in a defensive line awaiting a massive Chinese offensive toward Seoul. The 3rd Infantry Division was aligned along the Imjin and Hant'an rivers with the 7th Infantry Regiment holding the high ground on the Uijongbu-Seoul highway. Miyamura and the rest of the 2nd Battalion were in a central position south of where the two rivers joined. On the night of April 24, 1951, Miyamura and his machine gun squad were sent to a hill near Taejon-ni to occupy a defensive position and delay the Chinese attack.

During the night, the Chinese crossed the river in force. As the Chinese attacked the hill, Miyamura's machine gun squad opened fire. With the enemy still approaching, Miyamura told his squad to stay in place, and he charged down the hill, breaking up the enemy attack. Returning to his position, he broke up the next attack with deadly and accurate machine gun fire. With ammunition low, he ordered his men to fall back while he stayed to cover their withdrawal. Miyamura then made his way to another position and again ordered the men to fall back when that position was close to being overrun. He covered their withdrawal until his ammunition was low, at which time he too fell back. Wounded along the way, he collapsed and passed out.

Due to his courage although unbeknownst to him, many of his squad survived and were able to make it back to American lines. When he awoke, Miyamura pretended to be dead until he was discovered by a Chinese soldier. After his capture and despite his wounds, he was forced to march with other prisoners to captivity with no medical treatment and little food or water. He spent the next 28 months in captivity, where he endured exposure, mental and physical abuse, limited food and water, and limited shelter. His captors tried to break his spirit, but he endured. Undernourished, he lost 50 pounds while in captivity.

On August 20, 1953, as part of Operation Big Switch, the exchange of prisoners of war (POWs), Miyamura arrived at Freedom Village near Panmunjom. He received medical care and expected to be court-martialed for the loss of his squad; Miyamura instead was told by Brig. Gen. Ralph Osborne in front of the press that he was going to be awarded the Medal of Honor for his actions on April 24 and 25. Osborne explained to the press that Miyamura's award had been kept top secret because of concern that if the Chinese had known what he had done there would have been reprisals against him.

Miyamura was repatriated back to the United States and discharged. On October 27, 1953, President Dwight D. Eisenhower awarded him and six other soldiers and marines the Medal of Honor in a White House ceremony. At the time, he was only the second Japanese American to receive the award. He returned to Gallup and began a career selling household and automotive items and subsequently became a service station owner. He eventually retired and lives in Gallup. Miyamura serves as the honorary sergeant major for the 7th Infantry Regiment.

Robert J. Rielly

Further Reading

Blair, Clay. *The Forgotten War: America in Korea, 1950–1953*. New York: Anchor Books Doubleday, 1987.

Collier, Peter, and Nick Del Calzo. *Medal of Honor: Portraits of Valor beyond the Call of Duty*. New York: Artisan, 2006.

Mikaelian, Allen, and Mike Wallace. *Medal of Honor: Profiles of America's Military Heroes from the Civil War to the Present*. New York: Hyperion, 2003.

Murphy, Edward F. *Korean War Heroes*. Novato, CA: Presidio Press, 1992.

Smith, Larry. *Beyond Glory: Medal of Honor Heroes in Their Own Words—Extraordinary Stories of Courage from WWII to Vietnam*. New York: W. W. Norton, 2003.

Mize, Ola L.

Born: August 28, 1931
Died:
Home State: Alabama
Service: Army
Conflict: Korean War
Age at Time of Award: 23

Ola Lee Mize was born on August 28, 1931, in Albertville, Alabama, the son of a sharecropper. He dropped out of high school in 1946 after his freshman year to work and help support his family. Realizing he could bring in more money joining the Army, he went to enlist. Due, however, to the fact that he weighed a mere 120 pounds, he was turned away. Mize would not take no for an answer. He persisted and eventually was allowed to join.

Upon finishing basic training, he was assigned to the 82nd Airborne Division. Just as Mize's enlistment was up, war broke out in Korea and thwarted his plans to return to school. His desire for combat experience was too great, and he reenlisted for frontline infantry duty. He was assigned to Company K, 15th Infantry Regiment, 3rd Infantry Division under the command of Col. William Westmoreland, who would later serve as the senior US commander during the Vietnam War.

In the summer of 1953, Company K was assigned to defend a strategically important elevation near Surang-ni and the main line of resistance. The position was also in close proximity to United Nations Command (UNC) positions and critical lines of communication and supply. The position was dubbed Outpost Harry. In the early days of June 1953, aerial reconnaissance revealed a significant buildup of Chinese forces, indicating that an offensive was imminent.

On the night of June 10, the Chinese opened with a murderous artillery barrage on Company K. Mize, having learned of a comrade wounded at a forward listening post, set out with a medic amid the artillery fire to retrieve and treat the wounded soldier. As the barrage lifted, the remnants of the reeling unit were vastly outnumbered and swarmed by the Chinese assault. Mize, with a carbine he had recently swapped out for his older M-1 (unbeknownst to the carbine's owner), mowed down an estimated 40 Chinese. Throughout the course of the fighting, he was blown off his feet three times from artillery and grenade explosions that shredded his uniform. Nevertheless, Mize remained determined. He was able to regroup the company, utilizing destroyed American bunkers to fashion a defensible position. The American soldiers collected their wounded comrades and prepared for the coming hours of close-quarters and brutal hand-to-hand combat. During lapses in the Chinese assault, Mize ingeniously organized a small group who ran from one bunker to another, laying down fire and tossing grenades from advantageous positions, inflicting casualties and giving the enemy the impression that there remained a much larger contingent in front of them than there actually was. On one occasion, Mize saved the life of another comrade by shooting an enemy soldier who had crept up from behind. In another instance that night, he seized a friendly machine gun nest that had been overrun and killed 10 Communist soldiers, in the process rescuing several more wounded comrades.

In the early morning hours, Mize and a small group of men made their way back to the company command post. On the way, Mize and his men found several more wounded and a radio, which he used to call in an artillery strike on the Chinese position. When they finally reached the command post, the men there were astonished to see Mize, as they believed him to have been killed in the fighting. As the new day dawned, Mize assisted in coordinating a successful counterattack that recaptured Outpost Harry.

Upon discovering that he was to be awarded the Medal of Honor for his super-human efforts, Mize on several occasions attempted to refuse the recognition, insisting that it should go to his platoon. Finally, he was ordered to accept the medal, and, on September 7, 1954, in Denver, Colorado, he was decorated with the Medal of Honor by President Dwight D. Eisenhower.

After Korea, Mize eventually joined the fledgling the Army Special Forces (Green Berets). He would serve three tours in Vietnam with the 5th Special Forces Group, which worked closely with the Central Intelligence Agency (CIA) in the South Vietnamese Central Highlands, arming and training the Montagnard minority to oppose the Viet Cong as a part of the Civilian Irregular Defense Group (CIDG) program. Mize went on to command the 3rd Mobile Strike Command comprised of Cambodian troops.

In 1981, Ola Mize retired from his long and illustrious military career with the rank of colonel, having overseen Special Forces training at Fort Bragg, North Carolina, following his time in Vietnam. In 2004, Mize, along with numerous other Medal of Honor recipients, publicly endorsed George W. Bush's candidacy for president. In 2008, the US House of Representatives passed a bill naming the Veteran Affairs outpatient clinic in Gadsden, Alabama, where Mize currently resides, the "Colonel Ola Lee Mize Veterans Clinic" in his honor.

Jason C. Engle

Further Reading

Anderson, David L. *Columbia Guide to the Vietnam War*. New York: Columbia University Press, 2002.

Collier, Peter, and Nick Del Calzo. *Medal of Honor: Portraits of Valor beyond the Call of Duty*. New York: Artisan, 2006.

Moffett, William A.

Born: October 31, 1869
Died: April 4, 1933
Home State: South Carolina
Service: Navy
Conflict: Mexican Campaign (Veracruz)
Age at Time of Award: 46

Born in Charleston, South Carolina, on October 31, 1869, to George Hall Moffett and Elizabeth Moffet, William A. Moffett had an ordinary early childhood with the lone exception of losing his father in an accident on June 27, 1875. After attending

Charleston High School, Moffett's uncle, George H. Simonton, convinced him to apply to the US Naval Academy in Annapolis, Maryland. After passing the entrance examination, Moffett enter the academy on September 20, 1886. He graduated from the academy on June 10, 1890, and, after two years of sea duty, received his commission as an ensign on July 14, 1892.

During his early career, he served aboard various vessels including the cruiser USS *Baltimore*, wooden frigate USS *Portsmouth*, and the cruiser USS *Chicago* (commanded by Capt. Alfred Thayer Mahan), and he attended the Naval War College in Newport, Rhode Island. During the Spanish-American War, Moffett served aboard the USS *Charleston*, which took part in Adm. George Dewey's blockade of Manila Harbor.

By 1905, Moffett had risen to the rank of lieutenant commander and made a name for himself as a dedicated and highly competent naval officer. In 1911, the Navy promoted him to commander, and, in 1913, he took command of the light cruiser USS *Chester*.

In April 1914, the USS *Chester*, under the command of Moffett, was part of Adm. Frank E. Fletcher's US Navy task force detailed to preserve American interests in the burgeoning Mexican Revolution. On the evening of April 21–22, following the earlier landing of the initial US contingent at Veracruz, Moffett single-handedly navigated the USS *Chester*, without benefit of a pilot, into a position where the ship provided critical coverage of landing parties as well as fire support for US forces on shore. Throughout the engagement, the USS *Chester* remained under constant small arms fire and fired 160 rounds onto inshore positions.

On December 4, 1915, Moffett received the Medal of Honor. It is important to note that the actions in Veracruz were the first military action in which officers were eligible for the Medal of Honor. In addition to Moffett, 36 officers and 18 enlisted men also demonstrated gallantry and bravery that earned them the Medal of Honor.

After the events in Veracruz, Moffett continued to serve in the US Navy and was promoted to captain in August 1916, while he served as commander of the Great Lakes Naval Training Center. In the years 1918 to 1921, he achieved the pinnacle of a 20th-century naval career by commanding the battleship USS *Mississippi*.

Despite having commanded a battleship, Moffett had become increasingly convinced that aviation had a future in the US Navy. In March 1921, he became director of naval aviation with the temporary rank of rear admiral, which the US Navy made a permanent rank in 1923 as Moffett oversaw the creation of the Navy's Aviation Bureau. Moffett served as head of the bureau until his death, a result of the crash of the Navy's Airship USS *Akron*, on which he was a passenger, on April 4, 1933. During his tenure at the Aviation Bureau, Moffett worked to establish aviation as a critical component of the US Navy. For his steadfast support and tireless dedication, he is widely acknowledged at the "Father of Naval Aviation."

Moffett is buried in Arlington National Cemetery. The naval air station he helped establish at Sunnyvale, California, was renamed Moffett Field in his honor shortly after his death.

Sean N. Kalic

Further Reading

Coletta, Paolo, and Bernarr B. Coletta. *Admiral William A. Moffett and U.S. Naval Aviation.* Lewiston, NY: Edmin Mellen Press, 1997.

Trimble, William F. *Admiral William A. Moffett: Architect of Naval Aviation.* Annapolis, MD: Bluejacket Books, 2007.

Monsoor, Michael A.

Born: April 5, 1981
Died: September 29, 2006
Home State: California
Service: Navy
Conflict: Iraq
Age at Time of Award: 25

Born in Long Beach, California, on April 5, 1981, Michael Anthony Monsoor graduated from Garden Grove High School, in Garden Grove, California, in 1999. Enlisting in the US Navy in March 2001, Monsoor attended basic training at the Recruit Training Command, Great Lakes, Illinois. Forced to drop out of Basic Underwater Demolition/SEAL (BUD/S) training because of an injury, Monsoor reentered that program and, in September 2004, graduated as one of the top members of his class. He then completed basic airborne school; cold weather training in Kodiak, Alaska; and, in March 2004, SEAL Qualification Training at Coronado, California. Master-at-Arms Monsoor was then assigned to SEAL Team 3.

Seal Team 3 arrived in Ramadi, Iraq, in April 2006. There, Monsoor was regularly on patrol and was involved in frequent clashes with Iraqi insurgents. Monsoor was awarded a Silver Star for an action on May 9, 2006, in which he braved insurgent fire to rescue a wounded comrade.

On September 29, Monsoor was manning a machine gun with three SEAL and several Iraqi Army snipers assigned to a rooftop sniper detail when they became engaged in a firefight with insurgents, killing several. Fighting continued, and the sniper element came under insurgent small arms and rocket-propelled grenade attack. An insurgent from an unseen location then hurled a grenade on the roof. It bounced off Monsoor's body. As the only member of the detail to have easy access to an escape route, he might have saved himself but instead yelled "Grenade!" and covered the explosive device with his own body. Monsoor was badly wounded in the blast seconds later; although soon evacuated, he died 30 minutes later.

On March 31, 2008, Master-at-Arms Second Class Michael Monsoor was awarded the Medal of Honor for his selfless action in saving the lives of several of his colleagues. President George W. Bush presented the award to his family at the White House on April 8. Monsoor was the first Navy recipient of the Medal of Honor for the Iraq War and the third member of the US Armed Forces to receive the medal for Iraq. In October, the Navy Department announced that the *DDG-1001*, the second ship in the Zumwalt-class of destroyers, would be named in Monsoor's honor.

Spencer C. Tucker

Further Reading

Abruzzese, Sarah. "Bush Gives Medal of Honor to Slain Navy SEALs Member." *New York Times*, April 9, 2008.

Perry, Tony. "Destroyer to Bear O.C. SEAL's Name." *Los Angeles Times,* October 30, 2008.

Monti, Jared C.

Born: September 20, 1975
Died: June 21, 2006
Home State: Massachusetts
Service: Army
Conflict: Afghanistan
Age at Time of Award: 30

Born in Abington, Massachusetts, on September 20, 1975, Jared Christopher Monti grew up in Raynham, Massachusetts. He enlisted in the National Guard as a high school junior in March 1993 under the Delayed Entry Program. He graduated from Bridgewater-Raynham High School in 1994 and switched to active duty. Monti attended both basic and advanced training at Fort Sill, Oklahoma. He also received artillery observer training and earned the Parachutist Badge and Air Assault Badge. His initial duty assignment was at Fort Riley, Kansas. Monti was then assigned in Korea as part of 1st Battalion, 506th Infantry Regiment, in the demilitarized zone. Upon return from Korea, he was reassigned to Fort Bragg, North Carolina. From there, he went back to Korea and then to Fort Drum, New York.

In February 2006, Monti was assigned to Afghanistan as a targeting noncommissioned officer in the 3rd Squadron, 71st Cavalry Regiment, 3rd Brigade Combat Team of the 10th Mountain Division (Light Infantry) stationed at Fort Drum, New York. On June 21, 2006, Staff Sergeant Monti was the assistant leader of a 16-man

Jared C. Monti, US Army (US Army).

reconnaissance force that came under fire in a mountainous area near Gowardesh, Nuristan Province. In the ensuing firefight, two of the members of Monti's unit were separated from the rest, and both were wounded. Monti dragged one to safety under fire. He returned to assist the other wounded soldier but was killed by a rocket-propelled grenade. Monti was posthumously promoted to sergeant first class.

Monti was the second US service member to be awarded the Medal of Honor for actions in Afghanistan, and Monti's medal was the sixth for service in either Iraq or Afghanistan. Eight Medals of Honor have been awarded, all but one posthumously.

President Barack Obama signed the award in July 2009 and presented the Medal of Honor to Jared Monti's parents in a White House ceremony on September 17, 2009.

Spencer C. Tucker

Further Reading

Cavallaro, Gina. "Fallen Soldier to Receive Medal of Honor." *Army Times,* July 23, 2009.

"SGT 1st Class Jared C. Monti." *Soldiers* 65, no. 3 (March 2010): 8–9.

Weinstein, Susan Parkou. "Raynham's Jared C. Monti Posthumously Awarded Medal of Honor." *The Daily News Tribune* (Waltham, MA), July 23, 2009.

Munemori, Sadao S.

Born: August 17, 1922
Died: April 5, 1945
Home State: California
Service: Army
Conflict: World War II
Age at Time of Award: 22

Sadao S. Munemori was born on August 17, 1922, in Los Angeles and grew up near Glendale, California. His father, Kametaro, and mother, Nawa, were immigrants from Hiroshima. Their first child, Yuriko, had been born in Japan, but the rest of their children were born in Los Angeles. Sadao, nicknamed Spud, was a middle child.

At age 19, Munemori volunteered to join the Army and was inducted a month before Pearl Harbor was attacked on December 7, 1941. He was in training when over 100,000 Japanese Americans were sent to detention centers in the remote western United States. His family was sent to the Manzanar relocation center, which was located 230 miles northeast of Los Angles in the Owen's Valley at the foot of the Sierra Nevada range.

The first two years of Munemori's military service were spent at installations in Arkansas, Illinois, and Minnesota. In January 1944, he was sent to Camp Shelby, located a few miles south of Hattiesburg, Mississippi, where he was assigned to Company A of the 442nd Regimental Combat Team. In a letter from Camp Shelby to his family at Manzanar, Munemori stated that his decision to join the Army was the right thing to do because his home was in America.

Munemori arrived in Italy in April of 1944 as a replacement in the 100th Infantry Battalion, which had been fighting in Italy for nine months. It had landed at Salerno Bay south of Naples in September 1943 and participated in the battle for Monte Cassino.

The Anzio landing was launched in order to execute a flanking movement that would cut off the Nazis and open the way to Rome. The 100th Battalion joined the defense of the beachhead at Anzio and then participated in the push for Rome, which fell on June 5, 1944.

Later that month, the 100th Battalion was attached to the 442nd Regimental Combat Team, a larger Nisei unit that had just arrived in theater. After fighting at the Arno River in August 1944, the 442nd moved to France for an attack in the Vosges Mountains. There, Munemori and his unit participated in the rescue of the "Lost Battalion" from the 36th Division in the forests near Bruyeres.

After several months of light patrol duty, Munemori's unit was returned to Italy to aid in a breakthrough of the Gothic Line. The Apennines Mountains formed a defensive barrier to the Po Valley. The Nazis had fortified it so effectively that the 5th Army had not been able to break through it. The job was given to the 100th/442nd.

The assault on the Gothic Line began early on the morning of April 5, 1945. By 5:00 a.m., the 100th/442nd had reached the mountain heights undetected. A massive artillery barrage was laid down onto its objectives—the hills named Georgia and Florida.

Munemori's Company A was in the lead and advanced several hundred yards before being halted by intense enemy machine fire that inflicted heavy casualties on Company A. With his squad leader injured, Private First Class Munemori led his squad toward a Nazi machine gun emplacement. The Nazis counter attacked with grenades, but none were effective. Munemori took out the machine guns with grenades in a one man attack, but as he was crawling back under fire to the shell hole where men in his squad were taking cover, a grenade hit him in the helmet. It bounced off into the shell hole. Munemori immediately threw himself onto the grenade; the explosion killed him, but his action saved the lives of two others who suffered concussions and partial deafness.

The Medal of Honor was awarded posthumously to Sadao Munemori for "conspicuous gallantry." His family was informed of his heroic death at their residence at the Manzanar relocation center. He was buried in the veterans' section of the Evergreen Cemetery in Los Angeles. Munemori was the first Nisei (second-generation Japanese American) to receive the award.

In 1948, the troop transport *Wilson Victory* was renamed the *Private Sadao S. Munemori*. The ship saw extensive action during the Korean War, receiving four battle stars.

Andrew J. Waskey

Further Reading

Asahina, Robert. *Just Americans: The Story of the 100th Battalion/442nd Regimental Combat Team in World War II*. New York: Gotham Books, 2007.

Chang, Thelma, and Daniel K. Inouye. *I Can Never Forget: Men of the 100th/442nd*. Honolulu: SIGI Productions, 1995.

Crost, Lyn. *Honor by Fire: Japanese Americans at War in Europe and the Pacific*. Novato, CA: Presidio Press, 1997.

Holland, James. *Italy's Sorrow: A Year of War: 1944–1945*. New York: St. Martin's Press, 2008.

Proft, R. J., ed. *United States of America's Congressional Medal of Honor Recipients and Their Official Citations*. 4th ed. Columbia Heights, MN: Highland House, 2002.

Sterner, C. Douglas. *Go for Broke: The Nisei Warriors of World War II Who Conquered Germany, Japan, and American Bigotry*. Clearfield, UT: American Legacy Historical Press, 2008.

Tanaka, Chester. *Go for Broke*. New York: Random House, 1997.

Munro, Douglas Albert

Born: October 11, 1919
Died: September 27, 1942
Home State: Washington
Service: Coast Guard
Conflict: World War II
Age at Time of Award: 22

Douglas Albert Munro was born to James and Edith Munro on October 11, 1919, in Vancouver, British Columbia. Subsequently, he spent most of his early life in

Cle Elum, Washington. After graduating from Cle Elum High School in 1937, he attended Central Washington College of Education for a year. Not finding that to his liking, he enlisted in the Coast Guard in 1939. As an enlisted coastguardsman, he thrived and was promoted to first class petty officer rank (today E-6) in only three years on active duty. Munro was initially assigned to serve aboard the Coast Guard cutter *Spencer,* where he was promoted to signalman third class.

In the summer of 1941, he was transferred, no doubt due to his valuable skills as a signalman and the rapidly expanding Navy buildup prompted by gathering war clouds, to the transport fleet. He specifically requested that his executive officer on *Spencer* transfer him to the largest ship in a group of transports bound for the South Pacific, the *USS Hunter Liggett* (APA-17). This ship included numerous small boats as well as two of a new type of landing craft, the Landing Craft Tank (LCT). These were larger landing craft of British design, and it is unclear as to whether Munro knew of them. He certainly figured that getting aboard a transport heading for the active theater of war might put him into actual combat.

Douglas Albert Munro, US Coast Guard (Naval History and Heritage Command).

On August 7, 1942, the United States embarked on its first major amphibious assault of the Pacific War in the Solomon Islands. The primary goal was to seize a completed Japanese seaplane base on the island of Tulagi, but recent air intelligence photographs of a nearly completed Japanese airstrip on the nearby island of Guadalcanal resulted in the commitment of most of the landing forces to seize that island. Of the 22 ships in Rear Admiral R. K. Turner's invasion flotilla, 18 included Coast Guard personnel. The coastguardsmen were highly prized for their superior abilities as coxswains (skilled small-boat pilots), and they played a prominent role in the initial landings at Guadalcanal and other nearby islands. Munro, by now a signalman first class, was assigned to Transport Division 17.

At the time of the actual invasion, he was attached to the staff of Admiral Turner on board USS *McCawley* (APA-4) due to his abilities with radios. Munro actually landed on Tulagi with the first assault waves but two weeks later was transferred across "Iron Bottom Sound" to Guadalcanal, where the 1st Marine Division under Maj. Gen. Alexander A. Vandegrift was coming under increasing pressure by the Japanese attempting to recapture the airfield, now named Henderson Field. Munro and 24 other Coast Guard and Navy personnel were attached to the marines and stationed in an old coconut plantation known as Lunga Point Base. They provided all the small-boat services for the marines during this portion of the campaign.

On Sunday, Sept. 27, 1942, Marine lieutenant colonel Lewis B. "Chesty" Puller embarked three companies of his 7th Marines in landing craft. They planned to land west of the Matanikau River. Munro took charge of 10 LCPs (also known as Higgins Boats) and LCTs to transport Puller's men from Lunga Point to a small cove west of Point Cruz. The 500 marines landed and pushed inland unopposed and reorganized on a ridge about 500 yards from the beach. About the time they reached the ridge, they were attacked by an overwhelming Japanese force to the west of the river. Munro and the boats had already returned to Lunga Point when they got word that the marines were in trouble. Munro volunteered to lead the boats back to the beach to extract the marines. His Higgins Boat had a plywood hull, was slow and vulnerable, and was armed only with two .30 caliber machine guns.

As Munro led the boats ashore, the Japanese fired on the small boats, causing a number of casualties. Munro led the other boats to the beach two or three at a time to pick up the marines, who had withdrawn to the beach under heavy fire, and extract them on the landing craft. Munro, under constant fire, organized the evacuation of the marines and their wounded and provided covering fire from his Higgins Boat, which was interposed between the withdrawing marines and the Japanese. The citation for his Medal of Honor lists him being killed nearly simultaneously with this covering fire, but he was actually completing the supervision of the rescue of some additional marines trapped on a grounded LCT. Shortly after these marines escaped, a Japanese machine gun bullet hit him in the head. Munro died before reaching Lunga. In two weeks, he would have been 23. A month after his death, his parents were notified by the Navy Department that their son would be awarded the Medal of Honor, which was formally presented to them by President Franklin D. Roosevelt in a ceremony at the White House in May 1943. His mother, in honor of her son, was commissioned later that year as a lieutenant (junior grade) in the Coast Guard Women's Reserve and served on active duty until the end of the war.

Douglas Munro was buried on September 28, 1942, on Guadalcanal, but his remains were brought home after the war, and he was reinterred at the Laurel Hill Memorial Park in his hometown of Cle Elum. Two ships, the Coast Guard's USCGC *Munro* (WHEC-724) and the Navy's USS *Douglas A. Munro* (DE-422); a barracks building on the US Coast Guard Training Center Cape May; and an administrative and guest quarters building at the US Coast Guard Academy in New London, Connecticut, were named in his honor.

John T. Kuehn

Further Reading

Hargis, Robert, and Ramiro Bujeiro. *World War II Medal of Honor Recipients: Navy & USMC*. Oxford, UK: Osprey, 2003.

Kuehn, John T., and D. M. Giangreco. *Eyewitness Pacific Theater*. New York: Sterling Books, 2008.

Murphy, Audie L.

Born: June 20, 1924 (some sources say June 20, 1925)
Died: May 28, 1971
Home State: Texas
Service: Army
Conflict: World War II
Age at Time of Award: 20

On June 20, 1924, Audie L. Murphy became the 7th of 12 children to be born into a family of poor Texas sharecroppers. When Murphy was young, his father deserted the family, leaving them to fend for themselves. Seven months later, his mother died suddenly. With his mother's death and his father's departure, Murphy had to find work while his younger siblings relocated to an orphanage. When the United States entered World War II, he attempted to enter the Marine Corps. Since he weighed roughly 110 pounds and stood only five feet, six inches tall, the Marines quickly rejected him. However, a determined Murphy decided to put on weight and attempt to join the US Army. On June 30, 1942, he entered the Army and left home for infantry training soon after.

In February of 1943, Audie Murphy joined Company B, 15th Infantry Regiment of the 3rd Infantry Division in North Africa. Although he saw little combat in Africa, Murphy found plenty of action with his unit in Sicily, Italy, and Southern France. He also excelled in combat, heroically working his way up the enlisted ranks, and eventually received a battlefield promotion to second lieutenant. Rank advancements were not the only thing Murphy received due to his combat actions. By the time his unit reached Germany in January of 1945, Murphy had earned nearly every American combat medal and several medals from other countries. Even so, his actions in Germany on January 26, 1945, earned him his highest decoration of the war, the Medal of Honor.

Murphy, although wounded in combat the previous day, assumed command of Company B as the only surviving officer in the unit during combat operations in the Colmar Pocket region of Germany. He ordered his men to hold their positions and wait for reinforcement while two tank destroyers supported their position. A few hours later, six German Mark VI Tiger tanks with at least 200 infantrymen headed toward Murphy and his men. As he prepared his soldiers for the coming fight, one of the two tank destroyers mistakenly maneuvered into a ditch while trying to get a better firing position on the oncoming Germans. Murphy telephoned a nearby supporting artillery battalion to call for artillery fire in front of his position. Immediately, the German tanks opened fire on the remaining tank destroyer supporting Company B and disabled it.

As Murphy phoned corrections to his supporting artillery, the German tanks and troops continued toward his position. Realizing that his men were in danger, he quickly ordered his sergeant to move the men deeper in the woods to a safer position. As his men fell back, Murphy continued to call in artillery fire and immediately opened fire with his carbine at the advancing enemy soldiers roughly 200 yards from his position. After he fired all his ammunition, Murphy rushed to the burning tank destroyer and fired at the enemy with the .50-caliber machine gun mounted on the vehicle's turret. He continued to call in artillery support from his new position and eventually requested the shells to land right on top of his position. As the artillery rounds inched closer, Murphy pulled back in the direction of his men and was soon knocked to the ground by the explosion of the tank destroyer from which he had just been firing.

For his actions in single-handedly turning back an enemy armor force and saving his outnumbered company, Murphy received the Medal of Honor on June 2, 1945, in a ceremony near Salzburg, Austria. By the war's end, Murphy was America's most decorated soldier, and yet he still was not old enough to vote. Throughout the war he earned not only the Medal of Honor, but the Distinguished Service Cross, two Silver Stars, the Legion of Merit, three Purple Hearts, and two Bronze Stars, along with campaign medals, unit citations, and foreign decorations of the countries in which he served.

Audie Murphy quickly became popular back in the United States. He appeared on the cover of *Life* magazine and eventually gained so much attention that he received an invitation from Hollywood actor James Cagney to retreat to his home to avoid the public for a while. In following years, Murphy became an actor in several dozen films and eventually starred as himself in his autobiographical movie, *To Hell and Back*. Sadly, as time progressed, his popularity diminished, he failed with various business ventures, and he constantly faced problems with "battle fatigue," or post traumatic stress disorder (PTSD), as it is known today.

After many years in the public eye, America's most decorated soldier of World War II died tragically at a young age. On May 28, 1971, Audie Murphy flew on a private plane to Virginia with an investment group. The small plane carrying the group crashed just before reaching their destination of Martinsville, Virginia. Murphy was laid to rest at Arlington National Cemetery, where he received a burial with full military honors.

Thomas D. Lofton Jr.

Further Reading

Murphy, Audie. *To Hell and Back*. New York: Henry Holt, 1949.

Murphy, Edward F. *Heroes of World War II*. New York: Ballantine Books, 1990.

Tillman, Barrett. *Heroes: U.S. Army Medal of Honor Recipients*. New York: The Berkley Group, 2006.

Murphy, Michael P.

Born: May 7, 1976
Died: June 28, 2005
Home State: New York
Service: Navy
Conflict: Afghanistan
Age at Time of Award: 29

Born in Smithtown, New York, on May 7, 1976, Michael Patrick Murphy grew up on Long Island. He graduated from Pennsylvania State University in 1998 with bachelor's degrees in political science and psychology.

Although accepted to several law schools, Murphy decided to enter the Navy, and, in December 2000, he graduated from the US Navy's officer candidate school in Pensacola, Florida, and was commissioned an ensign. He then underwent Basic Underwater Demolition/SEAL (BUD/S) training at Coronado, California. On graduation from BUD/S, Murphy underwent further training at the US Army Airborne School, SEAL Qualification Training, and SEAL Delivery Vehicle (SDV) school. He then served in Hawaii, Florida, Qatar, and Djibouti.

In early 2006, Murphy was assigned to Afghanistan as a member of SDV Team 1. On June 27, 2005, Murphy took part in Operation Red Wing, leading a four-man reconnaissance unit that was inserted by helicopter east of Asadabad in Kunar Province near the border with Pakistan in an attempt to capture a top Taliban leader. Murphy and his men were soon discovered by Afghans cooperating with the insurgents, and, on June 28, the reconnaissance unit was surrounded and came under attack by 30–40 insurgents. In the ensuing firefight, Murphy's team inflicted numerous casualties on the attackers, but all of his team members were wounded. Disregarding his own wounds, Murphy knowingly left his relatively secure position and moved to an exposed area in order to get a clear signal to notify headquarters of events. He calmly continued to report his position and request assistance while under fire and then returned to his original position and continued to fight until mortally wounded. A helicopter dispatched to the scene with reinforcements was shot down with the loss of all 16 aboard. Two other members of Murphy's team, Gunner's Mate Second Class Danny Dietz and Sonar Technician (Surface) Second

Class Matthew Axelson, also perished in the firefight. Only Hospital Corpsman First Class Marcus Luttrell survived. All members of the team were awarded the Navy Cross for their actions that day.

Michael Murphy's actions were subsequently recognized by the award of the Medal of Honor. He was the first US serviceman to be so honored in the Afghanistan war and the first member of the US Navy to receive the award since the Vietnam War. On October 22, 2007, President George W. Bush presented the award to Murphy's family at the White House. On May 7, 2008, the Navy Department announced that *DDG-112*, the last planned ship in the Arleigh Burke–class of destroyers, would be named in Murphy's honor.

Spencer C. Tucker

Further Reading

Evans, Martin C. "Slain Patchogue Sailor to Get Medal of Honor." *Newsday,* October 11, 2007.

Hernandez, Raymond. "A Protector as a Child, Honored as a Hero." *New York Times,* October 22, 2007.

Murphy, Raymond G.

Born: January 14, 1930
Died: April 6, 2007
Home State: Colorado
Service: Marine Corps
Conflict: Korean War
Age at Time of Award: 23

Born on January 14, 1930, in Pueblo, Colorado, Raymond G. Murphy attended Adams State College, where he excelled in football, basketball, and baseball on his way to a degree in physical education. Upon graduating in 1951, Murphy enlisted in the Marine Corps Reserve. Murphy attended the Marine Corps' officer candidate school at Parris Island and, upon his graduation in September, received his commission as a second lieutenant.

After his commissioning, Murphy underwent further officer training throughout 1951 and 1952. By mid-1952, Murphy completed his officer training and found himself in command of a Marine infantry platoon Korea. As an officer, Second Lieutenant Murphy led the 3rd Platoon of Able Company, a part of the distinguished 5th Marine Regiment. While on patrol in November 1952, Murphy encountered enemy fire, and, with several of his men wounded, he successfully led his platoon back to base. For his actions, Murphy received the Silver Star.

In February 1953, Able Company was assigned to partake in Operation Clambake, a raid against two hills in the Ungok area of Korea. Murphy's platoon stood as a reserve and evacuation element as the operation commenced in the early hours of February 3, 1953. Despite the element of surprise, the marines assaulting Ungok found the Chinese forces strongly entrenched. Against troops in well-supplied, deep caves, the marines' advance soon stalled with many troops pinned down from enemy fire. Amid the confusion, Lieutenant Murphy personally scouted the front lines. Seeing the other platoons under fire, Murphy ordered the 3rd Platoon to advance on an enemy location in order to relieve the other units. Under fire from entrenched Chinese forces, Murphy led his platoon from position to position in order to rescue troops from the original assault.

During the action, Murphy attempted to remove an injured marine. As he was doing so, Murphy sustained injuries to his left side from a mortar blast that struck near him. Despite his wounds, Murphy continued to aid the marine, finally managing to move him to safety. Despite his own wounds, Murphy returned up the hill to continue his relief efforts. Making several trips up the hill, Murphy saw to it that his platoon provided covering fire during the evacuation while he personally led injured troops to safety. Under constant fire, Murphy took part of his platoon to support the assault teams. During the battle, Murphy killed two enemy soldiers. After the decision was made to call off the attack, Murphy continued to direct the evacuation of the wounded and also provided covering fire as the units withdrew from the hill.

At the conclusion of the battle, Murphy led a search-and-rescue team in an effort to locate any remaining troops. While carrying an injured marine down the hill on a stretcher, Murphy was hit in the hand from a piece of shrapnel from enemy artillery fire. Despite his various injuries, Murphy managed to carry the stretcher down the hill. He refused to be treated until he was sure all the wounded were accounted for.

Lieutenant Murphy was treated for his injuries aboard various medical ships and at a hospital in Japan before finally being transferred to the Mare Island Naval Hospital in California. During his recovery, Murphy was promoted to the rank of first lieutenant. Due to his injuries, the Marine Corps released Murphy from active duty in April 1953.

President Dwight D. Eisenhower presented Murphy the Medal of Honor on October 27, 1953, at a White House ceremony. Despite his injuries, Murphy remained in the Marine Corps Reserve until retiring in 1959. After serving in Korea, Murphy obtained a master's degree from Springfield College and briefly worked as a director of recreation in Massachusetts. Murphy then operated a bowling alley in Santa Fe, New Mexico, before taking a job at the New Mexico Veterans Administration (VA), where he retired as director in 1997. He continued to volunteer his services to assist veterans for the next seven years. In 2005, Murphy returned to his hometown of Pueblo.

Raymond Murphy passed away in Pueblo on April 6, 2007, at the age of 77. He was buried at the Santa Fe National Cemetery. In June 2008, the Albuquerque VA Hospital was officially renamed the Raymond G. Murphy VA Medical Center.

John Sager

Further Reading

Ballenger, Lee. *The Final Crucible: U.S. Marines in Korea.* Vol. 2, *1953.* Washington, D.C.: Brassey's, 2001.

Collier, Peter, and Nick Del Calzo. *Medal of Honor: Portraits of Valor beyond the Call of Duty.* New York: Artisan, 2006.

Jacobs, Bruce. *Korea's Heroes: The Medal of Honor Story.* New York: Berkeley Publishing, 1961.

Smith, Larry. *Beyond Glory: Medal of Honor Heroes in Their Own Words—Extraordinary Stories of Courage from WWII to Vietnam.* New York: W. W. Norton, 2003.

Norris, Thomas R.

Born: January 14, 1944
Died:
Home State: Florida
Service: Navy
Conflict: Vietnam War
Age at Time of Award: 32

Thomas R. Norris was born January 14, 1944, in Jacksonville, Florida. During his youth, his family moved several times, finally ending up in Washington, D.C. In 1963, Norris entered the University of Maryland, where he majored in sociology with an emphasis in criminology and was a two-time Atlantic Coast Conference wrestling champion in the 115-pound weight class. When he graduated in 1967, he enlisted in the Navy with the hopes of becoming a pilot. Unfortunately, his eyesight prevented Norris's desire to fly from being realized. Instead, he decided to volunteer for the Navy SEALs, graduating in BUD/S (Basic Underwater Demolition/SEAL) Class 45.

On April 10, 1972, during his second tour of duty in Vietnam, he received orders to rescue two pilots whose aircraft had been shot down deep into the North Vietnamese province of Quang Tri. He led a four-man team of Lein Doi Nguoi Nhai (LDNNs—US-trained South Vietnamese frogmen). The downed pilots were given instructions on where to meet Norris and his team. They found pilot Lt. Mark Clark just before dawn on April 11 and successfully evacuated him. On April 12, Norris's team suffered two casualties in a North Vietnamese Army (NVA) attack.

The following day, Norris and his team were notified of the location of the second pilot, Lt. Col. Gene Humbleton. After two unsuccessful attempts to reach Humbleton, they were forced to take a more daring approach. Norris, with LDNN Nguyen Van Kiet, dressed as peasant fishermen, paddled up the Song Mieu Giang River on a sampan, found Humbleton, loaded him into the boat, and covered him with leaves from a banana tree. With Humbleton on board, they cautiously headed back downstream toward their forward operating base (FOB), calling in air strikes on NVA patrols as they encountered them. The air strikes also provided a violent and chaotic diversion, allowing Norris and his team to close in on the FOB. However, before they arrived safely at their FOB, they came under intense NVA machine gun fire. Norris wisely called for another air strike on the NVA position, enabling them to reach the FOB and prepare Humbleton for evacuation.

Several years later, after the details of the mission were declassified, the successful rescue of these two pilots earned Norris the Medal of Honor, which was awarded to him on March 6, 1976, by President Gerald R. Ford. Additionally, Nguyen Van Kiet was decorated with the Navy Cross, becoming the only Vietnamese of the war to receive the honor.

Just six months after the Clark and Humbleton rescue mission, on October 31, 1972, Norris nearly lost his life leading an intelligence-gathering mission back into the Quang Tri Province. His team consisted of SEAL Engineman Second Class Michael Thornton and three Vietnamese LDNNs. Their mission was to capture an NVA soldier in an effort to gain information on the formerly South Vietnamese Cua Viet Naval River Base. The team, having departed on a small inflatable boat (IBS) from a South Vietnamese naval vessel, landed on shore and began their trek inland. Two hours later, they were informed that the vessel they departed from had been too far north and that they were outside of the intended location. In order to gain a more accurate fix on their location, Norris and company returned to their landing point. At this time, they came under heavy fire from a large NVA patrol. During the course of the intense firefight, Norris was shot in the head and was believed to be dead. Thornton, having suffered shrapnel wounds himself, was determined to retrieve Norris's body and dashed out under fire, slung Norris over his shoulder, and dashed back to their position. Eventually, the large NVA force overwhelmed the team, forcing them out to sea to swim back to the ship from which they had originally departed. With Norris on his back, Thornton and the LDNNs swam for two hours before arriving back at the ship. Thornton, too, received the Medal of Honor for his Herculean rescue of Norris. In all, Lieutenant Norris served three years in the Navy SEALs before being medically retired because of the wounds he suffered during this mission.

After several years of surgeries and medical procedures, Norris recovered from his wounds and, in 1979, joined the Federal Bureau of Investigation (FBI). During his time in the FBI, he served in its original Hostage Rescue Team. The 1988 film

BAT-21 was based on Norris's 1972 rescue mission. After 20 years of service in the FBI, Thomas R. Norris retired and now lives in Idaho.

Jason C. Engle

Further Reading

Bosiljevic, T. L. *SEALs: UDT/SEAL Operations in Vietnam.* Boulder, CO: Paladin Press, 1990.

Collier, Peter, and Nick Del Calzo. *Medal of Honor: Portraits of Valor beyond the Call of Duty.* New York: Artisan, 2006.

Dockery, Kevin. *Navy SEALs: A Complete History from World War II to the Present.* New York: Berkley Publishing, 2004.

Zimmerman, Dwight Jon, and John D. Gresham. *Beyond Hell and Back: How America's Special Forces Became the World's Greatest Fighting Unit.* New York: St. Martin's Press, 2007.

Novosel, Michael J.

Born: September 3, 1922
Died: April 2, 2006
Home State: Pennsylvania
Service: Army
Conflict: Vietnam War
Age at Time of Award: 47

Born in Etna, Pennsylvania, on September 3, 1922, Michael J. Novosel joined the US Army as an enlisted man in 1941, just months before the United States entered World War II. He "grew" a quarter inch to meet the aviator height requirement, passed flight school, and was commissioned in December 1942 in the Army Air Corps. Early in the war, he was an instructor; he then became a B-29 pilot in the last months of the war, flying missions over Japan.

Returning home at war's end, Novosel married his high school sweetheart and became an operational test pilot at Eglin Air Force Base. Because the newly created Air Force had too many officers, Novosel left the service. He opened a restaurant, rejoined the Air Force Reserve during the 1950–1953 Korean War, and became a pilot for Southern Airways. He retired from the Reserves in 1953.

Ten years later, President John F. Kennedy's assassination motivated Novosel to again enter military service. Turned down by the Air Force, at 42 he volunteered with the US Army as a warrant officer in June 1964. Drawing on his civilian helicopter training, he became a UH-1 (Huey) helicopter pilot. Novosel expected to become an instructor but was assigned to Fort Bragg, North Carolina, where he flew for Special Forces units and deployed to the Dominican Republic in 1965.

Novosel's first assignment to Vietnam in 1966 occurred 21 years after his last combat experience, and his assignment to a medevac unit was by happenstance; he had never heard of "dustoff," the slang designation for the aerial evacuation helicopters. As the only instrument-qualified pilot in the 283rd Medical Detachment (Helicopter Ambulance), he flew many of the night flights and often in thunderstorms. In his first Vietnam tour, he flew about 600 hours and received three Distinguished Flying Crosses. Back home in 1968, he was planning to leave the Army and return to airline flying but was diagnosed with glaucoma. Federal Aviation Administration rules would have prohibited him from flying as an airline pilot, but the Army was willing to keep him on, so he remained in the service.

Michael J. Novosel, US Army (US Army Medical Department Regiment).

During 1969–1970, Novosel returned to Vietnam, this time with the 82nd Medical Detachment (Helicopter Ambulance) flying in the Delta region of the Republic of Vietnam. With six helicopters, the 82nd supported all riverine elements and most South Vietnamese military forces, covering thousands of square miles.

At 4:00 p.m. on October 2, 1969, after already flying seven hours that day, Novosel received a message that South Vietnamese troops were cut off and pinned down by heavy communist ground fire, and there were an unknown number of wounded who needed to be evacuated. Novosel flew through choppy weather and rain to the area, parallel to the Cambodian border. Quickly evaluating the situation, he was told he was on his own with no covering fire (fighter-bombers and helicopter gunships turned up just before dark). His helicopter took hits on his first two runs in, and the fire was too intense to land. Novosel flew ovals while his crew grabbed wounded South Vietnamese. For the entire two-and-a-half-hour mission, Novosel flew by instinct and experience. Leaving the wounded at a Special Forces base camp, he repeatedly refueled so he could fly until dark. On his last run, a Viet Cong jumped up and emptied a magazine into the cockpit. Bullets hit each side of the pilot's seat, chest high, but only fragments hit Novosel. He saved 29 South Vietnamese soldiers that day and was nominated for the Medal of Honor by Gen. Creighton Abrams.

Later in his tour, Novosel's son, Michael Jr., was also assigned to the 82nd. During one week in late 1969, each rescued the other. Overall, in his two Vietnam tours, Novosel flew 2,038 hours in 2,543 missions and rescued 5,589 wounded. He completed his final tour in Vietnam in 1970 and returned to the United States.

On June 15, 1971, President Richard Nixon awarded the Medal of Honor to Novosel in a White House ceremony. The ceremony had been delayed so Novosel's son could finish his tour in Vietnam and be present.

After holding a number of posts, Michael Novosel's final assignment was at Fort Rucker as senior tactical adviser and counseling officer for pilot training. In his lengthy career, Novosel also received the Distinguished Flying Cross (with two oak leaf clusters), the Bronze Star, the Air Medal (with 60 oak leaf clusters), the Purple Heart, and five service or campaign medals. When Novosel retired from the Army in 1985, he had been a military aviator for 42 years and was the last World War II military aviator in the US to remain on active flying duty. While residing in Enterprise, Alabama, he remained active in the military community during retirement. He published a book on his experiences in 1999. Novosel died of complications from cancer in Washington, D.C., on April 2, 2006, and was buried with full military honors in Arlington National Cemetery.

Sanders Marble

Further Reading

Collier, Peter, and Nick Del Calzo. *Medal of Honor: Portraits of Valor beyond the Call of Duty.* New York: Artisan, 2006.

Novosel, Michael. *Dustoff: The Memoir of an Army Aviator.* Novato, CA: Presidio Press, 1999.

Reece, Beth. "Father and Son at War." *Soldiers Magazine* 58, no. 11 (2003): 16–17.

O'Hare, Edward Henry

Born: March 13, 1914
Died: November 26, 1943
Home State: Missouri
Service: Navy
Conflict: World War II
Age at Time of Award: 29

Edward H. O'Hare was born on March 13, 1914, in St. Louis, the son of E. J. O'Hare, a wealthy businessman and attorney. Ed had always been interested in flying; his father thought the Navy would be a fine career for him and secured him an appointment to the Naval Academy. O'Hare earned the nickname Butch during some joking around in his sophomore year at Annapolis. Upon graduation from the Naval

Academy, he received choice duty on the battleship USS *New Mexico* (BB-40). In 1939, shortly after he had started flight training at Naval Air Station (NAS) Pensacola, his father was murdered, probably assassinated by Al Capone's henchmen as a result of providing the government information that had been used to put Capone away.

Upon the eve of World War II, O'Hare was assigned to VF-3 ("Fighting Three") at NAS North Island, San Diego, California. It was here in the summer of 1941 that he and his innovative commanding officer, Lt. Cdr. James "Jimmie" Thach, developed the famous fighter tactic known as the "Thach Weave." Shortly afterward, in September, O'Hare married Rita Wooster. The Japanese attack on Pearl Harbor found O'Hare and Rita living in Coronado as O'Hare's squadron desperately worked up in preparation for war. O'Hare's squadron was loaded aboard the carrier *Saratoga,* which then proceeded to Hawaii.

On February 20, 1942, the carrier *Lexington*, with O'Hare onboard, had been assigned the dangerous task of penetrating enemy-held waters north of New Ireland in the south Pacific. Late in the day, the Japanese attacked. Nine Japanese G4M1 "Betty" bombers, detected by CXAM radar, were reported on the way. Six F4F Wildcats, two piloted by O'Hare and Thach, roared off to intercept them. O'Hare and his wingman actually worked against the second wave of attackers. The other F4Fs were too far away to reach most of the enemy planes before they released their bombs, and O'Hare's wingman discovered his guns were jammed. O'Hare stood alone between *Lexington* and the threat.

Using careful and controlled bursts of fire, O'Hare started to shoot up the enemy formation from the rear first, making every shot count and coming incredibly close to each of his targets. One by one, he attacked the oncoming bombers until five had been downed. Thach later reported that at one point he saw three of the bombers falling in flames at the same time. By now, Thach and the other pilots had joined the fight. This was lucky because O'Hare was out of ammunition. The Wildcats took care of several more bombers, and *Lexington* managed to evade the few bombs that were released. Afterward, Thach figured out that O'Hare had used only 60 rounds of ammunition for each plane he destroyed. He had single-handedly saved the *Lexington*. He was promoted to lieutenant commander and awarded the Medal of Honor by President Roosevelt.

O'Hare, against his own desires, toured the United States after the award promoting the sale of war bonds. Shortly after the critical battle of Midway, he returned to the Pacific, not to combat but to train new pilots and stand up various fighter squadrons and even air groups. He was to spend most of his time on the Island of Maui until returning to combat in late 1943. In November of that year, the central Pacific drive began in the Gilbert Islands (Tarawa and Makin), and the carriers were covering the landings. O'Hare and his comrades were now equipped with the new F6F Hellcats. From their bases in the Caroline and Mariana islands, the Japanese developed tactics that sent torpedo-armed Bettys on night missions against the US fleet. In late November, they launched these low-altitude strikes almost nightly in a deadly attempt to get at the carriers and other American ships.

O'Hare was now the air group commander (CAG) aboard the USS *Enterprise*, one of the most storied ships in the Pacific. He was involved in developing night fighting countertactics, the first of their kind in Navy, involving tandem flight operations by radar-equipped torpedo bombers (TBF Avengers) and the smaller, faster Hellcats.

On the night of November 26–27, 1943, the Japanese attacked Rear Admiral Arthur Radford's carriers as they steamed south from Makin Island. Aboard *Enterprise*, fighter direction officers (FDOs) attempted to vector O'Hare's two sections, each composed of two TBFs and one Hellcat, against the attackers. The goal was for the Avengers to find the target and send the Hellcat in to destroy it. In the confusion of the engagement, O'Hare was probably lost to friendly fire from an Avenger that thought it was engaging another Japanese bomber. Nonetheless, O'Hare's "Black Panthers" had broken up the Japanese night air attack, downing several bombers (out of total force of around 30). Butch O'Hare died in much the same way he had earned his Medal of Honor—protecting his carrier from an overwhelming air attack. On September 19, 1949, the Chicago airport was renamed O'Hare International Airport in his honor.

John T. Kuehn

Further Reading

Ewing, Steve, and John Lundstrom. *Fateful Rendezvous*. Annapolis, MD: Naval Institute Press, 1997.

Morison, Samuel Eliot. *The Two-Ocean War*. Boston, MA: Little, Brown, 1963.

O'Kane, Richard Hetherington

Born: February 2, 1911
Died: February 16, 1994
Home State: New Hampshire
Service: Navy
Conflict: World War II
Age at Time of Award: 33

Born in Dover, New Hampshire, on February 2, 1911, Richard Hetherington O'Kane graduated from the US Naval Academy in 1934 and began a series of tours aboard cruisers and destroyers. He entered the submarine service in 1938. After duty aboard the mine-laying submarine *Argonaut*, O'Kane reported to the submarine *Wahoo* in early 1942. When Lt. Cdr. Dudley W. Morton took command of the *Wahoo* after her second war patrol, O'Kane became her executive officer. Morton and O'Kane then worked closely to develop more aggressive submarine tactics, which proved to be some of the most effective of the war. The *Wahoo* was soon the Navy's most effective submarine, sinking 16 Japanese vessels totaling 45,000 tons between May and July 1943.

In July 1943, O'Kane was ordered to fit out and take command of the new submarine *Tang.* He commanded the *Tang* throughout her career, implementing and improving on the tactics he and Morton had previously developed. During her fifth war patrol on October 24, 1944, while between Taiwan and the Philippines in an attack on a Japanese convoy, one of the *Tang*'s own Mark XVIII torpedoes malfunctioned, circled back, and sank her. Only O'Kane and eight of his crew survived the sinking; they were picked up by Japanese ships. The *Tang* was credited with sinking 24 Japanese ships totaling 93,285 tons.

O'Kane spent the duration of the war in a Japanese prisoner-of-war camp. For the *Tang*'s final patrol, O'Kane was awarded the Medal of Honor. O'Kane remains the highest-scoring submarine commander in US naval history.

In 1949, Richard O'Kane commanded Submarine Division 32. Promoted to captain in 1953, he attended the Naval War College and then commanded Submarine Division 7 at Pearl Harbor. O'Kane held various commands after the war, including the Navy submarine school at New London and Submarine Squadron 7. O'Kane retired from active duty in 1957 as a rear admiral. He died at Petaluma, California, on February 16, 1994.

Edward F. Finch

Further Reading

Beach, Edward L. *Submarine!* New York: Holt, 1952.

Blair, Clay. *Silent Victory: The Submarine War against Japan.* Philadelphia: Lippincott, 1975.

O'Kane, Richard H. *Clear the Bridge! The War Patrols of the USS* Tang. Chicago: Rand McNally, 1977.

Tuohy, William. *The Bravest Man: The Story of Richard O'Kane and the U.S. Submariners in the Pacific War.* Phoenix Mill, UK: Sutton, 2001.

Okubo, James K.

Born: May 30, 1920
Died: January 29, 1967
Home State: Washington
Service: Army
Conflict: World War II
Age at Time of Award: 24

James K. Okubo, US Army (US Army Medical Department Regiment).

James K. Okubo was born on May 30, 1920, in Anacortes, Washington. After the attack on Pearl Harbor, he was sent with his family to the Heart Mountain War Relocation Center in Wyoming. The camp, 1 of 10 in which Japanese Americans were interned, was located in Park County between Cody and Powell on a Bureau of Reclamation site that was upgraded to house over 10,000 internees.

Although incarcerated, the internees were still subject to the draft, which sparked the Heart Mountain Fair Play Committee, an antiwar organization. Some of its members were convicted of conspiracy to violate the Selective Service Act, and 85 Japanese Americans were convicted of draft evasion. However, 799 Japanese Americans either volunteered or were drafted into military service. One of those who served was James Okubo. He was inducted at Bellingham, Washington, and, after completing training as a medic, was assigned to the 442nd Regimental Combat Team (RCT), a unit made up mostly of second-generation Japanese Americans (Nisei) that would become one of the most highly decorated American units of the war.

In October 1944, the 442nd RCT had relocated from the Italian front to the new front in southern France and was attached to the 36th Infantry Division. Okubo was serving in the 442nd as a combat medic with the Medical Detachment with a rank of technician fifth grade.

On October 28, 1944, Okubo's unit was near Biffontaine, eastern France, in the Foret Domaniale de Champ. During the battle that day, Okubo distinguished himself by rescuing a number of his wounded buddies. When the unit came under heavy fire from entrenched German positions, Okubo crawled 150 yards to a place that was within 40 yard of enemy lines. The Germans threw two grenades in his direction, but he was uninjured. Leaving this last covered position, he repeatedly braved the incoming fire to carry back his wounded comrades.

Okubo continued to treat the wounded while under intense enemy fire from small arms and machine guns; that day he treated 17 men, and the next day he repeated these actions, again braving enemy fire to treat 7 more wounded men in forward positions.

On November 4, 1944, Okubo ran 75 yards while under intense enemy fire to pull a severely wounded man from a burning tank, no doubt saving the man from certain death.

For his valor in late October and early November, Okubo was recommended for the Medal of Honor. However, he received the Silver Star instead under the mistaken belief that medics were not eligible to receive the Medal of Honor.

At the end of World War II, Okubo was mustered out while still at his rank of technician fifth grade. He attended college on the GI Bill and subsequently became a dentist. On January 29, 1967, Doctor Okubo was killed in an automobile accident in Detroit, Michigan. He was buried in Woodlawn Cemetery in Detroit. He was survived by his wife, Nobuyo Okubo of Walled Lake, Michigan.

In 1966, Congress, concerned about racial prejudice during wartime, directed the secretary of the army to conduct a review of the service records of Asian Americans and Pacific Islanders who had been awarded the Distinguished Service Cross in World War II. Ultimately, the investigation resulted in a recommendation to upgrade 21 of these awards to the Medal of Honor. The review also concluded that James Okubo should also have been awarded the Medal of Honor. However, it took a special act of Congress sponsored by Senator Daniel K. Akaka (D-HI) to authorize the awarding of the Medal of Honor to Okubo.

In a special White House ceremony on June 21, 2000, President Bill Clinton awarded the Medal of Honor to the 22 Asian Americans and Pacific Islanders whose earlier medals had been upgraded, all but 7 posthumously. James Okubo's medal was presented to his surviving family. In 2002 the U.S Army named a military medical clinic in Okubo's honor at Fort Lewis, Washington.

Andrew J. Waskey

Further Reading

Chang, Thelma, and Daniel K. Inouye. *I Can Never Forget: Men of the 100th/442nd.* Honolulu: SIGI Productions, 1995.

Holland, James. *Italy's Sorrow: A Year of War: 1944–1945.* New York: St. Martin's Press, 2008.

Proft, R. J., ed. *United States of America's Congressional Medal of Honor Recipients and their Official Citations.* 4th ed. Columbia Heights, MN: Highland House, 2002.

Tanaka, Chester. *Go for Broke.* New York: Random House, 1997.

Olive, Milton L., III

Born: November 7, 1946
Died: October 22, 1965
Home State: Illinois

Service: Army
Conflict: Vietnam War
Age at Time of Award: 18

Born in Chicago, Illinois, on November 7, 1946, Milton Lee Olive III enlisted in the US Army right after high school graduation. By 1965, Olive was serving in Vietnam as a private first class in Company B of the 2nd Battalion (Airborne), 503rd Infantry Regiment, 173rd Airborne Brigade.

Olive had served less than five months in country when, on October 22, 1965, his platoon became temporarily pinned down under heavy Viet Cong gunfire while conducting combat operation near Phu Cuong in III Corps Tactical Zone. The platoon retaliated and scattered the enemy, who fled the area. Olive's platoon broke into small squads in pursuit. Olive and four fellow soldiers were making their way through the dense jungle when the Viet Cong suddenly threw a grenade into their group. Upon seeing the grenade, Olive immediately grabbed it, pulled it to his body, and fell to the ground with it, using his body to shield the explosion from the other four soldiers, saving their lives. For his selfless act of bravery, Olive was nominated for the Medal of Honor.

At a ceremony on the steps of the White House, President Lyndon B. Johnson presented Olive's Medal of Honor to his father and stepmother, citing Olive's conspicuous gallantry and intrepidity at the risk of his life above and beyond the call of duty. Two of the four soldiers whose lives Olive saved on that October day attended the ceremony.

Milton Olive was the first African American of the Vietnam War to receive the Medal of Honor. Olive's body was returned to the United States; he was buried in West Grove Cemetery in Holmes County, Mississippi. His home state of Illinois has paid tribute to Olive, naming a park and a college in his honor.

Debra J. Sheffer

Further Reading

Curtis, Arthur S. *Thirty-Seven Greatest Army Heroes.* N.p., 1969.

Murphy, Edward F. *Vietnam Medal of Honor Heroes.* New York: Ballantine Books, 2005.

US Congress. Senate. Committee on Veterans Affairs. *Medal of Honor Recipients, 1863–1978: "In the Name of the Congress of the United States."* Washington, D.C.: Government Printing Office, 1979.

O'Neill, Richard W.

Born: August 28, 1898
Died: April 9, 1982
Home State: New York

Service: Army
Conflict: World War I
Age at Time of Award: 20

Richard W. O'Neill was born in New York City on August 28, 1898. He lived in Harlem and was a professional boxer, winning 12 fights. In June 1916, he joined the famed 69th Infantry, a mostly Irish Catholic New York National Guard regiment, where he rose to the rank of sergeant. The regiment was later redesignated as the 165th Infantry after it joined the Rainbow Division in August 1917. From September 1 to October 25, 1917, the unit trained at Camp Mills, New York. In November, the regiment sailed for France; in February, the regiment trained with the French 32nd Battalion of Chasseurs. From March to June, the regiment conducted defensive operations in the Baccarat sector of Lorraine. Then, in June, they moved to the Champagne region, where the 165th participated in the defense against the last major German offensive on July 15.

Three days later, the Allied counteroffensive, known as the Aisne-Marne Offensive, began. On July 25, the 42nd Division was attached to the American I Corps, part of the French 6th Army southwest of Reims, and relieved the US 26th Division. Elements of the 42nd Division advanced on July 26 and maintained contact with the enemy as they withdrew to the Ourcq River. O'Neill's unit occupied a supporting role until July 28. On that day, they crossed the Ourcq.

By July 30, his regiment was bogged down in front of Meurcy Farm about a mile north of the river. They eventually made the fortified farm untenable for the Germans but then had to advance through the Brulé forest, which was littered with German machine gun positions. Sergeant O'Neill was in command of a platoon in Company D. O'Neill was ordered to take charge of the company, which only had 42 men remaining out of 250, and clear out the machine guns blocking the regiment's advance.

O'Neill had quickly outpaced his men when his rifle was shot from his hands; he found himself locked in fierce hand-to-hand fighting. He was completely isolated from his men with only a pistol and a handful of grenades. Noticing a camouflage-covered pit nearby, he dove toward it. To his surprise, O'Neill dropped among a machine gun nest with 25 startled Germans. Reacting quickly, the sergeant threw a grenade at them and began firing with his pistol. Three went down before the others charged toward him. O'Neill was hit several times during the ensuing exchange, but he stoically continued discharging his weapon. Then, to his amazement, about 20 Germans threw up their hands and surrendered. As he marched them back toward the American lines, another set of German machine guns opened up on them. Several of the prisoners were killed, and O'Neill was hit again. Unable to walk or crawl, he rolled down the hill toward safety, all the while being peppered by more bullets. As his men wrapped him in a blanket to carry him to an aid station, O'Neill demanded to make a report to his commanding officer, Maj. William Donovan. While he was relaying vital information, he passed out.

Just a few months after this action, in October 1918, when O'Neill was convalescing at a hospital on the Spanish border, he browbeat his doctor into releasing him so he could make his way back to his unit. The 165th was participating in the Meuse-Argonne Offensive. O'Neil was shot in the right hand, and his arm became partially paralyzed.

In 1919, he returned to the United States and studied at Columbia University to become an electrical engineer. In 1921, O'Neill was awarded the Medal of Honor by President Warren G. Harding for his actions in the Brulé forest that day in July 1918. Altogether, he received 14 awards for his valor in combat, including several from foreign nations, making him one of New York's most decorated soldiers of the war.

In 1975, a hall was named after him at Camp Smith in Peekskill, New York. Richard O'Neill died on April 9, 1982, and is buried in Gate of Heaven Cemetery, Hawthorne, New York.

Lon Strauss

Further Reading

American Battle Monuments Commission. *42nd Division, Summary of Operations in the World War*. Washington, D.C.: Government Printing Office, 1944.

Demeter, Richard. *The Fighting 69th: A History*. Pasadena, CA: Cranford Press, 2002.

Duffy, Francis P. *Father Duffy's Story: A Tale of Humor and Heroism, of Life and Death with the Fighting 69th*. New York: George H. Doran, 1919.

Harris, Stephen L. *Duffy's War: Fr. Francis Duffy, Wild Bill Donovan, and the Irish Fighting 69th in World War I*. Dulles, VA: Potomac Books, 2006.

Page, John U. D.

Born: February 8, 1904
Died: December 11, 1950
Home State: Philippines
Service: Army
Conflict: Korean War
Age at Time of Award: 46

Born in Malahi Islands, Luzon, Philippines, on February 8, 1904, John Upshur Dennis Page graduated from Princeton University in 1926. Page enlisted in the US Army in St. Paul, Minnesota. Although Page served in the Army during World War II, he did not see combat. Throughout the war, Page was stationed at Fort Sill, Oklahoma, where he helped train troops.

CHOSIN (CHANGJIN) RESERVOIR CAMPAIGN

As part of MacArthur's goal to finish the Korean War by Christmas 1950, the United Nations Command (UNC) drove past the 38th parallel and made a push toward the Yalu River. In support of this offensive, on October 25, UNC forces made an administrative amphibious landing at Wonson on the east side of the peninsula. Once ashore, UNC troops moved north to the city of Hamhung and were tasked to relieve a Korean Army corps and then occupy both the Chosin and Fusen reservoir areas. Once these areas were secured, UNC forces were then expected to advance north to the Yalu River. Key to the operation was a 78-mile, narrow main supply route (MSR) stretching from the town of Yudanm-ni, west of the Chosin Reservoir, south to the city of Hungnam on the shores of the Sea of Japan.

Days before, on October 19, and unknown to the UNC forces, Communist Chinese Forces (CCF) secretly crossed the Yalu River in support of the North Korean Army. Facing the UNC in the Chosin area was the 9th CCF Army Group comprising approximately 60,000 men. As a result, UNC forces, consisting of the 1st Marine Division's 25,000 men plus 2,500 US Army, UK, and Korean troops, were facing 12 divisions of Chinese regulars with the communists' sole mission being the destruction of the UNC forces. In early November, captured CCF soldiers reported that large Chinese units were already in the vicinity of the Chosin Reservoir preparing to assault UNC formations. As the UNC pushed cautiously north, they were probed by CCF forces that began encircling elements of the 1st Marine Division in the channelized and mountainous terrain.

During the first part of November, the weather in Korea started to turn for the worse, and subzero temperatures became the norm. Temperatures continued to fall throughout the campaign and reached as low as −35°F. In such conditions, automatic weapons malfunctioned, canteens froze, vehicles stopped working, and cases of frostbite were common. Compounding the cold temperatures were 35- to 40-mile-per-hour winds that made the experience even more miserable. Digging a decent fighting position was next to impossible as nearly frostbitten hands struggled to break ground frozen some 18 inches down.

By November 18, marines pushed up to the Chosin Reservoir, began improving the MSR, and started building a C-47 capable airstrip just south of the reservoir at Hagaru-ri. On Thanksgiving, the marines continued north to the town of Yudam-ni west of the reservoir, while on November 25 an Army task force under Lt. Col. Don Faith took up a position on the reservoir's eastern edge. In the afternoon of November 28, after the Chinese assaulted the Army position, Faith was visited by the X Corps commander, Maj. Gen. Ned Almond, who reported that there was nothing beyond the Army perimeter except retreating enemy. Almond's quip proved woefully wrong as, hours later, Faith's command was assaulted by CCF forces. For five days during the enemy assault, Faith personally led defensive actions, saw to the evacuation of the wounded, and was killed during an attack he was personally leading against a CCF roadblock. For his actions during this period, he was posthumously awarded the Medal of Honor.

Similarly, at Yudam-ni, the CCF sprung a trap that sent three divisions to envelop and destroy the marines. Additionally, CCF forces attacked the MSR near Koto-ri and Hagaru-ri while also assaulting other UNC positions. Essentially surrounded, the UNC's only option was to withdraw. Despite the overwhelming odds, the UNC then conducted offensive operations in a different direction. Supported by effective US close air support flying in dangerous mountain terrain, UNC troops moved at night. Attacking CCF forces in the hills surrounding the MSR, the marines from Yudam-ni made an orderly march south. On the same day as Faith's action, Marine first lieutenant Frank Mitchell repulsed a CCF attack while covering the marines' withdraw from Yudam-ni. Additionally, he organized a recovery team to extract marine casualties stuck behind enemy lines. Despite his own wounds, Mitchell led the recovery effort until he was mortally wounded by enemy small arms fire. Because of his actions, Mitchell was awarded the Medal of Honor. As a result of acts like Mitchell's, and many others, the marines reached Hagaru-ri on December 3.

After evacuating their wounded at the Hagaru-ri airfield and replenishing supplies, UNC forces continued their movement south toward Koto-ri despite CCF roadblocks and other obstacles. On November 29, as the CCF attacked the UNC position at Hagaru-ri, Marine major Reginald Myers collected a group of soldiers and marines and conducted a series of counterattacks on the east side of the UNC defensive perimeter. While leading these attacks, Myers directed mortar and artillery fire for 14 hours in the subzero temperatures, resulting in over 1,100 enemy casualties. For his action, he too was awarded the Medal of Honor.

Upon reaching Koto-ri, UNC troops evacuated the men wounded en route, and, on December 8, they continued south. As the UNC forces continued on the MSR, they were continuously attacked by CCF forces. On the night of December 10, Army lieutenant colonel John Page was with a convoy when it was stopped by enemy fire. Making his way to the front of the column, he led an attack that disrupted the enemy position, resulting in several CCF casualties. He continued his assault single-handedly until mortally wounded. As a result of this action and several others he had conducted over a 10-day period, he was posthumously awarded the Medal of Honor.

When reaching the lowland littorals, CCF attacks abated as relief columns coming north from Hamhung met the UNC troops. Conducting an amphibious withdrawal, all UNC units were evacuated through the Hungnam port by Christmas Eve. In all, UNC forces claim some 25,000 Chinese were killed and over 12,500 wounded. Conversely, the UNC forces suffered over 1,000 casualties with 9,000 wounded or missing in action. Indicative of the bravery exhibited throughout this campaign, 17 soldiers and marines earned Medals of Honor for their actions.

John M. Curatola

Page got his chance to prove his mettle in combat shortly after he arrived in Korea in November 1950. Assigned to X Corps Artillery, Lieutenant Colonel Page was attached to the 52nd Transportation Battalion. At dawn on November 29, Page led a nine-jeep convoy north from Hamhung to Koto-ri in order to establish communications points for regulating traffic along the main supply route to 1st Marine Division positions in the north. Having accomplished his mission, Page and his driver began their return trip to Hamhung. As darkness fell, they came upon a force of Chinese troops preparing to ambush a 96th Field Artillery radio relay unit. Page and his driver attempted to return to Koto-ri for help. However, the Chinese forces fired at Page and his driver, whereupon both men promptly took cover in a ditch along the side of the road. Lieutenant Colonel Page told his driver that he would provide suppressing fire while the driver was to get in the jeep and withdraw to a position around a bend in the road. The driver, Cpl. David E. Klepsig, jumped in the jeep and looked up to see Page standing in the middle of the road firing at the Chinese with his M-1 carbine. The startled Chinese fled, and Page and Klepsig continued their trip to Koto-ri.

By the following day, Chinese forces had succeeded in surrounding the entire Koto-ri region. Although separated from his unit, Page took the initiative and organized an infantry company composed of assorted available Army troops, most of them separated from their parent units. Calling upon his experience training troops, Page managed to create an effective fighting force and drew up battle plans and had them approved by the Marines, who controlled the area.

Over the next 12 days, Page and his men, along with the Marine units at Koto-ri, held off the Chinese while also supporting the retreat of X Corps units from the Chosin River area. During this time, Page supervised the construction of a small airstrip for evacuating wounded. He also took part in a reconnaissance flight during which he dropped hand grenades down onto enemy positions.

Page flew to the secure location of Hamhung in early December in order to arrange for artillery support to cover the withdrawal from Koto-ri. However, rather than remain in the rear, Page flew back in order to be with the men he had trained. With the troops from Koto-ri providing a rear guard, units from the 1st Marines and 7th Infantry Division began the march back to Hungnam harbor. During the withdrawal, a Chinese ambush threatened to cut off the rear guard forces. Page, realizing the danger, manned a machine gun on an abandoned tank while the Koto-ri convoy made its escape.

On the night of December 10, a small group of Chinese troops came upon a Marine company guarding a supply truck column. Page and a marine, Pfc. Marvin Wasson, stormed the Chinese position in order to break up their attack. Despite being outnumbered, Page and Wasson managed to halt the attack long enough for a larger relief force to arrive. However, prior to reinforcements appearing, Wasson was wounded and Page was killed by enemy fire. The following morning, Page's body was recovered. His position was surrounded by 16 enemy dead.

Lt. Col. John Page had been killed by enemy fire on December 11, 1950, after 12 days of bitter fighting. He was buried in Arlington National Cemetery and posthumously received the Navy Cross for his gallant actions. Despite this, Page would not be posthumously awarded the Medal of Honor until 1957, after Congress had passed special legislation authorizing the awarding of the medal despite the number of years since Page's actions. Page was the second most senior man to be awarded the Medal of Honor during the Korean War. Page was further honored when the military named Camp Page, Korea, in his honor. Camp Page housed US troops until its closure in 2005.

John Sager

Further Reading

Blair, Clay. *The Forgotten War: America in Korea 1950–1953*. New York: Times Books, 1987.

Jacobs, Bruce. *Korea's Heroes: The Medal of Honor Story*. New York: Berkeley Publishing, 1961.

Mossman, Billy C. *United States Army in the Korean War: Ebb and Flow November 1950–July 1951*. Washington, D.C.: Government Printing Office, 1990.

Tillman, Barrett. *Heroes: U.S. Army Medal of Honor Recipients*. New York: Berkley Publishing Group, 2006.

Wise, James E., Jr., and Scott Barron. *The Navy Cross: Extraordinary Heroism in Iraq, Afghanistan, and Other Conflicts*. Annapolis, MD: Naval Institute Press, 2007.

Paige, Mitchell

Born: August 31, 1918
Died: November 15, 2003
Home State: Pennsylvania
Service: Marine Corps
Conflict: World War II
Age at Time of Award: 24

Born August 31, 1918, in Charleroi, Pennsylvania, Mitchell Paige served 28 years in the US Marine Corps and held almost every rank and assignment in an infantry battalion from private to commanding officer. Paige tried to enlist at the age of 17 but was initially turned away from the Marines because of his youth. After another year, and following graduation from high school in 1936 in McKeesport, Pennsylvania, he enlisted in the Marines and went to boot camp at Parris Island, South Carolina.

After boot camp, he saw service in both the Caribbean and on the West Coast. Subsequently, he was assigned duties in the Far East, first serving in Cavite, in the Philippines. Once the Sino-Japanese war started, Paige was reassigned to duty in China at Shanghai and Teinsen. In 1940, he was sent stateside and eventually stationed at Guantánamo Bay, Cuba, and was part of the initial forming of the 1st Marine Division.

After World War II began and while serving with the 1st Marine Division, Paige participated in America's first offensive action in the Pacific War, Operation Watchtower—the invasion of Guadalcanal. During this operation, Paige was assigned as a platoon sergeant for a .30 caliber machine gun section. On October 25, 1942, Paige's battalion was ordered to defend the all-important Henderson Airfield, which was surrounded by thick jungle foliage and steep terrain, making for a poorly defensible position. The battalion arrived at the field in a driving rain under heavy artillery fire. Paige set his machine guns up on the perimeter with fields of fire to protect the rifle companies on his right and left flanks.

Knowing the importance of the airfield, Paige fully expected an attack that evening. Around 2:00 a.m., Paige heard Japanese forces moving into attack positions in the jungle. When the Japanese assaulted, Paige's platoon began throwing hand grenades at the attackers. Eventually, the marines opened up with machine gun fire as up to 75 Japanese soldiers screamed "Banzai" and "Blood for the Emperor." After the Americans beat back this initial wave of attackers, a second Japanese assault engulfed the American position, and Paige ended up manning one of the guns himself. After killing a number of attackers, he ran from position to position to encourage his marines. However, at each position he found only casualties.

Finding marines from an adjacent company, Paige made his way back to his unit's positions as a third wave of attackers came upon him. While under fire, and with Japanese soldiers crawling upon the American positions, Paige jumped into one of the defensive positions and took charge of the machine gun. Well forward of any other marines, he fired the machine gun at the assailants. Resupplied by three other marines, Paige moved from position to position in order to avoid enemy fire and single-handedly cleared the area of the enemy.

As dawn was breaking, he spotted 30 Japanese soldiers hidden in tall kunai grasses located near his position. He called out to them in Japanese; the enemy soldiers looked to Paige out of curiosity, and he then dispatched all of them. As more marines arrived at his location, Paige threw two belts of ammunition over his shoulder, removed the machine gun from its tripod, took the 80-pound weapon in his hands, and directed a counterattack. Moving forward, Paige continued to spray the area with automatic fire. He continued his assault until he reached the jungle's edge from where the Japanese attackers had first come. When the fighting was over, and due to Paige's quick actions, hundreds of Japanese soldiers lay dead with the airfield still in American hands.

As a result of his actions, Paige was awarded a battlefield commission as a second lieutenant and went on to serve in New Guinea, Cape Gloucester, and New Britain. Gen. Alexander Vandegrift presented Paige the Medal of Honor for his actions on Guadalcanal in a special ceremony in Balcombe, Australia, on May 21, 1943.

After his tour in the Pacific, Mitchell Paige was sent stateside in 1944 and went on the Bond Tour circuit to raise funds for the war effort. Following VJ Day, Paige saw further service in Korea and retired from the Marines as a colonel in 1964. After his service in the Corps, he worked in the research and development field. He remained active in many veterans' and service organizations and made his home in

LaQuinta, California. Paige died at the age of 85 from consumptive heart failure on November 15, 2003. He was buried with full military honors at the Riverside National Cemetery in Riverside, California.

John M. Curatola

Further Reading

Collier, Peter, and Nick Del Calzo. *Medal of Honor: Portraits of Valor beyond the Call of Duty.* New York: Artisan, 2006.

The Guadalcanal Legacy. Paducah, KY: Turner Publishing, 1987.

Hammel, Eric. *Guadalcanal: Starvation Island.* New York: Crown Publishing. 1987.

Paige, Mitchell. *A Marine Named Mitch.* New York: Vantage Press. 1975.

Shaw, Henry I., Jr. *First Offensive: The Marine Campaign for Guadalcanal.* Marines in World War II Commemorative Series. Washington, D.C.: Marine Corps Historical Center, 1992.

Parker, Samuel I.

Born: October 17, 1891
Died: December 1, 1975
Home State: North Carolina
Service: Army
Conflict: World War I
Age at Time of Award: 26

Born in Monroe, Union County, North Carolina, on October 17, 1891, Samuel Iredell Parker graduated from the University of North Carolina at Chapel Hill. He labored during summers at a ranch in Kansas where he became proficient at quickly shooting from the hip. He claimed this skill saved his life many times in World War I. Immediately upon America's entry into the war in April 1917, Parker volunteered for officer's training at Fort Oglethorpe, Georgia. He deployed to France in September of that year and trained with the British Army on the Somme River until November 11, 1917. At that time, he joined Company K, 3rd Battalion, 28th Infantry Regiment, 1st Division at Gondrecourt, France.

As a platoon leader, he first fought in the battle of Seicheprey in April 1918. At Cantigny on May 28, 1918, Parker skillfully and calmly led his men under intense small arms fire to establish an outpost within German lines. He would continue to perform superbly during the battle of Noyan-Montdidier, June 9 to July 5, 1918. However, these battles took a bloody toll on the regiment's men and officers, and by the Battle of Soissons during the Aisne-Marne campaign, the 2nd and 3rd battalions of the 28th Infantry Regiment were consolidated.

Parker had made an impression on the senior officers of the regiment, and, as a second lieutenant, Parker suddenly found himself second in command of a newly formed consolidated battalion just before the battle of Soissons. At Soissons, Parker's battalion "went over the top" at 5:30 p.m. on July 18, 1918, in support of the first battalion to capture the heights near Ploissy. Casualties mounted quickly due to intense fire from the heights, and the battalion commander, Maj. Clarence R. Huebner, was wounded and out of action soon after the battle began, leaving Parker in command of the battalion. He quickly grasped the situation, realizing that the French 153rd Division on the left had veered to their left, leaving the 28th Regiment to deadly enfilading fire from German machine gun nests in a rock quarry on the heights. While maneuvering his battalion to close the gap, he was severely wounded in the right foot. He administered first aid to himself, wrapping his foot and tying a tourniquet around his ankle. Without a shoe on his right foot, he assembled his men, along with some French Colonials he found wandering leaderless. Parker led the charge up the steep hill and took the enemy position by storm, capturing approximately 40 Germans and six machine guns. Amazingly, Parker refused to be evacuated. He remained in command of the battalion through the next day, continuing the attack much like the first day until his objective had been reached. By that point, he was crawling on his hands and knees due to the pain from his right foot.

Parker was back in action with his newly rebuilt platoon for the battle of St. Mihiel on September 12, 1918. He continued to fight through the Meuse-Argonne campaign, September 26 through October 25, 1918. During this campaign, Parker earned the Distinguished Service Cross for extraordinary heroism on October 5, 1918, near Exermont, France. Again, Parker led an attack on a machine gun strongpoint. He and his men continued to fight even while surrounded by the inevitable enemy counterattack. They held out, although only a few men remained alive in his platoon by the end of the battle.

Parker finally made first lieutenant by the war's end, and he was discharged on September 25, 1919. He entered the Reserves in 1923 until 1939, reaching the rank of captain. During the mid-1930s, Gen. Douglas MacArthur, Army chief of staff, believing Parker might not have been appropriately recognized for his performance during the war, appointed a committee to examine Parker's wartime service. In 1937, President Franklin D. Roosevelt awarded Parker the nation's 100th Medal of Honor for his gallantry and intrepidity above and beyond the call of duty at Soissons.

On August 24, 1942, Samuel Parker reentered the active Army as a major, teaching military leadership for the infantry school at Fort Benning, Georgia. He left the service for the last time on September 20, 1945, as a lieutenant colonel. After a successful career in business, he retired in 1956, remaining very active in the community. He died December 1, 1975, at Walter Reed Army Medical Center and is buried in Oakwood Cemetery, North Carolina.

Scott A. Porter

Further Reading

Johnson, Douglas V., and Rolfe L. Hillman Jr. *Soissons, 1918*. College Station: Texas A&M University Press. 1999.

Wheeler, James Scott. *The Big Red One: America's Legendary 1st Infantry Division from World War I to Desert Storm*. Lawrence: University Press of Kansas. 2007.

Pennypacker, Galusha

Born: June 1, 1842
Died: October 1, 1916
Home State: Pennsylvania
Service: Army
Conflict: Civil War
Age at Time of Award: 22

Galusha Pennypacker was born on June 1, 1842, in Valley Forge, Pennsylvania, in the house that served as Washington's headquarters during the Continental Army's winter encampment of 1777 to 1778. His lineage and upbringing seemed to destine him for military service. Pennypacker's great-grandfather was a German nobleman who served as a British officer and fought alongside General Wolfe at the Battle of Quebec in 1759 during the French and Indian War. His paternal grandfather fought in both the Revolutionary War and the War of 1812, and Pennypacker was a fourth cousin to another famous Civil War general and Indian fighter—George Armstrong Custer.

Effectively orphaned at an early age by his mother's death and his father's departure out West to seek a fortune, Pennypacker was left in the care of his paternal grandmother. The greatest influence on his young life was undoubtedly his uncle, Elijah F. Pennypacker, a Quaker whose farm in Phoenixville was a central station on the Underground Railroad, moving slaves from the south, through Pennsylvania, and further north to freedom. In addition to assisting his uncle, Pennypacker worked as a printer, studied law, and was deciding whether to accept an appointment to West Point when the Civil War broke out.

Pennypacker's wartime service was marked by a steady rise through the ranks and an unswerving desire to be at the forefront of any action. He helped raise Company A of the 97th Pennsylvania Volunteers Regiment; he was elected its captain on August 22, 1861, at the age of 19 and only two months later was promoted to major. From 1862 through early 1864, Pennypacker bravely led his men through battles, sieges, and skirmishes in Georgia, Florida, and South Carolina as part of the Union X Corps in the Department of the South.

In April 1864, Pennypacker was promoted to lieutenant colonel and second in command as the regiment prepared to move north to Virginia and support the

Army of the James. Pennypacker led part of the regiment in several engagements during Grant's march on Richmond in early May of 1864. He was hit three times and severely wounded on May 20 while leading an assault to retake lost ground at Bermuda Hundred. Upon recuperation from his wounds, he returned to the regiment in August, when he was promoted to colonel and took command of the 97th Pennsylvania. In September, he was elevated to command of the 2nd Brigade, 2nd Division, of X Corps—the youngest brigade commander in the Union Army.

In December of 1864, the five regiments of Pennypacker's 2nd Brigade (76th, 97th, and 203rd Pennsylvania; 47th and 48th New York) became part of the XXIV Corps. Maj. Gen. Alfred Terry deployed the corps to the North Carolina coast to capture Fort Fisher in January 1865. The fort, considered to be the Confederate's most impregnable stronghold on the eastern coast, guarded the entrance to the city of Wilmington, the last major port still open for the South.

Pennypacker's brigade was designated as the second wave of the assault force and went ashore on January 13 near Fort Fisher. Late in the afternoon of January 15, he led his brigade through deadly shot, shell, and canister fire to revive the initial stalled attack. His men swarmed over Shepard's Battery of the fort's defenses. As the color bearer for the 97th Pennsylvania went down, Pennypacker caught up the regiment's colors and charged to the top of the third traverse, where he defiantly planted the flag. At that instant, a Confederate minie ball entered his right hip and exited his lower back, causing severe internal damage to his pelvis and nerves. Though Fort Fisher did not fall until later that night, Pennypacker's war was over.

Pennypacker was carried from the fort by his men, although he refused to leave the battlefield until he had reported on his brigade's success to General Terry. Believing Pennypacker's wound to be mortal, General Terry requested a battlefield promotion for him from Secretary of War Stanton. Effective January 15, 1865, Pennypacker was promoted to the rank of brevet brigadier general of US Volunteers to be followed a month later by promotion to full brigadier general. At the age of 22, he was (and remains) the youngest general officer ever in the US Army.

Following additional surgeries to repair damage from his grievous wound at Fort Fisher, Pennypacker returned to the Army as a colonel, and, in 1869, he became the first commander of the newly formed 16th Infantry Regiment. He led the regiment through eight years of service in the South during Reconstruction and by all accounts was a fair and just military administrator, admired by both Southern whites and African Americans. After six years on the frontier in command of Fort Riley, Kansas, Pennypacker retired from active duty on July 3, 1883, and returned home to Philadelphia. Though begged by Pennsylvania citizens to run for higher political office, he quietly demurred. Supporters petitioned Congress, and, on August 17, 1891, he was awarded the Medal of Honor for "gallantly leading the charge over a traverse and planting the colors of one of his regiments."

Galusha Pennypacker died at the age of 74 on October 1, 1916, of complications from his old Fort Fisher wound that had never fully healed even after a half century.

Allan S. Boyce

Further Reading

Gragg, Rod. *Confederate Goliath: The Battle of Fort Fisher.* New York: Harper-Collins, 1991.

Stackhouse, Eugene Glenn. "General Galusha Pennypacker: American Hero and Descendent of the Early Germantown Settlers." *German Town Crier* 1, no. 1 (Spring 1999).

Warner, Ezra J. *Generals in Blue: Lives of the Union Commanders.* Baton Rouge: University of Louisiana Press, 1964.

Penry, Richard A.

Born: November 18, 1948
Died: May 9, 1994
Home State: California
Service: Army
Conflict: Vietnam War
Age at Time of Award: 19

Born in Petaluma, California, on November 18, 1948, Richard Allen Penry joined the US Army on March 5, 1969, in Oakland, California. He completed basic and advanced infantry training at Fort Lewis, Washington. He was reassigned to Vietnam, arriving in August 1969.

On January 31, 1970, he was a sergeant serving in Company C, 4th Battalion, 12th Infantry Regiment, 199th Infantry Brigade, in Binh Tuy Province, Republic of Vietnam. That day, he was helping his platoon prepare a nighttime ambush mission position when they came under intense enemy mortar, rocket, and automatic weapons fire that seriously wounded most of the platoon members and Penry's company commander. With the commander incapacitated, Penry found himself in charge of several small, isolated, and wounded groups of soldiers. Under heavy fire, Penry administered what immediate first aid he could to the company commander and the other wounded soldiers and then proceeded to move the command post to a better-protected area, which also provided a position from which to communicate and direct the other platoon elements. Once again exposing himself to heavy enemy fire, Penry scouted the area in search of an operable radio, which he needed to communicate with the battalion headquarters. Although under fire, he retrieved one radio, only to find it damaged and inoperable.

Focusing on organizing the platoon's defense, he continued to expose himself to heavy enemy fire to gather up scattered weapons and ammunition to distribute to those wounded who could still operate a weapon. A group of 30 enemy soldiers launched a determined attack, but Penry poured accurate rifle fire and grenades into the attackers, almost single-handedly turning the enemy back.

Penry continued to administer first aid to the wounded and retrieved yet another needed radio, finally successfully establishing communications with battalion headquarters. Also during this time, Penry discovered five additional wounded soldiers outside the perimeter and led them to safety, despite sniper fire. With the approach of evacuation helicopters, Penry left the perimeter to guide the helicopters, supervised the evacuation, and personally carried 18 wounded men to the evacuation site. Once the wounded were safely evacuated, Penry continued with another platoon in pursuit of the enemy. For his actions that day, Penry would receive the Medal of Honor in 1971. His other awards included the Distinguished Service Cross, the Bronze Star, and an Air Medal.

Penry returned to the United States in August 1970 and was assigned to 1st Squadron, 3rd Armored Cavalry Regiment at Fort Lewis, Washington, where he served until he was honorably discharged from the Army on March 4, 1971.

Richard Penry died at age 45 on May 9, 1994, and is buried in Cypress Hill Memorial Park in Petaluma, California. His hometown of Petaluma renamed a park in his honor and created the Sgt. Richard Penry Medal of Honor Memorial Military Museum, which houses his Medal of Honor.

Debra J. Sheffer

Further Reading

The Congressional Medal of Honor: The Names, the Deeds. Forest Ranch, CA: Sharp & Dunnigan, 1984.

Murphy, Edward F. *Vietnam Medal of Honor Heroes.* New York: Ballantine Books, 2005.

Pitsenbarger, William H.

Born: July 8, 1944
Died: April 11, 1966
Home State: Ohio
Service: Air Force
Conflict: Vietnam War
Age at Time of Award: 21

William H. Pitsenbarger was born on July 8, 1944, and grew up in Piqua, Ohio, a small town near Dayton. In his junior year of high school, he tried to enlist in the Army's Special Forces, but he was not old enough, and his parents refused to sign the consent forms. He remained in school one more year, graduating in the spring of 1962. After graduation, he continued to work as a stockboy at a local grocery supermarket for a time. However, he joined the Air Force, departing Piqua for basic training in San Antonio, Texas, on New Year's Eve, 1962.

After completing basic training, Pitsenbarger attended a number of special schools, including the Army's parachute school at Fort Benning, Georgia, the Navy's underwater swimmers course, the rescue and survival medical course, the combat survival course, and the Tropical Survival School at Albrook Air Base in the Panama Canal Zone. Having completed all the special training, he emerged as one of the Air Force's elite pararescuemen, more commonly known as PJs. He first served as a pararescue-medic in the NASA space program, working on the Gemini and Mercury space vehicle recoveries.

In August 1965, Pitsenbarger went to Vietnam and was assigned to Detachment 6, 38th Air Rescue and Recovery Squadron at Bien Hoa Air Base near Saigon. His unit flew HH-43F Kaman Huskie helicopters and were responsible for rescuing downed pilots and, when required, evacuating friendly ground troops. Pitsenbarger went to work immediately and soon had logged over 300 rescue missions, facing enemy fire over and over, while helping rescue hundreds of men. In March 1966, he received the Airman's Medal for rescuing a South Vietnamese soldier who had lost a foot and was trapped inside an old mine field. The government of South Vietnam awarded him Vietnam's Medal of Military Merit and the Cross of Gallantry with Bronze Palm.

On April 11, 1966, Pitsenbarger was on board one of two Huskies dispatched to assist in extracting several Army casualties from a unit pinned down near the village of Cam My, a few miles east of Saigon. Pitsenbarger and a wire mesh Stokes litter were lowered through the jungle canopy to the ground, where he attended to the wounded before strapping them into the litter basket to be lifted to the hovering helicopter by cable. Six wounded men were loaded onto the helicopters this way and were flown to the aid station while Pitsenbarger remained on the ground with the rest of the wounded.

Upon returning for the second load, the hovering helicopter had lowered the litter basket to Pitsenbarger when the aircraft was hit by enemy small arms fire. Rather than climbing into the litter basket and departing with the damaged aircraft, Pitsenbarger, disregarding his own safety, waved off the pilot and remained on the ground with the wounded. As the helicopter flew away to safety, the enemy intensified its attack on the American unit. Amid incoming mortar and small arms fire, Pitsenbarger tended to the wounded, redistributed ammunition, and joined in the fight to hold off the Viet Cong (VC), despite being wounded three times during the battle. Pitsenbarger was killed by VC snipers during the night; reportedly, when his body was recovered the next day, one hand still held his rifle and the other clutched a medical aid kit.

For his bravery and determination under fire, Pitsenbarger was nominated for the Medal of Honor, but it was downgraded to the Air Force Cross. His parents accepted the medal on behalf of their son on September 22, 1966. William Pitsenbarger became the first enlisted airman in history to receive the Air Force Cross posthumously.

Four years after Pitsenbarger received the Air Force Cross, Airman First Class John Levitow became the only enlisted airman to receive the Medal of Honor. By the 1990s, Pitsenbarger and his valor that day in 1966 had become a legend in the Air Force. No doubt encouraged by Levitow's receipt of the Medal of Honor, several private citizens and a number of federal officials launched a campaign to have Pitsenbarger's nomination for the medal revisited. Subsequent reviews agreed that the level of his valor and sacrifice warranted the higher award.

On December 8, 2000, Secretary of the Air Force Whit Peters presented Pitsenbarger's Medal of Honor to his father in a ceremony at Wright-Patterson Air Force Base in Pitsenbarger's home state of Ohio. It had taken 34 years, but Pitsenbarger's uncommon valor was finally fully recognized.

William Pitsenbarger is buried in Miami Memorial Park Cemetery in Covington, Ohio. Several buildings have been named in his honor at Wright-Patterson Air Force Base in Ohio, Randolph Air Force Base and Sheppard Air Force Base in Texas, and Spangdahlem Air Base in Germany. Pitsenbarger's hometown of Piqua, Ohio, renamed a recreational park in his honor.

James H. Willbanks

Further Reading

Caubarreaux, Eric R. *Recipients of the Air Force Medal of Honor and the Air Force Cross*. Scotts Valley, CA: CreateSpace, 2009.

Gomez-Granger, Julissa. *CRS Report for Congress: Medal of Honor Recipients: 1979–2008*. Washington, D.C.: Congressional Research Service, RL 30011, June 4, 2008.

Murphy, Edward F. *Vietnam Medal of Honor Heroes*. New York: Ballantine Books, 2005.

Pittman, John A.

Born: October 15, 1928
Died: April 8, 1995
Home State: Mississippi
Service: Army
Conflict: Korean War
Age at Time of Award: 22

John Albert Pittman was born on October 15, 1928, at Carrollton, Mississippi. Raised in a rural area of central Mississippi, Pittman learned the meaning of hard work and responsibility. After high school, Pittman enlisted in the US Army in 1947. He was assigned to Company C, 23rd Infantry Regiment, 2nd Division. When the North Korean Army crossed the 38th parallel into South Korea on June 25, 1951, the 2nd Division was quickly alerted to prepare for combat. Only a month later, the first elements of the division set sail from Seattle, headed for Pusan. By August 20, the entire division had arrived at the UN bridgehead around Pusan. After a series of defensive battles, the division spearheaded an offensive that broke out of the Pusan perimeter and headed north to join forces landed at Inchon.

By November 1950, the war in Korea seemed to have been won. UN forces had driven into North Korea and were poised to drive to the Yalu. Resistance from the remaining North Korean units was light. Pittman, by this time a sergeant, was a squad leader in the 2nd Platoon of Company C, 23rd Infantry. The 2nd Division held the right flank of IX Corps and was in the middle of the 8th Army line. It was advancing from Kunu-ri towards the Yalu River, with a goal of linking up with X Corps, advancing along the east coast of Korea. The American advance, however, collapsed when Chinese communist forces attacked during the night of November 25. When daylight broke on November 26, the Chinese disappeared, leaving behind their dead.

Company C had advanced to Kujangdong. That night, advanced elements of the regiment were attacked around 8:30 p.m. by large numbers of Chinese soldiers. Two companies of the 23rd were driven off the high ground. Pittman volunteered to lead his squad in an immediate counterattack to regain the lost territory. Despite intense artillery, mortar, and small arms fire being laid down by the Chinese, Pittman led his men forward. He was quickly knocked down by a mortar shell that exploded nearby. Despite being wounded by fragments from the mortar, Pittman struggled to his feet and continued to lead the advance.

The squad reached the crest of the hill they were attacking and drove the Chinese defenders off the summit. One of the retreating enemy soldiers threw a hand grenade back at the Americans. When Pittman saw it land among his squad, he did not hesitate. Throwing himself on the grenade, Pittman absorbed the explosion and debris with his own body. When a medical aid man reached him, Pittman's first words were to ask how many of his men had been hurt. His courageous action had in fact prevented the injury or death of his squad members. Pittman was stabilized and evacuated to a hospital in the rear, where his actions became widely known.

Pittman was recommended for the Medal of Honor for conspicuous gallantry and intrepidity in volunteering to lead the counterattack and in risking his own life to prevent harm to his men.

Pittman was evacuated to the United States because of his wounds. On June 4, 1951, Pittman received the Medal of Honor from President Harry S. Truman in a ceremony at the White House in which the president also presented the Medal of Honor to 1st Lt. Carl H. Dodd and M.Sgt. Ernest R. Kouma. In recognition of

Pittman's courage, *Life* put his picture on their July 2, 1951, issue, while *Time* covered the awards ceremony.

Of the 32 men who received the Medal of Honor in Korea before Pittman, only he and one other man were not dead or missing in action as a result of their actions. He was also the third man in Korea up to that time to receive the Medal of Honor for throwing himself on a grenade, but the first to survive. In comparison, during World War II, 13 men won the same award for covering up a grenade, with only one man surviving.

John Pittman left the Army in 1951 and returned to civilian life in Carrollton. He died there on April 8, 1995, at the age of 66. He is buried in the New Hope Cemetery in Carroll County.

Tim J. Watts

Further Reading

Fehrenbach, T. R. *This Kind of War: A Study in Unpreparedness*. New York: Macmillan Company, 1963.

Jacobs, Bruce. *Korea's Heroes: The Medal of Honor Story*. New York: Berkley Publishing, 1961.

Murphy, Edward F. *Korean War Heroes*. Novato, CA: Presidio Press, 1992.

Pittman, Richard A.

Born: May 26, 1945
Died:
Home State: California
Service: Marine Corps
Conflict: Vietnam War
Age at Time of Award: 21

Richard A. Pittman was born May 26, 1945, in San Joaquin, California. He attended Hazilton Elementary School and Freemont Junior High School and graduated from Franklin High School in Stockton in June 1964.

Although classified 4-F because of a traumatic eye ailment, and thus not acceptable for military service, Pittman longed to follow in the footsteps of his older brother, who was then serving in the Marine Corps. He subsequently petitioned his local draft board to reconsider their decision and, as a result, was reclassified to 1-A, allowing him unrestricted military service. After enlisting in the Marine Corps Reserves at Stockton, he received his wish to enter the regular Marine Corps, enlisting on November 1, 1965.

After completing recruit training at the Marine Corps Recruit Depot, San Diego, in December 1965, he completed individual combat training with the 1st Battalion,

2nd Infantry Training Regiment at Camp Pendleton, California, graduating in February 1966. Upon graduation, he was promoted to private first class.

He then deployed to the Republic of Vietnam, where he served until February 1967 as a rifleman, and later squad leader, with Company I, 3rd Battalion, 5th Marines, 1st Marine Division. He was promoted to lance corporal on July 1, 1966.

On July 24 1966, Corporal Pittman's unit was engaged in Operation Hastings in Quang Tri Province when intelligence confirmed the presence of a large enemy force near the demilitarized zone.

As Company I approached a narrow jungle trail, the leading elements came under heavy and sustained enemy fire, which resulted in numerous casualties. Corporal Pittman immediately exchanged his rifle for a machine gun, left the relative safety of his platoon, and unhesitatingly rushed forward to aid his comrades. Taken under intense small arms fire from the well-entrenched North Vietnamese force, he returned fire and silenced the enemy positions. Later, learning that there were wounded marines further along the trail, he braved a withering hail of enemy mortar and small arms fire to reach his wounded comrades. As he approached the position where the leading marines had fallen, he was suddenly confronted with a bold frontal attack by over 30 enemy soldiers. Totally disregarding his own safety, he calmly established a position in the middle of the trail and raked the advancing enemy with devastating machine gun fire. After the rapid succession of fire caused his weapon to jam, he picked up an enemy AK-47, firing that weapon until he ran out of ammunition. Corporal Pittman then retrieved a .45 caliber pistol left behind by a fallen marine and killed two more enemy soldiers at point-blank range. In a final act of valor, he threw his only grenade in the direction of the now-retreating North Vietnamese soldiers. Corporal Pittman's daring initiative, bold fighting spirit, and selfless devotion to the welfare of his fellow marines disrupted an enemy attack and saved the lives of many of his wounded comrades.

Following his discharge from the Marine Corps in 1968, Richard Pittman returned home to Stockton, California, where he learned that he would be awarded the Medal of Honor for his heroic actions in Vietnam, the 11th Marine to be so honored in the Vietnam War. Pittman was presented the nation's highest award for valor by President Lyndon B. Johnson at a White House ceremony on May 14, 1968. In 1970, he decided to reenlist in his beloved Marine Corps, where he served 18 more years, finally retiring in 1988 at the rank of master sergeant. He now lives in Stockton, California.

Heather Leahy

Further Reading

Cerasini, Marc. *U.S. Marine Corps Medal of Honor Winners.* New York: Berkley Books, 2002.

Collier, Peter, and Nick Del Calzo. *Medal of Honor: Portraits of Valor beyond the Call of Duty*. New York: Artisan, 2006.

Dunstan, Simon. *1st Marine Division in Vietnam*. Minneapolis, MN: Zenith Press, 2008.

Lowry, Timothy. *And Brave Men, Too*. New York: Crown Publishers, 1985.

Murphy, Edward F. *Semper Fi: Vietnam: From Da Nang to the DMZ: Marine Corps Campaigns, 1965–1972*. Novato, CA: Presidio Press, 1997.

Pope, Everett Parker

Born: July 16, 1919
Died: July 16, 2009
Home State: Massachusetts
Service: Marine Corps
Conflict: World War II
Age at Time of Award: 25

Everett P. Pope was born July 16, 1919, in Milton, Massachusetts, the son of Lawrence and Ruth Pope. He attended North Quincy High School, matriculating to Bowdoin College, where he studied French. Not only was Pope a first-rate scholar, graduating magna cum laude, he was also an accomplished athlete and led his college tennis team to win the state championship. Not content to settle for an outstanding academic and athletic career, Pope was also an active member of the Beta Theta Pi fraternity. Upon his graduation in June 1941, Pope joined the US Marine Corps; shortly thereafter he married his high school sweetheart, Eleanor Hawkins.

Like many Marine Corps officers, Pope was a "mustang" advancing from enlisted man to officer by attending the officer candidate school at Quantico, Virginia. He was commissioned a second lieutenant in the Marine Corps Reserves on November 1, 1941. After the attack on Pearl Harbor, Pope trained at Quantico, Virginia, and New River, North Carolina, before going overseas with Company C, 1st Battalion, 1st Marines. In the first of his two major campaigns, he led his machine gun platoon into action at Guadalcanal on August 7, 1942, and participated in the battle to secure the island. His actions on Guadalcanal earned him the Bronze Star.

Following time off the line in Australia during 1943, Pope and the 1st Marines were assigned to help take Peleliu Island in the western Pacific. On September 15, Pope, then a captain, and his company of marines landed on the island and began the bloody fight to dislodge the Japanese from the elaborate network of caves and defensive positions they had built to defend the island.

After four days of almost constant fighting, Pope and his company were given the mission of taking Hill 154, a nearly coverless coral outcrop near the aptly named

Suicide Ridge. In the face of point-blank enemy cannon fire that caused heavy casualties and badly disorganized his company as they assaulted the steep hill, Pope rallied his men and led them to the summit in the face of machine gun, mortar, and sniper fire. In order to hold the ground they had taken, Pope deployed the remnants of his company in a thin defensive perimeter against Japanese counterattack. With his machine guns out of order and insufficient water and ammunition, Pope with 12 men and 1 wounded officer remained on the exposed hill determined to hold through the night.

On the night of September 20, the Japanese attacked from three sides, completely surrounding Pope and his men. The marines fought them off until they ran out of ammunition. Then they were forced into hand-to-hand combat. With no ammunition, they had to resort to throwing rocks and empty ammunition containers at the attackers. During the battle, Captain Pope was wounded and later received the Purple Heart, but he remained overseas until November 1944.

Despite the fearlessness of Company C, Pope was ordered to take the eight remaining men and withdraw from the hill. One would be mistaken to interpret the attack on the hill as futile. Because Company C held the hill, they possibly saved thousands of lives of young men below from the onslaught of Imperial Japanese forces who would have held an elevated position.

Pope was promoted to major in January 1945 and sent to study Japanese at Yale University in preparation for the invasion of Japan. However, the atomic bombing of Hiroshima and Nagasaki in August would make the invasion unnecessary.

In the spring of 1945, Pope was ordered to the White House to receive the Medal of Honor. At the presentation ceremony, President Harry Truman, who was awarding his first Medal of Honor, remarked that he would rather have the Medal of Honor than be president of the United States.

Pope was released from active service in July 1946 and returned to Massachusetts. He remained in the Marine Corps Reserve and commanded the 2nd Infantry Battalion, US Marine Corps Reserve, in Hingham, Massachusetts, until 1950, when he was recalled to active duty. He served as executive officer of 3rd Battalion, 2nd Marines in Camp Lejeune, North Carolina, until he finally resigned from the Corps in 1951.

Everett Pope returned to Massachusetts, where he worked in the banking industry and was a major proponent of the Federal Student Loan program. Upon his return to Bowdoin College, Pope established a leadership award for his friend Andrew Haldane, who gave his life at Peleliu. Also of note is the book by one of Pope's men, Eugene B. Sledge, author of possibly the most acclaimed and best book on the Pacific Theater, *With the Old Breed on Peleliu and Okinawa*. Everett Pope passed away on his 90th birthday on July 16, 2009, in Bath, Maine. He is buried in Arlington National Cemetery.

Jason Everitt Foster

Further Reading

Collier, Peter, and Nick Del Calzo. *Medal of Honor: Portraits of Valor beyond the Call of Duty.* New York: Artisan, 2006.

Sledge, E. B. *With the Old Breed: Peleliu and Okinawa.* London, UK: Oxford University Press, 1990.

Pope, Thomas A.

Born: December 15, 1894
Died: June 14, 1989
Home State: Illinois
Service: Army
Conflict: World War I
Age at Time of Award: 23

Thomas A. Pope was born in Chicago, Illinois, on December 15, 1894. He joined the 1st Illinois Regiment of the National Guard before the war. That unit went on to form part of the nucleus of the 33rd Infantry Division when that division was activated in July 1917. The regiment, which was redesignated the 131st Infantry, largely was recruited from some of the roughest areas in Chicago. The 33rd Division spent the first months after its activation training in Texas before traveling to Europe in May 1918. In France, the division underwent further training with their Australian allies in the sector behind Amiens and participated in some minor actions, as well as manned positions in the sector's reserve line.

Pope's unit, Company E, 131st Regiment, was one of six US companies assigned to work with the 4th and 11th Australian Infantry brigades, which were scheduled for an attack on the village of Le Hamel on July 4. Company E was detailed to the 43rd Australian Infantry Battalion. The assault was an exceptionally successful combined arms battle. A creeping artillery barrage was closely followed up by the infantry, who coordinated with battle tanks, supply tanks, and air-dropped supplies of ammunition and water. The victory also witnessed some tremendous heroism. One Medal of Honor and two Victoria Crosses were awarded for the action.

Interestingly, the action at Le Hamel almost did not involve any American soldiers at all. On July 3, Gen. John Pershing had requested that the American units be pulled out of the attack. However, the commander on the spot contacted the British commander-in-chief, who, in turn, spoke with Pershing and the four companies already in the line who were left to participate in the Australian advance. This attack was the first real action in the war for the 33rd Division.

Pope moved forward with his company at 3:10 a.m. after a very heavy, but short, barrage. The men followed the artillery fire, moving forward at a steady pace—100 yards every three minutes. As they approached Hamel, the village was shelled for a solid 10 minutes before the attack was launched. After a stiff fight, the town was taken. Throughout the day, the Germans intermittently shelled and gassed the Allied troops, and that night, they launched a strong counterattack against the town, capturing some of the Allied trenches. During the confusion of battle, Pope was seen going forward alone to attack an enemy machine gun that had pinned down his unit. He rushed the machine gun, killing the crew with his bayonet, and then was seen astride the gun while he fought off other Germans until support came up. The Allied troops then retook the position and captured a number of Germans. For the action that day, Pope would receive the Medal of Honor.

It is not entirely clear in which unit Pope was fighting at the time of these actions. Some men had become separated from their units, and others some had been seconded to other companies for a specific task. The official US report indicates that he was with American troops, yet the Australians presented his unit with a machine gun captured through the tremendous bravery of an American soldier. His subsequent receipt of American, British, and French medals of valor indicate that probably he was with the Australians when he carried out his heroic actions.

Overall, the operation was a complete success. The Allies killed, wounded, and captured 3,500 Germans. The Allies received over 1,000 casualties, with the Americans losing about 175 men, many to German gas. Through the terrific bravery of its men, the 33rd Division acquitted itself well.

Contrary to what is often written, Pope was not the first recipient of a Medal of Honor during World War I. However, he was the Army's first Medal of Honor recipient to receive his medal during the war; General Pershing presented the medal to Pope on April 22, 1919. Previously, on August 12, 1918, King George V personally had presented Pope with the British Distinguished Conduct Medal, and Pope also received both the Croix de Guerre and Medaille Militaire from France.

Thomas Pope was the last surviving recipient of the Medal of Honor from World War I. He passed away on June 14, 1989, aged 94, at the Edward Hines Jr. VA Hospital in Chicago. He is buried at Arlington National Cemetery.

Nicholas A. Murray

Further Reading

Pease, Theodore Calvin, ed. *Illinois in the World War*, vol. 2. Springfield: Illinois State Historical Library, 1921.

Sanborn, Col. Joseph B. *The 131st U.S. Infantry in the World War*. Chicago: Illinois National Guard, 1919.

33rd Division A.E.F. From Its Arrival in France until the Armistice with Germany November 11, 1918. Diekirch, Luxembourg: Gustave Soupert, 1919.

US Congress. Senate. *Medal of Honor Recipients, 1863–1978*. Washington: Government Printing Office, 1979.

Rascon, Alfred V.

Born: September 10, 1945
Died:
Home State: California
Service: Army
Conflict: Vietnam War
Age at Time of Award: 21

Alfred V. Rascon, son of Alfredo and Andrew Rascon, was born on September 10, 1945, in Chihuahua, Mexico. His family immigrated to the United States when he very young, briefly settling in east Los Angeles before moving to Oxnard, California, a coastal community about 40 miles northwest of Los Angeles.

From an early age, Rascon knew he wanted to be a paratrooper. Before age 10, Rascon made a parachute and jumped off the roof of his house, breaking his wrist. Undaunted, he thrilled to the departure of soldiers and marines from nearby Port Hueneme Naval Station on their way to the Korean War, a sight that further whetted his appetite for the military life. Rascon enlisted in the Army after graduation from high school at age 17—his parents signed a waiver. He completed basic training at Fort Ord, California, and went on to Fort Sam Houston to train as a medic.

Subsequently, Rascon obtained his paratrooper wings at Fort Benning and was assigned to Okinawa with the 173rd Airborne Brigade, a unit serving as a rapid reaction force in the Pacific.

The 173rd was the first large combat unit sent to Vietnam in early 1965. Rascon was wounded that fall. He recovered and rejoined his unit to serve during the spring of 1966 in Operation Silver City, a series of major actions that drew in elements of the US 1st Infantry Division and 10th Army of the Republic of Vietnam (ARVN) Division. The operation was a search-and-destroy mission in War Zone D, Long Khanh Province, in the Republic of Vietnam's III Corps area.

Alfred V. Rascon, US Army (US Army Medical Department Regiment).

On March 16, 1966, the 2nd Battalion of the 503rd Infantry Regiment established heavy contact with the enemy. Specialist Rascon moved up to provide medical care for the wounded despite being told to wait for covering fire. While working his way forward, he positioned his body between enemy machine gun fire and a wounded machine gunner and, in the process, sustained shrapnel wounds and a bullet wound to the hip. After dragging the machine gunner to safety, Rascon determined that the man was mortally wounded. Meanwhile, Rascon heard another machine gunner yelling for ammunition. Under heavy enemy fire, Rascon crawled back to the now-deceased soldier he had dragged to safety and peeled off his ammunition bandoleers, successfully delivering them to the requesting machine gunner.

Rascon now feared the dead machine gunner's weapon would fall into enemy hands. While attempting to retrieve the gun and its ammunition, several grenades exploded nearby, and he suffered a shrapnel wound to the face. Despite accumulated wounds, Rascon recovered the weapon and passed it to another soldier, who promptly put it to good use. Resuming his treatment of casualties, Rascon grabbed a wounded comrade and threw him flat on the ground as a grenade detonated nearby, striking both men with shrapnel. Rascon next made his way to the wounded point squad leader and covered him with his body, absorbing still more grenade fragments. By now wounded many times, Rascon remained on the battlefield and inspired his fellow soldiers to stay in the fight. Once the enemy broke contact, Rascon denied himself aid to continue treating and evacuating the wounded. Only when safely aboard an evacuation helicopter did he submit to treatment.

After recuperating in Japan, he was discharged to the Reserves. Rascon became a naturalized citizen in 1967 and attended college. In 1970, he was commissioned a second lieutenant upon completion of officer candidate school. He returned to Vietnam that same year to serve as an advisor. In 1976, Rascon received posting as a US Army military liaison officer in Panama.

During a reunion in the 1980s, several of Rascon's comrades discovered that he had never received the Medal of Honor for which he had been nominated. In 1997, they approached Congressman Lane Evans of Illinois, who served on the House Veterans Affairs Committee. Evans, in turn, passed the information on Rascon to President Bill Clinton, who persuaded the Pentagon to reopen Rascon's case. On February 8, 2000, Rascon was awarded the Medal of Honor during a ceremony at the White House.

In May 2002, Alfred Rascon was named the 10th director of the Selective Service. The same year, he returned to military service as a major in the US Army Reserve. Rascon subsequently served in Iraq and Afghanistan with the Medical Service Corps and retired as a lieutenant colonel. He currently resides in Maryland.

Anton A. Menning

Further Reading

Collier, Peter, and Nick Del Calzo. *Medal of Honor: Portraits of Valor beyond the Call of Duty*. New York: Artisan, 2006.

Smith, Larry. *Beyond Glory: Medal of Honor Heroes in Their Own Words—Extraordinary Stories of Courage from WWII to Vietnam*. New York: W. W. Norton, 2003.

173rd Airborne Brigade: Sky Soldiers. Nashville, TN: Turner Publishing, 2006.

Ray, Ronald Eric

Born: December 7, 1941
Died:
Home State: Georgia
Service: Army
Conflict: Vietnam War
Age at Time of Award: 28

Born on December 7, 1941, in Cordele, Georgia, Ronald E. Ray left high school in 1959 and enlisted in the US Army. He served three years and then was discharged, but, two months later, he reenlisted for Special Forces. After completing training, he excelled in his new assignment, and his battalion commander recommended him for officer candidate school. Upon graduation, he was commission a second lieutenant of infantry.

In June 1966, he went to Vietnam, where he was assigned to the 25th Infantry Division operating in the Ia Drang Valley in the Central Highlands. The valley had already been the site of difficult and costly combat in 1965 when elements of the 1st Cavalry Division had fought North Vietnamese regulars there.

Ray was serving as a platoon leader in Company A, 2nd Battalion, 35th Infantry Regiment, which was engaged in Operation Paul Revere I, designed to interdict North Vietnamese Army (NVA) units in the Ia Drang Valley infiltrating Vietnam from Cambodia. During the early days of the operation, Ray's company commander divided his company in two and placed Ray's platoon augmented with one mortar north of the Ia Drang River, while the remainder of the company occupied positions south of the river.

Ray located his platoon on a small hill largely devoid of underbrush. To provide security and early warning, Ray established a series of listening posts along likely enemy avenues of approach while at the same time sending out patrols. One of his patrols discovered a new trail in an area initially marked as a possible enemy avenue of approach.

Moving along the trail toward the Cambodian border, the patrol came upon a smaller NVA detachment. A brief firefight ensued in which the Americans killed one of the NVA soldiers and took another prisoner. Ray began to suspect that larger NVA movements were occurring in the area.

With the Cambodian border only three kilometers away, Ray pushed his patrols closer to the border. On June 19, one of the patrols came under intense small arms and crew-served weapons fire. Fearing that the enemy would overrun his small element, Ray ordered his men to detonate their claymores and make their way back to the platoon perimeter. It was Ray's intention to move forward with another patrol and extricate the engaged element. Ray requested reinforcements from his company commander, but none were available.

The situation was worsening; the engaged patrol reported receiving fire from all sides, wounding the radio operator. First Lieutenant Ray left his mortar squad to secure the base and led the rest of his platoon to relieve the beleaguered patrol. Ray's men fought their way to the cut-off patrol. As the enemy regrouped, the medic and two additional men prepared the wounded soldier for evacuation and started for the anticipated landing zone (LZ). They did not get far before enemy fire pinned them down.

Believing that the enemy was now in the process of surrounding his force, Ray tried to reach the three soldiers and the wounded radio operator. He regained contact with his men and attempted to push past them to the LZ. Before he could make progress, an enemy grenade landed next to the medic and radio operator. Ray dove over the men, using his body to shield them. The blast sent shrapnel into his legs. Several rounds from a machine gun struck him in the legs. Ray was momentarily paralyzed from the waist down by the trauma but managed to return fire, silencing the machine gun with a grenade.

Ray planned to stay behind to cover his men's withdrawal, but his medic carried him to the LZ, where a helicopter extracted Ray and the other wounded soldier. Ray was taken to Pleiku, where he was operated on, before further evacuation to Womack Army Hospital at Fort Bragg, North Carolina. Some of the damage from the enemy grenade would plague him throughout the rest of his Army career.

In 1970, he was stationed at Fort Benning, Georgia, when he was notified that he would receive the Medal of Honor. It was presented to him by President Richard Nixon on May 14, 1970.

Ray's career in the US Army lasted until 1980. He had been ably serving as battalion commander of 1st Battalion, 7th Special Forces Group (Airborne) at the time he made his decision to retire. The men of his battalion remembered him as the personification of the Special Forces soldier. Supremely confident and exceptionally talented, he was nonetheless one of the most humble of men, electing on more than one occasion to place his men in the limelight while he deliberately avoided it.

His civilian career proved noteworthy. In 1989, President George W. Bush nominated and Congress approved his appointment as assistant secretary of veterans affairs, where he served from 1989 to 1993. Moving back into the business world, he became president of MedicaSoft LLC, a company dedicated to the production of software for medical services. He remains active in various veterans' organizations, including the Veterans of Foreign Wars and the American Legion, and now resides in Tarpon Springs, Florida.

Joseph R. Fischer

Further Reading

Collier, Peter, and Nick Del Calzo. *Medal of Honor: Portraits of Valor beyond the Call of Duty.* New York: Artisan, 2006.

Jordon, Kenneth N. *Heroes of Our Time: 239 Men of the Vietnam War Awarded the Medal of Honor 1964–1972.* Atglen, PA: Schiffer Publishing, 2004.

Red Cloud, Mitchell, Jr.

Born: July 2, 1924
Died: November 5, 1950
Home State: Wisconsin
Service: Army
Conflict: Korean War
Age at Time of Award: 26

Mitchell Red Cloud Jr. was born July 2, 1924, in Hatfield, Wisconsin. The eldest son of Mitchell Red Cloud and his wife, Lillian, Mitchell Jr. was born a member of the Ho Chunk (Winnebago) Native American Tribe.

Red Cloud dropped out of high school at age 16 and, with his father's permission, enlisted in the Marine Corps on August 11, 1941. He served as a member of the 2nd Marine Raider Battalion under Lt. Col. Evans Carlson. This elite unit only accepted the most physically and mentally tough marines, and Red Cloud fit right in. He deployed with the unit to Guadalcanal, and, during the period November 6– December 4, 1942, he participated in the 2nd Battalion's mission to cut

Mitchell Red Cloud Jr., US Army (Library of Congress).

off escaping Japanese forces. The mission was highly successful and earned the unit a Presidential Unit Citation.

After contracting a variety of tropical diseases while on Guadalcanal, Red Cloud was sent back to the United States to recuperate. Refusing a medical discharge, he recovered and was assigned to the 29th Marines, 6th Marine Division. The 6th Marine Division was unique because it was activated on Guadalcanal and then deactivated overseas following the war, thus never serving in the United States. While assigned to the 29th Marines, Red Cloud participated in the invasion of Okinawa, where his unit saw some of the most intense fighting of the battle.

Following World War II, Red Cloud returned to the United States and separated from the Marine Corps. After two years, he enlisted in the Army and was assigned to the 19th Infantry Regiment, 24th Infantry Division stationed on the Japanese Island of Kyushu. The 24th was one of the four US divisions that constituted the occupation force for Japan. All four of the divisions were filled with green, inexperienced troops. In addition, occupation duty in Japan was not challenging, and training opportunities were limited.

When North Korea invaded South Korea in June 1950, the 24th Infantry Division was one of the first divisions to be sent to Korea as part of the US response. Red Cloud and the rest of the members of E Company, 2nd Battalion, 19th Infantry Regiment entered Korea in the first weeks of July 1950, and, trading time for space, the US forces tried to delay the communist advance with a fighting withdrawal. When conducting a complex military operation like this, a combat veteran like Red Cloud was a great asset to his unit. The withdrawal was confusing and bloody, with the battalion barely escaping encirclement and destruction along the Kum River outside Taejon. Red Cloud and his unit eventually withdrew to the Pusan Perimeter, where they participated in the bitter battles to hold on to the US foothold in Korea.

Following the Inchon landings and the breakout from Pusan in September 1950, members of the 24th Infantry, now assigned to I Corps, participated in the pursuit of the North Korean Army into North Korea. After the capture of the North Korean capital of Pyongyang, the US forces prepared to advance to the Yalu River. Unbeknownst to Red Cloud and his men, Chinese communist forces were preparing to enter the war. Although there was evidence of Chinese intervention, US forces believed victory was in their grasp. The Chinese struck the 8th Army on October 26, fighting at night and surrounding the forward-most forces. The 8th Army commander, Gen. Walton Walker, ordered his forces into a defensive line along the Chongchon River.

Red Cloud and the 2nd Battalion occupied positions north of the river. Beginning on November 3, the Chinese launched their attack on the Chongchon defenses. On the night of November 5, Companies E and G occupied Hill 123 near the hamlet of Chongyou. Corporal Red Cloud was positioned in a forward listening post when he heard and then saw the Chinese troops as they advanced on the

American positions. He immediately gave warning to his comrades and returned fire with his Browning Automatic Rifle (BAR). During the fighting, Corporal Red Cloud was wounded by enemy fire, but he continued to engage the enemy. His devastating and accurate fire prevented his company from being overrun. Weak from his wounds, Red Cloud propped himself against a tree until Chinese forces overran his position. Red Cloud was reportedly struck by as many as eight bullets before he died. When his comrades recovered his body the next day, his position was surrounded by "a string of dead Chinese soldiers" in front of his position. Red Cloud's warning and devastating fire had allowed his company time to hold their position.

In April 1951, at a ceremony in the Pentagon, Cpl. Mitchell Red Cloud Jr. was posthumously awarded the Medal of Honor, which was presented to his mother by Gen. Omar N. Bradley. In 1955, his remains were moved from the UN Cemetery in Korea to Wisconsin, where he was buried in accordance with tribal custom.

In 1957, the US Army named the home of the 2nd Infantry Division in Korea after Red Cloud. In addition, the US Navy honored him by naming one of its new roll-on roll-off ships in his name; USNS *Red Cloud* (T-AKR-1313) was commissioned in 1999.

Robert J. Rielly

Further Reading

Benna, Dana. "After a World War II Stint in the Marines, Mitchell Red Cloud Jr. Became an Army Hero in Korea." *Military History* 23, no. 4 (June 2006): 24–80.

Blair, Clay. *The Forgotten War: America in Korea, 1950–1953*. New York: Anchor Books Doubleday, 1987.

Murphy, Edward F. *Korean War Heroes*. Novato, CA: Presidio Press, 1992.

Rickenbacker, Edward V.

Born: October 8, 1890
Died: July 23, 1973
Home State: Ohio
Service: Army
Conflict: World War I
Age at Time of Award: 27

Edward Vernon Rickenbacker was born on October 8, 1890, in Columbus, Ohio, where he received little formal education. In 1905, he worked as a laborer in a railroad car firm but quickly developed an interest in gasoline engines and cars. At the age of 16, Rickenbacker began professional racing, and, commencing in 1911, he regularly drove at the Indianapolis 500. By 1917, he was America's most famous daredevil racer and established a land speed record of 134 miles per hour at Daytona Beach, Florida. That May, Rickenbacker tried enlisting in the Army but was turned down for want of education. Nonetheless, he persisted and was eventually allowed to join as a driver on the staff of Gen. John J. Pershing.

Despite his prestigious staff position, Rickenbacker wanted a combat assignment. While in France, he met and was befriended by Col. Billy Mitchell, who arranged a transfer to the Air Service for him. Rickenbacker underwent flight training at the Aviation Training School at Tours, gaining his wings in October 1917. His first assignment came as engineering officer with the 3rd Aviation Instruction Center at Issoudun under Maj. Carl A. Spaatz. Rickenbacker pressed Spaatz for a fighter assignment, and, in March 1918, he was posted with the 94th Aero Pursuit Squadron as a captain.

This outfit, known through its famed "Hat-in-the-Ring" insignia, was the first American squadron to see combat. Rickenbacker accompanied unit commander Maj. Raoul Lufbery on several dangerous forays over enemy lines and scored his first kill on April 25, 1918. The Americans were then flying cast-off Nieuport 28s donated by the French. These were maneuverable fighters but had a tendency to shed their upper wing while diving and had to be flown carefully. Nevertheless, when pitted against the "flying circus" of Baron Manfred von Richthofen, Rickenbacker scored several kills and became an ace on May 30, 1918.

Following Lufbery's death that same month, Rickenbacker succeeded him as commander of the 94th with the rank of major. A natural flier, he continued racking up victories through late spring until a severe ear infection grounded him for several months. Rickenbacker resumed flying in September, only this time in fast and rugged SPAD XIIIs, which had replaced the rickety Nieuports. He immediately added to his tally of kills, and, on September 25, 1918, for single-handedly attacking seven German aircraft and shooting down two, Rickenbacker received the Medal of Honor. He also acquired eight Distinguished Flying Crosses, the French Legion of Honor, and two Croix de Guerres. By war's end in November 1918, Rickenbacker's score stood at 26, making him the highest-ranking American ace of the war. His 94th Aero Squadron also claimed 69 victories, another record.

Rickenbacker returned to the United States in 1919 as a war hero. He then began his own automobile firm in Detroit, the Rickenbacker Motor Company, which pioneered such innovative technology as four-wheel brakes. When the company was dissolved in 1926, Rickenbacker bought controlling interest in the Indianapolis Speedway before beginning a new career as an engineer at General Motors Corporation (GM). In 1935, he was appointed general manager of a failing GM subsidiary, Eastern Airlines, which he turned around and made profitable in short order.

Within three years, Rickenbacker was president and director of Eastern. During World War II, his aviation knowledge and technical expertise led to his appointment as special representative of Henry L. Stimson, the secretary of war. He was dispatched to the Pacific on an inspection tour of fighter bases, but, in October 1942, his B-17 bomber ditched 600 miles north of Samoa. Rickenbacker and seven survivors then drifted for three weeks, subsisting on fish and rainwater before being rescued. After two weeks in a hospital, he boarded another plane and completed his assignment.

After the war, Edward Rickenbacker resumed his corporate activities with Eastern Airlines, rising to chairman of the board in 1954, and oversaw a period of tremendous growth. He retired in 1963 and, two years later, was inducted into the National Aviation Hall of Fame in Dayton, Ohio. Rickenbacker died in Zurich, Switzerland, on July 23, 1973, the seventh-ranking American ace of all time.

John C. Fredriksen

Further Reading

Adamson, Hans Christian. *Eddie Rickenbacker.* New York: The Macmillan Company, 1946.

Farr, Finis. *Rickenbacker's Luck—An American Life.* Boston: Houghton-Mifflin, 1979.

Lewis, W. David. *Eddie Rickenbacker: An American Hero in the 20th Century.* Baltimore: Johns Hopkins University Press, 2005.

Rickenbacker, Capt. Edward V. *Seven Came Through.* Garden City, NY: Doubleday, Doran, 1943.

Rickenbacker, Edward V. *Rickenbacker: An Autobiography.* Englewood Cliffs, NJ: Prentice-Hall, 1967.

Roberts, Gordon R.

Born: June 14, 1950
Died:
Home State: Ohio
Service: Army
Conflict: Vietnam War
Age at Time of Award: 19

Gordon R. Roberts was born on June 14, 1950, in Middletown, Ohio. On June 14, 1968, three days after graduating from high school, Roberts left his home in Lebanon, Ohio, and enlisted in the US Army. He trained as a rifleman with the 8th Infantry Division in Germany and earned the nickname Bird Dog. In April of 1969, he was transferred to South Vietnam. There he joined Company B, 1st Battalion, 506th Infantry in the 101st Airborne Division as a specialist fourth class. This division was the same division his father had served in during World War II. Roberts fought in the A Shau Valley at the Battle for Ap Bia Mountain, or "Hamburger Hill," from May 10 to 20 in 1969. For his performance there, he earned a Silver Star. For the rest of the month, Roberts's unit attempted to block the enemy's main supply route from Laos in Thua Thien Province.

On July 11, 1969, around noon, another US infantry company was engaged in heavy combat with a large enemy force about three miles from Roberts's unit. The company had lost their battalion commander in the intense fighting and were outnumbered, with 78 out of the 80 soldiers already wounded or killed.

Roberts's company loaded on helicopters and went to assist their beleaguered comrades. After landing, they were moving along a ridgeline when the North Vietnamese Army (NVA), entrenched on a nearby hill, opened fire on them with rocket-propelled grenades and small arms. Roberts and his platoon dove for cover and were soon pinned down. However, Roberts realized that something had to be done and crawled toward the nearest enemy bunker. He then jumped up and charged the position, firing his rifle as he ran forward. He killed two North Vietnamese who has been manning the machine gun. He reloaded his M-16 with a new clip and moved toward the second bunker as enemy fire knocked Roberts's rifle from his hands. He grabbed a rifle that was lying on the ground as he continued toward the North Vietnamese position. Roberts successfully destroyed the second bunker and, with accurate grenade throws, also destroyed a third enemy bunker. Isolated from the majority of his platoon, Roberts continued his assault and took out the fourth North Vietnamese bunker. Still under continuous enemy fire, Roberts fought his way to the company that had been surrounded and assisted wounded soldiers from this exposed position back to an evacuation area. He made multiple trips before returning to his own company.

In April 1970, Roberts finished his one-year tour in South Vietnam. While stationed at Ford Meade, Maryland, he received news that he was to receive the Medal of Honor. President Richard Nixon presented Roberts with the medal on March 2, 1971.

Three weeks later, he was discharged from the Army and enrolled in college. He graduated from the University of Dayton in 1974 with a bachelor's degree in sociology. He later received his master's degree from the University of Cincinnati in social work. He enjoyed a career as a social worker and served as the director for a residential treatment facility for behaviorally handicapped children.

After 18 years away from the military, Gordon Roberts joined the Ohio Army National Guard in 1988 and received a direct commission as an officer, serving initially with the 112th Medical Brigade. In 1991, he went on active duty. For the next eight years, Roberts served in various company and field grade assignments in the United States, Korea, Haiti, Iraq, and Kuwait. As of this writing, Roberts is a colonel on active duty based at Walter Reed Army Medical Center.

Denise M. Carlin

Further Reading

Collier, Peter, and Nick Del Calzo. *Medal of Honor: Portraits of Valor beyond the Call of Duty.* New York: Artisans, 2006.

US Congress. Senate. Committee on Veterans Affairs. *Medal of Honor Recipients, 1863–1978: "In the Name of the Congress of the United States."* Washington, D.C.: Government Printing Office, 1979.

Rocco, Louis R.

Born: November 19, 1938
Died: October 31, 2002
Home State: California
Service: Army
Conflict: Vietnam War
Age at Time of Award: 31

Louis Richard Rocco was born in Albuquerque, New Mexico, on November 19, 1938. One of nine children of an Italian American father and a Mexican American mother, he had a troubled youth following the family's 1948 move to a housing project in the San Fernando Valley of California. A gang member and high school dropout, Rocco was only 16 years old when he was arrested for armed robbery. With the assistance of a US Army recruiter, he persuaded a judge to give him a suspended sentence—provided that he enlist as soon as he turned 17.

After joining the Army in 1955, Rocco earned his high school general equivalency diploma (GED) during his first assignment in Germany and became an Army medic. Some years later, when working as a medic at Fort Mac-Arthur in San Pedro, California, the recruiter who had assisted him with the judge and helped him join the Army arrived at a hospital for treatment; Rocco made sure that the recruiter received special, round-the-clock care for his injuries.

Rocco served two tours in South Vietnam; his first was from 1965 to

Louis R. Rocco, US Army (US Army Medical Department Regiment).

1966. In 1970, during his second tour, he was a sergeant first class assigned to Advisory Team 162, US Military Assistance Command Vietnam. On May 24, 1970, Rocco was part of a medical evacuation team sent to pick up eight critically wounded South Vietnamese soldiers near the village of Katum. His helicopter came under heavy enemy fire as it approached the landing zone, and he manned the helicopter's door-mounted machine gun to apply suppressive fire on the enemy positions.

"We started taking fire from all directions," he recalled in a 1998 interview with the American Forces Information Service. "The pilot was shot through the leg. The helicopter spun around and crashed in an open field, turned on its side and started burning. The co-pilot's arm was ripped off—it was just hanging." Despite the best efforts of the pilots, the helicopter sustained significant damage and crash-landed outside of the South Vietnam–controlled lines.

Although Rocco, the two pilots, the crew chief, and the medic had all survived the crash, he was the only individual who had not lost consciousness. Despite a fractured wrist and hip and a severely bruised spine, he carried his four comrades away from the burning helicopter to the safety of a perimeter established by South Vietnamese soldiers. "I guess I was going on reflexes," he said. "I jumped out and pulled the pilot out first. I looked for cover and saw a big tree lying on the ground. I dragged him to the tree, knowing that any time I was going to get shot." After getting all the wounded to the safety of the South Vietnamese position, Rocco administered first aid until the pain from his wounds and burns caused him to lose consciousness.

In March 1971, Lt. Lee Caubarreaux, the copilot rescued by Rocco that day in 1970, received a Medal of Honor recommendation for Rocco in the mail from a warrant officer in the 1st Cavalry Division awards office in South Vietnam, who had found it in a desk drawer. Caubarreaux pressed Army authorities to approve the award and even enlisted the help of his congressman. Caubarreaux, his shattered arm saved by doctors, stated that if not for Rocco, "we would have burned to death in the helicopter. I can't screw in a light bulb with my arm, but I can still hug my wife." On December 12, 1974, President Gerald R. Ford presented the Medal of Honor to Rocco in a ceremony held at the White House.

Rocco retired from the Army as a chief warrant officer in 1978 after 22 years of active service. Named the director of New Mexico's Veterans Service Commission, he persuaded New Mexico legislators and voters to let veterans attend state colleges for free and started a nursing home for homeless veterans. Rocco returned to active duty during Operation Desert Shield/Desert Storm, spending six months at Fort Sam Houston, Texas, recruiting medical personnel.

In 2002, Louis Rocco was diagnosed with terminal lung cancer. He died on October 31, 2002, at his home in San Antonio. He was buried at the Fort Sam Houston National Cemetery. In his honor, the city of San Antonio named a youth center the Louis Rocco Youth and Family Center.

Alexander M. Bielakowski

Further Reading

Bernstein, Jonathan. *US Army AH-1 Cobra Units in Vietnam.* Oxford, UK: Osprey, 2003.

Collier, Peter, and Nick Del Calzo. *Medal of Honor: Portraits of Valor beyond the Call of Duty.* New York: Artisan, 2006.

Faranacci, Donald. *Last Full Measure of Devotion: A Tribute to America's Heroes of the Vietnam War.* Bloomington, IN: AuthorHouse, 2007.

Rodriguez, Joseph C.

Born: November 14, 1928
Died: November 1, 2005
Home State: California
Service: Army
Conflict: Korean War
Age at Time of Award: 23

Born on November 14, 1928, Joseph C. Rodriguez was raised in San Bernardino, California. He graduated from San Bernardino Valley College in 1950 with a major in architecture. Rodriguez was working for an architect when he was drafted in the fall of 1950. He received his basic training at Fort Carson, Colorado, where he was assigned to H Company, 2nd Battalion of the 196th Regimental Combat Team. Upon completion of basic infantry training in February 1951, Private Rodriguez volunteered for duty in the Korean theater of operations. Promoted to private first class, he was deployed overseas with F Company, 17th Infantry Regiment of the 7th Infantry Division.

Part of the 8th Army that was attacked by the combined North Korean and Chinese Communist Forces (CCF) in May 1951, Private Rodriguez's unit was ordered to capture and occupy the strategic high ground located near the village of Munye-ri, 30 miles north of the 38th Parallel.

Three times, F Company tried to take the high ground, and three times they were repelled. As enemy forces began to roll hand grenades downhill toward the 2nd and 3rd platoons of F Company, Rodriguez took it upon himself to eliminate the enemy positions. He leaped to his feet, ran up the hill a distance of 60 yards, and charged their emplacements, hurling grenades into each of the enemy foxholes, destroying the emplacements and killing 15 enemy soldiers in the process. Rodriguez's actions had single-handedly broken the enemy defense, and the high ground near the village of Munye-ri was subsequently secured.

Following the battle at Munye-ri, Private Rodriguez was promoted to sergeant. A week later, Rodriguez was hit by small arms fire and evacuated to a hospital in Japan, where he spent three months in rehabilitation. When he finally returned to his old unit in the fall of 1951, he learned that he had been nominated for the Medal of Honor. For that reason, he was restricted from further combat. After being notified that he was to receive the medal, he flew home to the United States. On February 5, 1952, President Harry S. Truman presented Sergeant Rodriguez with the Medal of Honor in a ceremony held in the Rose Garden at the White House.

His next assignment was in the ROTC department at his alma mater, San Bernardino Valley College. During his tenure there, Sergeant Rodriguez indicated his interest in pursuing the military as a career to his superiors. He was subsequently commissioned an officer and promoted to rank of second lieutenant in the US Army Corps of Engineers. His first assignment involved engineering support of an Air Force unit stationed in northern Maine. Subsequent assignments included tours of duty in South Korea and Vietnam. Other assignments took him to Bolivia, Argentina, Puerto Rico, and the Panama Canal Zone. His duties involved working with military missions in those countries with further special assignments in Puerto Rico, where he was an advisor to the National Guard of Puerto Rico, and in the Panama Canal Zone, where he was director of the Technology Department at the School of the Americas and where he later served four years with the Inter-American Geodetic Survey Department.

His last assignment was at Fort Bliss, Texas, as facilities engineer. In 1980, after serving 30 years in the US Army, Colonel Rodriquez retired and settled in El Paso, Texas. After retiring from the military, he became the director of the Physical Plant at the University of Texas at El Paso for 10 years.

Joseph Rodriguez died on November 1, 2005, of an apparent heart attack in El Paso, Texas. He was buried with full military honors at Mountain View Cemetery in San Bernardino, California.

Keith A. Leitich

Further Reading

Collier, Peter, and Nick Del Calzo. *Medal of Honor: Portraits of Valor beyond the Call of Duty*, New York: Artisan Books, 2006.

Samora, Julian, and Patricia Vandel Simon. *A History of the Mexican-American People*. South Bend, IN: University of Notre Dame Press, 1977.

Roosevelt, Theodore

Born: October 27, 1858
Died: January 6, 1919
Home State: New York
Service: Army

Conflict: Spanish-American War
Age at Time of Award: 40

Born to an aristocratic family on October 27, 1858, in New York City, Theodore Roosevelt overcame a series of childhood maladies and had a distinguished career as a civil servant prior to his service during the Spanish-American War. After graduating magnum cum laude from Harvard in 1880, he wrote the first of his 26 books and was nominated as a state assemblyman in New York. Following a brief stint as a Dakota cattleman, Roosevelt served as the New York City Police commissioner and subsequently as a US Civil Service commissioner. In 1897, he was appointed as assistant secretary of the Navy in the McKinley Administration. When war with Spain broke out in 1898, Roosevelt resigned his Navy post and raised the regiment of the 1st US Volunteer Cavalry, known as the "Rough Riders."

The Rough Riders were composed of soldiers from a myriad of backgrounds, including cowboys, miners, socialites, ranchers, policemen, and associated men of fortune. The unit was described as "a society page, a financial column, a sports section, and a Wild West show all rolled into one." While offered command of the regiment by Secretary of War Russell Alger, Roosevelt turned the command down due to his own military inexperience and deferred to his close friend, veteran soldier Leonard Wood.

In Cuba, near the town of Santiago de Cuba on July 1, 1898, the Rough Riders attacked Spanish forces in prepared defensive positions situated on high ground. Lieutenant Colonel Roosevelt led successive charges up both Kettle and San Juan hills. While on horseback and under enemy fire, Roosevelt led his troops, along with troops from other units, up Kettle Hill. Upon reaching a barbed wire fence, he dismounted and continued on foot, routing the defenders, and reached the crest of the hill. Looking to his left, Roosevelt saw American troops advancing on San Juan Hill. In support of this advance, he leaped toward the Spanish defenses on the adjacent hill. Without regard for his own safety, and under heavy enemy fire, he started toward the Spanish position. With the rest of the regiment eventually following him, he was the first to enter the enemy's defenses while personally dispatching one of the Spaniards with his revolver. Roosevelt was recommended for the Medal of Honor for his actions on San Juan Hill, where his inspirational leadership led to the successful defeat of the Spanish defenders.

However, Roosevelt's actions during the battle were not officially recognized by the awarding of the medal. While stationed in the malaria-ridden island, many soldiers suffered from the illness, and the delay in withdrawing the military from Cuba drew the ire of the future president and other senior officers. In response, Roosevelt authored a report outlining troop conditions and penned a letter asking the War Department to quickly redeploy the Army. The letter was signed by fellow officers and sent to the War Department. Additionally, a copy of the letter was given to an

Associated Press correspondent and subsequently published in American news-papers. Roosevelt was considered the prime suspect for the "Round Robin" letter press leak, as it became known.

The press report was severely critical of the McKinley Administration's manage-ment of the war and proved an embarrassment for the president and the secretary of war. While Secretary Alger considered court-martialing Roosevelt for insub-ordination and his supposed role in the press leak, he decided against it. How-ever, revenge for the public embarrassment came when Alger declined to endorse Roosevelt's Medal of Honor recommendation despite endorsement from Wood and other members of the expedition. Interestingly, other accounts of Roosevelt's actions concluded that his deeds were not necessarily worthy of the award and that he merely executed his duties as was expected. Roosevelt called the denial of the award "one of the bitterest disappointments in my life."

Following the war, Theodore Roosevelt was elected governor of New York and ironically named vice president by McKinley, and then elected chief executive in 1901. Roosevelt died January 6, 1919. However, the issue regarding Roosevelt's medal surfaced again in 1998 when congressional legislation forced a review of the late president's actions in Cuba. As a result of the inquiry, on January 16, 2001, 103 years after the fact, President Bill Clinton presented the award posthumously to Tweed Roosevelt, Theodore's great-grandson, in the Roosevelt Room in the White House. As a result, Roosevelt remains the only president to have been awarded both the Medal of Honor and the Nobel Peace prize.

John Curatola

Further Reading

Jeffers, Paul, H. *Colonel Roosevelt: Theodore Roosevelt Goes to War, 1897–1898*. New York: John Wiley and Sons, 1996.

Miller, Nathan. *Theodore Roosevelt, A Life*. New York: Morrow and Co, 1992.

Tillman, Barrett. *Heroes: U.S. Army Medal of Honor Recipients*. New York: The Berkley Group, 2006.

Rosser, Ronald E.

Born: October 24, 1929
Died:
Home State: Ohio
Service: Army
Conflict: Korean War
Age at Time of Award: 22

Ronald Eugene Rosser was born October 24, 1929, in Columbus, Ohio. The old-est of 17 children in the family of John and Edith Marie Rosser, he grew up in the

PYRAMID OF HONOR

In 1918, following the Medal of Honor review board findings made public the previous year, Congress passed legislation that established several other medals, constituting what became known as the "pyramid of honor," a hierarchy of military awards for combat valor and meritorious service. The Medal of Honor would be the apex of this hierarchy, and lower-precedence awards would be established in ascending order to recognize heroism or distinguished service of a "lesser degree" than that recognized by the Medal of Honor.

Second in order of precedence was the Distinguished Service Cross, established in 1918 to recognize extraordinary heroism rising to a level just below that required for the Medal of Honor. The Navy Cross (for Navy, Marines, and Coast Guard) was established in 1919 and made a combat-only decoration in 1942. The Air Force Cross was established in 1960.

Also established by the 1918 legislation was the Distinguished Service Medal, which is awarded for exceptionally meritorious service. It is the highest nonvalorous award and can be awarded to civilians as well as military personnel.

Next in precedence comes the Silver Star, the third highest military award for valor in combat. It was established in 1918 as the Citation Star and was originally a device added to a campaign ribbon to recognize valor. However, in 1932, the Silver Star was redesignated as a medal with retroactive provision that allowed servicemen as far back as the Spanish-American War to receive it for gallant actions.

The Distinguished Flying Cross (DFC), awarded for heroism or extraordinary achievement in aerial flight, was established by an act of Congress in 1926 and made retroactive for actions after 1918; Charles A. Lindberg was the first recipient of the DFC. However, in December 1928, Congress passed a special act awarding the Distinguished Flying Cross retroactively to Wilbur and Orville Wright for the first manned flight at Kitty Hawk, North Carolina, in 1903.

The Bronze Star was established by executive order on February 4, 1944. It is awarded for heroism, outstanding achievement or meritorious service not involving aerial flight in connection with operations against an opposing armed force. When the award is for an act of combat heroism or valor, a bronze "V" device is affixed to the ribbon holding the Bronze Star.

The Purple Heart is the oldest American military award. The predecessor for the Purple Heart was George Washington's "Badge of Military Merit," which was first authorized in 1782. It was resurrected in 1932 as the Purple Heart, which is awarded for wounds or death as a result of any opposing armed force, as a result of an international terrorist attack, or as a result of military operations while serving as part of a peacekeeping force.

The Air Medal was established in 1942 for meritorious achievement while participating in aerial flight, for a single act of heroism in aerial operations against an armed enemy, or for merit in operational activities. During the Vietnam War, a single award of the Air Medal denoted participation by ground troops in a requisite number of combat air assaults. As of February 29, 1964, the bronze "V" device is authorized when the Air Medal is awarded for acts of heroism involving conflict with an armed enemy.

Each service also has a medal that is awarded for valor and heroism not involving armed conflict with an enemy. They are the Soldier's Medal (Army), the Navy and Marine Corps Medal, and the Airman's Medal. In precedence, they rank above the Bronze Star.

James H. Willbanks

Roseville/Crooksville area of Ohio. Spurning traditional family employment in the coalmines, Rosser delivered papers as a teenager for the *Zanesville News*. He spent his summers on a family farm with his grandparents, often hunting for days on end with his .22 caliber rifle. In 10th grade, Rosser left school to work in a pottery factory. In 1946, at the age of 17, he joined the US Army.

After enlisting at Crooksville, he trained at Camp Atterbury, Indiana, and then at Fort Benning, Georgia. After jump school, he was assigned to the 82nd Airborne Division, where he received training in a heavy weapons platoon as a mortar man. He left the army in 1949 and worked in a coal mine until 1951, when his brother Richard was killed in the Korean War. To avenge his brother's death, Rosser reenlisted in the Army in May 1951, requesting a combat assignment. Instead, he was sent to the 187th Airborne Combat Regiment in Japan. Dissatisfied with this posting, Rosser requested Korea. He was reassigned to the 38th Infantry Regiment of the 2nd Division, the first unit to arrive in Korea directly from the United States.

In Korea, Rosser was posted to a heavy mortar company in which he initially saw action as a forward observer. In November 1951, his parent unit relieved the Turkish Brigade after fierce battles at Bloody Ridge and Heart Break Ridge. In December 1951 and January 1952, Rosser was involved in heavy fighting in the vicinity of the Kumwha Valley. In early January, Corporal Rosser joined Love Company, 38th Regiment. On January 12, his unit was ordered to take Hill 472 near the town of Ponggilli.

During the initial assault, more than half the unit was killed or wounded. The commanding officer, badly wounded himself, radioed for instructions but was told to continue the attack to take the hill. Seeing that his commander was in no shape to lead a renewed attack, Rosser took it upon himself to organize the survivors and lead the charge.

As he pushed up the hill, he realized that the rest of the soldiers had halted their advance and that he was alone. Driven by desire to avenge his brother's death, he elected to continue the attack on his own, charging the objective with only a carbine and a grenade. Reaching the first bunker, Rosser killed the defenders with a burst from his carbine. At the top of the hill, he killed two more enemy soldiers and then moved down the trench line, killing another five enemies. At this point, he lobbed his grenade into another bunker and shot two soldiers who emerged. Out of ammunition, Rosser braved enemy fire to run downhill, obtain more magazines and grenades, and then charge the hill once again. As he exhorted others to join him, Rosser assaulted two more bunkers and once again found himself without ammunition. He returned downhill again, grabbed more ammunition, and assaulted enemy fortifications for the third time. Single-handedly, Rosser killed at least 13 enemy soldiers. During his platoon's withdrawal under fire, Rosser, now also wounded, helped more seriously wounded comrades to safety.

In April 1952, Rosser's unit was pulled off the line to guard prisoners on Koji-do, an island off the coast of Korea. After Koji-do, Rosser's unit rotated to Pusan, then to Japan, and finally back to the United States. There, he learned he would receive the Medal of Honor for his actions on January 12. Rosser was awarded the medal by President Harry Truman in a ceremony at the White House on June 27, 1952.

After returning to the United States from Korea, Rosser decided to stay in the Army and obtained his general equivalency diploma (GED). He later took classes at Florida Atlantic University, earning a BA in history. He served as an advisor to the Army Reserve and then was stationed in Germany as a platoon sergeant with the 370th Armored Infantry. During 1956–1958, Rosser was an instructor at Fort Benning. Before his retirement in 1968, Rosser served as a reenlistment noncommissioned officer in West Palm Beach, Florida. After his brother Gary was killed in Vietnam, Rosser once again sought a combat assignment. However, he was turned down, and he subsequently retired, becoming chief of police in Haverhill, Florida.

In 1987, Ronald Rosser married Sandy Smith, settling in Roseville, Florida. His daughter, Pamela, also served in the military for nearly 10 years, most of it in the 101st Airborne Division. Rosser donated his Medal of Honor to the Ohio State House.

Anton A. Menning

Further Reading

Collier, Peter, and Nick Del Calzo. *Medal of Honor: Portraits of Valor beyond the Call of Duty.* New York: Artisan, 2006.

Coy, Jimmie Dean. *Valor: A Gathering of Eagles.* Mobile, AL: Evergreen Press, 2003.

Schott, Joseph. *Above and Beyond: The Story of the Congressional Medal of Honor.* New York: Putnam, 1963.

Rubin, Tibor

Born: June 18, 1929
Died:
Home State: New York
Service: Army
Conflict: Korean War
Age at Time of Award: 21

Tibor Rubin was born in Pásztó, Hungary, on June 18, 1929, the son of a shoemaker. His father, Ferenz, had been a soldier in the Hungarian Army during World War I and a prisoner of war in Russia. Rubin was only 13 when he was deported to the Mauthausen concentration camp, where American troops subsequently liberated him. During the war, his father died at Buchenwald concentration camp; his mother and 10-year-old sister died at Auschwitz concentration camp; and his older brother served with Free Czech armed forces based in the United Kingdom.

In 1948, Rubin immigrated to the United States and settled in New York. The following year, he tried to enlist in the US Army, but his poor English caused him to fail the language test. In 1950, Rubin again attempted to enlist and, with some help from two fellow volunteers, this time passed the language exam.

By July 1950, Rubin was serving in combat with I Company, 8th Cavalry Regiment, 1st Cavalry Division in the Korean War. Fellow soldiers in Korea would later describe Rubin's immediate superior, Sgt. Artice V. Watson, as "an anti-Semite who gave Rubin dangerous assignments in hopes of getting him killed." In one such assignment, Rubin single-handedly defended a hill for 24 hours against waves of North Korean soldiers.

While two of his commanding officers recommended Rubin for the Medal of Honor, both were killed in action before any paperwork could be processed. Nearly a dozen men who served under Watson submitted lengthy affidavits in support of Rubin, but nothing came of their efforts.

In October 1950, the 1st Cavalry Division was badly mauled when large numbers of Chinese communist "volunteers" crossed the Yalu River into North Korea to prevent a victory for UN forces. On October 30, 1950, Chinese forces attacked Rubin's unit. During that night and throughout the next day, he manned a .30 caliber machine gun at the extreme end of the unit's line. Severely wounded, he continued to man his machine gun until his ammunition was exhausted. The Chinese captured him as he attempted to return to friendly lines. As if Rubin's actions in combat were not enough, his bravery continued during the next 30 months in a prisoner-of-war (POW) camp.

As a POW, Rubin refused preferential treatment and his captors' repeated offers of repatriation to Hungary. He frequently stole food from the Chinese and North Koreans in order to aid his comrades. "He shared the food evenly among the GIs," wrote one fellow prisoner. "He also took care of us, nursed us, carried us to the latrine....He did many good deeds, which he told us were mitzvahs in the Jewish tradition....He was a very religious Jew and helping his fellow men was the most important thing to him." Many survivors of the camp credit Rubin with keeping them alive.

After repatriation to the United States at the end of the Korean War, Rubin became a US citizen. "I always wanted to become a citizen of the United States and when I became a citizen it was one of the happiest days in my life," he said. "I think about the United States and I am a lucky person to live here. When I came to America, it was the first time I was free. It was one of the reasons I joined the US Army because I wanted to show my appreciation."

Despite the best efforts of those who served with Tibor Rubin, it was not until 2001 that the US Army officially reviewed Rubin's case. In that year, Congress passed the Leonard Kravitz Jewish War Veterans Act, named for the uncle and namesake of rock musician Lenny Kravitz who was killed in action while manning a machine gun against attacking Chinese troops, thereby allowing the rest of his platoon to retreat to safety. While Kravitz's action was almost identical to that of several non-Jewish Medal of Honor winners, he had only received the Distinguished Service Cross. The bill allowed for the reexamination of Medal of Honor recommendations in cases of apparent anti-Semitism. Under the provisions of the bill, Rubin's case was reopened, and, ultimately, he was presented the Medal of Honor by President George W. Bush on September 23, 2005.

Alexander M. Bielakowski

Further Reading

Collier, Peter, and Nick Del Calzo. *Medal of Honor: Portraits of Valor beyond the Call of Duty*. New York: Artisan, 2006.

Tillman, Barrett. *Heroes: U.S. Army Medal of Honor Recipients*. New York: The Berkley Group, 2006.

Rudolph, Donald E.

Born: November 14, 1921
Died: May 25, 2006
Home State: Minnesota
Service: Army
Conflict: World War II
Age at Time of Award: 24

Donald E. Rudolph, born on November 14, 1921, in South Haven, Minnesota, believed he had enlisted for a one-year term of service in 1941. However, the Japanese attack on Pearl Harbor changed his one-year enlistment into an indefinite term of service. Assigned to the 6th Infantry Division, Rudolph originally trained in Yuma, Arizona, preparing for desert warfare. The unit's orders changed, and it began preparations to fight in the jungles of the Pacific Theater.

After seeing combat in New Guinea and the Philippines, Rudolph earned a rotation to the rear while his unit was in Luzon. While assisting the wounded in the rear area, several injured men from his unit came from the front. Without orders, Rudolph moved to the front lines to be with his men and take part in the fighting.

Rudolph, then a technical sergeant, took over his platoon on February 3, 1945, after an injury incapacitated his platoon leader. The unit came under heavy enemy fire two days later from well-constructed fighting positions in an area the unit previously thought lightly defended. While rendering aid to wounded soldiers, Rudolph noticed that the heaviest fire was coming from a nearby canal. With his rifle and grenades, Rudolph maneuvered toward the enemy and took it under fire, killing the three Japanese soldiers manning the position. After this initial success, Rudolph continued to move to the line of enemy pillboxes that inhibited another company's advance. Opening the roof of the first position he encountered, Rudolph threw in a grenade and killed the gunners inside. At the second position, he used a pickax to open the bunker; then he used a grenade and his rifle to eliminate the enemy inside. Rudolph continued to attack nearby enemy positions, eventually eliminating six more enemy bunkers.

Later, when his unit came under attack from a Japanese tank, Rudolph advanced under covering fire, mounted the tank, opened a hatch on the turret, and used a white phosphorous grenade to destroy the tank and kill its crew. Rudolph's actions contributed to "one of the most decisive victories of the Philippine campaign." For his actions that day, he received a battlefield commission.

Several weeks later, an artillery shell sent shrapnel into Rudolph's nose, and it lodged under his eye. After his release from the hospital, he learned he was under consideration for a medal. Later, while serving as a military policeman, he learned he would receive the Medal of Honor. On August 23, 1945, in one of the largest such ceremonies, President Truman awarded Rudolph and 27 others the Medal of Honor in the East Room of the White House.

Donald Rudolph retired from the Army in 1963. After his retirement, he continued to serve as a benefits counselor for the Veterans Administration (VA) until he retired from the VA in 1976. In 1995, Rudolph attended the reenactment of the Philippine landings; he was one of three Medal of Honor recipients who had served in the Philippines to attend the 50th-anniversary ceremonies celebrating the landings. During the anniversary celebration, Rudolph received a certificate of recognition from the government of the Philippines for his gallantry during the war. During his lifetime, Rudolph attended seven presidential inaugurations. He wrote a series of articles for the *Minneapolis Star Tribune* describing his service and his Medal of Honor ceremony at the White House. He died at the age of 85 on May 25, 2006, at a nursing home in Grand Rapids, Minnesota, from complications of Alzheimer's disease. He is buried at the Fort Snelling National Cemetery in Minneapolis, Minnesota.

Gates M. Brown

Further Reading

Above and Beyond: A History of the Medal of Honor from the Civil War to Vietnam. Boston: Boston Publishing Company, 1985.

Collier, Peter, and Nick Del Calzo. *Medal of Honor: Portraits of Valor beyond the Call of Duty.* New York: Artisan, 2006.

Ruiz, Alejandro R. Renteria

Born: June 26, 1924
Died: November 20, 2009
Home State: New Mexico
Service: Army
Conflict: World War II
Age at Time of Award: 20

Alejandro R. Renteria Ruiz was born June 26, 1924, in Loving, New Mexico, the son of a Mexican immigrant who had served in Pancho Villa's army. Ruiz joined the US Army in 1944 after getting involved in a legal matter while driving to see his girlfriend in Texas. When he went before the judge, Ruiz was given the option to enlist in the Army or go to jail. Ruiz chose the Army. After basic training, Ruiz became a member of the 165th Infantry Regiment, 27th Infantry Division and eventually was shipped out for combat duty in the Pacific.

In April 1945, Ruiz and his unit landed on the island of Okinawa. Immediately, they were engaged in heavy fighting with the Japanese. On April 28, Ruiz and his company worked their way down a ravine when a hidden Japanese pillbox opened fire on them. Amazingly, Ruiz and his squad leader were the only men to escape injury. He soon realized the pillbox needed to be silenced.

Ruiz grabbed a Browning Automatic Rifle (BAR) to provide him with more firepower and quickly charged the enemy pillbox. Upon reaching the pillbox, Ruiz climbed on top just as his weapon jammed. At that same moment, a Japanese soldier charged at him, forcing Ruiz to use the BAR as a club in hand-to-hand combat. Once the Japanese soldier was down, Ruiz tossed the weapon aside and ran back through heavy enemy fire in order to retrieve another BAR and more ammunition. Again, he raced back toward the pillbox while the enemy concentrated all their fire on him. Ruiz retook his position back on top of the pillbox and fired multiple bursts into open apertures. He killed 12 Japanese soldiers inside of the structure and silenced the enemy machine gun.

After the gun was silenced, Ruiz sat down to light a cigarette only to have difficulty due to his shaking hands. Surprisingly, Ruiz escaped with only a minor flesh wound despite running through enemy fire. For the next several weeks, Ruiz continued fighting on Okinawa. After returning to the United States in May 1946, Ruiz learned that he was to receive the Medal of Honor for his actions in saving the pinned-down soldiers and destroying the enemy machine gun.

On June 12, 1946, with members of his family present, Ruiz was presented the medal by President Harry S. Truman. Regardless of the hard combat he had endured, his service did not stop with World War II. Ruiz went on to fight in Korea and eventually retired from the US Army as a sergeant in 1964.

In retirement, Alejandro Ruiz resided in Visalia, California, and was active in active in Medal of Honor activities. He died at the age of 85 from congestive heart failure at a hospital in Napa, California, on November 20, 2009. The town of Visalia named a park in his honor.

Thomas D. Lofton Jr.

Further Reading

Collier, Peter, and Nick Del Calzo. *Medal of Honor: Portraits of Valor beyond the Call of Duty*. New York: Artisan, 2006.

Rush, Robert S. *GI: The US Infantryman in World War II*. Oxford, UK: Osprey, 2003.

Tillman, Barrett. *Heroes: U.S. Army Medal of Honor Recipients*. New York: Berkley Caliber, 2006.

Sakato, George T.

Born: February 19, 1921
Died:
Home State: California
Service: Army
Conflict: World War II
Age at Time of Award: 23

George T. Sakato was born in Colton, California, on February 19, 1921. In early 1942, Sakato and his family relocated from California to Arizona in order to avoid the Japanese American internment camps created after the attack on Pearl Harbor. Soon after, Sakato attempted to enlist in the Army Air Corps but was denied due to his draft status being 4-C, an undesirable alien. By 1943, the government changed its policy to allow Japanese Americans to enter the service largely due to the highly publicized exploits of the 100th Infantry Battalion of the Hawaiian National Guard, a primarily Japanese American (Nisei) unit fighting in the Mediterranean Theater.

Sakato immediately entered the US Army, joining his brother who had enlisted just before Pearl Harbor. By the summer of 1944, both brothers had completed their training and were sent to Naples, Italy, as replacements for the "Go for Broke" 442nd Regimental Combat Team (RCT), another Nisei outfit that would become the most decorated unit of the war. In August, Sakato and the 442nd boarded ships in preparation for landing at Marseille, France.

For the next two months, Sakato and his unit fought northward through France. By late October, the 442nd reached the town of Biffontaine in the Vosges Mountains, where German troops had established a strong defensive line in the high ground nearby. One of the German positions, known as Hill 617, overlooked an open valley cut by a railroad line in the center. The Germans used this position to protect the rail line and fire downward on the American troops as they advanced.

On October 28, Private Sakato and his company were ordered to move out just before midnight and attempt to flank the German position. At dawn, Sakato led an assault on the Germans, killing five with a recently acquired Thompson sub-machine gun. Before long, Sakato and his company had secured Hill 617 and captured a number of German prisoners in the process. However, other German forces nearby mounted a counterattack. During the ensuing battle, one of Sakato's closest friends was hit and died in his arms. An angry Sakato took charge of his squad and continued to fire on the enemy with his submachine gun until he no longer had any ammunition. Then, grabbing an enemy pistol and rifle he picked up from the battlefield, Sakato proceeded to kill seven more Germans, inspiring his fellow soldiers. During the battle, Sakato and his platoon captured 34 enemy soldiers and held their position until they were relieved.

After a few days in the area, the 442nd received word that a nearby battalion of Americans in the 141st Infantry Regiment had been cut off from Allied lines and surrounded by Germans. They were ordered to break through the German lines in order to rescue the trapped men. It was during this rescue attempt that Sakato was knocked down by a mortar shell; the bulky winter overcoat he was wearing prevented him from being killed, but he was seriously wounded by shrapnel that struck both his spine and lungs.

For the next eight months, Sakato was hospitalized for treatment from his wounds. During his time in the hospital, Sakato received word that he had been recommended for the Medal of Honor, but he eventually received the Distinguished Service Cross (DSC) instead.

After the war, George Sakato eventually became a postal worker in Denver, Colorado. Some 55 years after the war, Sakato received an unexpected phone call from the Pentagon asking him to report to Washington, D.C., to receive the Medal of Honor. It was explained to him that his Distinguished Service Cross was being upgraded as part of a review of the records of Asian American DSC recipients. On June 21, 2000, President Bill Clinton presented Sakato with the Medal of Honor. Twenty-one other Asian American veterans also received the Medal of Honor that day, all but seven of them posthumously.

Thomas D. Lofton Jr.

Further Reading

Asahina, Robert. *Just Americans: The Story of the 100th Battalion/442nd Regimental Combat Team in World War II*. New York: Gotham Books, 2007.

Chang, Thelma, and Daniel K. Inouye. *I Can Never Forget: Men of the 100th/442nd*. Honolulu: SIGI Productions, 1995.

Collier, Peter, and Nick Del Calzo. *Medal of Honor: Portraits of Valor beyond the Call of Duty.* New York: Artisan, 2006.

Crost, Lyn. *Honor by Fire: Japanese Americans at War in Europe and the Pacific.* Novato, CA: Presidio Press, 1997.

Moulin, Pierre. *U.S. Samurais in Bruyeres.* Luxembourg: Peace and Freedom Trail, 1993.

Sterner, C. Douglas. *Go for Broke: The Nisei Warriors of World War II Who Conquered Germany, Japan, and American Bigotry.* Clearfield, UT: American Legacy Historical Press, 2007.

Salomon, Ben L.

Born: September 1, 1914
Died: July 7, 1944
Home State: Wisconsin
Service: Army
Conflict: World War II
Age at Time of Award: 29

Born in Milwaukee, Wisconsin, on September 1, 1914, Benjamin Lewis Salomon graduated from Shorewood High School and attended Marquette University. He completed his undergraduate education at the University of Southern California (USC). He went on to the USC Dental College, graduating in 1937, and started a dental practice. He was drafted as a private in the US Army in 1940 but was notified that he was to be transferred to the Army Dental Corps; he was commissioned a first lieutenant on August 14, 1942. He became the regimental dental officer for the 2nd Battalion, 105th Infantry Regiment, 27th Infantry Division, where he was still serving in 1944 when he was promoted to captain. In June 1944, he went ashore with his battalion in the invasion of Saipan in the Marianas Islands in the Pacific Theater. Once ashore, he volunteered to replace the 2nd Battalion's wounded regimental surgeon. He soon became very busy as the American casualties mounted as they pushed inland.

On July 7, Salomon's aid station was set up only 50 yards behind the forward line of US positions. The Japanese launched an overwhelming offensive involving approximately 3,000 to 5,000 Japanese troops. Salomon's aid station was soon full of wounded Americans, with attacking enemy soldiers following close behind. Salomon fended off the first Japanese troops who entered the aid station but quickly realized it would soon be overrun. Grabbing a rifle, he gave orders for the wounded to be evacuated to safety while he provided cover. Salomon left the tent and took over a machine gun whose crew had been killed. No survivors witnessed Salomon's actions from that point, but evidence suggested the following: Salomon used the machine gun to take out large numbers of approaching enemy troops. He had apparently moved the machine gun at least three times to regain a clear field of fire, even though the blood trail from one position to another proved he was seriously injured at the time. When his body was found, 98 enemy troops lay dead in front of his position. Examiners determined that Salomon had suffered 76 bullet wounds and many bayonet wounds, up to 24 of which could have been received while he was still alive, moving and operating the machine gun.

Three men were nominated for the Medal of Honor for their acts in this engagement. The other two were quickly approved, but Salomon's nomination, which was submitted by Capt. Edmund G. Love, the 27th Division historian, was returned by the division commander, Maj. Gen. George Griner, who said that according to the Geneva Convention no medical officer could bear arms against an enemy. Additionally, he believed that Salomon, as a medical noncombatant, was outside the Medal of Honor guidelines. In the end, Salomon received no recognition for his valorous acts, not even a Purple Heart for his wounds.

In 1951, Love, by then working as a civilian historian with the US Army, again submitted the recommendation, this time through the Office of the Chief of Military History, but it was returned without action because the time limit for submitting World War II awards had passed. In 1969, another recommendation was submitted by Lt. Gen. Hal B. Jennings, the surgeon general of the Army. After a legal review by the Army judge advocate general that determined the Geneva Convention did allow medical personnel to bear arms in self-defense or in defense of the wounded and sick, the secretary of the Army recommended approval and forwarded the recommendation to the secretary of defense, but it was returned without action.

In 1998, Dr. Robert West, University of Southern California (USC) School of Denistry, resubmitted the nomination through his congressman, Representative Brad Sherman. This time the nomination made it before the Senior Army Decorations Board for processing. After the nomination was favorably considered by the board, the recommendation was approved by the secretary of the Army and the Defense Department. Finally, after legislation was passed in Congress to waive the time limitation, in May 2002 President George W. Bush posthumously awarded Benjamin Salomon the Medal of Honor many felt he had long deserved; the medal was presented to Dr. West. It is on display at the USC School of Dentistry. Salomon is one of the few medical officers to receive the award; he is also one of only 17 Jewish Americans to receive the award.

Debra J. Sheffer

Further Reading

Brody, Seymour. *Jewish Heroes and Heroines of America*. Hollywood, FL: Lifetime Books, 1996.

Tillman, Barrett. *Heroes: U.S. Army Medal of Honor Recipients*. New York: The Berkley Group, 2006.

Sandlin, Willie

Born: January 1, 1890
Died: May 29, 1949
Home State: Kentucky
Service: Army
Conflict: World War I
Age at Time of Award: 28

Willie Sandlin was born in Jackson, Kentucky, on New Year's Day, 1890. He grew up around Buckhorn. Having lost his mother at an early age and without many advantages growing up, Sandlin joined the Regular Army in 1914 and served along the Mexican border.

In 1917, as a sergeant, he joined the 132nd Regiment, 33rd Division, which was an Illinois National Guard division. In order to bring the unit up to full strength, it was merged with three draftee, or National Army, divisions: the 86th, another Illinois unit; the 88th from Iowa; and the 84th from Kentucky. The 33rd Division trained from September 1917 to May 1918 at Camp Logan, Houston, Texas. Sandlin's regiment left Hoboken, New Jersey, on May 16 and arrived at Brest, France, on May 24. By the end of June, they arrived at Oisemont, where they trained with the British.

Then, on July 4, the 132nd participated in an attack on Hamel. This was the first time Americans and Australian soldiers had fought together. Elements of the regiment were attached to the 4th Australian Infantry Brigade. By August 6, the regiment had assumed responsibility for its own sector of the front. On August 19, the regiment was transferred to the 1st American Army in the Toul sector. Sandlin's unit relieved a French division north of Verdun in preparation for the Meuse-Argonne Offensive, which would begin on September 26, 1918.

The 33rd Division was adjacent to the Meuse River. Their attack would run approximately four miles north, following the river and clearing the west bank of Germans before veering east to cross it. Sergeant Sandlin's regiment held the extreme right flank of the entire offensive. Directly in their path was the daunting Bois de Forges, just four miles east of the formidable Montfaucon where German crown prince Rupprecht had overseen the Battle of Verdun in 1916. Bois de Forges was defended by no fewer than five belts of machine gun nests.

Crossing the hastily built bridges over the Forges River, Sandlin's unit immediately came under intense machine gun fire. Sandlin observed a narrow gap where the machine gun fire was not overlapping. Grabbing a handful of grenades, he single-handedly charged through the gap. He threw a couple of grenades, one within about 40 yards of the nests, which fell among the German gunners. After lobbing a couple more for good measure, he leaped into the emplacement. Out of eight Germans, two remained unharmed, and, as they unloaded their revolvers at him, Sandlin bayoneted them. After his actions, he and his men continued their advance.

It was not long before they encountered the second line of machine guns, where Sandlin charged and repeated his previous performance. Without pausing, he continued onto the third line in the same manner. Single-handedly, Willie Sandlin destroyed three machine gun nests and killed 24 Germans.

Ultimately, the 33rd Division cleared the forest and reached their objective overlooking the Meuse in three-and-a-half hours with 86 wounded and 24 killed.

On July 9, 1919, Sandlin received the Medal of Honor for his actions in the Bois de Forges. He is the only native-born Kentuckian to have received this honor in World War I.

After the war, Willie Sandlin moved back to Kentucky, where he bought a farm near Hyden. He and his wife had five children. On May 29, 1949, at the age of 59, he died from a lingering lung infection from a gas attack in the Meuse-Argonne. He was buried in Hurricane Cemetery near Hyden. In 1990, his remains were moved to Zachary Taylor National Cemetery in Louisville, Kentucky.

Lon Strauss

Further Reading

American Battle Monuments Commission. *33rd Division, Summary of Operations in the World War*. Washington, D.C.: Government Printing Office, 1944.

Federal Writers' Project of the Work Projects Administration for the State of Kentucky. *Military History of Kentucky, Chronologically Arranged*. Frankfort, KY: Printed by the State Journal, 1939.

Huidekoper, Frederic Louis. *The History of the 33rd Division, A.E.F.* Springfield: Illinois State Historical Society, 1921.

Rand, Fred E. *132nd Infantry, 66th Brigade, 33rd Division: 50th Anniversary, March 13, 1926*. S.I: s.n., 1926.

33rd Division A.E.F. From Its Arrival in France until the Armistice with Germany November 11, 1918. Diekirch, Luxembourg: Gustave Soupert, 1919.

Sasser, Clarence Eugene

Born: September 12, 1947
Died:
Home State: Texas
Service: Army
Conflict: Vietnam War
Age at Time of Award: 20

Clarence Eugene Sasser, US Army (US Army Medical Department Regiment).

Clarence Eugene Sasser was born on September 12, 1947, in Chenango, Texas. He was drafted after losing his college deferment at the University of Houston, but because of his education he was trained as a combat medic. Sasser's tour of duty in Vietnam with Headquarters Company, 3rd Battalion, 60th Infantry Regiment, 9th Infantry Division, lasted only 51 days.

On January 10, 1968, Sasser was attached to the 3rd Battalion's Company A, which was part of a "reconnaissance in force" being inserted into an area of reported Viet Cong (VC) activity. As the Americans approached the landing zone (LZ), the lead helicopter was heavily damaged by enemy small arms fire and crashed. The remaining helicopters quickly disgorged the company's other soldiers, not realizing that the enemy occupied fortified positions on three sides of the LZ and that the single American company was facing an entire VC regiment. The American soldiers came under fire from VC small arms, mortar, and rocket fire, and, in less than five minutes, more than 30 American soldiers were wounded.

Sasser immediately began to aid the wounded soldiers around him. He crawled in the muck of rice paddies from soldier to soldier through enemy fire. As he carried a comrade to safety, shrapnel from a VC mortar wounded Sasser in the left shoulder and side. Refusing assistance, he bandaged himself and returned to the rice paddy to assist more wounded soldiers. VC machine gun fire subsequently wounded him in both legs. Despite this injury, he pulled himself through the mud 100 meters with his hands to help another soldier. Then, peering over the top of the dike that separated him from a neighboring rice paddy, Sasser received a glancing blow on the head from a VC sniper. Bleeding from his scalp, he lay unconscious for some time before more mortar rounds woke him.

Despite the pain and loss of blood from his wounds, Sasser not only continued to treat wounded Americans, but also encouraged others in the fight against the VC. Finding a group of soldiers pinned down by enemy fire 200 meters from the main American element, he convinced them to make their way back to the rest of the Americans. "I felt that if I could get the guys up and fighting," he said later, "we might all get out of there somehow."

Despite the best efforts of American higher command, the main support lent to the trapped company was airpower. "All we got was air support from the [US Air Force F-4] Phantoms. My respect for the Phantoms went up immediately," he said. "Man they were dropping napalm on the wood lines, laying it in there so close that a lot of times you'd think the pilot was going to get his tail caught in it when he pulled up, it was that close."

After returning to he American lines, Sasser continued to treat the wounded for five hours until they were safely evacuated. In the course of that day, 34 Americans were killed and 59 wounded—and doubtless more Americans would have died had it not been for his efforts.

After three months in a hospital at Camp Zama, Japan, the Army initially intended to return Sasser to combat in Vietnam. Thankfully, an Army doctor arranged for him to be reassigned to the camp dispensary. While still at Camp Zama, Sasser was informed that he would receive the Medal of Honor.

On March 7, 1969, in a ceremony held at the White House, President Richard Nixon presented Sasser and two others with the Medal of Honor.

After leaving the Army, Clarence Sasser attended Texas A&M University to study chemistry but left after he married. After working for Dow Chemical Company and Amoco for five years, he began working for the Veterans Administration, where he still works at the time of the writing.

Alexander M. Bielakowski

Further Reading

Collier, Peter, and Nick Del Calzo. *Medal of Honor: Portraits of Valor beyond the Call of Duty*. New York: Artisan, 2006.

Smith, Larry. *Beyond Glory: Medal of Honor Heroes in Their Own Words—Extraordinary Stories of Courage from World War II to Vietnam*. New York: W. W. Norton, 2003.

Schofield, John M.

Born: September 29, 1831
Died: March 4, 1906
Home State: New York
Service: Army
Conflict: Civil War
Age at Time of Award: 29

John McAllister Schofield was born September 29, 1831, in Gerry, New York, but, at the age of 12, was taken by his father, a Baptist minister, to Freeport, Illinois. He received an appointment to the US Military Academy at West Point in 1849 from Illinois and graduated seventh of 52 cadets in his class in 1853. He was commissioned in the artillery and served in Florida before returning to West Point as an instructor in natural and experimental philosophy. In 1860, he took a leave of absence from the Army and taught at Washington University in St. Louis, Missouri.

When the Civil War began, he first served as mustering officer for the state of Missouri. Receiving a promotion to major of the 1st Missouri Infantry, Schofield served as chief of staff to Brig. Gen. Nathaniel Lyon. He saw action at Wilson's Creek, where Lyon was killed. During the battle, Schofield led a regiment in a charge against Confederate troops. For his "conspicuous gallantry" in this action, he would be awarded the Medal of Honor on July 2, 1892.

Schofield was promoted to brigadier general in November 1861 and was placed in command of all Federal militia in Missouri until April 1862, when he assumed command of the Army of the Frontier, Department of Missouri. He was promoted to major general in November 1962. Requesting to be relieved from duty due to an altercation with his superior, Samuel R. Curtis, Schofield departed Missouri. On April 17, 1863, he assumed command of the 3rd Division in the XIV Corps of the Army of the Cumberland. He returned to Missouri later that year as commander of the Department of Missouri. In 1864, as commander of the Army of the Ohio, he took part in the Atlanta Campaign under Maj. Gen. William T. Sherman.

When Sherman set off on his "March to the Sea" after the fall of Atlanta, Schofield's Army of the Ohio was detached to join Maj. Gen. George H. Thomas in blocking Confederate general John Bell Hood's invasion of Tennessee. On November 30, 1864, Schofield's forces engaged Hood at the Battle of Franklin, repulsing the Confederate attack and crippling his army. Two weeks later, Schofield's troops participated in the destruction of what was left of Hood's army at the Battle of Nashville. Schofield was then ordered to move his army to North Carolina to join forces with Sherman's army. His troops occupied Wilmington on February 22, 1865, and fought a battle at Kinton on March 10 before joining Sherman at Goldsboro. He was still serving under Sherman in North Carolina when the Civil War ended.

After the war, Schofield was sent on a special diplomatic mission to France to negotiate the removal of French troops from Mexico. During Reconstruction, he served as military governor of Virginia. From June 1868 to March 1869, he served as President Andrew Johnson's interim secretary of war, replacing Edwin M. Stanton.

In 1873, Schofield was given a secret mission by Secretary of War William Belknap to investigate the strategic potential of the Hawaiian Islands. Schofield subsequently recommended that the US establish a naval port at Pearl Harbor.

From 1876 to 1881, Schofield served as superintendent of the Military Academy at West Point. In 1888, after serving in successive assignments as commander of the Pacific, Missouri, and Atlantic departments, Schofield succeeded Philip H. Sheridan as commanding general of the Army upon Sheridan's death. As the general in charge, Schofield was instrumental in clarifying lines of authority and achieving harmony between staff and line. He also supported increases in pay for noncommissioned officers, advanced a plan to reduce desertions, initiated efficiency reports for officers, and recommended that incompetent officers be denied promotion.

Lt. Gen. John Schofield retired from the army on September 29, 1895, at the age of 64 and published his memoirs, *Forty-Six Years in the Army*, two years later. He died at St. Augustine, Florida, on March 4, 1906. He was buried at Arlington National Cemetery. The military installation at Schofield Barracks, Hawaii, about 30 miles north of Honolulu, was named in his honor.

James H. Willbanks

Further Reading

Connolly, John B. *John M. Schofield and the Politics of Generalship*. Durham: University of North Carolina Press, 2006.

Eicher, John H., and David J. Eicher. *Civil War High Commands*. Palo Alto, CA: Stanford University Press, 2001.

McDonough, James L. *Schofield: Union General in the Civil War and Reconstruction*. Tallahassee: University Press of Florida, 1972.

Schofield, John M. *Forty-Six Years in the Army*. New York: The Century Company, 1897.

Shafter, William R.

Born: October 16, 1835
Died: November 13, 1906
Home State: Michigan
Service: Army
Conflict: Civil War
Age at Time of Award: 26

William Rufus Shafter was born outside Galesburg, Michigan, on October 16, 1835. The eldest of four children, Shafter was a bright student who attended local schools and enrolled in the Prairie Seminary in Richland, Michigan, in 1861. The start of the Civil War in the spring of 1861 upset Shafter's plans. He waited until the end of the spring semester and then traveled to Galesburg to enlist in the 7th Michigan Volunteer Infantry as a private. On the way to camp in Fort Wayne, Michigan, Shafter received word he had been promoted to first lieutenant by the 7th's colonel, Ira B. Grosvenor. The Federal debacle at the first Battle of Bull Run on July 21, 1861, accelerated the pace of training and led to the 7th Michigan shipping out for the Eastern Theater and the Union Army of the Potomac.

Shafter and the 7th Michigan participated in the Peninsula Campaign of May–July 1862. During the Battle of Fair Oaks on June 1, Shafter was wounded in the hip and had his horse killed beneath him. The wound was serious but not fatal.

Nevertheless, Shafter refused treatment until three days later, continuing to perform his duties. It took close to two months for the wound to heal, but for his actions that day, Shafter later received the Medal of Honor (he did not receive the award until June 12, 1895). Shafter later resigned his post with the 7th Michigan to take a commission as a major with the 19th Michigan Volunteer Infantry.

The rest of Shafter's Civil War experience saw his fortunes continue to rise. Shafter accepted a commission as a colonel of the 17th United States Colored Infantry (USCT) in June 1863 and moved to the Western Theater. The 17th USCT performed creditably at the Battle of Nashville on December 15–16, 1864, and Maj. Gen. George H. Thomas noticed Shafter. With the war winding down, Shafter received a promotion to brevet brigadier general.

Shafter's experience commanding black troops paid off handsomely after the Civil War's conclusion. Thomas recommended Shafter for command of the 24th US Infantry, a regiment of regular African American troops with white officers. Shafter, who was given the nickname Pecos Bill, spent the next 10 years fighting Native Americans in West Texas. That decade was characterized by tough combat against a number of Indian tribes, and Shafter performed well in the harsh environment. He also stirred controversy in 1881 when Shafter, in command of Fort Davis, began the court-martial proceedings against 2nd Lt. Henry O. Flipper, the first African American graduate of West Point, that led to Flipper's dismissal.

In 1879, Shafter was promoted to colonel of the 1st Infantry Regiment and moved to the Department of the Columbia. For the bulk of the next two decades, Shafter's service in the departments of Columbia and California proved uneventful. The outbreak of the Spanish-American War in 1898 gave Shafter another chance to distinguish himself.

Shafter was promoted to major general of volunteers and tasked with command of the US expeditionary force to Cuba in 1898. The expeditionary force was headquartered in Tampa, Florida, and the job of preparing for an overseas campaign—even if it was just off the Florida coast—proved to be enormous. The US military was ill prepared for a war with Spain, or anyone else for that matter. Still, Shafter waded through mountains of red tape and brought order out of chaos in getting the 16,000 men of the expeditionary force to Cuba on June 14, 1898.

The campaign in Cuba proved ultimately successful, but due to Shafter's lack of media savvy, many Americans viewed it as a fiasco. One of the many criticisms Shafter endured during the Cuban campaign was that he was not aggressive enough. Shafter refused to attack strongly fortified positions, instead using negotiations to secure the surrender of Santiago de Cuba. The American force suffered from disease, spoiled food, and a host of other issues. Although victorious, Shafter was portrayed in the media as a bumbling leader, which has clouded his reputation.

After the Spanish-American War, William Shafter was assigned to command the Department of California with his headquarters in San Francisco. Shafter retired from the US Army in 1901 as a major general. He died on November 13, 1906, and was laid to rest in the San Francisco National Cemetery. Fort Shafter, Hawaii, is named for him, as is the city of Shafter, California.

Terry L. Beckenbaugh

Further Reading

Carlson, Paul Howard. "*Pecos Bill*": *A Military Biography of William R. Shafter*. College Station: Texas A&M University Press, 1989.

Vandiver, Frank E. *Black Jack: The Life and Times of John J. Pershing*. 2 vols. College Station: Texas A&M University Press, 1977.

Shoup, David Monroe

Born: December 30, 1904
Died: January 13, 1983
Home State: Indiana
Service: Marines
Conflict: World War II
Age at Time of Award: 38

David M. Shoup was born December 30, 1904, on a small farm near Battle Ground, Indiana, a few miles north of Lafayette, and grew up a typical Indiana farm boy. He graduated from DePauw University at Greencastle, Indiana, in 1926, where he had participated in the ROTC program. After a short stint as an Army Reserve officer, he was commissioned in the US Marine Corps on July 20, 1926.

Over the next 17 years, Shoup served in many locations, including several assignments in China; Quantico, Virginia; Pensacola, Florida; San Diego, California; with the Marine detachment aboard the USS *Maryland*; and at Puget Sound Naval Shipyard, Seattle, Washington. He also served on temporary duty with the Civilian Conservation Corps and with the 1st Marine Brigade in Iceland. His Marine Corps schools included the Marine officers basic course at the Philadelphia Navy Yard and, later, the junior course at the Marine Corps school at Quantico, Virginia. In August 1942, he was promoted to lieutenant colonel and, in September, sailed to New Zealand with the 2nd Marine Division as the assistant operations and training officer.

During the next year, Shoup was closely involved with the training and preparations of the 2nd Marine Division for landing operations in the Pacific. He saw service as an observer on Guadalcanal and New Georgia, where he earned the Purple Heart.

Promoted to colonel on November 9, 1943, he was given command of the 2nd Marines (Reinforced) and designated to lead the landing on Betio Island, Tarawa Atoll. On the morning of November 20, 1943, Shoup went ashore with the first wave of landing craft and was wounded for the first time before reaching the beach. For the next 48 hours, he directed the battle from a precarious and exposed position a few yards up the beach. Although wounded and suffering from a concussion, he continued to coordinate the battle ashore, communicate with fleet support units, direct the incoming landing elements, and inspire his marines as they fought for every square foot of the island. After two days and nights without sleep and in considerable discomfort due to his wounds, Shoup turned command over to Col. Merritt Edson and caught some well-deserved sleep. For his untiring leadership under constant enemy fire, his selfless devotion to accomplishing his mission in spite of numerous personal wounds, and "his indomitable fighting spirit," Gen. Julian Smith recommended Shoup for the Medal of Honor.

Colonel Shoup subsequently participated in the landings at Saipan and Tinian before returning to the United States in October 1944 to work on the logistics planning staff at Headquarters Marine Corps. In December 1944, President Franklin Roosevelt presented Shoup the Medal of Honor at a White House ceremony.

After the war, Shoup would hold a number of increasingly important positions, including commander of the basic school in Quantico, Virginia; inspector general of recruit training; inspector general of the Marine Corps; and commanding general of the Marine Corps Recruit Depot at Parris Island, South Carolina. He was promoted to brigadier general in April 1953. Upon his nomination by President Dwight Eisenhower, General Shoup became the 22nd commandant of the Marine Corps on January 1, 1960. As commandant, Shoup headed the Marine Corps during two major crises of the John F. Kennedy presidency—the Bay of Pigs (April 1961) and the October (1962) Missile Crisis.

Shoup retired from the Marine Corps on December 31, 1963. During his distinguished career, in addition to the Medal of Honor, he also received two Legions of Merit with combat "V" devices, two Purple Hearts, the Distinguished Service Medal, the World War II Victory Medal, the British Distinguished Service Order, the Letter of Commendation with Commendation Ribbon, and a Presidential Unit Citation.

After his retirement from the Marine Corps, General Shoup became an outspoken and controversial critic of the United States's role in the Vietnam War, speaking at numerous public gatherings and testifying before Congress in opposition to further US involvement.

David Shoup died on January 13, 1983, after a lengthy illness and is interred at Arlington National Cemetery.

Jerold E. Brown

Further Reading

Jablon, Howard. *David M. Shoup: A Warrior against War*. Lanham, MD: Rowman & Littlefield, 2005.

Russ, Martin. *Line of Departure: Tarawa*. Garden City, NY: Doubleday, 1975.

Shughart, Randall D.

Born: August 13, 1958
Died: October 13, 1993
Home State: Nebraska
Service: Army
Conflict: Somalia
Age at Time of Award: 35

Randall David Shughart was born on August 13, 1958, in Lincoln, Nebraska. While still in high school, Shughart enlisted in the US Army; he entered into active duty upon graduation in 1976.

Shughart subsequently graduated from Ranger school and was assigned to the 2nd Ranger Battalion, 75th Infantry (Airborne) at Fort Lewis, Washington. After briefly leaving the Army, Shughart reenlisted and qualified for Special Forces. He was then assigned to the premier army Special Forces unit, the 1st Special Forces Operational Detachment-Delta, better known as Delta Force.

Shughart served in Operation Just Cause, the invasion of Panama, in 1989. In the summer of 1993, Sergeant First Class Shughart was ordered to Somalia with other Delta Force members to participate in Operation Restore Hope, designed to help bring stability to the troubled country. As part of Task Force Ranger, Shughart was assigned to a three-man sniper team. His teammates were Sergeant First Class Brad Hallings and M.Sgt. Gary Gordon, the team leader. On October 3, 1993, they were part of Operation Gothic Serpent, an assault mission designed to capture key advisers to Somali warlord Mohamed Farrah Aidid in the part of Mogadishu still controlled by Aidid.

During the operation, one of the Sikorsky UH-60 Black Hawk helicopters transporting the assault teams was shot down and crashed into Aidid-held territory. The Combat Search and Rescue (CSAR) team on standby was dispatched to secure the crash site and to rescue any survivors. While they were fighting their way through to the crash site, a second Black Hawk was shot down. The crew of four survived, but they were soon threatened by Aidid's militia and civilian supporters. The CSAR was still engaged in trying to reach the first crash site.

Shughart's team was aboard another Black Hawk, and they were attempting to cover the second crashed helicopter. Gordon requested permission to land so his team could take position to protect the injured crew, but his field commander twice refused permission, believing that their position in the air would better allow them to target hostile Somalis. On Gordon's third request, the commander gave in and allowed the sniper team to land.

Before landing, the mini-gun operator on the Black Hawk was wounded, so Hallings was assigned to man it and provide cover. Shughart and Gordon then landed

BLACK HAWK DOWN

Mogadishu, Somalia, was the setting for a battle between US forces and Somali militia during Operation Gothic Serpent, October 3–4, 1993. In the preceding months, widespread starvation had claimed the lives of hundreds of thousands of Somali civilians as rival militia clans stole and then sold international relief supplies. American forces (3rd Battalion, 75th Ranger Regiment/1st Special Forces Operational Detachment-Delta [SFOD-D]/160th Special Operations Aviation Regiment/10th Mountain Division) were attached to UNOSOM II (United Nations Operations in Somalia). Pursuant to UN National Security Council Resolution 837, US forces were directed to capture and bring to trial those hostile Somalis responsible for a fatal attack on Pakistani peacekeepers in June 1993. Until the violence against UN personnel stopped, an effective humanitarian relief operation was impossible.

On October 3, as part of an effort to capture and isolate Mohamed Farrah Aidid, whose Habar Gidir militia controlled significant portions of Mogadishu and who was responsible for disrupting food distribution to the starving populace and implicated in the Pakistani attack, American forces launched a raid to arrest Aidid's "foreign minister" and other high-value targets. The plan was for a team of SFOD-D operators to raid the Olympic Hotel in the Aidid-controlled portion of the city, capture the targets, and then deliver them to a ground convoy that would arrive immediately thereafter. Bravo Company, 3rd Battalion, 75th Rangers was to fast-rope from UH-60 Black Hawk helicopters to secure the building perimeter and await the ground convoy.

The plan went awry when a Ranger was critically injured after he fell from a UH-60; immediately afterward, the Black Hawk piloted by Chief Warrant Officer (CW3) Cliff Wolcott was downed by a rocket-propelled grenade (RPG). An Air Force combat search-and-rescue team arrived at the site, but their Black Hawk helicopter was then damaged by another RPG strike. Shortly after, yet another Black Hawk—this one piloted by CW3 Michael Durant—was struck by an RPG and crashed.

With the ground convoy blocked from reaching either of the crash sites, Rangers and SFOD-D operators made their way to the first site, where they were heavily engaged by large numbers of heavily armed militia. With the fate of Durant and his crew unknown, two airborne SFOD-D operators—Sergeant First Class Randy Shughart and M.Sgt. Gary Gordon—volunteered to land and secure the site against oncoming militia forces. Shughart and Gordon were landed near the crash site, and they made their way to the downed helicopter. There they extracted the surviving Durant from the aircraft and established defensive positions around the aircraft. In the ensuing desperate battle, the Somalis eventually overran the Americans. Shughart and Gordon were killed, and Durant was beaten and captured (he would be released two weeks later). The Somalis suffered 24 casualties in this battle and many others wounded who may have died from their wounds.

During an intense overnight battle, the Rangers and SFOD-D operators trapped near the Wolcott crash site held off repeated, determined attacks. They were supported by AH-6J fire and managed to hold their position until a mixed force (UN and US) reached their position the next morning. During the course of the two-day engagement, 18 American soldiers were killed and another 83 wounded. Estimates of Somali militia casualties vary from several hundred to several thousand. Following the raid and images of American bodies being dragged through Mogadishu's streets, the US ended its active military role in Somalia and completely withdrew from the conflict in March 2004.

On May 23, 1994, Shughart and Gordon were posthumously awarded Medals of Honor. They were the first Americans to receive the Medal of Honor since Vietnam.

Mark M. Hull

alone. Debris and ground fire prevented their Black Hawk from landing at the crash site, so they found an open area some 100 yards away. The pair made their way through buildings to the crash site, taking Somali fire along the way. When they arrived at the downed helicopter, Gordon and Shughart managed to remove the crew, including Chief Warrant Officer (CWO) Mike Durant and three others. Shughart and Gordon established a perimeter around the helicopter, moving from place to place to keep the attacking Somalis away. Armed only with their personal weapons, the pair managed to kill or disable numerous attackers. Finally, their ammunition ran low, and the Somali attackers were able to move closer.

Accounts vary as to whether Gordon or Shughart was killed first by Somali gunfire. Shughart's citation for the Medal of Honor indicates he was killed first, but some authorities believe he was the last to die. Durant survived, and he testified that after one of the Rangers had been killed, the other gave him the extra weapon. Durant could not identify if it was Shughart or Gordon, but the weapon he had was not Shughart's distinctive M14, but rather Gordon's weapon. Other Rangers did not believe Gordon would have given another soldier his own weapon, indicating that it was Shughart's. In any event, after Shughart and Gordon were killed, Durant was captured by the Somalis. The other three members of the crew died, leaving Durant the only American survivor. In all, 18 American servicemen died in Operation Gothic Serpent. The failure led to a loss of public support for operations in Somalia, eventually causing the Clinton administration to withdraw American troops from that country.

On May 23, 1994, Randall Shughart and Gordon were decorated posthumously with Medals of Honor for their sacrifice in attempting to save fellow Americans. They were the only soldiers in Operation Gothic Serpent to receive the medal and its first recipients since the Vietnam War. The heroics of Gordon and Shughart were featured in the book and movie *Black Hawk Down*. Shughart was further honored by having a US Navy ship named after him. The ship, the USNS *Shughart*, was the Navy's first large, medium-speed, roll-on roll-off ship, intended to hasten the rapid deployment of forces overseas.

Tim J. Watts

Further Reading

Bowden, Mark. *Black Hawk Down*. London: Corgi, 2002.

DeLong, Kent, and Steven Tuckey. *Mogadishu! Heroism and Tragedy*. Westport, CT: Praeger, 1994.

Eversmann, Matt Schilling. *The Battle of Mogadishu: Firsthand Accounts from the Men of Task Force Ranger*. Novato, CA: Presidio Press, 2004.

Sickles, Daniel E.

Born: October 20, 1819
Died: May 3, 1914
Home State: New York
Service: Army
Conflict: Civil War
Age at Time of Award: 43

Born into a prosperous New York City family on October 20, 1819, Daniel E. Sickles studied law as a young man and was admitted to the bar in 1843. He also entered politics, quickly becoming one of the leading figures in New York's notorious Tammany Hall faction of the Democratic Party. His personal magnetism and gift for oratory served him well both in the courtroom and in politics. He also gained a reputation as an extravagant spendthrift and womanizer. Sickles represented New York in the US House of Representatives from 1857 to 1861 and seemed poised for even greater accomplishments. His ambitions came crashing down in 1859 when Sickles shot and killed his wife's lover, Philip Barton Key, a prominent Maryland aristocrat and son of the author of "The Star Spangled Banner." Although acquitted of murder, Sickles's political career appeared to be over.

The outbreak of the Civil War gave Sickles an opportunity to repair his ruined reputation. He helped raise a brigade of US volunteers and was given command of the formation with the rank of brigadier general. Sickles and his brigade performed well in the Peninsula Campaign of 1862, resulting in his elevation to division command. However, he saw little action as division commander. Nonetheless, Sickles was given command of III Corps and won promotion to major general early in 1863. At the battle of Chancellorsville that May, Sickles contributed to the Federal debacle by reporting that the Confederates to his front were retreating when in fact they were marching around the Federal flank. Sickles and his corps did, however, fight stubbornly when the Confederate blow fell and helped prevent the defeat from becoming a rout.

Two months later, Sickles played a central role in the battle of Gettysburg. Ordered to occupy a position on Cemetery Ridge, with his left on Little Round Top and his right linked to II Corps, Sickles instead advanced his corps nearly half a mile to the now-famous Peach Orchard. The new position was unsupported on either flank and involved the removal of troops from Little Round Top, setting the stage for Joshua Chamberlain and the 20th Maine to win their place in history.

In the fighting of July 2, elements of two Confederate corps mauled III Corps in its exposed position and drove it back to the original line on Cemetery Ridge. Sickles himself suffered a severe wound when a cannonball struck his right leg. After surgeons amputated the mangled limb, Sickles had it sent to the Army Medical Museum, where the shattered bones are still on display in the renamed National Museum of Health and Medicine.

Sickles never commanded in battle after Gettysburg, though he served as military governor and department commander in the Carolinas after the war. Retired with the rank of major general in the Regular Army in 1869, Sickles spent four years as the ambassador to Spain, with scandal and intrigue accompanying him as always. In 1893, he returned to the House of Representatives for one term, where he was instrumental in having the Gettysburg battlefield made into a federally controlled military park.

Aside from his official duties, Sickles's great obsession after July 1863 was to get himself recognized as the hero of Gettysburg who saved the Army of the Potomac by advancing his corps to the Peach Orchard. When Sickles received the Medal of Honor in 1897 for his role at Gettysburg, many contemporaries viewed the award as a blatant act of self-promotion accomplished through intrigue and pulling strings.

To this day, students of the battle dispute the wisdom and impact of his actions at Gettysburg. Most historians would agree, however, with Alexander Webb, who commanded a brigade in another corps and who himself received the Medal of Honor for action at Gettysburg. Regarding Sickles, Webb observed: "He could fight, yes; as a tactician, no." But Sickles outlasted most of his contemporary critics. Living to the ripe old age of 94, Daniel Sickles, who died on May 3, 1914, was the last surviving corps commander, Federal or Confederate, from the great battle at Gettysburg.

Christopher R. Gabel

Further Reading

Hessler, James A. *Sickles at Gettysburg.* New York: Savas Beatie, 2009.

Swanberg, W. A. *Sickles the Incredible.* New York: Charles Scribner's Sons, 1956.

Sijan, Lance P.

Born: April 13, 1942
Died: January 22, 1968
Home State: Wisconsin

Service: Air Force
Conflict: Vietnam War
Age at Time of Award: 25

Born on April 13, 1942, in Milwaukee, Wisconsin, Lance Peter Sijan grew up in Milwaukee and entered the US Air Force Academy in Colorado Springs, Colorado, in 1961. After graduating in 1965, he was trained to fly the F-4 Phantom II fighter-bomber.

On July 1, 1967, First Lieutenant Sijan was assigned to the 480th Tactical Fighter Squadron of the 366th Tactical Fighter Wing operating out of Da Nang Airbase, Republic of Vietnam (RVN, South Vietnam). On November 9, 1967, during a mission against the Ban Loboy ford located along the Ho Chi Minh Trail in Laos, Sijan was the back-seat pilot in Lt. Col. John William Armstrong's F-4C. Shrapnel, evidently from a premature bomb detonation during the attack, destroyed their plane. Sijan was able to bail out of the aircraft but suffered severe injuries, including a broken leg, that restricted his mobility. Search-and-rescue units initiated a rescue attempt involving more than 100 aircraft, yet difficulties in pinpointing Sijan's exact position, his inability to move quickly, and heavy hostile fire prevented his rescue.

It is not known whether Armstrong got out of the aircraft, and he and Sijan were listed as missing in action (MIA). During the next 45 days, Sijan successfully evaded capture. Upon being caught, he temporarily escaped after overpowering a guard but was quickly recaptured. Although Sijan was now a prisoner of war (POW) in Vinh, Democratic Republic of Vietnam (DRV, North Vietnam), the North Vietnamese government did not inform the US government of his capture. He was placed under the care of two other Air Force officers—Capt. Guy Gruters and Maj. Robert Craner—while the three men were being transferred to Hoa Lo Prison, nicknamed the Hanoi Hilton by American POWs.

Throughout his interrogation sessions, which included torture, Sijan refused to provide any information that was not required by the Geneva Convention or the US Military Code of Conduct. Furthermore, despite suffering from severe illness and injuries suffered during the bailout and inflicted by his captors, he continually plotted to escape from his captivity.

Lance Sijan died on January 22, 1968, in Hanoi, North Vietnam, probably from the effects of his injuries. Still classified as MIA by the military, Sijan was promoted to captain on June 13, 1968. News of his death, as well as his heroic conduct while a POW, did not surface until after the repatriation of American POWs in 1973. His remains were returned, identified, and reinterred in 1974 in Milwaukee. Craner nominated Sijan for the Medal of Honor posthumously, and, on March 4, 1976, President Gerald R. Ford presented the medal to Sijan's parents. Sijan was the only Air Force Academy graduate to earn the Medal of Honor for his actions during the

Vietnam War. In addition to service and campaign medals, Sijan's other decorations included the Air Medal, a Purple Heart, and the Prisoner of War Medal.

Wyndham E. Whynot

Further Reading

Howes, Craig. *Voices of the Vietnam POWs: Witnesses to their Fight.* New York: Oxford University Press, 1993.

McConnell, Malcolm. *Into the Mouth of the Cat: The Story of Lance Sijan: Hero of Vietnam.* New York: W. W. Norton, 2004.

Simanek, Robert E.

Born: April 26, 1930
Died:
Home State: Michigan
Service: Marine Corps
Conflict: Korean War
Age at Time of Award: 22

Robert Ernest Simanek was born on April 26, 1930, in Detroit, Michigan. After graduating from high school in Detroit in 1948, he worked for Ford Motor Company and later for General Motors. On August 13, 1951, Simanek enlisted in the Marine Corps. He went on to complete boot camp at Parris Island, South Carolina, in October 1951 and then moved to Camp Pendleton, California, for further training in November of that year. Shortly after completing training at Camp Pendleton, Private First Class Simanek sailed for Korea in April 1952 to join Company F, 2nd Battalion, 5th Marines, 1st Marine Division under command of Capt. Clarence G. Moody Jr., arriving on May 6, 1952.

The action for which Simanek was to receive his Medal of Honor occurred on August 17, 1952, in a place called the Hook, near Panmunjom in South Korea, the location of a series of bloody engagements for outposts along what was known as the Jamestown main line of resistance. Combat between communist forces and US Marines had been building up that summer along the entire Jamestown defensive line.

Typically, at this point in the war, the marines did not occupy the outposts in front of their lines at night. Unfortunately, the Chinese figured out this procedure and began to occupy the temporarily vacant marine positions during the night and then attempted to ambush marines coming up for outpost duty after daybreak.

Just after dawn on August 17, 1952, Private First Class Simanek, along with a 20-man patrol from his company, moved forward to occupy outpost Irene, a ridgeline just ahead of 2nd Battalion's main line of resistance. However, upon arrival, Simanek and his fellow marines found that the Chinese had already taken possession of the area. Almost immediately, the patrol came under heavy small arms and mortar fire from the Chinese. Twelve of the Marines were able to pull back, but Simanek and five others were trapped in a narrow trench halfway down the hill. Pinned down by intense enemy fire from Chinese above and below them, Simanek and his fellow marines fired back but had little effect on the intensity of the enemy fire. During the attack, the Chinese threw several grenades into the trench. Simanek and his fellow marines frantically kicked them away before they exploded. Seconds later, two more grenades were thrown into the trench. Simanek, acting quickly, was able to throw one of them out of his position. However, there was no time to grab the second grenade. Without hesitation, Simanek jumped sideways onto the grenade, trying to press it into the dirt with his body weight. The grenade exploded and took most of the blast in his legs and lower body, gravely wounding him. Simanek exhibited a high degree of courage and a resolute spirit of self-sacrifice that saved the lives of his fellow marines. Despite his wounds, he continued to fight until the Chinese finally retreated and Simanek was able to crawl down from the outpost to safety.

Seriously wounded and near death, Robert Simanek was initially hospitalized aboard the hospital ship USS *Haven* anchored off the coast of Korea. He was later transferred to several different hospitals in Japan before being returned to the United States in September 1952. It took him six months to recuperate from his wounds and learn how to walk again. It was during this time that he learned he had been nominated for the Medal of Honor. On October 27, 1953, President Dwight D. Eisenhower presented the medal to Simanek in a White House ceremony. Simanek was the 33rd of 36 marines to be honored with this special award for action in Korea. In addition to the Medal of Honor, Simanek was also awarded the Purple Heart, the Korean Service Medal with two bronze stars, the United Nations Service Medal, and the National Defense Service Medal. He currently resides in Detroit, Michigan.

Heather M. Leahy

Further Reading

Collier, Peter, and Nick Del Calzo. *Medal of Honor: Portraits of Valor beyond the Call of Duty.* New York: Artisan, 2006.

DeLong, Kent. *War Heroes: True Stories of Congressional Medal of Honor Recipients.* Westport, CT: Praeger, 1993.

Meid, Lt. Col. Pat , USMCR, and Maj. James M. Yingling, USMC. *U.S. Marine Operations in Korea 1950–1953.* Vol. 5. Washington, D.C.: Historical Division, Headquarters Marine Corps, 1972.

Smith, Charles. *U.S. Marines in the Korean War.* Washington, D.C.: US Marine Corps History Division, 2007.

Sitter, Carl L.

Born: December 2, 1921
Died: April 4, 2000
Home State: Colorado
Service: Marine Corps
Conflict: Korean War
Age at Time of Award: 30

Carl Leonard Sitter was born December 2, 1921, at Syracuse, Missouri. Growing up in Pueblo, Colorado, he graduated from Pueblo's Central High School in 1940. Sitter enlisted in the Marine Corps on June 22, 1940, and initially was assigned to duty in Iceland with Company F, 2nd Battalion, 6th Marine Regiment, 1st Marine Brigade.

Ordered to the Pacific area with his unit in 1941, he was offered a commission in the Marine Corps Reserve and was appointed a platoon commander in Company K, 3rd Battalion, 22nd Marine Regiment. He participated in the assault on Eniwetok in the Marshall Islands and later at Guam in the Marianas. Sitter was slightly wounded in action at Eniwetok but was not evacuated. During the fighting on Guam, Sitter was again wounded when he fearlessly exposed himself to heavy enemy fire while leading his rifle platoon. For his conspicuous gallantry in combat, he was awarded the Silver Star. However, Sitter's wounds were so serious he had to be medically evacuated.

Following the end of World War II, he was briefly assigned as the commanding officer of the Marine Barracks at the Brooklyn Navy Yard. He then served as a commanding officer of a Marine Guard company in the Panama Canal Zone and later served at the naval base in Key West, Florida.

Soon after fighting broke out in Korea, Sitter, now a captain, was assigned as the commanding officer of George Company, 3rd Battalion, 1st Marine Regiment, 1st Marine Division. During the historic retreat of the 1st Marine Division at Chosin Reservoir, Sitter's company fought a vicious two-day action against communist Chinese forces on November 29 and 30, 1950, in and around the town of Hagaru-ri. Ordered to break through enemy-held territory to reinforce his battalion, Sitter's conspicuous courage, despite losing over 25 percent of his company, was once again evident as he drove through to achieve his objective. Quickly assuming responsibility to seize an enemy entrenchment on a hill that commanded a valley southeast of Hagaru-ri as well as the 1st Marine Division line of retreat out of town, Sitter led his marines and those of other units up the hillside in the face of withering enemy fire. During the night, Sitter and his marines withstood violent enemy counterattacks, often in hand-to-hand combat. Sitter repulsed each enemy attack, and, although painfully wounded in the face, arms, and chest by hand grenades, he refused evacuation and continued to fight on and successfully defended the area while inflicting over 50 percent casualties on the Chinese attackers. After the battle, Sitter remained in Korea until February 1951 and then returned to the United States.

For "his valiant leadership, superb tactics, and great personal valor," Sitter was presented the Medal of Honor for his actions at Hagaru-ri by President Harry S. Truman during ceremonies at the White House on October 29, 1951.

Following the Korean conflict, Sitter served in a variety of posts and stations and was an instructor at Quantico, Virginia; he later served as the Marine representative to the director of the Naval Security Group in London. While in the United Kingdom, he earned his bachelor of arts degree from the University of Maryland (European Division). In 1967, Sitter served as the chief of staff, Force Troops, Fleet Marine Force, Pacific, and he retired from active duty at Richmond, Virginia, in 1970 after having served in the Marine Corps for 30 years and achieving the rank of colonel.

Following his retirement from the Marine Corps, Carl Sitter worked for the Virginia Department of Social Services until he fully retired from public service in 1985. In 1998, at age 75, Sitter attended divinity school in Richmond, Virginia, and graduated on May 28, 1999. He subsequently served as a lay minister in his church. He passed away on April 4, 2000, in Richmond and was buried in Arlington National Cemetery.

Huong T. D. Nguyen

Further Reading

Anderson, Burton F. *We Claim the Title: Korean War Marines*. Aptos, CA: Tracy Publishing, 2000.

Collier, Peter, and Nick Del Calzo. *Medal of Honor: Portraits of Valor beyond the Call of Duty*. New York: Artisan, 2006.

Martin, Robert J. *First Marine Division*. Paducah, KY: Turner Publishing, 1997.

Russ, Martin. *Breakout: The Chosin Reservoir Campaign, Korea 1950*. New York: Penguin Books, 2000.

Smith, Andrew Jackson

Born: September 3, 1842
Died: March 4, 1932
Home State: Kentucky
Service: Army
Conflict: Civil War
Age at Time of Award: 21

Andrew Jackson Smith was born into slavery on or about September 3, 1842. His mother, Susan, was a slave, and his father was Elijah Smith, a slave owner. When he was 10 years old, his owner assigned him to run a ferry transporting people and supplies across the Cumberland River. He continued this task for almost eight years, becoming an accomplished boatman in the process.

When the Civil War broke out, Andrew's father and owner, Elijah Smith, immediately enlisted in the Confederate Army. After a year's absence, he returned home on leave and indicated that he planned to take Andrew back with him. When Andrew, 19 at the time, overheard the plans, he and another slave decided to run away.

They made their way 25 miles through a freezing rain to seek protection from a Union Army regiment, the 41st Illinois Infantry, near Smithland, Kentucky. Andrew became a servant to Maj. John Warner. The two agreed that if Warner fell in battle, Jackson would take his belongings to Warner's home in Clinton, Illinois. The regiment moved on to battle at Fort Henry, where the Union forces captured Confederate general Lloyd Tillingham. The regiment then moved on to Fort Donelson, where it lost 200 soldiers during the heavy fighting there.

In March 1862, Smith's regiment moved to Pittsburg Landing and participated in the Battle of Shiloh in April. During the battle, Major Warner had two horses shot out from under him, and Smith provided him fresh mounts. During the course of the battle, Smith was struck with a Confederate minie ball that entered his left temple, rolled just under the skin, and stopped in the middle of his forehead. The ball was removed by the regimental surgeon, leaving Smith with only a scar.

After the battle, Major Warner, accompanied by Smith, returned to Clinton, Illinois. Smith was there when he heard that President Abraham Lincoln had authorized black troops to join the Union forces to fight for their freedom.

Smith left Illinois to enroll in the Massachusetts Colored Volunteers. On May 16, 1863, he and 55 other Illinois volunteers were mustered into Company B of the 55th Regiment. After the 54th Regiment of Colored Volunteers, the sister regiment of the 55th, fought at Fort Wagner, South Carolina, it was joined by the 55th Regiment, and they fought five major engagements together over the next two years.

In the late afternoon of November 30, 1864, the 54th and 55th regiments were involved in a bloody battle to take Honey Hill, near Boyd's Landing in South Carolina. The Confederates, in fortified entrenchments, occupied an elevated position on a rise fronted by swampy ground. As the Union troops advanced through the swamp, they came under withering fire from the Confederates. When the lead Union forces were thrown back, the 55th Regiment was ordered forward into the furious fight. Forced into a narrow gorge in the face of the enemy position, the Union troops took heavy casualties. The 55th regimental color sergeant was killed by an exploding shell, and Smith, now a corporal, took the state and federal flags from his hand and carried them forward through the heavy canister and rifle fire.

Although half the officers and a third of the enlisted men in his unit were killed or wounded, Corporal Smith continued to expose himself to enemy fire by carrying the colors throughout the battle. As the color bearer, he presented a conspicuous target to the Confederates, but he pressed forward, disregarding his own safety and inspiring his fellow soldiers in the attack.

Smith was promoted to color sergeant soon after the battle at Honey Hill. He was discharged on August 29, 1865, and was sent to Boston on the steamer *Karnac* for his formal mustering out. After the war, he went back to Clinton, Illinois, for a short period of time but returned to Kentucky, where he lived out his days as a leader in the local community. He died at age 88 on March 4, 1932, and was buried in Mount Pleasant Cemetery in Grand Rivers, Kentucky.

Andrew Smith was nominated for the Medal of Honor in 1916, but the Army denied the nomination, citing a lack of official records documenting the case. It was not until January 16, 2001, 137 years after the fact, that Smith's valor at Honey Hill was finally recognized; on that day, President Bill Clinton presented the Medal of Honor to several of Smith's descendants, including his 93-year-old daughter, during a White House ceremony. Smith's Medal of Honor set a record for the longest period between a soldier's valorous act and the official recognition of that act by presentation of the medal. Also during that ceremony, the president presented the Medal of Honor posthumously to the relatives of former president Theodore Roosevelt for his action during the Spanish-American War.

James H. Willbanks

Further Reading

Gomez-Granger, Julissa. *CRS Report for Congress: Medal of Honor Recipients: 1979–2008.* Washington, D.C.: Congressional Research Service, RL 30011, June 4, 2008.

Hanna, Charles W. *African American Recipients of the Medal of Honor: A Biographical Dictionary, Civil War through Vietnam War.* Jefferson, NC: McFarland, 2002.

Reef, Catherine. *African Americans in the Military.* New York: Facts on File, 2004.

Smith, Paul R.

Born: September 24, 1969
Died: April 4, 2003
Home State: Florida
Service: Army
Conflict: Iraq
Age at Time of Award: 33

Paul Ray Smith was born in El Paso, Texas, on September 24, 1969, but grew up primarily in Tampa, Florida, where he moved at the age of nine. After graduating from Tampa Bay Technical High School in 1989, he joined the Army. He completed basic training and advanced individual training at Fort Leonard Wood, Missouri, and became a combat engineer. Smith served in both Germany and the United States—with the 82nd Engineer Battalion in Bamberg, Germany; in the 1st Engineer Battalion at Fort Riley, Kansas; in the 317th Engineer Battalion at Fort Benning, Georgia; and in the 9th Engineer Battalion in Schweinfurt, Germany. While in Germany, he met and married his wife, Birgit, and they had two children.

Smith served in Iraq during the Persian Gulf War and in Bosnia. In 1999, Smith joined the 11th Engineer Battalion based at Fort Stewart, Georgia, which was deployed to Kosovo in May 2001.

By March 2003, Smith, by then a sergeant first class with 14 years of service, was a member of Bravo Company, 11th Engineer Battalion, of the 3rd Infantry Division. Smith and his unit deployed to Kuwait as part of the buildup for Operation Iraqi Freedom. Crossing the border into Iraq on March 19, Smith's unit was assigned to support the 7th Infantry Regiment's 2nd Battalion, which was advancing toward Saddam International Airport in Baghdad. They advanced more than 300 kilometers in the first 48 hours of the war. Passing through the Karbala Gap, the battalion encountered resistance on its way to the airport on April 4, 2003, and the fight resulted in the taking of a number of Iraqi prisoners.

To hold these prisoners, Smith and his unit had to create a makeshift prisoner-of-war camp. He and his men employed an earthmover to create a hole in a nearby enclosed courtyard with a tower. Just outside the gate of the courtyard was a company-sized Iraqi force, with perhaps as many as 100 Iraqi Republican Guards, in entrenched positions. Smith, along with two platoons, a Bradley Fighting Vehicle, and three armored personnel carriers (APCs), attacked the Iraqi position. During the fighting, the Bradley was damaged and ran low on ammunition and fuel, requiring it to withdraw. The APCs were hit by a rocket-propelled grenade and a mortar round, injuring three crew members whom Smith helped to safety.

Given the withdrawal of the Bradley and the damage inflicted on the APCs, Smith could have ordered a partial withdrawal, but he instead chose to continue to fight lest the Iraqis overrun his position and take a nearby aid station treating battle casualties. Some Iraqis, meanwhile, were able to take up position in the tower, and they began firing down into the courtyard on the Americans. Smith then took charge of one of the damaged APCs and used its .50 caliber machine gun to fire on the tower and the Iraqis in the nearby trenches. Meanwhile, a team under 1st Sgt. Tim Campbell attacked the tower. In order for Campbell to accomplish this, Smith had to place himself in an exposed position and provide covering fire. As Campbell's men made their move against the rear of the tower, Smith was shot in the neck and head and killed instantly. His flak jacket had been hit 13 times.

Although Paul Smith's actions were immediately hailed as heroic, the process of recognizing them with the Medal of Honor took several years. Lt. Col. Thomas Smith, Smith's battalion commander, first recommended him for the Medal of

Honor in May 2003. Two years later, Smith's bravery was recognized with the award of the Bronze Star, the Purple Heart, and the Medal of Honor, which President George W. Bush presented to Smith's son David at a White House ceremony on April 4, 2005. This was the first Medal of Honor awarded for the Iraq War.

Michael Beauchamp

Further Reading

Collier, Peter, and Nick Del Calzo. *Medal of Honor: Portraits of Valor beyond the Call of Duty*. New York: Artisan, 2006.

Keegan, John. *The Iraq War*. New York: Knopf, 2004.

"Sgt. 1st Class Paul Ray Smith." *Soldiers* 65, no. 3 (March 2010): 4–5.

Spurrier, Junior J.

Born: December 14, 1922
Died: February 25, 1984
Home State: Virginia
Service: Army
Conflict: World War II
Age at Time of Award: 22

James I. Spurrier Jr. was born in Castlewood, Virginia, on December 14, 1922. One of six Spurrier children, he lived in the heart of the economically depressed Appalachian area of western Virginia. Spurrier left school in the seventh grade in order to work on a neighboring farm and provide for his family. Spurrier eventually moved to Bluefield, West Virginia, where he found work at a Civilian Conservation Corps camp. He enlisted in the US Army in September 1940. He filled out the name on his Army application incorrectly, henceforth becoming Junior James Spurrier in the Army's eyes. He did not take to well to the discipline of Army life and received several reprimands and accrued many hours of stockade time. Spurrier initially served as a baker but transferred to the infantry in fall of 1943, joining Company G, 134th Infantry Regiment, 35th Division. He joined the unit in England and participated in the Normandy landings on June 6, 1944.

Spurrier proved to be a very capable combat soldier. He rose to the rank of staff sergeant but was made a company runner instead of being given command of a squad. His lack of discipline often meant he went on his own to hunt for Germans, and his company commander felt Spurrier was better suited to the more independent runner position. As part of Patton's 3rd Army, the 134th Regiment and Spurrier received many opportunities to hone their fighting skills. Spurrier displayed these skills on September 16, 1944, near Lay St. Christopher, France. He earned the Distinguished Service Cross for his actions in the capture of a heavily defended German hill position. Spurrier mounted a tank destroyer during the fighting and used the .50 caliber machine gun on the vehicle to kill the enemy. On two occasions, he climbed off the tank destroyer to throw grenades and fire into German bunker positions. In all, Spurrier captured 22 Germans and killed at least a dozen.

Spurrier was not finished, as he soon demonstrated in subsequent action on November 13, 1944, in Moselle, France. At 2:00 p.m., Company G attacked the village of Achain from the east. Staff Sergeant Spurrier, armed with a Browning Automatic Rifle (BAR), passed around the village and advanced alone. Attacking from the west, he immediately killed three Germans. From this time until dark, Spurrier—using at different times his BAR, his Ml rifle, American and German rocket launchers, a German automatic pistol, and hand grenades—continued his solitary attack despite all types of enemy small arms and automatic weapons fire. He killed 1 officer and 24 enlisted men and captured 2 officers and 2 enlisted men. His unofficial capture total for the day was around 60 German soldiers, which differs slightly from the official records but does not diminish the heroics of Spurrier's actions. The men of Company G began referring to Spurrier as the "One Man Army" as a result of his actions during the fighting in Achain.

Spurrier fought with the 35th Division during the Battle of the Bulge and into Germany. However, Spurrier's lack of discipline and his problems with alcohol got him into trouble several times. Nevertheless, Spurrier received the Medal of Honor from Lt. Gen. William H. Simpson on March 6, 1945. Spurrier and his fellow Medal of Honor recipients were among the first servicemen to be sent home at the conclusion of the war.

Spurrier left the Army but reenlisted after having trouble adjusting to civilian life. Spurrier's drinking troubles continued to haunt him, and he was reduced to the rank of private by the time the Korean War started in June 1950. He refused to go to Korea, stating that he had seen enough combat. The Army decided to give Spurrier a general discharge in 1951 rather than court-martial a holder of America's two highest decorations.

Junior Spurrier continued to have a severe problem with alcohol and served three jail terms for various crimes, including attempted murder. When he was released from jail in 1969, he vowed never to touch alcohol again. He retired to an isolated cabin in eastern Tennessee, remaining sober and isolated. He died in peaceful obscurity on February 25, 1984, and is buried in Mountain Home National Cemetery in Johnson City, Tennessee.

Jason M. Sokiera

Further Reading

Murphy, Edward F. *Heroes of World War II*. Novato, CA: Presidio Press, 1990.

US Senate. Committee on Veterans Affairs. *Medal of Honor Recipients, 1863–1973*. Washington, D.C.: Government Printing Office, 1973.

Stockdale, James B.

Born: December 23, 1923
Died: July 5, 2005
Home State: Illinois
Service: Navy
Conflict: Vietnam War
Age at Time of Award: 52

James Bond Stockdale was born December 23, 1923, as the only child to Vernon and Mabel Stockdale of Abingdon, Illinois. Vernon, known as Stock, had enlisted in the US Navy during World War I. In 1935, when Jim was seven years old, his father took him to visit Annapolis during a trip back east; according to Stockdale, this was where he decided to attend the Naval Academy. Four years later, his father took him to see the famous polar explore Adm. Richard Byrd in Mount Pleasant, Illinois. Stockdale got an autograph for his troubles and a lifelong fascination with naval aviation.

True to his youthful vow, Stockdale gained an appointment to Annapolis in 1943 after a year of college in Illinois. He graduated academically at the top of his company and so received diplomas on their behalf personally from Fleet Admiral Chester Nimitz. After three years of surface line officer duty in destroyers, he reported to Pensacola, Florida, for naval pilot training, earning the wings of gold of a naval aviator in the summer of 1950. In 1947, he married Sybil, the sweetheart he had met while on a blind date at Annapolis. Stockdale thrived as a "tailhook" aviator and was selected for Naval Test Pilot School at Patuxent ("Pax") River, Maryland, in 1954, where he flew jet aircraft for the first time.

While instructing at Pax River, Stockdale had helped test the brand new F-8 Crusader jet fighter. In the early 1960s, Jim attended graduate school at Stanford University, earning a master's degree in international relations. Not long after, he was selected for squadron command of VF-51 aboard USS *Ticonderoga* (CV-14), still flying Crusaders. Stockdale personally led a division of four F-8s in repulsing the August 2, 1964, attack of several North Vietnamese gunboats on the destroyer USS *Maddox*. Subsequent events led to the fateful Gulf of Tonkin resolution by President Johnson that effectively committed the country to war. On August 6, Stockdale led one of the first strategic strikes by the Navy in the war against the North Vietnamese petroleum facilities at Vinh.

After the *Ticonderoga* cruise, Stockdale and his squadron were transferred on a short turnaround to the USS *Oriskany* (CV-34). Since Stockdale was the most experienced and senior squadron commander of the squadron, he was selected to command Carrier Air Wing (or Group) 16 (CAG-16).

By mid-year 1965, CAG-16 and *Oriskany* were back in action in the Gulf of Tonkin. However, the North Vietnamese had used the interim wisely, building up their air defenses as the Americans launched Operation Rolling Thunder. On September 9, 1965, while leading a strike over North Vietnam, Stockdale was shot down by antiaircraft guns near Tinh Gia. He successfully ejected from the aircraft but broke his back and dislocated his knee when he landed. Stockdale was as well prepared as anyone for the ordeal ahead, having gone through prisoner-of-war (POW) training twice in his career.

Stockdale was housed in the infamous Hoa Lo prison, known better to history as the Hanoi Hilton. For the next seven years, Jim endured hell. The North Vietnamese had decided to use the POWs as a form of political warfare, but, as the senior Navy POW, Jim organized and led his fellow prisoners under the most severe conditions of isolation and torture. Similarly, his wife Sybil, now a single mother of four, suspected (and then became convinced) that her husband and his men were being tortured. She organized the National League of Families of American Prisoners and Missing in Southeast Asia in 1968 as an advocacy group for political action.

Meanwhile, the world had no idea of the conditions and violations of the laws of war taking place in Hanoi. Stockdale's most heroic acts took place during 1969, when first he mutilated himself to avoid being used as an example of how "well" the Americans were being treated. Then, in an act of sheer heroism, he cut his wrists and almost killed himself after several of his fellow POWs died after torture. His high visibility as the most senior officer, and his death, would have embarrassed his captors to no end, and they realized he would never submit. Slowly but surely, the maltreatment began to subside. There is no telling how many lives Commander Stockdale saved by his actions.

Meanwhile, Sybil's efforts had brought the POW issue to the fore, and the safe return of the POWs became one of the United States's official war aims, codified in the Paris Peace Accords of 1973. That year, Stockdale was repatriated. On March 6, 1976, President Gerald Ford presented Stockdale with the Medal of Honor for his courage and valor as a prisoner of war in North Vietnam.

Jim Stockdale was later promoted to admiral (having already been promoted to captain while incarcerated) and, as befitting a man of his intellect and character, closed out his career as the president of the Naval War College. He later ran for vice president on the ticket of his old Annapolis friend H. Ross Perot in 1992. During his last years, he suffered from Alzheimer's disease and died on July 5, 2005. He was buried at the US Naval Academy Cemetery. The Navy has named its annual leadership prize awarded to active duty officers in his honor.

John T. Kuehn

Further Reading

Collier, Peter, and Nick Del Calzo. *Medal of Honor: Portraits of Valor beyond the Call of Duty*. New York: Artisan, 2006.

Smith, Larry. *Beyond Glory: Medal of Honor Heroes in Their Own Words—Extraordinary Stories of Courage from WWII to Vietnam.* New York: W. W. Norton, 2003.

Stockdale, Jim, and Sybil Stockdale. *In Love and War.* New York: Harper & Row, 1984.

Stone, James L.

Born: December 27, 1922
Died:
Home State: Texas
Service: Army
Conflict: Korean War
Age at Time of Award: 28

James Lamar Stone was born December 27, 1922, in Pine Bluff, Arkansas, later moving to Hot Springs. As a child, he recalled once seeing Lou Gehrig and Babe Ruth play baseball. As a young man, he matriculated at the University of Arkansas, where he studied zoology and chemistry and enrolled in ROTC. Stone graduated in 1947 and worked briefly for General Electric in Houston, Texas, before entering active military service from that city in 1948.

During the Korean War, Stone first saw action in March 1951 as a first lieutenant with the 8th Cavalry Regiment, 1st Cavalry Division. The regiment had landed in Korea during the summer of 1950, executing the first amphibious operation of the war. By late October, the unit was located some 50 miles south of the Chinese/Korean border when the Chinese entered the war in force, pushing UN forces inexorably south. The 3rd Battalion, 8th Cavalry, unable to break through enveloping Chinese forces, was virtually wiped out. Elements of the regiment would go on to see more than 500 days of combat, including action at "Old Baldy," before rotation back to Japan.

In service with the 8th Regiment on November 22, 1951, near Sokkogae, overlooking the Imjin River, Stone's platoon was attacked by battalion-size elements of Chinese soldiers. Stone exposed himself repeatedly to enemy fire while directing his platoon's defense. With Bangalore torpedoes blowing holes in the wire fortification around his position, he relocated a flamethrower that was poorly emplaced and returned it to action after repairing a malfunction. Wounded during a second enemy assault, Stone personally repositioned a machine gun to fire on attackers pressing his position from two directions. Hit a second time, Stone continued to direct his platoon's defense and inspire his soldiers by personal example. Finally, with only his carbine for self-defense, Stone could be heard exhorting his men until they were overrun.

Suffering by now from three separate wounds—two in the leg and one in the neck—Stone led a handful of soldiers to cover the withdrawal of his platoon's survivors to positions held by F Company. Just before dawn on November 23, the remainder of the platoon was overrun, and he lost consciousness. A subsequent body count indicated that his platoon had left more than 500 enemy dead around its position.

Captured by the Chinese, Stone spent 22 months in a prisoner-of-war camp on the Yalu River. On September 3, 1953, Stone was repatriated in Operation Big Switch, a prisoner-exchange program initiated the previous month.

Returning stateside, Stone was informed he was to receive the Medal of Honor for his actions on November 21–22, 1951. On October 27, 1953, Stone and six other recipients were presented the medal by President Dwight D. Eisenhower at the White House. Stone was 1 of 38 troopers of the 1st Cavalry to receive the Medal of Honor, including 8 during the Korean War. He was also one of five University of Arkansas graduates to be so honored.

James Stone stayed in the military, eventually retiring as a colonel. He served in Germany and with ROTC units in the Fort Worth area and eventually served a tour of duty in Vietnam in 1971. After retiring in 1976, Stone moved to Arlington, Texas, to assist his son, James L. Stone Jr., in his home-building business. Still active, Stone is a member of the Walton H. Walker Chapter 215 Korean War Veterans Association. He still participates in various Memorial Day and Veterans Day activities and still enjoys watching baseball.

Anton A. Menning

Further Reading

Collier, Peter, and Nick Del Calzo. *Medal of Honor: Portraits of Valor beyond the Call of Duty.* New York: Artisan, 2006.

The Congressional Medal of Honor: The Names, the Deeds. Forest Ranch, CA: Sharp & Dunnigan, 1984.

Ecker, Richard. *Korean Battle Chronology.* Jefferson: McFarland, 2005.

First Cavalry Division. Paducah, KY: Turner Publishing, 2002.

Halberstam, David. *The Coldest Winter.* New York: Hyperion Books, 2007.

Stowers, Freddie

Born: 1896
Died: September 28, 1918
Home State: South Carolina
Service: Army
Conflict: World War I
Age at Time of Award: 22

The grandson of a slave, Freddie Stowers was born in 1896 and raised on a farm in Sandy Springs, South Carolina. Drafted in 1917, he was inducted in the newly formed 1st Provisional Infantry Regiment (Colored) at Camp Jackson, South Carolina. In December 1917, the 1st Provisional Infantry Regiment (Colored) was redesignated the 371st Infantry and assigned to the 186th Infantry Brigade (Colored) of the 93rd Division (Provisional). The division was composed of four African American regiments, three from the National Guard and the 371st composed of draftees from the National Army.

At Camp Jackson, the 93rd spent many long days drilling and training basic soldier skills. British officers and noncommissioned officers arrived to train the men on trench warfare tactics, along with rifle practice, bayonet drill, grenade throwing, and even training on foreign mortars and machine guns. The 371st deployed with the division on April 5th, 1918, arriving at their final destination of Vaubecourt, France, by the end of the month. Although part of the American Expeditionary Force, upon reaching France all four African American regiments of the 93rd were permanently assigned to different French divisions. The 371st Infantry Regiment became a permanent unit of the French 157th "Red Hand" Division under the command of Gen. Mariano Goybet. The men of the 371st Infantry Regiment exchanged their American equipment for all French equipment except the US-issue brown woolen uniform. General Goybet even reorganized the 371st to the structure of a French infantry regiment.

By early June 1918, the men of the 371st were in the trenches in the Verrières sector between the Aire and Meuse rivers. Throughout the rest of the summer, the 371st made numerous raids on German positions, some small and some large, but all bloody. During this fighting, Stowers was recognized early on for his initiative and leadership abilities. Promoted to corporal and squad leader in Company C of the 1st Battalion, his leadership qualities would soon be put to the ultimate test in one of the largest battles of the war.

On September 28, 1918, the 371st jumped off in the Champagne-Marne sector as part of the immense Meuse-Argonne Offensive. Attacking across a front of 500 meters, the objective was Hill 188, a heavily fortified defense including massive barbed wire entanglements. Under intense machine gun and artillery fire, Stowers's company penetrated the barbed wire and were closing in on the German positions. Suddenly, the Germans ceased fire and crawled out of their positions with their hands in the air. As the Americans moved forward to take prisoners, the Germans jumped back into their trenches and opened fire. Exposed in the open approximately 100 meters from the German positions, C Company was devastated by a withering fire from interlocking machine guns and mortars. Corporal Stowers's platoon lost all of its leaders within seconds, and he immediately took charge by reorganizing the survivors in order to continue the attack. With complete disregard for his own safety, Stowers crawled forward toward a machine gun nest that was causing heavy casualties to his company. After destroying the machine gun nest, Stowers continued to lead his men forward to take the German positions. Stowers was struck by machine gun fire, and although mortally wounded, he continued to lead and encourage his fellow soldiers onward through heavy fire. Because of his extraordinary and inspirational courage, Stowers and his men captured the German trenches and all the machine gun positions. Stowers collapsed while organizing defensive positions to prepare for the inevitable enemy counterattack. He later died of his wounds.

Recommended by his company commander for the Medal of Honor, the paperwork was lost for over 70 years. Found among Army records in 1990, the Army dispatched a team to France to investigate Freddie Stowers's actions. As a result of this investigation, the Army Decorations Board approved the only African American to be awarded the Medal of Honor in World War I. On April 24, 1991, in a White House ceremony, President George Bush presented the Medal of Honor to Stowers's surviving sisters, Georgina Palmer and Mary Bowens. Corporal Stowers is buried in the Meuse-Argonne American Cemetery and Memorial east of the village of Romagne-sous-Montfaucon in France.

Scott A. Porter

Further Reading

Aster, Gerald. *The Right to Fight: A History of African Americans in the Military*. Cambridge, MA: Da Capo Press, 1998.

Franklin, John Hope, and Alfred A. Moss Jr. *From Slavery to Freedom: A History of African Americans*. 8th ed. 2 vols. in one. New York: Random House, 2004.

Lengel, Edward G. *To Conquer Hell: The Meuse-Argonne, 1918: The Epic Battle That Ended the First World War*. New York: Henry Holt, 2008.

Roberts, Frank E. *The American Foreign Legion: Black Soldiers of the 93d in World War I*. Annapolis, MD: Naval Institute Press, 2004.

Thornton, Michael Edwin

Born: March 23, 1949
Died:
Home State: South Carolina
Service: Navy
Conflict: Vietnam War
Age at Time of Award: 23

Born in Greenville, South Carolina, on March 23, 1949, Michael E. Thornton joined the Navy upon graduation from high school in 1967. Thornton served on destroyers and was accepted into Underwater Demolition Recruit class 49 at Coronado in the winter of 1968. Upon completion of his training, Thornton became a member of the elite SEALs and was deployed to Vietnam. Thornton was assigned to the I Corps area in Vietnam in Quang Tri Province northeast of Hue at Tuy Not.

By the fall of 1972, North Vietnamese Army units were regularly moving south, and the SEALS at Tuy Not were assisting in reconnaissance and intelligence-gathering operations to assess enemy troop strength in the area. Petty Officer Thornton was chosen to join a five-man team that was to be inserted by boat to a coastal position in Quang Tri Province near the mouth of the Cua Viet River on October 31, 1972. Two enlisted members, Quon and Tai, and their commanding officer, Dang of the Lien Doc Nguoi Nhai (LDNN), the South Vietnamese equivalent of the Navy SEALs, joined Thornton and Navy lieutenant Tom Norris on the mission. Norris had been recommended for the Medal of Honor for an action earlier that spring.

The team was transported to the insertion point by junk, but upon arrival, Lieutenant Norris realized the junk was out of position and too far north from the objective area. Thornton and Norris decided to land anyway and conduct a reconnaissance of the area, during which they discovered a North Vietnamese Army unit. Lieutenant Norris made radio contact with an escorting destroyer trying to verify their position while Thornton and Dang established a perimeter.

The team's position was threatened when two North Vietnamese soldiers came toward the team on the beach, which required the soldiers to be silenced; Thornton managed to sneak up on one of the soldiers and knocked him out with the butt of his carbine. The other soldier was confronted by Dang, who had a silenced pistol. Instead of shooting the soldier, Dang challenged the soldier and demanded his surrender. The soldier opened fire on Dang, who took cover behind a sand dune. The soldier ran back up the beach to report the encounter, but Thornton gave chase and shot him. The gunfire alerted the North Vietnamese unit, and a force of approximately 75 men was assembled and moved down the beach toward the team's position. A five-hour pitched battle ensued.

The team quickly interrogated the enemy soldier Thornton had knocked out. The soldier revealed the team's exact location, and Lieutenant Norris radioed the position to the destroyers offshore. The destroyers moved in and began providing gunfire support to the team. The destroyers and artillery began exchanging fire, and the cruiser *Newport News* moved into position to provide support.

The destroyers radioed Norris about the *Newport News,* and Norris called for the heavy naval gunfire to be used on the team's position while the rest of the team moved to the shore to escape. Shortly after Thornton reached the beach, Dang, who had stayed behind with Norris, arrived and informed Thornton that Norris had been shot in the head and killed. Thornton decided to retrieve Norris dead or alive to prevent him from falling into North Vietnamese hands. Thornton made it to Norris's location and realized Norris, while badly wounded, was still alive. Thornton carried Norris back just as the heavy naval gunfire landed on their previous position; Thornton was knocked down by the concussion. Thornton got up and continued carrying Norris to the beach.

Thornton treated Norris's head wound as best he could and rigged an inflatable life vest to float Norris into the surf. Thornton also found Quon wounded near the beach. While still under enemy fire, he managed to float Norris and Quon into the surf and swam toward the open sea. Thornton reached the junk that had brought them after four hours in the water. Dang and Tai had managed to swim out to the junk separately. Norris was flown to the Philippines and then the United States for surgery.

Michael Thornton was informed that he was to report to the White House on October 15, 1973, to receive the Medal of Honor for his heroism in his rescue of Lieutenant Norris almost a year before, on Halloween 1972. Thornton and Norris had the honor of attending each other's awards ceremonies at the White House. Thornton continued serving in the Navy and retired in 1992 as a lieutenant; Thornton was one of three US Navy SEALs to receive the Medal of Honor during the Vietnam War. Since his retirement, he has given speeches and spoken of his experiences to schools and other organizations.

Steven F. Marin

Further Reading

Collier, Peter, and Nick Del Calzo. *Medal of Honor: Portraits of Valor beyond the Call of Duty.* New York: Artisan, 2006.

Dockery, Kevin. *Navy SEALs: A History.* Part 2, *The Vietnam Years.* New York: Berkley, 2002.

Dockery, Kevin. *SEALs in Action.* New York: Avon, 1991.

Thorsness, Leo K.

Born: February 14, 1932
Died:
Home State: Minnesota
Service: Air Force
Conflict: Vietnam War
Age at Time of Award: 35

Leo K. Thorsness was born on February 14, 1932, in Walnut Grove, Minnesota. He enlisted in the Air Force in 1951 and earned his commission three years later through the aviation cadet program. His first operational flying assignment was in F-84 Thunderstreaks with the 31st Strategic Fighter Wing in Albany, Georgia. He later flew F-100 Super Sabres before transitioning to the F-105 Thunderchief.

By 1966, Thorsness had completed F-105F "Wild Weasel" training and was assigned to the 357th Tactical Fighter Wing at Takhli Royal Thai Air Base, Thailand. The Weasels' job was to precede a strike force into the assigned target area in North Vietnam, entice enemy surface-to-air missiles (SAMs) and antiaircraft radars to come on the air, and then knock them out with bombs or missiles that honed in on their radar emissions.

On April 19, 1967, Thorsness was leading a flight of four on a SAM-suppression mission deep in enemy territory near Hanoi. Arriving in the target area, he directed the second element of his flight to patrol north while his element swept south. Subsequently, he and his wingman took out two SAM sites, but on the second run, his wingman was hit by flak; he and his backseater (electronic warfare officer) successfully ejected from the damaged aircraft. Unknown to Thorsness, the other element of his flight had been attacked by North Vietnamese MiG fighters; when the afterburner on one of the F-105s would not light, the element disengaged and returned to base, leaving Thorsness to fight on alone.

Thorsness circled the parachutes of the crewmembers who had ejected, relaying their position to the search-and-rescue center. Suddenly, his backseater, Capt. Harold Johnson, spotted a MiG-17 off their left wing. Although the F-105 Wild Weasel was not designed for air-to-air combat, Thorsness attacked and shot down the MiG with his 20-mm cannon. Another MiG closed on his tail, but Thorsness, low on fuel, had to break off the battle and rendezvous with a tanker.

In the meantime, two A-1E Sandies and a rescue helicopter arrived to look for the downed crewmen. Upon being advised of that fact, Thorsness, with only 500 rounds of ammunition left, turned back from the tanker to fly cover over the rescue force, knowing there were still a number of MiGs in the area. He spotted four MiG-17s and initiated an attack on them, damaging one (although he did not get credit for the kill because his gun camera had run out of film) and driving the other away from the rescue scene. While this was happening, another pair of MiGs shot down one of the Sandies. Although he was now of ammunition, Thorsness headed back to the area, hoping in some way to draw the MiGs away from the surviving Sandy. Just then, a US strike force arrived to take on the remaining enemy fighters.

Again low on fuel, Thorsness headed back to the tanker just as one of the strike force pilots, almost out of fuel himself, radioed for help. Thorsness knew he could not make Takhli without refueling, but he quickly determined that he could make it to Udorn, 200 miles closer, so he directed the tanker toward the strike fighter and headed for Udorn. As he crossed the Mekong River and neared the base, he throttled back to idle and glided toward Udorn, touching down just as his tanks went dry and his engine shut down.

Eleven days later, on his 93rd mission, just seven days short of returning home, Thorsness and Johnson were shot down by a heat-seeking missile from a MiG-21 over North Vietnam. Both men ejected from the crippled aircraft, Thorsness suffering severe injuries. Both men were captured and spent the next six years in North Vietnam prisons, where they ran into the F-105 crew they had been trying to rescue. Because of his "uncooperative attitude," Thorsness was denied medical attention, spent a year in solitary confinement, and suffered severe back injuries during torture. While he was in captivity, Thorsness learned he had been nominated for the Medal of Honor; the officer in charge of writing the nomination had been shot down himself and was brought to the same prison where Thorsness was held.

In March 1973, Thorsness, Johnson, and the other prisoners of war (POWs) were released from prison, with Thorsness on crutches. On October 15, 1973, President Richard Nixon presented the Medal of Honor to Thorsness for his heroism that day in April 1967. The medal had actually been approved while he was still a POW, but to keep the North Vietnamese from using the information against him, the award was not announced publicly until Thorsness returned home. Johnson was later awarded the Air Force Cross.

Thorsness completed 23 years in the Air Force and retired in 1973, 10 days after he received the Medal of Honor, because he was no longer medically qualified to fly fighters due to the injuries sustained during his ejection and torture during captivity.

After retirement, Leo Thorsness worked for Litton Industries for six years. In 1986, he and his wife, Gaylee, moved to Seattle, Washington, where he served as a Washington State senator from 1988 to 1992. In 1993, he and his wife built a waterfront home in Indianola, Washington, where they retired and were involved in aquaculture. They later moved to Saddlebrooke, Arizona, and then, in 2008, to Huntsville, Alabama, to be close to family. Thorsness is on the Board of Directors of the Congressional Medal of Honor Foundation and currently serves as president of the Congressional Medal of Honor Society.

James H. Willbanks

Further Reading

Broughton, Col. Jack. *Thud Ridge: F-105 Missions over Vietnam*. Sussex, UK: Crecy Publishing, 2006.

Collier, Peter, and Nick Del Calzo. *Medal of Honor: Portraits of Valor beyond the Call of Duty*. New York: Artisan, 2006.

DeLong, Kent. *War Heroes: True Stories of the Congressional Medal of Honor Recipients*. Westport, CT: Praeger, 1993.

Faranacci, Donald. *Last Full Measure of Devotion: A Tribute to America's Heroes of the Vietnam War*. Bloomington, IN: AuthorHouse, 2007.

Lowry, Timothy. *And Brave Men, Too*. New York: Crown Publishers, 1985.

Thorsness, Leo. *Surviving Hell: A POW's Journey*. New York: Encounter Books, 2008.

Titus, Calvin Pearl

Born: September 22, 1879
Died: May 27, 1966
Home State: Iowa
Service: Army
Conflict: China Relief Expedition
Age at Time of Award: 21

Calvin Pearl Titus was born on September 22, 1879, in Vinton, Iowa. At age 11, his mother passed away, and he moved to Oklahoma with his father. Later, he moved to Kansas, where he took up residence with an aunt and uncle. Having developed a love for music, Titus taught himself how to play the violin and coronet. He also frequently traveled around the country with his uncle, a Salvation Army minister, playing music during prayer meetings. While in Vermont with his uncle, Titus was recruited by the Vermont National Guard as news of the sinking of the USS *Maine* swept across the country. He enlisted, not surprisingly, as a bugler. After fighting a case of malaria contracted during training, Titus was released from his obligation. In 1899, he enlisted in the Army once more, again as a bugler and (unofficially) chaplain's assistant, and was assigned to the US 14th Infantry Regiment, which was headed to the recently acquired Philippines.

In the summer of 1900, the 14th Infantry found itself in China as part of the International Relief Expedition during the Boxer Rebellion. On August 14, the expeditionary force had marched from Tientsin to Peking and halted in front of the massive walls surrounding the city. Col. A. S. Daggett, Titus's commander, asked for a volunteer to try to climb the 30-foot wall. Titus answered the call and successfully scaled the massive facade, coming under fire at the top. His courageous action inspired his fellow soldiers, who assaulted and penetrated the walls of the city.

For his bravery, it was decided on March 11, 1902, that Titus was to be recommended for the Medal of Honor. In addition to being recommended for the nation's highest military honor, Titus was granted admission into the US Military Academy at West Point by President William McKinley. During the academy's 100th-anniversary celebration in June 1902, Titus was presented the Medal of Honor by President Theodore Roosevelt, becoming the only freshman cadet to ever wear the Medal of Honor.

After graduating from West Point in 1905, Titus left the Army and undertook evangelical work for several years. In 1908, he reenlisted, returning to the 14th US Infantry, stationed in the Philippines, this time as a second lieutenant. In 1909, he became an ordained minister in the People's Mission Church and applied for chaplaincy. However, his application was denied due to the fact that the denomination was not recognized by the US Army. Throughout the next five years, he was assigned to various duty stations training National Guard officers. This fateful assignment took Titus to the Mexican border in 1916, where he took part in John J. Pershing's famous Mexican Expedition to capture Pancho Villa.

By the time America had entered World War I, Titus had risen to the rank of major. He was assigned to administrative duties that kept him in America throughout the course of the war. It was only after the war's conclusion that Titus was assigned to duties in France and Germany. After returning from Europe in 1922, he was assigned to the ROTC program at Coe College in Cedar Rapids, Iowa. Titus was also an honor graduate from the Army Command and General Staff College in 1926. In 1930, Lieutenant Colonel Titus retired from Coe College as professor of military science and tactics. Titus passed away on May 27, 1966, in San Fernando, California. In 1999, the US Navy named container ship MV *Ltc. Calvin P. Titus* in his honor.

Calvin Titus's military career spanned three decades, involving him in some of the most storied conflicts in US military history: the Philippine-American War, the Boxer Rebellion, the Mexican Expedition, and World War I. Few soldiers throughout American military history can claim such an illustrious career.

Jason C. Engle

Further Reading

Boot, Max. *The Savage Wars of Peace: Small Wars and the Rise of American Power*. New York: Basic Books, 2002.

Houlihan, William J. "Before the Chaplain Assistant." *The Army Chaplaincy*, Spring 1999.

King, Brig. Gen. Edward L. "Annual Report of the Commandant: The General Service Schools, Fort Leavenworth, Kansas 1926–1927." Fort Leavenworth, KS: US Army Command and General Staff College, 1927.

Owens, Ron. *Medal of Honor: Historical Facts and Figures*. Paducah, KY: Turner Publishing, 2004.

Turner, George B.

Born: June 27, 1899
Died: June 29, 1963
Home State: Texas
Service: Army
Conflict: World War II
Age at Time of Award: 46

Born in Longview, Texas, on June 27, 1899, George Benton Turner studied liberal arts at Wentworth Military Academy in Lexington, Missouri, but did not graduate with a degree. He joined the Marine Corps in World War I but saw no fighting. When World War II erupted, he was working as a law secretary in Los Angeles County, California, but joined the Army in 1942.

By early 1945, Turner had served more than two years in the European Theater with Battery C of the 499th Armored Field Artillery Battalion, 14th Armored Division. Fellow soldiers in Turner's unit looked to him for leadership and guidance, partly because of his age and partly because of the example he set for others. At 42, Turner was the oldest private in his unit. His dedication to the defense of his country was apparent. Officers recognized his leadership qualities and repeatedly encouraged him to accept a promotion, which he refused. He wanted to remain on the front lines in the fighting, and promotion would deny him that opportunity. He remained a private first class until the war ended.

On January 3, 1945, at Philippsbourg, France, an enemy armored infantry attack cut him off from his unit. Unwilling to miss the action, he had joined a retreating infantry company when he noticed two German tanks and as many as 75 German soldiers advancing down the main street of the village in their direction. Under heavy fire from the German soldiers, he fired at the tanks with a rocket launcher, taking them both out of action. Standing in the open and firing a light machine gun from the hip, he killed or wounded many of the advancing German soldiers, foiling the German attack.

In the American counterattack that followed, enemy antitank fire disabled two supporting American tanks. Turner held off the Germans so the trapped crews could extricate themselves. He ran toward one of the burning tanks to help free an American who could not free himself. As he approached the tank, the onboard ammunition exploded, wounding him.

Despite his wounds, he refused to be evacuated and remained with his temporary unit through the next day, fighting an enemy patrol, capturing an enemy-held position, and driving a truck full of wounded under fire to an aid station. His courage under fire and actions even though wounded and cut off from his own unit played a key role in the successful defense of the French town.

On September 14, 1945, Turner was awarded the Medal of Honor for his actions at Philippsbourg. President Truman presented him the medal in a White House ceremony. Turner was one of the oldest Americans to receive the Medal of Honor, and he was the 14th Armored Division's only recipient of the Medal of Honor.

After the war, he lived in Encino, California, with his wife until his death on June 29, 1963. He is buried at Arlington National Cemetery.

Members of the 14th Armored Division Association Annual Reunion in 1979 dedicated the gathering to George Turner, not only because he was the unit's only Medal of Honor recipient, but also because of the dedication to duty and commitment to country they had seen Turner consistently demonstrate through his years in the war. Letters from fellow soldiers and officers paid tribute to Turner for his leadership and for the example he set for others.

Debra J. Sheffer

Further Reading

The Congressional Medal of Honor: The Names, the Deeds. Forest Ranch, CA: Sharp & Dunnigan, 1984.

Desiderio, Tim. *Into the Fire: The 275th Infantry Regiment in WWII.* Victoria, BC, Canada: Trafford Publishing, 2005.

Murphy, Edward F. *Heroes of World War II.* Novato, CA: Presidio Press, 1990.

Urban, Matt

Born: August 25, 1919
Died: March 20, 1995
Home State: New York
Service: Army
Conflict: World War II
Age at Time of Award: 25

Matt Louis Urban was born in Buffalo, New York, on August 25, 1919, the son of Polish immigrants originally named Urbanowicz. He graduated from Buffalo Public High School before going on to study history and government at Cornell University. Following graduation from Cornell, he was commissioned a second lieutenant of infantry through ROTC.

With the outbreak of World War II, Urban deployed to North Africa with the 60th Infantry Regiment, 9th Infantry Division and fought with the division throughout campaigns in North Africa, Sicily, France, and Germany.

On June 14, 1944, Captain Urban, while leading his infantry company in the vicinity of Renouf, France, performed the first in a series of heroic actions that would eventually result in the belated award of the Medal of Honor. That day, Urban's company was under intense fire from enemy tanks and supporting infantry. Recognizing the danger to his unit, Urban armed himself with a bazooka, and he and an ammo bearer worked their way into a firing position from which he destroyed both enemy tanks, paving the way for his company's advance. In action later that same day, Urban was wounded in the leg by fire from an enemy 37-mm tank gun. He refused to be evacuated and organized his unit into a night defensive position. The next morning, he led the company in another attack. He was wounded again. Having been wounded twice, one time seriously, he could no longer refuse medical treatment and was evacuated to England.

While recuperating a month later, he learned of his unit's shortage of combat leaders following engagements in the hedgerows of France and left the hospital to rejoin his unit. Shortly after the commencement of Operation Cobra on July 25, Urban found his unit near St. Lo, France, but it was already in the attack. He made his way forward and reassumed command of the company. They were soon held up by strong enemy opposition that had succeeded in knocking out two supporting tanks. Though hampered by his wound from the engagement in June, Urban mounted the remaining tank under heavy enemy fire and destroyed the enemy strongpoint with precise fire from the tank's machine gun. Following Urban's lead, his company moved forward and overcame the enemy forces.

Urban was once again wounded on August 2, this time by shell fragments to the chest, but refused to leave his unit. On August 6, he took command of the 2nd Battalion, sustaining yet another wound in action on August 16. His battalion was given the mission of establishing a crossing point on the Meuse River near Heer, Belgium, to facilitate the forward movement of follow-on units. On September 3, the battalion's advance stalled as it approached the Meuse River, and Urban moved forward to join the battalion's lead elements to survey the situation. Seizing an opportunity, he personally reorganized and led elements of the battalion in a charge of the enemy strongpoint that had stopped the advance. As he advanced, he was wounded in the neck and lost his ability to speak above a whisper. Yet again, Urban refused evacuation until the battalion had completed its mission and the crossing point was secured.

Urban was nominated for the Medal of Honor for his actions in France and Belgium during the period June 14 to September 3, but for a number of reasons, nothing came of the nomination. His commanding officer had been killed during the fighting in France, and the formal recommendation letter from S.Sgt. Earl G. Evans, written in July 1945, was somehow overlooked. Despite the fact that he did not received the Medal of Honor immediately after World War II, Lieutenant Colonel Urban earned an impressive number of awards for valor, including two Silver Stars, three Bronze Stars, and seven Purple Hearts.

Retired for medical disability in 1947, Urban returned to Michigan and worked in the public sector for the remainder of his life. He held successive positions as recreation director at Port Huron, Monroe, and Holland, Michigan.

As public law only requires the original recommendation to have been made within two years of the event for which the individual is recommended, once the original letter nominating Urban for the Medal of Honor was found in Urban's personnel file, the investigation went forward and resulted in the belated award. In July of 1980, President Jimmy Carter presented the medal to Urban in a White House ceremony, calling him "the greatest soldier in American History." Urban, a well-known hero among the Polish American community, has often been called the most highly decorated US soldier from World War II. This is arguable, but there is little doubt that Urban earned a place on a list of the most decorated soldiers in American military history.

Matt Urban died on March 25, 1995, in Holland, Michigan, at the age of 75. He was buried with full military honors at Arlington National Cemetery.

James B. Martin

Further Reading

Boven, Robert W. *Most Decorated Soldier in World War II: Matt Urban*. Victoria, BC, Canada: Trafford Publishing, 2000.

Urban, Matt. *The Matt Urban Story*. Holland, MI: Matt Urban Story, Inc., 1989.

Vandegrift, Alexander Archer

Born: March 13, 1887
Died: May 8, 1973
Home State: Virginia
Service: Marine Corps
Conflict: World War II
Age at Time of Award: 42

Alexander Archer Vandegrift was born in Charlottesville, Virginia, on March 13, 1887, and remained there through his elementary and secondary education years. Growing up in Charlottesville, surrounded by history, Vandegrift's interest in the military and history began to grow. He secured an appointment to the US Military Academy at West Point but was refused admission following a failed physical exam. Vandegrift attended the University of Virginia while seeking a second appointment to West Point. At age 21, Vandegrift again tried to obtain an officer's appointment in the Army. However, he was convinced to take the examination for an officer's commission in the US Marine Corps. After taking and passing the exam, Vandegrift left the University of Virginia to receive his commission as a second lieutenant in the Marine Corps on January 22, 1909.

Vandegrift's early years in the Marine Corps were spent in the Central and South American theaters including participation in the capture of Coyotepe, Nicaragua; the occupation of Veracruz, Mexico; and the pacification efforts in Haiti beginning in 1915. He was also deployed to China during his early career.

Vandegrift graduated from the Marine Corps Field Officers' Course at Quantico in May of 1926 and then was assigned to Marine Corps Base, San Diego to serve as assistant chief of staff. Thereafter, Vandegrift served at a number of posts in the United States and overseas between 1926 and 1941, when he became the assistant commander of the newly formed 1st Marine Division. In April 1940, Vandegrift was promoted to the rank of brigadier general.

Alexander Archer Vandegrift, US Marine Corps (Naval History and Heritage Command).

In May 1942, the 1st Marine Division was deployed to the South Pacific with Vandegrift, who had just been promoted to major general in March, serving as commanding general. The division was tasked with seizing and holding Guadalcanal, an island viewed by the military as critical to the Pacific War effort. This was to be the first large-scale operation offensive of the Pacific War.

On August 7, 1942, Maj. Gen. Vandegrift led the 1st Marine Division's attack on the island of Guadalcanal. During the long, harsh, but ultimately successful campaign to seize and hold Guadalcanal between August and December 1942, Vandegrift would command all air, sea, and ground forces in the area. For his "tenacity, courage and resourcefulness" during the operation, Vandegrift was awarded the Medal of Honor.

In July 1943, Vandegrift was promoted and assumed command of the 1st Marine Amphibious Corps. The 1st Marine Amphibious Corps began to train for the invasion of Bougainville in the Solomon Island chain. On November 1, 1943, Lt. Gen. Vandegrift commanded the initial landing on Bougainville. Shortly after the establishment of the beachhead, he relinquished command upon announcement of his appointment as commandant-designee of the US Marine Corps.

On January 1, 1945, Vandegrift became the 18th commandant of the Marine Corps. Promoted to the rank of four-star general in March of 1945, he continued to serve as commandant until 1948, retiring from the Marine Corps in April of 1949. During his tenure, he played a major role in the discussions to restructure the American defense establishment, arguing forcefully for the continued existence of the Marine Corps.

Following his retirement, Alexander Vandegrift returned to Charlottesville, Virginia, with his wife, Kathryn. Following a period in Charlottesville, they moved to Florida. General Vandegrift died at the National Naval Medical Center in Bethesda, Maryland, on May 8, 1973, after a long illness. He was buried on May 10, 1973, at Arlington National Cemetery. Vandegrift's son, Col. Alexander A. Vandegrift Jr., also served as an officer in the US Marine Corps in World War II, was wounded at the Battle of Iwo Jima, and later saw service in the Korean Conflict. The guided missile frigate *Vandegrift* (FFG-48), which entered service in 1984, is named in honor of General Vandegrift, as is the main street at Camp Pendleton.

Christopher S. Trobridge

Further Reading

Millett, Allan Reed, and Jack Shulimson, eds. *Commandants of the Marine Corps*. Annapolis, MD: Naval Institute Press, 2006.

Shaw, Henry I., Jr. *First Offensive: The Marine Campaign for Guadalcanal*. Marines in World War II Commemorative Series. Washington, D.C.: Marine Corps Historical Center, 1992.

Vandegrift, Alexander. *Once a Marine: The Memoirs of General A. A. Vandegrift*. New York: W. W. Norton, 1964.

Vargas, Jay R.

Born: July 29, 1937
Died:
Home State: Arizona
Service: Marine Corps
Conflict: Vietnam War
Age at Time of Award: 30

Jay R. Vargas was born in Winslow, Arizona, on July 29, 1937. Vargas spent his youth in Arizona up through his graduation from Northern Arizona University, where he earned a bachelor of science degree in education in 1961. Following in the footsteps of his three older brothers who had also served in the armed forces, Vargas joined the Marine Corps, completing officer candidate school and the basic school by June 1962.

Vargas's first assignment was as a platoon commander with Company C, 1st Battalion, 5th Marines, 1st Marine Division, at Camp Pendleton, California. In 1963, he served a tour with the 3rd Marine Division in Okinawa, Japan, and was reassigned to the Recruit Training Regiment in San Diego, California. Following this assignment, Vargas transferred to the 1st Battalion, 27th Marines then located at Twentynine Palms, California, where he served as a staff officer and as the commanding officer of Company B, 1st Battalion, 27th Marines.

Upon completion of reconnaissance training at the Marine Corps schools at Camp Pendleton, in December 1967, Vargas was once again assigned to the 3rd Marine Division, which was by this time serving in the Republic of Vietnam. He assumed command of Company G, 2nd Battalion, 4th Marines as part of the 9th Marine Amphibious Brigade. For his heroic action against elements of three North Vietnamese battalions on March 18, 1968, in Quang Tri Province, Vargas received the Silver Star for gallantry in combat.

Just a month and a half later, on April 30, Vargas's unit was inserted into an ongoing battle near the village of Dai Do, south of the demilitarized zone, where two other Marine companies were doing battle with a North Vietnamese Army regiment. Maneuvering across 700 meters of open rice paddies, Vargas and his marines advanced under intense enemy fire. When one of his platoons became pinned down, Vargas led his reserve platoon to the aid of his beleaguered men, and, although wounded by a grenade, he took out three machine gun emplacements himself. Vargas organized his men in a defensive perimeter around the edge of the village. Shortly afterward, the enemy launched a series of savage counterattacks, but Vargas and his men stood firm, fighting throughout the night and into the next morning, when the bodies of more than 300 enemy soldiers were found around the position.

Early in the morning of May 2, Company E under Capt. James Livingston was ordered to link up with Vargas's dangerously exposed company, and both companies were able to largely secure Dai Do by 0930. The fighting was intense as Livingston, Vargas, and their marines used flamethrowers, grenades, satchel charges, and rockets to destroy numerous fortified enemy bunkers in and around the village itself.

Later that afternoon, when an attack by a sister company faltered, Vargas was ordered to continue the assault with his company and that of Company F. However, after having advanced to the edge of the village of Thuong Do, the marines began taking fire from the front and flank and even from the rear of their exposed position; Vargas was ordered to withdraw his forces back to Dai Do.

Coolly directing the withdrawal, Vargas remained in the open and encouraged his marines throughout the intense fighting that took place, but, in the process, he was wounded for a third time in three days. When his battalion commander was shot in the back three times, Vargas, disregarding his own wounds, crossed the fire-swept area and dragged his commander to a covered location where he could be evacuated. Vargas continued to fight until the North Vietnamese forces withdrew. Vargas's leadership and personal example during the intense three days of fighting in and around the village of Dai Do resulted in him being recommended for the Medal of Honor. He received the medal from President Richard M. Nixon on May 14, 1970.

Vargas later served as the Marine officer instructor at the University of New Mexico and was a graduate of both the Marine Corps Command and Staff College and National Defense University. He retired from the Marine Corps as a colonel in 1992. After retirement, from 1992 to 1998, he was the secretary of the California Department of Veterans Affairs and in 2001 was appointed the regional veterans liaison for the Department of Veterans Affairs.

Jay Vargas is one of a few recipients in the United States to be awarded the American Academy of Achievement's "Golden Plate Award" presented to national leaders in all professional fields. He has also received the National Collegiate Athletic Association's Commemorative Plaque presented by the United States Collegiate Athletic Directors and Coaches, in Houston, Texas, for excelling in collegiate athletics and having made a significant contribution to his country.

Heather M. Leahy

Further Reading

Collier, Peter, and Nick Del Calzo. *Medal of Honor: Portraits of Valor beyond the Call of Duty.* New York: Artisan, 2006.

Murphy, Edward F. *Semper Fi: Vietnam: From Da Nang to the DMZ: Marine Corps Campaigns, 1965–1972.* Novato, CA: Presidio Press, 1997.

Nolan, Keith. *The Magnificent Bastards: The Joint Army-Marine Defense of Dong Ha, 1968.* Novato, CA: Presidio Press, 2007.

Shulimson, Jack, and Leonard A. Blaisol, Charles R. Smith, and David A. Dawson. *U.S. Marines in Vietnam: The Defining Year, 1968*. Washington, D.C.: Headquarters Marine Corps, History and Museums Division, 1997.

Smith, Larry. *Beyond Glory: Medal of Honor Heroes in Their Own Words—Extraordinary Stories of Courage from WWII to Vietnam*. New York: W. W. Norton, 2003.

Versace, Humbert R.

Born: July 2, 1937
Died: September 26, 1965
Home State: Virginia
Service: Army
Conflict: Vietnam War
Age at Time of Award: 27

Humbert Roque "Rocky" Versace was born in Honolulu, Hawaii, on July 2, 1937. He was the eldest of five children born to Col. Humbert Joseph Versace, a US Army officer, and Marie Teresa Rios, a noted author whose book *The Fifteenth Pelican* inspired the 1960's television series *The Flying Nun*. Versace grew up in Alexandria, Virginia, and attended the first two years of high school in Washington, D.C., but graduated from Norfolk Catholic High School in Norfolk, Virginia.

Like his father before him, Versace attended the US Military Academy at West Point, entering in 1955. He graduated in 1959 and was commissioned a second lieutenant in the US Army with armor as his branch specialty. After completing Airborne and Ranger training at Fort Benning, Georgia, he served in Korea as a tank platoon leader in the 1st Cavalry Division. Upon returning to the United States in April 1961, he was assigned to the 3rd US Infantry (Old Guard) at Fort Meyer, Virginia.

Less than enamored with his ceremonial duties in the Old Guard, he volunteered for duty in Vietnam. After attending advisor training at Fort Bragg, North Carolina; an intelligence course at Fort Holabid, Maryland; and Vietnamese language school at the Presidio of San Francisco, he arrived in South Vietnam in May of 1962. He began his first tour as an intelligence advisor in Xuan Loc, Long Khanh Province, III Corps Tactical Zone. In November of 1962, he moved to Bien Hoa to become the assistant G-2 advisor, 5th Infantry Division, III ARVN Corps.

In May 1963, Versace volunteered to stay in South Vietnam as an advisor for another 6 months beyond his 12-month tour. Upon completion of that extension, he planned to leave the service and attend seminary with the intent to join the priesthood and return to Vietnam as a missionary.

When his extension was approved, he joined Advisory Team 70, An Xuyen Province, IV Corps, as the team intelligence advisor. On October 29, 1963, less than two weeks before the end of his tour, during a liaison mission to Army Special

Forces Detachment A-23, Versace decided to accompany a Civilian Irregular Defense Group (CIDG) operation against the 306th Main Force Viet Cong Battalion. While in the U Minh forest, Viet Cong troops ambushed the CIDG force, causing numerous casualties. Versace, 1st Lt. Nick Rowe, and Sergeant First Class Dan Pitzer reacted to the ambush by trying to rally the South Vietnamese forces, but they were quickly overrun by the Viet Cong, and Versace sustained multiple bullet wounds in the leg. All three Americans and numerous CIDG troops were captured.

The prisoners were bound, stripped of their boots, and led into the U Minh forest to a Viet Cong prisoner camp. For much of the next two years, their home would be bamboo cages, six feet long, two feet wide, and three feet high. They were given little to eat and little protection from the elements.

Versace, as the ranking officer, took command of the Americans and provided inspiration to his fellow captives while at the same time making it clear to the Viet Cong that they were bound to honor the Geneva Convention. Versace's untreated leg became badly infected, but within three weeks he tried to escape; guards soon discovered him crawling in the surrounding swamp, and they placed him in irons and locked him in an isolation cage.

The prisoners were forced to attend indoctrination classes, but Versace argued continuously with their captors in English, French, and Vietnamese, quickly earning the ire of his captors. During this period, Versace tried three more times to escape. Because of his vocal protests, recalcitrance, and repeated escape attempts, Versace was thrown into solitary confinement and tortured by the Viet Cong. Through his actions, resistance, and adherence to the Code of Conduct, he forced the Viet Cong to focus their efforts on him rather than the other American prisoners. The last the other prisoners heard from him, Versace was signing "God Bless America" at the top of his lungs from his isolation cage. On September 26, 1965, Versace's struggle came to an end when the Viet Cong executed him.

Although his remains were never recovered, Rocky Versace was awarded the Purple Heart and Silver Star posthumously during the war. After escaping the Viet Cong and returning to friendly forces, Rowe helped write the Medal of Honor nomination for Versace, but the nomination was subsequently misplaced or lost. His family and friends did not forget Versace, and they continued to lobby for the award of the Medal of Honor. After much pressure, Versace's Medal of Honor was finally approved in 2002. On July 8, President George W. Bush presented the medal to Versace's surviving family members in a ceremony in the East Room of the White House. This was the first time that the Army, unlike the Air Force, Navy, and Marines, had ever awarded the Medal of Honor to a prisoner of war from Vietnam for actions during captivity.

James M. Cloninger

Further Reading

Carhart, Tom. *West Point Warriors: Profiles of Duty, Honor, and Country in Battle.* New York: Grand Central Publishing, 2002.

Faranacci, Donald. *Last Full Measure of Devotion: A Tribute to America's Heroes of the Vietnam War.* Bloomington, IN: AuthorHouse, 2007.

Murphy, Edward F. *Vietnam Medal of Honor Heroes.* New York: Ballantine Books, 2005.

Rowe, James N. *Five Years to Freedom.* New York: Ballantine Books, 1984.

Wahlen, George Edward

Born: August 8, 1924
Died: June 5, 2009
Home State: Utah
Service: Navy
Conflict: World War II
Age at Time of Award: 21

George Edward Wahlen was born on August 8, 1924, to Albert and Doris Wahlen of West Ogden, Utah. Immediately upon completion of high school, Wahlen enlisted in the Navy. He wanted more than anything to go to the front line—which to him was the aircraft carriers. He was disappointed when selected as a Navy hospital corpsman but was promised by his commanding officer that if he did well in his medical training he might be considered for reassignment to aircraft mechanic training. Ironically, Wahlen did so well in his medical training that he was considered too valuable to lose. Accordingly, Wahlen immediately volunteered for service with the Marines and was assigned to the 2nd Battalion of the 26th Marine Regiment.

Wahlen's desire to get into combat was frustrated yet again when the 26th Marines, en route to Guam, got word they were no longer needed for the fighting there and were shipped back to Hawaii. Meanwhile, the 5th Marine Division, the parent unit for Wahlen's outfit, trained intensely for the invasion of Iwo Jima.

The Navy's leadership decided that the small volcanic island, approximately halfway between the Army Air Force bomber bases in Saipan and Tinian and the Japanese mainland, must be captured in order to eliminate it as an early warning station against Gen. Curtis Lemay's bombing raids and as an emergency divert field for damaged and low-fuel-state B-29 bombers. Additionally, fighters could be based on it to escort the bombers. The operation was planned for February and involved the commitment of an entire amphibious corps to take the island.

On D-Day, February 19, 1945, Wahlen landed with his unit to secure the island, and they soon found themselves in a bloody fight. As Wahlen prepared to hit the beach, knowing what awaited him, he had prayed, "Please help me not let one of my buddies down; please help me do my job." Over the next few days, he was in constant action and, on February 26, received the first of three wounds he would receive; the wound was from grenade shrapnel to his face, which temporarily blinded him. Wahlen continued to render critical aid to his platoon as well as the others in his company. In one instance, he carried a wounded comrade on his back under fire to the safety of an aid station. Not long after, he moved over to an adjacent platoon that had lost its corpsman and treated 14 marines before returning to his platoon; all the while, he was under fierce enemy fire, including mortars.

His company was one of the most heavily engaged in the battle, with only 5 men out of 240 coming out without being wounded or killed. Including replacements, the company had a 125 percent casualty rate. On March 2, Wahlen was painfully wounded in the back but refused evacuation in order to continue treating wounded marines. Finally, on March 3, he received a wound in his leg and could no longer walk. Nevertheless, he continued to provide emergency medical treatment, crawling a final 50 yards to treat a wounded comrade. He was finally evacuated to a hospital ship later that day and remained hospitalized at Camp Pendleton in California for the treatment of his multiple wounds for the remainder of the war and until discharged.

While still recovering, Pharmacist Second Class Wahlen was transported to Washington, D.C., where President Harry Truman presented him the Medal of Honor on October 5, 1945, for his bravery during the battle of Iwo Jima. Truman reputedly said, "I'm sure glad a pill pusher finally made it up here."

After the war, George Wahlen quietly married Melba Holley, and for several years she did not even know he had earned his nation's highest commendation for bravery. During this period, he attended Weber College in Utah, earning an associate's degree. In 1948, he joined the Army medical service branch and served in both Korea and Vietnam, retiring as a major in 1968. During his time on active duty with the Army, he earned his bachelor of science degree, graduating magna cum laude from Church College in Hawaii. After retirement, he continued to serve his country in the Veterans Administration for 12 more years. He was the penultimate "silent hero," never giving interviews about Iwo Jima until late in his life. He passed away after a short bout with cancer on June 5, 2009, at the age of 84.

John T. Kuehn

Further Reading

Alexander, Joseph H. *Closing In: Marines in the Seizure of Iwo Jima.* Washington, D.C.: Marine Corps Historical Center, 1994.

Collier, Peter, and Nick Del Calzo. *Medal of Honor: Portraits of Valor beyond the Call of Duty.* New York: Artisan, 2006.

Toyn, Gary W. *The Quiet Hero: The Untold Medal of Honor Story of George E. Wahlen at the Battle of Iwo Jima.* Clearfield, UT: American Legacy Media, 2006.

Wai, Francis B.

Born: April 14, 1917
Died: October 20, 1944
Home State: Hawaii
Service: Army
Conflict: World War II
Age at Time of Award: 27

Francis B. Wai was born in Honolulu, Hawaii, on April 14, 1917, the son of a Chinese father and a native Hawaiian mother. He attended Punahou School in Honolulu. Like many young boys in Honolulu, he learned to surf with Duke Kahanamoku and Buster Crabbe.

After high school, Wai entered Sacramento Junior College, later transferring to the University of California at Los Angeles (UCLA). Very athletic, he participated in four sports at UCLA. He graduated in 1939 with a degree in banking and finance. Returning to Honolulu, he intended to work with his father in real estate but instead joined the Hawaii National Guard.

In 1941, Wai was commissioned a lieutenant after successfully completing officer candidate school (OCS). His achievement was significant at the time because few Asian Americans were assigned to combat leadership roles.

Wai was assigned to the 34th Infantry Regiment of the 24th Infantry Division based at Schofield Barracks on Oahu. He was among those who fought back against the Japanese during their surprise attack on Pearl Harbor and other military installations on December 7, 1941.

Between 1941 and 1943, Wai's unit was kept on Oahu to guard against a Japanese invasion. In 1943, Wai, now a captain, and his regiment embarked with the 24th Division to Australia, where they trained for Operation Reckless, the upcoming New Guinea campaign. On April 22, 1944, the division participated in the assault on New Guinea, capturing the Hollandia Airdrome. Wai's regiment was directed to move to Biak Island to reinforce the 41st Infantry Division in its effort to liberate the island from Japanese control. During this operation, Wai and his regiment captured two more airfields.

In October 1944, Wai's division was assigned to X Corps of the 6th US Army in preparation for the upcoming invasion of the Philippines. The plan called for the 1st Cavalry Division to join the 24th in an assault landing at Leyte. The objective of this operation was to separate the Japanese forces in Luzon from those in Mindanao. The latter were to be left isolated and Luzon saved for liberation at a later date.

The 6th Army invasion force was commanded by Gen. Douglas McArthur, whose wading ashore onto Leyte was the setting for his famous "I have returned" speech.

The landings on Leyte occurred on October 20, 1944, and were preceded by a massive air campaign that reduced Japanese air assets to a handful of planes. The plan called for a pincer movement with US forces in the Northern Transport Area landing on White and Red beaches in San Pedro Bay near the town of San Jose. Meanwhile, in the Southern Transport Area, more US troops would land a dozen miles to the south on four other landing zones.

Captain Wai's unit landed on Red Beach with great difficulty because of the shallow water. Four landing craft were stranded and subsequently destroyed or damaged by Japanese mortars. When the American forces reached the beach, they came under intense Japanese fire from a coconut grove bounded by rice paddies on both sides.

Captain Wai landed in the fifth wave only to find that earlier waves were pinned down and leaderless. Taking command, he advanced through the rice paddies with total disregard for his own safety. His courage under fire provided an example for the other men. As he advanced, he drew intense enemy fire, exposing the locations of the entrenched Japanese to the attackers. One by one, the Japanese positions were overcome. Captain Wai, leading the assault, was killed taking out the last active Japanese pillbox.

For his conspicuous bravery, Wai was posthumously awarded the Distinguished Service Cross. After the war, his remains were buried in the National Memorial Cemetery of the Pacific in Honolulu in the Punch Bowl Crater.

In 1996, Congress directed Louis Caldera, the secretary of the Army, to review records to determine if Asian Americans had been denied full recognition because of racial prejudice. After the review, 22 Asian Americans were determined to have not received full consideration for the award of the Medal of Honor. On June 20, 2000, the medals previously awarded to these 22 Asian Americans were upgraded to the Medal of Honor by President Bill Clinton in a White House ceremony. Francis Wai was only one of two from this group who did not belong to the predominantly Japanese American 442nd Regimental Combat Team/100th Infantry Battalion; the other was Rudolph B. Davila of the 7th Infantry. To date, Wai is the only Chinese American and the first Asian American officer to receive the Medal of Honor.

Andrew J. Waskey

Further Reading

Cutler, Thomas J. *The Battle of Leyte Gulf: 23–26 October 1944*. Annapolis, MD: Naval Institute Press, 1997.

Ireland, Bernard. *Leyte Gulf 1944: The World's Greatest Sea Battle*. Oxford, UK: Osprey, 2006.

Jordan, Kenneth N. *Yesterday's Heroes: 433 Men of World War II Awarded the Medal of Honor, 1941–1945*. Atglen, PA: Schiffer Military History, 1996.

Marston, Daniel. *The Pacific War Companion: From Pearl Harbor to Hiroshima*. Oxford, UK: Osprey, 2005.

Proft, R. J., ed. *United States of America's Congressional Medal of Honor Recipients and their Official Citations*. 4th ed. Columbia Heights, MN: Highland House, 2002.

Sear, David. *The Last Epic Naval Battle: Voices from Leyte*. New York: Penguin Books, 2007.

Wainwright, Jonathan M.

Born: August 23, 1883
Died: September 3, 1953
Home State: Washington
Service: Army
Conflict: World War II
Age at Time of Award: 58

Born on August 23, 1883, at Fort Walla Walla, Washington Territory, Jonathan Mayhew Wainwright graduated from the US Military Academy in 1906 and was commissioned in the cavalry. During his early career, he fought against Moro rebels in the Philippines (1906–1908) and was assigned to various military posts in the western United States. Following the US entry into World War I, he served with the American Expeditionary Forces in France and participated in the Saint-Mihiel and Meuse-Argonne offensives. He ended the war as a lieutenant colonel.

Wainwright then reverted to his permanent rank of captain and held a variety of command and staff slots. Promoted to lieutenant colonel in 1929, he graduated from the Command and General Staff School, Fort Leavenworth (1931), and the Army War College (1936). Promoted to colonel, he commanded the 3rd Cavalry Regiment at Fort Myer, Virginia (1936–1938). After being made a temporary brigadier general (1938), he was put in charge of the 1st Cavalry Brigade. In September 1940, Wainwright was advanced to temporary major general and assigned to the Philippines to command the Philippine Division.

Following the Japanese landings there on December 8, Wainwright commanded the North Luzon Force. Gen. Douglas MacArthur, confident his forces could throw back any Japanese invasion, had scrapped the original plan to meet a Japanese invasion by withdrawing into the Bataan Peninsula. Wainwright's Filipino and US forces fought well but were ultimately forced from the Lingayen Gulf onto Bataan. Much of their equipment and supplies were lost in the withdrawal.

With a Japanese victory in sight, Washington ordered MacArthur to leave the Philippines for Australia. MacArthur was then awarded the Medal of Honor. On MacArthur's departure on March 11, 1942, Wainwright took over as commander of US forces in the Far East, with the rank of lieutenant general. Forced off Bataan to Corregidor, he had no choice but to surrender on May 6, 1942. MacArthur protested Army chief of staff Gen. George C. Marshall's recommendation that Wainwright receive the Medal of Honor.

Treated harshly as a prisoner of war in camps in northern Luzon, Formosa, and Manchuria for the next three years, Wainwright was liberated by the Soviets in August 1945. He witnessed the formal Japanese surrender on September 2 on the USS *Missouri* and traveled to the Philippines to receive the surrender of Japanese forces there.

Jonathan Wainwright returned to the United States and, despite MacArthur's opposition, was awarded the Medal of Honor. In September 1945, he was promoted to full general. He took command of 4th Army at Fort Sam Houston, Texas, in 1946 but retired in August 1947. Wainwright died in San Antonio, Texas, on September 3, 1953.

T. Jason Soderstrum

Further Reading

Beck, John Jacob. *MacArthur and Wainwright: Sacrifice of the Philippines.* Albuquerque: University of New Mexico Press, 1974.

Schultz, Duane P. *Hero of Bataan: The Story of General Jonathan M. Wainwright.* New York: St. Martin's Press, 1981.

Wainwright, Jonathan Mayhew. *General Wainwright's Story: The Account of Four Years of Humiliating Defeat, Surrender, and Captivity.* Garden City, NY: Doubleday, 1946.

Walker, Dr. Mary E.

Born: November 26, 1832
Died: February 21, 1919
Home State: New York
Service: Civilian
Conflict: Civil War
Age at Time of Award: 32

Mary Edwards Walker was born in Oswego, New York, on November 26, 1832. Encouraged by her parents to pursue her education beyond the primary level, for a brief time she worked as a teacher before deciding on a career as a medical doctor, a profession that at the time was almost completely closed to women. Through sheer perseverance, she gained acceptance at the Syracuse Medical College and graduated with an MD degree in 1855, only the second American woman to achieve the degree. Married while in medical school, she refused to adopt her husband's surname. She opened a medical practice in Rome, New York, that soon failed because most people refused to accept a female physician. From there she went to Cincinnati, Ohio, to practice medicine but enjoyed little success.

When the Civil War began in 1861, Walker volunteered her services to the Union Army, which permitted her to work as a nurse but not as a physician. She worked mostly in a hospital in Washington, D.C. In early 1864, the 52nd Ohio Infantry Regiment hired her as a contract surgeon for a period of six months, and, in October 1864, the Union Army hired her as an assistant surgeon, a commission she held until she resigned in June 1865. Her position enabled her to move freely between Union and Confederate lines, and she actively sought to treat civilians on both sides. There is conjecture that she performed espionage work for the Union, but this has never been sub-

Dr. Mary E. Walker, Contract Surgeon (National Archives).

stantiated. Nevertheless, as she was treating a wounded Confederate soldier in 1864, she was charged with spying. She spent four months as a prisoner before being released. During her war service, Walker adopted the Union officer's uniform but wore her hair in curls to ensure she was not mistaken for a man.

On November 11, 1865, Walker became the first woman to be awarded the Medal of Honor, thanks to the recommendations of major generals William T. Sherman and George Thomas, for her meritorious work during the war. Following the war, Walker continued to work as a physician; published two books; and actively campaigned for women's rights, improved health care, and temperance. She also advocated the direct election of US senators.

Walker was known for her adoption of the bloomer costume, an outfit that incorporated both a skirt and trousers. Arrested many times because of her penchant for wearing male attire, she later wore men's suits exclusively. In 1897, Walker tried unsuccessfully to establish an all-female "colony," which she called "Adamless Eden." Because she spurned the prescribed gender roles of the era, she was considered highly controversial and militant. Most women did not support her activities, and even her own family ostracized her.

In 1917, the federal government revoked Mary Walker's Medal of Honor, along with those of five Indian scouts, including "Buffalo Bill" Cody, because they were deemed ineligible for the award due to their civilian status. Despite demands by the US Army that she return the medal, Walker refused, responding, "You can have it, over my dead body." She died alone and penniless on February 21, 1919, in Oswego, New York. In 1977, President Jimmy Carter signed a proclamation posthumously restoring her Medal of Honor. In 1982, Walker was depicted on a US postal stamp, which listed her title as Army surgeon and Medal of Honor recipient.

Wendy A. Maier

Further Reading

Graf, Mercedes. *A Woman of Honor: Dr. Walker and the Civil War.* Gettysburg, PA: Thomas Publications, 2001.

Mikaelian, Allen, and Mike Wallace. *Medal of Honor: Profiles of America's Military Heroes from the Civil War to the Present.* New York: Hyperion, 2003.

Walker, Dale. *Mary Edwards Walker: Above and Beyond.* New York: Forge Books, 2005.

Ware, Keith L.

Born: November 23, 1915
Died: September 13, 1968
Home State: California
Service: Army
Conflict: World War II
Age at Time of Award: 38

Born in Denver, Colorado, on November 23, 1915, Keith L. Ware was inducted into the Army in July 1941. He completed officer candidate school (OCS) at Fort Benning, Georgia, and was commissioned a second lieutenant of infantry in 1942. He participated in the Allied invasion of North Africa, the campaigns in Sicily and Italy, and the invasion of southern France. In December 1944, near Sigolsheim, France, Lieutenant Colonel Ware led a patrol against four machine gun positions, killing many defenders. Half of his patrol members, including himself, were wounded, but Ware refused medical attention until the enemy positions had been captured. For this action, he received the Medal of Honor.

After World War II, Ware attended Army professional schools, served on the Army staff in Washington, D.C., and was an instructor at West Point. Promoted to colonel in 1953, he commanded an infantry regiment in Korea (1955–1956) and then attended the National War College. Other assignments included service at Supreme Headquarters Allied Powers Europe (SHAPE). He was promoted to brigadier general in 1963 while serving with the 2nd Armored Division at Fort Hood, Texas. In September 1964, Ware was appointed deputy chief of information (public affairs) for the Army and then chief in February 1966. In July 1966, he was promoted to major general.

Ware reported to Vietnam for assignment as deputy commanding general, II Field Force, Vietnam (IFFV) in December 1967. When the Communists launched the Tet Offensive in early 1968, he was dispatched to Saigon to assume command of all US ground forces in the area. Forming Task Force Ware, he stabilized the situation after several weeks of heavy fighting. In March 1968, he assumed command of the 1st Infantry Division ("Big Red One"). Ware was an inspirational leader whose dream had been to command the division in combat.

On September 13, 1968, Gen. Keith Ware was killed in action when his command helicopter was hit by hostile ground fire and crashed in the jungle southeast of Loc Ninh. His command sergeant major, Joseph A. Venable; six other members of the general staff; and the general's canine companion, King, died with him. Ware was the fourth general officer killed in Vietnam. His name now honors a scholarship program for the 1st Infantry Division. Additionally, the Army's annual award for journalism is named after him as are the parade ground and an elementary school at Fort Riley, Kansas.

John F. Votaw

Further Reading

First Infantry Division in Vietnam. Vol. 2, *May 1, 1967–31 Dec. 1968.* Vietnam: 1st Infantry Division, n.d.

Official Biography of Major General Keith L. Ware. Washington, D.C.: Department of the Army, n.d.

Wheeler, James Scott. *The Big Red One: America's Legendary 1st Infantry Division from World War I to Desert Storm.* Lawrence: University Press of Kansas, 2007.

Warren, Francis E.

Born: June 20, 1844
Died: November 24, 1929
Home State: Massachusetts
Service: Army
Conflict: Civil War
Age at Time of Award: 18

Francis Emroy Warren was born on June 20, 1844, in Hinsdale, Massachusetts. He attended Hillsdale Academy prior to his enlistment as a private in the 49th Massachusetts Volunteer Infantry in 1862. The following year, the 49th Massachusetts traveled to Louisiana, where it participated in the siege of Port Hudson, Louisiana.

Shortly after the siege started on May 21, 1863, the recently promoted Corporal Warren volunteered for duty on a forlorn hope to storm the Confederate defenses protecting Port Hudson. The storming party's task was to fill the ditches in front of the Rebel lines, and then level the works to pave the way for follow-up troops assaulting the fortifications.

The attack went forward on May 27, 1863. The desperate attack failed, and virtually every member of the party was killed or wounded, including Warren, who was wounded. Warren survived and served for the remainder of the Civil War as a noncommissioned officer and received his discharge from the Union Army in 1865.

Warren returned to Massachusetts following the Civil War and served in the Massachusetts Militia. Warren farmed and raised livestock in his home state before moving west in 1868 to Cheyenne, in the Dakota Territory, what is now the state of Wyoming. The move west opened a myriad of business possibilities for the young Civil War veteran. Warren engaged in the mercantile business, farming, livestock, and land speculation and shrewdly invested in the infant lighting business. These moves paid off handsomely for Warren, and, by 1873, he gained enough prominence to secure election as president of the recently formed Wyoming Territorial Senate and served as a member of the Cheyenne City Council. Marked as an up-and-comer in the Republican Party, Warren continued his rise by securing the territorial treasurer's office in 1876, 1879, 1882, and 1884. He was elected mayor of Cheyenne in 1885 and was appointed governor of the Territory of Wyoming by President Chester Arthur in 1885. Warren was removed from the governorship by Democratic president Grover Cleveland in 1886 and then accepted reappointment to the same post by Republican president Benjamin Harrison in 1889. Wyoming gained full statehood in 1890, and Warren was elected its first governor that same year. Warren served as governor for roughly a month before he resigned because he won one of Wyoming's two US Senate seats and left for Washington, D.C. in 1891 to start a long career as a US senator.

Warren's career in the Senate proved to be a distinguished one. With the exception of a short break from 1893 to 1895, Warren won reelection five times before he died in office in 1929, serving longer than any other senator to that date. Warren served on a variety of important Senate committees, most notably the Senate Committee on Military Affairs, the Senate Foreign Affairs Committee, and the Senate Appropriations Committee. Warren's daughter, Helen Frances Warren, married a young army officer named John J. "Black Jack" Pershing in 1905. Pershing eventually rose to command the American Expeditionary Force (AEF) in France during World War I.

Francis Warren did not receive his Medal of Honor until September 30, 1893, one of a flood of medals awarded during that decade. Warren complained about the poor record keeping, which he believed prevented him from receiving his

Medal of Honor earlier, but Warren's status as a sitting US senator undoubtedly aided his quest for recognition. Warren died in Washington, D.C. on November 24, 1929, and is buried in Lakeview Cemetery, Cheyenne, Wyoming.

Terry L. Beckenbaugh

Further Reading

The Congressional Medal of Honor: The Names, the Deeds. Forest Ranch, CA: Sharp & Dunnigan, 1984.

Mitchell, Lt. Col. Joseph B., and James Otis. *The Badge of Gallantry: Recollections of Civil War Congressional Medal of Honor Winners.* New York: Macmillan, 1968.

Watson, George

Born: ca. 1915
Died: March 8, 1943
Home State: Colorado
Service: Army
Conflict: World War II
Age at Time of Award: 28

Raised in Birmingham, Alabama, George Watson graduated from Colorado A&M College (now known as Colorado State University) in 1942 and was drafted on September 1, 1942. Despite his university education, Watson—an African American—was assigned as a private to the US Army's 2nd Battalion, 29th Quartermaster Regiment.

On March 8, 1943, Watson was aboard the transport USAT *Jacob* near Porlock Harbor, New Guinea, when Japanese aircraft attacked the ship. With the vessel sinking and still under attack by the Japanese, the order was given to abandon ship. In the chaos that followed, Watson, rather than saving himself, assisted many soldiers who could not swim into the life rafts. Swimming back and forth from the sinking ship to the life rafts, he continued to rescue his comrades until he himself was so exhausted that he was pulled down by the tow of the sinking ship. It is believed that Watson drowned since his body was never recovered.

Watson was the first African American to earn the Distinguished Service Cross (DSC) during World War II. In the late 1990s, the Army conducted a three-year review of the records of 10 African Americans heroes to determine if they met the standards for award of the Medal of Honor. Of these, seven names were submitted to Congress and the president. On January 13, 1997, in a crowded White House ceremony, President Bill Clinton awarded the Medal of Honor to these seven African American veterans of World War II. Only one of the men, 77-year-old Vernon Baker, who had been a platoon leader with the 92nd Infantry Division, was alive and present for the ceremony. The others, including Watson, were awarded the Medal of Honor posthumously. While some of the other departed were represented by next of kin, Watson's wife had passed away by this time and no other living next of kin could be found.

When Watson's DSC was upgraded to the Medal of Honor, he became the only African American to earn the medal while serving in the Pacific Theater. He has been memorialized at the Manila American Cemetery in the Philippines and by the George Watson Memorial Field at Fort Benning, Georgia. In addition, in 1997, the US Navy named USNS *Watson* (T-AKR-310) in Private Watson's honor. The *Watson* is the lead ship of a class of large, medium-speed, roll-on roll-off (LMSR) ships.

George Watson's Medal of Honor now resides in the US Army Quartermaster Museum at Fort Lee, Virginia.

Alexander M. Bielakowski

Further Reading

Bruning, John R., Jr. *Elusive Glory: African-American Heroes of World War II*. Greensboro, NC: Avisson Press, 2001.

Moore, Christopher. *Fighting for America: Black Soldiers—The Unsung Heroes of World War II*. New York: Presidio Press, 2005.

Watters, Charles Joseph

Born: January 17, 1927
Died: November 3, 1967
Home State: New Jersey
Service: Army
Conflict: Vietnam War
Age at Time of Award: 40

Born in Jersey City, New Jersey, on January 17, 1927, Charles J. Watters attended Seton Hall College and Immaculate Conception Seminary. He was ordained a priest in the Roman Catholic Church in 1953 and served in parishes in Jersey City, Rutherford, Crawford, and Paramus. In 1962, Watters joined the New Jersey Air National Guard and then joined the Regular Army in 1964 and trained at Fort Dix. The young priest hardly cut a figure as a soldier. Slight and bespectacled, Watters liked to remark that he was "of the peaceful kind. All I shoot is my camera. If they start shooting at me, I yell 'tourist!' " Nonetheless, he won respect as both a soldier and chaplain.

CHAPLAINS AND THE MEDAL OF HONOR

Only seven military chaplains have earned the Medal of Honor—three during the Civil War and four during the 20th century. Six of these seven chaplains received their medals for heroic aid to the wounded and dying without regard to their own safety.

All four 20th-century recipients were Roman Catholic priests. Navy chaplain Joseph T. O'Callahan was the only chaplain awarded the medal during World War II. Army chaplains Angelo J. (Charles) Liteky and Charles J. Watters, along with Navy chaplain Vincent R. Capodanno, received their awards for actions in Vietnam. Both Watters's and Capodanno's medals were posthumous.

On December 31, 1862, John M. Whitehead, chaplain to the 15th Indiana Infantry, dodged enemy fire to carry Union soldiers to safety during the Battle of Murfreesboro. For his courage, Whitehead was issued the Medal of Honor in 1898. Francis B. Hall, chaplain for the 16th New York Infantry, received the medal for carrying "wounded men to the rear for treatment . . . during the thickest of the fight" in the Battle of Salem Church on May 3, 1863; he was awarded the medal in 1897.

As ordained clergy who are also commissioned military officers, chaplains are prohibited from carrying weapons. Despite this tradition of noncombatant status, the Civil War's third chaplain recipient was awarded the Medal of Honor for taking up arms. During a Union counterattack outside of Atlanta on July 22, 1864, Milton L. Haney, chaplain to the 55th Illinois Infantry, distinguished himself by carrying "a musket in the ranks of his regiment." Haney was awarded the Medal of Honor in 1896.

Joseph T. O'Callahan's Medal of Honor was the first awarded to a Navy chaplain and the only one awarded to any military chaplain during World War II. A Jesuit priest and Massachusetts native, O'Callahan entered the Navy Chaplain Corps in 1940. He was awarded the medal for his actions aboard the USS *Franklin* following its attack by Japanese kamikazes on March 19, 1945.

Wounded by shrapnel in the attack, O'Callahan tended to the wounded and dead while organizing and leading fire-fighting crews, supervising the jettisoning of live ammunition, and providing leadership in inferno-like conditions that was credited with saving the badly damaged aircraft carrier. He was awarded the medal by President Harry S. Truman on January 23, 1945. His memoir, *I Was Chaplain on the Franklin*, was published in 1957.

The Medal of Honor was awarded posthumously to Vincent R. Capodanno on January 7, 1968. A Maryknoll Order priest from Staten Island, New York, Capodanno became the second Navy chaplain to receive the medal. Following service as a missionary in Taiwan, Capodanno joined the Navy as a chaplain in 1965. Assigned to the 3rd Battalion of the 5th Marines in 1966, Capodanno volunteered to extend his yearlong tour in Vietnam by another six months. On September 4, 1967, Capodanno was in the company command post (CP) of a Marine outpost in the Queson Valley, Quang Tin Province. When the unit's 2nd Platoon came under attack, Capodanno left the CP, exposing himself to enemy fire in order to provide spiritual and medical aid to the beleaguered unit. Although sustaining serious shrapnel wounds, he refused medical attention in order to continue to aid others. Finally, in an attempt to rescue a wounded medical corpsman "in the direct line of fire of an enemy machine gunner," Capodanno was fatally wounded.

Chaplain Charles Joseph Watters's Medal of Honor was also awarded posthumously. A New Jersey native and Catholic priest, Watters had previously served as chaplain to the Air National Guard before becoming an Army chaplain in 1964. Sent to Vietnam as chaplain to the 173rd Support Battalion of the 173rd Airborne Brigade in 1966, Watters, like Chaplain Capodanno, volunteered to extend his yearlong tour by six months. On November 19, 1967, the company Watters was in made contact with an enemy battalion near Dak To. During the ensuing battle, Watters repeatedly moved to the forward-most point of contact in order to minister to the wounded and dying. While giving aid to the wounded, Watters himself was mortally wounded. He was posthumously awarded the Medal of Honor on November 4, 1969.

Chaplain Angelo J. (Charles) Liteky was awarded the Medal of Honor for his actions on December 6, 1967, in Vietnam. A Roman Catholic priest and Navy brat from Florida, Liteky was on his first combat patrol, accompanying elements of the 199th Light Infantry Brigade on a search-and-destroy mission near the village of Phuoc Lac, in Bien Hoa Province. In an ensuing battle, Liteky personally evacuated 20 soldiers under intense hostile fire, physically carrying many despite his own neck and foot wounds sustained during the battle. During that same fight, Liteky repeatedly exposed himself to enemy fire in order to tend to the wounded and dying, administer last rites, and direct the movement of medical evacuation helicopters. He was awarded the medal by President Lyndon B. Johnson on November 19, 1968.

Liteky is the only nonposthumous chaplain recipient during the Vietnam War. Moreover, Liteky is also the only recipient to publicly renounce and return his medal, having done so in 1986 in protest of US foreign policy.

Perhaps the best-known account of extraordinary chaplain heroism is that of the collective action of the "Four Chaplains" on board the troopship *Dorchester* on February 3, 1943. While the ship had been torpedoed by a German submarine in the North Atlantic and was rapidly sinking, chaplains George L. Fox, Alexander D. Goode, Clark V. Poling, and John P. Washington were credited with bringing a calming presence to a panicked evacuation. Survivors reported that Chaplain Goode gave up his gloves, and Chaplain Washington and, reportedly, the others gave away their own lifebelts. The chaplains were last seen arms linked, united in prayer, as the ship sank. The story of the Four Chaplains, as they become known, quickly became a symbol of both extraordinary heroism and interfaith sacrifice—Chaplain Fox was a Methodist minister, Chaplain Goode a rabbi, Chaplain Poling a Dutch Reformed minister, and Chaplain Washington a Catholic priest. In December 1944, all four chaplains were posthumously awarded the Distinguished Service Cross. They were commemorated in 1948 on a US postage stamp. However, contrary to popular belief, the Four Chaplains were never awarded the Medal of Honor. Instead, at the direction of Congress, on January 18, 1961, the Army posthumously awarded a special "Medal for Heroism" to the chaplains. This was a one-time award that was intended to have the same weight and importance as the Medal of Honor.

Bradley Carter

As a spiritual guide and morale officer, Watters commanded respect because of his generosity and willingness to help in any way. One soldier, Carlos Lozada, went off to Vietnam married outside of the church but with a young child. When he and his wife encountered financial difficulties, Watters made out a personal check for $130. Then, he blessed both the marriage and the child. Although Lozada later died in combat, his widow never forgot the act.

In 1966, the Army sent Watters to Vietnam as chaplain of Company A, 173rd Support Battalion, 173rd Airborne Brigade. In a prelude of what was to come, Watters was awarded the Bronze Star for retrieving a wounded man from beyond the perimeter and then voluntarily extended his tour by six months in 1967 because of the shortage of chaplains to the troops.

On November 3, 1967, Watters was accompanying the 1st Battalion, 502nd Infantry on combat operations in Kontum Province in the Central Highlands when it became involved in a pitched battle with North Vietnamese Army forces on Hill 875 near Dak To. As the battle unfolded, commanders admonished Watters to return to the rear, but he remained with his men. He disregarded his own safety and rushed unarmed and completely exposed among as well as in front of the advancing troops, giving aid to the wounded, assisting in their evacuation, giving words of encouragement, and administering last rites to the dying. When Watters saw a wounded paratrooper standing in shock in front of the assaulting forces, the chaplain ran forward, picked up the man on his shoulders, and carried him to safety. In the first assault against an enemy entrenchment, he ran through intense enemy fire to aid a fallen comrade. Three more times, Watters ignored attempts to restrain him and repeatedly exposed himself to both friendly and enemy fire to recover wounded soldiers.

Satisfied that all the wounded were inside the perimeter, Watters aided the medics in applying field bandages, getting food and water to the men, and giving spiritual strength and comfort. During this ministering, he moved out to the perimeter from position to position, redistributing food and water and tending to the needs of his men. He was giving aid to the wounded when an errant American bomb mortally wounded him and 42 other men.

Watters was posthumously awarded the Distinguished Service Cross (DSC). Maj. Gen. Francis Sampson, a chaplain who won renown in World War II, delivered Watters's funeral sermon on December 11, 1967, at Fort Myer, Virginia; Watters was buried in Arlington National Cemetery.

The DSC that Charles Watters received for his actions on Hill 875 in 1967 was upgraded to the Medal of Honor. Vice President Spiro T. Agnew presented the medal to Chaplain Watters's two brothers in a ceremony on November 4, 1969.

John D. Fitzmorris

Further Reading

Ackermann, Henry F. *He Was Always There: The U.S. Army Chaplain Ministry in the Vietnam Conflict.* Washington, D.C.: Office of the Chief of Chaplains, Department of the Army, 1989.

Atkinson, Rick. *The Long Gray Line.* New York: Houghton Mifflin, 1989.

Clark, David. "Chaplain (Maj) Charles J. Watters." *On Point: The Journal of Army History* 11, no. 1 (Summer 2005): 25.

Murphy, Edward F. *Vietnam Medal of Honor Heroes.* New York: Ballantine Books, 2005.

Tillman, Barrett. *Heroes: U.S. Army Medal of Honor Recipients.* New York: The Berkley Group, 2006.

Webb, Alexander S.

Born: February 15, 1835
Died: February 12, 1911
Home State: New York
Service: Army
Conflict: Civil War
Age at Time of Award: 28

Alexander S. Webb was born February 15, 1835, in Carroll Place, New York City. He came from a prominent family with a strong military lineage. Webb's father was a newspaper owner and diplomat who had been an Army officer. His grandfather, Samuel Blatchley Webb, was wounded at the Battle of Bunker Hill and served on George Washington's staff during the Revolutionary War.

Webb graduated from the US Military Academy at West Point in 1855, 13th out of 34 cadets. He was commissioned a brevet second lieutenant in the 4th US Artillery and was sent to Florida to fight in the Seminole War. After that assignment, he went back to West Point to serve as a mathematics instructor.

At the outbreak of the Civil War, Webb took part in the defense of Fort Pickens, Florida, and was present at the First Battle of Bull Run. From July 1861 to June 1862, he served in the Army of the Potomac and later as chief of staff to Maj. Gen. Fitz John Porter in V Corps during the Maryland Campaign and the Battle of Antietam. After a short stint in Washington, D.C. as the inspector of artillery, he was again assigned to V Corps as chief of staff to Maj. Gen. George G. Meade, who had assumed command from Porter. During the Battle of Chancellorsville, Meade gave Webb temporary command of Brig. Gen. Erastus B. Tyler's brigade; he served well in battle and was commended by General Meade.

On July 3, 1863, Webb was in command of the 2nd Brigade, 2nd Division of II Corps at Gettysburg. Webb's brigade was occupying the center of the Union line near the famous "Copse of Trees," preparing to defend against the impending Confederate attack. When the Confederates launched a massive artillery barrage on the Union position, Webb made himself conspicuous to his men, impressing them with his personal bravery under fire.

When Confederate major general Pickett's Virginia division launched its charge, part of his force made it to within a few hundred yards of the Union position when two companies from Webb's 71st Pennsylvania broke and ran away. Webb tried to get the neighboring 72nd Pennsylvania to counterattack the Confederates, but, not recognizing him, they refused to move. Webb then braved the intense enemy fire and raced to the adjacent 69th Pennsylvania, ordering them to fire across the front of the 72nd to catch the attacking Confederates who had been led across a low stone wall by Confederate general Lewis Armistead. This resulted in a crossfire that inflicted heavy casualties on the attackers and repulsed the attack. Webb's dynamic leadership and disregard for his own personal safety played a critical role in the Union defense even though he was so new to command that many of the soldiers in the brigade did not know who he was. For his "distinguished personal gallantry in leading his men forward at a critical period" during the Battle of Gettysburg, Webb would be presented the Medal of Honor on September 28, 1891.

For his service at Gettysburg, Webb was promoted to major general of volunteers, effective August 1, 1863. Webb subsequently received command of a division, replacing John Gibbon, who had been wounded during the fighting in July 1863. Webb led the division throughout the subsequent fall campaigns, playing a significant role in the Battle of Bristoe Station.

In the spring of 1864, Gibbon returned to assume command of his division, and Webb went back to command a brigade for the Overland Campaign. At the Battle of Spotsylvania Court House in May, he was hit by a bullet that passed through the corner of his right eye and came out his ear but left him with no permanent disabilities. After recovering from his wounds, he returned to the Army in January 1865 as chief of staff for the Army of the Potomac. At the end of hostilities, he became the assistant inspector general of the Military Division of the Atlantic.

General Webb stayed in the Army until 1870, reverting to the permanent rank of lieutenant colonel in first the 44th US Infantry and later the 5th US Infantry. He served his final tour as an instructor at West Point.

From 1869 to 1902, General Webb served as the second president of the City College of New York. He wrote extensively on the Civil War, publishing a book titled *The Peninsula: McClellan's Campaign of 1862* in 1881.

Alexander Webb died on February 12, 1911, in Riverdale, New York. He is buried in the West Point Cemetery at the US Military Academy. A statue of General Webb was dedicated in the Gettysburg National Military Park in 1915.

James H. Willbanks

Further Reading

Coddington, Edwin B. *The Gettysburg Campaign: A Study in Command*. New York: Scribner's, 1968.

Eicher, John H., and David J. Eicher. *Civil War High Commands*. Palo Alto, CA: Stanford University Press, 2001.

Warner, Ezra J. *Generals in Blue: Lives of the Union Commanders*. Baton Rouge: Louisiana State University Press, 1964.

Webb, Alexander S. *The Peninsula: McClellan's Campaign of 1862*. New York: Charles Scribner's Sons, 1881.

Wetzel, Gary George

Born: September 9, 1947
Died:
Home State: Wisconsin
Service: Army
Conflict: Vietnam War
Age at Time of Award: 20

Gary George Wetzel, a native of South Milwaukee, Wisconsin, was born on September 9, 1947, as the second oldest of nine children. He enlisted in the US Army in Milwaukee at the age of 18. After attending basic and advanced individual training, he was assigned as an instructor at Fort Leonard Wood in a heavy equipment unit. Wetzel volunteered for assignment to Vietnam and had just turned 19 when he arrived in country in October 1966. He served his first tour with an ordnance unit near Vung Tau.

Wetzel reenlisted in the Army after one year with the hope that someday he would become a helicopter pilot. He served his second tour in Vietnam as a door gunner with the 173rd Assault Helicopter Company (the Robin Hoods), 11th Combined Aviation Battalion, 1st Aviation Brigade, which operated primarily out of Lai Khe in the Iron Triangle region.

On January 8, 1968, Private First Class Wetzel was a mere 10 days from finishing his second tour. That day, the Robin Hoods were in support of the 9th Infantry Division, flying what were popularly known as Eagle Flights. During these flights, unplanned insertions were conducted in hopes of surprising enemy forces. Wetzel's UH-1D helicopter was part of a flight of 14 aircraft carrying 80 men who were to be inserted into a landing zone (LZ) east of the Can Giouc River, near Ap Dong An, hoping to prevent enemy forces from reaching prepared defensive positions. As Wetzel's helicopter approached the hot LZ, it was shot down by a rocket-propelled grenade, marking the fifth time the aircraft in which he was riding had been shot down. Two crew members were lost.

Going to the aid of his wounded pilot, Capt. William F. Dismukes, Wetzel was hit by a grenade; though badly wounded in both arms, left leg, and chest, Wetzel returned to his door gun and returned fire. Seemingly the only one returning effective fire, and with a useless left arm, Wetzel's relentless effort suppressed enemy automatic fire and destroyed an enemy bunker that had prevented an American counterattack on the enemy positions. He then returned to try to help his flight commander but passed out from his serious wounds. After regaining consciousness, he aided his crew chief in getting the pilot to the safety of a dike, though he again lost consciousness. He was evacuated the next morning.

Wetzel spent five months in hospitals recovering from his wounds. His left arm was amputated as a result of his wounds, thus ending his military career and his dream of becoming a pilot. For his heroic efforts at Ap Dong An, Wetzel was originally awarded the Distinguished Service Cross. Upon his return to the United States and civilian life, a surprised and disbelieving Wetzel learned he would be awarded the Medal of Honor. He received his award from President Lyndon B. Johnson in a White House ceremony on November 19, 1968.

In private life, Gary Wetzel returned home to Wisconsin and found work as a heavy equipment operator and time to ride his Harley-Davidson. A longtime supporter of Vietnam veterans' groups, Wetzel was a founder of the Wisconsin Vietnam Veterans committee and remains active with the Vietnam prisoner-of-war/missing-in-action (POW/MIA) organization. He currently resides in his native Milwaukee. He was inducted into the Army Aviation Hall of Fame in 1990.

Thomas Dwight Veve

Further Reading

Collier, Peter, and Nick Del Calzo. *Medal of Honor: Portraits of Valor beyond the Call of Duty*. New York: Artisan, 2006.

Lowry, Timothy S. *And Brave Men, Too*. New York: Crown Publishers, 1985.

Whiteley, Eli

Born: December 10, 1913
Died: December 2, 1986
Home State: Texas
Service: Army
Conflict: World War II
Age at Time of Award: 31

Eli L. Whiteley was born on December 10, 1913, and grew up on his family's farm in Georgetown, Texas. He graduated from high school in 1932 and attended the Agricultural and Mechanical College of Texas (Texas A&M University), where he received a bachelor of science in agronomy upon graduation in 1941. Whitely was six months into his master's degree at North Carolina State University when he was drafted into the Army in 1942.

Whiteley was a first lieutenant with Company L, 15th Infantry, 3rd Infantry Division when he arrived in France. On December 27, 1944, Whiteley led his platoon in house-to-house fighting in the fortified town of Sigolsheim, France. Advancing on a building through mortar and small arms fire, Whiteley was severely wounded in the arm and shoulder. Despite his wounds, he charged into the house alone and killed two enemy soldiers. Hurling smoke and fragmentation grenades before him, he reached the next house and stormed inside, killing 2 more enemy soldiers and capturing 11 more. Whiteley continued to lead his platoon in the house-to-house advance until he came upon a building held by fanatical Nazi troops. Although his left arm was useless, he destroyed one of the building's walls with a bazooka. With a submachine gun wedged under his uninjured arm, he charged into the building in the face of a hail of enemy bullets. Whiteley killed 5 enemy soldiers and forced an additional 12 soldiers to surrender. He was wounded in the eye by an exploding shell fragment as he left the house but continued his advance. Despite his injuries, Whiteley continued to lead his platoon in the attack until he was forcibly evacuated. For his leadership and courage, Whiteley was awarded the Medal of Honor.

After the war, Whiteley returned to North Carolina State, where he completed his degree in 1948. In 1949, he married Anna Morris of Laurinburg, North Carolina; they had two sons and three daughters. Whiteley returned to Texas A&M University, where he received a doctorate in soil physics. He taught at Texas A&M while researching plants and soil management. Whiteley was eventually named a professor emeritus of the Department of Soil and Crop Sciences.

Eli Whiteley died on December 2, 1986, in College Station, Texas, and was buried in College Station City Cemetery. Texas A&M named the Eli Whiteley Memorial Medal of Honor Park on its grounds in his honor.

James H. Willbanks

Further Reading

Dethloff, Henry C. *Texas Aggies Go to War in Service of Their Country.* College Station: Texas A&M University Press, 2006.

Neal, Charles M., Jr. *Valor across the Lone Star: The Congressional Medal of Honor in Frontier Texas.* Austin: Texas State Historical Association, 2002.

Taggart, Donald G., ed. *History of the Third Infantry Division in World War II.* Washington, D.C.: Infantry Journal Press, 1947. Reprint, Nashville, TN: Battery Press, 1987.

Woodall, James R. *Texas Aggie Medals of Honor: Seven Heroes of World War II.* College Station: Texas A&M University Press, 2010.

Whittington, Hulon B.

Born: July 9, 1921
Died: January 17, 1969
Home State: Louisiana
Service: Army
Conflict: World War II
Age at Time of Award: 22

Born in Bogalusa, Louisiana, on July 9, 1921, Hulon B. Whittington entered active service on August 21, 1940. Upon completion of initial entry training, Whittington served in Sicily with the 41st Armored Infantry Regiment, 2nd Armored Division, where he received minor wounds in an action that earned him both the Silver Star and promotion to sergeant. After recuperating from his wounds, Whittington proceeded with his unit to England, where he spent five months preparing for the invasion of France.

Sergeant Whittington remained with the 41st during the Army's operations in Normandy, seeing his first action in France while participating in the breakout during Operation Cobra. The operation began inauspiciously with a poorly executed preparatory bombing that resulted in nearly 160 American casualties on July 24, 1944. Much more successful carpet-bombing operations conducted on the following two days caused devastating damage to the defending German units, including the vaunted Panzer Lehr Division, opening the way for a major breakout of American forces and encirclement of large numbers of German troops.

On July 29, 1944, Sergeant Whittington found himself assigned to a small task force ordered to maintain an outpost on the Countances-Gavray road near Cambray with orders to interdict any retreating German units trapped by the rapidly advancing Americans. Shortly after midnight, a force of about 2,500 Germans mounted a counterattack in an attempt to break through American lines to safety. The German force quickly overran a tank roadblock, and, with his platoon leader and platoon sergeant both missing in action, Sergeant Whittington suddenly found himself in command of a platoon in desperate circumstances.

Whittington quickly reorganized the defense, moving between defensive positions under intense enemy fire to direct his men's efforts. Observing an enemy advance that threatened to penetrate another roadblock and outflank his small force, Sergeant Whittington, moving through intense enemy fire in complete disregard of his personal safety, mounted a Sherman tank and shouted orders through the turret, directing point-blank fire against the lead Mark V Panther Tank. The Sherman's shot disabled the German tank, allowing Whittington to block the movement of a column of more than 100 German vehicles and enabling his force to destroy them with hand grenades, antitank weapons, and supporting tank and artillery fire. As it became apparent to the Germans that their armored column faced complete annihilation, they dismounted their vehicles and attacked on foot, but Sergeant Whittington forestalled their attack by leading a well-timed bayonet charge. After completing the destruction of the German column, Whittington administered medical aid to his men in place of the platoon medic, who had himself become a casualty.

For his actions that day, Sergeant Whittington was awarded the Medal of Honor, the first awarded to a soldier in a tank formation in France. Whittington continued leading his platoon after this action, but a stomach wound inflicted only seven days later by fragments from a mortar round took him out of action for the remainder of the war. Whittington remained in the Army, earning an officer's commission and eventually retiring as a major.

In a fitting memorial to his bravery and selfless service, the American Legion selected Major Whittington as the model for "G.I. Joe: American Legion Soldier," a 13-foot-tall limestone statue that can be seen at the entry to American Legion Headquarters in Washington, D.C. The US Army Ordnance Corps selected Major Whittington as a 1969 inductee into the Ordnance Corps Hall of Fame.

Hulon Whittington died on January 17, 1969. He is buried at Arlington National Cemetery.

Mark T. Calhoun

Further Reading

Blumenson, Martin. *Breakout and Pursuit. US Army in World War II: European Theater of Operations*. Reprint, Washington, D.C.: Historical Division, Department of the Army, 2005.

Lang, George, Raymond L. Collins, and Gerard F. White. *Medal of Honor Recipients, 1863–1994*. 2 vols. New York: Facts on File, 1995.

Tillman, Barrett. *Heroes: U.S. Army Medal of Honor Recipients*. New York: Berkley Publishing, 2006.

Weigley, Russell F. *Eisenhower's Lieutenants: The Campaign of France and Germany, 1944–1945*. Bloomington: Indiana University Press, 1981.

Zaloga, Steven J. *Operation Cobra, 1944: Breakout from Normandy*. Westport, CT: Praeger, 2004.

Williams, Hershel Woodrow

Born: October 2, 1923
Died:
Home State: West Virginia
Service: Marine Corps

Conflict: World War II
Age at Time of Award: 21

Born in Quiet Dell, West Virginia, on October 2, 1923, Hershel Woodrow Williams grew up working on his family's dairy farm during the Great Depression. The youngest of 11 children, Williams joined the Civilian Conservation Corps (CCC) as a teenager and was stationed at White Hall, Montana. After the Japanese attacked Pearl Harbor in December of 1941, Williams requested and received his discharge from the CCC in order to return home and enlist in the US Marine Corps. However, he was denied entry into the Marines in November of 1942 because, at only 5 feet,

Hershel Woodrow Williams, US Marine Corps (Naval History and Heritage Command).

6 inches tall, he failed to meet the 5-foot, 8-inch height requirement. Williams then worked as a truck driver in Fairmont, West Virginia, until May of the following year. On May 26, 1943, Williams successfully enlisted in the Marine Corps Reserve after the height requirement had been removed.

For three months, Williams remained on a waiting list before being assigned to the US Marine Corps recruit training facilities in San Diego, California. During that time, Williams met and courted his future wife, Ruby. Just before his deployment to San Diego, Williams's fiancée gave him a ruby ring to serve as a reminder of her love for him; he carried the ring throughout his duty in the South Pacific.

After infantry training, Williams was assigned to train as a flamethrower operator and demolitions expert. Trained to work in two-man teams, Williams operated a 70-pound apparatus that spewed a combination of diesel fuel and high-octane gasoline while his assistant carried his field pack and extra supplies. In addition to using a flamethrower, Williams learned how to use and detonate Composition C-2 explosives.

In December of 1943, Private Williams traveled, as part of 32nd Replacement Battalion, to Guadalcanal, where he joined the 3rd Marine Division. Originally assigned to Charlie Company, 1st Battalion, 21st Marines, Williams later transferred to the battalion's Headquarters Company, where he served as leader of a six-man demolition team. As section leader, Williams divided his men into three two-man teams to act as demolition specialists in companies A, B, and C. In July and August of 1944, Williams and his teams saw action at Guam. The following February, they were part of the forces that attacked the island of Iwo Jima.

The first wave of marines landed on Iwo Jima on February 19, 1945; then corporal Williams's reserve division landed two days later, on February 21. After two days of heavy fighting, all six members of Williams's teams were out of action, leaving him to fulfill their duties by himself.

Although his unit had only advanced about 50 yards in the two days of fighting, the sight of the American flag waving on the top of Mount Suribachi galvanized the marines, and they surged forward, sweeping over the initial positions. However, the advance of the marines was again halted by a series of enemy pillboxes.

Williams grabbed a flamethrower and went forward in an attempt to take out the Japanese positions. For four hours on February 23, 1945, Williams slowly crawled back and forth from his supply area to the enemy emplacements despite the fact that only four riflemen covered his moves. Using the technique of "rolling" the explosive mixture from his flamethrower along the ground, Williams knocked off the pillboxes one by one. As he approached one pillbox, bullets from the machine gun inside ricocheted off his pressurized tank. Knowing that he could not safely return to his own lines until he had disabled the pillbox, Williams crawled to side of the bunker, jumped onto the roof, and fired his flamethrower into the ventilation shaft, quickly silencing the guns inside. He repeatedly returned to friendly lines to get new flamethrowers and demolition charges, which he used as he methodically took out the pillboxes. Ultimately, he forged a path through the Japanese lines, enabling his fellow marines to advance.

After the battle of Iwo Jima, he went back to Guam to help train the Marine force for the planned invasion of Japan.

On October 5, 1945, President Harry S. Truman presented Williams with the Medal of Honor for his heroic actions on Iwo Jima; Williams also received the Purple Heart for wounds sustained on March 6, 1945, during the Iwo Jima campaign.

After his discharge in November 1945, Hershel Williams reenlisted in the Marine Corps Reserves several times, serving for 17 years and rising to the rank of chief warrant officer 4 (CWO4) until his retirement in 1969. After his service, Williams and his late wife, Ruby, ran a boarding and training barn for horses in Ona, West Virginia. In retirement, Williams became active in his church as a lay minister and also served as chaplain of the Medal of Honor Society.

Matthew R. McGrew

Further Reading

Collier, Peter, and Nick Del Calzo. *Medal of Honor: Portraits of Valor beyond the Call of Duty.* New York: Artisan, 2006.

Hammel, Eric M. *Iwo Jima: Portrait of a Battle: United States Marines at War in the Pacific.* St. Paul, MN: Zenith Imprint, 2006.

Newcomb, Richard F., and Harry Schmidt. *Iwo Jima.* New York: Macmillan, 2002.

Wilson, Louis Hugh, Jr.

Born: February 11, 1920
Died: June 21, 2005
Home State: Mississippi
Service: Marine Corps
Conflict: World War II
Age at Time of Award: 24

Louis Hugh Wilson was born on February 11, 1920, in Brandon, Mississippi. He earned a bachelor of arts degree in 1941 from Millsaps College. He enlisted in the Marine Corps Reserve in May 1941 and was commissioned a second lieutenant in November of that year. Following completion of officer candidate school in early 1942, he was assigned to the 9th Marine Regiment, 3rd Marine Division.

Wilson was transferred to the Pacific Theater with the 9th Marines in February 1943, making stops at Guadalcanal, Efate, and Bougainville. He was promoted to captain in April 1943. In the assault on Guam on July 25, 1944, he was in command of Company F, 2nd Battalion, 9th Marines, 3rd Marine Division.

As commanding officer, Wilson led his infantry company against overwhelming odds in a battle for Fonte Hill during the struggle to retake Guam from the Japanese. Wilson advanced his company over 300 yards of rugged and broken terrain, all the while under intense enemy machine gun fire, and took his objective. Although wounded three times, Wilson took command of numerous marines from other units disorganized during the violent assault and prepared for the inevitable enemy counterattack he was sure would take place that first night on Fonte Hill. During the night, the Japanese launched a series of savage counterattacks, but Wilson and his marines retained control of the hill. During the fighting, Wilson repeatedly exposed himself to enemy fire and at one time dashed over 50 yards of open terrain to rescue a wounded marine. Fighting for over 10 hours, often in hand-to-hand combat with the enemy, Wilson and his marines succeeded in halting the last efforts of the Japanese to retake this important strategic hill.

The following morning, Wilson organized a 17-man patrol and advanced on a ridge that was being used by the Japanese to direct mortar fire on his position. Despite losing 13 of his 17 men, Wilson succeeded in seizing this vital ground and denying it to the enemy. In the two-day battle, Wilson and his marines killed over 350 of the enemy. His action significantly contributed to the success of the

9th Marines during the early phase of the battle for Guam. For his extraordinary and heroic performance on the battlefield, Wilson was nominated for the Medal of Honor.

After the battle, he was evacuated to the US Naval Hospital, San Diego, California, and remained there until October 1944. Transferred to Washington, D.C., Wilson served as detachment commander at the Marine Barracks in the national capital. He was promoted to major in March 1945. On October 5, 1945, Wilson received the Medal of Honor from President Harry S. Truman in a White House ceremony.

Immediately after the war, Wilson served in a number of successive assignments, including aide-de-camp to the commanding general, Fleet Marine Force, Pacific, at Pearl Harbor and officer-in-charge of the district recruiting headquarters in New York City.

He served during the Korean War as assistant G-3, 1st Marine Division. After the armistice, he served in a number of critical billets, including commander of 2nd Battalion, 5th Marines, 1st Marine Division and several assignments at Headquarters Marine Corps.

Wilson deployed with the 1st Marine Division in August 1965 to Vietnam, where he served as assistant chief of staff, G-3. He was promoted to brigadier general in December 1966. After service as legislative assistant to the commandant of the Marine Corps and chief of staff, Headquarters, Fleet Marine Force, Pacific, he was promoted to major general in 1970. Wilson's next duty was a one-year tour as the commanding general, I Marine Amphibious Force, 3rd Marine Division on Okinawa.

Louis Wilson was promoted to lieutenant general in August 1972 before assuming command of Fleet Marine Force, Pacific one month later. After this assignment, he was promoted to general on July 1, 1975, and named the commandant of the Marine Corps, the fourth Marine commandant to have earned the Medal of Honor. Retiring on June 30, 1979, he returned to his home in Mississippi. General Wilson passed away peacefully at his home in Birmingham, Alabama, on June 21, 2005. He was laid to rest in Arlington National Cemetery, Arlington, Virginia.

Huong T. D. Nguyen

Further Reading

Bartlett, Merrill L., and Jack Sweetman. *Leathernecks: An Illustrated History of the United States Marine Corps.* Annapolis, MD: Naval Institute Press, 2008.

Collier, Peter, and Nick Del Calzo. *Medal of Honor: Portraits of Valor beyond the Call of Duty.* New York: Artisan, 2006.

Hargis, Robert, and Ramiro Bujeiro. *World War II Medal of Honor Recipients: Navy & USMC.* Oxford, UK: Osprey, 2003.

Lodge, O. R. *The Recapture of Guam.* Washington, D.C.: US Marine Corps Historical Branch, Headquarters Marine Corps, 1954.

Rottman, Gordon. *Guam 1941 and 1944: Loss and Reconquest.* Oxford, UK: Osprey, 2004.

Wood, Leonard

Born: October 9, 1860
Died: August 7, 1927
Home State: Massachusetts
Service: Army
Conflict: Indian Campaigns
Age at Time of Award: 26

Leonard Wood was born on October 9, 1860, in Winchester, New Hampshire, the son of a marginally trained and generally unsuccessful family doctor who died before his children reached adulthood. He attended Pierce Academy in Middleborough, Massachusetts, and earned a medical degree from Harvard in 1884. Wood was accepted as an intern at Boston City Hospital but was fired for generally insubordinate behavior before completing his internship.

Wood joined the Army as a contract surgeon in 1885 and participated in a protracted pursuit of Apache leader Geronimo through the mountains of southern Arizona and northern Mexico. He was awarded the Medal of Honor for carrying dispatches 100 miles through hostile territory and for assuming command of an infantry detachment that was without officers.

In 1890, he married Louise Conditt-Smith, favorite niece of Supreme Court Justice Stephen Field. In 1895, after a time at Fort McPherson in Atlanta during which he helped organize and served as the first coach of the Georgia Tech football team, Wood was assigned to Washington, D.C. With the assistance of his wife's guardian, Wood became friends with President Grover Cleveland. When

Leonard Wood, US Army (US Army Medical Department Regiment).

William McKinley was elected president, Wood became personal physician to his hypochondriacal wife. He also became a close friend of the new assistant secretary of the Navy, Theodore Roosevelt.

Wood and Roosevelt encouraged McKinley to support war with Spain in 1898, and, when he did, they received permission to recruit their friends from both the western territories and the eastern aristocracy into the 1st Volunteer Cavalry Regiment, which, after a number of less attractive alternatives, was nicknamed the Rough Riders. Wood was colonel and commander, and Roosevelt was lieutenant colonel and second in command.

Wood commanded the Rough Riders in their first skirmish of the war at Las Guasimás, after which he was promoted brigadier general. Wood commanded the 2nd Cavalry Brigade in the Battle of San Juan Hill. Shortly after the Spanish surrendered Santiago, Wood was made first military governor of the city and then of the province. He used his medical training to bring disease and starvation under control and proved an exceptional and exceptionally stern administrator. His success, coupled with his Washington ties and talent for political machinations, led to his nomination as military governor of Cuba in December 1899. As governor, he made notable strides in education, public health, and prison reform, and he established a fiscally responsible republican government. Perhaps his most notable accomplishment was his sponsorship of, and acceptance of responsibility for, Walter Reed's yellow fever experiments. Immediately after Reed demonstrated the mosquito's role as a vector for the disease, Wood used his autocratic power to authorize draconian insect control measures carried out by his chief surgeon, Maj. William Gorgas. The campaign transformed Havana from one of the most dangerous cities in the world to one of the healthiest.

Wood had attained the rank of major general in the Volunteer Army but was still a captain in the medical corps until 1901, when, in a controversial move, Roosevelt, now president, secured Wood's promotion to brigadier general in the Regular Army over 509 more senior officers.

Wood turned the government of Cuba over to an elected government in 1902 and was named commander of the Department of Mindanao, where he fought to control Islamic insurgents. He was promoted major general in 1904 and was named commander of the Division of the Philippines in 1906. During his tenure with the army in the Philippines, Wood was involved in a number of actions against insurgents, several of which resulted in the deaths of large numbers of civilians.

In 1908, Wood was named commander of the Eastern Division and, in 1910, chief of staff of the Army. In the latter office, he rescued the general staff system from department heads determined to prevent its implementation, introduced techniques of scientific management to the military, and worked to professionalize the officer corps.

From 1910 to 1917, Wood, convinced the United States would participate in a European war, became a vocal advocate of military preparedness and led the Plattsburg Movement designed to train civilians who could be officers in such a war. He advocated universal military training and was a vocal opponent of Woodrow Wilson's pacifism. In 1916, Wood, who repeatedly crossed the traditional line separating military officers from politics, was briefly considered as a Republican candidate for president.

When the United States entered World War I, Wood was passed over for command of the American Expeditionary Force in favor of his former subordinate, Gen. John J. Pershing. Wood was relegated to training the 89th Division at Camp Funston, and, when that unit was sent to Europe in May 1918, Wood was (at Pershing's specific request) relieved and reassigned to train the 10th Division. In January 1918, while on an inspection tour of the Western Front, Wood received a minor injury from a mortar shell. In spite of the fact that he never was formally assigned a combat role, he was the most senior American officer actually wounded by hostile fire.

When Theodore Roosevelt died unexpectedly in 1919, Leonard Wood became his political heir and narrowly missed receiving the Republican nomination for president in 1920. After the election, he was returned to the Philippines as governor-general, a post he occupied until 1927. He died in Boston on August 7, 1927, during surgery to remove a benign brain tumor.

Jack McCallum

Further Reading

Hagedorn, Hermann. *Leonard Wood: A Biography*. New York: Harper & Brothers, 1931.

Lane, Jack. *Armed Progressive: General Leonard Wood*. San Rafael, CA: Presidio Press, 1978.

McCallum, Jack. *Leonard Wood: Rough Rider, Surgeon, and Architect of American Imperialism*. New York: New York University Press, 2006.

Woodfill, Samuel

Born: January 6, 1883
Died: August 10, 1953
Home State: Indiana
Service: Army
Conflict: World War I
Age at Time of Award: 35

Born on January 6, 1883, in Jefferson County, Indiana, Samuel Woodfill learned to hunt at an early age and was a good shot by the age of 10. After attending local schools, he enlisted in the US Army in 1901, serving in the Philippines, Alaska, and Texas. While in Texas, he completed officer training school and was commissioned a second lieutenant. Woodfill went to Europe in April 1918 as part of the 60th Infantry Regiment of the US 5th Division of the American Expeditionary Forces (AEF).

The 5th Division participated in the Meuse-Argonne Offensive, and, on the morning of October 12 near Cunel, France, First Lieutenant Woodfill was leading his company as it advanced through thick fog. The unit was soon pinned by German machine gun fire ahead and on both flanks. Using shell holes for cover, Woodfill moved forward and silenced the machine gun emplacements on both flanks. He continued to advance despite receiving a dose of mustard gas in one shell hole. Finding cover in a roadside ditch, Woodfill shot and killed six members of a German machine gun crew to the front of his position. Woodfill then stalked a fourth German machine gun crew and killed them as well. German fire drove him into a trench. Switching to his pistol, Wooodfill killed five members of that machine gun crew with single headshots and two more with a pick after his pistol jammed. In all, Lieutenant Woodfill single-handedly eliminated five machine gun emplacements and killed more than 20 German soldiers.

For this action, Woodfill was awarded the Medal of Honor. He also received the French Croix de Guerre with palm and Italy's Meriot di Guerra and the Cross of Prince Danilo, First Class, and was also made a chevalier of the French Legion of Honor. AEF commander Gen. John Pershing later called Woodfill America's most outstanding soldier of the war.

In 1921, Samuel Woodfill was one of three Medal of Honor recipients selected as pallbearers for the Unknown Soldier at Arlington National Cemetery. Having taken a reduction in rank to stay in the service after the war, Sergeant Woodfill left the Army in 1922 to farm in northwestern Kentucky. Commissioned a major in 1942, he taught marksmanship until his retirement in 1943 at the mandatory age of 60. He lived alone in Vevay, Indiana, until his death there on August 10, 1953.

Douglas M. Doss

Further Reading

Mikaelian, Allen, and Mike Wallace. *Medal of Honor: Profiles of America's Military Heroes from the Civil War to the Present.* New York: Hyperion, 2002.

Thomas, Lowell. *Woodfill of the Regulars: A True Story of Adventure from the Arctic to the Argonne.* Garden City, NY: Doubleday, Doran, 1929.

York, Alvin C.

Born: December 13, 1887
Died: September 2, 1964
Home State: Tennessee

Service: Army
Conflict: World War I
Age at Time of Award: 30

Born in a one-room log cabin in Pall Mall, Tennessee, on December 13, 1887, Alvin Cullum York was drafted shortly after America's entry into World War I. After his draft notice arrived on June 5, 1917, York was conflicted between his obligations to his God and to his country. York applied four times for exemption based on his religious beliefs but was denied each time; he was inducted into the Army on November 15 and set off for Camp Gordon, Georgia, for training.

Lost in his strange surroundings and still plagued by his lingering doubts, York finally went to his company commander, Capt. Edward Danforth, to explain his situation. Impressed with York's sincerity, Captain Danforth sent him to see the battalion commander, Maj. George Edward Buxton. After a long night discussing the Biblical implications of the war, Buxton granted York a 10-day leave to go home and reflect. Buxton assured York that if he returned unconvinced about the righteousness of the war, he would grant him a noncombat assignment. After much soul-searching, York reconciled the differences in his mind and returned to Camp Gordon determined to do his duty to the best of his abilities.

York embarked with the rest of Company G, 328th Infantry Regiment, 82nd Infantry Division for France on May 1, 1918. His regiment saw little action in France until September 28, when the 82nd was committed to the Battle of the Argonne. On the morning of October 8, York, a corporal by this time, was part of a 17-man detachment with orders to infiltrate around the rear of Hill 223 to destroy the machine gun positions on the crest. The detachment initially encountered two German medics; one surrendered and the other was chased back to the German lines. The medic led them to a band of about 15 to 20 Germans, including one officer; the startled Germans immediately surrendered at the sight of the Americans. Before the Americans could consolidate their tenuous position, the machine guns up the hill shifted their fire onto the small band of soldiers huddled below. The initial fusillade from the German guns killed or wounded nine Americans, including three other noncommissioned officers, leaving York as the ranking soldier.

Lying between the Americans and the German machine guns, York began to pick off the German gunners as they raised their heads. After determining York's position, a handful of Germans tried to rush him with fixed bayonets. York held his ground and calmly shot the Germans bearing down him. With the onslaught stopped, York called for the remaining Germans to surrender. A German officer stood up and offered to surrender his position. York accepted, and the officer blew a whistle to signal his men to a cease-fire. As the Germans began to file out, one soldier threw a grenade in York's direction; he shot the man as the grenade passed over his head.

York's next problem was how to get the dozens of prisoners and several wounded Americans back to friendly lines. With only seven able-bodied Americans, York led his band back through the German position. On the way out, York and his command ran into several more machine gun positions, and at each one the senior German prisoner ordered them to surrender. By the time York got his prisoners back to American lines, he had captured 128 enlisted and 4 officers.

Credited with killing 25 Germans, capturing 132 more, and silencing 35 machine guns, York's feat was one of outstanding personal heroism, and he was originally awarded the Distinguished Service Cross. It was later upgraded to the Medal of Honor, which was presented to him by Gen. John J. Pershing, commander of the American Expeditionary Force. Additionally, France bestowed upon him the Croix de Guerre and Legion of Honor. York returned to a hero's welcome May 22, 1919, and was given a ticker tape parade through New York. A much-bemused but homesick York only wanted to get back home. Discharged on May 29, York quickly headed back to Pall Mall and his family.

Alvin York only wanted to return to his life as before the war, but he could not escape his wartime experience. Always a devout man, he eventually concluded that God had protected him during the war for a bigger purpose. York decided that his mission in life was to end the isolation of the hill people and bring education to the children. For the rest of his life, he worked to break down barriers and open up opportunities in the Cumberland Mountains. Though he was not always successful, York never stopped working toward his goal until his health broke down in the 1950s. York eventually succumbed to his ailments and died peacefully on September 2, 1964. He was laid to rest in a simple gravesite in Pall Mall, Tennessee.

Marlyn R. Pierce

Further Reading

Lee, David D. *Sergeant York: An American Hero.* Lexington: University Press of Kentucky, 1985.

Skeyhill, Thomas. *Sergeant York: His Own Life Story and War Diary.* New York: Doubleday, Doran, 1928.

Young, Rodger W.

Born: April 28, 1918
Died: July 31, 1943
Home State: Ohio
Service: Army
Conflict: World War II
Age at Time of Award: 25

Rodger Wilton Young was born in Tiffin, Ohio, on April 28, 1918. At 5 feet, 2 inches tall and 125 pounds, Young was not a physically imposing man when he signed up for the National Guard. Joining Company B, 148th Infantry Regiment in the Ohio National Guard with his older brother Webster, Young quickly gained a reputation for excellence. When his unit was federalized in 1942, Young was promoted to the rank of sergeant during his predeployment training. This was a significant achievement for the small man who tried hard, and he was very proud of this promotion.

The 37th Infantry Division, of which Young was a member, shipped to the Southwest Pacific in the late spring of 1943, arriving on freshly captured Guadalcanal for more training. During training on Guadalcanal, Young noticed increased difficulty in hearing and seeing. As a teenager, Young had suffered a traumatic head injury and was forced to wear thick glasses for the rest of his life. It also had affected his hearing. These combined disabilities had forced him to drop out of high school and go to work, unable to complete his schooling. Now, in the summer of 1943, these injuries were not just nuisances, but began to affect Young's abilities to lead his squad.

As proud as he was to be a new squad leader, Staff Sergeant Young approached his company commander and requested a voluntary reduction in rank to private. For the man who had worked so hard to obtain the stripes of a noncommissioned officer and train his squad, this had to have been heart wrenching. His wish was granted, and, after several weeks, the 37th Infantry Division was sent on to New Georgia, another island in the Solomon chain. Young came under the command of his old boyhood friend, S.Sgt. Walter Rigby.

The 148th Infantry Regiment was assigned to seize Munda Airfield on New Georgia Island. Landing on New Georgia beginning June 30, 1943, US forces began the desperate jungle fight across the island toward Munda Airfield. By July 27, the 148th Infantry reached Horseshoe Hill, the last significant terrain feature before Munda Airfield. Patrols were sent forward to reconnoiter approaches to the airfield. On July 31, Young found himself part of a platoon patrol attempting to find the Japanese main line of defense.

By mid-afternoon, the platoon leader determined the platoon should return to friendly lines before being caught deep in enemy lines during darkness. Unfortunately, the platoon then encountered an enemy ambush. A well-hidden enemy machine gun bunker waited until the platoon entered its kill zone, opening a withering fire on the 20 US soldiers and killing two in the first burst. Two more soldiers were killed as the platoon attempted to maneuver against the enemy. The platoon leader decided to extricate the platoon by withdrawing from contact, but the platoon was pinned down by Japanese machine gun fire. Seeing that the situation was desperate, Young decided that only the destruction of the machine gun could save his friends. As he began crawling forward toward the gun, the platoon leader yelled for Young to come back. Young retorted that the lieutenant knew he had bad hearing and continued toward the machine gun. The Japanese turned their gun on Young, hitting him in the left shoulder and severely wounding him. Young refused to quit, even when the platoon leader continued to implore him to stop.

Pushing forward again, Young was hit in the left leg and foot but managed to gain a position below the muzzle of the machine gun and within grenade range. In a tremendous effort, Young rose up and, with his good right arm, flung a grenade into the enemy bunker as he was shot by a final burst into his face, which killed him.

Young's sacrifice saved the lives of the remaining 15 men of his platoon. For his actions that day, he was nominated for the Medal of Honor. The medal was presented posthumously to his mother. After the war, Young's remains were returned to Clyde, Ohio, where he was interred in McPherson Cemetery.

Rodger Young left a profound legacy of sacrifice and valor. A fellow soldier, Pvt. Frank Loesser, wrote a song about Young, the only ballad written about a Medal of Honor recipient. The song was very popular for the following few decades, particularly among infantry soldiers, but sadly is largely unknown today. However, the words to the song "The Ballad of Rodger Young" are featured prominently in Robert A. Heinlein's science fiction novel *Starship Troopers,* and Young is epitomized in the book as a model of soldierly virtues.

Edwin L. Kennedy Jr.

Further Reading

Lang, George, Raymond L. Collins, and Gerard F. White. *Medal of Honor Recipients, 1863–1994.* Vol. 2, *WWII to Somalia.* New York: Facts on File, 1995.

Phillips, Col. James H., and Maj. John F. Kane, eds. *The Medal of Honor of the United States Army.* Washington, D.C.: Government Printing Office, 1948.

Schott, Joseph L. *Above and Beyond: The Story of the Congressional Medal of Honor.* New York: G. P. Putnam's Sons, 1963.

Sowash, Rick. *Heroes of Ohio: 23 True Tales of Courage and Character.* Bowling Green, OH: Gabriel's Horn Publishing Company, 1998.

War Department. *Combat Lessons No. 7: Rank and File in Combat: What They Are Doing—How They Do It.* Washington, D.C.: War Department, 1944.

Zabitosky, Fred William

Born: October 27, 1942
Died: January 8, 1996

Home State: New Jersey
Service: Army
Conflict: Vietnam War
Age at Time of Award: 26

Born in the industrial town of Trenton, New Jersey, on October 27, 1942, Fred W. Zabitosky entered the Army out of high school in November 1957. His early Army years were spent in infantry and artillery units, with service in the 11th Infantry at Fort Benning, Georgia; the 2nd Field Artillery Missile Training Battalion at Fort Still, Oklahoma; and the 34th Field Artillery in the Federal Republic of Germany. Attracted by the growing reputation of Special Forces, Zabitosky volunteered for Special Forces. After completing the required training, he joined the 1st Special Forces Group in Okinawa. He would eventually serve with the 5th, 7th, and 20th Special Forces groups between the years 1963 and 1972.

By February 1968, Staff Sergeant Zabitosky was serving in Vietnam with the highly classified Military Assistance Command Vietnam (MACV) Studies and Operations Group (SOG). SOG was responsible for conducting long-range reconnaissance operations in the area of the tri-border region of Vietnam, Cambodia, and Laos focused on collecting information, particularly regarding the movement of men and material down the Ho Chi Minh Trail. The highly complex and exceptionally risky intelligence-gathering operation called for highly skilled soldiers. Zabitosky had proven himself just such a man while serving as the noncommissioned officer in charge of the school that trained soldiers for these kinds of missions. In early 1968 at the time of the Tet Offensive, Zabitosky was the assistant team leader for Recon Team (RT) Maine.

Earlier reconnaissance teams operating in Laos reported signs of North Vietnamese Army (NVA) tank units. Although most of the information suggested the presence of PT-76 light tanks, much heavier T-54s seemed a possibility as well. Headquarters SOG ordered increased emphasis on corroborating the presence of the vehicles as well as indications of bivouac sites and supply/maintenance facilities.

Team Maine's entry into Laos on February 19, 1968, proved uneventful. After they were inserted into the area of operations, the helicopters carrying the nine-man team departed the landing zone (LZ) without taking fire. Working on the assumption that the enemy had not detected them, the team headed toward its surveillance area. Cresting a low ridge not far from the LZ, the team came under heavy fire from an NVA unit operating in the area. Calling for air support as well as an emergency exfiltration, the team fought its way back to the LZ. Zabitosky personally covered the final move to the LZ, exposing himself to concentrated enemy automatic weapons fire in the process.

At the LZ, Zabitosky formed the men into a defensive perimeter, directing fire as necessary to keep the enemy at bay. Tactical air support arrived to keep the enemy from seizing the LZ in order for the helicopters to extract the beleaguered team. Almost as if on cue, the sound of arriving helicopters spurred the NVA to step up their assault.

Zabitosky repeatedly organized and adjusted the defense to meet the threat and then, once on one of the helicopters, directed fire on the rapidly closing enemy. The helicopter carrying Zabitosky and most of his team did not lift far from the LZ before enemy small arms fire damaged the connections to the tail rotor. The spinning helicopter threw Zabitosky to the ground before crashing. Zabitosky, now in intense pain from several cracked ribs, made his way back to the flaming wreckage and pulled the severely injured pilot from the inferno. He made repeated but unsuccessful attempts to save other members of the team. Returning to the injured and unconscious pilot, Zabitosky dragged the pilot to another waiting helicopter before himself collapsing. For his actions that day, he was nominated for the Medal of Honor.

Promoted to sergeant first class, Zabitosky received the Medal of Honor from President Richard M. Nixon during a White House ceremony in March 1969. At the time, Zabitosky was serving on the faculty at the US Army Special Warfare School at Fort Bragg. He would return to Vietnam for one final tour, this time with 101st Airborne Division, from July 1971 to January 1972. During the final years of his military career, his service included assignments to both the 50th and 35th Signal Battalions at Fort Bragg and a final assignment with the 68th Air Defense Artillery at Homestead Air Force Base, Florida.

Retirement from the Army did not end his service. Fred Zabitosky actively participated in prisoner-of-war/missing-in-action (POW/MIA) recovery from Southeast Asia and later served as the military services coordinator and military liaison for the Veterans Affairs Regional Office in Winston-Salem, North Carolina. He remained active in the Special Forces Association throughout the rest of his life. Zabitosky died on January 8, 1996, and was buried in Lumbee Memorial Park in Lumberton, North Carolina.

Joseph R. Fischer

Further Reading

Plaster John L. *Secret Commandos: Behind Enemy Lines with the Elite Warriors of SOG*. New York: Simon & Schuster, 2004.

Saal, Harve. *SOG: MACV Studies and Observations Group*, Vol. 3. Ann Arbor, MI: Edwards Brothers, 1990.

Sutherland, Lt. Col. Ian D. W. *Special Forces of the United States Army*. San Jose, CA: R. James Bender Publishing, 1990.

Zeamer, Jay, Jr.

Born: July 25, 1918
Died: March 22, 2007
Home State: Maine
Service: Army
Conflict: World War II
Age at Time of Award: 24

Jay Zeamer Jr. was born in Carlisle, Pennsylvania, on July 25, 1918. He grew up in Orange, New Jersey, but ultimately made Maine his home. His schooling included Culver Military Academy in Indiana and Massachusetts Institute of Technology (MIT), where he earned a degree in civil engineering. While at MIT, Zeamer also completed ROTC training and was commissioned an infantry second lieutenant in the Army Reserve. Subsequently, Zeamer left the Reserves and signed on as an aviation cadet in the Regular Army. He received his wings and a commission in March 1941.

The American entry into World War II found Zeamer serving in the 22nd Bombardment Group flying the B-26 twin-engine bomber. The 22nd deployed to the southwest Pacific, where Zeamer first saw combat. In September 1942, he transferred to the 43rd Bombardment Group, which flew four-engine B-17 bombers out of Port Moresby, New Guinea. By June 1943, Zeamer had flown a total of 47 combat missions and earned two Silver Stars.

On June 16, 1943, Captain Zeamer and his crew from the 65th Squadron volunteered to fly a reconnaissance mission in preparation for the invasion of Bougainville in the Solomon Islands. The mission involved a 1,200-mile round trip from Port Moresby to the small island of Buka, where Zeamer's men would photograph Japanese installations and then map the west coast of Bougainville itself on the return home. Zeamer's B-17 would be flying alone the entire way. Having volunteered for such hazardous missions before, Zeamer and his men had modified their aircraft by adding extra armament, including a fuselage-mounted .50 caliber machine gun operated by the pilot himself.

The flight to Buka was uneventful, as was the photo run over the Japanese-held island. Ominously, however, the crew could see an estimated 22 Japanese aircraft rising from the Buka airstrip 28,000 feet below. The B-17 had nearly completed the mapping run along Bougainville when the mission turned into a fight for survival. Eight Japanese A6M ("Zero") aircraft launched head-on attacks against Zeamer's craft, inflicting damage and taking hits in return. Zeamer later credited 2nd Lt. Joseph R. Sarnoski, the bombardier, for breaking up the initial Japanese attack with machine gun fire from the nose of the bomber. One of the damaged Zeros, accompanied by a wingman, dropped out of the fight. The remaining six

Zeros engaged in a running gunfight with the lone B-17 that lasted approximately 40 minutes. Sarnoski, mortally wounded by Japanese shell fragments, stayed at his nose gun until he died. Zeamer was also riddled by shell fragments, but not before he damaged a Japanese attacker with fire from the special machine gun he operated. His skillful evasive maneuvering frustrated other attacks. When the last Japanese fighter finally broke away, the badly damaged B-17 was without an operable oxygen system, flaps, or brakes. Five of the nine crew members were wounded, and Sarnoski was dead. Although Zeamer's men claimed two Japanese planes destroyed and two probables, the Japanese themselves reported three aircraft damaged and a fourth Zero that ditched due to engine trouble. The Japanese had expended a total of 1,257 rounds of ammunition in shredding Zeamer's B-17, but the plane flew on.

Bleeding profusely from no fewer than 120 puncture wounds, Zeamer remained in command of the mission as the copilot, 2nd Lt. John T. Britton, nursed the battered B-17 back to New Guinea. Realizing that the plane could never clear the towering Owen Stanley Mountains on the return route to Port Moresby, Zeamer directed Britton to a fighter strip at Dobodura on the near side of the mountains. Britton made a successful downwind landing without either flaps or brakes, running off the runway but successfully "ground looping" the big bomber to a halt.

The medics who attended to the wounded men at first gave Jay Zeamer up for dead. It took more than a year for him to recover from his wounds. On January 16, 1944, Zeamer received the Medal of Honor from Gen. Henry H. Arnold, chief of the Army Air Forces. Lieutenant Sarnoski received the medal posthumously, and the remaining crew members were awarded the Distinguished Service Cross, making it the most decorated aircrew in American history. Out of 38 Medals of Honor awarded within the Army Air Forces in World War II, 2 were bestowed upon this one crew in a single mission but for separate actions, another unique event. Zeamer returned to active duty before the end of the war, but the lingering effects of his wounds forced him to retire in 1945. At the time of his death at the age of 88 on March 22, 2007, Zeamer was the last surviving Medal of Honor winner from the US Army Air Forces of World War II.

Christopher R. Gabel

Further Reading

Collier, Peter, and Nick Del Calzo. *Medal of Honor: Portraits of Valor beyond the Call of Duty.* New York: Artisan, 2006.

Frisbee, John L. "Valor: Battle over Bougainville." *Air Force Magazine* 68, no. 12 (1985): 119.

Kenney, George C. *General Kenney Reports.* New York: Duell, Sloan, and Pierce, 1949.

Tillman, Barrett. *Above and Beyond: The Aviation Medals of Honor.* Washington, D.C.: Smithsonian Institution Press, 2002.

RECIPIENTS OF THE MEDAL OF HONOR

Listed Alphabetically
Asterisk (*) indicates posthumous award

A

*Abrell, Charles G.
US Marine Corps
Korean War

Adams, James F.
US Army
Civil War

Adams, John G. B.
US Army
Civil War

Adams, John Mapes
US Marine Corps
China Relief Expedition

Adams, Lucien
US Army
World War II

Adams, Stanley T.
US Army
Korean War

*Adams, William E.
US Army
Vietnam War

Adkinson, Joseph B.
US Army
World War I

Adriance, Harry Chapman
China Relief Expedition

*Agerholm, Harold Christ
US Marine Corps
World War II

Aheam, Michael
US Navy
Civil War

Ahern, William
US Navy
Interim Awards,
   1871–1898

*Albanese, Lewis
US Army
Vietnam War

Albee, George E.
US Army
Indian Campaigns

Alber, Frederick
US Army
Civil War

Albert, Christian
US Army
Civil War

Alchesay
US Army
Indian Campaigns

Allen, Abner P.
US Army
Civil War

Allen, Edward
US Navy
China Relief
   Expedition

Allen, James
US Army
Civil War

Allen, Nathaniel M.
US Army
Civil War

Allen, William
US Army
Indian Campaigns

Allex, Jake
US Army
World War I

Allworth, Edward C.
US Army
World War I

Ames, Adelbert
US Army
Civil War

Ammerman, Robert W.
US Army
Civil War

Anders, Frank L.
US Army
Philippine Insurrection

Anderson, Beaufort T.
US Army
World War II

Anderson, Bruce
US Army
Civil War

Anderson, Charles W.
US Army
Civil War

Anderson, Edwin A.
US Navy
Mexican Campaign
   (Veracruz)

Anderson, Everett W.
US Army
Civil War

Anderson, Frederick C.
US Army
Civil War

Anderson, James
US Army
Indian Campaigns

*****Anderson, James, Jr.**
US Marine Corps
Vietnam War

Anderson, Johannes S.
US Army
World War I

Anderson, Marion T.
US Army
Civil War

Anderson, Peter
US Army
Civil War

*****Anderson, Richard A.**
US Marine Corps
Vietnam War

*****Anderson, Richard Beatty**
US Marine Corps
World War II

Anderson, Robert
US Navy
Civil War

Anderson, Thomas
US Army
Civil War

Anderson, Webster
US Army
Vietnam War

Anderson, William
US Navy
Interim Awards,
   1871–1898

Andrews, John
US Navy
1871 Korean Campaign

Angling, John
US Navy
Civil War

*****Antolak, Sylvester**
US Army
World War II

Antrim, Richard N.
US Navy
World War II

Apple, Andrew O.
US Army
Civil War

Appleton, Edwin Nelson
US Marine Corps
China Relief Expedition

Appleton, William H.
US Army
Civil War

Archer, James W.
US Army
Civil War

Archer, Lester
US Army
Civil War

Archinal, William
US Army
Civil War

Armstrong, Clinton L.
US Army
Civil War

Arnold, Abraham K.
US Army
Civil War

Arther, Matthew
US Navy
Civil War

*Ashley, Eugene, Jr.
US Army
Vietnam War

Asten, Charles
US Navy
Civil War

Aston, Edgar R.
US Army
Indian Campaigns

Atkins, Daniel
US Navy
Interim Awards,
   1871–1898

Atkins, Thomas E.
US Army
World War II

Atkinson, Thomas E.
US Navy
Civil War

Auer, John F.
US Navy
Interim Awards,
   1871–1898

*Austin, Oscar P.
US Marine Corps
Vietnam War

Austin, William G.
US Army
Indian Campaigns

Avery, James
US Navy
Civil War

Avery, William B.
US Army
Civil War

Ayers, David
US Army
Civil War

Ayers, James F.
US Army
Indian Campaigns

Ayers, John G. K.
US Army
Civil War

B

Babcock, John B.
US Army
Indian Campaigns

Babcock, William J.
US Army
Civil War

Baca, John P.
US Army
Vietnam War

Bacon, Elijah W.
US Army
Civil War

Bacon, Nicky Daniel
US Army
Vietnam War

Badders, William
US Navy
Interim Awards,
   1920–1940

Badger, Oscar Charles
US Navy
Mexican Campaign
   (Veracruz)

*Baesel, Albert E.
US Army
World War I

Bailey, James E.
US Army
Indian Campaigns

*Bailey, Kenneth D.
US Marine Corps
World War II

Baird, Absalom
US Army
Civil War

Baird, George W.
US Army
Indian Campaigns

*Baker, Addison E.
US Army Air Corps
World War II

Baker, Benjamin F.
US Navy
Spanish-American War

Baker, Charles
US Navy
Civil War

Baker, Edward L., Jr.
US Army
Spanish-American War

Baker, John
US Army
Indian Campaigns

Baker, John F., Jr.
US Army
Vietnam War

*Baker, Thomas A.
US Army
World War II

Baker, Vernon
US Army
World War II

Balch, John Henry
US Navy
World War I

Baldwin, Charles
US Navy
Civil War

**Baldwin, Frank D.
(First Award)**
US Army
Civil War

**Baldwin, Frank D.
(Second Award)**
US Army
Indian Campaigns

Ballard, Donald E.
US Navy
Vietnam War

Ballen, Frederick
US Army
Civil War

Bancroft, Neil
US Army
Indian Campaigns

Banks, George L.
US Army
Civil War

Barber, James A.
US Army
Civil War

Barber, William E.
US Marine Corps
Korean War

Barfoot, Van T.
US Army
World War II

Barger, Charles D.
US Army
World War I

*Barkeley, David B.
US Army
World War I

*Barker, Charles H.
US Army
Korean War

*Barker, Jedh Colby
US Marine Corps
Vietnam War

Barker, Nathaniel C.
US Army
Civil War

Barkley, John L.
US Army
World War I

***Barnes, John
Andrew, III**
US Army
Vietnam War

Barnes, Will C.
US Army
Indian Campaigns

Barnes, William H.
US Army
Civil War

Barnum, Harvey C., Jr.
US Marine Corps
Vietnam War

Barnum, Henry A.
US Army
Civil War

Barnum, James
US Navy
Civil War

Barrell, Charles L.
US Army
Civil War

Barrett, Carlton W.
US Army
World War II

Barrett, Edward
US Navy
Interim Awards,
    1871–1898

Barrett, Richard
US Army
Indian Campaigns

Barrick, Jesse T.
US Army
Civil War

Barringer, William H.
US Army
Civil War

Barrow, David O.
US Navy
Spanish-American War

Barry, Augustus
US Army
Civil War

Bart, Frank J.
US Army
World War I

Barter, Gurdon H.
US Navy
Civil War

Barton, Thomas
US Navy
Civil War

Basilone, John
US Marine Corps
World War II

Bass, David L.
US Navy
Civil War

**Batchelder,
Richard N.**
US Army
Civil War

Bates, Delavan
US Army
Civil War

Bates, Norman F.
US Army
Civil War

Bates, Richard
US Navy
Interim Awards,
    1866–1870

Batson, Matthew A.
US Army
Philippine Insurrection

*Bauer, Harold William
US Marine Corps
World War II

*Baugh, William B.
US Marine Corps
Korean War

*Bausell, Lewis Kenneth
US Marine Corps
World War II

Baybutt, Philip
US Army
Civil War

Bazaar, Philip
US Navy
Civil War

Bearss, Hiram Iddings
US Marine Corps
Philippine Insurrection

Beasley, Harry C.
US Navy
Mexican Campaign
    (Veracruz)

Beatty, Alexander M.
US Army
Civil War

Beaty, Powhatan
US Army
Civil War

***Beaudoin,
Raymond O.**
US Army
World War II

Beauford, Clay
US Army
Indian Campaigns

Beaufort, Jean J.
US Army
Civil War

Beaumont, Eugene B.
US Army
Civil War

Bebb, Edward J.
US Army
Civil War

Beckwith, Wallace A.
US Army
Civil War

Beddows, Richard
US Army
Civil War

Beebe, William S.
US Army
Civil War

Beech, John P.
US Army
Civil War

Begley, Terrence
US Army
Civil War

Behne, Frederick
US Navy
Interim Awards,
    1901–1911

Behnke, Heinrich
US Navy
Interim Awards,
    1901–1911

Beikirch, Gary B.
US Army
Vietnam War

*Belcher, Ted
US Army
Vietnam War

Belcher, Thomas
US Army
Civil War

Bell, Bernard P.
US Army
World War II

Bell, Dennis
US Army
Spanish-American
  War

Bell, George
US Navy
Civil War

Bell, Harry
US Army
Philippine Insurrection

Bell, J. Franklin
US Army
Philippine Insurrection

Bell, James
US Army
Indian Campaigns

Bell, James B.
US Army
Civil War

***Bellrichard, Leslie
Allen**
US Army
Vietnam War

Belpitt, W. H.
US Navy
Interim Awards,

Benavidez, Roy P.
US Army
Vietnam War

Bender, Stanley
US Army
World War II

Benedict, George G.
US Army
Civil War

*Benfold, Edward C.
US Navy
Korean War

***Benjamin,
George, Jr.**
US Army
World War II

Benjamin, John F.
US Army
Civil War

Benjamin, Samuel N.
US Army
Civil War

Bennett, Edward A.
US Army
World War II

*Bennett, Emory L.
US Army
Korean War

Bennett, Floyd
US Navy
Interim Awards,
  1920–1940

Bennett, James H.
US Navy
Spanish-American War

Bennett, Orren
US Army
Civil War

Bennett, Orson W.
US Army
Civil War

*Bennett, Steven L.
US Air Force
Vietnam War

*Bennett, Thomas W.
US Army
Vietnam War

***Bennion, Mervyn
Sharp**
US Navy
World War II

Bensinger, William
US Army
Civil War

Benson, James
US Navy
Interim Awards,
  1871–1898

Benyaurd, William H. H.
US Army
Civil War

Berg, George
US Army
Spanish-American War

Bergendahl, Frederick
US Army
Indian Campaigns

Berkeley, Randolph Carter
US Marine Corps
Mexican Campaign
    (Veracruz)

*Berry, Charles Joseph
US Marine Corps
World War II

Bertoldo, Vito R.
US Army
World War II

Bertram, Heinrich
US Army
Indian Campaigns

Bessey, Charles A.
US Army
Indian Campaigns

Betham, Asa
US Navy
Civil War

Betts, Charles M.
US Army
Civil War

Beyer, Albert
US Navy
Spanish-American War

Beyer, Arthur O.
US Army
World War II

Beyer, Hillary
US Army
Civil War

*Bianchi, Willibald C.
US Army
World War II

Bibber, Charles J.
US Navy
Civil War

Bickford, Henry H.
US Army
Civil War

Bickford, John F.
US Navy
Civil War

Bickford, Matthew
US Army
Civil War

Bickham, Charles G.
US Army
Philippine Insurrection

Biddle, Melvin E.
US Army
World War II

Bieger, Charles
US Army
Civil War

Biegler, George W.
US Army
Philippine Insurrection

*Bigelow, Elmer Charles
US Navy
World War II

Binder, Richard
US Marine Corps
Civil War

Bingham, Henry H.
US Army
Civil War

Birdsall, Horatio L.
US Army
Civil War

Birkhimer, William E.
US Army
Philippine Insurrection

Bishop, Charles Francis
US Navy
Mexican Campaign
    (Veracruz)

Bishop, Daniel
US Army
Indian Campaigns

Bishop, Francis A.
US Army
Civil War

Bjorklund, Arnold L.
US Army
World War II

Bjorkman, Ernest H.
US Navy
Interim Awards,
    1901–1911

Black, John C.
US Army
Civil War

Black, William P.
US Army
Civil War

Blackmar, Wilmon W.
US Army
Civil War

*Blackwell, Robert L.
US Army
World War I

Blackwood, William R. D.
US Army
Civil War

Blagheen, William
US Navy
Civil War

Blair, James
US Army
Indian Campaigns

Blair, Robert M.
US Navy
Civil War

Blake, Robert
US Navy
Civil War

*Blanchfield, Michael R.
US Army
Vietnam War

Blanquet
US Army
Indian Campaigns

Blasdel, Thomas A.
US Army
Civil War

Bleak, David B.
US Army
Korean War

*Bleckley, Erwin R.
US Army Air Corps
World War I

Blickensderfer, Milton
US Army
Civil War

Bliss, George N.
US Army
Civil War

Bliss, Zenas R.
US Army
Civil War

Bloch, Orville Emil
US Army
World War II

Blodgett, Welis H.
US Army
Civil War

Blucher, Charles
US Army
Civil War

Blume, Robert
US Navy
Spanish-American War

Blunt, John W.
US Army
Civil War

*Bobo, John P.
US Marine Corps
Vietnam War

Boehler, Otto
US Army
Philippine Insurrection

Boehm, Peter M.
US Army
Civil War

Boers, Edward William
US Navy
Interim Awards, 1901–1911

Bois, Frank
US Navy
Civil War

Bolden, Paul L.
US Army
World War II

Bolton, Cecil H.
US Army
World War II

Bond, William
US Navy
Civil War

Bondsteel, James Leroy
US Army
Vietnam War

Bonebrake, Henry G.
US Army
Civil War

Bong, Richard I.
US Army Air Corps
World War II

Bonnaffon, Sylvester, Jr.
US Army
Civil War

Bonney, Robert E.
US Navy
Interim Awards, 1901–1911

*Bonnyman, Alexander, Jr.
US Marine Corps
World War II

Boody, Robert
US Army
Civil War

*Booker, Robert D.
US Army
World War II

Boon, Hugh P.
US Army
Civil War

Boone, Joel T.
US Navy
World War I

Boquet, Nicholas
US Army
Civil War

*Bordelon, William James
US Marine Corps
World War II

Boss, Orlando
US Army
Civil War

Bourke, John G.
US Army
Civil War

Bourne, Thomas
US Navy
Civil War

Boury, Richard
US Army
Civil War

Boutwell, John W.
US Army
Civil War

Bowden, Samuel
US Army
Indian Campaigns

Bowen, Chester B.
US Army
Civil War

Bowen, Emmer
US Army
Civil War

*Bowen, Hammett L., Jr.
US Army
Vietnam War

Bowman, Alonzo
US Army
Indian Campaigns

Bowman, Edward R.
US Navy
Civil War

Box, Thomas J.
US Army
Civil War

*Boyce, George W. G., Jr.
US Army
World War II

Boydston, Erwin Jay
US Marine Corps
China Relief Expedition

Boyington, Gregory
US Marine Corps
World War II

Boyne, Thomas
US Army
Indian Campaigns

Boynton, Henry V.
US Army
Civil War

Bradbury, Sanford
US Army
Indian Campaigns

Bradley, Alexander
US Navy
Interim Awards,
   1871–1898

Bradley, Amos
US Navy
Civil War

Bradley, Charles
US Navy
Civil War

Bradley, George
US Navy
Mexican Campaign
   (Veracruz)

Bradley, Thomas W.
US Army
Civil War

Bradley, Willis Winter, Jr.
US Navy
World War I

Brady, George F.
US Navy
Spanish-American War

Brady, James
US Army
Civil War

Brady, Patrick Henry
US Army
Vietnam War

Branagan, Edward
US Army
Indian Campaigns

Brandle, Joseph E.
US Army
Civil War

Brannigan, Felix
US Army
Civil War

Brant, Abram B.
US Army
Indian Campaigns

Brant, William
US Army
Civil War

Bras, Edgar A.
US Army
Civil War

Bratling, Frank
US Army
Indian Campaigns

Brazell, John
US Navy
Civil War

Breault, Henry
US Navy
Interim Awards,
 1920–1940

Breeman, George
US Navy
Interim Awards,
 1901–1911

Breen, John
US Navy
Civil War

Brennan, Christopher
US Navy
Civil War

Bresnahan, Patrick Francis
US Navy
Interim Awards,
 1901–1911

Brest, Lewis F.
US Army
Civil War

Brett, Lloyd M.
US Army
Indian Campaigns

Brewer, William J.
US Army
Civil War

Brewster, Andre W.
US Army
China Relief Expedition

Breyer, Charles
US Army
Civil War

Briggs, Elijah A.
US Army
Civil War

Bright, George Washington
US Navy
Spanish-American War

Briles, Herschel F.
US Army
World War II

Bringle, Andrew
US Army
Civil War

Brinn, Andrew
US Navy
Civil War

Britt, Maurice L.
US Army
World War II

*Brittin, Nelson V.
US Army
Korean War

Brock, George F.
US Navy
Interim Awards,
 1901–1911

Brogan, James
US Army
Indian Campaigns

Bronner, August F.
US Army
Civil War

Bronson, Deming
US Army
World War I

Bronson, James H.
US Army
Civil War

Brookin, Oscar
US Army
Spanish-American War

Brophy, James
US Army
Indian Campaigns

Brosnan, John
US Army
Civil War

*Brostrom, Leonard C.
US Army
World War II

Brouse, Charles W.
US Army
Civil War

Brown, Benjamin
US Army
Indian Campaigns

Brown, Bobbie E.
US Army
World War II

Brown, Charles
US Army
Civil War

Brown, Charles
US Marine Corps
1871 Korean Campaign

Brown, Edward, Jr.
US Army
Civil War

Brown, Henri Le Fevre
US Army
Civil War

Brown, James
US Navy
Civil War

Brown, James
US Army
Indian Campaigns

Brown, Jeremiah Z.
US Army
Civil War

Brown, John
US Navy
Civil War

Brown, John H.
US Army
Civil War

Brown, John Harties
US Army
Civil War

Brown, John
US Navy
Interim Awards,
1866–1870

Brown, Lorenzo D.
US Army
Indian Campaigns

*Brown, Melvin L.
US Army
Korean War

*Brown, Morris, Jr.
US Army
Civil War

Brown, Robert
US Navy
Civil War

Brown, Robert B.
US Army
Civil War

Brown, Uriah
US Army
Civil War

Brown, William H.
US Navy
Civil War

Brown, Wilson
US Navy
Civil War

Brown, Wilson W.
US Army
Civil War

Brownell, Francis E.
US Army
Civil War

Brownell, William P.
US Navy
Civil War

*Bruce, Daniel D.
US Marine Corps
Vietnam War

Bruner, Louis J.
US Army
Civil War

Brush, George W.
US Army
Civil War

**Bruton (Braton),
Christopher C.**
US Army
Civil War

Brutsche, Henry
US Navy
Civil War

Bryan, William C.
US Army
Indian Campaigns

Bryant, Andrew S.
US Army
Civil War

***Bryant, William
Maud**
US Army
Vietnam War

Bucha, Paul William
US Army
Vietnam War

Buchanan, Allen
US Navy
Mexican Campaign
(Veracruz)

Buchanan, David M.
US Navy
Interim Awards,
1871–1898

*Buchanan, George A.
US Army
Civil War

Buck, F. Clarence
US Army
Civil War

Buck, James
US Navy
Civil War

Buckingham, David E.
US Army
Civil War

Buckles, Abram J.
US Army
Civil War

Buckley, Dennis
US Army
Civil War

Buckley, Howard Major
US Marine Corps
Philippine Insurrection

Buckley, John C.
US Army
Civil War

Bucklyn, John K.
US Army
Civil War

Buffington, John E.
US Army
Civil War

Buffum, Robert
US Army
Civil War

Buhrman, Henry G.
US Army
Civil War

*Buker, Brian L.
US Army
Vietnam War

Bulkeley, John Duncan
US Navy
World War II

Bumgarner, William
US Army
Civil War

Burbank, James H.
US Army
Civil War

Burger, Joseph
US Army
Civil War

Burk, E. Michael
US Army
Civil War

Burk, Thomas
US Army
Civil War

Burkard, Oscar
US Army
Indian Campaigns

Burke, Daniel W.
US Army
Civil War

Burke, Frank (also known as Francis X. Burke)
US Army
World War II

Burke, Lloyd L.
US Army
Korean War

Burke, Patrick J.
US Army
Indian Campaigns

Burke, Richard
US Army
Indian Campaigns

*Burke, Robert C.
US Marine Corps
Vietnam War

Burke, Thomas
US Army
Civil War

Burke, Thomas
US Navy
Interim Awards,
1866–1870

Burnes, James
US Marine Corps
China Relief Expedition

Burnett, George R.
US Army
Indian Campaigns

Burns, James M.
US Army
Civil War

Burns, John M.
US Navy
Civil War

*Burr, Elmer J.
US Army
World War II

Burr, Herbert H.
US Army
World War II

*Burris, Tony K.
US Army
Korean War

Burritt, William W.
US Army
Civil War

Burt, James M.
US Army
World War II

Burton, Albert
US Navy
Civil War

Bush, Richard Earl
US Marine Corps
World War II

Bush, Robert Eugene
US Navy
World War II

Butler, Edmond
US Army
Indian Campaigns

Butler, Smedley Darlington (First Award)
US Marine Corps
Mexican Campaign (Veracruz)

Butler, Smedley Darlington (Second Award)
US Marine Corps
Haitian Campaign 1915

Butterfield, Daniel
US Army
Civil War

Butterfield, Frank G.
US Army
Civil War

Button, William Robert
US Marine Corps
Haitian Campaign 1919 to 1920

Butts, George
US Navy
Civil War

*Butts, John E.
US Army
World War II

Buzzard, Ulysses G.
US Army
Spanish-American War

Byrd, Richard Evelyn, Jr.
US Navy
Interim Awards, 1920–1940

Byrne, Bernard A.
US Army
Philippine Insurrection

Byrne, Denis
US Army
Indian Campaigns

Byrnes, James
US Navy
Civil War

C

Cable, Joseph A.
US Army
Indian Campaigns

*Caddy, William Robert
US Marine Corps
World War II

Cadwallader, Abel G.
US Army
Civil War

Cadwell, Luman L.
US Army
Civil War

Cafferata, Hector A., Jr.
US Marine Corps
Korean War

Cahey, Thomas
US Navy
Interim Awards, 1901–1911

Caldwell, Daniel
US Army
Civil War

Calkin, Ivers S.
US Army
Civil War

Call, Donald M.
US Army
World War I

*Callaghan, Daniel Judson
US Navy
World War II

Callahan, John H.
US Army
Civil War

Callen, Thomas J.
US Army
Indian Campaigns

Calugas, Jose
US Army
World War II

Calvert, James S.
US Army
Indian Campaigns

Camp, Carlton N.
US Army
Civil War

Campbell, Albert Ralph
US Marine Corps
China Relief Expedition

Campbell, Daniel
US Marine Corps
Spanish-American War

Campbell, James A.
US Army
Civil War

Campbell, William
US Navy
Civil War

Campbell, William
US Army
Civil War

Canfield, Heth
US Army
Indian Campaigns

Cann, Tedford H.
US Navy
World War I

*Cannon, George Ham
US Marine Corps
World War II

Cantrell, Charles P.
US Army
Spanish-American War

Capehart, Charles E.
US Army
Civil War

Capehart, Henry
US Army
Civil War

*Capodanno, Vincent R.
US Navy
Vietnam War

Capron, Horace, Jr.
US Army
Civil War

*Carey, Alvin P.
US Army
World War II

*Carey, Charles F., Jr.
US Army
World War II

Carey, Hugh
US Army
Civil War

Carey, James
US Navy
Interim Awards,
    1866–1870

Carey, James L.
US Army
Civil War

Carlisle, Casper R.
US Army
Civil War

Carman, Warren
US Army
Civil War

Carmin, Isaac H.
US Army
Civil War

Carney, William H.
US Army
Civil War

*Caron, Wayne Maurice
US Navy
Vietnam War

Carpenter, Louis H.
US Army
Indian Campaigns

Carr, Chris (name legally changed from Christos H. Karaberis, under which name the medal was awarded)
US Army
World War II

Carr, Eugene A.
US Army
Civil War

Carr, Franklin
US Army
Civil War

Carr, John
US Army
Indian Campaigns

Carr, William L.
US Marine Corps
China Relief
    Expedition

Carr, William M.
US Navy
Civil War

Carroll, Thomas
US Army
Indian Campaigns

Carson, Anthony J.
US Army
Philippine Insurrection

Carson, William J.
US Army
Civil War

*Carswell, Horace S., Jr.
US Army Air Corps
World War II

Cart, Jacob
US Army
Civil War

*Carter, Bruce W.
US Marine Corps
Vietnam War

*Carter, Edward A., Jr.
US Army
World War II

Carter, George
US Army
Indian Campaigns

Carter, John J.
US Army
Civil War

Carter, Joseph E.
US Navy
Spanish-American War

Carter, Joseph F.
US Army
Civil War

Carter, Mason
US Army
Indian Campaigns

Carter, Robert G.
US Army
Indian Campaigns

Carter, William H.
US Army
Indian Campaigns

Caruana, Orlando E.
US Army
Civil War

Cary, Robert W.
US Navy
Interim Awards,
  1915–1916

Casamento, Anthony
US Marine Corps
World War II

Casey, David
US Army
Civil War

Casey, Henry
US Army
Civil War

Casey, James S.
US Army
Indian Campaigns

Cassidy, Michael
US Navy
Civil War

*Castle, Frederick W.
US Army Air Corps
World War II

**Castle, Guy Wilkinson
Stuart**
US Navy
Mexican Campaign
  (Veracruz)

**Catherwood, John
Hugh**
US Navy
Philippines 1911

**Catlin, Albertus
Wright**
US Marine Corps
Mexican Campaign
  (Veracruz)

Catlin, Isaac S.
US Army
Civil War

Cavaiani, Jon R.
US Army
Vietnam War

Cavanaugh, Thomas
US Navy
Spanish-American War

Cawetzka, Charles
US Army
Philippine Insurrection

Cayer, Ovila
US Army
Civil War

Cecil, Josephus S.
US Army
Philippine Insurrection

Chadwick, Leonard
US Navy
Spanish-American War

Chamberlain, Joshua L.
US Army
Civil War

Chamberlain, Orville T.
US Army
Civil War

Chambers, Joseph B.
US Army
Civil War

Chambers, Justice M.
US Marine Corps
World War II

*Champagne, David B.
US Marine Corps
Korean War

Chandler, Henry F.
US Army
Civil War

Chandler, James B.
US Navy
Civil War

Chandler, Stephen E.
US Army
Civil War

Chandron, August
US Navy
Interim Awards,
    1871–1898

Chapin, Alaric B.
US Army
Civil War

Chapman, Amos
US Army
Indian Campaigns

Chapman, John
US Army
Civil War

Chaput, Louis G.
US Navy
Civil War

Charette, George
US Navy
Spanish-American War

Charette, William R.
US Navy
Korean War

*Charlton, Cornelius H.
US Army
Korean War

Chase, John F.
US Army
Civil War

Chatham, John Purnell
US Navy
China Relief Expedition

Cheever, Benjamin H., Jr.
US Army
Indian Campaigns

*Cheli, Ralph
US Army Air Corps
World War II

Child, Benjamin H.
US Army
Civil War

Childers, Ernest
US Army
World War II

*Chiles, Marcellus H.
US Army
World War I

Chiquito
US Army
Indian Campaigns

Chisman, William W.
US Army
Civil War

Choate, Clyde L.
US Army
World War II

*Cholister, George Robert
US Navy
Interim Awards,
    1920–1940

*Christensen, Dale Eldon
US Army
World War II

*Christian, Herbert F.
US Army
World War II

Christiancy, James I.
US Army
Civil War

*Christianson, Stanley R.
US Marine Corps
Korean War

Church, James Robb
US Army
Spanish-American War

Churchill, Samuel J.
US Army
Civil War

*Cicchetti, Joseph J.
US Army
World War II

Cilley, Clinton A.
US Army
Civil War

Clancy, James T.
US Army
Civil War

Clancy, John E.
US Army
Indian Campaigns

Clancy, Joseph
US Navy
China Relief Expedition

Clapp, Albert A.
US Army
Civil War

Clark, Charles A.
US Army
Civil War

Clark, Francis J.
US Army
World War II

Clark, Harrison
US Army
Civil War

Clark, James G.
US Army
Civil War

Clark, John W.
US Army
Civil War

Clark, Wilfred
US Army
Indian Campaigns

Clark, William A.
US Army
Civil War

Clarke, Dayton P.
US Army
Civil War

Clarke, Powhatan H.
US Army
Indian Campaigns

Clary, Edward Alvin
US Navy
Interim Awards,
    1901–1911

Clausen, Charles H.
US Army
Civil War

Clausen, Claus Kristian
US Navy
Spanish-American War

Clausen, Raymond M.
US Marine Corps
Vietnam War

Clausey, John J.
US Navy
Interim Awards,
    1901–1911

Clay, Cecil
US Army
Civil War

Cleveland, Charles F.
US Army
Civil War

Clifford, Robert T.
US Navy
Civil War

Clopp, John E.
US Army
Civil War

Clute, George W.
US Army
Civil War

Coates, Jefferson
US Army
Civil War

Cockley, David L.
US Army
Civil War

Cody, William F.
US Army
Indian Campaigns

Coey, James
US Army
Civil War

Coffey, Robert J.
US Army
Civil War

Cohn, Abraham
US Army
Civil War

*Coker, Ronald L.
US Marine Corps
Vietnam War

Colalillo, Michael
US Army
World War II

Colbert, Patrick
US Navy
Civil War

Colby, Carlos W.
US Army
Civil War

*Cole, Darrell Samuel
US Marine Corps
World War II

Cole, Gabriel
US Army
Civil War

*Cole, Robert G.
US Army
World War II

Coleman, John
US Marine Corps
1871 Korean Campaign

*Collier, Gilbert G.
US Army
Korean War

*Collier, John W.
US Army
Korean War

Collins, Harrison
US Army
Civil War

Collins, Thomas D.
US Army
Civil War

Collis, Charles H. T.
US Army
Civil War

Colwell, Oliver
US Army
Civil War

*Colyer, Wilbur E.
US Army
World War I

Comfort, John W.
US Army
Indian Campaigns

Commiskey, Henry A., Sr.
US Marine Corps
Korean War

Compson, Hartwell B.
US Army
Civil War

Conaway, John W.
US Army
Civil War

Conboy, Martin
US Army
Civil War

Condon, Clarence M.
US Army
Philippine Insurrection

Congdon, James
US Army
Civil War

Conlan, Dennis
US Navy
Civil War

Connell, Trustrim
US Army
Civil War

Conner, Richard
US Army
Civil War

Connolly, Michael
US Navy
Interim Awards,
   1871–1898

Connor, James P.
US Army
World War II

Connor, John
US Army
Indian Campaigns

*Connor, Peter S.
US Marine Corps
Vietnam War

Connor, Thomas
US Navy
Civil War

Connor,
William C.
US Navy
Civil War

Connors, James
US Army
Civil War

*Cook, Donald Gilbert
US Marine Corps
Vietnam War

Cook, John
US Army
Civil War

Cook, John H.
US Army
Civil War

Cooke, Walter H.
US Army
Civil War

Cooley, Raymond H.
US Army
World War II

Coolidge, Charles H.
US Army
World War II

Cooney, James
US Marine Corps
China Relief
   Expedition

Cooney, Thomas C.
US Navy
Spanish-American
   War

Coonrod, Aquilla
US Army
Indian Campaigns

Cooper, John
(First Award)
US Navy
Civil War

**Cooper, John
(Second Award)**
US Navy
Civil War

Copp, Charles D.
US Army
Civil War

**Corahorgi,
Demetri**
US Navy
Interim Awards,
1901–1911

Corcoran, John
US Army
Civil War

Corcoran, Michael
US Army
Indian Campaigns

Corcoran, Thomas E.
US Navy
Civil War

Corey, William
US Navy
Interim Awards,
1871–1898

Corliss, George W.
US Army
Civil War

Corliss, Stephen P.
US Army
Civil War

***Corry, William
Merrill, Jr.**
US Navy
Interim Awards,
1920–1940

Corson, Joseph K.
US Army
Civil War

**Co-Rux-Te-Chod-Ish
(Mad Bear)**
US Army
Indian Campaigns

Cosgriff, Richard H.
US Army
Civil War

Cosgrove, Thomas
US Army
Civil War

Costello, John
US Navy
Interim Awards,
1871–1898

*Costin, Henry G.
US Army
World War I

Cotton, Peter
US Navy
Civil War

Coughlin, John
US Army
Civil War

*Coursen, Samuel S.
US Army
Korean War

***Courtney, Henry
Alexius, Jr.**
US Marine Corps
World War II

Courtney, Henry C.
US Navy
Interim Awards,
1871–1898

**Courts, George
McCall**
US Navy
Mexican Campaign
(Veracruz)

**Covington, Jesse
Whitfield**
US Navy
World War I

***Cowan,
Richard Eller**
US Army
World War II

**Cox, Robert
Edward**
US Navy
Interim Awards,
1901–1911

Cox, Robert M.
US Army
Civil War

Coyne, John N.
US Army
Civil War

Craft, Clarence B.
US Army
World War II

*Craig, Gordon M.
US Army
Korean War

*Craig, Robert
US Army
World War II

Craig, Samuel H.
US Army
Indian Campaigns

*Crain, Morris E.
US Army
World War II

Cramen, Thomas
US Navy
Interim Awards,
    1871–1898

Crandall, Bruce P.
US Army
Vietnam War

Crandall, Charles
US Army
Indian Campaigns

Crandall, Orson L.
US Navy
Interim Awards,
    1920–1940

Cranston, William W.
US Army
Civil War

*Craw, Demas T.
US Army Air Corps
World War II

Crawford, Alexander
US Navy
Civil War

Crawford, William J.
US Army
World War II

Creed, John
US Army
Civil War

*Creek, Thomas E.
US Marine Corps
Vietnam War

Creelman, William J.
US Navy
Interim Awards,
    1871–1898

Cregan, George
US Navy
Mexican Campaign
    (Veracruz)

*Crescenz, Michael J.
US Army
Vietnam War

Crews, John R.
US Army
World War II

Crilley, Frank William
US Navy
Interim Awards,
    1915–1916

Cripps, Thomas
US Navy
Civil War

Crist, John
US Army
Indian Campaigns

Criswell, Benjamin C.
US Army
Indian Campaigns

Crocker, Henry H.
US Army
Civil War

Crocker, Ulric L.
US Army
Civil War

Croft, James E.
US Army
Civil War

*Cromwell, John Philip
US Navy
World War II

Cronan, Willie
US Navy
Interim Awards,
    1901–1911

Cronin, Cornelius
US Navy
Civil War

Crosier, William H. H.
US Army
Civil War

Cross, James E.
US Army
Civil War

**Crouse, William
Adolphous**
US Navy
Spanish-American War

Crowley, Michael
US Army
Civil War

Crump, Jerry K.
US Army
Korean War

Cruse, Thomas
US Army
Indian Campaigns

Cubberly, William G.
US Army
Indian Campaigns

**Cukela, Louis
(Army Medal)**
US Marine Corps
World War I

**Cukela, Louis
(Navy Medal)**
US Marine Corps
World War I

Cullen, Thomas
US Army
Civil War

Cummings, Amos J.
US Army
Civil War

Cummins, Andrew J.
US Army
Spanish-American War

Cumpston, James M.
US Army
Civil War

Cunningham, Charles
US Army
Indian Campaigns

**Cunningham,
Francis M.**
US Army
Civil War

Cunningham, James S.
US Army
Civil War

Curran, Richard
US Army
Civil War

Currey, Francis S.
US Army
World War II

Curtis, John C.
US Army
Civil War

Curtis, Josiah M.
US Army
Civil War

Curtis, Newton Martin
US Army
Civil War

**Custer, Thomas W.
(First Award)**
US Army
Civil War

**Custer, Thomas W.
(Second Award)**
US Army
Civil War

Cutcheon, Byron M.
US Army
Civil War

*Cutinha, Nicholas J.
US Army
Vietnam War

Cutter, George W.
US Navy
Interim Awards,
   1871–1898

Cutts, James M.
US Army
Civil War

D

*Dahl, Larry G.
US Army
Vietnam War

Dahlgren, Edward C.
US Army
World War II

Dahlgren, John Olof
US Marine Corps
China Relief Expedition

Daily, Charles
US Army
Indian Campaigns

Dalessondro, Peter J.
US Army
World War II

**Daly, Daniel Joseph
(First Award)**
US Marine Corps
China Relief Expedition

**Daly, Daniel Joseph
(Second Award)**
US Marine Corps
Haitian Campaign 1915

Daly, Michael J.
US Army
World War II

***Damato, Anthony
Peter**
US Marine Corps
World War II

Daniels, James T.
US Army
Indian Campaigns

Darrough, John S.
US Army
Civil War

*Davenport, Jack A.
US Marine Corps
Korean War

*David, Albert Leroy
US Navy
World War II

Davidsizer, John A.
US Army
Civil War

Davidson, Andrew
US Army
Civil War

Davidson, Andrew
US Army
Civil War

Davila, Rudolph B.
US Army
World War II

Davis, Charles C.
US Army
Civil War

Davis, Charles P.
US Army
Philippine Insurrection

Davis, Charles W.
US Army
World War II

Davis, Freeman
US Army
Civil War

***Davis, George A., Jr.**
US Air Force
Korean War

Davis, George E.
US Army
Civil War

***Davis, George Fleming**
US Navy
World War II

Davis, Harry
US Army
Civil War

Davis, John
US Army
Civil War

Davis, John
US Navy
Civil War

Davis, John
US Navy
Spanish-American War

Davis, John
US Navy
Interim Awards,
1871–1898

Davis, Joseph
US Army
Civil War

Davis, Joseph H.
US Navy
Interim Awards,
1871–1898

Davis, Martin K.
US Army
Civil War

Davis, Raymond E.
US Navy
Interim Awards,
1901–1911

Davis, Raymond G.
US Marine Corps
Korean War

***Davis, Rodney Maxwell**
US Marine Corps
Vietnam War

Davis, Sammy L.
US Army
Vietnam War

Davis, Samuel W.
US Navy
Civil War

Davis, Thomas
US Army
Civil War

Dawson, Michael
US Army
Indian Campaigns

Day, Charles
US Army
Civil War

Day, David F.
US Army
Civil War

Day, George E.
US Air Force
Vietnam War

Day, James
US Marine Corps
World War II

Day, Matthias W.
US Army
Indian Campaigns

Day, William L.
US Army
Indian Campaigns

Deakin, Charles
US Navy
Civil War

***Dealey, Samuel David.**
US Navy
World War II

Dean, William F.
US Army
Korean War

Deane, John M.
US Army
Civil War

De Armond, William
U.S. Army
Indian Campaigns

Deary, George
US Army
Indian Campaigns

DeBlanc, Jefferson Joseph
US Marine Corps
World War II

De Castro, Joseph H.
US Army
Civil War

Decker, Percy A.
US Navy
Mexican Campaign
   (Veracruz)

Deetline, Frederick
US Army
Indian Campaigns

*****De Franzo, Arthur F.**
US Army
World War II

*****DeGlopper, Charles N.**
US Army
World War II

Deignan, Osborn
US Navy
Spanish-American War

De Lacey, Patrick
US Army
Civil War

*****De La Garza, Emilio A., Jr.**
US Marine Corps
Vietnam War

Deland, Frederick N.
US Army
Civil War

Delaney, John C.
US Army
Civil War

De Lavie, Hiram H.
US Army
Civil War

*****Deleau, Emile, Jr.**
US Army
World War II

Dempsey, John
US Navy
Interim Awards,
   1871–1898

Dempster, John
US Navy
Civil War

Deneef, Michael
US Navy
Interim Awards,
   1871–1898

Denham, Austin
US Navy
Interim Awards,
   1871–1898

Denig, J. Henry
US Marine Corps
Civil War

Denning, Lorenzo
US Navy
Civil War

Dennis, Richard
US Navy
Civil War

Denny, John
US Army
Indian Campaigns

Densmore, William
US Navy
Civil War

De Puy, Charles H.
US Army
Civil War

Dervishian, Ernest H.
US Army
World War II

*****Desiderio, Reginald B.**
US Army
Korean War

DeSomer, Abraham
US Navy
Mexican Campaign
   (Veracruz)

De Swan, John F.
US Army
Spanish-American War

Dethlefsen, Merlyn Hans
US Air Force
Vietnam War

*****DeVore, Edward A., Jr.**
US Army
Vietnam War

*Dewert, Richard David
US Navy
Korean War

Dewey, Duane E.
US Marine Corps
Korean War

De Witt, Richard W.
US Army
Civil War

*Diamond, James H.
US Army
World War II

*Dias, Ralph E.
US Marine Corps
Vietnam War

Di Cesnola, Louis P.
US Army
Civil War

Dickens, Charles H.
US Army
Indian Campaigns

*Dickey, Douglas E.
US Marine Corps
Vietnam War

Dickey, William D.
US Army
Civil War

Dickie, David
US Army
Civil War

*Dietz, Robert H.
US Army
World War II

Diggins, Bartholomew
US Navy
Civil War

*Dilboy, George
US Army
World War I

Dilger, Hubert
US Army
Civil War

Dillon, Michael A.
US Army
Civil War

Ditzenback, John
US Navy
Civil War

Dix, Drew Dennis
US Army
Vietnam War

Dixon, William
US Army
Indian Campaigns

*Doane, Stephen Holden
US Army
Vietnam War

Dockum, Warren C.
US Army
Civil War

Dodd, Carl H.
US Army
Korean War

Dodd, Robert F.
US Army
Civil War

Dodds, Edward E.
US Army
Civil War

Dodge, Francis S.
US Army
Indian Campaigns

Doherty, Thomas M.
US Army
Spanish-American War

Dolby, David Charles
US Army
Vietnam War

Dolloff, Charles W.
US Army
Civil War

Donahue, John L.
US Army
Indian Campaigns

Donaldson, John
US Army
Civil War

Donaldson, Michael A.
US Army
World War I

Donavan, Cornelius
US Army
Indian Campaigns

Donelly, John S.
US Army
Indian Campaigns

Donlon, Roger Hugh C.
US Army
Vietnam War

Donnelly, John
US Navy
Civil War

Donoghue, Timothy
US Army
Civil War

Donovan, William Joseph
US Army
World War I

Doody, Patrick
US Army
Civil War

Doolen, William
US Navy
Civil War

Doolittle, James H.
US Army Air Corps
World War II

Doran, John J.
US Navy
Spanish-American War

Dore, George H.
US Army
Civil War

Dorley, August
US Army
Civil War

Dorman, John
US Navy
Civil War

Dorsey, Daniel A.
US Army
Civil War

Dorsey, Decatur
US Army
Civil War

Doss, Desmond T.
US Army
World War II

Dougall, Allan H.
US Army
Civil War

Dougherty, James
US Marine Corps
1871 Korean Campaign

Dougherty, Michael
US Army
Civil War

Dougherty, Patrick
US Navy
Civil War

Dougherty, William
US Army
Indian Campaigns

Dow, George P.
US Army
Civil War

Dow, Henry
US Navy
Civil War

Dowling, James
US Army
Indian Campaigns

Downey, William
US Army
Civil War

Downs, Henry W.
US Army
Civil War

Downs, Willis H.
US Army
Philippine
    Insurrection

Dozier, James B. (a.k.a. James B. Doshier)
US Army
Indian Campaigns

Dozier, James C.
US Army
World War I

Drake, James M.
US Army
Civil War

*Drexler, Henry C.
US Navy
Interim Awards,
    1920–1940

Drowley, Jesse R.
US Army
World War II

Drury, James
US Army
Civil War

Drustrup, Niels
US Navy
Mexican Campaign
    (Veracruz)

Duffey, John
US Army
Civil War

*Duke, Ray E.
US Army
Korean War

Du Moulin, Frank
US Navy
Interim Awards,
    1866–1870

Dunagan, Kern W.
US Army
Vietnam War

Duncan, Adam
US Navy
Civil War

Duncan, James K. L.
US Navy
Civil War

*Dunham, Jason L.
US Marine Corps
War in Iraq

Dunham, Russell E.
US Army
World War II

Dunlap, Robert Hugo
US Marine Corps
World War II

Dunlavy, James
US Army
Civil War

*Dunn, Parker F.
US Army
World War I

Dunn, William
US Navy
Civil War

Dunne, James
US Army
Civil War

Dunphy, Richard D.
US Navy
Civil War

Du Pont, Henry A.
US Army
Civil War

*Durham, Harold Bascom, Jr.
US Army
Vietnam War

Durham, James R.
US Army
Civil War

Durham, John S.
US Army
Civil War

Durney, Austin J.
US Navy
Spanish-American War

*Dutko, John W.
US Army
World War II

Dyer, Jesse Farley
US Marine Corps
Mexican Campaign
   (Veracruz)

*Dyess, Aquilla James
US Marine Corps
World War II

E

Eadie, Thomas
US Navy
Interim Awards,
   1920–1940

Eckes, John N.
US Army
Civil War

Eddy, Samuel E.
US Army
Civil War

Edgerton, Nathan H.
US Army
Civil War

Edson, Merritt Austin
US Marine Corps
World War II

Edwards, Daniel R.
US Army
World War I

Edwards, David
US Army
Civil War

Edwards, John
US Navy
Civil War

*Edwards, Junior D.
US Army
Korean War

Edwards, Walter Atlee
US Navy
Interim Awards,
   1920–1940

Edwards, William D.
US Army
Indian Campaigns

Eggers, Alan Lewis
US Army
World War I

Eglit, John
US Navy
Spanish-American War

Ehle, John W.
US Navy
Spanish-American War

Ehlers, Walter D.
US Army
World War II

Eilers, Henry A.
US Navy
Interim Awards,
    1871–1898

Eldridge, George H.
US Army
Indian Campaigns

Elliott, Alexander
US Army
Civil War

**Elliott, Middleton
Stuart**
US Navy
Mexican Campaign
    (Veracruz)

Elliott, Russell C.
US Army
Civil War

Ellis, Horace
US Army
Civil War

Ellis, Michael B.
US Army
World War I

Ellis, William
US Army
Civil War

Ellsworth, Thomas F.
US Army
Civil War

Elmore, Walter
US Navy
Interim Awards,
    1871–1898

***Elrod, Henry
Talmadge**
US Marine Corps
World War II

Elsatsoosu
US Army
Indian Campaigns

Elson, James M.
US Army
Civil War

Elwood, Edwin L.
US Army
Indian Campaigns

Embler, Andrew H.
US Army
Civil War

Emmet, Robert Temple
US Army
Indian Campaigns

Enderlin, Richard
US Army
Civil War

*Endl, Gerald L.
US Army
World War II

Engle, James E.
US Army
Civil War

English, Edmund
US Army
Civil War

*English, Glenn H., Jr.
US Army
Vietnam War

English, Thomas
US Navy
Civil War

Ennis, Charles D.
US Army
Civil War

Enright, John
US Navy
Interim Awards,
    1871–1898

***Epperson, Harold
Glenn**
US Marine Corps
World War II

Epps, Joseph L.
US Army
Philippine Insurrection

Erickson, John P.
US Navy
Civil War

Erickson, Nick
US Navy
Spanish-American War

Erwin, Henry E.
US Army Air Corps
World War II

*Essebagger, John, Jr.
US Army
Korean War

Estes, Lewellyn G.
US Army
Civil War

*Estocin, Michael J.
US Navy
Vietnam War

*Etchberger, Richard L.
US Air Force
Vietnam War

*Eubanks, Ray E.
US Army
World War II

Evans, Coron D.
US Army
Civil War

*Evans, Donald W., Jr.
US Army
Vietnam War

*Evans, Ernest Edwin
US Navy
World War II

Evans, Ira H.
US Army
Civil War

Evans, James R.
US Army
Civil War

*Evans, Rodney J.
US Army
Vietnam War

Evans, Thomas
US Army
Civil War

Evans, William
US Army
Indian Campaigns

Everetts, John
US Navy
Interim Awards,
  1871–1898

Everhart, Forrest E.
US Army
World War II

Everson, Adelbert
US Army
Civil War

Ewing, John C.
US Army
Civil War

F

Factor, Pompey
US Army
Indian Campaigns

Fadden, Harry D.
US Navy
Interim Awards,
  1901–1911

*Faith, Don C., Jr.
US Army
Korean War

Falconer, John A.
US Army
Civil War

Falcott, Henry
US Army
Indian Campaigns

Fall, Charles S.
US Army
Civil War

Fallon, Thomas T.
US Army
Civil War

*Falls, Benjamin F.
US Army
Civil War

Fanning, Nicholas
US Army
Civil War

*Fardy, John Peter
US Marine Corps
World War II

Farley, William
US Navy
Civil War

Farnsworth, Herbert E.
US Army
Civil War

Farquhar, John M.
US Army
Civil War

Farrell, Edward
US Navy
Civil War

Farren, Daniel
US Army
Indian Campaigns

Fasnacht, Charles H.
US Army
Civil War

Fassett, John B.
US Army
Civil War

Fasseur, Isaac L.
US Navy
Interim Awards,
  1871–1898

Feaster, Mosheim
US Army
Indian Campaigns

Fegan, James
US Army
Indian Campaigns

*Femoyer, Robert E.
US Army Air Corps
World War II

Ferguson, Arthur M.
US Army
Philippine
Insurrection

Ferguson, Frederick Edgar
US Army
Vietnam War

Fernald, Albert E.
US Army
Civil War

*Fernandez, Daniel
US Army
Vietnam War

Ferrari, George
US Army
Indian Campaigns

Ferrell, John H.
US Navy
Civil War

Ferrier, Daniel T.
US Army
Civil War

Ferris, Eugene W.
US Army
Civil War

Fesq, Frank
US Army
Civil War

Fichter, Hermann
US Army
Indian Campaigns

Field, Oscar Wadsworth
US Marine Corps
Spanish-American War

Fields, James H.
US Army
World War II

Finkenbiner, Henry S.
US Army
Civil War

Finn, John William
US Navy
World War II

Fisher, Almond E.
US Army
World War II

Fisher, Bernard Francis
Vietnam War

Fisher, Frederick Thomas
US Navy
Philippine Insurrection

*Fisher, Harry
US Marine Corps
China Relief Expedition

Fisher, John H.
US Army
Civil War

Fisher, Joseph
US Army
Civil War

Fitz, Jospeh
US Navy
Philippine Insurrection

Fitzgerald, John
US Marine Corps
Spanish-American War

Fitzmaurice, Michael John
US Army
Vietnam War

Fitzpatrick, Thomas
US Navy
Civil War

*Flaherty, Francis C.
US Navy
World War II

Flanagan, Augustin
US Army
Civil War

Flannagan, John
US Navy
Interim Awards,
1871–1898

Flannigan, James
US Army
Civil War

*Fleek, Charles Clinton
US Army
Vietnam War

Fleetwood, Christian A.
US Army
Civil War

Fleming, James P.
US Air Force
Vietnam War

*Fleming, Richard E.
US Marine Corps
World War II

Fletcher, Frank Friday
US Navy
Mexican Campaign
(Veracruz)

Fletcher, Frank Jack
US Navy
Mexican Campaign
(Veracruz)

Flood, Thomas
US Navy
Civil War

Floyd, Edward
US Navy
Interim Awards,
    1901–1911

Fluckey, Eugene Bennett
US Navy
World War II

Flynn, Christopher
US Army
Civil War

Flynn, James E.
US Army
Civil War

Foley, Alexander Joseph
US Marine Corps
China Relief Expedition

Foley, John H.
US Army
Indian Campaigns

Foley, Robert F.
US Army
Vietnam War

*Folland, Michael Flemming
US Army
Vietnam War

Follett, Joseph L.
US Army
Civil War

Folly, William H.
US Army
Indian Campaigns

Foran, Nicholas
US Army
Indian Campaigns

Forbeck, Andrew P.
US Navy
Philippine Insurrection

Force, Manning F.
US Army
Civil War

Ford, George W.
US Army
Civil War

Forman, Alexander A.
US Army
Civil War

Forrest, Arthur J.
US Army
World War I

Forsterer, Bruno Albert
US Marine Corps
Philippine Insurrection

Forsyth, Thomas H.
US Army
Indian Campaigns

Foss, Herbert Louis
US Navy
Spanish-American War

Foss, Joseph Jacob
US Marine Corps
World War II

Foster, Gary Evans
US Army
World War I

Foster, Paul Frederick
US Navy
Mexican Campaign
    (Veracruz)

*Foster, Paul Hellstrom
US Marine Corps
Vietnam War

Foster, William
US Army
Indian Campaigns

*Foster, William Adelbert
US Marine Corps
World War II

*Fournet, Douglas B.
US Army
Vietnam War

Fournia, Frank O.
US Army
Spanish-American War

*Fournier, William G.
US Army
World War II

*Fous, James W.
US Army
Vietnam War

Fout, Frederick W.
US Army
Civil War

Fowler, Christopher
US Navy
Interim Awards,
    1871–1898

*Fowler, Thomas W.
US Army
World War II

Fox, Henry
US Army
Civil War

Fox, Henry M.
US Army
Civil War

*Fox, John R.
US Army
World War II

Fox, Nicholas
US Army
Civil War

Fox, Wesley L.
US Marine Corps
Vietnam War

Fox, William R.
US Army
Civil War

Foy, Charles H.
US Navy
Civil War

Francis, Charles Robert
US Marine Corps
China Relief Expedition

Franklin, Frederick
US Navy
1871 Korean Campaign

Franklin, Joseph John
US Marine Corps
Spanish-American War

Franks, William J.
US Navy
Civil War

Frantz, Joseph
US Army
Civil War

**Fraser, William W.
(Frazier)**
US Army
Civil War

*Fratellenico, Frank R.
US Army
Vietnam War

Frazer, Hugh Carroll.
US Navy
Mexican Campaign
   (Veracruz)

Fredericksen, Emil
US Navy
Interim Awards,
   1901–1911

Freeman, Archibald
US Army
Civil War

Freeman, Ed W.
US Army
Vietnam War

Freeman, Henry B.
US Army
Civil War

Freeman, Martin
US Navy
Civil War

Freeman, William H.
US Army
Civil War

Freemeyer, Christopher
US Army
Indian Campaigns

French, Samuel S.
US Army
Civil War

Frey, Franz
US Army
Civil War

Frick, Jacob G.
US Army
Civil War

Frisbee, John B.
US Navy
Civil War

Fritz, Harold A.
US Army
Vietnam War

**Frizzell (Frazell),
Henry F.**
US Army
Civil War

Fry, Isaac N.
US Marine Corps
Civil War

*Fryar, Elmer E.
US Army
World War II

Fryer, Eli Thompson
US Marine Corps
Mexican Campaign
   (Veracruz)

Fuger, Frederick
US Army
Civil War

Funk, Jesse N.
US Army
World War I

Funk, Leonard A., Jr.
US Army
World War II

Funk, West
US Army
Civil War

Funston, Frederick
US Army
Philippine Insurrection

Fuqua, Samuel Glenn
US Navy
World War II

Furlong, Harold A.
US Army
World War I

Furman, Chester S.
US Army
Civil War

Furness, Frank
US Army
Civil War

G

Gaffney, Frank
US Army
World War I

Gage, Richard J.
US Army
Civil War

Gaiennie, Louis Rene
US Marine Corps
China Relief Expedition

Galbraith, Robert
US Navy
Philippine Insurrection

Galer, Robert Edward
US Marine Corps
World War II

Galloway, George N.
US Army
Civil War

Galloway, John
US Army
Civil War

Galt, Sterling A.
US Army
Philippine Insurrection

***Galt, William Wylie**
US Army
World War II

***Gammon, Archer T.**
US Army
World War II

***Garcia, Fernando Luis**
US Marine Corps
Korean War

García, Macario
US Army
World War II

Gardiner, James
US Army
Civil War

Gardiner, Peter W.
US Army
Indian Campaigns

Gardner, Charles
US Army
Indian Campaigns

Gardner, Charles N.
US Army
Civil War

***Gardner, James A.**
US Army
Vietnam War

Gardner, Robert J.
US Army
Civil War

Gardner, William
US Navy
Civil War

Garland, Harry
US Army
Indian Campaigns

Garlington, Ernest A.
US Army
Indian Campaigns

Garman, Harold A.
US Army
World War II

Garrett, William
US Army
Civil War

Garrison, James R.
US Navy
Civil War

Garvin, William
US Navy
Civil War

Gary, Donald Arthur
US Navy
World War II

***Gasson, Richard**
US Army
Civil War

Gates, George
US Army
Indian Campaigns

Gaughan, Philip
US Marine Corps
Spanish-American War

Gaujot, Antoine A.
US Army
Philippine Insurrection

Gaujot, Julien E.
US Army
Mexican Campaign
(Veracruz)

Gaunt, John C.
US Army
Civil War

Gause, Isaac
US Army
Civil War

Gay, Thomas H.
US Army
Indian Campaigns

Gaylord, Levi B.
US Army
Civil War

Gedeon, Louis
US Army
Philippine Insurrection

Geiger, George
US Army
Indian Campaigns

*George, Charles
US Army
Korean War

George, Daniel G.
US Navy
Civil War

Georgian, John
US Army
Indian Campaigns

Gerber, Frederick W.
US Army
Indian Campaigns

Gere, Thomas P.
US Army
Civil War

Gerstung, Robert E.
US Army
World War II

*Gertsch, John G.
US Army
Vietnam War

Geschwind, Nicholas
US Army
Civil War

Gibbons, Michael
US Navy
Spanish-American War

Gibbs, Wesley
US Army
Civil War

Gibson, Edward H.
US Army
Philippine Insurrection

*Gibson, Eric G.
US Army
World War II

Gidding, Charles
US Navy
Interim Awards,
1871–1898

Gifford, Benjamin
US Army
Civil War

Gifford, David L.
US Army
Civil War

Gile, Frank S.
US Navy
Civil War

Gill, Freeman
US Navy
Spanish-American War

Gillenwater, James R.
US Army
Philippine Insurrection

Gillespie, George L.
US Army
Civil War

Gillick, Matthew
US Navy
Interim Awards,
1871–1898

Gilligan, Edward L.
US Army
Civil War

*Gilliland, Charles L.
US Army
Korean War

*Gilmore, Howard Walter
US Navy
World War II

Gilmore, John C.
US Army
Civil War

Ginley, Patrick
US Army
Civil War

Gion, Joseph
US Army
Civil War

Girandy, Alphonse
US Navy
Interim Awards,
1901–1911

Gisburne, Edward A.
US Navy
Mexican Campaign
(Veracruz)

Giunta, Salvatore A.
US Army
Afghanistan

*Given, John J.
US Army
Indian Campaigns

Glavinski, Albert
US Army
Indian Campaigns

Glover, T. B.
US Army
Indian Campaigns

**Glowin, Joseph
Anthony**
US Marine Corps
Dominican Campaign

Glynn, Michael
US Army
Indian Campaigns

Godfrey, Edward S.
US Army
Indian Campaigns

Godley, Leonidas M.
US Army
Civil War

Goettel, Philip
US Army
Civil War

***Goettler, Harold
Ernest**
US Army Air Service
World War I

Goheen, Charles A.
US Army
Civil War

Golden, Patrick
US Army
Indian Campaigns

Goldin, Theodore W.
US Army
Indian Campaigns

Goldsbery, Andrew E.
US Army
Civil War

*Gomez, Edward
US Marine Corps
Korean War

*Gonsalves, Harold
US Marine Corps
World War II

*Gonzales, David M.
US Army
World War II

*Gonzalez, Alfredo
US Marine Corps
Vietnam War

Goodall, Francis H.
US Army
Civil War

*Goodblood, Clair
US Army
Korean War

Goodman, David
US Army
Indian Campaigns

Goodman, William E.
US Army
Civil War

Goodrich, Edwin
US Army
Civil War

*Gordon, Gary I.
US Army
Somalia

**Gordon, Nathan
Green**
US Navy
World War II

*Gott, Donald J.
US Army Air Corps
World War II

Gould, Charles G.
US Army
Civil War

Gould, Newton T.
US Army
Civil War

Gouraud, George E.
US Army
Civil War

**Gowan, William
Henry**
US Navy
Interim Awards,
1901–1911

*Grabiarz, William J.
US Army
World War II

Grace, Patrick H.
US Navy
1871 Korean Campaign

Grace, Peter
US Army
Civil War

Grady, John
US Navy
Mexican Campaign
   (Veracruz)

*Graham, James A.
US Marine Corps
Vietnam War

Graham, Robert
US Navy
Civil War

Graham, Thomas N.
US Army
Civil War

*Grandstaff, Bruce Alan
US Army
Vietnam War

Grant, Gabriel
US Army
Civil War

Grant, George
US Army
Indian Campaigns

*Grant, Joseph Xavier
US Army
Vietnam War

Grant, Lewis A.
US Army
Civil War

Graul, William
US Army
Civil War

Graves, Ora
US Navy
World War I

*Graves, Terrence Collinson
US Marine Corps
Vietnam War

Graves, Thomas J.
US Army
Spanish-American War

Gray, John
US Army
Civil War

Gray, Robert A.
US Army
Civil War

*Gray, Ross Franklin
US Marine Corps
World War II

Grbitch, Rade
US Navy
Interim Awards,
   1901–1911

Greaves, Clinton
US Army
Indian Campaigns

Grebe, M. R. William
US Army
Civil War

Greely, Adolphus W.
US Army
Interim Awards,
   1920–1940

Green, Francis C.
US Army
Indian Campaigns

Green, George
US Army
Civil War

Green, John
US Army
Indian Campaigns

Greenawalt, Abraham
US Army
Civil War

Greene, John
US Navy
Civil War

Greene, Oliver D.
US Army
Civil War

Greer, Allen J.
US Army
Philippine Insurrection

Gregg, Joseph O.
US Army
Civil War

Gregg, Stephen R.
US Army
World War II

Gregory, Earl D.
US Army
World War I

Greig, Theodore W.
US Army
Civil War

Gresham, John C.
US Army
Indian Campaigns

Gresser, Ignatz
US Army
Civil War

Gribben, James H.
US Army
Civil War

Griffiths, John
US Navy
Civil War

Grimes, Edward P.
US Army
Indian Campaigns

Grimshaw, Samuel
US Army
Civil War

Grindlay, James G.
US Army
Civil War

Griswold, Luke M.
US Navy
Civil War

Gross, Samuel (real name is Marguilies, Samuel)
US Marine Corps
Haiti 1915

Grove, William R.
US Army
Philippine Insurrection

Grueb, George
US Army
Civil War

*Gruennert, Kenneth E.
US Army
World War II

*Guenette, Peter M.
US Army
Vietnam War

Guerin, Fitz W.
US Army
Civil War

*Guillen, Ambrosio
US Marine Corps
Korean War

Guinn, Thomas
US Army
Civil War

Gumpertz, Sydney G.
US Army
World War I

Gunther, Jacob
US Army
Indian Campaigns

*Gurke, Henry
US Marine Corps
World War II

Gwynne, Nathaniel
US Army
Civil War

H

Hack, John
US Army
Civil War

Hack, Lester G.
US Army
Civil War

Haddoo, John
US Army
Indian Campaigns

Hadley, Cornelius M.
US Army
Civil War

Hadley, Osgood T.
US Army
Civil War

Haffee, Edmund
US Navy
Civil War

Hagemeister, Charles Chris
US Army
Vietnam War

*Hagen, Loren D.
US Army
Vietnam War

Hagerty, Asel
US Army
Civil War

Haight, John H.
US Army
Civil War

Haight, Sidney
US Army
Civil War

Hajiro, Barney F.
US Army
World War II

Haley, James
US Navy
Civil War

Halford, William
US Navy
Interim Awards,
    1866–1870

Hall, Francis B.
US Army
Civil War

Hall, George J.
US Army
World War II

Hall, Henry Seymour
US Army
Civil War

Hall, John
US Army
Indian Campaigns

*__*Hall, Lewis__*
US Army
World War II

Hall, Newton H.
US Army
Civil War

*__*Hall, Thomas Lee__*
US Army
World War I

Hall, William E.
US Navy
World War II

Hall, William P.
US Army
Indian Campaigns

Halling, Luovi
US Navy
Interim Awards,
    1901–1911

*__*Hallman,__*
Sherwood H.
US Army
World War II

Hallock, Nathan M.
US Army
Civil War

Halstead, William
US Navy
Civil War

*__*Halyburton, William__*
David, Jr.
US Navy
World War II

Ham, Mark G.
US Navy
Civil War

Hamberger, William F.
US Navy
China Relief Expedition

Hamilton, Frank
US Army
Indian Campaigns

Hamilton, Hugh
US Navy
Civil War

Hamilton, Mathew H.
US Army
Indian Campaigns

Hamilton,
Pierpont M.
US Army Air Corps
World War II

Hamilton, Richard
US Navy
Civil War

Hamilton, Thomas W.
US Navy
Civil War

Hammann, Charles
Hazeltine
US Navy
World War I

Hammel, Henry A.
US Army
Civil War

*__*Hammerberg, Owen__*
Francis Patrick
US Navy
World War II

*__*Hammond, Francis C.__*
US Navy
Korean War

*__*Hammond, Lester, Jr.__*
US Army
Korean War

Hand, Allexander
US Navy
Civil War

Handran, John
US Navy
Interim Awards,
    1871–1898

*__*Handrich, Melvin O.__*
US Army
Korean War

Haney, Milton L.
US Army
Civil War

Hanford, Burke
US Navy
China Relief Expedition

Hanford, Edward R.
US Army
Civil War

Hanks, Joseph
US Army
Civil War

Hanley, Richard P.
US Army
Indian Campaigns

Hanna, Marcus A.
US Army
Civil War

Hanna, Milton
US Army
Civil War

Hanneken, Herman Henry
US Marine Corps
Haitian Campaign
 1919–1920

Hanscom, Moses C.
US Army
Civil War

*Hansen, Dale Merlin
US Marine Corps
World War II

Hansen, Hans A.
US Navy
China Relief Expedition

*Hanson, Jack G.
US Army
Korean War

*Hanson, Robert Murray
US Marine Corps
World War II

Hapeman, Douglas
US Army
Civil War

Harbourne, John H.
US Army
Civil War

Harcourt, Thomas
US Navy
Civil War

Hardaway, Benjamin F.
US Army
Spanish-American War

*Hardenbergh, Henry M.
US Army
Civil War

Harding, Mosher A.
US Army
Indian Campaigns

Harding, Thomas
US Navy
Civil War

Haring, Abram P.
US Army
Civil War

Harley, Bernard
US Navy
Civil War

Harmon, Amzi D.
US Army
Civil War

*Harmon, Roy W.
US Army
World War II

Harner, Joseph Gabriel
US Navy
Mexican Campaign
 (Veracruz)

*Harr, Harry R.
US Army
World War II

Harrell, William George
US Marine Corps
World War II

Harrington, Daniel
US Navy
Civil War

Harrington, David
US Navy
Interim Awards,
 1871–1898

Harrington, Ephraim W.
US Army
Civil War

Harrington, John
US Army
Indian Campaigns

Harris, Charles D.
US Army
Indian Campaigns

Harris, David W.
US Army
Indian Campaigns

Harris, George W.
US Army
Civil War

Harris, James H.
US Army
Civil War

*Harris, James L.
US Army
World War II

Harris, John
US Navy
Civil War

Harris, Moses
US Army
Civil War

Harris, Sampson
US Army
Civil War

Harris, William M.
US Army
Indian Campaigns

Harrison, Bolden Reush
US Navy
Philippines 1911

Harrison, George H.
US Navy
Civil War

Harrison, William Kelly
US Navy
Mexican Campaign
(Veracruz)

Hart, John W.
US Army
Civil War

Hart, William
US Navy
Spanish-American War

Hart, William E.
US Army
Civil War

*Hartell, Lee R.
US Army
Korean War

Hartigan, Charles Conway
US Navy
Mexican Campaign
(Veracruz)

Hartranft, John F.
US Army
Civil War

*Hartsock, Robert W.
US Army
Vietnam War

Hartzog, Joshija B.
US Army
Indian Campaigns

*Harvey, Carmel Bernon, Jr.
US Army
Vietnam War

Harvey, Harry
US Army
Civil War

Harvey, Harry
US Marine Corps
Philippine Insurrection

Harvey, Raymond
US Army
Korean War

*Hasemoto, Mikio
US Army
World War II

Haskell, Frank W.
US Army
Civil War

Haskell, Marcus M.
US Army
Civil War

*Hastings, Joe R.
US Army
World War II

Hastings, Smith H.
US Army
Civil War

Hatch, John P.
US Army
Civil War

Hathaway, Edward W.
US Navy
Civil War

Hatler, M. Waldo
US Army
World War I

*Hauge, Louis James, Jr.
US Marine Corps
World War II

Haupt, Paul
US Army
Indian Campaigns

Havron, John H.
US Army
Civil War

Hawk, John D.
US Army
World War II

Hawkins, Charles
US Navy
Civil War

Hawkins, Gardner C.
US Army
Civil War

Hawkins, Martin J.
US Army
Civil War

Hawkins, Thomas R.
US Army
Civil War

*Hawkins, William Dean
US Marine Corps
World War II

Hawks, Lloyd C.
US Army
World War II

Hawthorne, Harris S.
US Army
Civil War

Hawthorne, Harry L.
US Army
Indian Campaigns

Hay, Fred S.
US Army
Indian Campaigns

*Hayashi, Joe
US Army
World War II

Hayashi, Shizuya
US Army
World War II

Hayden, Cyrus
US Navy
1871 Korean Campaign

Hayden, David E.
US Navy
World War I

Hayden, John
US Navy
Interim Awards,
 1871–1898

Hayden, Joseph B.
US Navy
Civil War

Hayes, John
US Navy
Civil War

Hayes, Thomas
US Navy
Civil War

Hayes, Webb C.
US Army
Philippine Insurrection

Haynes, Asbury F.
US Army
Civil War

Hays, George Price
US Army
World War I

Hays, John H.
US Army
Civil War

Healy, George W.
US Army
Civil War

Heard, John W.
US Army
Spanish-American War

Heartery, Richard
US Army
Indian Campaigns

Hedges, Joseph
US Army
Civil War

*Hedrick, Clinton M.
US Army
World War II

Heermance, William L.
US Army
Civil War

Heisch, Henry William
US Marine Corps
China Relief Expedition

Heise, Clamor
US Army
Indian Campaigns

Heller, Henry
US Army
Civil War

Helms, David H.
US Army
Civil War

Helms, John Henry
US Marine Corps
Interim Awards,
 1901–1911

Henderson, Joseph
US Army
Philippine Insurrection

Hendrickson, Henry
US Navy
Spanish-American War

Hendrix, James R.
US Army
World War II

Henrechon, George Francis
US Navy
Philippines 1911

*Henry, Frederick F.
US Army
Korean War

Henry, Guy V.
US Army
Civil War

Henry, James
US Army
Civil War

*Henry, Robert T.
US Army
World War II

Henry, William W.
US Army
Civil War

Herda, Frank A.
US Army
Vietnam War

Herington, Pitt B.
US Army
Civil War

*Heriot, James D.
US Army
World War I

Hernández, Rodolfo P.
US Army
Korean War

Herrera, Silvestre S.
US Army
World War II

Herring, Rufus G.
US Navy
World War II

Herron, Francis J.
US Army
Civil War

Herron, Leander
US Army
Indian Campaigns

Hesseltine, Francis S.
US Army
Civil War

Heyl, Charles H.
US Army
Indian Campaigns

*Hibbs, Robert John
US Army
Vietnam War

Hibson, Joseph C.
US Army
Civil War

Hickey, Dennis W.
US Army
Civil War

Hickman, John
US Navy
Civil War

Hickok, Nathan E.
US Army
Civil War

Higby, Charles
US Army
Civil War

Higgins, Thomas J.
US Army
Civil War

Higgins, Thomas P.
US Army
Indian Campaigns

High, Frank C.
US Army
Philippine Insurrection

Highland, Patrick
US Army
Civil War

Hill, Edward
US Army
Civil War

*Hill, Edwin Joseph
US Navy
World War II

Hill, Frank
US Marine Corps
Spanish-American War

Hill, Frank E.
US Army
Indian Campaigns

Hill, Frank E.
US Navy
Interim Awards,
 1901–1911

Hill, George
US Navy
Interim Awards,
 1871–1898

Hill, Henry
US Army
Civil War

Hill, James
US Army
Civil War

Hill, James
US Army
Civil War

Hill, James M.
US Army
Indian Campaigns

Hill, Ralyn M.
US Army
World War I

Hill, Walter Newell
US Marine Corps
Mexican Campaign
    (Veracruz)

Hill, William L.
US Navy
Interim Awards,
    1871–1898

Hilliker, Benjamin F.
US Army
Civil War

Hillock, Marvin C.
US Army
Indian Campaigns

Hills, William G.
US Army
Civil War

Hilton, Alfred B.
US Army
Civil War

Hilton, Richmond H.
US Army
World War I

Himmelsback, Michael
US Army
Indian Campaigns

Hincks, William B.
US Army
Civil War

Hinemann, Lehmann
US Army
Indian Campaigns

Hinnegan, William
US Navy
Civil War

Hoban, Thomas
US Navy
Spanish-American War

Hobday, George
US Army
Indian Campaigns

Hobson, Richmond Pearson
US Navy
Spanish-American War

Hodges, Addison J.
US Army
Civil War

Hoffman, Charles F. (Army Medal)
US Marine Corps
World War I

Hoffman, Henry
US Army
Civil War

Hoffman, Thomas W.
US Army
Civil War

Hogan, Franklin
US Army
Civil War

Hogan, Henry (First Award)
US Army
Indian Campaigns

Hogan, Henry (Second Award)
US Army
Indian Campaigns

Hogarty, William P.
US Army
Civil War

Holcomb, Daniel I.
US Army
Civil War

***Holcomb, John Noble**
US Army
Vietnam War

Holden, Henry
US Army
Indian Campaigns

Holderman, Nelson M.
US Army
World War I

Holehouse, James J.
US Army
Civil War

Holland, David
US Army
Indian Campaigns

Holland, Lemuel F.
US Army
Civil War

Holland, Milton M.
US Army
Civil War

Hollat, George
US Navy
Civil War

Holmes, Lovilo N.
US Army
Civil War

Holmes, William T.
US Army
Civil War

Holt, George
US Navy
Interim Awards,
    1871–1898

Holton, Charles M.
US Army
Civil War

Holton, Edward A.
US Army
Civil War

Holtz, August
US Navy
Interim Awards,
    1901–1911

Holyoke, William E.
US Navy
China Relief Expedition

Homan, Conrad
US Army
Civil War

*****Hooker, George**
US Army
Indian Campaigns

Hooker, George W.
US Army
Civil War

Hooper, Joe R.
US Army
Vietnam War

Hooper, William B.
US Army
Civil War

Hoover, Samuel
US Army
Indian Campaigns

Hopkins, Charles F.
US Army
Civil War

Horan, Thomas
US Army
Civil War

Hornaday, Simpson
US Army
Indian Campaigns

Horne, Samuel B.
US Army
Civil War

Horner, Freeman V.
US Army
World War II

Horsfall, William H.
US Army
Civil War

Horton, James
US Navy
Civil War

Horton, James
US Navy
Interim Awards,
    1871–1898

Horton, Lewis A.
US Navy
Civil War

Horton, William Charlie
US Marine Corps
China Relief Expedition

*****Hosking, Charles Ernest, Jr.**
US Army
Vietnam War

Hottenstine, Solomon J.
US Army
Civil War

Hough, Ira
US Army
Civil War

Houghton, Charles H.
US Army
Civil War

Houghton, Edward J.
US Navy
Civil War

Houghton, George L.
US Army
Civil War

Houlton, William
US Army
Civil War

Howard, Henderson C.
US Army
Civil War

Howard, Hiram R.
US Army
Civil War

Howard, James
US Army
Civil War

Howard, James H.
US Army Air Corps
World War II

Howard, Jimmie E.
US Marine Corps
Vietnam War

Howard, Martin
US Navy
Civil War

Howard, Oliver O.
US Army
Civil War

Howard, Peter
US Navy
Civil War

Howard, Robert L.
US Army
Vietnam War

Howard, Squire E.
US Army
Civil War

***Howe, James D.**
US Marine Corps
Vietnam War

Howe, Orion P.
US Army
Civil War

Howe, William H.
US Army
Civil War

Howze, Robert L.
US Army
Indian Campaigns

Hubbard, Thomas
US Army
Indian Campaigns

Hubbell, William S.
US Army
Civil War

Huber, William Russel
US Navy
Interim Awards, 1920–1940

Hudner, Thomas Jerome, Jr.
US Navy
Korean War

Hudson, Aaron R.
US Army
Civil War

Hudson, Michael
US Marine Corps
Civil War

Huff, James W.
US Army
Indian Campaigns

Huff, Paul B.
US Army
World War II

Huggins, Eli L.
US Army
Indian Campaigns

Hughes, John Arthur
US Marine Corps
Mexican Campaign (Veracruz)

***Hughes, Lloyd H.**
US Army Air Corps
World War II

Hughes, Oliver
US Army
Civil War

Hughey, John
US Army
Civil War

Huidekoper, Henry S.
US Army
Civil War

Hulbert, Henry Lewis
US Marine Corps
Philippine Insurrection

Hull, James L.
US Navy
Spanish-American War

Humphrey, Charles F.
US Army
Indian Campaigns

Hunt, Fred O.
US Army
Indian Campaigns

Hunt, Louis T.
US Army
Civil War

Hunt, Martin
US Marine Corps
China Relief Expedition

Hunter, Charles A.
US Army
Civil War

Hunterson, John C.
US Army
Civil War

Huntsman, John A.
US Army
Philippine Insurrection

Huse, Henry McClaren Pinckney
US Navy
Mexican Campaign (Veracruz)

Huskey, Michael
US Navy
Civil War

*Hutchins, Carlton Barmire
US Navy
Interim Awards,
    1920–1940

*Hutchins, Johnnie David
US Navy
World War II

Hutchinson, Rufus D.
US Army
Indian Campaigns

Hyatt, Theodore
US Army
Civil War

Hyde, Henry J.
US Army
Indian Campaigns

Hyde, Thomas W.
US Army
Civil War

Hyland, John
US Navy
Civil War

Hymer, Samuel
US Army
Civil War

I

Iams, Ross Lindsey
US Marine Corps
Haiti 1915

Ilgenfritz, Charles H.
US Army
Civil War

Immell, Lorenzo D.
US Army
Civil War

*Ingalls, George Alan
US Army
Vietnam War

Ingalls, Lewis J.
US Army
Civil War

Ingman, Einar H., Jr.
US Army
Korean War

Ingram, Jonas Howard
US Navy
Mexican Campaign
    (Veracruz)

*Ingram, Osmond K.
US Navy
World War I

Ingram, Robert R.
US Navy
Vietnam War

Inouye, Daniel K.
US Army
World War II

Inscho, Leonidas H.
US Army
Civil War

Irlam, Jospeh
US Navy
Civil War

Irsch, Francis
US Army
Civil War

Irving, John
US Navy
Civil War

Irving, Thomas
US Navy
Civil War

Irwin, Bernard J. D.
US Army
Indian Campaigns

Irwin, Nicholas
US Navy
Civil War

Irwin, Patrick
US Army
Civil War

Itrich, Franz Anton
US Navy
Spanish-American War

Izac, Edouard Victor Michel
US Navy
World War I

J

*Jachman, Isadore S.
US Army
World War II

Jackson, Arthur J.
US Marine Corps
World War II

Jackson, Frederick R.
US Army
Civil War

Jackson, James
US Army
Indian Campaigns

Jackson, Joe M.
US Air Force
Vietnam War

Jacobs, Jack H.
US Army
Vietnam War

Jacobson, Douglas Thomas
US Marine Corps
World War II

Jacobson, Eugene P.
US Army
Civil War

James, Isaac
US Army
Civil War

James, John
US Army
Indian Campaigns

James, John H.
US Navy
Civil War

James, Miles
US Army
Civil War

*James, Willy F., Jr.
US Army
World War II

Jamieson, Walter
US Army
Civil War

Janson, Ernest August (Navy Medal)
US Marine Corps
World War I

Jardine, Alexander
US Navy
Spanish-American War

Jardine, James
US Army
Civil War

Jarrett, Berrie H.
US Navy
Mexican Campaign (Veracruz)

Jarvis, Frederick
US Army
Indian Campaigns

*Jecelin, William R.
US Army
Korean War

Jellison, Benjamin H.
US Army
Civil War

Jenkins, Don J.
US Army
Vietnam War

*Jenkins, Robert H., Jr.
US Marine Corps
Vietnam War

Jenkins, Thomas
US Navy
Civil War

Jennings, Delbert O.
US Army
Vietnam War

Jennings, James T.
US Army
Civil War

Jensen, Gotfred
US Army
Philippine Insurrection

*Jerstad, John L.
US Army Air Corps
World War II

Jetter, Bernhard
US Army
Indian Campaigns

Jewett, Erastus W.
US Army
Civil War

Jim
US Army
Indian Campaigns

*Jimenez, Jose Francisco
US Marine Corps
Vietnam War

Joel, Lawrence
US Army
Vietnam War

Johannessen, Johannes J.
US Navy
Interim Awards, 1901–1911

Johanson, John P.
US Navy
Spanish-American War

Johansson, Johan J.
US Navy
Spanish-American War

John, William
US Army
Civil War

Johndro, Franklin
US Army
Civil War

Johns (Jones), Elisha
US Army
Civil War

Johns, Henry T.
US Army
Civil War

Johnsen, Hans
US Navy
Spanish-American War

Johnson, Andrew
US Army
Civil War

Johnson, Dwight H.
US Army
Vietnam War

*Johnson, Elden H.
US Army
World War II

Johnson, Follett
US Army
Civil War

Johnson, Henry
US Navy
Civil War

Johnson, Henry
US Army
Indian Campaigns

*Johnson, James E.
US Marine Corps
Korean War

Johnson, John
US Army
Civil War

Johnson, John
US Navy
Interim Awards,
    1871–1898

Johnson, Joseph E.
US Army
Civil War

Johnson, Leon W.
US Army Air Corps
World War II

*Johnson, Leroy
US Army
World War II

Johnson, Oscar G.
US Army
World War II

Johnson, Peter
US Navy
Spanish-American War

*Johnson, Ralph H.
US Marine Corps
Vietnam War

Johnson, Ruel M.
US Army
Civil War

Johnson, Samuel
US Army
Civil War

Johnson, Wallace W.
US Army
Civil War

Johnson, William
US Navy
Interim Awards,
    1871–1898

Johnston, David
US Army
Civil War

*Johnston, Donald R.
US Army
Vietnam War

Johnston, Edward
US Army
Indian Campaigns

Johnston, Gordon
US Army
Philippine Insurrection

Johnston, Harold I.
US Army
World War I

Johnston, Rufus Zenas
US Navy
Mexican Campaign
    (Veracruz)

Johnston, William J.
US Army
World War II

Johnston, William P.
US Navy
Civil War

Johnston, Willie
US Army
Civil War

Jones, Andrew
US Navy
Civil War

Jones, Claud Ashton
US Navy
Interim Awards,
    1915–1916

Jones, David
US Army
Civil War

*Jones, Herbert Charpoit
US Navy
World War II

Jones, John
US Navy
Civil War

Jones, John E.
US Navy
Civil War

Jones, Thomas
US Navy
Civil War

Jones, William
US Army
Civil War

Jones, William
US Navy
Civil War

*Jones, William A., III
US Air Force
Vietnam War

Jones, William H.
US Army
Indian Campaigns

Jordan, Absalom
US Army
Civil War

Jordan, George
US Army
Indian Campaigns

Jordan, Robert
US Navy
Civil War

Jordan, Thomas
US Navy
Civil War

*Jordon, Mack A.
US Army
Korean War

Josselyn, Simeon T.
US Army
Civil War

Judge, Francis W.
US Army
Civil War

*Julian, Joseph Rudolph
US Marine Corps
World War II

K

Kaiser, John
US Army
Civil War

Kaltenbach, Luther
US Army
Civil War

*Kandle, Victor L.
US Army
World War II

Kane, John R.
US Army Air Corps
World War II

Kane, John
US Army
Civil War

Kane, Thomas
US Navy
Civil War

*Kanell, Billie G.
US Army
Korean War

Kappesser, Peter
US Army
Civil War

Karaberis, Christos H. (name legally changed to Carr, Chris)
US Army
World War II

Karnes, James E.
US Army
World War I

*Karopczyc, Stephen Edward
US Army
Vietnam War

Karpeles, Leopold
US Army
Civil War

Kates, Thomas Wilbur
US Marine Corps
China Relief
    Expedition

Katz, Phillip C.
US Army
World War I

Kaufman, Benjamin
US Army
World War I

*Kaufman, Loren R.
US Army
Korean War

Kauss (Kautz), August
US Army
Civil War

*Kawamura, Terry
Teruo
US Army
Vietnam War

Kay, John
US Army
Indian Campaigns

Kays, Kenneth
Michael
US Army
Vietnam War

Kearby, Neel E.
US Army Air Corps
World War II

Kearney, Michael
US Marine Corps
Spanish-American War

*Keathley, George D.
US Army
World War II

Keating, Daniel
US Army
Indian Campaigns

*Kedenburg, John J.
US Army
Vietnam War

*Keeble, Woodrow W.
US Army
Korean War

Keefer, Philip B.
US Navy
Spanish-American War

Keele, Joseph
US Army
Civil War

Keen, Joseph S.
US Army
Civil War

Keenan,
Bartholomew T.
US Army
Indian Campaigns

Keenan, John
US Army
Indian Campaigns

Keene, Joseph
US Army
Civil War

*Kefurt, Gus
US Army
World War II

*Keith, Miguel
US Marine Corps
Vietnam War

Keller, Leonard B.
US Army
Vietnam War

Keller, William
US Army
Spanish-American War

Kelley, Andrew J.
US Army
Civil War

Kelley, Charles
US Army
Indian Campaigns

Kelley, George V.
US Army
Civil War

Kelley, John
US Navy
Civil War

*Kelley, Jonah E.
US Army
World War II

Kelley, Leverett M.
US Army
Civil War

*Kelley, Ova A.
US Army
World War II

Kelley, Thomas G.
US Navy
Vietnam War

Kellogg, Allan Jay, Jr.
US Marine Corps
Vietnam War

Kelly, Alexander
US Army
Civil War

Kelly, Charles E.
US Army
World War II

Kelly, Daniel
US Army
Civil War

Kelly, Francis
US Navy
Spanish-American War

Kelly, Thomas
US Army
Civil War

*Kelly, John D.
US Army
World War II

*Kelly, John D.
US Marine Corps
Korean War

**Kelly, John Joseph
(Army Medal)**
US Marine Corps
World War I

**Kelly, John Joseph
(Navy Medal)**
US Marine Corps
World War I

Kelly, John J. H.
US Army
Indian Campaigns

Kelly, Thomas
US Army
Civil War

Kelly, Thomas
US Army
Indian Campaigns

Kelly, Thomas
US Army
Spanish-American War

Kelly, Thomas J.
US Army
World War II

Kelsay
US Army
Indian Campaigns

*Kelso, Jack William
US Marine Corps
Korean War

Kemp, Joseph
US Army
Civil War

Kendall, William W.
US Army
Civil War

Kendrick, Thomas
US Navy
Civil War

Kenna, Barnett
US Navy
Civil War

Kennedy, John
US Army
Civil War

Kennedy, John T.
US Army
Philippine Insurrection

Kennedy, Philip
US Army
Indian Campaigns

Kennemore, Robert S.
US Marine Corps
Korean War

Kenyon, Charles
US Navy
Civil War

Kenyon, John S.
US Army
Civil War

Kenyon, Samuel P.
US Army
Civil War

Keough, John
US Army
Civil War

Kephart, James
US Army
Civil War

***Keppler, Reinhardt
John**
US Navy
World War II

Kerr, John B.
US Army
Indian Campaigns

Kerr, Thomas R.
US Army
Civil War

Kerrey, Joseph R.
US Navy
Vietnam War

Kerrigan, Thomas
US Army
Indian Campaigns

Kersey, Thomas
US Navy
Interim Awards,
1871–1898

Kerstetter, Dexter J.
US Army
World War II

*Kessler, Patrick L.
US Army
World War II

*Kidd, Isaac Campbell
US Navy
World War II

Kiggins, John
US Army
Civil War

**Kilbourne,
Charles E.**
US Army
Philippine Insurrection

Killackey, Joseph
US Navy
China Relief Expedition

Kilmartin, John
US Army
Indian Campaigns

*Kilmer, John E.
US Navy
Korean War

Kimball, Joseph
US Army
Civil War

*Kimbro, Truman
US Army
World War II

Kindig, John M.
US Army
Civil War

*Kiner, Harold G.
US Army
World War II

King, Horatio C.
US Army
Civil War

King, Hugh
US Navy
Interim Awards,
  1871–1898

**King, John (First
Award)**
US Navy
Interim Awards,
  1901–1911

**King, John (Second
Award)**
US Navy
Interim Awards,
  1901–1911

King, Robert H.
US Navy
Civil War

King, Rufus, Jr.
US Army
Civil War

*Kingsley, David R.
US Army Air Corps
World War II

Kinnaird, Samuel W.
US Navy
Civil War

Kinne, John B.
US Army
Philippine Insurrection

*Kinser, Elbert Luther
US Marine Corps
World War II

Kinsey, John
US Army
Civil War

**Kinsman, Thomas
James**
US Army
Vietnam War

Kirby, Dennis T.
US Army
Civil War

Kirk, John
US Army
Indian Campaigns

Kirk, Jonathan C.
US Army
Civil War

Kirkwood, John A.
US Army
Indian Campaigns

Kisters, Gerry H.
US Army
World War II

Kitchen, George K.
US Army
Indian Campaigns

Klein, Robert
US Navy
Interim Awards,
  1901–1911

Kline, Harry
US Army
Civil War

Kloth, Charles H.
US Army
Civil War

Knaak, Albert
US Army
Indian Campaigns

**Knappenberger,
Alton W.**
US Army
World War II

Knight, Charles H.
US Army
Civil War

*Knight, Jack L.
US Army
World War II

Knight, Joseph F.
US Army
Indian Campaigns

*Knight, Noah O.
US Army
Korean War

*Knight, Raymond L.
US Army Air Corps
World War II

Knight, William J.
US Army
Civil War

Knowles, Abiather J.
US Army
Civil War

Knox, Edward M.
US Army
Civil War

Knox, John W.
US Army
Indian Campaigns

Kobashigawa, Yeiki
US Army
World War II

*Kocak, Matej (Army Medal)
US Marine Corps
World War I

*Kocak, Matej (Navy Medal)
US Marine Corps
World War I

Koelpin, William
US Army
Indian Campaigns

*Koelsch, John Kelvin
US Navy
Korean War

Koogle, Jacob
US Army
Civil War

Kosoha
US Army
Indian Campaigns

Kouma, Ernest R.
US Army
Korean War

Kountz, John S.
US Army
Civil War

Kramer, Franz
US Navy
Spanish-American War

Kramer, Theodore L.
US Army
Civil War

*Kraus, Richard Edward
US Marine Corps
World War II

Krause, Ernest
US Navy
Spanish-American War

Kreher, Wendelin
US Army
Indian Campaigns

Kretsinger, George
US Army
Civil War

*Krotiak, Anthony L.
US Army
World War II

*Krzyzowski, Edward C.
US Army
Korean War

Kuchneister, Hermann William
US Marine Corps
Spanish-American War

Kuder, Andrew
US Army
Civil War

Kuder, Jeremiah
US Army
Civil War

*Kuroda, Robert T.
US Army
World War II

*Kyle, Darwin K.
US Army
Korean War

Kyle, John
US Army
Indian Campaigns

Kyle, Patrick J.
US Navy
Interim Awards,
    1871–1898

L

*La Belle, James Dennis
US Marine Corps
World War II

Labill, Joseph S.
US Army
Civil War

Ladd, George
US Army
Civil War

Lafferty, John
US Navy
Civil War

Laffey, Bartlett
US Navy
Civil War

Laing, William
US Army
Civil War

Lakin, Daniel
US Navy
Civil War

Lakin, Thomas
US Navy
Interim Awards,
    1871–1898

Lambers, Paul Ronald
US Army
Vietnam War

Landis, James P.
US Army
Civil War

Lane, Morgan D.
US Army
Civil War

Lanfare, Aaron S.
US Army
Civil War

Lang, George C.
US Army
Vietnam War

Langbein, J. C. Julius
US Army
Civil War

*Langhorn, Garfield M.
US Army
Vietnam War

Langhorne, Gary DeVall
US Navy
Mexican Campaign
    (Veracruz)

Lann, John S.
US Navy
Civil War

Lannon, James Patrick
US Navy
Mexican Campaign
    (Veracruz)

*LaPointe, Joseph G., Jr.
US Army
Vietnam War

Larimer, Smith
US Army
Civil War

Larkin, David
US Army
Indian Campaigns

Larrabee, James W.
US Army
Civil War

Lassen, Clyde Everett
US Navy
Vietnam War

Latham, John Cridland
US Army
World War I

*Lauffer, Billy Lane
US Army
Vietnam War

Laverty, John
US Navy
Interim Awards,
    1871–1898

*Law, Robert D.
US Army
Vietnam War

Lawley, William R., Jr.
US Army Air Corps
World War II

Lawrence, James
US Army
Indian Campaigns

Laws, Robert E.
US Army
World War II

Lawson, Gaines
US Army
Civil War

Lawson, John
US Navy
Civil War

Lawton, Henry W.
US Army
Civil War

Lawton, John S.
US Army
Indian Campaigns

Lawton, Louis B.
US Army
China Relief Expedition

Leahy, Cornelius J.
US Army
Philippine Insurrection

Lear, Nicholas
US Navy
Civil War

Lee, Daniel W.
US Army
World War II

Lee, Fitz
US Army
Spanish-American War

Lee, Howard V.
US Marine Corps
Vietnam War

Lee, Hubert L.
US Army
Korean War

Lee, James H.
US Navy
Civil War

*Lee, Milton A.
US Army
Vietnam War

Leims, John Harold
US Marine Corps
World War II

*Leisy, Robert Ronald
US Army
Vietnam War

Lejeune, Emile
US Navy
Interim Awards,
 1891–1898

Leland, George W.
US Navy
Civil War

*Lemert, Milo
US Army
World War I

Lemon, Peter C.
US Army
Vietnam War

Lenihan, James
US Army
Indian Campaigns

Leon, Pierre
US Navy
Civil War

Leonard, Edwin
US Army
Civil War

Leonard, Joseph
US Marine Corps
Philippine Insurrection

*Leonard, Matthew
US Army
Vietnam War

Leonard, Patrick J.
US Army
Indian Campaigns

Leonard, Patrick T.
US Army
Indian Campaigns

*Leonard, Turney W.
US Army
World War II

Leonard, William
US Army
Indian Campaigns

Leonard, William E.
US Army
Civil War

Leslie, Frank
US Army
Civil War

*Lester, Fred Faulkner
US Navy
World War II

Levery, William
US Navy
Spanish-American War

Levitow, John L.
US Air Force
Vietnam War

Levy, Benjamin
US Army
Civil War

Lewis, DeWitt Clinton
US Army
Civil War

Lewis, Henry
US Army
Civil War

Lewis, Samuel E.
US Army
Civil War

Lewis, William B.
US Army
Indian Campaigns

Libaire, Adolphe
US Army
Civil War

*Libby, George D.
US Army
Korean War

Lilley, John
US Army
Civil War

Lindbergh, Charles A.
US Army Air Corps
Interim Awards,
   1920–1940

*Lindsey, Darrell R.
US Army Air Corps
World War II

Lindsey, Jake W.
US Army
World War II

*Lindstron, Floyd K.
US Army
World War II

Lipscomb, Harry
US Navy
Interim Awards,
   1901–1910

Liteky, Angelo J.
US Army
Vietnam War

Little, Henry F. W.
US Army
Civil War

Little, Thomas
US Army
Indian Campaigns

Littlefield, George H.
US Army
Civil War

*Littleton, Herbert A.
US Marine Corps
Korean War

Littrell, Gary Lee
US Army
Vietnam War

Livingston, James E.
US Marine Corps
Vietnam War

Livingston, Josiah O.
US Army
Civil War

Lloyd, Benjamin
US Navy
Civil War

*Lloyd, Edgar H.
US Army
World War II

Lloyd, John W.
US Navy
Civil War

*Lobaugh, Donald R.
US Army
World War II

Locke, Lewis
US Army
Civil War

*Logan, Hugh
US Navy
Civil War

Logan, James M.
US Army
World War II

*Logan, John A.
US Army
Philippine Insurrection

Lohnes, Francis W.
US Army
Indian Campaigns

Loman, Berger
US Army
World War I

Lonergan, John
US Army
Civil War

*Long, Charles Russell
US Army
Korean War

*Long, Donald Russell
US Army
Vietnam War

Long, Oscar F.
US Army
Indian Campaigns

Longfellow, Richard M.
US Army
Philippine Insurrection

Longshore, William H.
US Army
Civil War

Lonsway, Joseph
US Army
Civil War

*Lopez, Baldomero
US Marine Corps
Korean War

Lopez, Jose M.
US Army
World War II

Lord, William
US Army
Civil War

***Loring, Charles J., Jr.**
US Air Force
Korean War

Lorish, Andrew J.
US Army
Civil War

Love, George M.
US Army
Civil War

Lovering, George M.
US Army
Civil War

Low, George
US Navy
Interim Awards,
   1871–1898

Lower, Cyrus B.
US Army
Civil War

Lower, Robert A.
US Army
Civil War

Lowry, George Maus
US Navy
Mexican Campaign
   (Veracruz)

Lowthers, James
US Army
Indian Campaigns

Loyd, George
US Army
Civil War

Loyd, George
US Army
Indian Campaigns

***Lozada, Carlos James**
US Army
Vietnam War

***Lucas, Andre C.**
US Army
Vietnam War

Lucas, George W.
US Army
Civil War

Lucas, Jacklyn Harold
US Marine Corps
World War II

Luce, Moses A.
US Army
Civil War

Lucy, John
US Navy
Interim Awards,
   1871–1898

Ludgate, William
US Army
Civil War

Ludwig, Carl
US Army
Civil War

***Luke, Frank, Jr.**
US Army Air Service
World War I

Lukes, William F.
US Navy
1871 Korean Campaign

***Lummus, Jack**
US Marine Corps
World War II

Lunt, Alphonso M.
US Army
Civil War

Lutes, Franklin W.
US Army
Civil War

Luther, James H.
US Army
Civil War

Luty, Gotlieb
US Army
Civil War

***Lyell, William F.**
US Army
Korean War

Lyle, Alexander Gordon
US Navy
World War I

Lyman, Joel H.
US Army
Civil War

Lynch, Allen James
US Army
Vietnam War

Lyon, Edward E.
US Army
Philippine Insurrection

Lyon, Frederick A.
US Army
Civil War

Lyons, Thomas
US Navy
Civil War

Lytle, Leonidas S.
US Army
Indian Campaigns

Lytton, Jeptha L.
US Army
Indian Campaigns

M

Mabry, George L., Jr.
US Army
World War II

MacArthur, Arthur, Jr.
US Army
Civil War

MacArthur, Douglas
US Army
World War II

MacGillivary, Charles A.
US Army
World War II

Machol
US Army
Indian Campaigns

Machon, James
US Navy
Civil War

Mack, Alexander
US Navy
Civil War

Mack, John
US Navy
Civil War

MacKenzie, John
US Navy
World War I

Mackie, John F.
US Marine Corps
Civil War

Maclay, William P.
US Army
Philippine Insurrection

MacNeal, Harry Lewis
US Marine Corps
Spanish-American War

Madden, Michael
US Army
Civil War

Madden, William
US Navy
Civil War

Maddin, Edward
US Navy
Interim Awards,
    1871–1898

Madison, James
US Army
Civil War

Madison, James Jonas
US Navy
World War I

Magee, John W.
US Navy
Interim Awards,
    1871–1898

Magee, William
US Army
Civil War

Mager, George F.
US Navy
Spanish-American War

*Magrath, John D.
US Army
World War II

Mahers, Herbert
US Army
Indian Campaigns

Mahoney, George
US Navy
Spanish-American War

Mahoney, Gregory
US Army
Indian Campaigns

Mahoney, Jeremiah
US Army
Civil War

Mallon, George H.
US Army
World War I

Mandusich, Jake A.
US Army
World War I

Mandy, Harry J.
US Army
Civil War

Mangam, Richard C.
US Army
Civil War

*Mann, Joe E.
US Army
World War II

Manning, Henry J.
US Navy
Interim Awards,
    1871–1898

Manning, Joseph S.
US Army
Civil War

Manning, Sidney E.
US Army
World War I

Marland, William
US Army
Civil War

Marm, Walter Joseph, Jr.
US Army
Vietnam War

Marquette, Charles
US Army
Civil War

Marsh, Albert
US Army
Civil War

Marsh, Charles H.
US Army
Civil War

Marsh, George
US Army
Civil War

Martin, Edward S.
US Navy
Civil War

Martin, George (service rendered under name of Martin Schwenk)
US Army
Civil War

*Martin, Harry Linn
US Marine Corps
World War II

Martin, James
US Marine Corps
Civil War

Martin, Patrick
US Army
Indian Campaigns

Martin, Sylvester H.
US Army
Civil War

Martin, William
US Navy
Civil War

Martin, William
US Navy
Civil War

*Martinez, Benito
US Army
Korean War

*Martinez, Joe P.
US Army
World War II

*Martini, Gary W.
US Marine Corps
Vietnam War

Mason, Elihu H.
US Army
Civil War

*Mason, Leonard Foster
US Marine Corps
World War II

Mathews, George W.
US Army
Philippine Insurrection

Mathews, William H. (service rendered under name of Henry Sivel)
US Army
Civil War

Mathias, Clarence Edward
US Marine Corps
China Relief
  Expedition

*Mathies, Archibald
US Army Air Corps
World War II

*Mathis, Jack W.
US Army Air Corps
World War II

*Matthews, Daniel P.
US Marine Corps
Korean War

Matthews, David A.
US Army
Indian Campaigns

Matthews, John C.
US Army
Civil War

Matthews, Joseph
US Navy
Interim Awards,
  1871–1898

Matthews, Milton
US Army
Civil War

Mattingly, Henry B.
US Army
Civil War

Mattocks, Charles P.
US Army
Civil War

Maus, Marion P.
US Army
Indian Campaigns

***Mausert,
Frederick W., III**
US Marine Corps
Korean War

***Maxam, Larry
Leonard**
US Marine Corps
Vietnam War

Maxham, Lowell M.
US Army
Civil War

Maxwell, John
US Navy
Spanish-American War

Maxwell, Robert D.
US Army
World War II

May, John
US Army
Indian Campaigns

*May, Martin O.
US Army
World War II

May, William
US Army
Civil War

Mayberry, John B.
US Army
Civil War

Mayes, William B.
US Army
Civil War

Mayfield, Melvin
US Army
World War II

Maynard, George H.
US Army
Civil War

Mays, Isaiah
US Army
Indian Campaigns

McAdams, Peter
US Army
Civil War

McAllister, Samuel
US Navy
China Relief Expedition

McAlwee, Benjamin F.
US Army
Civil War

McAnally, Charles
US Army
Civil War

McBride, Bernard
US Army
Indian Campaigns

McBryar, William
US Army
Indian Campaigns

McCabe, William
US Army
Indian Campaigns

McCall, Thomas E.
US Army
World War II

**McCammon,
William W.**
US Army
Civil War

McCampbell, David
US Navy
World War II

McCandless, Bruce
US Navy
World War II

McCann, Bernard
US Army
Indian Campaigns

***McCard, Robert
Howard**
US Marine Corps
World War II

McCarren, Bernard
US Army
Civil War

McCarter, Lloyd G.
US Army
World War II

**McCarthy, Joseph
Jeremiah**
US Marine Corps
World War II

McCarthy, Michael
US Army
Indian Campaigns

McCarton, John
US Navy
Interim Awards,
    1871–1898

McCauslin, Joseph
US Army
Civil War

McCleary, Charles H.
US Army
Civil War

McCleery, Finnis D.
US Army
Vietnam War

McClelland, James M.
US Army
Civil War

McClelland, Matthew
US Navy
Civil War

McClernand, Edward J.
US Army
Indian Campaigns

McCloy, John (First Award)
US Navy
China Relief Expedition

McCloy, John (Second Award)
US Navy
Mexican Campaign
(Veracruz)

McConnell, James
US Army
Philippine Insurrection

McConnell, Samuel
US Army
Civil War

McCool, Richard Miles, Jr.
US Navy
World War II

McCormick, Michael
US Navy
Civil War

McCormick, Michael
US Army
Indian Campaigns

McCornack, Andrew
US Army
Civil War

McCullock, Adam
US Navy
Civil War

McDonald, Franklin M.
US Army
Indian Campaigns

McDonald, George E.
US Army
Civil War

McDonald, James
US Army
Indian Campaigns

McDonald, James Harper
US Navy
Interim Awards,
1920–1940

McDonald, John
US Navy
Civil War

McDonald, John W.
US Army
Civil War

***McDonald, Phill G.**
US Army
Vietnam War

McDonald, Robert
US Army
Indian Campaigns

McDonnell, Edward Orrick
US Navy
Mexican Campaign
(Veracruz)

McElhinny, Samuel O.
US Army
Civil War

McEnroe, Patrick H.
US Army
Civil War

McFall, Daniel
US Army
Civil War

McFarland, John
US Navy
Civil War

McGaha, Charles L.
US Army
World War II

McGann, Michael A.
US Army
Indian Campaigns

McGar, Owen
US Army
Indian Campaigns

McGarity, Vernon
US Army
World War II

***McGee, William D.**
US Army
World War II

*McGill, Troy A.
US Army
World War II

McGinn, Edward
US Army
Civil War

*McGinnis, Ross A.
US Army
Iraq

McGinty, John J., III
US Marine Corps
Vietnam War

McGonagle, William L.
US Navy
Vietnam Era

McGonagle, Wilson
US Army
Civil War

McGonnigle,
Andrew J.
US Army
Civil War

McGough, Owen
US Army
Civil War

*McGovern, Robert M.
US Army
Korean War

McGowan, John
US Navy
Civil War

McGrath, Hugh J.
US Army
Philippine Insurrection

*McGraw, Francis X.
US Army
World War II

McGraw, Thomas
US Army
Civil War

McGuire, Fred Henry
US Navy
Philippines 1911

McGuire, Patrick
US Army
Civil War

*McGuire,
Thomas B., Jr.
US Army Air Corps
World War II

McGunigal, Patrick
US Navy
World War I

McHale, Alexander U.
US Army
Civil War

McHugh, John
US Army
Indian Campaigns

McHugh, Martin
US Navy
Civil War

McIntosh, James
US Navy
Civil War

McKay, Charles W.
US Army
Civil War

McKee, George
US Army
Civil War

McKeen, Nineveh S.
US Army
Civil War

McKeever, Michael
US Army
Civil War

McKenzie, Alexander
US Navy
1871 Korean
   Campaign

*McKibben, Ray
US Army
Vietnam War

McKinley, Daniel
US Army
Indian Campaigns

McKinney, John R.
US Army
World War II

McKnight, William
US Navy
Civil War

McKown, Nathaniel A.
US Army
Civil War

McLaughlin, Alford L.
US Marine Corps
Korean War

McLennon, John
US Army
Indian Campaigns

McLeod, James
US Navy
Civil War

McLoughlin, Michael
US Army
Indian Campaigns

McMahon, Martin T.
US Army
Civil War

*****McMahon, Thomas J.**
US Army
Vietnam War

McMasters, Henry A.
US Army
Indian Campaigns

McMillen, Francis M.
US Army
Civil War

McMillian, Albert W.
US Army
Indian Campaigns

McMurtry, George G.
US Army
World War I

**McNair, Frederick
Vallette., Jr.**
US Navy
Mexican Campaign
(Veracruz)

McNally, James
US Army
Indian Campaigns

**McNally, Michael
Joseph**
US Marine Corps
Philippine Insurrection

McNamara, Michael
US Marine Corps
1871 Korean Campaign

McNamara, William
US Army
Indian Campaigns

McNerney, David H.
US Army
Vietnam War

McPhelan, Robert
US Army
Indian Campaigns

*****McTureous, Robert
Miller, Jr.**
US Marine Corps
World War II

McVeagh, Charles H.
US Army
Indian Campaigns

*****McVeane, John P.**
US Army
Civil War

*****McVeigh, John J.**
US Army
World War II

*****McWethy,
Edgar Lee, Jr.**
US Army
Vietnam War

McWhorter, Walter F.
US Army
Civil War

*****McWhorter, William A.**
US Army
World War II

McWilliams, George W.
US Navy
Civil War

Meach, George E.
US Army
Civil War

Meagher, John
US Army
World War II

Meagher, Thomas
US Army
Civil War

Meaher, Nicholas
US Army
Indian Campaigns

Mears, George W.
US Army
Civil War

Mechlin, Henry W. B.
US Army
Indian Campaigns

Melville, Charles
US Navy
Civil War

*****Mendonca, Leroy A.**
US Army
Korean War

Menter, John W.
US Army
Civil War

Meredith, James
US Marine Corps
Spanish-American War

Merli, Gino J.
US Army
World War II

*Merrell, Joseph F.
US Army
World War II

Merriam, Henry C.
US Army
Civil War

Merrifield, James K.
US Army
Civil War

Merrill, Augustus
US Army
Civil War

Merrill, George
US Army
Civil War

Merrill, John
US Army
Indian Campaigns

Merritt, John G.
US Army
Civil War

Merton, James F.
US Navy
1871 Korean Campaign

***Messerschmidt,
Harold O.**
US Army
World War II

***Mestrovitch,
James I.**
US Army
World War I

*Metzger, William E., Jr.
US Army Air Corps
World War II

Meyer, Henry C.
US Army
Civil War

Meyer, William
US Navy
Spanish-American War

*Michael, Don Leslie
US Army
Vietnam War

Michael, Edward S.
US Army Air Corps
World War II

*Michael, Harry J.
US Army
World War II

Mifflin, James
US Navy
Civil War

Mihalowski, John
US Navy
Interim Awards,
    1920–1940

Miles, L. Wardlaw
US Army
World War I

Miles, Nelson A.
US Army
Civil War

Miller, Andrew
US Marine Corps
Civil War

*Miller, Andrew
US Army
World War II

Miller, Archie
US Army
Philippine Insurrection

Miller, Daniel H.
US Army
Indian Campaigns

Miller, Frank
US Army
Civil War

Miller, Franklin D.
US Army
Vietnam War

*Miller, Gary L.
US Army
Vietnam War

Miller, George
US Army
Indian Campaigns

Miller, George W.
US Army
Indian Campaigns

Miller, Henry A.
US Army
Civil War

Miller, Harry Herbert
US Navy
Spanish-American War

Miller, Hugh
US Navy
Interim Awards,
    1871–1898

Miller, Jacob C.
US Army
Civil War

Miller, James
US Navy
Civil War

Miller, James P.
US Army
Civil War

Miller, John
US Army
Civil War

Miller, John
US Army
Civil War

***Miller, Oscar F.**
US Army
World War I

***Miller, Robert J.**
US Army
Afghanistan

Miller, Willard
US Navy
Spanish-American War

Miller, William E.
US Army
Civil War

Millett, Lewis L.
US Army
Korean War

Milliken, Daniel
US Navy
Civil War

Millmore, John
US Navy
Interim Awards,
   1871–1898

Mills, Albert L.
US Army
Spanish-American War

Mills, Charles
US Navy
Civil War

Mills, Frank W.
US Army
Civil War

Mills, James H.
US Army
World War II

Mindil, George W.
US Army
Civil War

***Minick, John W.**
US Army
World War II

***Minue, Nicholas**
US Army
World War II

**Mitchell,
Alexander H.**
US Army
Civil War

***Mitchell, Frank N.**
US Marine Corps
Korean War

Mitchell, John
US Army
Indian Campaigns

Mitchell, John J.
US Army
Indian Campaigns

Mitchell, Joseph
US Navy
China Relief
   Expedition

Mitchell, Theodore
US Army
Civil War

Mitchell, Thomas
US Navy
Interim Awards,
   1871–1898

***Mitchell, William**
US Army
Special Act of Congress,
   1946

Miyamura, Hiroshi H.
US Army
Korean War

Mize, Ola L.
US Army
Korean War

Modrzejewski, Robert J.
US Marine Corps
Vietnam War

Moffett, William A.
US Navy
Mexican Campaign
   (Veracruz)

Moffitt, John H.
US Army
Civil War

Molbone, Archibald
US Army
Civil War

Molloy, Hugh
US Navy
Civil War

***Molnar, Frankie Zoly**
US Army
Vietnam War

Monaghan, Patrick
US Army
Civil War

*Monegan, Walter C., Jr.
US Marine Corps
Korean War

*Monroe, James H.
US Army
Vietnam War

Monssen, Mons
US Navy
Interim Awards,
    1901–1911

*Monsoor, Michael A.
US Navy
Iraq

Montague, Daniel
US Navy
Spanish-American War

***Monteith,
Jimmie W., Jr.**
US Army
World War II

Montgomery, Jack C.
US Army
World War II

Montgomery, Robert
US Navy
Civil War

*Monti, Jared C.
US Army
Afghanistan

Montrose, Charles H.
US Army
Indian Campaigns

*Moon, Harold H., Jr.
US Army
World War II

Moore, Albert
US Marine Corps
China Relief Expedition

Moore, Charles
US Navy
Civil War

Moore, Charles
US Navy
Civil War

Moore, Daniel B.
US Army
Civil War

Moore, Francis
US Navy
Interim Awards,
    1871–1898

Moore, George
US Navy
Civil War

Moore, George G.
US Army
Civil War

Moore, Philip
US Navy
Interim Awards,
    1871–1898

Moore, Wilbur F.
US Army
Civil War

Moore, William
US Navy
Civil War

Moquin, George
US Army
Indian Campaigns

Moran, John
US Army
Indian Campaigns

Moran, John E.
US Army
Philippine Insurrection

*Moreland, Whitt L.
US Marine Corps
Korean War

Morelock, Sterling
US Army
World War I

Morey, Delano
US Army
Civil War

Morford, Jerome
US Army
Civil War

Morgan, George H.
US Army
Indian Campaigns

Morgan, James H.
US Navy
Civil War

Morgan, John C.
US Army Air Corps
World War II

Morgan, Lewis
US Army
Civil War

Morgan, Richard H.
US Army
Civil War

*Morgan, William D.
US Marine Corps
Vietnam War

Moriarity, John
US Army
Indian Campaigns

Morin, William H.
US Navy
Spanish-American War

Morrill, Walter G.
US Army
Civil War

Morris, Charles B.
US Army
Vietnam War

Morris, James L.
US Army
Indian Campaigns

Morris, John
US Marine Corps
Interim Awards,
   1871–1898

Morris, William
US Army
Civil War

Morris, William W.
US Army
Indian Campaigns

Morrison, Francis
US Army
Civil War

Morrison, John G.
US Navy
Civil War

Morse, Benjamin
US Army
Civil War

Morse, Charles E.
US Army
Civil War

Morse, William
US Navy
Interim Awards,
   1871–1898

Morton, Charles W.
US Navy
Civil War

Mosher, Louis C.
US Army
Philippine Insurrection

***Moskala, Edward J.**
US Army
World War II

Mostoller, John W.
US Army
Civil War

***Moto, Kaoru**
US Army
World War II

Mott, John
US Army
Indian Campaigns

***Mower, Charles E.**
US Army
World War II

***Moyer, Donald R.**
US Army
Korean War

Moylan, Myles
US Army
Indian Campaigns

Mulholland, St. Clair A.
US Army
Civil War

**Mullen, Patrick (First
Award)**
US Navy
Civil War

**Mullen, Patrick (Second
Award)**
US Navy
Civil War

Muller, Frederick
US Navy
Spanish-American War

***Muller, Joseph E.**
US Army
World War II

Mullin, Hugh P.
US Navy
Philippine Insurrection

Mundell, Walter L.
US Army
Civil War

***Munemori, Sadao S.**
US Army
World War II

***Munro, Douglas Albert**
US Coast Guard
World War II

Munsell, Harvey M.
US Army
Civil War

Munson, Alexander D.
US Army
Indian Campaigns

***Muranaga, Kiyoshi K.**
US Army
World War II

Murphy, Audie L.
US Army
World War II

Murphy, Charles J.
US Army
Civil War

Murphy, Daniel J.
US Army
Civil War

Murphy, Dennis J. F.
US Army
Civil War

Murphy, Edward
US Army
Indian Campaigns

Murphy, Edward F.
US Army
Indian Campaigns

***Murphy, Frederick C.**
US Army
World War II

Murphy, James T.
US Army
Civil War

Murphy, Jeremiah
US Army
Indian Campaigns

**Murphy, John
Alphonsus**
US Marine Corps
China Relief Expedition

Murphy, John Edward
US Navy
Spanish-American War

Murphy, John P.
US Army
Civil War

Murphy, Michael C.
US Army
Civil War

***Murphy, Michael P.**
US Navy
Afghanistan

Murphy, Patrick
US Navy
Civil War

Murphy, Philip
US Army
Indian Campaigns

Murphy, Raymond G.
US Marine Corps
Korean War

Murphy, Robinson B.
US Army
Civil War

Murphy, Thomas
US Army
Civil War

Murphy, Thomas
US Army
Indian Campaigns

Murphy, Thomas C.
US Army
Civil War

Murphy, Thomas J.
US Army
Civil War

Murray, Charles P., Jr.
US Army
World War II

***Murray, Robert C.**
US Army
Vietnam War

Murray, Thomas
US Army
Indian Campaigns

Murray, William H.
US Marine Corps
China Relief Expedition

Myers, Fred
US Army
Indian Campaigns

Myers, George S.
US Army
Civil War

Myers, Reginald R.
US Marine Corps
Korean War

Myers, William H.
US Army
Civil War

N

***Nakae, Masato**
US Army
World War II

***Nakamine, Shinyei**
US Army
World War II

***Nakamura,
William K.**
US Army
World War II

Nannasaddie
US Army
Indian Campaigns

Nantaje (Nantahe)
US Army
Indian Campaigns

***Nash, David P.**
US Army
Vietnam War

Nash, Henry H.
US Army
Civil War

Nash, James J.
US Army
Spanish-American War

Naylor, David
US Navy
Civil War

Neahr, Zachariah C.
US Army
Civil War

Neal, Solon D.
US Army
Indian Campaigns

Neder, Adam
US Army
Indian Campaigns

Nee, George H.
US Army
Spanish-American War

Neibaur, Thomas C.
US Army
World War I

Neil, John
US Navy
Civil War

Neilon, Frederick S.
US Army
Indian Campaigns

Nelson, Lauritz
US Navy
Spanish-American War

Nelson, Oscar F.
US Navy
Interim Awards,
    1901–1911

***Nelson, William L.**
US Army
World War II

Neppel, Ralph G.
US Army
World War II

Nett, Robert P.
US Army
World War II

Neville, Edwin M.
US Army
Civil War

Neville, Wendell Cushing
US Marine Corps
Mexican Campaign
    (Veracruz)

***New, John Drury.**
US Marine Corps
World War II

Newland, William
US Navy
Civil War

***Newlin, Melvin Earl**
US Marine Corps
Vietnam War

Newman, Beryl R.
US Army
World War II

Newman, Henry
US Army
Indian Campaigns

Newman, Marcellus J.
US Army
Civil War

Newman, William H.
US Army
Civil War

Nibbe, John H.
US Navy
Civil War

Nichols, Henry C.
US Army
Civil War

Nichols, William
US Navy
Civil War

Nickerson, Henry Nehemiah
US Navy
Mexican Campaign
    (Veracruz)

Nihill, John
US Army
Indian Campaigns

***Nininger, Alexander R., Jr.**
US Army
World War II

***Nishimoto, Joe M.**
US Army
World War II

Nisperos, Jose B.
US Army
Philippines 1911

Niven, Robert
US Army
Civil War

Noble, Daniel
US Navy
Civil War

Noil, Joseph B.
US Navy
Interim Awards,
 1871–1898

Nolan, John J.
US Army
Civil War

Nolan, Joseph A.
US Army
Philippine Insurrection

Nolan, Richard J.
US Army
Indian Campaigns

Noll, Conrad
US Army
Civil War

***Noonan,
Thomas P., Jr.**
US Marine Corps
Vietnam War

**Nordsiek, Charles
Luers**
US Navy
Mexican Campaign
 (Veracruz)

Nordstrom, Isidor
US Navy
Interim Awards,
 1901–1911

Norris, J. W.
US Navy
Interim Awards,
 1871–1898

Norris, Thomas R.
US Navy
Vietnam War

North, Jasper N.
US Army
Civil War

Norton, Elliott M.
US Army
Civil War

Norton, John R.
US Army
Civil War

Norton, Llewellyn P.
US Army
Civil War

Novosel, Michael J.
US Army
Vietnam War

Noyes, William W.
US Army
Civil War

Nugent, Christopher
US Marine Corps
Civil War

Nutting, Lee
US Army
Civil War

O

Oakley, William
US Navy
Spanish-American War

O'Beirne, James R.
US Army
Civil War

***Obregon, Eugene
Arnold**
US Marine Corps
Korean War

O'Brien, George H., Jr.
US Marine Corps
Korean War

O'Brien, Henry D.
US Army
Civil War

O'Brien, Oliver
US Navy
Civil War

O'Brien, Peter
US Army
Civil War

*O'Brien, William J.
US Army
World War II

O'Callaghan, John
US Army
Indian Campaigns

**O'Callahan, Joseph
Timothy**
US Navy
World War II

O'Connell, Thomas
US Navy
Civil War

O'Conner, James F.
US Navy
Interim Awards,
 1871–1898

O'Connor, Albert
US Army
Civil War

O'Connor, Timothy
US Army
Civil War

O'Dea, John
US Army
Civil War

O'Donnell, Menomen
US Army
Civil War

O'Donoghue, Timothy
US Navy
Civil War

Ogden, Carlos C.
US Army
World War II

O'Hare, Edward Henry
US Navy
World War II

*Ohata, Allan M.
US Army
World War II

Ohmsen, August
US Navy
Interim Awards,
    1871–1898

**O'Kane, Richard
Hetherington**
US Navy
World War II

*Okubo, James K.
US Army
World War II

Okutsu, Yukio
US Army
World War II

*Olive, Milton L., III
US Army
Vietnam War

Oliver, Charles
US Army
Civil War

Oliver, Francis
US Army
Indian Campaigns

Oliver, Paul A.
US Army
Civil War

Olsen, Anton
US Navy
Spanish-American War

*Olson, Arlo L.
US Army
World War II

*Olson, Kenneth L.
US Army
Vietnam War

*Olson, Truman O.
US Army
World War II

O'Malley, Robert E.
US Marine Corps
Vietnam War

O'Neal, John
US Navy
Interim Awards,
    1871–1898

O'Neill, Richard W.
US Army
World War I

O'Neill, Stephen
US Army
Civil War

O'Neill, William
US Army
Indian Campaigns

*Ono, Frank H.
US Army
World War II

Opel, John N.
US Army
Civil War

Orbansky, David
US Army
Civil War

O'Regan, Michael
US Army
Indian Campaigns

Oresko, Nicholas
US Army
World War II

**Ormsbee, Francis
Edward, Jr.**
US Navy
World War I

**Orndoff, Henry
Westley**
US Marine Corps
China Relief Expedition

Orr, Charles A.
US Army
Civil War

Orr, Moses
US Army
Indian Campaigns

Orr, Robert L.
US Army
Civil War

Ortega, John
US Navy
Civil War

Orth, Jabob G.
US Army
Civil War

Osborne, John
US Navy
Interim Awards,
    1871–1898

***Osborne, Weedon E.**
US Navy
World War I

Osborne, William
US Army
Indian Campaigns

Osborne, William H.
US Army
Civil War

Osepins, Christian
US Navy
Interim Awards,
    1871–1898

***O'Shea, Thomas E.**
US Army
World War I

Oss, Albert
US Army
Civil War

Ostermann, Edward Albert
US Marine Corps
Haiti 1915

O'Sullivan, John
US Army
Indian Campaigns

***Otani, Kazuo**
US Army
World War II

***Ouellet, David G.**
US Navy
Vietnam War

***Ouellette, Joseph R.**
US Army
Korean War

Overturf, Jacob H.
US Army
Civil War

Oviatt, Miles M.
US Marine Corps
Civil War

Owens, Michael
US Marine Corps
1871 Korean Campaign

***Owens, Robert Allen**
US Marine Corps
World War II

***Ozbourn, Joseph William**
US Marine Corps
World War II

P

Packard, Loron F.
US Army
Civil War

***Page, John U. D.**
US Army
Korean War

Paige, Mitchell
US Marine Corps
World War II

Paine, Adam
US Army
Indian Campaigns

Palmer, George H.
US Army
Civil War

Palmer, John G.
US Army
Civil War

Palmer, William J.
US Army
Civil War

Parker, Alexander
US Navy
Interim Awards,
    1871–1898

Parker, James
US Army
Philippine Insurrection

Parker, Pomeroy
US Marine Corps
Spanish-American War

Parker, Samuel I.
US Army
World War I

Parker, Thomas
US Army
Civil War

Parker, William
US Navy
Civil War

Parks, George
US Navy
Civil War

Parks, Henry Jeremiah
US Army
Civil War

Parks, James W.
US Army
Civil War

*Parle, John Joseph
US Navy
World War II

Parnell, William R.
US Army
Indian Campaigns

*Parrish, Laverne
US Army
World War II

Parrott, Jacob
US Army
Civil War

Parsons, Joel
US Army
Civil War

Patterson, John H.
US Army
Civil War

Patterson, John T.
US Army
Civil War

Patterson, Robert Martin
US Army
Vietnam War

*Paul, Joe C.
US Marine Corps
Vietnam War

Paul, William H.
US Army
Civil War

Pay, Byron E.
US Army
Civil War

Payne, Irvin C.
US Army
Civil War

Payne, Isaac
US Army
Indian Campaigns

Payne, Thomas H. L.
US Army
Civil War

Pearsall, Platt
US Army
Civil War

Pearson, Alfred L.
US Army
Civil War

*Pease, Harl, Jr.
US Army Air Corps
World War II

Pease, Joachim
US Navy
Civil War

Peck, Archie A.
US Army
World War I

Peck, Cassius
US Army
Civil War

Peck, Oscar E.
US Navy
Civil War

Peck, Theodore S.
US Army
Civil War

*Peden, Forrest E.
US Army
World War II

Peirsol, James K.
US Army
Civil War

Pelham, William
US Navy
Civil War

*Pendleton, Charles F.
US Army
Korean War

*Pendleton, Jack J.
US Army
World War II

Pengally, Edward
US Army
Indian Campaigns

Penn, Robert
US Navy
Spanish-American War

Pennsyl, Josiah
US Army
Indian Campaigns

Pennypacker, Galusha
US Army
Civil War

Penry, Richard A.
US Army
Vietnam War

Pentzer, Patrick H.
US Army
Civil War

*Peregory, Frank D.
US Army
World War II

*Perez, Manuel, Jr.
US Army
World War II

*Perkins, Michael J.
US Army
World War I

*Perkins, William Thomas, Jr.
US Marine Corps
Vietnam War

Perry, Thomas
US Navy
Civil War

Pesch, Joseph
US Army
Civil War

Peters, Alexander
US Navy
Interim Awards,
    1901–1911

*Peters, George J.
US Army
World War II

Peters, Henry C.
US Army
Civil War

*Peters, Lawrence David
US Marine Corps
Vietnam War

Petersen, Carl Emil
US Navy
China Relief Expedition

*Petersen, Danny J.
US Army
Vietnam War

Peterson, Alfred
US Navy
Civil War

*Peterson, George
US Army
World War II

*Peterson, Oscar Verner
US Navy
World War II

*Petrarca, Frank J.
US Army
World War II

Petty, Orlando Henderson
US Navy
World War I

Petty, Philip
US Army
Civil War

Pfeifer, Louis Fred
US Marine Corps
Interim Awards,
    1901–1911

Pfisterer, Herman
US Army
Spanish-American War

Pharris, Jackson Charles
US Navy
World War II

Phelps, Charles E.
US Army
Civil War

*Phelps, Wesley
US Marine Corps
World War II

Phife, Lewis
US Army
Indian Campaigns

Philipsen, Wilhelm O.
US Army
Indian Campaigns

*Phillips, George
US Marine Corps
World War II

Phillips, George F.
US Navy
Spanish-American War

Phillips, Josiah
US Army
Civil War

*Phillips, Lee H.
US Marine Corps
Korean War

Phillips, Reuben Jasper
US Marine Corps
China Relief Expedition

Phillips, Samuel D.
US Army
Indian Campaigns

Phinney, William
US Navy
Civil War

*Phipps, Jimmy W.
US Marine Corps
Vietnam War

Phisterer, Frederick
US Army
Civil War

Phoenix, Edwin
US Army
Indian Campaigns

Pickle, Alonzo H.
US Army
Civil War

Pierce, Charles H.
US Army
Philippine Insurrection

Pierce, Francis Junior
US Navy
World War II

*Pierce, Larry S.
US Army
Vietnam War

Pike, Edward M.
US Army
Civil War

*Pike, Emory J.
US Army
World War I

Pile, Richard
US Navy
Interim Awards,
    1871–1898

*Pililaau, Herbert K.
US Army
Korean War

*Pinder, John J., Jr.
US Army
World War II

Pingree, Samuel E.
US Army
Civil War

Pinkham, Charles H.
US Army
Civil War

Pinn, Robert
US Army
Civil War

Pipes, James
US Army
Civil War

Pitman, George J.
US Army
Civil War

*Pitsenbarger, William H.
US Air Force
Vietnam War

Pittinger, William H.
US Army
Civil War

Pittman, John A.
US Army
Korean War

Pittman, Richard A.
US Marine Corps
Vietnam War

*Pitts, Riley L.
US Army
Vietnam War

Plant, Henry E.
US Army
Civil War

Platt, George C.
US Army
Civil War

Platten, Frederick
US Army
Indian Campaigns

Pless, Stephen W.
US Marine Corps
Vietnam War

Plimley, William
US Army
Civil War

Plowman, George H.
US Army
Civil War

Plunkett, Thomas
US Army
Civil War

Polond, Alfred
US Army
Spanish-American War

*Pomeroy, Ralph E.
US Army
Korean War

Pond, George F.
US Army
Civil War

Pond, James B.
US Army
Civil War

Poole, William B.
US Navy
Civil War

Pope, Everett Parker
US Marine Corps
World War II

Pope, Thomas A.
US Army
World War I

Poppe, John A.
US Army
Indian Campaigns

*Port, William D.
US Army
Vietnam War

Porter, Ambrose
US Army
Civil War

Porter, David Dixon
US Marine Corps
Philippine Insurrection

*Porter, Donn F.
US Army
Korean War

Porter, Horace
US Army
Civil War

Porter, John R.
US Army
Civil War

Porter, Samuel
US Army
Indian Campaigns

Porter, William
US Army
Civil War

Post, Philip Sidney
US Army
Civil War

Postles, James Parke
US Army
Civil War

Potter, George W.
US Army
Civil War

Potter, Norman F.
US Army
Civil War

Powell, William H.
US Army
Civil War

Power, Albert
US Army
Civil War

*Power, John Vincent
US Marine Corps
World War II

*Powers, John James
US Navy
World War II

Powers, Leo J.
US Army
World War II

Powers, Thomas
US Army
Indian Campaigns

Powers, Wesley J.
US Army
Civil War

*Poxon, Robert Leslie
US Army
Vietnam War

*Poynter, James I.
US Marine Corps
Korean War

Prance, George
US Navy
Civil War

Pratt, James
US Army
Indian Campaigns

Prendergast, Thomas Francis
US Marine Corps
Philippine Insurrection

Prentice, Joseph R.
US Army
Civil War

Preston, Arthur Murphy
US Navy
World War II

Preston, Herbert Irving
US Marine Corps
China Relief Expedition

Preston, John
US Navy
Civil War

Preston, Noble D.
US Army
Civil War

Price, Edward
US Navy
Civil War

*Prom, William R.
US Marine Corps
Vietnam War

Province, George
US Navy
Civil War

*Pruden, Robert J.
US Army
Vietnam War

*Pruitt, John Henry (Army Medal)
US Marine Corps
World War I

***Pruitt, John Henry
(Navy Medal)**
US Marine Corps
World War I

*Prussman, Ernest W.
US Army
World War II

*Pucket, Donald D.
US Army Air Corps
World War II

Purcell, Hiram W.
US Army
Civil War

Purman, James J.
US Army
Civil War

Purvis, Hugh
US Marine Corps
1871 Korean Campaign

Putnam, Edgar P.
US Army
Civil War

Putnam, Winthrop D.
US Army
Civil War

Pym, James
US Army
Indian Campaigns

Pyne, George
US Navy
Civil War

Q

Quay, Matthew S.
US Army
Civil War

Quick, John Henry
US Marine Corps
Spanish-American War

Quick, Joseph
US Navy
Interim Awards,
   1901–1911

Quinlan, James
US Army
Civil War

Quinn, Alexander M.
US Army
Spanish-American War

Quinn, Peter H.
US Army
Philippine Insurrection

R

*Rabel, Laszlo
US Army
Vietnam War

Raerick, John
US Army
Indian Campaigns

Rafferty, Peter
US Army
Civil War

Ragnar, Theodore
US Army
Indian Campaigns

**Ramage, Lawson
Patterson**
US Navy
World War II

*Ramer, George H.
US Marine Corps
Korean War

Ramsbottom, Alfred
US Army
Civil War

Rand, Charles F.
US Army
Civil War

Rankin, William
US Army
Indian Campaigns

Rannahan, John
US Marine Corps
Civil War

Ranney, George E.
US Army
Civil War

Ranney, Myron H.
US Army
Civil War

Rascon, Alfred V.
US Army
Vietnam War

Ratcliff, Edward
US Army
Civil War

Raub, Jacob F.
US Army
Civil War

*Ray, Bernard J.
US Army
World War II

Ray, Charles W.
US Army
Philippine Insurrection

*Ray, David Robert
US Navy
Vietnam War

Ray, Ronald Eric
US Army
Vietnam War

Raymond, William H.
US Army
Civil War

Read, Charles
US Navy
Civil War

Read, Charles A.
US Navy
Civil War

Read, George E.
US Navy
Civil War

Read, Morton A.
US Army
Civil War

*Reasoner, Frank S.
US Marine Corps
Vietnam War

Rebmann, George F.
US Army
Civil War

*Red Cloud, Mitchell, Jr.
US Army
Korean War

Reddick, William H.
US Army
Civil War

Reed, Axel H.
US Army
Civil War

Reed, Charles W.
US Army
Civil War

Reed, George W.
US Army
Civil War

Reed, James C.
US Army
Indian Campaigns

Reed, William
US Army
Civil War

Reeder, Charles A.
US Army
Civil War

*Reem, Robert Dale
US Marine Corps
Korean War

*Reese, James W.
US Army
World War II

*Reese, John N., Jr.
US Army
World War II

*Reeves, Thomas James
US Navy
World War II

Regan, Jeremiah
US Navy
Civil War

Regan, Patrick
US Navy
Interim Awards,
1871–1898

Regan, Patrick
US Army
World War I

Reid, George Croghan
US Marine Corps
Mexican Campaign
(Veracruz)

Reid, Patrick
US Navy
Interim Awards,
1901–1911

Reid, Robert
US Army
Civil War

Reigle, Daniel P.
US Army
Civil War

Reisinger, J. Monroe
US Army
Civil War

Renninger, Louis
US Army
Civil War

Ressler, Norman W.
US Army
Spanish-American War

Reynolds, George
US Army
Civil War

Rhodes, Julius D.
US Army
Civil War

Rhodes, Sylvester D.
US Army
Civil War

Rice, Charles
US Navy
Civil War

Rice, Edmund
US Army
Civil War

Rich, Carlos H.
US Army
Civil War

Richards, Louis
US Navy
Civil War

Richardson, William R.
US Army
Civil War

Richey, William E.
US Army
Civil War

Richman, Samuel
US Army
Indian Campaigns

Richmond, James
US Army
Civil War

Rickenbacker, Edward V.
US Army Air Service
World War I

*Ricketts, Milton Ernest
US Navy
World War II

Ricksecker, John H.
US Army
Civil War

Riddell, Rudolph
US Army
Civil War

Riley, Thomas
US Army
Civil War

Rilley, John Phillip
US Navy
Spanish-American War

Ringold, Edward
US Navy
Civil War

*Riordan, Paul F.
US Army
World War II

Ripley, William Y. W.
US Army
Civil War

*Rivers, Ruben
US Army
World War II

Roach, Hampton M.
US Army
Indian Campaigns

*Roan, Charles Howard
US Marine Corps
World War II

Roantree, James S.
US Marine Corps
Civil War

*Roark, Anund C.
US Army
Vietnam War

Robb, George S.
US Army
World War I

Robbins, Augustus J.
US Army
Civil War

Robbins, Marcus M.
US Army
Indian Campaigns

Roberts, Charles Church
US Navy
Interim Awards, 1901–1911

Roberts, Charles D.
US Army
Spanish-American War

Roberts, Gordon R.
US Army
Vietnam War

*Roberts, Harold W.
US Army
World War I

Roberts, James
US Navy
Civil War

Roberts, Otis O.
US Army
Civil War

Robertson, Marcus W.
US Army
Philippine Insurrection

Robertson, Robert S.
US Army
Civil War

Robertson, Samuel
US Army
Civil War

Robie, George F.
US Army
Civil War

Robinson, Alexander
US Navy
Civil War

Robinson, Charles
US Navy
Civil War

Robinson, Elbridge
US Army
Civil War

***Robinson,
James E., Jr.**
US Army
World War II

Robinson, James H.
US Army
Civil War

***Robinson,
James W., Jr.**
US Army
Vietnam War

Robinson, John
US Navy
Interim Awards,
   1866–1870

Robinson, John C.
US Army
Civil War

Robinson, John H.
US Army
Civil War

Robinson, Joseph
US Army
Indian Campaigns

Robinson, Robert Guy
US Marine Corps
World War I

Robinson, Thomas
US Army
Civil War

Robinson, Thomas
US Navy
Interim Awards,
   1866–1870

Rocco, Louis R.
US Army
Vietnam War

Roche, David
US Army
Indian Campaigns

Rock, Frederick
US Army
Civil War

Rockefeller, Charles M.
US Army
Civil War

**Rodenbough,
Theophilus F.**
US Army
Civil War

Rodenburg, Henry
US Army
Indian Campaigns

Rodriguez, Cleto
US Army
World War II

Rodriguez, Joseph C.
US Army
Korean War

*Roeder, Robert E.
US Army
World War II

Rogan, Patrick
US Army
Indian Campaigns

Rogers, Charles Calvin
US Army
Vietnam War

Rogers, Samuel F.
US Navy
1871 Korean Campaign

Rohm, Ferdinand F.
US Army
Civil War

Romeyn, Henry
US Army
Indian Campaigns

Rood, Oliver P.
US Army
Civil War

*Rooks, Albert Harold
US Navy
World War II

Rooney, Edward
US Army
Indian Campaigns

Roosevelt, George W.
US Army
Civil War

Roosevelt, Theodore
US Army
Spanish-American War

*Roosevelt, Theodore, Jr.
US Army
World War II

Rose, George
US Navy
China Relief Expedition

Ross, Donald Kirby
US Navy
World War II

Ross, Frank F.
US Army
Philippine Insurrection

Ross, Marion A.
US Army
Civil War

Ross, Wilburn K.
US Army
World War II

Rossbach, Valentine
US Army
Civil War

Rosser, Ronald E.
US Army
Korean War

Roth, Peter
US Army
Indian Campaigns

Rought, Stephen
US Army
Civil War

Rouh, Carlton Robert
US Marine Corps
World War II

Rounds, Lewis A.
US Army
Civil War

Rouning, Johannes
US Navy
Interim Awards,
    1871–1898

Rountry, John
US Navy
Civil War

Roush, J. Levi
US Army
Civil War

Rowalt, John F.
US Army
Indian Campaigns

**Rowand,
Archibald H., Jr.**
US Army
Civil War

Rowdy
US Army
Indian Campaigns

Rowe, Henry W.
US Army
Civil War

Roy, Stanislaus
US Army
Indian Campaigns

Rubin, Tibor
US Army
Korean War

*Rubio, Euripides
US Army
Vietnam War

*Rud, George William
US Navy
Interim Awards,
    1915–1916

Rudolph, Donald E.
US Army
World War II

*Ruhl, Donald Jack
US Marine Corps
World War II

**Ruiz, Alejandro R.
Renteria**
US Army
World War II

Rundle, Charles W.
US Army
Civil War

Rush, John
US Navy
Civil War

Rush, William Rees
US Navy
Mexican Campaign
    (Veracruz)

Russell, Charles L.
US Army
Civil War

Russell, Henry P.
US Navy
Spanish-American War

Russell, James
US Army
Indian Campaigns

Russell, John
US Navy
Interim Awards,
    1871–1898

Russell, Milton
US Army
Civil War

Rutherford, John T.
US Army
Civil War

Rutter, James M.
US Army
Civil War

Ryan, David
US Army
Indian Campaigns

Ryan, Dennis
US Army
Indian Campaigns

Ryan, Francis T.
US Navy
China Relief Expedition

Ryan, Peter J.
US Army
Civil War

Ryan, Richard
US Navy
Interim Awards,
    1871–1898

Ryan, Thomas John
US Navy
Interim Awards,
    1920–1940

S

Sacriste, Louis J.
US Army
Civil War

Sadler, William
US Navy
Interim Awards,
    1871–1898

*Sadowski, Joseph J.
US Army
World War II

Sage, William H.
US Army
Philippine Insurrection

Sagelhurst, John C.
US Army
Civil War

Sakato, George T.
US Army
World War II

Sale, Albert
US Army
Indian Campaigns

*Salomon, Ben L.
US Army
World War II

Sampler, Samuel M.
US Army
World War I

Sancrainte, Charles F.
US Army
Civil War

Sanderson, Aaron
US Navy
Civil War

Sandlin, Willie
US Army
World War I

Sands, William
US Army
Civil War

Sanford, Jacob
US Army
Civil War

***Santiago-Colon,
Hector**
US Army
Vietnam War

Sapp, Isaac
US Navy
Interim Awards,
    1871–1898

Sargent, Jackson
US Army
Civil War

*Sargent, Ruppert L.
US Army
Vietnam War

*Sarnoski, Joseph R.
US Army Air Corps
World War II

Sartwell, Henry
US Army
Civil War

Sasser, Clarence Eugene
US Army
Vietnam War

Saunders, James
US Navy
Civil War

*Savacool, Edwin F.
US Army
Civil War

Savage, Auzella
US Navy
Civil War

*Sawelson, William
US Army
World War I

Saxton, Rufus
US Army
Civil War

*Sayers, Foster J.
US Army
World War II

Scanlan, Patrick
US Army
Civil War

Scannell, David John
US Marine Corps
China Relief Expedition

Schaefer, Joseph E.
US Army
World War II

Schaffner, Dwite H.
US Army
World War I

Schauer, Henry
US Army
World War II

Scheibner, Martin E.
US Army
Civil War

Schenck, Benjamin W.
US Army
Civil War

Schepke, Charles S.
US Navy
Interim Awards,
    1901–1911

Schiller, John
US Army
Civil War

Schilt, Christian Franck
US Marine Corps
Second Nicaraguan
    Campaign

Schlachter, Philipp
US Army
Civil War

Schmal, George W.
US Army
Civil War

Schmauch, Andrew
US Army
Civil War

Schmidt, Conrad
US Army
Civil War

Schmidt, Oscar, Jr.
US Navy
World War I

Schmidt, Otto Diller
US Navy
Interim Awards,
    1901–1911

Schmidt, William
US Army
Civil War

Schneider, George
US Army
Civil War

Schnell, Christian
US Army
Civil War

Schnepel, Fred Jurgen
US Navy
Mexican Campaign
    (Veracruz)

Schnitzer, John
US Army
Indian Campaigns

Schofield, John M.
US Army
Civil War

**Schonland, Herbert
Emery**
US Navy
World War II

**Schoonmaker,
James M.**
US Army
Civil War

*Schoonover, Dan D.
US Army
Korean War

Schorn, Charles
US Army
Civil War

Schou, Julius
US Army
Indian Campaigns

**Schowalter,
Edward R., Jr.**
US Army
Korean War

Schroeder, Henry F.
US Army
Philippine Insurrection

Schroeter, Charles
US Army
Indian Campaigns

Schubert, Martin
US Army
Civil War

Schutt, George
US Navy
Civil War

*Schwab, Albert Ernest
US Marine Corps
World War II

Schwan, Theodore
US Army
Civil War

**Schwenk, Martin
(Martin, George)**
US Army
Civil War

Scofield, David H.
US Army
Civil War

Scott, Alexander
US Army
Civil War

Scott, George D.
US Army
Indian Campaigns

Scott, John M.
US Army
Civil War

Scott, John Wallace
US Army
Civil War

Scott, Joseph Francis
US Marine Corps
Spanish-American War

Scott, Julian A.
US Army
Civil War

*Scott, Norman
US Navy
World War II

Scott, Robert B
US Army
Indian Campaigns

*Scott, Robert R.
US Navy
World War II

Scott, Robert S.
US Army
World War II

Seach, William
US Navy
China Relief Expedition

Seaman, Elisha B.
US Army
Civil War

Seanor, James
US Navy
Civil War

Sears, Cyrus
US Army
Civil War

Seaver, Thomas O.
US Army
Civil War

*Seay, William W.
US Army
Vietnam War

*Sebille, Louis J.
US Air Force
Korean War

Seibert, Lloyd M.
US Army
World War I

Seitzinger, James M.
US Army
Civil War

Sellers, Alfred J.
US Army
Civil War

Semple, Robert
US Navy
Mexican Campaign
   (Veracruz)

*Seston, Charles H.
US Army
Civil War

Seward, Griffin
US Army
Indian Campaigns

Seward, Richard E.
US Navy
Civil War

Sewell, William J.
US Army
Civil War

**Shacklette, William
Sidney**
US Navy
Interim Awards,
   1901–1911

Shaffer, William
US Army
Indian Campaigns

Shafter, William R.
US Army
Civil War

Shahan, Emisire
US Army
Civil War

Shaler, Alexander
US Army
Civil War

Shambaugh, Charles
US Army
Civil War

Shanahan, Patrick
US Navy
Philippine Insurrection

Shanes, John
US Army
Civil War

Shapland, John
US Army
Civil War

Sharp, Hendrick
US Navy
Civil War

Sharpless, Edward C.
US Army
Indian Campaigns

Shaw, George C.
US Army
Philippine Insurrection

Shaw, Thomas
US Army
Indian Campaigns

Shea, Charles W.
US Army
World War II

*Shea, Daniel John
US Army
Vietnam War

Shea, Joseph H.
US Army
Civil War

*Shea, Richard T., Jr.
US Army
Korean War

Sheerin, John
US Army
Indian Campaigns

Shellenberger, John S.
US Army
Civil War

Shelton, George M.
US Army
Philippine Insurrection

Shepard, Irwin
US Army
Civil War

Shepard, Louis C.
US Navy
Civil War

Shepherd, Warren J.
US Army
Spanish-American War

Shepherd, William
US Army
Civil War

Sheppard, Charles
US Army
Indian Campaigns

*Sheridan, Carl V.
US Army
World War II

Sheridan, James
US Navy
Civil War

Sherman, Marshall
US Army
Civil War

Shiel (Shields), John
US Army
Civil War

Shields, Bernard
US Army
Civil War

*Shields, Marvin G.
US Navy
Vietnam War

Shiels, George F.
US Army
Philippine Insurrection

Shilling, John
US Army
Civil War

Shingle, John H.
US Army
Indian Campaigns

Shipley, Robert F.
US Army
Civil War

Shipman, William
US Navy
Civil War

Shivers, John
US Marine Corps
Civil War

*Shockley, William R.
US Army
World War II

Shoemaker, Levi
US Army
Civil War

Shomo, William A.
US Army Air Corps
World War II

Shopp, George J.
US Army
Civil War

*Shoup, Curtis F.
US Army
World War II

Shoup, David Monroe
US Marine Corps
World War II

Shubert, Frank
US Army
Civil War

*Shuck, William E., Jr.
US Marine Corps
Korean War

*Shughart, Randall D.
US Army
Somalia

Shutes, Henry
US Navy
Civil War

Sickles, Daniel E.
US Army
Civil War

Sickles, William H.
US Army
Civil War

Sidman, George E.
US Army
Civil War

Siegel, John Otto
US Navy
World War I

Sigler, Franklin Earl
US Marine Corps
World War II

*Sijan, Lance P.
US Air Force
Vietnam War

Silk, Edward A.
US Army
World War II

Silva, France
US Marine Corps
China Relief Expedition

Simanek, Robert E.
US Marine Corps
Korean War

Simkins, Lebbeus
US Navy
Civil War

Simmons, John
US Army
Civil War

Simmons, William T.
US Army
Civil War

Simonds, William E.
US Army
Civil War

Simons, Charles J.
US Army
Civil War

Simpson, Henry
US Navy
Interim Awards,
    1871–1898

*Sims, Clifford C.
US Army
Vietnam War

Singleton, Frank
(see **Frederick S.
Neilon**)

*Singleton, Walter K.
US Marine Corps
Vietnam War

Sinnett, Lawrence C.
US Navy
Mexican Campaign
    (Veracruz)

*Sisler, George K.
US Army
Vietnam War

*Sitman, William S.
US Army
Korean War

Sitter, Carl L.
US Marine Corps
Korean War

**Sivel, Henry
(see William H.
Mathews, true name)**

Sjogren, John C.
US Army
World War II

Skaggs, Luther, Jr.
US Marine Corps
World War II

Skellie, Ebenezer
US Army
Civil War

***Skidgel, Donald
Sidney**
US Army
Vietnam War

*Skinker, Alexander R.
US Army
World War I

Skinner, John O.
US Army
Indian Campaigns

***Skinner,
Sherrod E., Jr.**
US Marine Corps
Korean War

Slack, Clayton K.
US Army
World War I

Sladen, Joseph A.
US Army
Civil War

Slagle, Oscar
US Army
Civil War

Slaton, James D.
US Army
World War II

Slavens, Samuel
US Army
Civil War

Sletteland, Thomas
US Army
Philippine Insurrection

Sloan, Andrew J.
US Army
Civil War

Slusher, Henry C.
US Army
Civil War

Smalley, Reuben
US Army
Civil War

Smalley, Reuben S.
US Army
Civil War

*Smedley, Larry E.
US Marine Corps
Vietnam War

Smith, Albert Joseph
US Marine Corps
Interim Awards,
  1920–1940

Smith, Alonzo
US Army
Civil War

Smith, Andrew Jackson
US Army
Civil War

Smith, Andrew J.
US Army
Indian Campaigns

Smith, Charles E.
US Army
Indian Campaigns

*Smith, Charles H.
US Navy
Civil War

Smith, Charles H.
US Army
Civil War

Smith, Cornelius C.
US Army
Indian Campaigns

Smith, David L.
US Army
Civil War

*Smith, David M.
US Army
Korean War

Smith, Edwin
US Navy
Civil War

*Smith, Elmelindo R.
US Army
Vietnam War

Smith, Eugene P.
US Navy
Interim Awards,
  1915—1916

Smith, Francis M.
US Army
Civil War

Smith, Frank E.
US Navy
China Relief Expedition

*Smith, Fred E.
US Army
World War I

*Smith, Furman L.
US Army
World War II

*Smith, George W.
US Army
Indian Campaigns

Smith, Henry I.
US Army
Civil War

Smith, James (Ovid)
US Army
Civil War

Smith, James
US Navy
Civil War

Smith, James
US Navy
Interim Awards,
  1871–1898

Smith, James
US Navy
China Relief Expedition

Smith, John
US Navy
Civil War

Smith, John
US Navy
Civil War

Smith, John
US Navy
Interim Awards,
  1871–1898

Smith, John Lucian
US Marine Corps
World War II

Smith, Joseph S.
US Army
Civil War

Smith, Maynard H.
US Army Air Corps
World War II

Smith, Oloff
US Navy
Civil War

Smith, Otis W.
US Army
Civil War

Smith, Otto
US Army
Indian Campaigns

*Smith, Paul R.
US Army
Iraq

Smith, Richard
US Army
Civil War

Smith, Robert
US Army
Indian Campaigns

Smith, S. Rodmond
US Army
Civil War

Smith, Thaddeus S.
US Army
Civil War

Smith, Theodore F.
US Army
Indian Campaigns

Smith, Thomas
US Navy
Civil War

Smith, Thomas
US Army
Indian Campaigns

Smith, Thomas
US Navy
Interim Awards,
  1871–1898

Smith, Thomas J.
US Army
Indian Campaigns

Smith, Walter B.
US Navy
Civil War

Smith, Wilhelm
US Navy
Interim Awards,
  1915–1916

Smith, Willard M.
US Marine Corps
Civil War

Smith, William
US Navy
Civil War

Smith, William
US Army
Indian Campaigns

Smith, William H.
US Army
Indian Campaigns

Smith, Wilson
US Army
Civil War

Snedden, James
US Army
Civil War

Snow, Elmer A.
US Army
Indian Campaigns

Snyder, William E.
US Navy
Interim Awards,
  1901–1911

Soderman, William A.
US Army
World War II

Sorenson, Richard Keith
US Marine Corps
World War II

Southard, David
US Army
Civil War

Sova, Joseph E.
US Army
Civil War

Sowers, Michael
US Army
Civil War

Spalding, Edward B.
US Army
Civil War

*Specker, Joe C.
US Army
World War II

*Speicher, Clifton T.
US Army
Korean War

Spence, Orizoba
US Army
Indian Campaigns

Sperry, William J.
US Army
Civil War

Spicer, William
US Navy
Spanish-American War

Spillane, Timothy
US Army
Civil War

Sprague, Benona
US Army
Civil War

Sprague, John W.
US Army
Civil War

Sprayberry, James M.
US Army
Vietnam War

Springer, George
US Army
Indian Campaigns

Sprowle, David
US Marine Corps
Civil War

Spurling, Andrew B.
US Army
Civil War

Spurrier, Junior J.
US Army
World War II

*Squires, John C.
US Army
World War II

Stacey, Charles
US Army
Civil War

Stacy, William B.
US Navy
Interim Awards,
    1866–1870

Stahel, Julius
US Army
Civil War

Stance, Emanuel
US Army
Indian Campaigns

Stanley, David S.
US Army
Civil War

Stanley, Eben
US Army
Indian Campaigns

Stanley, Edward
US Army
Indian Campaigns

Stanley, Robert Henry
US Navy
China Relief Expedition

Stanley, William A.
US Navy
Civil War

Stanton, Thomas
US Navy
Interim Awards,
    1901–1911

Starkins, John H.
US Army
Civil War

Staton, Adolphus
US Navy
Mexican Campaign
    (Veracruz)

Stauffer, Rudolph
US Army
Indian Campaigns

Steele, John W.
US Army
Civil War

*Stein, Tony
US Marine Corps
World War II

*Steindam, Russell A.
US Army
Vietnam War

Steiner, Christian
US Army
Indian Campaigns

Steinmetz, William
US Army
Civil War

Stephens, William G.
US Army
Civil War

Sterling, James E.
US Navy
Civil War

Sterling, John T.
US Army
Civil War

Stevens, Daniel D.
US Navy
Civil War

Stevens, Hazard
US Army
Civil War

Stewart, Benjamin F.
US Army
Indian Campaigns

Stewart, George E.
US Army
Philippine Insurrection

Stewart, George W.
US Army
Civil War

Stewart, James A.
US Marine Corps
Interim Awards,
    1871–1898

*Stewart, Jimmy G.
US Army
Vietnam War

Stewart, Joseph
US Army
Civil War

Stewart, Peter
US Marine Corps
China Relief Expedition

Stickels, Joseph
US Army
Civil War

**Stickney, Herman
Osman**
US Navy
Mexican Campaign
    (Veracruz)

Stickoffer, Julius H.
US Army
Indian Campaigns

Stivers, Thomas W.
US Army
Indian Campaigns

Stockdale, James B.
US Navy
Vietnam War

***Stockham, Fred W.
(Army Medal)**
US Marine Corps
World War I

Stockman, George H.
US Army
Civil War

Stoddard, James
US Navy
Civil War

Stokes, Alonzo
US Army
Indian Campaigns

Stokes, George
US Army
Civil War

Stokes, John
US Navy
Philippine Insurrection

Stoltenberg, Andrew V.
US Navy
Philippine Insurrection

Stolz, Frank
US Army
Civil War

Stone, James L.
US Army
Korean War

*Stone, Lester R., Jr.
US Army
Vietnam War

Storey, John H. R.
US Army
Civil War

*Story, Luther H.
US Army
Korean War

*Stout, Mitchell W.
US Army
Vietnam War

Stout, Richard
US Navy
Civil War

*Stowers, Freddie
US Army
World War I

Strahan, Robert
US Navy
Civil War

Straub, Paul F.
US Army
Philippine Insurrection

**Strausbaugh,
Bernard A.**
US Army
Civil War

Strayer, William H.
US Army
Indian Campaigns

Street, George Levick, III
US Navy
World War II

Streile, Christian
US Army
Civil War

Strivson, Benoni
US Army
Indian Campaigns

Strong, James N.
US Army
Civil War

***Stryker, Robert F.**
US Army
Vietnam War

***Stryker, Stuart S.**
US Army
World War II

Stumpf, Kenneth E.
US Army
Vietnam War

Stupka, Loddie
US Navy
Interim Awards,
   1901—1911

Sturgeon, James K.
US Army
Civil War

***Sudut, Jerome A.**
US Army
Korean War

Sullivan, Daniel Augustine Joseph
US Navy
World War I

Sullivan, Edward
US Marine Corps
Spanish-American War

Sullivan, James
US Navy
Civil War

Sullivan, James F.
US Navy
Interim Awards,
   1871–1898

Sullivan, John
US Navy
Civil War

Sullivan, Thomas
US Army
Indian Campaigns

Sullivan, Thomas
US Army
Indian Campaigns

Sullivan, Timothy
US Navy
Civil War

Summers, James C.
US Army
Civil War

Summers, Robert
US Navy
Civil War

Sumner, James
US Army
Indian Campaigns

Sundquist, Axel
US Navy
Spanish-American War

Sundquist, Gustav A.
US Navy
Spanish-American War

Surles, William H.
US Army
Civil War

Sutherland, John A.
US Army
Indian Campaigns

Sutton, Clarence Edwin
US Marine Corps
China Relief Expedition

Swan, Charles A.
US Army
Civil War

Swanson, John
US Navy
Civil War

***Swanson, Jon E.**
US Army
Vietnam War

Swap, Jacob E.
US Army
Civil War

Swatton, Edward
US Navy
Civil War

Swayne, Wager
US Army
Civil War

Swearer, Benjamin
US Navy
Civil War

Sweatt, Joseph S. G.
US Army
Civil War

Sweeney, James
US Army
Civil War

Sweeney, Robert (First Award)
US Navy
Interim Awards,
1871–1898

Sweeney, Robert (Second Award)
US Navy
Interim Awards,
1871–1898

Sweeney, William
US Navy
Interim Awards,
1871–1898

Swegheimer, Jacob
US Army
Civil War

Swett, James Elms
US Marine Corps
World War II

Swift, Frederic W.
US Army
Civil War

Swift, Harlan J.
US Army
Civil War

Sype, Peter
US Army
Civil War

T

Tabor, William L. S.
US Army
Civil War

Taggart, Charles A.
US Army
Civil War

*Talbot, Ralph
US Marine Corps
World War I

Talbott, William
US Navy
Civil War

*Tallentine, James
US Navy
Civil War

Talley, Edward R.
US Army
World War I

Tanner, Charles B.
US Army
Civil War

*Tanouye, Ted T.
US Army
World War II

Taylor, Anthony
US Army
Civil War

Taylor, Bernard
US Army
Indian Campaigns

Taylor, Charles
US Army
Indian Campaigns

Taylor, Forrester L.
US Army
Civil War

Taylor, George
US Navy
Civil War

Taylor, Henry H.
US Army
Civil War

Taylor, James Allen
US Army
Vietnam War

Taylor, John
US Navy
Civil War

Taylor, Joseph
US Army
Civil War

*Taylor, Karl G., Sr.
US Marine Corps
Vietnam War

Taylor, Richard
US Army
Civil War

Taylor, Richard H.
US Navy
Interim Awards,
1871–1898

Taylor, Thomas
US Navy
Civil War

Taylor, Wilbur N.
US Army
Indian Campaigns

Taylor, William
US Army
Civil War

Taylor, William G.
US Navy
Civil War

Tea, Richard L.
US Army
Indian Campaigns

Terry, John D.
US Army
Civil War

*Terry, Seymour W.
US Army
World War II

Teytand, August P.
US Navy
Interim Awards,
    1901–1911

Thacker, Brian Mills
US Army
Vietnam War

Thackrah, Benjamin
US Army
Civil War

Thatcher, Charles M.
US Army
Civil War

Thaxter, Sidney W.
US Army
Civil War

Thayer, James
US Navy
Interim Awards,
    1871–1898

Thielberg, Henry
US Navy
Civil War

Thomas, Charles L.
US Army
Indian Campaigns

*Thomas, Charles L.
US Army
World War II

Thomas, Hampton S.
US Army
Civil War

*Thomas, Herbert Joseph
US Marine Corps
World War II

Thomas, Karl
US Navy
China Relief Expedition

Thomas, Stephen
US Army
Civil War

*Thomas, William H.
US Army
World War II

*Thomason, Clyde
US Marine Corps
World War II

Thompkins, George W.
US Army
Civil War

Thompkins, William H.
US Army
Spanish-American War

Thompson, Allen
US Army
Civil War

Thompson, Charles A.
US Army
Civil War

Thompson, Freeman C.
US Army
Civil War

Thompson, George W.
US Army
Indian Campaigns

Thompson, Henry
US Navy
Interim Awards,
    1871–1898

Thompson, Henry A.
US Marine Corps
Civil War

Thompson, J. (James) Harry
US Army
Civil War

Thompson, James
US Army
Civil War

Thompson, James B.
US Army
Civil War

Thompson, John
US Army
Civil War

Thompson, John
US Army
Indian Campaigns

Thompson, Joseph H.
US Army
World War I

Thompson, Max
US Army
World War II

Thompson, Peter
US Army
Indian Campaigns

Thompson, Thomas
US Army
Civil War

Thompson, William
US Navy
Civil War

*Thompson, William
US Army
Korean War

Thompson, William P.
US Army
Civil War

Thomson, Clifford
US Army
Civil War

Thordsen, William George
US Navy
Philippine Insurrection

Thorn, Walter
US Army
Civil War

*Thorne, Horace M.
US Army
World War II

Thornton, Michael
US Navy
Interim Awards, 1871–1898

Thornton, Michael Edwin
US Navy
Vietnam War

Thorsness, Leo K.
US Air Force
Vietnam War

*Thorson, John F.
US Army
World War II

Tibbets, Andrew W.
US Army
Civil War

Tilton, Henry R.
US Army
Indian Campaigns

Tilton, William
US Army
Civil War

*Timmerman, Grant Frederick
US Marine Corps
World War II

Tinkham, Eugene M.
US Army
Civil War

Titus, Calvin Pearl
US Army
China Relief Expedition

Titus, Charles
US Army
Civil War

Toban, James W.
US Army
Civil War

Tobie, Edward P.
US Army
Civil War

Tobin, John M.
US Army
Civil War

Tobin, Paul
US Navy
Interim Awards, 1871–1898

Todd, Samuel
US Navy
Civil War

Toffey, John J.
US Army
Civil War

Tolan, Frank
US Army
Indian Campaigns

*Tomich, Peter
US Navy
World War II

Tominac, John J.
US Army
World War II

Tomlin, Andrew J.
US Marine Corps
Civil War

Tompkins, Aaron B.
US Army
Civil War

Tompkins, Charles H.
US Army
Civil War

Toohey, Thomas
US Army
Civil War

Toomer, William
US Army
Civil War

Torgerson, Martin T.
US Navy
China Relief Expedition

Torgler, Ernst
US Army
Civil War

***Towle, John R.**
US Army
World War II

Townsend, Julius Curtis
US Navy
Mexican Campaign
  (Veracruz)

Toy, Frederick E.
US Army
Indian Campaigns

Tozier, Andrew J.
US Army
Civil War

Tracy, Amasa A.
US Army
Civil War

Tracy, Benjamin F.
US Army
Civil War

Tracy, Charles H.
US Army
Civil War

Tracy, John
US Army
Indian Campaigns

Tracy, William G.
US Army
Civil War

Trautman, Jacob
US Army
Indian Campaigns

Traynor, Andrew
US Army
Civil War

**Treadwell,
Jack L.**
US Army
World War II

Treat, Howell B.
US Army
Civil War

Tremain, Henry E.
US Army
Civil War

Trembley, William B.
US Army
Philippine Insurrection

Tribe, John
US Army
Civil War

Trinidad, Telesforo
US Navy
Interim Awards,
  1915–1916

Triplett, Samuel
US Navy
Spanish-American
  War

Tripp, Othniel
US Navy
Civil War

Trogden, Howell G.
US Army
Civil War

Trout, James M.
US Navy
Interim Awards,
  1871–1898

Troy, Jeremiah
US Navy
Interim Awards,
  1871–1898

Troy, William
US Navy
1871 Korean Campaign

Truell, Edwin M.
US Army
Civil War

***Truemper,
Walter E.**
US Army Air Corps
World War II

**Truesdell,
Donald Leroy
(name officially
changed to Truesdale)**
US Marine Corps
Second Nicaraguan
  Campaign

Truett, Alexander H.
US Navy
Civil War

Tucker, Allen
US Army
Civil War

Tucker, Jacob R.
US Army
Civil War

***Turner, Charles W.**
US Army
Korean War

*Turner, Day G.
US Army
World War II

Turner, George B.
US Army
World War II

Turner, Harold L.
US Army
World War I

*Turner, William B.
US Army
World War I

Turpin, James H.
US Army
Indian Campaigns

Turvelin, Alexander H.
US Navy
Interim Awards,
    1871–1898

Tweedale, John
US Army
Civil War

Twombly, Voltaire P.
US Army
Civil War

Tyrell, George
William
US Army
Civil War

U

Uhrl, George
US Army
Civil War

Upham, Oscar J.
US Marine Corps
China Relief Expedition

Upshur, William
Peterkin
US Marine Corps
Haiti 1915

Upton, Frank Monroe
US Navy
World War I

Urban, Matt
US Army
World War II

Urell, M. Emmet
US Army
Civil War

V

Vadas, Albert
US Navy
Spanish-American War

*Valdez, Jose F.
US Army
World War II

Vale, John
US Army
Civil War

Valente, Michael
US Army
World War I

Van Etten, Hudson
US Navy
Spanish-American War

Van Iersel,
Ludovicus M. M.
US Army
World War I

Van Matre, Joseph
US Army
Civil War

*Van Noy, Junior
US Army
World War II

Van Schaick, Louis J.
US Army
Philippine Insurrection

*Van Valkenburgh,
Franklin
US Navy
World War II

*Van Voorhis, Bruce
Avery
US Navy
World War II

Van Winkle, Archie
US Marine Corps
Korean War

Van Wrinkle, Edward
US Army
Civil War

*Vance, Leon R., Jr.
US Army Air Corps
World War II

Vance, Wilson
US Army
Civil War

Vandegrift, Alexander
Archer
US Marine Corps
World War II

Vanderslice, John M.
US Army
Civil War

Vantine, Joseph E.
US Navy
Civil War

Vargas, Jay R.
US Marine Corps
Vietnam War

Varnum, Charles A.
US Army
Indian Campaigns

Vaughn, Pinkerton R.
US Marine Corps
Civil War

Veal, Charles
US Army
Civil War

Veale, Moses
US Army
Civil War

Veazey, Wheelock G.
US Army
Civil War

Vernay, James D.
US Army
Civil War

Verney, James W.
US Navy
Civil War

*Versace, Humbert R.
US Army
Vietnam War

Veuve, Ernest
US Army
Indian Campaigns

*Viale, Robert M.
US Army
World War II

Vifquain, Victor
US Army
Civil War

*Villegas, Ysmael R.
US Army
World War II

Villepigue, John C.
US Army
World War I

*Vittori, Joseph
US Marine Corps
Korean War

Vlug, Dirk J.
US Army
World War II

Voit, Otto
US Army
Indian Campaigns

Vokes, Leroy H.
US Army
Indian Campaigns

Volz, Jacob
US Navy
Philippines 1911

Volz, Robert
US Navy
Spanish-American War

Von Medem, Rudolph
US Army
Indian Campaigns

*Von Schlick, Robert H.
US Army
China Relief Expedition

Von Vegesack, Ernest
US Army
Civil War

Vosler, Forrest T.
US Army Air Corps
World War II

W

Waaler, Reidar
US Army
World War I

Wageman, John H.
US Army
Civil War

Wagg, Maurice
US Navy
Civil War

Wagner, John W.
US Army
Civil War

Wahlen, George
Edward
US Navy
World War II

*Wai, Francis B.
US Army
World War II

Wainwright, John
US Army
Civil War

Wainwright,
Jonathan M.
US Army
World War II

Wainwright,
Richard, Jr.
US Navy
Mexican Campaign
   (Veracruz)

Walker, Allen
US Army
Indian Campaigns

Walker, Edward Alexander
US Marine Corps
China Relief Expedition

Walker, Frank O.
US Army
Philippine Insurrection

Walker, James C.
US Army
Civil War

Walker, John
US Army
Indian Campaigns

*Walker, Kenneth N.
US Army Air Corps
World War II

Walker, Dr. Mary E.
Contract Surgeon
Civil War

Wall, Jerry
US Army
Civil War

Wallace, George W.
US Army
Philippine Insurrection

*Wallace, Herman C.
US Army
World War II

Wallace, William
US Army
Indian Campaigns

Waller, Francis A.
US Army
Civil War

Walley, Augustus
US Army
Indian Campaigns

Walling, William H.
US Army
Civil War

*Walmsley, John S., Jr.
US Air Force
Korean War

Walsh, James A.
US Navy
Mexican Campaign
    (Veracruz)

Walsh, John
US Army
Civil War

Walsh, Kenneth Ambrose
US Marine Corps
World War II

Walsh, Michael
US Navy
Interim Awards,
    1901–1911

*Walsh, William Gary
US Marine Corps
World War II

Walton, George W.
US Army
Civil War

Wambsgan, Martin
US Army
Civil War

Wanton, George H.
US Army
Spanish-American War

Ward, Calvin John
US Army
World War I

Ward, Charles H.
US Army
Indian Campaigns

Ward, James
US Navy
Civil War

Ward, James
US Army
Indian Campaigns

*Ward, James Richard
US Navy
World War II

Ward, John
US Army
Indian Campaigns

Ward, Nelson W.
US Army
Civil War

Ward, Thomas J.
US Army
Civil War

Ward, William H.
US Army
Civil War

Warden, John
US Army
Civil War

Ware, Keith L.
US Army
World War II

Warfel, Henry C.
US Army
Civil War

*Warner, Henry F.
US Army
World War II

Warren, David
US Navy
Civil War

Warren, Francis E.
US Army
Civil War

***Warren,
John E., Jr.**
US Army
Vietnam War

Warrington, Lewis
US Army
Indian Campaigns

*Watkins, Lewis G.
US Marine Corps
Korean War

*Watkins, Travis E.
US Army
Korean War

*Watson, George
US Army
World War II

Watson, James C.
US Army
Indian Campaigns

Watson, Joseph
US Army
Indian Campaigns

**Watson, Wilson
Douglas**
US Marine Corps
World War II

***Watters, Charles
Joseph**
US Army
Vietnam War

*Waugh, Robert T.
US Army
World War II

Waybur, David C.
US Army
World War II

***Wayrynen, Dale
Eugene**
US Army
Vietnam War

Weaher, Andrew J.
US Army
Indian Campaigns

Weaver, Amos
US Army
Philippine Insurrection

Webb, Alexander S.
US Army
Civil War

Webb, James
US Army
Civil War

Webber, Alason P.
US Army
Civil War

*Weber, Lester W.
US Marine Corps
Vietnam War

Webster, Henry S.
US Navy
Civil War

Weeks, Charles H.
US Navy
Civil War

Weeks, John H.
US Army
Civil War

*Weicht, Ellis R.
US Army
World War II

Weinert, Paul H.
US Army
Indian Campaigns

Weir, Henry C.
US Army
Civil War

**Weisbogel, Albert
(First Award)**
US Navy
Interim Awards,
    1871–1898

**Weisbogel, Albert
(Second Award)**
US Navy
Interim Awards,
    1871–1898

Weiss, Enoch R.
US Army
Indian Campaigns

Weissel, Adam
US Navy
Interim Awards,
    1871–1898

Welborn, Ira C.
US Army
Spanish-American
    War

Welch, Charles H.
US Army
Indian Campaigns

Welch, George W.
US Army
Civil War

Welch, Michael
US Army
Indian Campaigns

Welch, Richard
US Army
Civil War

Welch, Stephen
US Army
Civil War

Weld, Seth L.
US Army
Philippine Insurrection

*Wells, Henry S.
US Army
Civil War

Wells, Thomas M.
US Army
Civil War

Wells, William
US Army
Civil War

Wells, William
US Navy
Civil War

Welsh, Edward
US Army
Civil War

Welsh, James
US Army
Civil War

Wende, Bruno
US Army
Spanish-American
  War

West, Chester H.
US Army
World War I

West, Ernest E.
US Army
Korean War

West, Frank
US Army
Indian Campaigns

West, Walter S.
US Marine Corps
Spanish-American
  War

Westa, Karl
US Navy
Interim Awards,
  1901–1911

Westerhold, William
US Army
Civil War

Westermark, Axel
US Navy
China Relief Expedition

Weston, John F.
US Army
Civil War

Wetherby, John C.
US Army
Philippine Insurrection

Wetzel, Gary George
US Army
Vietnam War

*Wetzel, Walter C.
US Army
World War II

*Wheat, Roy M.
US Marine Corps
Vietnam War

Wheaton, Loyd
US Army
Civil War

Wheeler, Daniel D.
US Army
Civil War

**Wheeler,
George Huber**
US Navy
Interim Awards,
  1901–1911

Wheeler, Henry W.
US Army
Civil War

Wherry, William M.
US Army
Civil War

Whitaker, Edward W.
US Army
Civil War

White, Adam
US Army
Civil War

White, Edward
US Army
Philippine Insurrection

White, J. Henry
US Army
Civil War

White, Joseph
US Navy
Civil War

White, Patrick H.
US Army
Civil War

Whitehead, John M.
US Army
Civil War

Whitehead, Patton G.
US Army
Indian Campaigns

Whiteley, Eli
US Army
World War II

Whitfield, Daniel
US Navy
Civil War

Whitman, Frank M.
US Army
Civil War

Whitmore, John
US Army
Civil War

Whitney, William G.
US Army
Civil War

Whittier, Edward N.
US Army
Civil War

Whittington, Hulon B.
US Army
World War II

Whittlesey, Charles W.
US Army
World War I

*Wickam, Jerry Wayne
US Army
Vietnam War

*Wickersham, J. Hunter
US Army
World War I

Widick, Andrew J.
US Army
Civil War

Widmer, Jacob
US Army
Indian Campaigns

Wiedorfer, Paul J.
US Army
World War II

*Wigle, Thomas W.
US Army
World War II

*Wilbanks, Hilliard A.
US Air Force
Vietnam War

Wilbur, William H.
US Army
World War II

Wilcox, Franklin L.
US Navy
Civil War

Wilcox, William H.
US Army
Civil War

Wilder, Wilber E.
US Army
Indian Campaigns

Wiley, James
US Army
Civil War

Wilhelm, George
US Army
Civil War

Wilke, Julius A. R.
US Navy
Spanish-American
  War

Wilkens, Henry
US Army
Indian Campaigns

Wilkes, Henry
US Navy
Civil War

Wilkes, Perry
US Navy
Civil War

*Wilkin, Edward G.
US Army
World War II

Wilkins, Leander A.
US Army
Civil War

*Wilkins, Raymond H.
US Army Air Corps
World War II

**Wilkinson, Theodore
Stark, Jr.**
US Navy
Mexican Campaign
  (Veracruz)

*Will, Walter J.
US Army
World War II

Willcox, Orlando B.
US Army
Civil War

*Willett, Louis E.
US Army
Vietnam War

Willey, Charles H.
US Navy
Interim Awards,
 1915–1916

Williams, Anthony
US Navy
Civil War

Williams, Antonio
US Navy
Interim Awards,
 1871–1898

Williams, Augustus
US Navy
Civil War

Williams, Charles Q.
US Army
Vietnam War

*Williams,
Dewayne T.
US Marine Corps
Vietnam War

Williams, Elwood N.
US Army
Civil War

Williams, Ernest Calvin
US Marine Corps
Dominican Campaign

Williams, Frank
US Navy
Spanish-American
 War

Williams, George C.
US Army
Civil War

Williams, Henry
US Navy
Interim Awards,
 1871–1898

Williams, Hershel
Woodrow
US Marine Corps
World War II

*Williams, Jack
US Navy
World War II

Williams,
James E.
US Navy
Vietnam War

Williams, Jay
US Navy
China Relief
 Expedition

Williams, John
US Navy
Civil War

Williams, John
US Navy
Civil War

Williams, John
US Navy
Civil War

Williams,
Le Roy
US Army
Civil War

Williams, Louis
(First Award)
US Navy
Interim Awards,
 1871–1898

Williams, Louis
(Second Award)
US Navy
Interim Awards,
 1871–1898

Williams, Moses
US Army
Indian Campaigns

Williams, Peter
US Navy
Civil War

Williams,
Robert
US Navy
Civil War

Williams, William
US Navy
Civil War

Williams,
William H.
US Army
Civil War

Williamson,
James A.
US Army
Civil War

Willis, George
US Navy
Interim Awards,
 1871–1898

*Willis, John
Harlan
US Navy
World War II

Willis, Richard
US Navy
Civil War

Williston, Edward B.
US Army
Civil War

Wills, Henry
US Army
Indian Campaigns

*Wilson, Alfred L.
US Army
World War II

*Wilson, Alfred M.
US Marine Corps
Vietnam War

Wilson, Arthur H.
US Army
Philippine Insurrection

Wilson, August
US Navy
Interim Awards,
    1871–1898

Wilson, Benjamin
US Army
Indian Campaigns

Wilson, Benjamin F.
US Army
Korean War

Wilson, Charles
US Army
Indian Campaigns

Wilson, Charles E.
US Army
Civil War

Wilson, Christopher W.
US Army
Civil War

Wilson, Francis A.
US Army
Civil War

Wilson, Harold E.
US Marine Corps
Korean War

Wilson, John
US Army
Civil War

Wilson, John A.
US Army
Civil War

Wilson, John M.
US Army
Civil War

Wilson, Louis Hugh, Jr.
US Marine Corps
World War II

Wilson, Milden H.
US Army
Indian Campaigns

*Wilson, Richard G.
US Army
Korean War

*Wilson, Robert L.
US Marine Corps
World War II

**Wilson, William
(First Award)**
US Army
Indian Campaigns

**Wilson, William
(Second Award)**
US Army
Indian Campaigns

Wilson, William O.
US Army
Indian Campaigns

Winans, Roswell
US Marine Corps
Dominican Campaign

*Winder, David F.
US Army
Vietnam War

Windolph, Charles
US Army
Indian Campaigns

*Windrich, William G.
US Marine Corps
Korean War

Windus, Claron A.
US Army
Indian Campaigns

Winegar, William W.
US Army
Civil War

**Winterbottom,
William**
US Army
Indian Campaigns

Wise, Homer L.
US Army
World War II

Wisner, Lewis S.
US Army
Civil War

Witcome, Joseph
US Army
Indian Campaigns

*Witek, Frank Peter
US Marine Corps
World War II

**Withington,
William H.**
US Army
Civil War

*Wold, Nels
US Army
World War I

Wollam, John
US Army
Civil War

*Womack, Bryant E.
US Army
Korean War

Wood, H. Clay
US Army
Civil War

Wood, Leonard
US Army
Indian Campaigns

Wood, Mark
US Army
Civil War

Wood, Richard H.
US Army
Civil War

Wood, Robert B.
US Navy
Civil War

Woodall, William H.
US Army
Civil War

Woodall, Zachariah
US Army
Indian Campaigns

Woodbury, Eri D.
US Army
Civil War

Woodfill, Samuel
US Army
World War I

***Woodford,
Howard E.**
US Army
World War II

Woodruff, Alonzo
US Army
Civil War

Woodruff, Carle A.
US Army
Civil War

Woods, Brent
US Army
Indian Campaigns

Woods, Daniel A.
US Army
Civil War

Woods, Samuel
US Navy
Civil War

Woodward, Evan M.
US Army
Civil War

Woon, John
US Navy
Civil War

Woram, Charles B.
US Navy
Civil War

*Worley, Kenneth L.
US Marine Corps
Vietnam War

**Wortick (Wertick),
Joseph**
US Army
Civil War

Wortman, George G.
US Army
Indian Campaigns

Wray, William J.
US Army
Civil War

Wright, Albert D.
US Army
Civil War

Wright, Edward
US Navy
Civil War

**Wright,
Raymond R.**
US Army
Vietnam War

Wright, Robert
US Army
Civil War

Wright, Samuel
US Army
Civil War

Wright, Samuel C.
US Army
Civil War

Wright, William
US Navy
Civil War

Y

*Yabes, Maximo
US Army
Vietnam War

*Yano, Rodney J. T.
US Army
Vietnam War

Yeager, Jacob F.
US Army
Civil War

*Yntema, Gordon Douglas
US Army
Vietnam War

York, Alvin C.
US Army
World War I

Young, Andrew J.
US Army
Civil War

Young, Benjamin F.
US Army
Civil War

Young, Calvary M.
US Army
Civil War

Young, Cassin
US Navy
World War II

Young, Edward B.
US Navy
Civil War

Young, Frank Albert
US Marine Corps
China Relief Expedition

Young, Gerald O.
US Air Force
Vietnam War

Young, Horatio N.
US Navy
Civil War

Young, James M.
US Army
Civil War

*Young, Marvin R.
US Army
Vietnam War

*Young, Robert H.
US Army
Korean War

*Young, Rodger W.
US Army
World War II

Young, William
US Navy
Civil War

Younker, John L.
US Army
Civil War

Yount, John P.
US Army
Indian Campaigns

Z

Zabitosky, Fred William
US Army
Vietnam War

Zeamer, Jay, Jr.
US Army
   Air Corps
World War II

Ziegner, Hermann
US Army
Indian Campaigns

Zion, William
US Marine Corps
China Relief
   Expedition

Zuiderveld, William
US Navy
Mexican Campaign
   (Veracruz)

*Zussman, Raymond
US Army
World War II

Medals of Honor Authorized by Special Acts of Congress

Belgium Unknown Soldier
Great Britain Unknown Soldier
France Unknown Soldier

Italy Unknown Soldier
Rumania Unknown Soldier
United States Unknown Soldier

References

Congressional Medal of Honor Society, Mt. Pleasant, South Carolina. http://www.cmohs.org/.

The Congressional Medal of Honor: The Names, the Deeds. Forest Ranch, CA: Sharp & Dunnigan, 1984.

Gomez-Granger, Julissa. *CRS Report for Congress: Medal of Honor Recipients: 1979–2008.* Washington, D.C.: Congressional Research Service, RL 30011, June 4, 2008.

Home of Heroes, Pueblo, Colorado. http://www.homeofheroes.com/.

US Army Center of Military History. "Medal of Honor." http://www.history.army.mil/moh.html.

US Senate. Committee on Veterans Affairs. *Medal of Honor Recipients: 1863–1978.* Washington, D.C.: Government Printing Office, 1979.

DOUBLE AWARD RECIPIENTS

Seven recipients received two Medals of Honor for separate actions during the same war or period:

2nd Lt. Thomas Ward Custer	Army	Civil War
Pvt. Henry Hogan	Army	Indian Campaigns
Sgt. William Wilson	Army	Indian Campaigns
Ordinary Seaman Robert A. Sweeney	Navy	Interim 1871–1898
Captain of the Mizzen Top Albert Weisbogel	Navy	Interim 1871–1898
Captain of the Hold Louis Williams	Navy	Interim 1871–1898
Watertender John King	Navy	Interim 1901–1910

Seven recipients received two Medals of Honor for separate actions during different wars or periods:

Frank Dwight Baldwin	Army	first award, Civil War	second award, Indian Campaigns
John Cooper	Navy	first award, Civil War	second award, Interim 1865–1870
John Lafferty (a.k.a. John Laverty)	Navy	first award, Civil War	second award, Interim 1871–1898
Patrick Mullen	Navy	first award, Civil War	second award, Interim 1865–1870
Daniel Joseph Daly	USMC	first award, China Relief Expedition	second award, Haiti, 1915

John McCloy	Navy	first award, China Relief Expedition	second award, Mexican Campaign (Veracruz)
Smedley Darlington Butler	USMC	first award, Mexican Campaign (Veracruz)	second award, Haiti, 1915

Five recipients received both the Army and Navy Medal of Honor for the same actions during World War I:

Gunnery Sgt. Charles F. Hoffman (a.k.a. Ernest August Janson), USMC
Sgt. Louis Cukela, USMC
Sgt. Matej Kocak, USMC
Pvt. John Joseph Kelly, USMC
Cpl. John Henry Pruitt, USMC

References

The Congressional Medal of Honor: The Names, the Deeds. Forest Ranch, CA: Sharp & Dunnigan, 1984.

Tassin, Ray. *Double Winners of the Medal of Honor.* Canton, OH: Daring Books, 1986.

Medals of Honor Awarded by Conflict and Service

War	Totals	Army	Navy	Marines	Air Force	Coast Guard	Posthumous
Civil War	1,522	1,198	307	17	0	0	32
Indian Campaigns	426	426	0	0	0	0	13
Korea 1871	15	0	9	6	0	0	0
Spanish-American War	110	31	64	15	0	0	1
Samoa	4	0	1	3	0	0	0
Philippine Insurrection	80	69	5	6	0	0	4
Philippine Outlaws	6	1	5	0	0	0	0
China Relief Expedition	59	4	22	33	0	0	1
Mexican Campaign (Veracruz)	56	1	46	9	0	0	0
Haiti Campaign 1915	6	0	0	6	0	0	0
Dominican Republic	3	0	0	3	0	0	0
World War I	124	95	21	8	0	0	33
Haiti 1919–1920	2	0	0	2	0	0	0
Nicaraguan Campaign	2	0	0	2	0	0	0
World War II	464	324	57	82	0	1	266
Korean War	133	80	7	42	4	0	95
Vietnam	247	160	16	57	14	0	155
Somalia	2	2	0	0	0	0	2
Afghanistan	4	3	1	0	0	0	3
Iraq	4	2	1	1	0	0	4
Noncombat	193	3	185	5	0	0	5
Unknowns	9	9	0	0	0	0	9
Totals	3,471	2,405	747	297	18	1	623

References

Gomez-Granger, Julissa. *CRS Report for Congress: Medal of Honor Recipients: 1979–2008.* Washington, D.C.: Congressional Research Service, RL 30011, June 4, 2008.

US Army Center of Military History. "Medal of Honor." http://www.history.army.mil/moh.html.

US Senate. Committee on Veterans Affairs. *Medal of Honor Recipients: 1863–1978.* Washington, D.C.: Government Printing Office, 1979.

BIBLIOGRAPHY

Above and Beyond: A History of the Medal of Honor from the Civil War to Vietnam. Boston, MA: Boston Publishing Company, 1985.

Ackermann, Henry F. *He Was Always There: The U.S. Army Chaplain Ministry in the Vietnam Conflict*. Washington, D.C.: Office of the Chief of Chaplains, Department of the Army, 1989.

Adamson, Hans Christian. *Eddie Rickenbacker*. New York: The Macmillan Company, 1946.

Adler, J. O., Leonard G. McAneny, and Kaiser August. *History of the 77th Division: August 25, 1917 to November 11, 1918*. New York: 77th Division Association, 1919.

Alexander, Joseph H. *Closing In: Marines in the Seizure of Iwo Jima*. Marines in World War II Commemorative Series. Washington, D.C.: Marine Historical Center, 1994.

Alexander, Joseph H. *The Final Campaign: Marines in the Victory on Okinawa*. Marines in World War II Commemorative Series. Washington, D.C.: Marine Historical Center, 1995.

Ambrose, Hugh. *The Pacific*. New York: NAL Caliber, 2010.

Ambrose, Stephen E. *The Victors: Eisenhower and His Boys: The Men of World War II*. New York: Simon & Schuster, 1998.

Amchan, Arthur J. *The Most Famous Soldier in America: A Biography of Lt. Gen. Nelson A. Miles, 1839–1925*. McLean, VA: Amchan Publications, 1989.

American Battle Monuments Commission. *33rd Division, Summary of Operations in the World War*. Washington, D.C.: Government Printing Office, 1944.

American Battle Monuments Commission. *42nd Division, Summary of Operations in the World War*. Washington, D.C.: Government Printing Office, 1944.

America's Medal of Honor Recipients: Complete Official Citations. Golden Valley, MN: Highland Publishers, 1980.

Amos, Preston E. *Above and Beyond in the West: Black Medal of Honor Winners, 1870–1890*. Washington, D.C.: Potomac Corral, the Westerners, 1974.

Ancell, R. Manning, and Christine M. Miller. *The Biographical Dictionary of World War II Generals and Flag Officers: The U.S. Armed Forces*. Westport, CT: Greenwood, 1996.

Anderson, Burton F. *We Claim the Title: Korean War Marines*. Aptos, CA: Tracy Publications, 2000.

Anderson, David L. *Columbia Guide to the Vietnam War*. New York: Columbia University Press, 2002.

Appleman, Roy E. *East of Chosin: Entrapment and Breakout in Korea, 1950*. College Station: Texas A&M University Press, 1987.

Appleman, Roy E. *South to the Naktong, North to the Yalu*. Washington, D.C.: Office of the Chief of Military History, Department of the Army, 1961.

Appleman, Roy E., et al. *Okinawa: The Last Battle*. Washington, D.C.: Historical Division, Department of the Army, 1948.

Asahina, Robert. *Just Americans: The Story of the 100th Battalion/442nd Regimental Combat Team in World War II*. New York: Gotham Books, 2007.

Astor, Gerald. *The Bloody Forest: Battle for the Huertgen: September 1944–January 1945*. Novato, CA: Presidio Press, 2000.

Astor, Gerald. *The Right to Fight: A History of African Americans in the Military*. Cambridge, MA: Da Capo Press, 1998.

Atkinson, Rick. *The Day of Battle: The War in Sicily and Italy, 1943–1944*. New York: Henry Holt, 2007.

Atkinson, Rick. *The Long Gray Line*. New York: Houghton Mifflin, 1989.

Baker, Vernon J., and Ken Olsen. *Lasting Valor*. Columbus, MS: Genesis Press, 1997.

Baldwin, Alice Blackwood, ed. *Memoirs of the Late Frank D. Baldwin, Major General, U.S.A.* Los Angeles: Wetzel, 1929.

Balkoski, Joseph. *Omaha Beach: D-Day, June 6, 1944*. Mechanicsburg, PA: Stackpole Books, 2004.

Ballenger, Lee. *The Final Crucible: U.S. Marines in Korea*. Vol. 2, *1953*. Washington, D.C.: Brassey's, 2001.

Bartlett, Merrill L., and Jack Sweetman. *Leathernecks: An Illustrated History of the United States Marine Corps*. Annapolis, MD: Naval Institute Press, 2008.

Bartley, Whiman S. *Iwo Jima: Amphibious Epic*. Washington, D.C.: U.S. Marine Corps Historical Branch, Headquarters Marine Corps, 1954.

Beach, Edward L. *Submarine!* New York: Holt, 1952.

Beck, John Jacob. *MacArthur and Wainwright: Sacrifice of the Philippines*. Albuquerque: University of New Mexico Press, 1974.

Belote, James H., and William M. Belote. *Typhoon of Steel: The Battle for Okinawa*. New York: Bantam Books, 1984.

Benavidez, Roy P., and John R. Craig. *Medal of Honor: A Vietnam Warrior's Story*. Washington, D.C.: Brassey's, 1995.

Benavidez, Roy P., and John R. Craig. *The Three Wars of Roy Benavidez*. San Antonio, TX: Corona Publishing, 1986.

Bergerud, Eric M. *Red Thunder, Tropic Lightning: The World of a Combat Division in Vietnam*. Boulder, CO: Westview Press, 1993.

Bernstein, Jonathan. *US Army AH-1 Cobra Units in Vietnam*. Oxford, UK: Osprey, 2003.

Beyer, Walter F., and Oscar F. Keydel, eds. *Deeds of Valor: How America's Heroes Won the Medal of Honor*. Detroit, MI: The Perrien-Keydel Company, 1902.

Beyer, Walter F., and Oscar F. Keydel, eds. *Deeds of Valor: How America's Heroes Won the Medal of Honor*. Vol. 2. Detroit, MI: The Perrien-Keydel Company, 1906.

Blair, Clay, Jr. *The Forgotten War: America in Korea, 1950–1953*. New York: Anchor Books Doubleday. 1987.

Blair, Clay, Jr. *Silent Victory: The U.S. Submarine War against Japan*. Philadelphia: J. B. Lippincott, 1975.

Blumenson, Martin. *Breakout and Pursuit. US Army in World War II: European Theater of Operations*. Reprint, Washington, D.C.: Historical Division, Department of the Army, 2005.

Bonds, Russell S. *Stealing the General: The Great Locomotive Chase and the First Medal of Honor*. Yardley, PA: Westholme Publishing, 2007.

Boot, Max. *The Savage Wars of Peace: Small Wars and the Rise of American Power*. New York: Basic Books, 2002.

Borts, Lawrence H., and Col. Frank Foster. *U.S. Military Medals: 1939 to Present*. Fountain Inn, SC: Medals of America Press, 1995.

Bosiljevic, T. L. *SEALs: UDT/SEAL Operations in Vietnam*. Boulder, CO: Paladin Press, 1990.

Boven, Robert W. *Most Decorated Soldier in World War II: Matt Urban*. Victoria, BC, Canada: Trafford Publishing, 2000.

Bowden, Mark. *Black Hawk Down: A Story of Modern War*. 1st ed. New York: Atlantic Monthly Press, 1999.

Boyington, Gregory. *Baa Baa, Black Sheep*. New York: G. P. Putnam, 1958.

Brady, James. *Hero of the Pacific: The Life of Marine Legend John Basilone*. Hoboken, NJ: John Wiley and Sons, 2010.

Broadwater, Robert P. *Civil War Medal of Honor Recipients*. Jefferson, NC: McFarland, 2007.

Brody, Seymour. *Jewish Heroes and Heroines of America*. Hollywood, FL: Lifetime Books, 1996.

Brokaw, Tom. *The Greatest Generation*. New York: Random House, 1998.

Brooks, Thomas. *The War North of Rome: June 1944–May 1945*. New York: Sarpedon, 1996.

Broughton, Col. Jack. *Thud Ridge: F-105 Missions over Vietnam*. Sussex, UK: Crecy Publishing, 2006.

Brown, Anthony Cave. *Wild Bill Donovan: The Last Hero*. New York: The New York Times Book Company, 1982.

Bruning, John R., Jr. *Elusive Glory: African-American Heroes of World War II*. Greensboro, NC: Avisson Press, 2001.

Buckley, Gail L. *American Patriots: The Story of Blacks in the Military from the Revolution to Desert Storm*. New York: Random House, 2001.

Canzola, Nicolas, and Lynn Motross. *U.S. Marine Operations in Korea, 1950–1953*. Vol. 3, *The Chosin Reservoir Campaign*. Washington, D.C.: Headquarters Marine Corps Historical Branch, 1957.

Carhart, Tom. *West Point Warriors: Profiles of Duty, Honor, and Country in Battle.* New York: Grand Central Publishing, 2002.

Carlson, Paul H. *Pecos Bill: A Military Biography of William R. Shafter.* College Station: Texas A&M University Press, 1989.

Carroll, John M. *The Medal of Honor: Its History and Recipients for the Indian Wars.* Bryan, TX: J. M. Carroll, 1979.

Carter, Allene G., and Robert L. Carter. *Honoring Sergeant Carter: Redeeming a Black World War II Hero's Legacy.* New York: Amistead, 2003.

Carter, Robert A. *Buffalo Bill Cody: The Man behind the Legend.* Hoboken, NJ: Wiley, 2000.

Castel, Albert. *Decision in the West: The Atlanta Campaign of 1864.* Lawrence: University Press of Kansas, 1992.

Caubarreaux, Eric R. *Recipients of the Air Force Medal of Honor and the Air Force Cross.* Scotts Valley, CA: CreateSpace, 2009.

Cavanagh, William C. C. *The Battle East of Elsenborn and the Twin Villages.* South Yorkshire, UK: Pen & Sword Books, 2004.

Cave Brown, Anthony. *The Last Hero: Wild Bill Donovan.* New York: Times Books, 1982.

Cerasini, Marc. *U.S. Marine Corps Medal of Honor Winners.* New York: Berkley Books, 2002.

Chang, Thelma, and Daniel K. Inouye. *I Can Never Forget: Men of the 100th/442nd.* Honolulu, HI: SIGI Productions, 1995.

Clark, George B., ed. *United States Marine Corps Medal of Honor Recipients.* New York: McFarland, 2005.

Claxton, Melvin. *Uncommon Valor: A Story of Race, Patriotism, and Glory in the Final Battles of the Civil War.* Hoboken, NJ: John Wiley & Sons, 2006.

Cody, William F. *The Life of Hon. William F. Cody Known as Buffalo Bill the Famous Hunter, Scout, and Guide. An Autobiography.* Lincoln: University of Nebraska Press, 1978.

Cohen, Stan, and James G. Bogle. *The General and the Texas: A Pictorial History of the Andrews Raid, April 12, 1862.* Missoula, MT: Pictorial Histories Publishing, 1999.

Coletta, Paolo, and Bernarr B. Coletta. *Admiral William A. Moffett and U.S. Naval Aviation.* Lewiston, NY: Edmin Mellen Press, 1997.

Collier, Peter, and Nick Del Calzo. *Medal of Honor: Portraits of Valor beyond the Call of Duty.* New York: Artisan, 2006.

Collins, Gen. J. Lawton. *Lightning Joe: An Autobiography.* Baton Rouge: Louisiana State University Press, 1980.

The Congressional Medal of Honor: The Names, the Deeds. Forest Ranch, CA: Sharp & Dunnigan, 1984.

Converse, Elliott V., III. *The Exclusion of Black Soldiers from the Medal of Honor in World War II.* Jefferson, NC: McFarland, 1997.

Conwell, Russell H. *Life and Public Service of Gov. Rutherford B. Hayes.* East Lansing: Michigan Historical Society, 2005.

Cooke, Donald E. *For Conspicuous Gallantry: Winners of the Medal of Honor.* Maplewood, NJ: C. S. Hammond, 1966.

Coram, Robert. *American Patriot: The Life and Wars of Colonel Bud Day*. New York: Little, Brown. 2007.

Cosmas, Graham. *An Army for Empire: The United States Army in the Spanish-American War*. College Station: Texas A&M University Press, 1998.

Coy, Jimmie Dean. *Valor: A Gathering of Eagles*. Mobile, AL: Evergreen Press, 2003.

Cozzens, Peter. *The Shipwreck of Their Hopes: The Battles for Chattanooga*. Urbana: University of Illinois Press, 1994.

Cozzens, Peter, and Robert Girardi. *The Military Memoirs of General John Pope*. Chapel Hill: University of North Carolina Press, 1998.

Crosby, Donald F. *Battlefield Chaplains: Catholic Priests in World War II*. Lawrence, KS: The University Press of Kansas, 1994.

Crost, Lyn. *Honor by Fire: Japanese Americans at War in Europe and the Pacific*. Novato, CA: Presidio Press, 1997.

Crouch, Thomas W. *A Leader of Volunteers: Frederick Funston and the 20th Kansas in the Philippines, 1898–1899*. Lawrence, KS: Coronado Press, 1984.

Crouch, Thomas W. *A Yankee Guerrillero: Frederick Funston and the Cuban Insurrection, 1896–1897*. Memphis, TN: Memphis State University Press, 1975.

Curtis, Arthur S. *Thirty-Seven Greatest Army Heroes*. N.p.: 1969.

Custer, Elizabeth. *"A Beau Sabreur" in Uncle Sam's Medal of Honor: Some of the Noble Deeds for Which the Medal Has Been Awarded. Described by Those Who Have Won It*. Edited by Theodore F. Rodenbaugh. New York, 1886.

Custer, Elizabeth. *Boots and Saddles, or Life in the Dakotas with General Custer*. Reprint, Norman: University of Oklahoma Press, 1977.

Custer, Elizabeth. *Tenting on the Plains*. Reprint, Norman: University of Oklahoma Press, 1971.

Cutler, Thomas J. *The Battle of Leyte Gulf: 23–26 October 1944*. Annapolis, MD: Naval Institute Press, 1997.

Day, Carl F. *Tom Custer: Ride to Glory*. Spokane, WA: Arthur H. Clark Company, 2002.

Day, George E. *Return with Honor*. Mesa, AZ: Champlin Museum Press, 1991.

Dean, William F., with William L. Worden. *General Dean's Story*. New York: Viking, 1954.

DeBlanc, Jefferson. *The Guadalcanal Air War*. Grenta, LA: Pelican Publishing, 2008.

DeKever, Andrew J. *Here Rests in Honored Glory: Life Stories of Our Country's Medal of Honor Recipients*. Burlington, VT: Merriam Press, 2008.

DeLong, Kent. *War Heroes: True Stories of the Congressional Medal of Honor Recipients*. Westport, CT: Praeger, 1993.

DeLong, Kent, and Steven Tuckey. *Mogadishu! Heroism and Tragedy*. Westport, CT: Praeger, 1994.

Demeter, Richard. *The Fighting 69th: A History*. Pasadena, CA: Cranford Press, 2002.

DeMontravel, Peter R. *A Hero to His Fighting Men: Nelson A. Miles, 1839–1925*. Kent, OH: Kent State University Press, 1998.

Department of the Army Public Information Division. *The Medal of Honor of the United States Army*. Washington, D.C.: Government Printing Office, 1948.

Desiderio, Tim. *Into the Fire: The 275th Infantry Regiment in WWII*. Victoria, BC, Canada: Trafford Publishing, 2005.

Desjardin, Thomas A. *Stand Firm Ye Boys from Maine: The 20th Maine and the Gettysburg Campaign*. New York: Oxford University Press, 1995.

D'Este, Carlo. *Bitter Victory: The Battle for Sicily, 1943*. New York: E. P. Dutton, 1988.

Dethloff, Henry C. *Texas Aggies Go to War in Service of Their Country*. College Station: Texas A&M University Press, 2006.

Dix, Drew. *The Rescue of River City*. Mimbres, NM: Drew Dix Publishing, 2000.

Dockery, Kevin. *Navy SEALs: A Complete History from World War II to the Present*. New York: Berkley Publishing, 2004.

Dockery, Kevin. *Navy SEALs: A History*. Part 2, *The Vietnam Years*. New York: Berkley Publishing, 2002.

Dockery, Kevin. *SEALs in Action*. New York: Avon, 1991.

Donlon, Roger. *Beyond Nam Dong*. Leavenworth, KS: Roon Publishers, 1998.

Donlon, Capt. Roger H. C., and Warren Rogers. *Outpost of Freedom*. New York: McGraw-Hill, 1965.

Donovan, Frank R. *The Medal: The Story of the Medal of Honor*. New York: Dodd, Mead, 1962.

Doolittle, James H., with Carroll V. Glines. *I Could Never Be So Lucky Again: An Autobiography by General James H. "Jimmy" Doolittle*. Atglen, PA: Schiffer, 1991.

Dorland, Peter, and James Nanney. *Dust Off: Army Aeromedical Evacuation in Vietnam*. Washington, D.C.: U.S. Army Center of Military History, 1982.

Duffy, Francis P. *Father Duffy's Story: A Tale of Humor and Heroism, of Life and Death with the Fighting 69th*. New York: George H. Doran, 1919.

Dunlop, Richard. *Donovan: America's Master Spy*. Chicago: Rand McNally, 1982.

Dunstan, Simon. *1st Marine Division in Vietnam*. Minneapolis, MN: Zenith Press, 2008.

Durant, Michael. *In the Company of Heroes*. New York: Signet Press, 2006.

Duus, Masao, and Peter Duus. *Unlikely Liberators: The Men of the 100th and 442nd*. Honolulu, HI: University of Hawaii Press, 2007.

Ecker, Richard. *Korean Battle Chronology*. Jefferson, NC: McFarland, 2005.

Eicher, John H., and David J. Eicher. *Civil War High Commands*. Palo Alto, CA: Stanford University Press, 2001.

Eversmann, Matt, and Dan Schilling, eds. *The Battle of Mogadishu: Firsthand Accounts from the Men of Task Force Ranger*. Novato, CA: Presidio Press, 2006.

Ewing, Steve, and John Lundstrom. *Fateful Rendezvous*. Annapolis, MD: Naval Institute Press, 1997.

Faranacci, Donald. *Last Full Measure of Devotion: A Tribute to America's Heroes of the Vietnam War*. Bloomington, IN: AuthorHouse, 2007.

Farr, Finis. *Rickenbacker's Luck—An American Life*. Boston: Houghton Mifflin, 1979.

Federal Writers' Project of the Work Projects Administration for the State of Kentucky. *Military History of Kentucky, Chronologically Arranged*. Frankfort, KY: Printed by the State Journal, 1939.

Fehrenbach, T. R. *This Kind of War: A Study in Unpreparedness*. London: Brassey's, 1963.

Field, Ron, and Richard Hook. *American Civil War Marines, 1861–1865*. New York: Osprey, 2004.

First Cavalry Division. Paducah, KY: Turner Publishing, 2002.

Flanagan, E. M. *Rakkasans: The Combat History of the 187th Airborne Infantry*. New York: Presidio Press, 1997.

Fluckey, Eugene B. *Thunder Below! The USS Barb Revolutionizes Submarine Warfare in World War II*. Urbana: University of Illinois Press, 1992.

Foley, Robert F. *Consideration of Others*. Washington, D.C.: U.S. Army Military District of Washington, 1997.

Ford, Corey. *Donovan of OSS*. Boston, MA: Little, Brown, 1970.

Foss, Joe, and Donna Wild Foss. *A Proud American: The Autobiography of Joe Foss*. Novato, CA: Presidio Press, 2002.

Frank, Richard B. *Guadalcanal*. New York: Random House, 1990.

Franklin, John Hope, and Alfred A. Moss Jr. *From Slavery to Freedom: A History of African Americans*. 8th ed. 2 vols. in one. New York: Random House, 2004.

Funston, Frederick. *Memories of Two Wars: Cuban and Philippine Experiences*. Introduction by Thomas Bruscino. Lincoln, NE: Bison Books, 2009.

Gamble, Bruce. *Black Sheep One: The Life of Gregory "Pappy" Boyington*. Novato, CA: Presidio Press, 2000.

Garfield, Brian. *The Thousand Mile War: World War II in Alaska and the Aleutians*. New York and Toronto: Bantam Books, 1988.

Giangreco, D. M., and John T. Kuehn. *Eyewitness Pacific Theater*. New York: Sterling Publishing, 2008.

Glines, Carroll V. *Doolittle's Tokyo Raiders*. Salem, NH: Ayer, 1964.

Gomez-Granger, Julissa. *CRS Report for Congress: Medal of Honor Recipients: 1979–2008*. Washington, D.C.: Congressional Research Service, RL 30011, June 4, 2008.

Graf, Mercedes. *A Woman of Honor: Dr. Walker and the Civil War*. Gettysburg, PA: Thomas Publications, 2001.

Gragg, Rod. *Confederate Goliath: The Battle of Fort Fisher*. New York: Harper-Collins, 1991.

Graham, Don. *No Name on the Bullet: A Biography of Audie Murphy*. New York: Viking, 1989.

Greer, Emily Apt. *First Lady: The Life of Lucy Webb Hayes*. Fremont, OH: Rutherford B. Hayes Presidential Center, 1995.

The Guadalcanal Legacy. Paducah, KY: Turner Publishing, 1987.

Gushwa, Robert L. *The Best and Worst of Times: The United States Army Chaplaincy 1920–1945*. Washington, D.C.: Office of the Chief of Chaplains, Department of the Army, 1977.

Hagedorn, Hermann. *Leonard Woods: A Biography*. New York: Harper & Brothers, 1931.

Haiber, William, and Robert Haiber. *Frank Luke: September Rage*. La Grangeville, NY: Info Devels Press, 2003.

Halberstam, David. *The Coldest Winter*. New York: Hyperion Books, 2007.

Hall, Norman S. *The Balloon Buster: Frank Luke of Arizona*. New York: Bantam Books, 1966.

Hammel, Eric. *Carrier Clash: The Invasion of Guadalcanal and the Battle of the Eastern Solomons, August 1942*. Pacifica, CA: Pacifica Press, 1997.

Hammel, Eric. *Chosin: Heroic Ordeal of the Korean War*. Novato, CA: Presidio Press, 1981.

Hammel, Eric. *Fire in the Streets: The Battle for Hue, Tet 1968*. Pacifica, CA: Pacifica Press, 1991.

Hammel, Eric. *Guadalcanal: Starvation Island*. New York: Crown Publishing, 1987.

Hammel, Eric. *Iwo Jima: Portrait of a Battle: United States Marines at War in the Pacific*. St. Paul, MN: Zenith Imprint, 2006.

Hammel, Eric. *Marines at War: 20 True Heroic Tales of U.S. Marines in Combat, 1942–1983*. Pacifica, CA: Pacifica Press, 1999.

Hanna, Charles W. *African American Recipients of the Medal of Honor: A Biographical Dictionary, Civil War through Vietnam War*. Jefferson, NC: McFarland, 2002.

Hargis, Robert, and Ramiro Bujeiro. *World War II Medal of Honor Recipients: Navy & USMC*. Oxford, UK: Osprey, 2003.

Hargrove, Hondon B. *Buffalo Soldiers in Italy: Black Americans in World War II*. Jefferson, NC: McFarland, 1985.

Harris, Barnett W. *33rd Division across No-Man's Land*. Whitefish, MT: Kessinger Publishing, 2006.

Harris, Stephen L. *Duffy's War: Fr. Francis Duffy, Wild Bill Donovan, and the Irish Fighting 69th in World War I*. Dulles, VA: Potomac Books, 2006.

Harrison, Gordon A. *Cross-Channel Attack. US Army in World War II: European Theater of Operations*. Reprint, Washington, D.C.: Historical Division, Department of the Army, 2007.

Heinl, Robert Debs, Jr. *Soldiers of the Sea: The United States Marine Corps, 1775–1962*. Baltimore: The Nautical & Aviation Publishing Company of America, 1991.

Hennessey, John. *Return to Bull Run: The Second Campaign and Battle of Manassas*. New York: Simon & Schuster, 1992.

Hessler, James A. *Sickles at Gettysburg*. New York: Savas Beatie, 2009.

Holland, James. *Italy's Sorrow: A Year of War: 1944–1945*. New York: St. Martin's Press, 2008.

Howard, Oliver O. *Autobiography of Oliver Otis Howard*. New York: Baker & Taylor, 1908.

Howes, Craig. *Voices of the American POWs: Witnesses to their Fight*. New York: Oxford University Press, 1993.

Huidekoper, Frederic Louis. *The History of the 33rd Division, A.E.F.* Springfield: Illinois State Historical Society, 1921.

Ireland, Bernard. *Leyte Gulf 1944: The World's Greatest Sea Battle*. Oxford, UK: Osprey, 2006.

Izac, Edouard. *Prisoner of the U-90*. Boston: Houghton Mifflin, 1919.

Jablon, Howard. *David M. Shoup: A Warrior against War*. Lanham, MD: Rowman & Littlefield Publishers, 2005.

Jacobs, Bruce. *Heroes of the Army: The Medal of Honor and Its Winners*. New York: W. W. Norton, 1956.

Jacobs, Bruce. *Korea's Heroes: The Medal of Honor Story*. New York: Berkley Publishing, 1961.

Jacobs, Jack, and Douglas Century. *If Not Now, When? Duty and Sacrifice in America's Time of Need*. New York: Berkley Publishing, 2008.

James, D. Clayton. *The Years of MacArthur*. 3 vols. Boston: Houghton Mifflin, 1970–1985.

James, D. Clayton, and Anne Sharp Wells. *From Pearl Harbor to V-J Day: The American Armed Forces in WWII*. Chicago: Ivan R. Dee, 1995.

Jeffers, Paul, H. *Colonel Roosevelt: Theodore Roosevelt Goes to War, 1897–1898*. New York: John Wiley and Sons, 1996.

Johnson, Douglas V., and Rolfe L. Hillman, Jr. *Soissons, 1918*. College Station: Texas A&M University Press, 1999.

Johnson, Virginia. *The Unregimented General: A Biography of Nelson A. Miles*. Boston: Houghton Mifflin, 1962.

Jones, Robert. *101st Airborne Division*. 2nd ed. Paducah, KY: Turner Publishing, 2001.

Jordan, Kenneth N. *Forgotten Heroes: 131 Men of the Korean War Awarded the Medal of Honor, 1950–1953*. Atglen, PA: Schiffer Publishing, 1995.

Jordan, Kenneth N. *Heroes of Our Time: 239 Men of the Vietnam War Awarded the Medal of Honor 1964–1972*. Atglen, PA: Schiffer Publishing, 2004.

Jordan, Kenneth N. *Men of Honor: 38 Highly Decorated Marines of World War II, Korea, and Vietnam*. Atglen, PA: Schiffer Publishing, 1997.

Jordan, Kenneth N. *Yesterday's Heroes: 433 Men of World War II Awarded the Medal of Honor, 1941–1945*. Atglen, PA: Schiffer Publishing, 1996.

Katz, Robert. *The Battle for Rome: The Germans, the Allies, the Partisans, and the Pope, September 1943–June 1944*. New York: Simon & Schuster, 2003.

Kayser, Hugh. *The Spirit of America: The Biographies of 40 Living Congressional Medal of Honor Recipients*. Palm Springs, CA: ETC Publications, 1982.

Keegan, John. *The Iraq War*. New York: Knopf, 2004.

Kelly, Charles E. *One Man's War*. New York: Knopf, 1944.

Keneally, Thomas. *American Scoundrel: The Life of the Notorious Civil War General Dan Sickles*. New York: Nan A. Talese/Doubleday, 2002.

Kenney, George C. *General Kenney Reports*. New York: Duell, Sloan, and Pierce, 1949.

Kerrey, Bob. *When I Was a Young Man*. New York: Harcourt, 2002.

King, Brig. Gen. Edward L. "Annual Report of the Commandant: The General Service Schools, Fort Leavenworth, Kansas 1926–1927." Fort Leavenworth, KS: U.S. Army Command and General Staff College, 1927.

Kingseed, Cole C. *Old Glory Stories: American Combat Leadership in World War II.* Annapolis, MD: Naval Institute Press, 2006.

Kuehn, John T., and D. M. Giangreco. *Eyewitness Pacific Theater.* New York: Sterling Books, 2008.

Lane, Jack. *Armed Progressive: General Leonard Wood.* San Rafael, CA: Presidio Press, 1978.

Lang, George, Raymond L. Collins, and Gerard F. White. *Medal of Honor Recipients, 1863–1994.* 2 vols. New York: Facts on File, 1995.

Lanning, Michael L. *African American Soldier: From Crispus Attucks to Colin Powell.* Secaucus, NJ: Carroll Publishing, 1997.

Lee, David D. *Sergeant York: An American Hero.* Lexington: The University Press of Kentucky, 1985.

Lee, Irvin H. *Negro Medal of Honor Men.* New York: Dodd, Mead, 1967.

Lemon, Peter C. *Beyond the Medal: A Journey from Their Hearts to Yours.* Golden, CO: Fulcrum Publishing, 1997.

Lengel, Edward G. *To Conquer Hell: The Meuse-Argonne, 1918: The Epic Battle That Ended the First World War.* New York: Henry Holt, 2008.

Levy, Debbie. *Rutherford B. Hayes.* Minneapolis, MN: Lerner Publishing Group, 2006.

Lewis, Adrian R. *Omaha Beach: A Flawed Victory.* Chapel Hill: University of North Carolina Press, 2001.

Lewis, W. David. *Eddie Rickenbacker: An American Hero in the 20th Century.* Baltimore: Johns Hopkins University Press, 2005.

Linn, Brian McAllister. *The Philippine War, 1899–1902.* Lawrence: University Press of Kansas, 2000.

Linn, Brian McAllister. *The U.S. Army and Counterinsurgency in the Philippine War, 1899–1902.* Chapel Hill: University of North Carolina Press, 1989.

Livingston, James E., Colin D. Heaton, and Anne-Marie Lewis. *Noble Warrior: The Life and Times of Maj. Gen. James E. Livingston, USMC (Ret.), Medal of Honor.* New York: Zenith Press, 2010.

Lodge, O. R. *The Recapture of Guam.* Washington, D.C.: U.S. Marine Corp Historical Branch, Headquarters Marine Corps, 1954.

Lowry, Timothy. *And Brave Men, Too.* New York: Crown Publishers, 1985.

Lucas, Jacklyn, with D. K. Drum. *Indestructible: The Unforgettable Story of a Marine Hero at Iwo Jima.* Cambridge, MA: Da Capo Press, 2006.

MacDonald, Charles B. *The Siegfried Line Campaign. US Army in World War II: European Theater of Operations.* Reprint, Washington, D.C.: Historical Division, Department of the Army, 2001.

Manchester, William Raymond. *American Caesar: Douglas MacArthur, 1880–1964.* Boston: Little, Brown, 1978.

Marston, Daniel. *The Pacific War Companion: From Pearl Harbor to Hiroshima.* Oxford, UK: Osprey, 2005.

Martin, Robert J. *First Marine Division.* Paducah, KY: Turner Publishing, 1997.

Maslowski, Peter, and Don Winslow. *Looking for a Hero: Staff Sergeant Joe Ronnie Hooper and the Vietnam War*. Lincoln: University of Nebraska Press, 2004.

Masuda, Mindora. *Letters from the 442nd: The World War II Correspondence of a Japanese American Medic*. Seattle: University of Washington Press, 2008.

Mayer, Sydney L. *The Biography of General of the Army, Douglas MacArthur*. Northbrook, IL: Book Value International, 1981.

McCallum, Jack. *Leonard Wood: Rough Rider, Surgeon, and Architect of American Imperialism*. New York: New York University Press, 2006.

McConnell, Malcolm. *Into the Mouth of the Cat: The Story of Lance Sijan, Hero of Vietnam*. New York: W. W. Norton, 2004.

McDonough, James Lee. *Chattanooga—A Death Grip on the Confederacy*. Knoxville: University of Tennessee Press, 1984.

McDonough, James Lee. *Schofield: Union General in the Civil War and Reconstruction*. Tallahassee: University Press of Florida, 1972.

McPherson, James M. *The American Heritage New History of the Civil War*. New York: Metro Books, 2001.

McPherson, James M. *Battle Cry of Freedom: The Civil War Era*. New York: Oxford University Press, 2003.

Medal of Honor: Historical Facts and Figures. Paducah, KY: Turner Publishing, 2004.

Meid, Lt. Col. Pat, USMCR, and Maj. James M. Yingling, USMC. *U.S. Marine Operations in Korea 1950–1953*. Vol. 5. Washington, D.C.: Historical Division, Headquarters Marine Corps, 1972.

Merrill, James M. *Target Tokyo: The Halsey-Doolittle Raid*. New York: Rand McNally, 1964.

Mersky, Peter. *Time of Aces: Marine Pilots in the Solomons, 1942–1944*. Washington, D.C.: Marine Corps Historical Center, 1993.

Mikaelian, Allen, and Mike Wallace. *Medal of Honor: Profiles of America's Military Heroes from the Civil War to the Present*. New York: Hyperion, 2003.

Miles, L. Wardlaw. *History of the 308th Infantry: 1917–1919*. New York and London: The Knickerbocker Press, 1927.

Miles, Nelson A. *Personal Recollections and Observations of General Nelson A. Miles*. 2 vols. Lincoln: University of Nebraska Press, 1992.

Miller, Donald L. *D-Days in the Pacific*. New York: Simon & Schuster, 2005.

Miller, John Jr. *Guadalcanal: The First Offensive*. Washington, D.C.: Historical Division, Department of the Army, 1949.

Miller, Nathan. *Theodore Roosevelt, A Life*. New York: Morrow and Co., 1992.

Millett, Allan R. *Semper Fidelis: The History of the United States Marine Corps*. New York: The Free Press, 1982.

Millett, Allan Reed, and Jack Shulimson, eds. *Commandants of the Marine Corps*. Annapolis, MD: Naval Institute Press, 2006.

Mills, Randy K. *Troubled Hero: A Medal of Honor, Vietnam, and the War at Home*. Bloomington: Indiana University Press, 2006.

Mitchell, Joseph B., and James Otis. *The Badge of Gallantry: Recollections of Civil War Congressional Medal of Honor Winners*. New York: Macmillan, 1968.

Montross, Lynn. *The Chosin Reservoir Campaign: U.S. Marine Corps Operations in Korea, 1950–1953*. Nashville, TN: Battery Press, 1987.

Moore, Christopher. *Fighting for America: Black Soldiers—The Unsung Heroes of World War II*. New York: Presidio Press, 2005.

Moore, Lt. Gen. (Ret) Harold G., and Joseph L. Galloway. *We Were Soldiers Once…and Young*. New York: Random House, 1992.

Moore, Lt. Gen. (Ret) Harold G., and Joseph L. Galloway. *We Are Soldiers Still: A Journey Back to the Battlefields of Vietnam*. New York: Harper, 2008.

Morison, Samuel E. *History of United States Naval Operations in World War II*. Vol. 3, *The Rising Sun in the Pacific, 1931–April 1942*; Vol. 4, *Coral Sea, Midway and Submarine Actions, May 1942–August 1942*. Boston: Little, Brown, 1948, 1949.

Morison, Samuel E. *The Two-Ocean War*. Boston: Little, Brown, 1963.

Morton, Louis. *The Fall of the Philippines. United States Army in World War II: The War in the Pacific*. Washington, D.C.: U.S. Army Office of the Chief of Military History, 1952.

Moskin, Robert J. *The U.S. Marine Corps Story*. 3rd rev. ed. New York: Little, Brown, 1992.

Mossman, Billy C. *United States Army in the Korean War: Ebb and Flow November 1950–July 1951*. Washington, D.C.: Government Printing Office, 1990.

Moulin, Pierre. *Dachau, Holocaust, and US Samurais: Nisei Soldiers First in Dachau*. Bloomington, IN: AuthorHouse, 2007.

Moulin, Pierre. *U.S. Samurais in Bruyeres*. Luxembourg: Peace and Freedom Trail, 1993.

Murphy, Audie Leon. *To Hell and Back*. New York: Henry Holt, 1949.

Murphy, Edward F. *Heroes of World War II*. Novato, CA: Presidio Press, 1990.

Murphy, Edward F. *Korean War Heroes*. Novato, CA: Presidio Press, 1992.

Murphy, Edward F. *Semper Fi: Vietnam: from Da Nang to the DMZ: Marine Corps Campaigns, 1965–1972*. Novato, CA: Presidio Press, 1997.

Murphy, Edward F. *Vietnam Medal of Honor Heroes*. New York: Ballantine Books, 2005.

Neal, Charles M., Jr. *Valor across the Lone Star: The Congressional Medal of Honor in Frontier Texas*. Austin: Texas State Historical Association, 2002.

Newcomb, Richard F., and Harry Schmidt. *Iwo Jima*. New York: Macmillan, 2002.

Newman, Rick, and Don Shepperd. *Bury Us Upside Down: The Misty Pilots and the Secret Battle for the Ho Chi Minh Trail*. Novato, CA: Presidio Press, 2007.

Nolan, Keith. *The Magnificent Bastards: The Joint Army-Marine Defense of Dong Ha, 1968*. Novato, CA: Presidio Press, 2007.

Novosel, Michael. *Dustoff: The Memoir of an Army Aviator*. Novato, CA: Presidio Press, 1999.

O'Brien, John, and Horace Herbert Smith. *A Captain Unafraid: The Strange Adventures of Dynamite Johnny O'Brien as Set Down by Horace Smith*. New York: Harper, 1912.

O'Kane, Richard H. *Clear the Bridge! The War Patrols of the USS Tang*. Chicago: Rand McNally, 1977.

173rd Airborne Brigade: Sky Soldiers. Nashville, TN: Turner Publishing, 2006.

Owens, Ron. *Medal of Honor: Historical Facts and Figures.* Paducah, KY: Turner Publishing, 2004.

Paige, Mitchell. *A Marine Named Mitch.* New York: Vantage Press. 1975.

Pardoe, Blaine. *Terror of the Autumn Skies: The True Story of Frank Luke, America's Rogue Ace of WWI.* New York: Skyhorse, 2008.

Pease, Theodore Calvin, ed. *Illinois in the World War.* Vol. 2. Springfield: Illinois State Historical Library, 1921.

Perret, Geoffrey. *Old Soldiers Never Die: The Life of Douglas MacArthur.* Holbrook, MA: Adams Media, 1996.

Perry, Mark. *Conceived in Liberty: Joshua Chamberlain, William Oates, and the American Civil War.* New York: Viking, 1997.

Phillips, Col. James H., and Maj. John F. Kane, eds. *The Medal of Honor of the United States Army.* Washington, D.C.: Government Printing Office, 1948.

Phillips, Michael M. *The Gift of Valor: A War Story.* New York: Broadway Books, 2005.

Pinchon, Edgcumb. *Dan Sickles, Hero of Gettysburg and "Yankee King of Spain."* Garden City, NY: Doubleday, Doran, 1945.

Plaster, John. *Secret Commandos: Behind Enemy Lines with the Elite Warriors of SOG.* New York: Simon & Schuster, 2004.

Plaster, John. *SOG: The Secret Wars of America's Commandos in Vietnam.* Boulder, CO: Paladin, 2008.

Proft, Robert J. *United States of America's Congressional Medal of Honor Recipients: Their Official Citations.* Columbia Heights, MN: Highland House II, 2007.

Pullen, John J. *A Shower of Stars: The Medal of Honor and the 27th Maine.* Mechanicsburg, PA: Stackpole Books, 1997.

Rand, Fred E. *132nd Infantry, 66th Brigade, 33rd Division: 50th Anniversary, March 13th, 1926.* S.I.: s.n., 1926.

Reck, Franklin M. *Beyond the Call of Duty.* New York: Thomas Y. Crowell, 1994.

Reeder, Red. *Medal of Honor Heroes.* New York: Random House, 1965.

Reef, Catherine. *African Americans in the Military.* New York: Facts on File, 2004.

Regan, Stephen. *In Bitter Tempest: The Biography of Frank Jack Fletcher.* Ames: Iowa State Press, 1994.

Rickenbacker, Edward V. *Rickenbacker: An Autobiography.* Englewood Cliffs, NJ: Prentice-Hall, 1967.

Rickenbacker, Capt. Edward V. *Seven Came Through.* Garden City, NY: Doubleday, Doran, 1943.

Ricks, Thomas E. *The Gamble.* New York: The Penguin Press, 2009.

Rielly, Robin L. *Kamikazes, Corsairs, and Picket Ships: Okinawa 1945.* Drexel Hill, PA: Casemate, 2008.

Robbins, Maj. Robert. *The 91st Infantry Division in World War II.* Washington, D.C.: Infantry Journal Press, 1947.

Roberts, David. *Once They Moved Like the Wind: Cochise, Geronimo, and the Apache Wars.* New York: Simon & Schuster, 1993.

Roberts, Frank E. *The American Foreign Legion: Black Soldiers of the 93d in World War I.* Annapolis, MD: Naval Institute Press, 2004.

Ross, Bill D. *Iwo Jima: Legacy of Valor.* New York: Vintage Books, 1986.

Rottman, Gordon. *Guam 1941 and 1944: Loss and Reconquest.* Oxford, UK: Osprey, 2004.

Rush, Robert S. *GI: The US Infantryman in World War II.* Oxford, UK: Osprey, 2003.

Russ, Martin. *Breakout: The Chosin Reservoir Campaign, Korea 1950.* New York: Penguin Books, 2000.

Russ, Martin. *Line of Departure: Tarawa.* Garden City, NY: Doubleday, 1975.

Saal, Harve. *SOG: MACV Studies and Observation Group.* Vol. 3. Ann Arbor, MI: Edwards Brothers, 1990.

Salter, Fred H. *Recon Scout.* New York: Ballantine Publishing, 2001.

Samora, Julian, and Patricia Vandel Simon. *A History of the Mexican-American People.* South Bend, IN: University of Notre Dame Press, 1977.

Sanborn, Col. Joseph B. *The 131st U.S. Infantry in the World War.* Chicago: Illinois National Guard, 1919.

Schmidt, Hans. *Maverick Marine: General Smedley D. Butler and the Contradictions of American Military History.* Lexington: University Press of Kentucky, 1987.

Schneider, Donald K. *Air Force Heroes in Vietnam.* Washington, D.C.: Office of Air Force History, U.S. Air Force, 1986.

Schott, Joseph D. *Above and Beyond: The Story of the Congressional Medal of Honor.* New York: G. P. Putnam's Sons, 1963.

Schubert, Frank N. *Black Valor: Buffalo Soldiers and the Medal of Honor, 1870–1898.* Wilmington, DE: Scholarly Resources, 1997.

Schultz, Duane P. *Hero of Bataan: The Story of General Jonathan M. Wainwright.* New York: St. Martin's Press, 1981.

Sear, David. *The Last Epic Naval Battle: Voices from Leyte.* New York: Penguin Books, 2007.

Shaffer, Duane E. *Men of Granite: New Hampshire's Soldiers in the Civil War.* Columbia: University of South Carolina Press, 2008.

Shaw, Henry I., Jr. *First Offensive: The Marine Campaign for Guadalcanal.* Marines in World War II Commemorative Series. Washington, D.C.: Marine Corps Historical Center, 1992.

Shulimson, Jack, Leonard A. Blaisol, Charles R. Smith, and David A. Dawson. *U.S. Marines in Vietnam: The Defining Year, 1968.* Washington, D.C.: Headquarters Marine Corps, History and Museums Division, 1997.

Simmons, Edwin H. *Frozen Chosin: U.S. Marines at the Changjin Reservoir.* Washington, D.C.: Headquarters Marine Corps, History and Museums Division, 2002.

Simmons, Thomas E. *Forgotten Heroes of World War II: Personal Accounts of Ordinary Soldiers.* Nashville, TN: Cumberland House Publishing, 2002.

Simmons, Walter. *Joe Foss, Flying Marine: The Story of His Flying Circus.* Whitefish, MT: Kessinger Publishing, 2008.

Sinton, Starr, and Robert Hargis. *World War II Medal of Honor Recipients.* Vol. 1, *Navy & USMC.* Oxford, UK: Osprey, 2003.

Sinton, Starr, and Robert Hargis. *World War II Medal of Honor Recipients.* Vol. 2, *Army & Air Corps.* Oxford, UK: Osprey, 2003.

Skeyhill, Thomas. *Sergeant York: His Own Life Story and War Diary.* New York: Doubleday, Doran, 1928.

Sledge, E. B. *With the Old Breed: Peleliu and Okinawa.* London: Oxford University Press, 1990.

Slotkin, Richard. *Lost Battalions: The Great War and the Crisis of American Nationality.* New York: Henry Holt, 2005.

Slotkin, Richard. *No Quarter: The Battle of the Crater, 1864.* New York: Random House, 2009.

Smith, Charles. *U.S. Marines in the Korean War.* Washington, D.C.: U.S. Marine Corps History Division, 2007.

Smith, Larry. *Beyond Glory: Medal of Honor Heroes in Their Own Words—Extraordinary Stories of Courage from World War II to Vietnam.* New York: W. W. Norton, 2003.

Smith, Perry M. *A Hero among Heroes: Jimmie Dyess and the 4th Marine Division.* Quantico, VA: Marine Corps Association, 1998.

Sowash, Rick. *Heroes of Ohio: 23 True Tales of Courage and Character.* Bowling Green, OH: Gabriel's Horn Publishing Company, 1998.

Spector, Ronald. *Eagle against the Sun: The American War with Japan.* New York: Vintage Books, 1985.

Spiller, Roger J., ed. *Dictionary of American Military Biography.* 3 vols. Westport, CT: Greenwood, 1984.

Stanton, Shelby L. *The Rise and Fall of an American Army: U.S. Ground Forces in Vietnam, 1965–1973.* New York: Presidio Press, 1985.

Steidl, Franz. *Lost Battalions: Going for Broke in the Vosges, Autumn 1944.* Novato, CA: Presidio Press, 2000.

Steinman, Ron. *The Soldiers' Story: Vietnam in Their Own Words.* New York: Barnes & Noble, 2002.

Sterner, C. Douglas. *Go for Broke: The Nisei Warriors of World War II Who Conquered Germany, Japan, and American Bigotry.* Clearfield, UT: American Legacy Historical Press, 2008.

Stewart, Adrian. *The Battle of Leyte Gulf.* New York: Scribner's, 1980.

Stinton, Starr, Robert Hargiss, and Ramiro Bujeiro. *World War II Medal of Honor Recipients: Army & Air Corps.* Oxford, UK: Osprey, 2003.

Stockdale, Jim, and Sybil Stockdale. *In Love and War.* New York: Harper & Row, 1984.

Sullivan, David M. *The United States Marine Corps in the Civil War.* 2 vols. Shippensburg, PA: White Mane Publishing Company, 1997.

Sutherland, Jonathan. *African Americans at War: An Encyclopedia*. Santa Barbara, CA: ABC-Clio, 2003.

Sutherland, Lt. Col. Ian D. W. *Special Forces of the United States Army*. San Jose, CA: R. James Bender Publishing, 1990.

Swanberg, W. A. *Sickles the Incredible*. New York: Charles Scribner's Sons, 1956.

Sweeney, Edwin R. *Cochise: Chiricahua Apache Chief*. Norman: University of Oklahoma Press, 1995.

Sword, Wiley. *Mountains Touched with Fire: Chattanooga Besieged, 1863*. New York: St. Martin's Press, 1995.

Taggart, Donald G., ed. *History of the Third Infantry Division in World War II*. Washington, D.C.: Infantry Journal Press, 1947. Reprint, Nashville, TN: Battery Press, 1987.

Tanaka, Chester. *Go for Broke*. New York: Random House, 1997.

Tassin, Ray. *Double Winners of the Medal of Honor*. Canton, OH: Daring Books, 1986.

33rd Division A.E.F. From Its Arrival in France until the Armistice with Germany November 11, 1918. Diekirch, Luxembourg: Gustave Soupert, 1919.

Thomas, Lowell. *Woodfill of the Regulars: A True Story of Adventure from the Arctic to the Argonne*. Garden City, NY: Doubleday, Doran, 1929.

Thomas, Lowell, and Edward Jablonski. *Doolittle: A Biography*. Garden City, NY: Doubleday, 1976.

Thorsness, Leo. *Surviving Hell: A POW's Journey*. New York: Encounter Books, 2008.

Tillman, Barrett. *Above and Beyond: The Aviation Medals of Honor*. Washington, D.C.: Smithsonian Institution Press, 2002.

Tillman, Barrett. *Heroes: U.S. Army Medal of Honor Recipients*. New York: The Berkley Group, 2006.

Tillman, Barrett. *Wildcat Aces of World War 2*. London: Osprey, 1995.

Townley, Alvin. *Legacy of Honor: The Values and Influence of America's Eagle Scouts*. New York: Thomas Dunne Books, 2007.

Toyn, Gary W. *The Quiet Hero: The Untold Medal of Honor Story of George E. Wahlen at the Battle of Iwo Jima*. Clearfield, UT: American Legacy Media, 2006.

Trimble, William F. *Admiral William A. Moffett: Architect of Naval Aviation*. Annapolis, MD: Bluejacket Books, 2007.

Troy, Thomas F. *Wild Bill and Intrepid: Donovan, Stephenson, and the Origin of CIA*. New Haven, CT: Yale University Press, 1996.

Tully, Anthony P. *Battle of Surigao Strait*. Bloomington: University of Indiana Press, 2009.

Tuohy, William. *The Bravest Man: The Story of Richard O'Kane and the U.S. Submariners in the Pacific War*. Phoenix Mill, UK: Sutton, 2001.

Urban, Matt. *The Matt Urban Story*. Holland, MI: Matt Urban Story, Inc., 1989.

US Senate. Committee on Veterans Affairs. *Medal of Honor Recipients, 1863–1973*. Washington, D.C.: Government Printing Office, 1973.

US Congress. Senate. Committee on Veterans Affairs. *Medal of Honor Recipients, 1863–1978: "In the Name of the Congress of the United States."* Washington, D.C.: Government Printing Office, 1979.

Vandegrift, Alexander. *Once a Marine: The Memoirs of General A. A. Vandegrift*. New York: W. W. Norton, 1964.

Vandiver, Frank E. *Black Jack: The Life and Times of John J. Pershing*. 2 vols. College Station: Texas A&M University Press, 1977.

Venzke, Rodger R. *Confidence in Battle, Inspiration in Peace: The United States Army Chaplaincy 1945–1975*. Washington, D.C.: Office of the Chief of Chaplains, Department of the Army, 1977.

Venzon, Anne Ciprion. *General Smedley Darling Butler: The Letters of a Leatherneck, 1898–1931*. New York: Praeger, 1992.

Wachtel, Roger. *The Medal of Honor: Cornerstones of Freedom*. New York: Scholastic, 2009.

Wainwright, Jonathan Mayhew. *General Wainwright's Story: The Account of Four Years of Humiliating Defeat, Surrender, and Captivity*. Garden City, NY: Doubleday, 1946.

Walker, Dale L. *The Boys of '98: Theodore Roosevelt and the Rough Riders*. New York: Forge Books, 1998.

Walker, Dale L. *Mary Edwards Walker: Above and Beyond*. New York: Forge Books, 2005.

Wallace, Willard R. *Soul of the Lion: A Biography of General Joshua L. Chamberlain*. New York: Thomas Nelson and Sons, 1960.

Walton, Frank E. *Once They Were Eagles*. Lexington: University Press of Kentucky, 1986.

War Department. *Combat Lessons No. 7: Rank and File in Combat: What They Are Doing—How They Do It*. Washington, D.C.: War Department, 1944.

Warner, Ezra J. *Generals in Blue: Lives of the Union Commanders*. Baton Rouge: University of Louisiana Press, 1964.

Warren, Louis S. *Buffalo Bill's America: William Cody and the Wild West Show*. New York: Knopf, 2005.

Webb, Alexander S. *The Peninsula: McClellan's Campaign of 1862*. New York: Charles Scribner's Sons, 1881.

Weigley, Russell F. *Eisenhower's Lieutenants: The Campaign of France and Germany, 1944–1945*. Bloomington: Indiana University Press, 1981.

Weir, William. *Encyclopedia of African American Military History*. Amherst, NY: Prometheus Books, 2004.

West, Bing. *The Strongest Tribe*. New York: Random House, 2009.

Wetmore, Helen Cody. *The Last of the Great Scouts: The Life Story of Col. William Cody "Buffalo Bill."* Lincoln: University of Nebraska Press, 1899.

Wheeler, James Scott. *The Big Red One: America's Legendary 1st Infantry Division from World War I to Desert Storm*. Lawrence: University Press of Kansas, 2007.

Whitehouse, Arthur G. *The Ace from Arizona: Frank Luke, the Hun Killer*. New York: Award Books, 1966.

Whiting, Charles. *Hero: The Life and Death of Audie Murphy*. Chelsea, MI: Scarborough House, 1990.

Williams, David. *A People's History of the Civil War: Struggles for the Meaning of Freedom*. New York: New Press, 2005.

Wise, James E., Jr., and Scott Barron. *The Navy Cross: Extraordinary Heroism in Iraq, Afghanistan, and Other Conflicts.* Annapolis, MD: Naval Institute Press, 2007.

Woodall, James R. *Texas Aggie Medals of Honor: Seven Heroes of World War II.* College Station: Texas A&M University Press, 2010.

Wooster, Robert. *Nelson A. Miles and the Twilight of the Frontier Army.* Lincoln: University of Nebraska Press, 1993.

Yeide, Harry, and Mark Stout. *First to the Rhine: The 6th Army Group in World War II.* St. Paul, MN: Zenith Press, 2007.

Yenne, Bill. *Rising Sons: The Japanese American GIs Who Fought for the United States in World War II.* New York: St. Martin's Press, 2007.

Young, Kenneth Ray. *The General's General: The Life and Times of Arthur MacArthur.* San Francisco: Westview Press, 1994.

Zabecki, David T. *American Artillery and the Medal of Honor.* Bennington, VT: Merriam Press, 1988.

Zaloga, Steven J. *Operation Cobra, 1944: Breakout from Normandy.* Westport, CT: Praeger, 2004.

Zimmerman, Dwight Jon, and John D. Gresham. *Beyond Hell and Back: How America's Special Forces Became the World's Greatest Fighting Unit.* New York: St. Martin's Press, 2007.

Zimmerman, Dwight Jon, and John D. Gresham. *Uncommon Valor: The Medal of Honor and the Six Warriors Who Earned It in Afghanistan and Iraq.* New York: St. Martin's Press, 2010.

INDEX

War or Conflict Period

Home States

Branch of Service

Awards and Medals Other Than Medal of Honor

Presenters of the Medal of Honor

Burial Grounds of Medal of Honor Recipients

About the Editor

Dr. James H. Willbanks is the General of the Army George C. Marshall Chair of Military History and director of the Department of Military History at the US Army Command and General Staff College, Fort Leavenworth, Kansas. He is the author of *Abandoning Vietnam*; *The Battle of An Loc*; *The Tet Offensive: A Concise History*; *Vietnam War Almanac*; and the editor of *The Vietnam War*, a volume in The International Library of Essays on Military History.

CONTRIBUTORS

Margaret L. Albert
US Marine Corps History Division

Alan M. Anderson
Military Historian
Minneapolis, MN

Michael Beauchamp
Texas A&M University

Terry L. Beckenbaugh, PhD
Department of Military History
US Army Command and General Staff
College

Claude G. Berube
US Naval Academy

Alexander M. Bielakowski, PhD
Department of Military History
US Army Command and General Staff
College

Edward L. Bowie
Department of Military History
US Army Command and General Staff
College

Allan S. Boyce
Assistant Professor
US Army Command and General Staff
College

Capt. Gates M. Brown
Department of Military History
US Army Command and General Staff
College

Jerold E. Brown, PhD
Department of Military History
US Army Command and General Staff
College

Thomas Bruscino
School of Advanced Military Studies
US Army Command and General Staff
College

Mark T. Calhoun
School of Advanced Military Studies
US Army Command and General Staff
College

Denise M. Carlin
Department of History
University of Southern Mississippi

Dr. Erik D. Carlson
History Program
Florida Gulf Coast University

Dr. Bradley L. Carter
Department of Military History
US Army Command and General Staff
College

James M. Cloninger
Department of History
Texas Tech University

Dr. Jeffrey B. Cook
North Greenville University

John M. Curatola, PhD
Lt. Col. USMC (Ret)
US Army Command and General Staff
  College

Louis A. DiMarco
Department of Military History
US Army Command and General Staff
  College

Douglas M. Doss
Department of History
Austin Peay State University

Sean K. Duggan
Research Associate
Center for American Progress

Jason C. Engle
Department of History
University of Southern Mississippi

Dr. Edward F. Finch
Executive Director
Stephenson Co. Historical Society

Dr. Joseph R. Fischer
Department of Military History
US Army Command and General Staff
  College

John D. Fitzmorris III
University of Southern Mississippi
Our Lady of Holy Cross College

Jason Everitt Foster
Independent Scholar

Dr. Ronald B. Frankum, Jr.
Department of History
Millersville Universtiy of Pennsylvania

Dr. John C. Fredriksen
Independent Scholar

Dr. Christopher R. Gabel
Department of Military History
US Army Command and General Staff
  College

Dr. Mark T. Gerges
Department of Military History
US Army Command and General Staff
  College

Dr. Prisco R. Hernández
Associate Professor
US Army Command and General Staff
  College

Gregory S. Hospodor, PhD
Department of Military History
US Army Command and General Staff
  College

Dr. Mark M. Hull
Department of Military History
US Army Command and General Staff
  College

Sean N. Kalic, PhD
Department of Military History
US Army Command and General Staff
  College

Lt. Col. (ret) Edwin L. Kennedy Jr.
Assistant Professor
US Army Command and General Staff
  College

Luke B. Kingree
Virginia Military Institute

Dr. John T. Kuehn
Department of Military History
US Army Command and General Staff
  College

Heather M. Leahy
US Marine Corps History Division

Keith A. Leitich
Business and Social Science
Pierce College Puyallup

Shawn Livingston
Public Service Librarian
University of Kentucky

Thomas D. Lofton Jr.
Historian/Curator
The National World War II
  Museum

Jeannine M. Loftus
Independent Scholar

Wendy A. Maier
Associate Professor of History
Oakton Community College

Dr. William Sanders Marble
US Army Office of Medical History

Steven F. Marin
Social Science Department
Victor Valley College

Dr. James B. Martin
Associate Dean
US Army Command and General Staff
  College

Jack McCallum
Adjunct Professor
Department of History and Geography
Texas Christian University

Matthew R. McGrew
Department of History
University of Southern Mississippi

William E. Meador Jr.
Department of Military History
US Army Command and General Staff
  College

Anton A. Menning
Department of Geography
University of Kansas

Dr. Ron Milam
Department of History
Texas Tech University

Dr. Malcolm Muir Jr.
Department of History
Virginia Military Institute

Nicholas A. Murray, D.Phil.
Department of Military History
US Army Command and General Staff
  College

Dr. Charles P. Neimeyer
Director, US Marine Corps History
Marine Corps University

Huong T. D. Nguyen
Southeast Asian Studies Program
Ohio University

Marlyn R. Pierce
Department of Military History
US Army Command and General Staff
  College

Paul G. Pierpaoli Jr.
Associate Editor
Military History, ABC-CLIO, Inc.

Scott A. Porter
Department of Command and
  Leadership
US Army Command and General Staff
  College

Jeremy Prichard
Department of History
University of Kansas

Robert J. Rielly
Department of Command and
  Leadership
US Army Command and General Staff
  College

John Sager
Department of History
Texas Tech University

Dr. Debra J. Sheffer
Associate Professor of History
Park University

Dr. Charles R. Shrader
Independent Scholar

T. Jason Soderstrum
Iowa State University

Jason M. Sokiera
Department of History
University of Southern Mississippi

Lon Strauss
Department of History
University of Kansas

Christopher S. Trobridge
Department of History
Texas Tech University

Dr. Spencer C. Tucker
Senior Fellow
Military History, ABC-CLIO, Inc.

Dr. Thomas Dwight Veve
Department of Social Sciences
Dalton State College

John F. Votaw
The Cantigny First Division
    Foundation

Stephen Patrick Ward
Virginia Military Institute

Dr. Andrew J. Waskey
Department of Social Sciences
Dalton State College

Tim J. Watts
Hale Library
Kansas State University

Wyndham E. Whynot
Assistant Professor of History
Livingston College

**Maj. Gen. David T. Zabecki, PhD,
    AUS (ret)**
University of Birmingham (UK)